# Lecture Notes in Computer Science 4229

Commenced Publication in 1973
Founding and Former Series Editors:
Gerhard Goos, Juris Hartmanis, and Jan van Leeuwen

Elie Najm  Jean-François Pradat-Peyre
Véronique Viguié Donzeau-Gouge (Eds.)

# Formal Techniques for Networked and Distributed Systems – FORTE 2006

26th IFIP WG 6.1 International Conference
Paris, France, September 26-29, 2006
Proceedings

 Springer

Volume Editors

Elie Najm
ENST
Dept. Informatique et Reseaux
46, rue Barrault, 75634 Paris, Cedex 13, France
E-mail: Elie.Najm@ENST.fr

Jean-François Pradat-Peyre
Véronique Viguié Donzeau-Gouge
Conservatoire National des Arts et Métiers
Lab. CEDRIC
292, rue Saint-Martin, 75 141 Paris Cedex 03, France
E-mail: {peyre,V.Viguie.Donzeau-Gouge}@cnam.fr

Library of Congress Control Number: 2006933226

CR Subject Classification (1998): C.2.4, D.2.2, C.2, D.2.4-5, D.2, F.3, D.4

LNCS Sublibrary: SL 2 – Programming and Software Engineering

ISSN        0302-9743
ISBN-10     3-540-46219-8 Springer Berlin Heidelberg New York
ISBN-13     978-3-540-46219-4 Springer Berlin Heidelberg New York

Springer is a part of Springer Science+Business Media

springer.com

© IFIP International Federation for Information Processing 2006
Printed in Germany

Typesetting: Camera-ready by author, data conversion by Scientific Publishing Services, Chennai, India
Printed on acid-free paper      SPIN: 11888116      06/3142      5 4 3 2 1 0

# Preface

This volume contains the proceedings of FORTE 2006, the 26$^{th}$ IFIP WG 6.1 International Conference on Formal Methods for Networked and Distributed Systems, which took place in Paris, September 26-29, 2006. FORTE denotes a series of international working conferences on formal description techniques applied to computer networks and distributed systems. The conference series started in 1981 under the name PSTV. In 1988 a second series under the name FORTE was set up. Both series were united to FORTE / PSTV in 1996. Five years ago the conference changed the name to its current form.

FORTE was held in Taiwan in 2005, in Madrid in 2004, in Berlin in 2003, in Houston in 2002, etc. The 2006 edition took place in Paris in the buildings of the CNAM (Conservatoire National des Arts et Métiers), which is a Public Scientific, Cultural and Professional Institution. FORTE 2006 was organized by CEDRIC, the computer science research laboratory of the CNAM, and by the Parisian multi-laboratories research group MeFoSyLoMa (Méthodes Formelles pour les Systèmes Logiciels et Matériels). The conference comprised a three-day technical program, during which papers contained in these proceedings were presented. The technical program was preceded by a tutorial day.

FORTE is dedicated to formal description techniques and their application to distributed systems and cooperating applications. The focus of FORTE 2006 was on the construction of middleware and services using formalized and verified approaches. In addition to the classic protocol specification, verification and testing problems, FORTE 2006 addressed the issues of composition of protocol functions and of algorithms for distributed systems.

In total 99 abstracts and 78 full papers were submitted covering the special focus of FORTE 2006 and also more usual topics such as testing, slicing, and verification techniques; highlighting different formalisms among them one can cite Petri Nets, processes algebra or unified modelling languages. Out of the submissions, 26 full papers and 4 shorts papers were selected by the Program Committee for presentation. We would like to express our deepest appreciation to the authors of all submitted papers, to the Program Committee and to external reviewers who did an outstanding job in selecting the best papers for presentation (more than 300 referee reports were completed before closing the selection phase). In addition to the submitted contributions, there were three invited lectures: one by Daniel Krob (Ecole Polytechnique, France), who gave his vision of complex systems in a talk entitled "Modelling of Complex Software Systems: A Reasoned Overview"; one by Leslie Lamport (Microsoft, USA), who presented a new way to describe algorithms with his talk entitled "The $^{+}$CAL Algorithm Language"; and one by Martin Wirsing (Institut fur Informatikr, Ludwig-Maximilians-Universität München, Germany), who presented the SENSORIA project in a talk entitled "Semantic-Based Service-Oriented Software

Development." We thank them for the quality of their talks and of their papers. Two very interesting tutorials were given on the first day, one by Rüdiger Valk (Univ. Hamburg, Germany) on the use of Petri Nets for modelling and verifying concurrent systems and one by Dominique Méry (Université Henri Poincaré Nancy & LORIA, France) on the event B method. We thank them for their help in disseminating knowledge in formal methods for system design.

We would like to thank the CNAM technical and organizational support, Philippe Auger, Joel Berthelin, Frederic Lemoine, Gilles Lepage and Stephen Robert. Special thanks to Kristina and Gabriele Santini (KSW), who designed the FORTE 2006 Web site (http://forte2006.cnam.fr). We are also grateful to Christine Choppy, who organized tutorials, Kirill Bogdanov for his work as Publicity Chair, and to the Steering Committee members for their advice. We thank also Joyce El Haddad, Sami Evangelista, Irfan Hamid, Christophe Pajault, Isabelle Perseil, Pierre Rousseau, and Emmanuel Paviot-Adet for all their work before and during the conference.

Last, but not least, we would like to express our appreciation to speakers and to all the participants who helped in achieving the goal of the conference: providing a forum for researchers and practitioners for the exchange of information and ideas about formal methods for modelling, testing and verifying protocols and distributed systems.

July 2006

Elie Najm
Jean-François Pradat-Peyre
Véronique Viguié Donzeau-Gouge

# Organization

## Organization Chairs

| | |
|---|---|
| General Chair | Véronique Viguié Donzeau-Gouge (CEDRIC-CNAM, France) |
| Program Chairs | Elie Najm (Infres-ENST, France) |
| | Jean-François Pradat-Peyre (CEDRIC-CNAM, France) |
| Tutorials Chair | Christine Choppy (LIPN Univ. Paris-Nord, France) |
| Publicity Chair | Kirill Bogdanov (University of Sheffield, UK) |

## Steering Committee

G. v. Bochmann (University of Ottawa, Canada)
T. Bolognesi (Istituto di Scienza e Tecnologie dell'Informazione, Italy)
J. Derrick (Department of Computer Science, University of Sheffield, UK)
K. Turner (University of Stirling, UK)

## Program Committee

G. v. Bochmann (University of Ottawa, Canada)
T. Bolognesi (IEI Pisa, Italy)
M. Bravetti (University of Bologna, Italy)
A. Cavalli (INT Evry, France)
D. de Frutos-Escrig (Complutense University of Madrid,Spain)
J. Derrick (University of Sheffield, UK)
L. Duchien (LIFL, France)
A. Fantechi (Università di Firenze, Italy)
C. Fidge (Australia)
H. Garavel (INRIA, France)
R. Gotzhein (University of Kaiserslautern, Germany)
S. Haddad (Lamsade-Paris Dauphine, France)
T. Higashino (University of Osaka, Japan)
D. Hogrefe (University of Göttingen, Germany)
P. Inverardi (University of L'Aquila, Italia)
C. Jard (IRISA, France)
G. J. Holzmann (NASA/JPL, USA)
M. Kim (ICU Taejon, Korea)
H. König (Brandenburg University of Technology, Germany)
L. Logrippo (Université du Québec en Outaouais, Canada)
J. Magee (Imperial College of London, UK)
E. Najm (Infres ENST, France) Co-chair
M. Núñez (Complutense University of Madrid, Spain)

D. A. Peled (University of Warwick, UK)
A. Petrenko (CRIM Montreal, Canada)
F. Plasil (Charles University, Prague)
J.-F. Pradat-Peyre (Cedric-Cnam, France) Co-chair
W. Reisig (Humboldt-Universität, Berlin)
J.B. Stefani (INRIA, France)
K. Suzuki (Kennisbron Co., Ltd, Japan)
P. Traverso (ITC-IRST, Italy)
K. Turner, (University of Stirling, UK)
H. Ural (University of Ottawa, Canada)
F. Wang (National Taiwan University, Taiwan)

# External Referees

Jiri Adamek
Daniel Amyot
Marco Autili
Mehdi BenHmida
Béatrice Berard
Piergiorgio Bertoli
Laura Bocchi
Luciano Bononi
Sergiy Boroday
Céline Boutrous-Saab
Manuel Breschi
Tomas Bures
Thomas Chatain
Cheng Chih-Hong
José Manuel Colom
Bassel Daou
John Derrick
Véronique Donzeau-
    Gouge
Arnaud Dury
Michael Ebner
Khaled El-Fakih
Edith Elkind
Emmanuelle Encrenaz
Sami Evangelista
Hubert Garavel
Andreas Glausch
Ruediger Grammes
Cyril Grepet
Andrey Gromyko
Hesham Hallal
Irfan Hamid

Toru Hasegawa
Wael Hassan
May Haydar
Viliam Holub
Kohei Honda
Geng-Dian Huang
Akira Idoue
Pavel Jezek
Rajeev Joshi
Guy-Vincent Jourdan
Sungwon Kang
Raman Kazhamiakin
Jan Kofron
Mounir Lallali
Frédéric Lang
Ranko Lazic
Stefan Leue
Li-Ping Lin
Cai Lin-Zan
Luis Llana-Díaz
Luigi Logrippo
Niels Lohmann
Natalia López
Savi Maharaj
Wissam Mallouli
Annapaola Marconi
Olga Marroqun
Fabio Martinelli
Mieke Massink
Franco Mazzanti
Mercedes G. Merayo
Fabrizio Montesi

Gerardo Morales
Isabelle Mounier
Tomohiko Ogishi
Jean-Marie Orset
Christophe Pajault
Emmanuel Paviot-Adet
Patrizio Pelliccione
Isabelle Perseil
Marinella Petrocchi
Pascal Poizat
Nicolas Rouquette
Pierre Rousseau
Gwen Salaün
Koushik Sen
Soonuk Seol
Carron Shankland
Marianne Simonot
Isabelle Simplot-Ryl
Rene Soltwisch
Christian Stahl
Jean-Marc Talbot
Francesco Tapparo
Maurice ter Beek
Yann Thierry-Mieg
Francesco Tiezzi
Alberto Verdejo
Friedrich H. Vogt
Stephan Waack
Daniela Weinberg
Huang Wen-Ting
Constantin Werner
Jung-Hsuan Wu

# Table of Contents

## Invited Talks

## Services

## Middleware

## Petri Nets

## Parameterized Verification

## Real Time

## Testing

# Modelling of Complex Software Systems:
# A Reasoned Overview[*]

Daniel Krob

Laboratoire d'Informatique de l'Ecole Polytechnique (LIX)
CNRS & École Polytechnique,
Ecole Polytechnique – LIX – 91128 Palaiseau Cedex – France
dk@lix.polytechnique.fr
http://www.lix.polytechnique.fr/~dk

**Abstract.** This paper is devoted to the presentation of the key concepts on which a mathematical theory of complex (industrial) systems can be based. We especially show how this formal framework can capture the realness of modern information technologies. We also present some new modelling problems that are naturally emerging in the specific context of complex software systems.

**Keywords:** Complex system, Information system, Integrated system, Modelling, Software system.

*This paper is dedicated to the memory of M.P. Schützenberger*

## 1  Introduction

In the modern world, complex industrial systems are just everywhere even if they are so familiar for us that we usually forgot their underlying technological complexity. Transportation systems (such as airplanes, cars or trains), industrial equipments (such as micro-electronic or telecommunication components) and information systems (such as commercial, production, financial or logistical software systems) are for instance good examples of complex industrial systems that we are using or dealing with in the everyday life.

At a superficial level, "complex" refers here to the fact that the design and the engineering of these industrial systems are incredibly complicated technical and managerial operations. Thousands of specialized engineers, dozens of different scientific domains and hundreds of millions of euros can indeed be involved in the construction of such systems. In the automobile industry, a new car project lasts for instance typically 4 years, requires a total human working effort of more than 1.500 years, involves 50 different technical fields and costs around 1 billion of euros ! In the context of software systems, important projects have also the same kind of complexity. Recently the unification of the information systems of

---

[*] This paper was supported by the Ecole Polytechnique and Thales' chair "Engineering of complex systems".

E. Najm et al. (Eds.): FORTE 2006, LNCS 4229, pp. 1–22, 2006.
© IFIP International Federation for Information Processing 2006

two important French financial companies that merged, needed for example 6 months of preliminary studies followed by 2 years of work for a team of 1.000 computer specialists, in order to rebuild and to mix consistently more than 250 different business applications, leading to a total cost of around 500 millions euros.

At a deeper level, complex industrial systems are characterized by the fact that they are resulting of a complex *integration process* (cf. [38,39] for more details). This means that such systems are obtained by integrating in a coherent way – that is to say assembling through well defined interfaces – altogether a tremendously huge number of heterogeneous sub-systems and technologies, that belong in practice to the three following main categories:

1. *Physical systems:* these types of systems are manipulating and transforming *physical quantities* (energy, momentum, etc.). The hardware components of transportation, micro-electronic or telecommunication systems are for instance typical physical systems.
2. *Software systems:* these systems are characterized by the fact that they are managing and transforming *data.* Operating systems, compilers, databases, Web applications and Business Intelligence (BI) systems are classical examples of software systems.
3. *Human systems:* human organizations[1] can be considered as systems as soon as their internal processes have reached a certain degree of normalization. They will then be identified to the business processes that are structuring them.

Note at this point that the difficulty of integrating coherently the different parts of a complex industrial system reflects of course in the difficulty of integrating coherently the heterogeneous formal and informal models – going from partial differential equations and logical specifications to business process modelling (BPM) methods (cf. [11]) – that one must handle in order to deal globally with such systems. There is in particular still no real formal general models that can be used for dealing with complex industrial systems from a global point of view. This lack can also be seen in the fact that there are no unified tools for managing all the aspects of the realization cycle of an industrial complex system (which goes from the analysis of needs and the specification phase up to the final integration, verification, validation and qualification processes).

More generally, one must clearly face a huge lack of theoretical tools that may help to clarify the question of complexity in practice. Very few research works are for instance studying directly "heterogeneous" systems *in their whole*, though a rather important research effort has been done during the last decades to understand better several important families of homogeneous systems (such as Hamiltonian systems, dynamical systems, embedded systems, distributed systems, business organizations, etc.) which are involved within larger industrial

---

[1] One must obligatory take into account these non technical systems in the modelling of a global system as soon as the underlying human organizations are strongly interacting with its physical and/or software components. This situation occurs for instance naturally in the context of complex software systems (see Section 4).

systems. The key point is here to understand that the problematics are absolutely not the same if one studies a complex industrial system at local levels (the only ones that the classical approaches are addressing) and at a global level. We however believe that the existing formal "local" theoretical frameworks can and should be redeployed to analyze complex industrial system at a holistic level.

An interesting fact that militates in favor of the possibility of progressing in these directions is the convergence, that can be currently observed in the industry, between the approaches used for managing the engineering phases[2] of physical and of software systems. This convergence can in particular be seen at a methodological level since system engineering (see [47,55]) and software engineering (see [48,51]) are more or more expressing their methods in the same way, but also at the level of the architectural principles used in physical and software contexts (see [33]) and of the quasi-formal specifying and modelling tools that are now taking into account both physical and software frameworks (cf. for instance [8,53] for the description of SysML that extends the classical Unified Modelling Language (UML) – [46] – for general systems).

The purpose of this short paper is to make a reasoned overview on what could be a general theory of systems. After some preliminaries, we therefore present in Section 3 a tentative formal framework, for approaching in a mathematical way the notion of "complex industrial system", that tries to capture the realness both of these systems and of their engineering design processes (which are very difficult to separate in practice). Section 4 is then devoted both to the analysis of the modern software industrial ecosystem using the analysis grid provided by our approach and to the illustration of new types of research problems – of practical interest – that are naturally emerging from this new point of view on complex software systems.

## 2 Preliminaries

As in the few previous attempts to discuss globally of systems (see for instance [14,50,59]), these objects will be defined here as mechanisms that are able to receive, transform and emit physical and/or informational quantities among time. This explains why we will first introduce two key definitions on which are respectively based time and quantity modelling in our approach.

### 2.1 Time Scales

A *time scale* $\mathbb{T}$ refers to any mode of modelling all the possible moments of time starting from some initial moment $t_0 \in \mathbb{R}$. Time scales can be of two different kinds, i.e. continuous or discrete. The *continuous* time scales are of the form $\mathbb{T} = t_0 + \mathbb{R}^+$. One has more various *(regular) discrete* time scales which are of the form $\mathbb{T} = t_0 + \mathbb{N}\tau$ where $\tau \in \mathbb{R}^+_*$ denotes their *time step*. One can consider as well *irregular discrete* time scales that are of the form $\mathbb{T} = \{ t_0 + \tau_1 + \cdots + \tau_n, \ n \in \mathbb{N} \}$

---

[2] I.e. design, architecture, integration and qualification processes.

where $(\tau_i)_{i \in \mathbb{N}}$ is a given family of strictly positive real numbers. Note finally that the above time scales were always *deterministic*, but that they could also be *probabilistic* if the parameters involved in their definitions are random variables with given probabilistic laws.

## 2.2 Quantity Spaces

A *quantity space* refers to any mode of modelling either physical quantities (like energy, temperature, speed, position, etc.) or informational quantities (that is to say data in the usual computer science meaning). There are therefore two types of quantity spaces, i.e. continuous and discrete ones. On one hand, a *continuous* quantity space can be any complete topological space such as $\mathbb{R}^n$ or $\mathbb{C}^m$. On the other hand, a *discrete* quantity space is either any finite set or a discrete infinite set such as $\mathbb{N}^n$, $\mathbb{Z}^m$ or $A^*$ (where $A$ stands for any finite alphabet). Note finally that a quantity space $Q$ must also always distinguish a special element – called the *missing quantity* – that represents the absence of quantity (which is typically 0 is $Q$ is a subset of $\mathbb{C}$).

## 3    Complex Systems

### 3.1    Abstract Systems

In order to move towards the formal modelling of *complex industrial systems*, let us introduce a first notion of system, identified here to an input/output behavior.

**Definition 1.** *An* abstract system $\mathcal{S}$ *is defined as a 5-uple* $\mathcal{S} = (\mathbb{I}, \mathbb{O}, \mathbb{T}_i, \mathbb{T}_o, \mathcal{F})$ *where*

- $\mathbb{I}$ *and* $\mathbb{O}$ *are two quantity spaces respectively called the* input *and* output spaces *of* $\mathcal{S}$,
- $\mathbb{T}_i$ *and* $\mathbb{T}_o$ *are two time scales, respectively called the* input *and* output time scales *of* $\mathcal{S}$,
- $\mathcal{F}$ *is a function from* $\mathbb{I}^{\mathbb{T}_i}$ *into* $\mathbb{O}^{\mathbb{T}_o}$ *which is called the* transfer function *of* $\mathcal{S}$.

Observe that the discrete or continuous structure of the input and output spaces and of the input and output time scales defines naturally different kinds of abstract systems in the meaning of Definition 1. To illustrate and understand better this last definition, let us now study several examples of such systems that are distinguished according to this new criterium.

*Example 1.* – *Discrete systems* – An abstract system will said to be *discrete* when its input and output time scales are discrete. Discrete abstract systems can for instance easily be described by means of finite automaton modelling approaches which capture quite well the event reacting dimension of a real system. These types of formalisms all basically rely on the use of rational transducers – or equivalently Mealy machines – (cf. [3,37]) for expressing the transfer function of a discrete system. Figure 1 shows a simple example of this kind of formalism for modelling the effect of the switch button of a lamp on its lighting performance. The input space of the abstract system that models the lamp is here $\mathbb{I} = \{\rho, \pi\}$ (where $\rho$ and $\pi$ respectively model the fact that the switch button is released or pressed – note that $\rho$ stands therefore for the empty quantity of $\mathbb{I}$) when its output space is $\mathbb{O} = \{0, e\} \subset \mathbb{R}^+$ (an output real value represents the amount of energy produced by the lamp). The corresponding input and output time scales can finally here be any discrete regular time scales that are relevant with respect to the modelling purposes (they are both re-normalized to $\mathbb{N}$ in our example for the sake of simplicity). Note in particular that the discrete structure of the output time scale is not a problem as soon as we are only interested by a computer model for simulation purposes (one just has to take a sufficiently small output time step). We will revisit this example in the sequel, especially to see how to get more realistic models with respect to the lamp real physical behavior (see Examples 2 and 3).

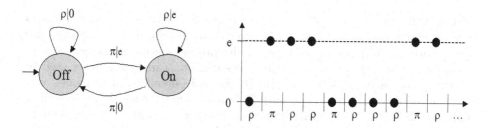

**Fig. 1.** Modelling the transfer function of a lamp by a rational transducer

Petri nets (cf. [42,45]), (min−max, +) systems (cf. [4]), Kahn networks (cf. [27]), etc. are other examples – among numerous others – of basic automaton-oriented formalisms that can be used (with slight modifications) for describing discrete abstract systems in our meaning.

There is also a purely logical approach for representing discrete abstract systems. The core modelling language in this direction is probably Lustre (cf. [22,13]). This programming language is indeed structurally devoted to express transformations of typed infinite sequences. The Lustre program that models the (simple) behavior of our lamp is for instance given below.

```
node Lamp(X:bool) returns (Y:real);
var E,Z:real;
let
E = e -> pre E;
Z = 0 -> pre Z;
Y = if X then E else Z;
tel
```

**Fig. 2.** Modelling the transfer function of a lamp by a Lustre program

In this example, $X$ stands for the infinite sequence of boolean entries a lamp receives (`false` and `true` modelling respectively the fact that the switch button of the lamp is released or pressed) when $Y$ represents the infinite sequence of the energy levels that can take the lamp (either 0 or $e$). The $E$ and the $Z$ variables are then just used here for defining the constant infinite real sequences $E = (e, e, e, \dots)$ and $Z = (0, 0, 0, \dots)$. The last line of the program expresses finally that the $n$-th entry of $Y$ is equal to the $n$-th entry of $E$ (resp. $Z$), i.e. to $e$ (resp. 0), when the $n$-th entry of $X$ is true (resp. false), i.e. when the button switch is pressed (resp. released), which models correctly the expected behavior of the lamp (initially switched off) we considered.

Other reactive languages such as Signal (see [32]) or Lucid (see [12]) are using too the same global flow manipulating approach. Note that one can of course also take any usual formal specification language such as B (cf. [1,57]), TLA+ (cf. [31]) or Z (cf. [52]), any modelling tool coming from the model checking approach (cf. [6,49]) or even any classical programming language, to describe the step-by-step behavior of an abstract system by a "logical" formalism.

*Example 2. Continuous systems* – An abstract system will said to be *continuous* when its input and output time scales are continuous. Since continuous systems occur naturally in physical contexts, all the various continuous models coming from control theory, physics, signal processing, etc. can therefore be used to represent continuous systems (see [14,50] for more details). These models rely more or less all on the use of (partial) differential equations which can be seen as the core modelling tool in such a situation. Going back again to the lamp system considered in Example 1, one can easily see that the lamp behavior can now for instance be modelled by a continuous signal $y(t)$ – giving the value of the lamp energy at each moment of time $t$ – that respects an ordinary differential equation of the following form:

$$y'(t) = e \times x(t) - k \times y(t), \qquad y(0) = 0, \tag{1}$$

where $x(t)$ stands for a continuous $\{0, 1\}$-signal that represents the behavior of the button switch – $x(t)$ being equal to 0 (resp. 1) at time $t$ iff the button switch is off (resp. on) at this moment of time – and where $k > 0$ is a real parameter which models the speed of reactivity of the lamp light to the opening/closing of the button switch. Figure 3 shows then the result (on the right side) of such a modelling (obtained here with $e = 2$ and $k = 1$) for a given $\{0, 1\}$-input signal (on the left side). Note that this model shows clearly the continuous initial or final evolutions of the energy of the lamp when the button is switched on or off (which are of course not immediate in reality as it was expressed in the discrete models considered in Example 1).

Mathlab and Simulink are the typical software tools that can be used for designing continuous systems (see [36]). Observe also that specific frameworks exist for dealing with several important families of continuous systems such as dynamical systems (cf. respectively [28] and [18] for the physical and the control theory point of views), Hamiltonian systems (cf. [40]), etc.

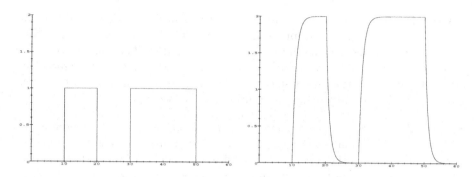

**Fig. 3.** Modelling the physical behavior of a lamp by a differential equation

*Example 3. Hybrid systems* – An abstract system will said to be *hybrid* when one of its input or output time scales is discrete when the other one is continuous. It is interesting to know that two types of approaches exist for studying hybrid systems, depending respectively whether one stresses on the discrete (see for instance [2,24]) or the continuous point of view (see for instance [58]) with respect to such systems. However hybrid systems will of course always be represented by hybrid formalisms that mix discrete and continuous frameworks. Hybrid automata (see [24]) are for instance classical models for representing abstract hybrid systems – in our meaning – with a discrete input time scale and a continuous output time scale (but not for the converse situation, which shows that our hybrid systems *must not be mixed up* with these last systems). Figure 4 shows an hybrid automaton that models the physical behavior of the lamp which was already considered in the two previous examples. Three modes of the lamp are modelled here: the "Init" mode (the switch button was never touched), the "On" mode (the lamp was switched on at least once) and the "Off" mode (the lamp was switched off at least once). The states corresponding to these three different modes contain then the three generic evolution modes – modelled by ordinary differential equations (see Figure 4) – of the continuous signal $y(t)$ that represents the output lamp energy at each moment of time $t$, taking here again the notations of Example 2. On the other hand, the inputs are here just sequences of $\pi$ and $\rho$ (that model respectively the fact that the switch button of the lamp is either pressed or released).

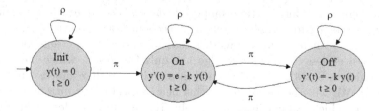

**Fig. 4.** Modelling the physical behavior of a lamp by an hybrid automaton

Other families of hybrid formalisms – in our meaning – can be typically found in signal processing (see [43]) for modelling demodulation or sampling (transformation of a continuous signal into a discrete one) and modulation (transformation of discrete signal into a continuous one). These last formalisms are radically different from the previous one since they are all based on complex analysis (i.e. $z$ or Laplace transforms) or on distribution theory (see again [43]).

*Example 4. Non functional properties are functional ...* – Let us now focus on how to express some engineering oriented system aspects. The key point we would like to stress is the fact that the classical non functional properties of a real system – that is to say response times, costs, delays of realization, availability, safety, quality of service, etc. – can easily be modelled by transfer functions in our framework. A non functional property $\mathcal{N}$ of a system can indeed typically always be measured either by some suited numerical indicator $f_N(t)$ or by an adapted boolean predicate $P_N(t)$ (see for instance [60]), depending on internal parameters of the considered system, that can be measured at each moment $t$ of the input time. Such non functional properties can then be expressed in our framework by extending the output space of the underlying system in order to send out the corresponding indicator or predicate values.

Note finally that the "real" systems that can be found in practice form only a "small" sub-family of the abstract systems covered by Definition 1 (which was only given here in such a generality for the sake of simplicity). One may found in [29,30] a formal definition of a "good" global more restricted family of abstract systems that tries to capture the full realness of systems, using a Turing machine type formalism mixed with non standard analysis (cf. [16]) for taking into account the continuous and discrete dimensions of systems in the same framework.

## 3.2   Abstract Integration

Up to now, we only focused on "simple" models for dealing with systems. Quite all these models are however not really very well adapted for describing hierarchical systems, i.e. systems – in our meaning – that are recursively defined as a coherent interfacing – i.e. an integration – of a collection of sub-systems of different nature. Very surprisingly, while there is a large modelling diversity for usual systems (as we saw in the previous subsection), it indeed appears that there are only a few models that support *homogeneous hierarchical* design (the key difficulty being to be able to take into account both quantities and temporal hierarchies) when the formal models that support *heterogeneous hierarchical* design are even less (to our knowledge, the only framework which handles this last situation is SysML – see [53] – which remains a rather informal modelling approach). We will therefore devote this new subsection to introduce the key concepts on which system integration rely. To this purpose, let us first define the notion of abstract multi-system that extends slightly the notion of system introduced in the previous section.

**Definition 2.** *An abstract $(n, m)$-system $\mathcal{S}$ is defined as a 5-uple $\mathcal{S} = (\mathcal{I}, \mathcal{O}, \mathcal{T}_i,$
$\mathcal{T}_o, \mathcal{F})$ where*

- *$\mathcal{I} = (\mathbb{I}_k)_{k=1...n}$ and $\mathcal{O} = (\mathbb{O}_l)_{l=1...m}$ are two families of quantity spaces, whose direct products are respectively called the input and output spaces of $\mathcal{S}$,*

- *$\mathcal{T}_i = (\mathbb{T}_i^k)_{k=1...n}$ and $\mathcal{T}_o = (\mathbb{T}_o^l)_{l=1...m}$ are two families of time scales, whose direct products are respectively called the input and output time scales of $\mathcal{S}$,*

- *$\mathcal{F}$ is a function from $\displaystyle\prod_{k=1}^{n} \mathbb{I}_k^{\mathbb{T}_i^k}$ into $\displaystyle\prod_{l=1}^{m} \mathbb{O}_l^{\mathbb{T}_o^l}$ which is called the transfer function of $\mathcal{S}$.*

This last definition just expresses that a $(n, m)$-system – or equivalently a *multi-system* – has several different typed and temporized input and output mechanisms (see Figure 5 for an example of "hybrid" multi-system with a mix of discrete and continuous input and output time scales). Note also that systems in the meaning of Definition 1 are now $(1, 1)$-multi-systems.

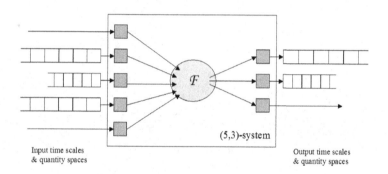

Input time scales
& quantity spaces

Output time scales
& quantity spaces

**Fig. 5.** Schematic description of a $(n, m)$-system

Multi-systems can easily be composed, using typed and temporized *interaction channels*, in a way that reflects the realness of system integration. An interaction channel stands for a medium between an output $O$ and an input $I$ of two multi-systems that can only transmit quantities of a given quantity space, at a time rate associated with some fixed time scale and with a constant temporal delay (for bringing a quantity from $O$ to $I$). This leads us to the following definition.

**Definition 3.** *An interaction channel is a triple $\mathcal{C} = (Q, \mathbb{T}, \tau)$ where $Q$ is a quantity space, $\mathbb{T}$ is a time scale (of initial moment $t_0$) and $\tau \in \mathbb{T} - t_0$ is a transmission delay.*

Multi-system composition makes only sense in the context of interacting system networks, another important notion that is defined below (see Figure 6 for a graphical vision).

**Definition 4.** *An* interacting system network $\mathcal{N}$ *is a triple* $\mathcal{N} = (\mathcal{S}, \chi, \mathcal{C})$ *where*

- $\mathcal{S} = (\mathcal{S}_i)_{i=1...N}$ *is a family of multi-systems,*
- $\chi : C^O \longrightarrow C^I$ *is a bijective mapping between a subset of the output indices of* $\mathcal{S}$ *into a subset of the input indices of* $\mathcal{S}^3$,
- $\mathcal{C} = \{ (\mathbb{OI}^c, \mathbb{T}_{io}^c, \tau^c), c \in C^O \}$ *is a family of interaction channels indexed by* $C^O$,

*such that the k-th output and l-th input quantity spaces and times scales of* $\mathcal{S}_i$ *and* $\mathcal{S}_j$ *are always equal – respectively to* $\mathbb{OI}^c$ *and* $\mathbb{T}_{io}^c$ *– for every* $c = (i, k) \in C^O$ *and* $(j, l) = \chi(c) \in C^I$.

The input and output indices of $\mathcal{S}$ that belong (resp. do not belong) to $C^I$ or to $C^O$ (with the above notations) are called *constrained* (resp. *free*) input or output indices within $\mathcal{S}$. Note also that an interacting system network will said to be *initialized* if it is equipped with a *initialization map* $\iota$ that associates with each constrained input index $c = (i, k) \in C^I$ of the underlying family $\mathcal{S}$ a quantity $q = \iota(c) \in \mathbb{I}_k^i$ where $\mathbb{I}_k^i$ is the $k$-th input quantity space of the $i$-th system of $\mathcal{S}$.

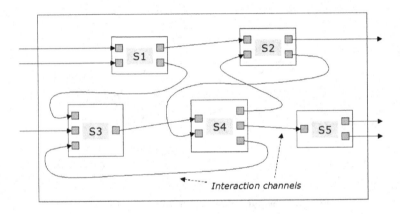

**Fig. 6.** Example of an interacting system network

Since we will be obliged for technical reasons to restrict composition to specific types of multi-systems defined topologically, let us equip any *flow space* $\mathbb{F}$, i.e. any set of the form $\mathbb{F} = \mathbb{I}^{\mathbb{T}}$ where $\mathbb{I}$ and $\mathbb{T}$ stand respectively for a quantity space and a time scale, with a sequential topology. We will indeed say that a sequence $(x_i)_{i \geq 0}$ of *flows* of $\mathbb{F} = \mathbb{I}^{\mathbb{T}}$, i.e. of elements of the form $x_i = (x_i^t)_{t \in \mathbb{T}} \in \mathbb{F}$, has a limit $x = (x^t)_{t \in \mathbb{T}}$ in $\mathbb{F}$ iff for every $t \in \mathbb{T}$, $x_i^t$ is always equal to $x^t$ for $i$ big enough. A multi-system is then said to be *continuous* if its transfer function $\mathcal{F}$ satisfies

$$\mathcal{F}(\lim_i x_i) = \lim_i \mathcal{F}(x_i) , \tag{2}$$

---

[3] $(i, k)$ is an input (resp. output) index within $\mathcal{S}$ iff $\mathcal{S}_i$ has a $k$-th input (resp. output) space.

for any sequence $(x_i)_{i\geq 0}$ of input multi-flows that has a limit in the previous meaning (naturally extended to products of flows). We can now introduce the notion of system composition, which is a bit tedious to define properly, but that is easily graphically depicted (see again Figure 6).

**Proposition 1.** *Let* $\mathcal{N} = (\mathcal{S}, \chi, \mathcal{C})$ *be an interacting system network constructed over a family* $\mathcal{S}$ *of continuous multi-systems which is equipped with an initialization map* $\iota$. *One defines then a new continuous multi-system* $S = (I, O, T_i, T_o, F)$ *– called the* composition of $\mathcal{S}$ through the interactions $\chi \times \mathcal{C}$ with initialization $\iota$ *– by setting:*

- *I and* $T_i$ *are respectively the families of all input quantity spaces and time scales that are associated with free input indices within* $\mathcal{S}$ *(whose set will be denoted by* $F^I$*),*

- *O and* $T_o$ *are respectively the families of all output quantity spaces and time scales that are associated with free output indices within* $\mathcal{S}$ *(whose set will be denoted by* $F^O$*),*

- *the function F associates with any possible input multi-flow* $x = (x_c)_{c \in F^I}$ *an output multi-flow* $y = (y_c)_{c \in F^O}$ *which is defined for each* $c = (i, k) \in F^O$ *by setting*

$$y_c = \mathcal{F}_i^k(X_{\chi^{-1}(i,1),(i,1)}, \dots, X_{\chi^{-1}(i,N_i),(i,N_i)})^4$$

*(* $N_i$ *denoting here the number of inputs of* $\mathcal{S}_i$*), where* $X = (X_{\chi^{-1}(c),c})_{c \in C^I \cup F^I}$ *is the smallest*[5] *solution of the equational system with flow variables*[6] *defined by setting*

$$\begin{cases} X_{(0,0),c} = x_c \text{ for } c \in F^I, \\[2mm] X^t_{\chi^{-1}(c),c} = \iota(c) \text{ for } c \in C^I \text{ and } t \in [t_0, t_0 + \tau^c[ \cap \mathbb{T}^i_k, \\[2mm] X^t_{\chi^{-1}(c),c} = \mathcal{F}_i^k(X_{\chi^{-1}(i,1),(i,1)}, \dots, X_{\chi^{-1}(i,N_i),(i,N_i)}))^{t-\tau^c} \text{ for } c \in C^I \text{ and } t \geq \tau^c \in \mathbb{T}^i_k, \end{cases}$$

*where we put* $c = (j, l)$ *and* $\chi^{-1}(c) = (i, k)$ *in all these last relations.*

*Proof.* The proof follows by using a classical argument of complete partial order theory (cf. [21]). Note that our result can be also seen as an extension of a classical result of Kahn (see [27]). □

This proposition translates now immediately in the following definition which gives a formal and precise meaning to the notion of system integration.

---

[4] We extend here $\chi^{-1}$ to $F^I$ by setting $\chi^{-1}(c) = (0,0)$ when $c$ is a free input index within $\mathcal{S}$.

[5] In the meaning of the product of the (complete) partial orders that are defined on each flow space $\mathbb{F} = \mathbb{I}^{\mathbb{T}}$ by setting $f \preceq g$ for two flows $f$ and $g$ of $\mathbb{F}$ iff the two following conditions are fulfilled: 1. $f$ and $g$ coincide up to some moment $t \in \mathbb{T}$; 2. $f^u$ is equal to the missing quantity of $\mathbb{I}$ for each moment $u > t$ in $\mathbb{T}$.

[6] Where $X_{\chi^{-1}(c),c}$ lies in the flow space $\mathbb{I}_k^{i \mathbb{T}_k^i}$ for every $c = (i,k) \in F^I \cup C^I$.

**Definition 5.** *A (continuous) multi-system will said to be an* integrated abstract multi-system *if it results of the composition of a series of other multi-systems.*

Integration leads naturally to the *fundamental design mechanism* for systems which consists in analyzing recursively any system as an *interfacing* of a series of sub-systems. This design process is quite simple to understand (in software context, it just reduces to the usual top-down design methodology), but rather difficult to realize in practice for complex heterogeneous systems (the key problem being to be sure to interface sub-systems both consistently and without any specification hole). The practical difficulty of integration reflects well in the fact that there is probably no existing formal framework for dealing with integrated systems at the generality level we tried to took here. As a consequence, one can also not really find any unique global design formal tool for real systems. To be totally complete, one should however stress that there are at least two interesting frameworks – presented in the two forthcoming examples – for helping the working engineers in his integration tasks, but which have both serious modelling limitations as soon as one arrives at a system level, and moreover quite deep semantical lacks.

*Example 5. Continuous oriented formalisms* – The most widely industrially used system design tool is probably the Mathlab & Simulink environment (see [36]). In this approach, systems are represented by "black boxes" whose transfer functions, inputs and outputs have to be explicitly given by the user (see Figure 7 for the graphical representation of a car window system modelled in this framework). The main problem of Mathlab & Simulink is however related to the fact that there is no unambiguous and/or crystal clear semantics behind the manipulated diagrams. The self loops in the graphical formalism provided by these tools does for instance not have a very well defined interpretation in this framework, which may typically create causality problems at the modelling level (i.e. lead to abstractly modelled systems whose past behavior depends on their future one ...[7]). The discrete formalism used by Mathlab & Simulink – i.e. Stateflow which is just the commercial name of the implementation of the Statecharts framework (see the next example) – is also semantically rather weak (one can find probably more than 20 different formal semantics in the literature that were proposed for Statecharts). Altogether this shows that Mathlab and Simulink, even if they are wonderful and efficient working tools for the engineer, still suffer from really fundamental flaws from a formal point of view (which limits in particular the possibility of automatically verifying and validating designs made in this formalism).

*Example 6. Discrete formalisms* – The last model that we would like to discuss in this section is Statecharts (see [23,35]). It is indeed probably the very first model – introduced in 1987 – that allowed hierarchical design, one of the key idea of this formalism. In Statecharts, it is indeed possible to deal with distributed

---

[7] Note that we totally avoided this problem in the formalism we introduced above, due to the fact that our interaction channels have always a response delay !

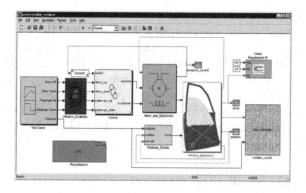

**Fig. 7.** A Matlab/Simulink $^{TM}$ integrated system model ©

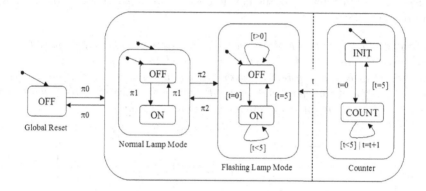

**Fig. 8.** The lamp revisited with Statechart

hierarchical Mealy machines (see again Example 1) which allow to model multi-flow production by *integrating* event oriented hierarchical mechanisms.

The example of Figure 8 illustrates these key aspects of Statecharts. We modelled here a lamp with two working modes: a normal one, where the usual lamp button switch – associated with $\pi_1$ – allows to switch on or off the lamp, and a flashing one, that one reachs or quits by pressing on a special button – represented by $\pi_2$. The lamp is also controlled by a global reset button – modelled by $\pi_0$ – which allow to stop or activate all the functions of the lamp when pressing on it. Note that from the point of view of this last button, the right state of the above figure is therefore just the "ON" state which is hierarchically decomposed into two states, corresponding to the two possible working modes for our lamp (in which one should continue to descend in order to arrive to the finer level of design in our example), plus a concurrent state representing a modulo 6 counter working totally independently from the other internal mechanisms, which gives permanently its value to the flashing mode management state[8].

---

[8] Which is not a very safe approach, as one may imagine, for obvious synchronization reasons ...

The problem of Statecharts is however its poor semantics with respect to distribution expressivity: the precise nature of the interactions between the two automata separated by the dashed line (which models concurrency) in Figure 8 is typically not totally clear. The Esterel language (see [7] or [5] where one can find a good overview of all so-called synchronous languages) was typically designed in order both to preserve the most interesting aspects of Statecharts' approach and to overcome its core flaws. For the sake of completeness, note finally that there are also other formal discrete formalisms that allow hierarchical design (see [9] and again [35]).

## 3.3   System Abstraction and Simulation

Abstraction and simulation are two classical notions that can also be re-adapted to systems (we take below all the flow notations of the previous section extended here to multi-flows).

**Definition 6.** *A multi-system $\mathcal{S}_1$ with input multi-flow space $\mathbb{F}_1^i$, output multi-flow space $\mathbb{F}_1^o$ and transfer function $\mathcal{F}_1$ is said to be an* abstraction *(resp. a* simulation*) of a multi-system $\mathcal{S}_2$ with input multi-flow space $\mathbb{F}_2^i$, output multi-flow space $\mathbb{F}_2^o$ and transfer function $\mathcal{F}_2$ iff there exists two injective functions $\sigma^i$ and $\sigma^o$ such that the following diagram is commutative:*

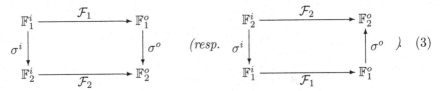

$$(3)$$

Hence $\mathcal{S}_1$ is an abstraction of $\mathcal{S}_2$ if these two systems have homomorphic functional behaviors, the first one being however less detailed than the second one. On the same way, $\mathcal{S}_1$ is a simulation of $\mathcal{S}_2$ if one can mimic all the functional behaviors of the second system by the first one.

*Example 7. Assembling and high level programs* – Let us fix a finite alphabet $A$ and a discrete time scale $\mathbb{T}$. One can then identify any halting Turing machine $M$ – i.e. any Turing machine that eventually stop on all its entries – with entries in $A$ with a discrete system $\mathcal{S}_M$ with $A^*$ as input and output quantity space, $\mathbb{T}$ as input and output time scale and a transfer function $\mathcal{F}_M$ defined as follows: 1. $\mathcal{F}_M$ transforms any flow of the form $F_x = (x, 1, 1, \dots)$, into the flow $F_{M,x} = (1, 1, \dots, Mx, 1, 1, \dots)$, where $Mx$ stands for the value computed by $M$ on $x$, produced at the moment given by the number of elementary steps of $M$ required to obtain it; 2. $\mathcal{F}_M$ transforms any input flow different from a flow of the form $F_x$ into the empty output flow. Looking on programs in this way, one can then easily check that each high level program $P$ is an abstraction of some assembling program $A$ (the one produced by the corresponding compiler) and that such an assembling program $A$ is then a simulation of the program $P$.

*Example 8. Interfaces* – The interface theory which was recently developed by de Alfaro and Henziger (see for instance [17]) can easily be transferred into the system framework as presented here (with of course again a number of slight reinterpretations). System interfaces provide then new generic interesting examples of system abstractions in our meaning . In this context, note that systems appear then as simulations of their interfaces.

Note finally that there are of course other less constrained abstraction notions, typically the ones coming from static analysis (see [15]), which are also of interest in the system context.

## 3.4   Concrete Systems

We are now in position to model formally the usual way a concrete system is designed.

**Definition 7.** *A concrete system $CS$ is a pair $(\mathcal{FS}, \mathcal{OS})$ of abstract integrated systems, the first one (resp. the second one) being an abstraction (resp. a simulation) of the other one, which are respectively called the functional behavior[9] and the organic structure[10] of $CS$.*

This definition reflects the fact that the design of a real system $S$ follows usually two main steps. The first one is a modelling step which defines the so-called *functional architecture* of $S$, i.e. in other words the recursive integration structure of a high level modelling of $S$ constructed by following the point of view of the external systems (hardware, software, users, etc.) that are interacting with $S$. When the functional architecture of $S$ is fixed, one can then define its *organic architecture*, i.e. the real internal structure of $S$, by respecting the requirements provided by the functional architecture (which appears as an abstraction of the organic architecture).

In classical software engineering, the two architectural notions involved in Definition 7 can be seen at different places. The pairs formed by a usual program and its machine or assembling code or, at a higher level, by a software specification and its programmed implementation are typical examples of concrete systems in our meaning. However the underlying conceptual separation does only take really all its importance when one is dealing with systems whose both functional and organic decompositions are complicated, which occurs typically when a system results from an highly heterogeneous integration process. Note that this last property can in fact be seen as an informal characterization of complex systems. Observe also finally that two totally different kinds of complex systems in this meaning, that is to say embedded systems and information systems, naturally arise in the software sphere (see below and Section 4.1).

---

[9] The functional behavior models the input/output behavior of $S$ as it can observed by an external observer.

[10] The organic structure models the intrinsic structure of the considered system.

*Example 9. Embedded system design* – When one deals with embedded system design, one must have an holistic approach that integrates in the same common framework the software, the hardware, the physical and the control theory points of views and constraints involved within such systems (see [25]). One therefore naturally divides the design in two separated, but completely interconnected, main parts: the functional design that corresponds here to the global environment and solution modelling where one will concentrate on the high level algorithmic and mathematical problems, the organic design related then with the low level system implementation where one must be sure to respect the physical and electronic constraints, the key difficulty being of course to have a good correspondence between these two levels of representation.

*Example 10. Information system design* – An information system can be seen as a global (enterprise) environment where software systems, hardware devices and human organizations interact in a coherent way (usually to fulfill a number of business missions). The complexity of these systems lead therefore classically to separate the corresponding design into two architectural levels: on one hand, the functional architecture which is devoted to the description of the user services, the business processes, the user and business data, the system environment, etc. that have to be managed by the information system; on the other hand, the associated organic architecture which is the concrete organization of the software applications, servers, databases, middleware, communication networks, etc. whose interactions will result in a working information system.

## 4    Complex Software Systems

### 4.1    Hierarchies of Complex Software Systems

Integration and abstraction mechanisms allow us to construct naturally a hierarchy of complexity – taken here in an informal way – on software systems which is organized around two axes, i.e. integration and abstraction complexity (see Figure 9). The idea consists in classifying families of software systems according both to their degree of integration, i.e. to their degree of internal systemic largeness and heterogeneity, or more formally to the size of the tree associated with their organic architecture, and to the degree of abstraction which is required to deal with them, i.e. equivalently to the size of the tree associated with their functional architecture.

Such a classification lead us to identify two main classes of complex software systems (the term complex referring here only at first analysis to the organic integration complexity):

1. the software systems where the integration and abstraction complexity comes from the mix of computer science frameworks with *physics, signal processing* and *control theory* environments and models, that is typically to say the so-called embedded systems,

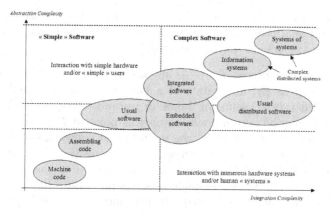

**Fig. 9.** The complex software hierarchy

2. the software systems where the integration and abstraction complexity comes from the mix of the computer science world with mainly *"human" systems and organizations* (plus possibly hardware components), which can be themselves separated into three main subclasses that are presented hereafter by increasing degree of integration and of abstraction (i.e. from the less to the most complex underlying organic and functional architectures):

   - *integrated softwares*: this corresponds to enterprise softwares that are specifically devoted either to some category of business activities – such as BI (global information consolidation inside a large company), CRM (customer relationship management), ERP (financial and production service management), SCM (supply chain management) or KM (documentation management) softwares – or to some type of technical integration purposes – such as B2Bi (external partner software integration), EAI (internal software integration), ETL (batch data consolidation) or EII (on the request data consolidation) softwares. We refer to [26] for an overview of these software technology (see also [54,34]).

   - *information systems*: an information system can be defined as a coherent integration of several integrated softwares – in the above meaning – that supports all the possible business missions of an organization, taken at a global level. An information system can therefore be seen as the integrated system that consists both of a human organization and of all the computer systems that are supporting the specific business processes of the considered organization (see [11,41] or Example 11 for more details).

   - *systems of systems*: this refers to an even higher level of integration, i.e. to the situation where a number of independently designed information systems have to cooperate in order to fulfill a common mission. Systems of systems are characterized by the loose couplings existing structurally between their organic components (that we will not discuss here since this would lead us too far with respect to the integration model we took within this survey paper). Network Centric Warfare (NCW) systems, airport platforms management systems, etc. can be typically seen as systems of systems in this meaning.

*Example 11. Information system* – As already pointed out, an information system can be seen as the integration of a human organization and a software system. The left side of Figure 10 shows for instance a very high level architecture of an information system focusing on this point of view: the sub-systems of the enterprise organization (i.e. the main business departments) are here at the border of this map when the technical sub-systems (i.e. the main integrated involved softwares) are in the center. One can also see on this map a number of arrows that are refering to the main business processes, that is to say to the main normalized interactions (or equivalently interfaces) existing between the corresponding human and software systems.

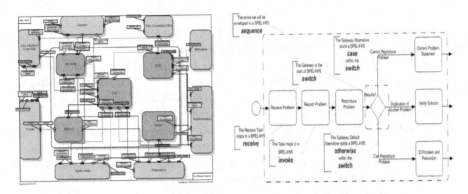

**Fig. 10.** An information system architecture (Sysoft ©) and a business process model (BPMN © – [56])

A business profess refers typically to an enterprise process such as billing, maintening, sourcing, producing, etc. Business process modelling (BPM) is therefore naturally one of the core methodology which is presently developed to represent better the functional behavior of an information system (see [10,41] or Figure 10 which gives an example of a software testing procedure modeling). Note however that BPM is not a formal approach in the line of the numerous models we presented in Section 3. It indeed rather belongs to the family of informal UML-like models, which limits seriously its theoretical potential (but leaves the door open for new research).

## 4.2   What Are the New Problems Emerging from This Framework ?

New types of problems are naturally arising with the most complex software systems. A rather important research effort is for instance presently done for understanding and designing better embedded systems, which are however probably the "most simple" complex systems due to the "nice" underlying mathematical environment in which they are living, even if they are already quite complex to handle (see [25]). We will therefore not focus here on these systems on which a lot was and continue to be made by numerous theoretical computer scientists, but rather on the "human"-oriented complex systems which were, quite surprisingly, not widely studied from a formal point of view, although they are at the center of important economic challenges and of a large technological and business literature (see for instance [11,41,48], etc.).

One of the key problems of these kind of software systems is clearly to be able to take more formally into account the "man in the loop", which appears to be their common denominator. There are therefore naturally several important research streams that could emerge in trying to develop operational modelling formalisms for business processes and more generally for organizational paradigms. We mean of course here formalisms with well defined semantics that would allow to express precisely and unambiguously characteristic properties of a business process (such as cost, speed of execution, probability of success, etc.) in order to be able to formally verify these properties. Such a modelling research effort could probably also help practically organizations to master better their structures and processes.

At a more global level, there is still in the same way an important high level formal modelling effort that must be done in order to give solid bases to a theory of complex software systems. If there is a real business consensus on the nature of an information system, no scientific consensus exists presently – at our knowledge – with respect to a *formal* – that is to say a mathematical – definition of an information system. For systems of systems, the situation is even worse since at this moment of time, there is even no clearly shared business definition of these more complex systems. The key point in this direction would therefore probably to be able to give sound formal definitions of information systems and systems of systems, taking of course integrated systems as primitive objects in such a modelling approach. Such a framework would probably result in the development of new methods for complex software quantitative analysis, an important subject which is still under-developed in the classical context of information systems (see [19,44]) and basically non existing for systems of systems.

One should finally not forget all the specific problems that are of course continuously emerging in the jungle of complex software systems. As a matter of conclusion to this paper, one can find such two problems – among many others – roughly and quickly presented below.

*Example 12. Information system degeneracy* – A classical operational problem that arises in a real information system corresponds typically to the situation where the system begins to emit too many information flows and crashes when it is not able anymore to support the resulting treatment charge. Usually such a crash is not immediate and appears as the consequence of a long intermediate period where nothing is made to prevent it. It is therefore of main interest to be able to predict it and to analyze its origins in order to react properly when it is still time. If one models at high level an information system as a network of multi buffered applications, one sees that the problem can be rephrased as a problem of queuing networks that can probably be attacked both from a static analysis and a distributed algorithmic point of view.

*Example 13. Interoperability of systems of systems* – When interoperability is a well known problem which is quite well mastered for usual information systems (see [20,34]), it is probably still an open subject at the level of systems of systems. The key difficulty at this level comes from the fact that one must interface in a coherent way a number of information systems that were not initially intended to work together. For technical reasons, the usual interoperability approaches can therefore not totally be applied in these contexts since it is typically not easy or even possible to interface these systems through an EAI layer. New methods – mixing semantical and syntactical approaches – are therefore required to solve in a generic way this key problem.

**Acknowledgements.** The author would sincerely like to thank Herman Kuilder, Matthieu Martel, Marc Pouzet and Jacques Printz for the numerous discussions we had together during the maturation period that preceded the writing of this paper, leading to several key evolutions of his point of view.

# References

1. ABRIAL J.R., *The B-book – Assigning programs to meanings*, Cambridge University Press, 1996.
2. ALUR R., COURCOUBETIS C., HALBWACHS N., HENZINGER T.A., HO P.H., NICOLLIN X., OLIVERO A., SIFAKIS J., YOVINE S., *The algorithmic analysis of hybrid systems*, Theor. Comp. Sci., 1995; **138** (1): 3–34.
3. AUTEBERT J.M., BOASSON L., *Transductions rationnelles – Applications aux langages algébriques*, Collection ERI, Masson, 1988.
4. BACCELLI F., COHEN G., OLSDER G.J., QUADRAT J.P., *Synchronization and linearity – An algebra for discrete event systems*, Wiley, 1992.
5. BENVENISTE A., CASPI P., EDWARDS S.A., HALBWACHS N., LE GUERNIC P., DE SIMONE R., *The Synchronous Languages Twelve years later*, Proc. of the IEEE, Special issue on Embedded Systems, 2003; **91** (1): 64–83.
6. BÉRARD B., BIDOIT M., LAROUSSINIE F., PETIT A., SCHNOEBELEN P., *Vérification de logiciels – Techniques et outils du model-checking*, Vuibert Informatique, 1999.
7. BERRY G., GONTHIER G., *The Synchronous Programming Language ESTEREL: Design, Semantics*, Implementation Science of Computer Programming, **19**, 83–152, 1992.
8. BOCK C., *SysML and UML2 Support for Activity Modeling*, Systems Engineering, **9**, (2), 160–186, 2006.
9. BÖRGER E., STÄRK R., *Abstract state machines – A method for high-level system design and analysis*, Springer, 2003.
10. BUSINESS PROCESS MANAGEMENT INITIATIVE – OBJECT MANAGEMENT GROUP, *Business Process Modeling Notation*, OMG, http://www.bpmn.org, 2006.
11. CASEAU Y., *Urbanisation et BPM : le point de vue d'un DSI*, Dunod, 2006.
12. CASPI P., HAMON G., POUZET M., *Lucid Synchrone, un langage de programmation des systèmes réactifs*, in "Systèmes Temps-réel : Techniques de Description et de Vérification - Théorie et Outils", 217–260, Hermes International Publishing, 2006.

13. CASPI P., POUZET M., *Synchronous Kahn networks*, Proc. of the first ACM SIG-PLAN Int. Conf. on Functional Programming, 226–238, 1996.

14. CHA D.P., ROSENBERG J.J., DYM C.L., *Fundamentals of Modeling and Analyzing Engineering Systems*, Cambridge University Press, 2000.

15. COUSOT P., COUSOT R., *Abstract interpretation: a unified lattice model for static analysis of programs by construction or approximation of fixpoints*, in "Conf. Record of the Sixth Annual ACM SIGPLAN-SIGACT Symp. on Principles of Programming Languages", Los Angeles, ACM Press, 238–252, 1977.

16. CUTLAND N., *Nonstandard analysis and its applications*, London Mathematical Society Student Texts, **10**, Cambridge University Press, 1988.

17. DE ALFARO L., HENZIGER T.A., *Interface-based design*, in "Engineering Theories of Software-intensive Systems", M. Broy, J. Gruenbauer, D. Harel, and C.A.R. Hoare, Eds., NATO Science Series: Mathematics, Physics, and Chemistry, Vol. 195, 83–104, Springer, 2005.

18. FLIESS M., *Fonctionnelles causales non linéaires et indéterminées non commutatives*, Bull. Soc. Math. France, 1981; **109**: 3–40.

19. GARMUS D., HERRON D., *Function Point Analysis: Measurement Practices for Successful Software Projects*, Addison-Wesley Information Technology Series, Addison-Wesley, 2000.

20. GOLD-BERNSTEIN B., RUH W., *Enterprise Integration: The Essential Guide to Integration Solutions*, Addison-Wesley Information Technology Series, Addsison-Wesley, 2004.

21. GUNTER C.A., SCOTT D., *Semantic domains*, in "Handbook of Theoretical Computer Science", Vol. B, 633–674, Elsevier, 1990.

22. HALBWACHS N., CASPI P., RAYMOND P., PILAUD D., *The synchronous data-flow programming language LUSTRE*, Proceedings of the IEEE, **79**, (9), 1305–1320, 1991.

23. HAREL D., *Statecharts: A visual formalism for complex systems*, Science of Computer Programming, **8**, (3), 231–274, 1987.

24. HENZINGER T.A., *The theory of hybrid automata*, in Proceedings of the 11th Annual IEEE Symposium on Logic in Computer Science, LICS'96, IEEE Society Press, 1996, pp. 278–292.

25. HENZINGER T.A., SIFAKIS J., *The embedded systems design challenge*, Proc. of the 14th Int. Symp. on Formal Methods (FM), LNCS, Springer, 2006 (to appear).

26. IT TOOL BOX, http://www.ittoolbox.com.

27. KAHN G., *The semantics of a simple language for paralell programming*, Proc. of the IFIP Congress 74, 471–475, 1974.

28. KATOK A., HASSELBLATT B., *Introduction to the modern theory of dynamical systems*, Cambridge, 1996.

29. KROB D., BLIUDZE S., *Towards a Functional Formalism for Modelling Complex Industrial Systems*, in "European Conference on Complex Systems (ECCS05), P. Bourgine, F. Kps, M. Schoenauer, Eds., (article 193), 20 pages, 2005.

30. KROB D., BLIUDZE S., *Towards a Functional Formalism for Modelling Complex Industrial Systems*, in "Complex Systems: Selected Papers", ComPlexUs (to appear).

31. LAMPORT L., *Specifying systems – The TLA+ Language and Tools for Hardware and Software Engineers*, Addison-Wesley, 2003.

32. LE GUERNIC P., GAUTIER T., *Data-Flow to von Neumann: the Signal approach*, in "Advanced Topics in Data-Flow Computing", Gaudiot J.-L. and Bic L., Eds., Prentice-Hall, 413–438, 1991.

33. MAIER M.W., *System and Software Architecture Reconciliation*, Systems Engineering, **9**, (2), 146–59, 2006.
34. MANOUVRIER B., *EAI – Intégration des applications d'entreprise*, Hermès, 2001.
35. MARWEDEL P., *Embedded systems design*, Kluwer, 2003.
36. MATHWORKS, *Mathlab and Simulink*; http://www.mathworks.com.
37. MEALY G.H., *A Method for Synthesizing Sequential Circuits*, Bell System Tech. J., **34**, 1045-1079, 1955.
38. MEINADIER J.P., *Ingénierie et intégration de systèmes*, Hermès, 1998.
39. MEINADIER J.P., *Le métier d'intégration de systèmes*, Hermès-Lavoisier, 2002.
40. MEYER K.R., HALL G.R., *Introduction to Hamiltonian Dynamical Systems and the N-Body Problem*, Applied Mathematical Sciences, **90**, Springer Verlag, 1992.
41. MORLEY C., HUGUES J., LEBLANC B., HUGUES O., *Processus métiers et systèmes d'information*, Dunod, 2005.
42. PETRI C.A., *Fundamentals of a Theory of Asynchronous Information Flow*, Proc. of IFIP Congress 1962, 386–390, North Holland, 1963.
43. PROAKIS J., *Digital Communications*, 3rd Edition, McGraw Hill, 1995.
44. PRINTZ J., DEH C., MESDON B., TRÈVES B., *Coûts et durée des projets informatiques – Pratique des modèles d'estimation*, Hermès Lavoisier, 2001.
45. REISIG W., *Petri nets*, Springer Verlag, 1985.
46. RUMBAUGH J., JACOBSON I., BOOCH G., *The Unified Modeling Language Reference Manual*, Addison Wesley, 1999.
47. SAGE A.P., ARMSTRONG J.E. JR., *Introduction to Systems Engineering*, John Wiley, 2000.
48. SATZINGER J.W., JACKSON R.B., BURD S., SIMOND M., VILLENEUVE M., *Analyse et conception de systèmes d'information*, Les éditions Reynald Goulet, 2003.
49. SCHNEIDER K., *Verification of reactive systems – Formal methods and algorithms*, Springer, 2004.
50. SEVERANCE F.L., *System modeling and simulation – An introduction*, John Wiley, 2001.
51. SOMMERVILLE I., *Software Engineering*, Addison Wesley, 6th Edition, 2001.
52. SPIVEY J.M., *The Z notation – A reference manual*, Prentice Hall, 1992.
53. SYSML, *Systems Modeling Language – Open Source Specification Project –* http://www.sysml.org.
54. TOMAS J.L., *ERP et progiciels de gestion intégrés – Sélection, déploiement et utilisation opérationnelle – Les bases du SCM et du CRM*, Dunod, 2002.
55. TURNER W.C., MIZE J.H., CASE K.E., NAZEMETZ J.W., *Introduction to industrial and systems engineering*, Prentice Hall, 1993.
56. WHITE S.A., *Introduction to BPMN*, IBM, http://www.bpmn.org, 2006.
57. WORDSWORTH J.B., *Software engineering with B*, Addison-Wesley, 1996.
58. ZAYTOON J., ED., *Systèmes dynamiques hybrides*, Hermès, 2001.
59. ZEIGLER B.P., PRAEHOFER H., GON KIM T., *Theory of modeling and simulation – Integrating discrete event and continuous complex dynamic systems*, Academic Press, 2000.
60. ZSCHALER S., *Formal Specification of Non-functional Properties of Component-Based Software*, in "Workshop on Models for Non-functional Aspects of Component-Based Software" (NfC'04), Bruel J.M., Georg G., Hussmann H., Ober I., Pohl C. Whittle J. and Zschaler S., Eds., Technische Universität Dresden, 2004.

# The +CAL Algorithm Language

Leslie Lamport

Microsoft Corporation
1065 La Avenida
Mountain View, CA 94043
U.S.A

Algorithms are different from programs and should not be described with programming languages. For example, algorithms are usually best described in terms of mathematical objects like sets and graphs instead of the primitive objects like bytes and integers provided by programming languages. Until now, the only simple alternative to programming languages has been pseudo-code.

+CAL is an algorithm language based on TLA+. A +CAL algorithm is automatically translated to a TLA+ specification that can be checked with the TLC model checker or reasoned about formally. +CAL makes pseudo-code obsolete.

E. Najm et al. (Eds.): FORTE 2006, LNCS 4229, p. 23, 2006.

# Semantic-Based Development of Service-Oriented Systems*

Martin Wirsing[1], Allan Clark[2], Stephen Gilmore[2], Matthias Hölzl[1],
Alexander Knapp[1], Nora Koch[1,3], and Andreas Schroeder[1]

[1] Ludwig-Maximilians-Universität München, Germany
[2] University of Edinburgh, United Kingdom
[3] F.A.S.T. GmbH, Germany

**Abstract.** Service-oriented computing is an emerging paradigm where services are understood as autonomous, platform-independent computational entities that can be described, published, categorised, discovered, and dynamically assembled for developing massively distributed, interoperable, evolvable systems and applications. The IST-FET Integrated Project SENSORIA aims at developing a novel comprehensive approach to the engineering of service-oriented software systems where foundational theories, techniques and methods are fully integrated in a pragmatic software engineering approach. In this paper we present first ideas for the SENSORIA semantic-based development of service-oriented systems. This includes service-oriented extensions to the UML, a mathematical basis formed by a family of process calculi, a language for expressing context-dependent soft constraints and preferences, qualitative and quantitative analysis methods, and model transformations from UML to process calculi. The results are illustrated by a case study in the area of automotive systems.

## 1 Introduction

Service-oriented computing is an emerging paradigm where services are understood as autonomous, platform-independent computational entities that can be described, published, categorised, discovered, and dynamically assembled for developing massively distributed, interoperable, evolvable systems and applications. These characteristics pushed service-oriented computing towards nowadays widespread success, demonstrated by the fact that many large companies invested a lot of efforts and resources to promote service delivery on a variety of computing platforms, mostly through the Internet in the form of Web services. Tomorrow, there will be a plethora of new services as required for e-government, e-business, and e-science, and other areas within the rapidly evolving Information Society. These services will run over "global computers", i.e., computational infrastructures available globally and able to provide uniform services with variable guarantees for communication, co-operation and mobility, resource usage, security policies and mechanisms, etc., with particular regard to exploiting their universal scale and the programmability of their services.

The aim of IST-FET Integrated Project SENSORIA is to develop a novel comprehensive approach to the engineering of service-oriented software systems where foundational theories, techniques and methods are fully integrated in a pragmatic software

---

* This work has been partially sponsored by the project SENSORIA, IST-2005-016004.

E. Najm et al. (Eds.): FORTE 2006, LNCS 4229, pp. 24–45, 2006.

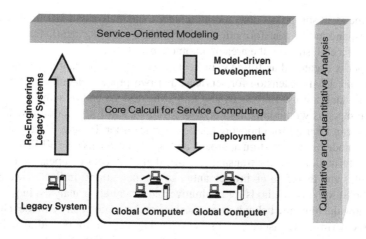

**Fig. 1.** The SENSORIA approach to service-oriented systems development

engineering approach. This includes a new generalised concept of service, new semantically well-defined modelling and programming primitives for services, new powerful mathematical analysis and verification techniques and tools for system behaviour and quality of service properties, and novel model-based transformation and development techniques.

In the envisaged software development process, services are modelled in a platform-independent architectural design layer; by using model transformations, these models are then transformed and refined to the service computing platform of SENSORIA which, in turn, can be used for generating implementations over different global computing platforms in a (semi-)automated way. On the other hand, legacy code is transformed systematically into service oriented software models (see Fig. 1).

The added value of SENSORIA to this widely used process comes from the deep mathematical foundations and their associated analysis methods. A typical scenario could be as follows: A service engineer will write her design of a service-oriented system for global computing in a precisely defined specialisation of UML for services on global computers. This UML extension will be carefully designed to be automatically connected with well-defined mathematical models of global computing services. These models come with mathematical theories, techniques and tools for analysing their qualitative and quantitative properties such as performance, security, costs, mobility, and distribution. By automatic translation of the analysis results back to UML the service engineer will get direct feedback on her system design from the mathematical models and can revise her models accordingly. Then she can use again mathematically well-founded transformation and refinement techniques for constructing the implementation or she can use the SENSORIA analysis techniques for checking the appropriateness of the offered or discovered services of other parties. She could also adopt the re-engineering techniques of SENSORIA for bringing legacy code in a service compatible format.

In this paper we present first ideas for the SENSORIA semantic-based development of service-oriented systems. This includes service-oriented extensions to the UML, a mathematical basis formed by a family of process calculi, a language for expressing context-dependent soft constraints and preferences, qualitative and quantitative analysis methods, and model transformations from UML to process calculi. The results are illustrated by a case study in the area of automotive systems.

The paper is organised as follows: In Sect. 2 we present the running example, (an excerpt of) the UML extension for services, and two process calculi PEPA [22] and Sagas [13] which are used for analysing the UML designs and as semantic basis for service transactions with compensation. Moreover, we show how soft constraints and preferences can be used for choosing the best service offer. In Sect. 3 we present the SENSORIA model transformation approach and show how we use the VIATRA2 [37,2] model transformation tool for translating UML diagrams with compensation into the Saga calculus and therefore giving semantics to compensations. In Sect. 4 we present some of the SENSORIA methods for qualitative and quantitative analysis; in particular, we show how the dynamic behaviour of a service orchestration can be model checked, and how the performance aspects of a service level agreement for providing help in an accident scenario can be analysed. We conclude the paper in Sect. 5 with some remarks on further SENSORIA results.

## 2  Languages for Service-Oriented Systems

Current service description and composition languages such as WSDL [40] and BPEL [9] are tailored to specific technological platforms such as Web Services and the Grid, and address low-level concerns.

The languages that have emerged for composing services into business processes such as WSFL [17], BizTalk [7], WSCI [39] and, most prominently, BPEL and BPEL4WS [10] have limited expressive power. They offer restricted support for concurrency and distribution and are mainly oriented towards programming workflows, making use of interconnection mechanisms that are far too rigid to support modelling business processes at the more abstract architectural layers.

SENSORIA aims at the definition of platform independent linguistic primitives for modelling and programming global service-oriented systems. Language primitives for services and their interactions are developed on two different abstraction levels, at the architectural design level and at the programming abstraction level for service overlay computing. The scientific tools used for the definition of programming-level primitives are category theory, process algebra and calculi as well as logics and constraints. A UML (Unified Modelling Language) [30] extension to service-oriented modelling makes the formal approaches available for practitioners and is the basis for many SENSORIA verification techniques. An additional soft-constraint-based language for service selection allows the declarative specification of orchestrations.

### 2.1  Automotive Case Study

Today's embedded computers in cars can access communication networks like the Internet and thereby provide a variety of new services for cars and drivers. A set of possible scenarios of the automotive domain are examined within the scope of the SENSORIA project, among which we select a car repair and an accident assistance scenario for illustrating the different techniques presented in this article.

In the car repair scenario, the diagnostic system reports a severe failure in the car engine so that the car is no longer drivable. The car's discovery system identifies garages, car rentals and towing truck services in the car's vicinity. The in-vehicle service platform selects a set of adequate offers taking into account personalised policies and preferences of the driver and tries to order them. We assume that the owner of the car has to deposit a security payment before being able to order services.

In the accident assistance scenario, the car's airbag is deployed after an accident. This causes the safety system to report the car's location to a accident report centre. This centre attempts to determine the severity of the accident and take appropriate actions.

## 2.2 Language for Service Orchestration

In the car repair scenario, it is necessary to invoke services in a specific order. It is not possible, e.g., to order any service before the security payment was deposited. Similarly, when undoing orders of repair assistance services, the security payment may be returned only after all orders were cancelled. That is to say, compensations of executed sequential forward actions must be performed in reverse order.

To address such compensation scenarios within SENSORIA, Bruni et al. [13] defined a calculus to provide a first semantic basis for service orchestration (a more elaborated calculus is under development). This calculus builds upon sagas [18], which is a formalism for long running transactions (LRT) with compensations initially developed for database systems. LRTs are transactions that require a very long time to complete (e.g. hours or days). In such cases, traditional database techniques to guarantee the ACID property, such as locking resources, are not suitable. Instead, sagas allow the specification of compensation actions which are installed dynamically when forward actions succeed.

As service orchestrations must be able to handle LRTs, most orchestration languages allow the specification of compensation actions. Hence, the saga calculus is a suitable semantic basis for service orchestrations. Within the calculus, one can specify compensation (%), sequential (;) and parallel (|) composition of actions, as well as sub-transactions ([ ]). The semantics of sub-transactions is elegant for the specification of orchestrations: if a sub-transaction fails and compensates successfully, the sub-transaction is considered successful. If the enclosing transaction fails however, the sub-transaction is required to compensate as well. This allows the specification of dependencies between, e.g., ordering of services, or the continuation of processes although other parallel processes fail.

The compensation strategy defined by the calculus is interruption based, that is to say, if a parallel branch fails all other branches are interrupted and compensate immediately. They do not need to execute forward actions until their control flow joins. In sequential composition, the compensation order is required to be the inverse of the forward action ordering. For the car repair scenario for example, we assume that the garage appointment is ordered next to the security payment deposit. This leads to the specification

$$ChargeCreditCard \% RevokeCharge \; ;$$
$$OrderGarageAppointment \% CancelGarageAppointment$$

If the forward flow *ChargeCreditCard* ; *OrderGarageAppointment* fails, it is compensated by executing *CancelGarageAppointment* ; *RevokeCharge* in exactly that ordering, which is the behaviour required by the scenario specification.

The saga calculus supports further constructs such as nondeterministic choice, exception and failure handling, and by this covers the semantics of common orchestration language constructs (see [13] for more details).

## 2.3 Language for Quantitative Analysis

Performance Evaluation Process Algebra (PEPA) [22] is a high-level language for quantitative analysis of systems. PEPA is a *stochastic process algebra* which extends classical process algebras by associating a duration with each activity used in a PEPA model. Thus where classical process algebras such as CCS and CSP deal with instantaneous actions which abstract away from time PEPA has instead continuous-time activities whose durations are quantified by exponentially-distributed random variables. PEPA models describe finite-state systems and via the operational semantics of the language a PEPA model gives rise to a continuous-time finite-state stochastic process called a Markov chain.

Continuous-time Markov Chains (CTMCs) are amenable to solution using standard procedures of numerical linear algebra such as Gaussian elimination or conjugate gradient methods. These can be applied to find the compute the *steady-state* or *equilibrium* probability distribution over the model. From this it is straightforward to compute conventional performance measures such as utilisation or throughput.

More advanced tools [27,11] can perform *transient* analysis of the CTMC where one considers the probability distribution at a chosen instant of time. It is possible to use these results to perform more complex quantitative analysis such as computing *response time* measures and *first passage time quantiles* as used in service-level agreements.

The PEPA process algebra is a compact formal language with a small number of combinators. Components perform activities. Activities have a type and rate specified using *prefix* (.). Alternative behaviours can be composed in a *choice* (+). Parallel composition of components uses CSP-style synchronisation over a set of activity types ($\bowtie$). Private behaviour can be hidden (/).

## 2.4 UML Extension for Service Oriented Architectures

Within the SENSORIA approach services are modelled with UML. For the static aspects of service-oriented software systems, this representation effort ranges from rather simple, stereotyped language extensions for introducing services to more complicated structures like dependency relations between services and their contextual relationships to resources and legacy systems. The dynamic parts of service-oriented software, in particular orchestration and choreography of services are supported by developing primitives for interaction and activity modelling that take into account possible failures and quality-of-service aspects. The extensions will incorporate structural and behavioural as well as functional and non-functional notions.

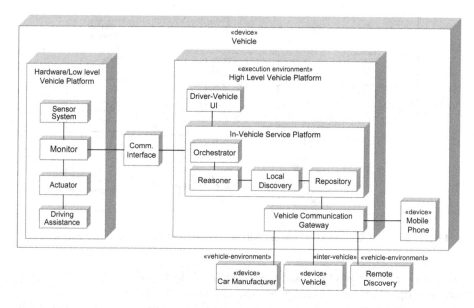

**Fig. 2.** Simplified architecture of car and car environment

The structure of a service oriented architecture can be visualised by UML deployment and composite structure diagrams. A deployment diagram is used to represent the—usually nested—nodes of the architecture, i.e. hardware devices or software execution environments. Fig. 2 shows a UML deployment diagram of the car and its environment as first approximation to an architecture model. The nodes are connected through communication paths that show the three types of communication that characterise the automotive domain: intra-vehicle communication, inter-vehicle communication, and communication among vehicle and environment such as communication with the car manufacturer or a remote discovery server. Note that the architecture comprises a local as well as a remote discovery service in order to find services in the local repository.

**Modelling Structural Aspects.** Service oriented architectures are highly dynamic because services are only loosely coupled, i.e., a service often needs to be discovered before it is connected and can be disconnected at run-time as well. Hence, different modelling features are required to express evolving connections. In addition to UML deployment diagrams, which give a static view of the architecture, a representation showing the evolution of an architecture is required. Baresi, Heckel, Thöne and Varró propose the construction of models visualising the functional aspects encapsulated in business-related components [3]. We use these UML structure diagrams to represent the evolving connections within the service oriented architecture of the vehicle and its environment. Fig. 3 shows the car internal components, a temporary connection to the discovery service of the car manufacturer, and a remote service (car rental) which knows the remote service discovery and will (later) publish its description to the remote service discovery. Other remote services such as tow truck and garage and their relationship to the discovery service can be modelled analogously. After publishing, the

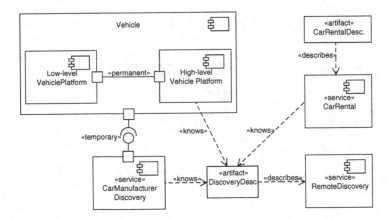

**Fig. 3.** Car components modelled with UML extension for SOA before service publishing

discovery service knows the description of the published services, so that it can pass these descriptions to service requesters at service discovery time.

Three different types of connections are identified: discovery connection, permanent connection (as in modelling of non service oriented architectures) and temporary connections. For more details about the last two types the reader is referred to [3]. The discovery connection is based on the information provided by a discovery service.

We can observe these three types of connections in the service oriented vehicle architecture. In order to be invoked services need to be discovered before the binding to the car's on-board system takes place. This type of connection using a discovery process is visualised with a «knows» stereotyped dependency, see Fig. 3. A temporary connection from the car on-board system to the car manufacturer discovery service is graphically represented by a UML connector with interfaces. For a permanent service we select a UML connector without interfaces as shown between components within the vehicle in Fig. 3.

Three components are involved in the execution of service orderings: a service discovery which may be local or external to the car, a reasoner for service selection and a service orchestrator, see Fig. 4.

**Modelling Behavioural Aspects.** The most interesting aspect when modelling the behaviour of a service oriented system is the workflow describing the orchestration of services. Modelling orchestration of services includes specifying non-functional properties of services such as performance and resource consumption, and also modelling transactional business processes that may require a very long period of time in order to complete. As discussed above, the key technique to handle long running transactions is to install compensations which are not directly available in UML.

We start with the modelling of the accident assistance scenario. The accident assistance scenario is concerned with road traffic accidents and dispatch of medical assistance to crash victims. Drivers wishing to use the service must have in-car GPS location tracking devices with communication capabilities and have pre-registered their mobile phone information with the service. If a road traffic accident occurs, the deployment of

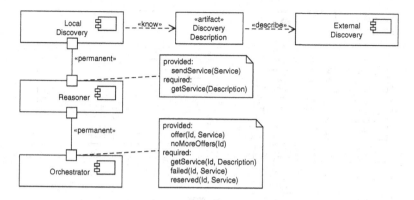

**Fig. 4.** Components for executing service orderings and their ports

the car airbag causes the on-board safety system to report the car's current location (obtained by GPS) to a pre-established accident report endpoint which in turn attempts to call the registered driver's mobile phone. If there is no answer to the call then medical assistance is dispatched to the reported location of the car (presuming that the driver has been incapacitated by injuries sustained in the accident).

We model this scenario in UML as state machine; to represent quantitative aspects (e.g., answer time) we use stereotypes to attach rates to transitions, see Fig. 5. Fig 6 explains the meaning of the rates.

Regarding the modelling of the second scenario, "car repair", the main focus lies on the specification of an appropriate transactional business process. As discussed in section 2.2, such a business process contains both forward actions and compensations. As UML activity diagrams lack such compensations, we define a set of modelling primitives and corresponding stereotypes for UML activity diagrams.

- Saga is an executable activity node that may have subordinate nodes as an ActivityGroup with the ability to compensate long running transactions.
- CompensableAction specialises UML Action to own exactly one pair of actions (forward action and compensation action).

To provide a more intuitive representation, both forward and compensation actions are drawn separated by a line within CompensableAction instances, although this is not completely UML compliant. The metamodel depicted in Fig. 7 shows how these compensation elements are related to UML elements StructuredActivityNode, ActivityNode and Action.

With these extensions, the orchestration for the car repair scenario can be compactly formulated (Fig. 8). In the modelled business process, the driver's credit card is charged with the security deposit payment, which will be revoked if ordering the services failed. Then, a garage appointment is searched for. The appointment with the garage will give coordinates to tow the broken down car to, and also a location constraint that restricts the car rental agency that may be ordered. If ordering the car rental fails, the overall process does not fail, as the activity is enclosed in a sub-transaction. However, if ordering a tow truck fails the garage appointment has to be cancelled as well. For this reason, the

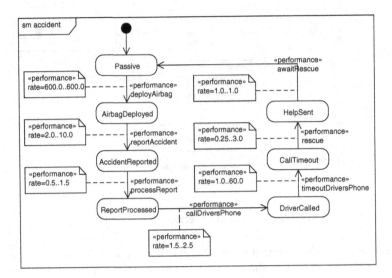

**Fig. 5.** State machine of the accident assistance scenario

| Rate | Value min | max | Meaning |
|------|-----------|-----|---------|
| $r_1$ | 600.0 | 600.0 | an airbag deploys in 1/10 of a second |
| $r_2$ | 2.0 | 10.0 | the car can transmit location data in 6 to 30 seconds |
| $r_3$ | 0.5 | 1.5 | it takes about one minute to register the incoming data |
| $r_4$ | 1.5 | 2.5 | it takes about thirty seconds to call the driver's phone |
| $r_5$ | 1.0 | 60.0 | give the driver from a second to one minute to answer |
| $r_6$ | 0.25 | 3.0 | vary about one minute to decide to dispatch medical help |
| $r_7$ | 1.0 | 1.0 | arbitrary value — the driver is now awaiting rescue |

**Fig. 6.** Table of minimum and maximum values of the rates from Fig. 5. All times are expressed in minutes. Thus a rate of 1.0 means that something happens once a minute (on average). A rate of 6.0 means that the associated activity happens six times a minute on average, or that its mean or expected duration is ten seconds, which is an equivalent statement.

orchestrator will try to order a tow truck service until either no more service offers are found or the ordering succeeds. If ordering a tow truck fails the rental car delivery will be redirected to the driver's actual location.

It is obviously possible to model the same orchestration with a plain UML activity diagram, and handle compensations as exceptions (Fig. 9). This requires explicit programming of the compensations and the conditions under which they are executed. In addition to actions, activities and control nodes, the specification requires an InterruptibleActivityRegion in order to terminate all active and pending activities of the region in case an interruption occurs. Even in this simple scenario, this approach requires the verification of three conditions. For larger scenarios the diagram's complexity will increase and its usefulness will decrease rapidly. Furthermore, it is difficult to explicitly model the silent failure of the car rental.

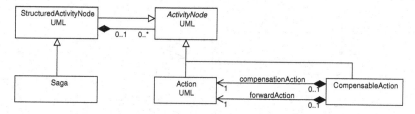

**Fig. 7.** UML extension for sagas

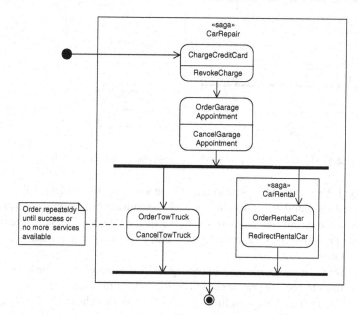

**Fig. 8.** Modelling car repair workflow with UML extension for sagas

## 2.5   Soft Constraints for Selecting the Best Service

In many cases service-oriented systems can utilise different combinations of services to achieve their goals. These combinations differ in functional and non-functional aspects like cost, reliability or performance. The reasoning component (cf. Fig. 4) of a service-oriented system decides how the available services are orchestrated so that the best compromise between different goals of the system is achieved. Soft constraints are a promising way to specify and implement reasoning mechanisms. In the case study, soft constraints are used for service selection only.

Soft constraints are an extension of classical constraints to deal with non-functional requirements, over-constrained problems and preferences. Instead of determining just a subset of admissible domain elements, a soft constraint assigns a grade—to be chosen from a set of finite or infinitely many "preference" values—to each element of the application domain. Bistarelli, Montanari and Rossi [6,5] have developed a very elegant semiring based theory of soft constraints where many different kinds of soft constraints can be represented and combined in a uniform way over so-called constraint semirings

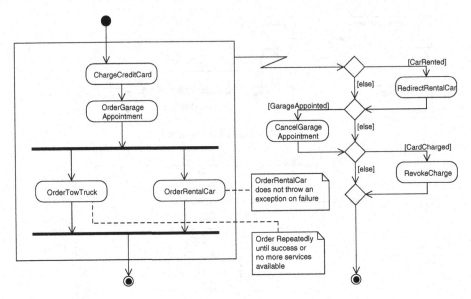

**Fig. 9.** Modelling car repair workflow with plain UML activity diagrams

(*c-semirings*). Examples for c-semirings are the semiring of Boolean values *Bool* or the "fuzzy natural numbers" *FuzzyNat*. The *Bool* semiring can be used to express hard constraints in the c-semiring framework; in the *FuzzyNat* semiring the value 0 is used to represent inadmissible solutions, higher values are used to represent increasingly preferred solutions.

In SENSORIA we are developing a language which extends the c-semiring approach with possibilities to specify preferences between constraints and to vary the constraints according to a *context*. This simplifies the description of behaviours of systems in a dynamically changing environment and with complex trade-offs between conflicting properties.

A context is an expression in a suitable logic (e.g., predicate logic or temporal logic) which can serve as a guard for a constraint. For example, the distance to the destination might determine whether the quick availability of a rental car is important or not. In this case, "*distance* < 20km" is a context that can restrict the applicability of a constraint to situations where we are close to our destination. Variables appearing in contexts are called *context variables*; variables appearing free in constraints but not in contexts are called *controlled variables*. In the car repair scenario the context variables will contain, among others, the distance to our destination, the time remaining until the appointment starts, or whether the journey is work related. The controlled variables represent properties of offers. Each offer is identified by a serial number (*offer-nr*), and other controlled variables are used to specify cost or quality of the offers, see Fig. 10.

A soft constraint is a mapping from (domains of) controlled variables into a c-semiring. An expression of the constraint language consists of (1) a set of labelled conditional rules where the constraints contained in the head of the rule depend on the guard, and (2) a set of conditional inequalities between constraint labels which specify preferences between constraints.

| Name | Type | Domain | Meaning |
|------|------|--------|---------|
| *distance* | *context* | $\mathbb{R}^+$ | The distance remaining to the target location (in km) |
| $\Delta_t$ | *context* | $\mathbb{N}$ | The time until the appointment starts (in minutes) |
| *work-related?* | *context* | $\mathbb{B}$ | Is the appointment work-related? |
| *offer-nr* | *controlled* | $\mathbb{N}$ | The unique serial number of an offer |
| *rental-car-cost* | *controlled* | $\mathbb{R}^+$ | The cost of the rental car in Euros |
| *rental-car-availability* | *controlled* | $\mathbb{N}$ | The estimated availability time of the rental car |
| *garage-cost* | *controlled* | $\mathbb{R}^+$ | The cost of the garage (in Euros) |
| *garage-duration* | *controlled* | $\mathbb{N}$ | The estimated duration that the garage needs for the repair (in hours) |

**Fig. 10.** Examples for context variables and controlled variables

In the car repair scenario we maintain hard constraints named *towTruckOffers*, *rental-CarOffers* and *garageOffers* containing disjunctions of the offers that the reasoner obtained from the discovery mechanism. If a new offer is provided to the reasoner the corresponding constraint or constraints are extended by another term.

Other constraints specify the preferences of the users. These constraints are soft constraints, for simplicity we use the fuzzy natural numbers as the domain of all these constraints.

This constraint prefers garages that can repair the car as quickly as possible:

$$fastRepair : [garage\text{-}duration \mid n \mapsto \lfloor 48/n \rfloor]$$

We also may want the repair to be done cheaply, but only if we are paying ourselves. Repairs costing more that 1000 Euros are still acceptable, but only barely.

$$cheapRepair : \textbf{in context } \neg work\text{-}related?$$
$$\textbf{assert } [garage\text{-}cost \mid n \mapsto \lceil 1000/n \rceil] \textbf{ end}$$

We are content to use any kind of car for short distances as long as it is cheap. In this case a cost of more than 100 Euros per day is unacceptable as the constraint evaluates to 0.

$$shortDistance1 : \textbf{in context } distance < 20\text{km}$$
$$\textbf{assert } [rental\text{-}car\text{-}cost \mid n \mapsto \lfloor 100/n \rfloor] \textbf{ end}$$

The following constraint means that we want to obtain a car as quickly as possible if the appointment is work-related, the distance is short and we have limited time to go to the appointment. If the rental car takes longer than $\Delta_t$ minutes we regard the offer as unacceptable. In this constraint the preference value depends on the context as $\Delta_t$ appears in the computation of a value.

$$shortDistance2 : \textbf{in context } work\text{-}related?$$
$$\wedge\, distance < 20\text{km} \wedge \Delta_t < 60\text{min}$$
$$\textbf{assert } [rental\text{-}car\text{-}availability \mid (n \mapsto \lfloor \Delta_t/n \rfloor)] \textbf{ end}$$

When determining the configuration of a system we might not consider all constraints to be equally important. For example, it might be most important that the car is repaired both quickly and cheaply, and that we consider the other constraints only if we have several offers that are equal in that respect. This can be expressed by taking the product of the grades computed by both constraints. On the other hand, we consider *shortDistance1* and *shortDistance2* to be incomparable, i.e., we compare the grades of these constraints individually and do not compute a combined value.

$$fastRepair * cheapRepair > shortDistance1, shortDistance2$$
$$shortDistance1, shortDistance2 > fastRepair$$
$$fastRepair > cheapRepair$$

From a set of constraints and preferences the reasoner can compute either the best solutions, or a set of all solutions that are better than a certain threshold. Two techniques that are used for solving soft constraint systems are branch and bound search [38] and dynamic programming [5].

## 3   Model Transformation

### 3.1   Use of Model Transformation in SENSORIA

In the field of service oriented computing, there is a large gain from using model transformation languages, since data formats from different services can be easily mapped to each other with the help of model transformation languages.

Model transformation is used in SENSORIA for several tasks such as e.g. model refinement, deployment, and model analysis. "Refinement" uses model transformations to add additional details to the model, and remove degrees of freedom left in the initial model, trading abstraction for determinism. In SENSORIA we see "deployment" as a special refinement mapping models from the SENSORIA platform level to platform specific software artifacts. This use of model transformations is similar to the transformation from PIMs to PSMs in the MDA approach [28]. Finally, "model analysis" uses model transformations to translate models to logics or languages tailor-made for model analysis, such as process algebras. With the help of these specific models, different crucial qualitative and quantitative properties of the modelled service oriented software system can be verified. Furthermore, model transformations can be used to back-annotate the initial model with analysis results provided by analysis tools. Thus, the fact that analysis is performed on an internal representation can be made transparent to the modeller.

There are several existing model transformation tools and frameworks, some of which are MOF QVT [31], ATLAS ATL [25] and IBM MTF [29]. Unfortunately, all of them have at best a partially defined formal semantics, which makes the use in semantic based engineering hard. Furthermore, MOF QVT still lacks an implementation.

The SENSORIA project comprises two model transformation languages, one with a pragmatic and easy usable programming model (VIATRA2) and one based on a declarative model with strong mathematical foundations (AGG). By having both languages, SENSORIA covers both pragmatical and formal mathematical approaches to model transformations.

VIATRA2 [37,2] (Visual Automated Model Transformations) is a model transformation language supporting graph transformation rules and imperative abstract state

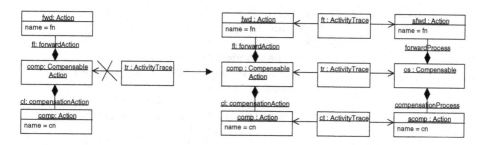

**Fig. 11.** Graph transformation rule for compensable actions

machine (ASM)-like code. VIATRA2 is a fully hybrid language since it allows to call graph transformation rules from imperative code through rule application calls, and also to call ASM code from declarative graph transformation rules. Nevertheless, VIATRA2 delivers a formal semantics of transformations along with the language. A big advantage of VIATRA2 over other solutions is that it offers a good combination of both imperative code with declarative graph patterns, as imperative constructs ease programming complex transformations considerably [19]. A recursive processing of the source model can be easily intertwined with graph transformation steps. In this way, the advantages from both the declarative and the imperative approach can be brought together.

AGG [1] (Attributed Graph Grammar System) uses an algebraic model transformation approach based on attributed graphs grammars. AGG has a strong mathematical basis in category theory, and follows a more declarative approach to transformation, which allows for easy mathematical analysis of transformation properties.

A graph transformation rule in both VIATRA2 and AGG consists of a left hand side and right hand side. The left hand side specifies the conditions under which the rule applies. The right hand side specifies which changes are made to the model if the rule applies. These changes reuse variables bound in the precondition and manipulates or remove the model elements to which the variables are bound (see, e.g., Fig. 11).

## 3.2 Model Transformation Examples

We discuss two examples of model transformation use in SENSORIA. The first, which was implemented in VIATRA2, shows how UML activity diagrams can be transformed to saga expressions. The activity diagram from the car repair scenario, Fig. 8, is transformed into the following corresponding sagas expression:

$[ChargeCreditCard \% RevokeCharge ;$
$OrderGarageAppointment \% CancelGarageAppointment ;$
$(OrderTowTruck \% CancelTowTruck \ | \ [OrderRentalCar\%RedirectRentalCar])]$

The abstract syntax tree of this expression is created via a VIATRA2 model transformation. We will now give a brief overview of the transformation implementation.

In the UML activity to sagas transformation example, all compensable actions are translated to simple sagas expressions with graph transformation rules (see Fig. 11).

```
rule nodeToSagas(in StartNode, out EndNode, out Sagas) =
    try choose with find p_activityNode(StartNode) do
        try choose NextNode
                with find p_nextNode(StartNode, NextNode) do
            try choose with find p_parseableNode(NextNode) do
                call handleSequence(StartNode, NextNode,
                                        EndNode, Sagas);
            else call handleActivity(StartNode, NextNode,
                                        EndNode, Sagas);
        else fail;
    else try choose with find p_sagaNode(StartNode) do
        call handleSagaNode(StartNode, EndNode, Sagas);
    else try choose with find p_parallelStartNode(StartNode) do
        call handleParallelNode(StartNode, EndNode, Sagas);
    else try choose with find p_finalNode(StartNode) do
        call handleFinalNode(StartNode, EndNode, Sagas);
    else
        call handleNOP(StartNode, EndNode, Sagas);
```

**Fig. 12.** Pattern Matching Dispatch. Called rules call nodeToSagas recursively

Non-compensable actions are translated with a similar graph transformation rule. These rules are called as long as applicable. Note that the creation of a trace prevents the repeated application of the rule (A second rule creates actions for activity nodes without compensations).

In a second step, the parallel nodes, nested sagas as well as sequential edges between activity nodes are translated into parallel, saga and sequence expressions respectively. This is done with a recursive imperative rule, since the transformation is complex in nature: saga's parallel expressions may be nested arbitrarily. Starting from the initial node, a node is transformed into a prefix of a saga expression and a recursive rule call is performed on successor nodes to transform the remaining subgraph. Different cases are distinguished by pattern matching (see Fig. 12). All names starting with p_ denote patterns to be matched, while names starting with handle denote imperative rules which call nodeToSagas recursively. After this second step terminates successfully, the transformation is complete.

Another example for the use of model transformations is the transformation from UML state and communication diagrams to PEPA. PEPA is, as elaborated above, an algebra for performance analysis. It is possible to extract PEPA models by model transformation from UML state and communication diagrams.

## 4    Qualitative and Quantitative Analysis

Qualitative and quantitative analysis methods for software systems aim at providing transparent support for the designer throughout the software construction phases based right on those notations used in development. However, proving the correctness of a design or measuring the performance, in general, relies on mathematical models and tool support that are not offered on the level of general software development notations, let alone using specialised extensions for particular domains. In SENSORIA, model transformations are employed to lift methods and tools from the well-founded, abstract, mathematical level to the concrete UML-based design level for service-oriented architectures. Furthermore, backward transformations project analysis results, delivered in terms of the underlying mathematical model, back to modelling notation (cf. section 3). We demonstrate how model checking (qualitative analysis) and performance evaluation (quantitative analysis) are applied to the automotive case study.

## 4.1   Model Checking Orchestration

The orchestration of services, like in the extended UML activity diagram description in Fig. 8, has to be implemented in an *orchestrator*. We transform the saga-based model into a conventional UML state machine model which details the handling of service allocation and compensation. Using model checking we can prove that the implementation model indeed preserves the compensation properties of the original UML model.

The state machine in Fig. 13 describes an implementation of the car repair workflow as depicted in Fig. 8. It relies on a *reasoner* for choosing services as in Fig. 4. The general idea of the implementation is that every service needed is first requested from the reasoner (getService). If the reasoner delivers an offer (offer) in a certain amount of time (after(T)), the service first is reserved and ordered afterwards. If the reasoner misses the deadline, or the reservation or the ordering fail the orchestrator terminates. In the latter cases the reasoner is informed of the failure (fail) such that it can avoid offering a failing service again. During the reservation phase the reasoner may send better offers for the requested service (offer). If a service can be reserved eventually, the reasoner is notified (reserved) and the offer is ordered. The compensation handling is done using a global compensation handler, like suggested by the UML activity diagram description in Fig. 9.

For the services "charge credit card", "order tow truck", and "order car rental", however, different implementation details are to be realised: On the one hand, the credit card charge need not be reserved; this is an implementation decision. Ordering the tow truck has been marked as to be done repeatedly until no more offers are available. Thus every possible offer has to be checked, that is, previous reservations may have to be compensated in the orchestration process (compensateReservation). Finally, the car rental may or may not fail without calling for overall compensation, as it is marked as a nested ≪saga≫.

In SENSORIA different tools are available for verifying the correct behaviour of the orchestrator implementation. The UML model checker UMC [35] (developed by ISTI) offers the verification of temporal properties described in the $\mu$-calculus directly on UML state machine. The UML model checking tool Hugo/RT [23] (developed by LMU) translates UML state machines and collaborations into different off-the-shelf model checkers like Spin [34] and UPPAAL [36] and also supports Java and SystemC code generation. Here, we used the UPPAAL option of Hugo/RT. By instrumenting the model, which we will not detail here, we checked, e.g., that whenever the global final state is reached all services indeed have been ordered; if an order fails all orders and reservations which have been done up to the point of failure of getting a service—i.e.,

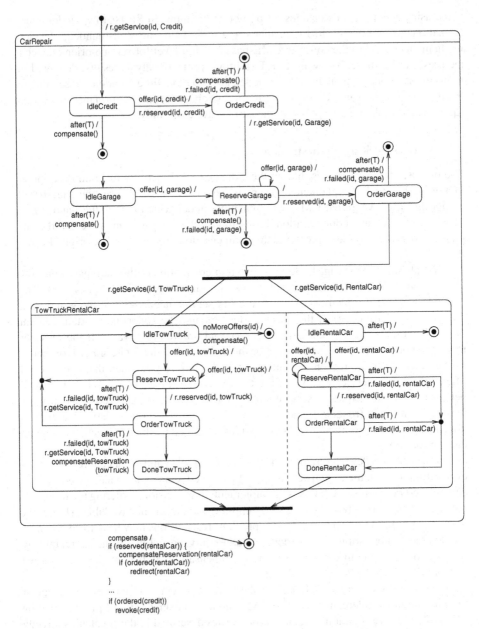

**Fig. 13.** Implementation state machine for car repair workflow

when one of the final states inside CarRepair is entered—are compensated. After behaviour verification, we have used Hugo/RT for generating Java code from the very same model that has been verified by UPPAAL.

## 4.2   Quantitative Analysis of the Accident Scenario

In this section we consider the assessment of a service level agreement offered by an automotive collision support service. The scenario with which these systems are concerned is road traffic accidents and dispatch of medical assistance to crash victims.

The Choreographer design platform [14] (developed by the DEGAS project [24]) can perform quantitative analysis via PEPA which starts and ends with UML models. A PEPA model is extracted from a UML model decorated with rate information such as the one shown in Fig. 5. This model is compiled into a CTMC and solved for its steady-state probability distribution. The results from this analysis are reflected back into a modified version of the input UML model with the quantitative analysis results recorded on the state diagrams in the model. Here we use the more computationally expensive but more informative method of transient analysis of the underlying CTMC and focus on the analysis of the PEPA model.

We represent in the model the sequence of events which begins with the deployment of the airbag after the crash and finishes with the dispatch of the medical response team. The first phase of the sequence is concerned with relaying the information to the remote service, reporting the accident. When the diagnostic report from the car is received the service processes the report and matches it to the driver information stored on their database.

$$Car_1 \stackrel{def}{=} (airbag, r_1).Car_2$$
$$Car_2 \stackrel{def}{=} (reportToService, r_2).Car_3$$
$$Car_3 \stackrel{def}{=} (processReport, r_3).Car_4$$

The second phase of this passage through the system focuses on the attempted dialogue between the service and the registered driver of the car. We consider the case where the driver does not answer the incoming call because this is the case which leads to the medical response team being sent.

$$Car_4 \stackrel{def}{=} (callDriversPhone, r_4).Car_5$$
$$Car_5 \stackrel{def}{=} (timeoutDriversPhone, r_5).Car_6$$

The service makes a final check on the execution of the procedure before the decision is taken to send medical help. At this stage the driver is awaiting rescue.

$$Car_6 \stackrel{def}{=} (rescue, r_6).Car_7$$
$$Car_7 \stackrel{def}{=} (awaitRescue, r_7).Car_1$$

We assess the service against the following compound service level agreement(SLA):

At least 40% of airbag deployments lead to medical help being sent within five minutes and at least 80% of airbag deployments lead to medical help being sent within ten minutes.

We assess this SLA using the passage-time quantile computation capabilities provided by the ipc/Hydra tool chain [11]. We vary rates $r_2$ to $r_6$ across five or six possible values leading to $5 \times 5 \times 5 \times 5 \times 6 = 3750$ experiments to be performed. The graphs of computed probability against experiment number for time bounds of five minutes and ten minutes for all 3750 experiments are shown in Fig. 14. Using both of these graphs we determine that the SLA is met across the values of the rates of the model.

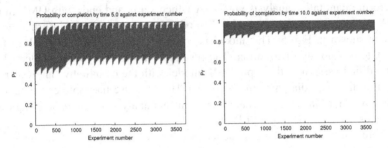

**Fig. 14.** Graph of probability of completing the passage from airbag deployment to medical assistance within five minutes and ten minutes plotted against experiment number over all 3750 experiments

We now consider how the cumulative distribution function for the passage from airbag deployment to dispatch of medical assistance is affected as the values of the rates $r_2$ to $r_6$ are varied as specified in the table in Fig. 6. The results for $r_2$ and $r_6$ are presented in Fig. 15.

These results show that variations in upstream rates (near the start of the passage of interest) such as $r_2$, $r_3$ and $r_4$ have less impact overall than variations in downstream rates (near the end of the passage of interest) such as $r_5$ and $r_6$. This is true even when the scale over which the upstream rates are varied is much more than the scale over which the downstream rates are varied (contrast variation in $r_2$ against variation in $r_6$).

The conclusion to be drawn from such an observation is that, if failing to meet a desired quality of service specified in an SLA then it is better to expend effort in making a faster decision to dispatch medical help (governed by rate $r_6$) than to expend effort in trying to transmit location data faster (governed by rate $r_2$), over the range of variability in the rates considered in the present study.

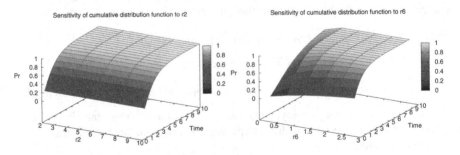

**Fig. 15.** Graphs of cumulative distribution function sensitivity to changes in rates for the passage from airbag deployment to dispatch of medical assistance

# 5   Concluding Remarks

In this paper we have presented some of the first results of the SENSORIA semantic-based development of service-oriented systems. We have shown service-oriented extensions to the UML, a first mathematical basis formed by process calculi such as PEPA and the saga calculus, a language for expressing soft constraints and preferences of services, qualitative and quantitative methods for analysing service orchstrations and service level agreements, and model transformations from UML to process calculi.

But these results represent only a small part of the SENSORIA project. In addition, the SENSORIA project is developing a comprehensive service ontology and a (SENSORIA) Reference Modelling Language (SRML) [16] for supporting service-oriented modelling at high levels of abstraction of "business" or "domain" architectures (similar to the aims of the service component architecture SCA [33]). To provide semantic foundations to the dynamic behaviour of services a new process calculus SCC [8] has been designed which features explicit notions of service definition, service invocation and session handling. Other research strands of SENSORIA comprise a probabilistic extension of a Linda-like language for service-oriented computing [12] and stochastic extensions of KLAIM [32] and beta-binders [15]. SENSORIA addresses security issues ranging from sandboxing for KLAIM [21], trust management for autonomic grid services [26], and security of service composition [4] to a formal framework for security and trust in the requirements phase of system development [20].

Moreover, SENSORIA is developing a model-driven approach for service-oriented software engineering and a suite of tools and techniques for deploying service-oriented systems and for re-engineering of legacy software into services. By integrating and further developing these results SENSORIA will achieve its overall aim: a comprehensive and pragmatic but theoretically well founded approach to software engineering for service-oriented systems.

# References

1. The Attributed Graph Grammar System (AGG). tfs.cs.tu-berlin.de/agg. Last visited: June 2006.
2. András Balogh and Dániel Varró. Advanced Model Transformation Language Constructs in the VIATRA2 Framework. In *Proc. ACM Symp. Applied Computing (SAC 2006) — Model Transformation Track*, 2006. To appear.
3. Luciano Baresi, Reiko Heckel, Sebastian Thöne, and Dániel Varró. Style-based Modelling and Refinement of Service-oriented Architectures. *Softw. Sys. Model.*, 2006. To appear.
4. M. Bartoletti, P. Degano, and Ferrari G.L. Security Issues in Service Composition. In *Proc. 8th IFIP International Conference on Formal Methods for Open Object-Based Distributed Systems (FMOODS)*, LNCS, 2006.
5. Stefano Bistarelli. *Semirings for Soft Constraint Solving and Programming*. LNCS 2962. Springer, Berlin, 2004.
6. Stefano Bistarelli, Ugo Montanari, and Francesca Rossi. Semiring-based constraint satisfaction and optimization. *J. ACM*, 44(2):201–236, 1997.
7. Microsoft BizTalk Server. www.microsoft.com/biztalk. Last visited: June 2006.
8. Michele Boreale, Roberto Bruni, Rocco DeNicola, Ivan Lanese, Michele Loreti, Ugo Montanari, Davide Sangiorgi, and Gianluigi Zavattaro. SCC: a Service Centered Calculus. Deliverable 2.2, SENSORIA, 2006.

9. Business Process Execution Language (BPEL). www.oasis-open.org. Last visited: June 2006.

10. BPEL for Web Services. www6.software.ibm.com/software/developer/library/ws-bpel.pdf. Last visited: June 2006.

11. Jeremy T. Bradley and William J. Knottenbelt. The ipc/HYDRA tool chain for the analysis of PEPA models. In *Proc. 1st Int. Conf. on the Quantitative Evaluation of Systems (QEST 2004)*, pages 334–335, Enschede, Netherlands, September 2004.

12. Mario Bravetti and Gianluigi Zavattaro. Service Oriented Computing from a Process Algebraic Perspective. *Journal of Logic and Algebraice Programming*, 2005. To appear.

13. Roberto Bruni, Hernan Melgratti, and Ugo Montanari. Theoretical Foundations for Compensations in Flow Composition Languages. In *Proc. 32nd ACM SIGPLAN-SIGACT Symp. Principles of Programming Languages (POPL'05)*, pages 209–220. ACM, 2004.

14. Mikael Buchholtz, Stephen Gilmore, Valentin Haenel, and Carlo Montangero. End-to-end integrated security and performance analysis on the DEGAS Choreographer platform. In I.J. Hayes J.S. Fitzgerald and A. Tarlecki, editors, *Proc. of the Int. Symposium of Formal Methods Europe (FM 2005)*, LNCS 3582, pages 286–301. Springer-Verlag, June 2005.

15. P. Degano, D. Prandi, C. Priami, and P. Quaglia. Beta-binders for biological quantitative experiments. *Proc. 4th Workshop on Quantitative Aspects of Programming Languages, QAPL'06, Electronic Notes in Theoretical Computer Science*, 2006. To appear.

16. José Luiz Fiadeiro, Antónia Lopes, and Laura Bocchi. A Formal Approach to Service Component Architecture. In *In Proc. 3rd International Workshop on Web Services and Formal Methods (WS-FM 06). 8-9 September 2006, Vienna, Austria*, 2006. To appear.

17. Frank Leymann. Web Services Flow Language, version 1.0. Specification, IBM, 2001. www-306.ibm.com/software/solutions/webservices/pdf/WSFL.pdf.

18. Hector Garcia-Molina and Kenneth Salem. Sagas. In *SIGMOD '87: Proc. of ACM SIGMOD Int. Conf. on Management of Data*, pages 249–259, New York, 1987. ACM Press.

19. Tracy Gardner, Catherine Griffin, Jana Koehler, and Rainer Hauser. A Review of OMG MOF 2.0 Query/Views/Transformations Submissions and Recommendations towards the Final Standard. In *Proc. Wsh. MetaModelling for MDA Workshop*, York, 2003. www.omg.org/docs/ad/03-08-02.pdf.

20. Paolo Giorgini, Fabio Massacci, and Nicola Zannone. Security and Trust Requirements Engineering. In *Foundations of Security Analysis and Design III - Tutorial Lectures*, volume 3655 of *LNCS*, pages 237–272. Springer-Verlag GmbH, 2005.

21. René Rydhof Hansen, Christian W. Probst, and Flemming Nielson. Sandboxing in myKlaim. In *The First International Conference on Availability, Reliability and Security, ARES 2006*, 2006.

22. Jane Hillston. *A Compositional Approach to Performance Modelling*. Cambridge University Press, 1996.

23. UML Model Translator for Model Checking (Hugo/RT). www.pst.ifi.lmu.de/projekte/hugo. Last visited: June 2006.

24. IST-FET Global Computing I Initiative Project DEGAS. www.omnys.it/degas/. Last visited: June 2006.

25. Frédéric Jouault and Ivan Kurtev. Transforming Models with ATL. In *MoDELS Satellite Events*, LNCS, pages 128–138. Springer, Berlin, 2005.

26. H. Koshutanski, F. Martinelli, P. Mori, and A. Vaccarelli. Fine-grained and history-based access control with trust management for autonomic grid services. In *Proc. of Internat. Conf. on Autonomic and Autonomous Systems (ICAS06), IEEE Computer Society*, 2006.

27. Marta Kwiatkowska, Gethin Norman, and David Parker. PRISM: Probabilistic symbolic model checker. In A.J. Field and P.G. Harrison, editors, *Proc. of the 12th Int. Conf. on Modelling Tools and Techniques for Computer and Communication System Performance Evaluation*, LNCS 2324, pages 200–204, London, UK, April 2002. Springer-Verlag.

28. Model Driven Architecture (OMG). www.omg.org/mda/. Last visited: June 2006.
29. Model Transformation Framework. www.alphaworks.ibm.com/tech/mtf. Last visited: June 2006.
30. Object Management Group (OMG). Unified Modeling Language: Superstructure, version 2.0. Specification, OMG, 2005. www.omg.org/cgi-bin/doc?formal/05-07-04.
31. Query/View/Transformation Specification Final Adopted Specification. www.omg.org/cgi-bin/doc?ptc/2005-11-01. Last visited: June 2006.
32. De Nicola R., Katoen J.P., Latella D., and Massink M. STOKLAIM: A Stochastic Extension of KLAIM. TR 2006-TR-01, ISTI, 2006.
33. SCA Consortium. Service Component Architecture, version 0.9. download.boulder.ibm.com/ibmdl/pub/software/dw/specs/ws-sca/SCA_White_Paper1_09.pdf. Specification, 2005. Last visited: June 2006.
34. SPIN Model Checker. www.spinroot.com. Last visited: June 2006.
35. Model Checker for UML Statechart Diagrams. fmt.isti.cnr.it/umc/. Last visited: June 2006.
36. UPPAAL Tool Environment. www.uppaal.com. Last visited: June 2006.
37. Dániel Varró and András Pataricza. Generic and Meta-Transformations for Model Transformation Engineering. In Thomas Baar et al., editor, *Proc. 7th Int. Conf. Unified Modeling Language (UML'04)*, LNCS 3273, pages 290–304. Springer, Berlin, 2004.
38. Martin Wirsing, Grit Denker, Carolyn Talcott, Andy Poggio, and Linda Briesemeister. A rewriting logic framework for soft constraints. In *WRLA 2006, 6th International Workshop on Rewriting Logic and its Applications*, April 2006. To appear in ENTCS, 2006.
39. Web Services Choreography Interface (WSCI). www.w3.org/TR/wsci. Last visited: June 2006.
40. Web Service Description Language (WSDL). www.w3.org/TR/wsdl. Last visited: June 2006.

# JSCL: A Middleware for Service Coordination*

Gianluigi Ferrari[1], Roberto Guanciale[2], and Daniele Strollo[1,2]

[1] Dipartimento di Informatica,
Università degli Studi di Pisa, Italy
{giangi, strollo}@di.unipi.it
[2] Istituto Alti Studi IMT Lucca, Italy
{roberto.guanciale, daniele.strollo}@imtlucca.it

**Abstract.** This paper describes the design and the prototype implementation of a middleware, called Java Signal Core Layer (JSCL), for coordinating distributed services. JSCL supports the coordination of distributed services by exploiting an *event notification* paradigm. The design and the implementation of JSCL has been inspired and driven by its formal specification given as a process calculus, the Signal Calculus (SC). At the experimental level JSCL has been exploited to implement Long Running Transactions (LRTs).

## 1   Introduction

One important challenge of the Software Engineering field is represented by the so called Service Oriented Architectures (SOAs) [20]. In the SOA approach applications are developed by coordinating the behavior of autonomous components distributed over an overlay network. Middleware for coordinating services are extremely important to the success of SOAs. Several research and implementation efforts are currently devoted to design and to implement middleware for coordinating distributes services (see ORC [18], BPEL [19], WS-CDL [23] and SIENA [12] to cite a few). However, research is still underway. The aim of this paper is to contribute to this theme of research by developing a middleware for coordinating services based upon a formal basis. The strict integration between theory and practice is the key feature of our proposal. In particular, this paper describes the design and the prototype implementation of the JSCL middleware. At the abstract level JSCL takes the form of a process calculus, SC, a dialect of the Ambient Calculus [11] with asynchronous communication facilities. At the implementation level, JSCL takes the form of a collection of Java APIs.

The starting point of our work is the event-notification paradigm. We assume to coordinate service behaviors through the exchange of (typed) signals. The basic building blocks of our middleware are called *components*. A component represents a "simple" service interacting though a signal passing mechanism. Components are basic computational units performing some internal operations and can be composed and distributed over a network. Composition of components, yields a new one that can be used in further compositions. Each component is identified by an unique *name*, which, intuitively, can be through as the URI of the published service. In this paper we assume as given

---

* Research partially supported by the EU, within the FET GC Project IST-2005-16004 Sensoria, and FIRB Project TOCAI.IT.

E. Najm et al. (Eds.): FORTE 2006, LNCS 4229, pp. 46–60, 2006.

the set of names of the components involved into a system with no assumption on the mechanisms adopted to retrieve them (e.g. UDDI service directories, registries, etc.).

The signals exchanged among components are basically messages containing information regarding the managed resources and the events raised during internal computations. Signals are tagged with a *meta type* representing the class of events they belong to. Such *meta type* information is often referred to, in the literature (e.g. [15]), with the term *topic*. Hence components are *reactive blocks* that declare the subset of signals they are interested in together with their *reactions* upon event notifications. The reactions are modeled by associating functional modules to topics of received signals. Once a signal of a well defined topic is received, the proper reaction is activated.

The way the events are notified to the subscribed components is strictly related to the specific coordination pattern chosen. Different *conversational styles* can be adopted to implement the way the participants are involved into a coordination, mainly split into two main groups: *orchestration* and *choreography* (as discussed in [4]). Briefly, the first solution defines an intermediate agent, the orchestrator, that is responsible to decide, at each step, which are the actions that must be performed by each component. The choreography, instead, identifies a more distributed scenario in which, each participant is responsible for its moves and the whole work-flow is executed following a pre-defined plan. Basically, the orchestration suggests a centralization point that is responsible for implementing the subscriptions and the notification forwarding. Such solution is closely related to the ideas of tuple space based systems and brokered event notification. Using the choreography, instead, each component can act both as publisher or subscriber for other components and the delivering of signals is implemented through *peer-to-peer* like structures. In this paper, we adopt the choreography approach since it better fits with the signal passing paradigm.

This paper is organized as follows. Section 2 introduces the Signal Calculus (SC). SC is a calculus for describing coordination primitives for components interacting through a signal passing mechanism. Section 3 describes JSCL APIs and the way components can be programmed. Basically, JSCL is a *ligthweight* framework for modeling distributed services by composing components that use signals for notifying events to other interested components in the style of SC. In section 4, as a case study, we describe the usage of JSCL as programming middleware for Long Running Transactions (LRTs) [10].

## 2   Signal Calculus: SC

The Signal Calculus (SC) is a process calculus in the style of [17, 11] specifically designed to describe coordination policies of services distributed over a network. SC describes computation via the choreography of local service behavior. In this section, we present the syntax and the operational semantics of SC.

### 2.1   SC Syntax

The main concepts of SC are signals, components, reactions, flows and networks. The data carried by a *signal* are the signal name and the conversation schema. A *signal name* represents an identifier of the current conversation (e.g. the session-id) and a *conversation schema* represents the kind of event (e.g. onMouseOver). New signals can be sent either by autonomous components or as reaction to other signals. In this paper, we present SC focusing only on the primitives needed to design coordination protocols. Hence, operations on conversation schemata are not defined, since they can be expressed at a higher level detail of abstraction. Of course, SC can be extended by adding types for conversation schemata (e.g. in the form of XML Schema) [2, 14, 8, 1]. A SC *component* is a wrapper for a *behavior*. Intuitively a SC component represents an autonomous service available over a network. Each SC component is uniquely identified by its name and contains a local behavior and an interface. Components can behave either as signal emitters or as signal handlers. Similarly to the event-notification pattern, signal handlers are associated to signals and are responsible for their management. The SC component *interface* is structured into *reactions* and *flows*. Reactions describe component behavior and the action of variable binding upon signal reception. Indeed, the reception of a signal acts like a trigger that activates the execution of a new behavior within the component.

Orchestration among components is implemented through flows. Flows represent the local view (component view) of the choreography, that is the set of local communications that have to be performed to satisfy the choreography demands. Each component flow declares the associations among signals, the conversation schema and the set of handlers. The connections among components are strictly related to a particular conversation schema thus offering the possibility to express different topologies of connectivity, depending on the schema of the outgoing signals. Both component reactions and flows are programmable, and they can be dynamically modified by the components.

Components are structured to build a *network* of services. A network provides the facility to transport envelopes containing the signals exchanged among components.

We now introduce the main syntactic categories of our calculus together with some notational machineries. We assume a finite set of conversation schemata ranged by $\tau_1, ..., \tau_k$, a finite set of component names ranged by $a, b, c...$ and a finite set of signal names ranged by $s_1, s_2, ....$ We also assume a set $Var$ of variable names whose typical elements are $x, y, z....$ We use $a$ to denote a set of names $a_1, ..., a_n$. Finally, we use $\sigma$ to denote a substitution from variable names to signal names.

Reactions $(R)$ are described by the following grammar:

$$(\text{REACTIONS}) \ R ::= 0 \qquad \text{Nil}$$
$$*(x : \tau \to B) \quad \text{Unit reaction}$$
$$R | R \qquad \text{Composition}$$

A reaction is a set (possibly empty) of unit reactions. A unit reaction $*(x : \tau \to B)$ triggers the execution of the behavior $B$ upon reception of a signal tagged by the schema $\tau$. Notice that $x : \tau$ acts as a binder for the variable $x$ within the behavior $B$. The syntax of behaviors will be given below. As usual we assume to work up-to alpha-conversion. Free and bound names are defined in the standard way.

Flows $(F)$ are described by the following grammar:

$$(\text{FLOWS}) \ F ::= 0 \qquad \text{Nil}$$
$$\tau \triangleright a \quad \text{Unit flow}$$
$$F \bullet F \quad \text{Composition}$$

A flow is a set (possibly empty) of unit flows. A unit flow $\tau \triangleright a$ describes the set of component names $a$ where outgoing signals having $\tau$ as conversation schema have to be delivered.

Reactions and flows are defined up-to a structural congruence ($\equiv$). Indeed, we assume that $\bullet$ and $|$ are associative, commutative and with 0 behaving as identity. Notice that such equations allow us to freely rearrange reactions and flows.

We define two auxiliary *schema* functions $S(R)$ and $S(F)$ that, respectively, return the set of conversation schemata on which the reaction $R$ and the flow $F$ are defined.

$$
\begin{aligned}
S(0) &= \emptyset \\
S(*(x : \tau \to B)) &= \{\tau\} \\
S(R_1 | R_2) &= S(R_1) \cup S(R_2)
\end{aligned}
\qquad\qquad
\begin{aligned}
S(0) &= \emptyset \\
S(\tau \triangleright a) &= \{\tau\} \\
S(F_1 | F_2) &= S(F_1) \cup S(F_2)
\end{aligned}
$$

We say that a reaction is *well-formed* (and we write $R\checkmark$) if there is no overlay among the conversation schemata triggered. The notion of well-formed reaction is inductively defined below.

$$
\frac{}{0\checkmark} \qquad \frac{}{*(x : \tau \to B)\checkmark} \qquad \frac{R_1\checkmark \quad R_2\checkmark \quad S(R_1) \cap S(R_2) \equiv \emptyset}{(R_1 | R_2)\checkmark}
$$

We also introduce two *projection* functions $R \downarrow_{s:\tau}$ and $F \downarrow_\tau$; the first takes a well-formed reaction $R$ and a signal $s$ of schema $\tau$ and returns a pair consisting of the variable substitution and the activated behavior. The second projection takes a flow $F$ and a schema $\tau$ and returns the set of component names linked to the flow having schema $\tau$. The two projections are defined below.

$$
\begin{aligned}
0 \downarrow_{s:\tau} &= (\{\}, 0) \\
(*(x : \tau \to B)|R) \downarrow_{s:\tau} &= (\{s/x\}, B) \\
(*(x : \tau_1 \to B)|R) \downarrow_{s:\tau} &= R \downarrow_{s:\tau} \quad \text{if } \tau_1 \neq \tau
\end{aligned}
\qquad
\begin{aligned}
0 \downarrow_\tau &= \{\} \\
(\tau \triangleright a \bullet F) \downarrow_\tau &= a \cup (F \downarrow_\tau) \\
(\tau_1 \triangleright a \bullet F) \downarrow_\tau &= F \downarrow_\tau \quad \text{if } \tau_1 \neq \tau
\end{aligned}
$$

Finally we say that a flow is well-formed (and we write $F\checkmark$) if there is no overlay among the linked components for all conversation schemata. The notion of well-formed flow is inductively defined below.

$$
\frac{}{0\checkmark} \qquad \frac{}{(\tau \triangleright a)\checkmark} \qquad \frac{F_1\checkmark \quad F_2\checkmark \quad \forall_{\tau \in (S(F_1) \cup S(F_2))}(F_1 \downarrow_\tau \cap F_2 \downarrow_\tau \equiv \emptyset)}{(F_1 \bullet F_2)\checkmark}
$$

Hereafter, we assume that reactions and flows are always well-formed.

Component behaviors ($B$) are defined by the following grammar:

| (BEHAVIORS) $B ::=$ | | |
|---|---|---|
| | $0$ | Nil |
| | $+R[x : \tau \to B]$ | Reaction update |
| | $+F[\tau \triangleright a]$ | Flow update |
| | $\bar{s} : \tau.B$ | Asynchronous signal emission |
| | $B|B$ | Parallel composition |
| | $!B$ | Bang |

A reaction update $+R[x : \tau \to B]$ extends the reaction part of the component interface, providing the ability to react to a signal of schema $\tau$ activating the behavior $B$. Such operation ensures that the resulting reaction is well-formed and permits to dynamically change the reaction interface. Similarly, a flow update $+F[\tau \triangleright a]$ extends the component flows, appending the component names in $a$ to the set of component names to which the signals of schema $\tau$ are delivered. An asynchronous signal emission $\bar{s} : \tau.B$ first spawns into the network a set of envelopes containing the signal $s$, one for each component name declared in the flow having schema $\tau$, and then activates $B$. As usual, the bang replication $!B$ represents a behavior that can always activate a new copy of the behavior $B$. When it is clear from the context, we will omit the Nil behavior, writing $\bar{s} : \tau$ for $\bar{s} : \tau.0$ and $B$ for $B|0$.

Networks ($N$) are defined by the following grammar:

$$
\begin{array}{llll}
(\text{NETWORKS}) \; N ::= & \mathbf{0} & & \text{Empty net} \\
& a[B]_F^R & & \text{Component} \\
& N \| N & & \text{Parallel composition} \\
& <s : \tau @ a> & & \text{Signal envelope}
\end{array}
$$

A component $a[B]_F^R$ describes a component of name $a$ with behavior $B$, reaction $R$ and flow $F$. A signal envelope $<s : \tau @ a>$ describes a message containing the signal $s$ of schema $\tau$ whose target component is the component named $a$. We use $\sum_{x \in a} B$ to denote the parallel composition of $B\{n/x\}$ for each name $n$ in the set $a$. A SC component is closely related to the notion of ambient [11] as it describes a behavior wrapped within a named context. Differently from the ambient calculus, SC networks are flat, that means there is no hierarchy of components.

**Examples.** To better present how the basic SC concepts can be used to model service coordination we introduce a simple example. Suppose to have a producer $p$ and a consumer $c$ both accessing a shared data space. We assume a synchronization policy, namely a consumer can get its resource only after a producer has produced it. The problem can be modeled as displayed in Figure 1. $P$ starts its execution performing the (internal) behavior $B_p$ that modifies the state of the data space that has to be read by $C$. When the data have been modified, $B_p$ executes a signal emission of a signal of schema *produced* ($\bar{s} : produced$) in order to inform $C$ that the required resources are now available. Upon notification, $C$ automatically starts and takes the resource in the data space performing its internal behavior $B_c$. We assume that $B_c$ executes a signal emission of a signal of schema *consumed* ($\bar{x} : consumed$) in order to inform $P$ that it can produce a new resource. Notice that the name of the signal emitted is the same of the signal received. Moreover $C$ is not a running process, it is an idle entity that is activated only at signal reception.

$$
P \triangleq p[\bar{s} : produced]_{produced \triangleright c}^{x:consumed \to \bar{x}:produced} \qquad C \triangleq c[0]_{consumed \triangleright p}^{x:produced \to \bar{x}:consumed} \qquad Net \triangleq P \| C
$$

**Fig. 1.** Components $p$ and $c$ share a data space

In the previous example, we presented two components with a statically defined choreography. However the producer and the consumer can be dynamically linked together (e.g. at the start up phase) using reaction update and flow update, thus providing a dynamic choreography scenario. This example is expressed in SC through the components and the network defined in Figure 2. Notice that, since component name passing has not been modeled in SC, we assume each component knows the names of the externally published components. We can enrich the SC core providing component name communication, thus yielding a true dynamic choreography in the style of the $\pi$-calculus [17].

$$
\begin{aligned}
P &\triangleq p[+F[produced \triangleright c]| + R[x : consumed \rightarrow \bar{x} : produced.0]|\bar{s} : produced]_0^0 \\
C &\triangleq c[+F[consumed \triangleright p]| + R[x : produced \rightarrow \bar{x} : consumed.0]]_0^0 \\
Net &\triangleq P\|C
\end{aligned}
$$

**Fig. 2.** Components $p$ and $c$ share a data space

## 2.2  SC Semantics

SC semantics is defined in a reduction style [5]. We first introduce a structural congruence over behaviors and networks. The structural congruence for component behaviors ($\equiv_B$) is defined by the following rules:

$$B_1|B_2 \equiv_B B_2|B_1 \qquad (B_1|B_2)|B_3 \equiv_B B_1|(B_2|B_3) \qquad 0|B \equiv_B B \qquad !B \equiv_B B|!B$$

As usual the bang operator allows us to express recursive behaviors.

Structural congruence for networks $\equiv_N$ is defined by the following rules:

$$N\|M \equiv_N M\|N \qquad (M\|N)\|O \equiv_N M\|(N\|O) \qquad 0\|N \equiv_N N$$

$$a[0]_F^0 \equiv_N 0 \qquad \frac{F^1 \equiv F^2 \ R^1 \equiv R^2 \ B^1 \equiv_B B^2}{a[B^1]_{F1}^{R^1} \equiv_N a[B^2]_{F2}^{R^2}}$$

A component having *nil* behavior and empty reaction can be considered as the empty network since it has no internal active behavior and cannot activate any behavior upon reception of a signal. Two components are considered structurally congruent if their internal behaviors, reactions and flows are structurally congruent. When it is clear from the context, we will use the symbol $\equiv$ for both $\equiv_B$ and $\equiv_N$.

The reduction relation of networks ($\rightarrow$) is defined by the rules in Figure 3. The rule (RUPD) extends the component reactions with a further unit reaction (the parameter of the primitive). The rule requires that the resulting reaction is well-formed. The rule (FUPD) extends the component flows with a unit flow. Also in this case a well-formed resulting flow is required. The rule (OUT) first takes the set of component names $a$ that are linked to the component for the conversation schema $\tau$ and then spawns into the network an envelope for each component name in the set. The rule (IN) allows a signal envelope to react with the component whose name is specified inside the envelope. Notice that signal emission rule (OUT) and signal receiving rule (IN) do not consume, respectively, the flow and the reaction of the component. This feature provides SC with a further form of recursion behavior. The rules (STRUCT) and (PAR) are standard rules. In the following, we use $N \rightarrow^+ N_1$ to represent a network $N$ that is reduced to $N_1$ after a finite number of steps.

$$\frac{R|*(x:\tau \to B)\checkmark}{a[+R[x:\tau \to B]|Q]_F^R \to a[Q]_F^{R|*(x:\tau \to B)}} \ (RUPD)$$

$$\frac{F \bullet \tau \rhd a \checkmark}{a[+F[\tau \rhd a]|Q]_R^F \to a[Q]_{F \bullet \tau \rhd a}^R} \ (FUPD)$$

$$\frac{F \downarrow_\tau = a}{a[\bar{s}:\tau.P|Q]_F^R \to a[P|Q]_F^R| \sum_{a_i \in a} <s:\tau@a_i>} \ (OUT)$$

$$\frac{R \downarrow_{s:\tau} = (\sigma, B)}{<s:\tau@a>|a[Q]_F^R \to a[Q|\sigma B]_F^R} \ (IN)$$

$$\frac{N \equiv N_1 \to M_2 \equiv N_3}{N \to N_3} \ (STRUCT)$$

$$\frac{N \to N_1}{N|N_2 \to N_1|N_2} \ (PAR)$$

**Fig. 3.** Semantic Rules

**Examples.** To describe how SC semantics rules work, we provide a short description of the execution of the examples given in Figure 1 and 2. As a shorthand, we write $\tau_p$ for the conversation schema *produced* and $\tau_c$ for *consumed*. The network in Figure 1 contains only one active component; namely the producer $p$ emits the signal, spawning into the network an envelope for the consumer $c$. This is represented by:

$$\frac{(\tau_p \rhd c) \downarrow_{\tau_p} = c}{p[\bar{s}:\tau_p]_{(\tau_p \rhd c)}^{(x:\tau_c \to \bar{x}:\tau_p)} \to p[0]_{(\tau_p \rhd c)}^{(x:\tau_c \to \bar{x}:\tau_p)}| <s:\tau_p@c>} \ (OUT)$$

The envelope reacts with the consumer component, activating inside the component the behavior of the corresponding reaction:

$$\frac{(x:\tau_p \to \bar{x}:\tau_c) \downarrow_{s:\tau_p} = (\{s/x\}, \bar{x}:\tau_c)}{<s:\tau_p@c>|c[0]_{(\tau_c \rhd p)}^{(x:\tau_p \to \bar{x}:\tau_c)} \to c[\bar{s}:\tau_c]_{(\tau_c \rhd p)}^{(x:\tau_p \to \bar{x}:\tau_c)}} \ (IN)$$

In a similarly way, the consumer component $c$ sends an envelope to the producer $p$, thus activating the proper internal behavior:

$$p[0]_{(\tau_p \rhd c)}^{(x:\tau_c \to \bar{x}:\tau_p)}|c[\bar{s}:\tau_c]_{(\tau_c \rhd p)}^{(x:\tau_p \to \bar{x}:\tau_c)} \to^+ p[\bar{s}:\tau_p]_{(\tau_p \rhd c)}^{(x:\tau_c \to \bar{x}:\tau_p)}|c[0]_{(\tau_c \rhd p)}^{(x:\tau_p \to \bar{x}:\tau_c)}$$

In the second example all the two components have active internal behaviors. The producer can update its flow by adding the link to the consumer for signals of schema $\tau_p$, as follows:

$$\frac{(0 \bullet \tau_p \rhd c)\checkmark}{p[+F[\tau_p \rhd c]\ |\ +R[x:\tau_c \to \bar{x}:\tau_p]\ |\ \bar{s}:\tau_p]_0^0 \to p[+R[x:\tau_c \to \bar{x}:\tau_p]\ |\ \bar{s}:\tau_p]_{(\tau_p \rhd c)}^0}$$

Then we apply the reduction rule for the reaction update of the producer:

$$\frac{(0|x:\tau_c \to \bar{x}:\tau_p)\checkmark}{p[+R[x:\tau_c \to \bar{x}:\tau_p]|\bar{s}:\tau_p]_{(\tau_p \rhd c)}^0 \to p[\bar{s}:\tau_p]_{(\tau_p \rhd c)}^{(x:\tau_c \to \bar{x}:\tau_p)}}$$

After these reductions the producer component has created a link to the consumer for signals of schema $\tau_p$ and can receive signals of schema $\tau_c$. In a similar way the consumer component updates its reaction and flow:

$$p[\bar{s}:\tau_p]_{(\tau_p \rhd c)}^{(x:\tau_c \to \bar{x}:\tau_p)}|c[+F[\tau_c \rhd p]|+R[x:\tau_p \to \bar{x}:\tau_c]]_0^0 \to^+ p[\bar{s}:\tau_p]_{(\tau_p \rhd c)}^{(x:\tau_c \to \bar{x}:\tau_p)}|c[0]_{(\tau_c \rhd p)}^{(x:\tau_p \to \bar{x}:\tau_c)}$$

## 3  Java Signal Core Layer

Java Signal Core Layer (JSCL) consists of a collection of Java API implementing the coordination primitives formally described by SC. In JSCL, known concepts of the event-based paradigm are considered in a distributed and open environment where components can be allocated on different execution sites and can join existing execution of other components. In the following, we often refer to components as *services* meaning that the current version of JSCL is specifically tailored to coordinate web services. However JSCL can be easily adapted to different technologies (e.g. CORBA). The essential ingredients of JSCL are *signals*, *components*, *signal links* and *input ports* corresponding, respectively, to the concepts of signals, components, flows and reactions defined in section 2. The notion of SC network is implemented by introducing an intermediate layer, the *Inter Object Communication Layer* (*IOCL*). The *IOCL* contains the set of primitives for creating, publishing, retrieving and connecting components. These operations are strictly related to the execution environment. To support multiple definitions of *IOCL*, these primitives have been developed as *plugins* that can be directly accessed at run-time. Such layer has been introduced to make JSCL more flexible and allows the interoperability of different technologies for inter object communication like CORBA, Web Services (see [22] for more details). In particular, the *IOCL* layer provides the mechanisms to implement the *data serialization* (e.g. SOAP message envelops for WSs, etc.) and the *deployment phase* (e.g. stub generation, dynamic proxy binding, etc.). Moreover each IOCL *plugin* defines the way components are identified by extending the basic interface ComponentAddress. The way components are named in JSCL strictly depends over the underlying overlay network adopted (e.g. an URL if the selected *iocl plugin* is based on WSs or CORBA, a couple $(IP, port)$ if sockets are used, an unique name if memory access is used etc.).

In JSCL, the set of information conveyed in each *signal* is split into two parts. The first contains information useful for coordination: the unique *name* of the signal instance and its *type*. The second part contains the payload of current request, the *session data*. Notice that the session data are not modeled in SC since the calculus only deals with the primitives needed for implementing the coordination among components. Signals are classified into *signal types* (*types* for short) that associate each signal to the class of events they belong to. Signal types are namely the SC conversation schemata. Signals have been modeled as *non persistent* entities; once the notification for an event has been delivered to all the interested handlers, the corresponding signal is *removed* from the system. This property is mandatory if we want to keep the distribution of the connections and their management. This feature, however, is not a limitation: persistent signals can be easily introduced in our middleware. Signals, in JSCL, are always sent in *non anonymous* way, meaning that it is always possible to know the sender of each signal. Such constraint is useful, at implementation level, if we want to extend the middleware with authoring primitives on the links.

The event notification mechanism of subscription is implemented through the creation of *input ports* and *signal links* connecting components. These operations correspond respectively to the primitives *reaction update* and *flow update* defined in SC.

An *input port* is a tuple $i = (sig_T, Task)$ meaning that the port can receive signals of type $sig_T$ whose handler is the process $Task$. Each component is able to specify only one input port for each $sig_T$. The notion of input port $i$, signal type $sig_T$ and handling task $Task$ map respectively the reaction $R$, the conversation schema $\tau$ and the behavior $B$ defined in SC. The component interface is obtained by taking the set of $sig_T$ for which there is a bound input port, and the set of $sig_T$ for which there is at least a signal link defined. Such sets in SC are given respectively by the auxiliary schema functions $S(R)$ and $S(F)$. Figure 4 shows a graphical notation for JSCL input ports.

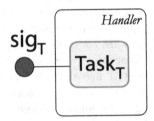

**Fig. 4.** JSCL input port

Connections between two components are implemented through *signal links*. A signal link is a tuple $l = (sig_T, S, R)$ and represents an virtual channel among the signals of type $sig_T$ emitted by $S$ and the handler $R$. Creating a new link between $S$ and $R$ requires that the input port corresponding to $sig_T$ has been previously created by $R$ with the right permissions for $S$. Basically, signal links are the linguistic device of JSCL for subscription/notification. We already pointed out that several receivers can be linked with the same signal type and the same sender. All the signal links created are *well formed* conforming to the rules defined in section 2.1. Namely further creations of links $(sig_T, S, R)$ are idempotent. The primitive for creating new signal links can be invoked outward the components by an external application that will connect all (or a subset of) the components among them and this will be the only agent conscious of the topology of the network. This assumption is useful to preserve the autonomy of the components from the particular system in which they are acting. The creation of a link is implemented through the *IOCL* component. Links in JSCL are *typed*, *unidirectional* and *"peer-to-peer"*. More complex scenarios (e.g., multi-casting, bi-directionality, etc.) can be obtained by introducing the suitable notions of links. For instance, multi-casting is achieved by connecting the same emitter to several handlers.

**Example.** We now describe how the *producer/consumer* example modeled in SC in section 2.2 can be implemented by exploiting the JSCL APIs. This provides a basic idea of the programmability offered by the middleware. The Figure 5 displays the choreography between two components $P$ and $C$ representing respectively the services implementing a *producer* and a *consumer*. The topics of signals exchanged in the system are $sig_{prod}$ and $sig_{cons}$ corresponding to notifications for events *produced* and *consumed* which can be raised respectively from $P$ and $C$.

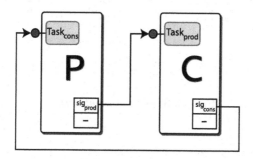

**Fig. 5.** JSCL: producer-consumer example

The designing of the whole application can be logically split into three phases: *i)* the creation of the components, *ii)* the declaration of the reactions associated to the components and *iii)* the publication of services and the designing of the connections. In the following, we assume to exploit the XSOAP [13] IOCL *plugin*, and to use the ServiceAddress[1] class, essentially an URL, to define component names.

```
IOCLPluginLoader loader = new IOCLPluginLoader ("jscl.core.IOCL.XSoap.IOCLImpl");
IOCLPluginI iocl = loader.getIOCLInstance ();
ServiceAddress Paddress = new ServiceAddress ("http", "jordie", 9092, "", "Producer");
ServiceAddress Caddress = new ServiceAddress ("http", "jordie", 9092, "", "Consumer");
GenericComponent producer = iocl.createComponent(Paddress);
GenericComponent consumer = iocl.createComponent(Caddress);
```

**Code 1.** Producer & consumer creation

The Code 1 illustrates the JSCL code for creating the needed services. First we instantiate a new IOCLPlugin that will be used to create the components. The creation of new components occurs by invoking the method *createComponent*, whose parameter is the address of the component itself. Alternatively, the *iocl* layer can be used to retrieve already published services by invoking the method *iocl.getComponent* which, given an address, returns a component proxy bound to it. Once our components have been built, we must program their reactions by binding them to new *input ports* as shown in Code 2. Roughly Code 2 describes the processes corresponding to the $Task_{cons}$ and $Task_{prod}$ depicted in Figure 5.

The last step is the publication of the created services and the creation of links as shown in Code 3.

Once the orchestration has been declared, we can start its execution by the signal emission of the producer component, which is the only active internal behavior. Here, for simplicity, the primitives for creating and publishing the components depicted in

---

[1] ServiceAddress is an implementation of ComponentAddress defined in section 3.

```
consumer.addInputPort(
  new SignalInputPort(SignalTypes.Sig_prod,
  new SignalHandlerTask(consumer){
    public Object handle(Signal signal){
      try{
        // Consumes the resource
        ...
        signal.setType(SignalTypes.Sig_cons);
        this.getParent().emitSignal(signal);
      } catch (GenericException e){
        e.printStackTrace();
      }
      return null;
    }
  }
)
);
```

```
producer.addInputPort(
  new SignalInputPort(SignalTypes.Sig_cons,
  new SignalHandlerTask(producer){
    public Object handle(Signal signal){
      try{
        // Produces the resource
        ...
        signal.setType(SignalTypes.Sig_prod);
        this.getParent().emitSignal(signal);
      } catch (GenericException e){
        e.printStackTrace();
      }
      return null;
    }
  }
)
);
```

**Code 2.** Binding of *input ports*

```
// Component publication
iocl.registerComponent(producer);
iocl.registerComponent(consumer);

// Creation of links
iocl.createLink(SignalTypes.Sig_prod, Paddress, Caddress);
iocl.createLink(SignalTypes.Sig_cons, Caddress, Paddress);
```

**Code 3.** Link creation

Code 1 and in Code 3, for simplicity, are collapsed into an unique block, using the same machine. Obviously more sophisticated strategies can be adopted, e.g. the component can be deployed into different machines, in such case the method `createComponent` is replaced by the `getComponent` method.

**JSCL Environment.** We have presented above the primitives provided by JSCL for declaring reactive components and for coordinating them via event notification. Other systems have been introduced in [22] to describe these issues (service declaration and coordination) in XML. On the one side, each component can be defined with an XML structure giving the signal types to which it reacts, the `iocl` support and the address to which it will be bound. These files are processed to obtain the corresponding Java skeleton code. On the other side, the coordination among components can be described in a separated XML document containing the definition of the services involved and their connections. Such file can be interpreted so to create the required coordination structure.

## 4    Long Running Transaction

JSCL has been adopted in [9] for implementing a framework for Long Running Transactions. The deployment phase has been driven by Naïve Sagas [10], a process calculus for compensable transactions, which defines Long Running Transactions in terms of logical blocks (*transactional flows*) orchestrating to reach a common goal. The building block of Naïve Sagas is the *compensation pair* construct. Given two actions $A$ and $B$, the compensation pair $A \div B$ corresponds to a process that uses $B$ as compensation for $A$. Intuitively, $A \div B$ yields two flows of execution: the *forward flow* and the *backward flow*. During the forward flow, $A \div B$ starts its execution by running $A$ and then, when $A$ finishes: $(i)$ $B$ is "installed" as compensation for $A$, and $(ii)$ the control is forwardly propagated to the other stages of the transactions. In case of a failure in the rest of the transaction, the backward flow starts so that the effects of executing $A$ must be rolled back. This is achieved by activating the installed compensation $B$ and afterward by propagating the rollback to the activities that were executed before $A$. Notice that $B$ is not installed if $A$ is not executed.

With JSCL the transactional blocks are obtained by suitable wrappers, Transactional Gates $(TG)$, that use signal passing for activating the flows. The possible signal types that can be exchanged are: $sig_{FW}$, which activates the *forward flow*, $sig_{RB}$, for activating the *backward flow* (rollback), $sig_{CM}$, propagated to notify that the whole orchestration has been successful executed (commit) and $sig_{EX}$, exchanged to notify that the rollback phase has failed and the state of the whole transaction is inconsistent (also referred as abnormal termination). When a $TG$ receives a signal typed $sig_{FW}$, it tries to execute the main activity $A$; whenever the execution of $A$ normally terminates, the signal is propagated to the next stage. On the contrary, if $A$ throws an exception, a signal typed $sig_{RB}$ is propagated to the previous stage (the rollback is propagated in backward way). Analogously when a $sig_{RB}$ is received by a $TG$, it tries to execute the *compensating activity* $B$, if it fails, throwing an exception, the signal is set to $sig_{EX}$ to notify that the rollback phase has failed and the state of the whole transaction is inconsistent, otherwise the rollback signal is propagated. The JSCL implementation of Naïve Sagas provides components implementing *parallel* and *sequential* structural composition of *transactional gates*. The composition constructs keep the structure of $TG$ and can be reused in further compositions. In Figure 6 it is shown how a Naïve Sagas compensable process $A_1 \div B_1; A_2 \div B_2; A_3 \div B_3$, is implemented using the JSCL graphical notation.

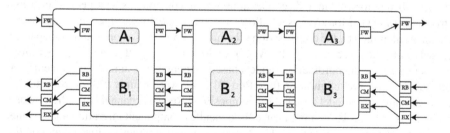

**Fig. 6.** JSCL Transactional Gates: an example

The JSCL implementation of transactional flows can be formally described in SC as follows. We assume given two functions $[\![A]\!]_{fw}(x)$ and $[\![A]\!]_{rb}(x)$ that translate the Naïve Sagas atomic activity $A$ to SC internal behaviors, working on signal named $x$. We assume that the first function translates the successful return statements into the signal emission $\bar{x} : fw.0$ and the exception rising into $\bar{x} : rb.0$, and that the second function translates the successful return statements into the signal emission $\bar{x} : rb.0$ and the exception rising into $\bar{x} : ex.0$. The example Naïve Sagas compensable process, previously described, is so represented by the SC network $[\![P]\!]$:

$$[\![A_1 \div B_1]\!] \triangleq p_1[0]_{fw \rhd p_2}^{x:fw \to [\![A_1]\!]_{fw}(x) \mid x:rb \to [\![B_1]\!]_{rb}(x)}$$

$$[\![A_2 \div B_2]\!] \triangleq p_2[0]_{fw \rhd p_3 \bullet rb \rhd p_1}^{x:fw \to [\![A_2]\!]_{fw}(x) \mid x:rb \to [\![B_2]\!]_{rb}(x)}$$

$$[\![A_3 \div B_3]\!] \triangleq p_3[0]_{rb \rhd p_2}^{x:fw \to [\![A_3]\!]_{fw}(x) \mid x:rb \to [\![B_3]\!]_{rb}(x)}$$

$$[\![P]\!] \qquad \triangleq [\![A_1 \div B_1]\!] \mid [\![A_2 \div B_2]\!] \mid [\![A_3 \div B_3]\!]$$

## 5   Concluding Remarks

We have introduced a core framework to formally describe coordination of distributed services. This framework has driven the implementation of a middleware for programming coordination policies by exploiting the event notification paradigm. In our approach the event notification paradigm supports fully distribution.

Unlike the current industrial technologies concerning service coordination (e.g. BPEL [19]), our solution is based on top of a clear foundational approach. This should provide strategies to prove coordination properties based on model checking or type systems. A semantic definition of the basic set of primitives can also drive the implementation of translators from industrial specification languages (e.g. WS-CDL [23]) to our framework. Our approach differs from other event based proposals (e.g. SIENA [12]), since focuses the implementation on the more distributed environment of services.

Our formal approach is based on process calculus literature (e.g. ccs [16], π-calculus [17]). Differently from π-calculus, the computation is boxed into components, in the style of Ambient Calculus [11]. Moreover we avoid components nesting, to model a flat topology of the network and to provide a more loose-coupled programming model. As described before, SC models connections among components with peer-to-peer like structures (*flows*). Moreover, such flows can be logically grouped into multicast-channels, identified by the conversation schema. This provides a communication pattern closed to the one presented in [21], even if SC does not deal with connection mobility.

There are several coordination models based on connection among components that provide dynamic reconfiguration (e.g. Reo [3]). Our work mainly differs from Reo on the communication model adopted for composition. Reo is a channel based framework, while SC is an event based one. Hence, Reo handles component migration and channel management as basic notions, while SC focuses on the activities performed and on the coordination over dynamic network topologies.

In this paper, we focused on the coordination aspects. However the calculus SC can be enriched by considering signals as tagged nested lists [2, 14], which represent XML documents, and conversation schemata as abstractions for XML Schema types [1]. This extension of conversation schemata lead to a more general notion of reaction based on pattern matching or unification in the style of [6]. A further extension can provide component and schema name passing, modelling a more dynamic scenario.

SC can describe dynamic orchestrations trough reaction and flow update primitives. These primitives have effects only on the component view of the choreography, namely a component cannot update the reaction or the flow of another component. Flow management can be enriched providing a primitive to update remote flows. This primitive should spawn a *flow update envelope* into the network. The update of remote reaction is more difficult, since a reaction contains code and than is necessary to formalize and implement the code migration.

## Bibliography

[1] Xml schema. Technical report, W3C, 2004.

[2] L. Acciai and M. Boreale. Xpi: A typed process calculus for xml messaging. In M. Steffen and G. Zavattaro, editors, *FMOODS*, volume 3535 of *Lecture Notes in Computer Science*, pages 47–66. Springer, 2005.

[3] F. Arbab. Reo: a channel-based coordination model for component composition. *Mathematical. Structures in Comp. Sci.*, 14(3):329–366, 2004.

[4] B. Benatallah, F. Casati, F. Toumani, and R. Hamadi. Conceptual modeling of web service conversations. In J. Eder and M. Missikoff, editors, *CAiSE*, volume 2681 of *Lecture Notes in Computer Science*, pages 449–467. Springer, 2003.

[5] G. Berry and G. Boudol. The chemical abstract machine. *Theoretical Comput. Sci.*, 96(1):217–248, April 1992.

[6] M. Boreale, M. G. Buscemi, and U. Montanari. A general name binding mechanism. In R. D. Nicola and D. Sangiorgi, editors, *TGC*, volume 3705 of *Lecture Notes in Computer Science*, pages 61–74. Springer, 2005.

[7] M. Bravetti, L. Kloul, and G. Zavattaro, editors. *Formal Techniques for Computer Systems and Business Processes, European Performance Engineering Workshop, EPEW 2005 and International Workshop on Web Services and Formal Methods, WS-FM 2005, Versailles, France, September 1-3, 2005, Proceedings*, volume 3670 of *Lecture Notes in Computer Science*. Springer, 2005.

[8] A. Brown, C. Laneve, and L. G. Meredith. Piduce: A process calculus with native xml datatypes. In Bravetti et al. [7], pages 18–34.

[9] R. Bruni, G. L. Ferrari, H. C. Melgratti, U. Montanari, D. Strollo, and E. Tuosto. From Theory to Practice in Transactional Composition of Web Services. In Bravetti et al. [7], pages 272–286.

[10] R. Bruni, H. C. Melgratti, and U. Montanari. Theoretical foundations for compensations in flow composition languages. In J. Palsberg and M. Abadi, editors, *POPL*, pages 209–220. ACM, 2005.

[11] L. Cardelli and A. D. Gordon. Mobile ambients. In M. Nivat, editor, *FoSSaCS*, volume 1378 of *Lecture Notes in Computer Science*, pages 140–155. Springer, 1998.

[12] A. Carzaniga, D. S. Rosenblum, and A. L. Wolf. Design of a scalable event notification service: Interface and architecture. Technical Report CU-CS-863-98, Department of Computer Science, University of Colorado, Aug. 1998.

[13] Department of Computer Science. Indiana University. XSoap. www.extreme.indiana. edu/xgws/xsoap/.

[14] H. Hosoya and B. C. Pierce. Xduce: A statically typed xml processing language. *ACM Trans. Internet Techn.*, 3(2):117–148, 2003.

[15] Y. Liu and B. Plale. Survey of publish subscribe event systems. Technical Report 574, Department of Computer Science, Indiana University.

[16] R. Milner. *Communication and Concurrency*. Printice Hall, 1989.

[17] R. Milner. The polyadic $\pi$-calculus: A tutorial. In F. L. Bauer, W. Brauer, and H. Schwichtenberg, editors, *Logic and Algebra of Specification, Proceedings of International NATO Summer School (Marktoberdorf, Germany, 1991)*, volume 94 of *Series F*. NATO ASI, 1993. Available as Technical Report ECS-LFCS-91-180, University of Edinburgh, October 1991.

[18] J. Misra. A programming model for the orchestration of web services. In *SEFM*, pages 2–11. IEEE Computer Society, 2004.

[19] OASIS Bpel Specifications. OASIS - BPEL. `http://www.oasis-open.org/cover/bpel4ws.html`.

[20] M. Papazouglou and D. Georgakopoulos. Special issue on service oriented computing. *Commun. ACM*, 46(10), 2003.

[21] F. Peschanski. Mobile agents in interaction space. In C. Canal and M. Viroli, editors, *FOCLASA'05*, volume 154(1), pages 63–82, 2005.

[22] D. Strollo. Java Signal Core Layer (JSCL). Technical report, Dipartimento di Informatica, Università di Pisa, 2005. Available at `http://www.di.unipi.it/~strollo`.

[23] W3C. Web Services Choreography Description Language (v.1.0). Technical report.

# Analysis of Realizability Conditions for Web Service Choreographies*

Raman Kazhamiakin and Marco Pistore

DIT, University of Trento
via Sommarive 14, 38050, Trento, Italy
{raman, pistore}@dit.unitn.it

**Abstract.** Web service choreography languages allow for the description of multipart collaborations from a global point of view, specifying the information exchanged by the participants in order to accomplish a common business goal. An important issue, emerging from the choreography modelling, is the protocol realizability, i.e., the possibility to extract the local specifications of the participants, so that their interactions preserve certain crucial properties of the global description.

In this paper, we present a formal framework for the definition of both the global protocols and the local specifications. The key feature of the approach is that it allows for arbitrary communication models (synchronous/asynchronous, with/without buffers) in the composition of the local specifications. We introduce a hierarchy of realizability notions that allows for capturing various properties of the global specifications, and associate specific communication models to each of them. We also present an approach, based on the analysis of the communication models, that allows to associate a particular level of realizability to the global protocol specification.

## 1  Introduction

Web service technology facilitates the development of complex distributed systems that span across the enterprise boundaries. It enables the specification, deployment, and enactment of heterogeneous software components accessible on the web via standardized protocols. One of the fundamental ideas underlying the Web service technology is the possibility to provide composite business applications by integrating existing services. To make this possibility realistic, it is necessary to address the problem of the specification and design of such compositions, taking into account the various aspects of a composition description.

One of the key aspects of this description is the ability to represent the stateful and coordinated behavior of the composite system. A wide range of standards and languages has been proposed for capturing these aspects [1,2,3]. Among them, the *choreography* specification languages, like e.g. Web Services Choreography Description Language (WS-CDL, [3]), are particularly relevant for the

---

* This work is partially funded by the MIUR-FIRB project RBNE0195K5, "KLASE", by the MIUR-PRIN 2004 project "STRAP", and by the EU-IST project FP6-016004 "SENSORIA".

E. Najm et al. (Eds.): FORTE 2006, LNCS 4229, pp. 61–76, 2006.

design phase of the composition, as they allow for the representation of the global observable behavior of the distributed business application.

The choreography languages open up the possibility of applying a range of formal techniques for the analysis of Web service compositions. Particularly relevant is the problem of *realizability* of the choreography specifications, that is, the possibility to automatically extract from the choreography the behavioral skeletons of the participants so that the concrete implementations, built on the basis of these skeletons, are guaranteed to satisfy the choreography specification.

This problem is made difficult by several crucial factors. First, the behavior of the application strongly depends on the way the services are exchanging the information, that is the *communication model* of the composition. The hypothesis of synchronous interactions, widely used for the analysis of service compositions, is not satisfied by many existing real-world applications. Moreover, the underlying interaction mechanism is not always known a priori, thus making problematic the usage of a particular model. Second, the strictness to which the application should satisfy the ordering constraints on messages and/or internal activities may differ from one scenario to another. In order to address this diversity, the realizability model has to be flexible, and should allow for an analysis which is parametric with respect to the set of requirements.

In this paper we address the problem of analyzing the realizability of choreographic protocols. We present a hierarchy of realizability notions that allows for capturing a variety of the choreography properties, thus providing a basis for a more flexible analysis. The presented approach is based on our previous work [4], where we give a formal model and analysis framework for the Web service compositions defined as composition of *local* participants specification. The key feature of that model is the definition of a parametric communication mechanism. More precisely, it is possible to specify different communication models for the interaction among the participants by changing the number of queues, their alphabets, and ordering rules. Using this formalism, it is possible to determine the communication model that is *adequate* for a given composition, that is the one that allows for the most complete description of the composition behavior.

In this work, we extend the approach of [4] and introduce a formalism for the *global* model that allows for the description of the compositions from a choreographic point of view. Furthermore, we express the problem of choreography realizability in terms of the composition of its local projections, and show how the hierarchy of the realizability notions is related to the hierarchy of communication models. Using this relation, we present an algorithm that allows to determine the appropriate level of the realizability, and the corresponding required conditions.

The paper is structured as follows. Section 2 introduces the realizability problem using variants of a simple example. Sections 3 and 4 define the formal models for the description of the underlying systems from the global perspective and as a composition of interacting local services respectively. In Sect. 5 the realizability problem is formalized and described, and various properties of the global protocols are discussed in terms of the composition of local models. Section 6 presents the algorithm that permits to reason on the realizability properties of the global

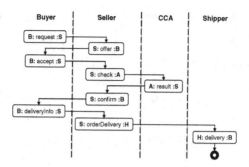

**Fig. 1.** RFQ case study: nominal case

protocols, which is based on the analysis of the communication models of the compositions. Conclusions and related works are discussed in Sect. 7.

## 2   Choreography Models

We illustrate the problem of modelling and analyzing Web service choreographies by means of an example. In this example we model a composition of Web services from the global point of view. We incrementally present several variants of the scenario, illustrating the approach presented in this paper. The global representation of the composition is modelled using the WS-CDL language that allows to describe the observable behavior of the composite protocol.

In our example we describe a simple business collaboration protocol for purchasing goods among a buyer, a seller, a credit card agency (CCA), and a shipper. The nominal case, defined as a UML activity diagram, is presented in Fig. 1. The protocol is defined as follows. First, the Buyer asks the Seller for a particular good, sending a request. The quote offer is prepared and sent back to the Buyer that accepts it (interaction **accept**). Given the payment details, the Seller asks the CCA to verify the information, and after receiving a positive **result** message, sends a confirmation to the Buyer. The Buyer sends the address information to the Seller, which forwards this data to the Shipper (**orderDelivery** message). Finally, the Shipper sends the delivery confirmation to the Buyer (**delivery**).

Given this global description, a straightforward step is to extract from it the local specifications of the participants. These specifications may be further detailed and serve as the basis for the composition implementation. In this example, the local specifications can be easily obtained by *projection* of the global model onto a particular participant. Moreover, the composition of these projections will behave exactly as the global specification, and therefore, the global model is *realizable*.

This is, however, not always the case. Consider a modification of the nominal case represented in Fig. 2(a). Here, after the **orderDelivery** interaction has been performed, the internal activity **prepareToDelivery** is invoked in the Buyer role. While the global model requires that the delivery is performed after this activity, the composition of projections is not able to guarantee this. Indeed,

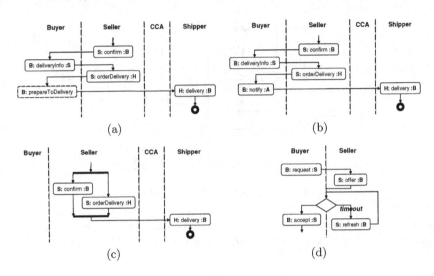

**Fig. 2.** RFQ case study: implementation variants

this internal activity of the Buyer is independent from the emission of delivery notification of the Shipper, and therefore the realizability is violated. In order to resolve this problem, either the specification should be modified and an additional synchronization interaction should be added, or the ordering requirement should be relaxed, allowing for interleaving internal activities and interactions.

A different modification of the nominal case is presented in Fig. 2(b). Here, after the **orderDelivery** interaction, the CCA is notified about the order by the **notify** message. In this case, also the ordering of interactions is violated, since the notification of CCA is independent from the emission of the delivery notification. We remark however that, while the order of actions specified in the global protocol is not respected, the states of the participants and the state of the protocol is not affected. That is, this scenario satisfies the property that, even if the actions are reordered, the outcome of the execution is the same.

In the implementation presented in Fig. 2(c) this property does not hold. In this scenario the addressing information of the Buyer is not required, and the confirmation and the order delivery activities may be invoked in parallel. This may lead to the following problem in the composition. The local specification of the Buyer requires that the delivery notification arrives after the confirmation from the Seller. Due to the fact that the Seller and the Shipper are independent, this order may be violated, and the final state of the Buyer depends on the implementation of the underlying communication system. Indeed, if the messages may be stored in queues, and, moreover, the messages from different partners are managed independently, then the Buyer process is not blocked, the messages are simply consumed in a different order. As a result, under certain assumptions on the middleware implementation and the usage of local variables, the global protocol may still be considered correct regardless the message ordering problems.

Contrary to the above examples, the acceptable conditions for the scenario presented in Fig. 2(d) are much more difficult to define. Here, if the Buyer does not provide an acceptance within a given period of time, the Seller refreshes the good information, sending a corresponding message `refresh`. The first problem is that the refresh message may be sent simultaneously with the acceptance message, even if the good is not in the stock anymore. The `refresh` message is ignored and the state of the protocol is incorrect. Second, if the time required for the offer processing by the Buyer exceeds the refreshment timeout, then the Seller will send more and more messages, and the queue of the Buyer will grow unboundedly. Finally, when the Buyer sends an acceptance message after several offer refresh messages, it is not clear which one is accepted due to possible reorderings and intersections of messages leading again to an incorrect state.

This example shows the complexity of defining realizability in a way that makes it possible to deal with scenarios like the ones illustrated above.

## 3   Global Model

In this section we introduce the formal model for representing the choreography specification. This global model defines the dynamic aspects of the service compositions from a global point of view by defining the involved participants and their interactions. The formalism follows the approach of [5,6] for modelling the global interaction protocols of Web service compositions.

The model is based on the notion of *roles* and *actions*. A role represents the behavior of a particular participant of the composed system. During the protocol execution, the $i^{th}$ role can be in one of its possible *states* $S_i$ (one of which is marked as an *initial state* $s_{0i}$) and can evolve to new states as a result of performing some actions.

We model message communications as *interactions* defined on a set of service operations (or message types) M. The signature of the interaction $a_o$ has the form $(r_s, r_d, \mu)$, where $r_s$ and $r_d$ are the roles of the sender and receiver respectively, $\mu$ is the service operation. The set of interactions is denoted as $\mathcal{A}_O$.

We also define *internal actions* $\mathcal{A}_\tau$, which are used to represent evolutions of the system that do not involve interactions between services. In particular, such an action may represent the internal decision branching of a particular participant (or even a group of participants[1]), or a modification of variables being performed by one or more partners in parallel. An internal action $a_\tau$ has the form $(\mathcal{R}_\tau, \tau)$, where $\mathcal{R}_\tau \subseteq \mathcal{R}$ denotes a subset of roles that perform an action, and $\tau$ is used to denote the internal action itself.

### 3.1   Global Protocol

We model choreography behavior as a *global protocol*. This behavior is defined by the *global transition relation* $\mathcal{T}$, which describes how the states of the participants

---

[1] The possibility of a group of participants to perform an internal action is used in [3] to model simultaneous evaluation of the branching condition by a group of roles.

can evolve on the basis of external and internal actions. We represent a *global state* of the choreography as a vector $\bar{s} = \langle s_1, \ldots, s_n \rangle$, where $s_i$ is a local state of the role $r_i$. We denote a vector $\bar{s}$ with component $s_i$ updated to $s_i'$ as $\bar{s}[s_i'/s_i]$.

**Definition 1 (Global Protocol).** *A global protocol representing the collaboration of $n$ roles is a tuple $P = \langle \mathcal{R}, \mathcal{S}, \bar{s}_0, \mathcal{A}, \mathcal{T} \rangle$, where*

- *$\mathcal{R}$ is a set of $n$ roles;*
- *$\mathcal{S} \subseteq \mathcal{S}_i \times \cdots \times \mathcal{S}_n$ is a set of global states, and $\bar{s}_0 \in \mathcal{S}$ is an initial state;*
- *$\mathcal{A} = \mathcal{A}_\tau \cup \mathcal{A}_O$ is a set of actions;*
- *$\mathcal{T} \subseteq \mathcal{S} \times \mathcal{A} \times \mathcal{S}$ is a global transition relation. A transition $(\bar{s}, a, \bar{s}') \in \mathcal{T}$ if*
  - *$a = (r_a, r_b, \mu)$ and $\bar{s}' = \bar{s}[s_a'/s_a, s_b'/s_b]$, or*
  - *$a = (\mathcal{R}_\tau, \tau)$ and $\bar{s}'$ agrees with $\bar{s}$ except for the state of the roles in $\mathcal{R}_\tau$.*

### 3.2    Behavior of the Global Model

We define the behavior of the global protocol using the notions of a *run* and a *conversation*. A run describes the evolution of the system by specifying, which actions were performed, and which global states were visited. The conversation, on the contrary, records only the sequences of interactions being performed during the evolution of the system.

More formally, the protocol behavior is defined as follows. We say that an action $a \in \mathcal{A}$ is *fireable* in a state $\bar{s}$, denoted as $\bar{s} \xrightarrow{a} \bar{s}'$, if there is a transition $(\bar{s}, a, \bar{s}') \in \mathcal{T}$. Let $\pi = \bar{s}_1, a_1, \bar{s}_2, a_2, \ldots$ be a (possibly infinite) sequence of states and actions. We say that the sequence is fireable from $\bar{s}_1$, written as $\bar{s}_1 \xrightarrow{\pi}{}^*$, if $\forall k \geq 1$, $\bar{s}_k \xrightarrow{a_k} \bar{s}_{k+1}$. Let us also denote as $\rho(\pi) = \mu_1, \mu_2, \ldots$ a sequence of all the interactions appeared on the sequence $\pi$.

**Definition 2.** *Let $P = \langle \mathcal{R}, \mathcal{S}, \bar{s}_0, \mathcal{A}, \mathcal{T} \rangle$ be a global protocol. A run of the protocol is a sequence $\pi = \bar{s}_0, a_0, \bar{s}_1, a_1, \ldots$ such that $\bar{s}_0 \xrightarrow{\pi}{}^*$. The behavior of the protocol is the set of all the runs of the protocol: $B = \{\pi \mid \bar{s}_0 \xrightarrow{\pi}{}^*\}$.*
*A conversation of the protocol $\rho(\pi)$ is a sequence of interactions performed on some run $\pi$. The set of all the conversations, denoted as $\Omega$, is called the conversation set of the protocol: $\Omega = \{\rho(\pi) \mid \bar{s}_0 \xrightarrow{\pi}{}^*\}$.*

## 4    Local Model

In the local model, the Web service composition is defined by a set of local protocols that separately describe the behavior of each participant of the composition. During their executions, the participants exchange messages with other participants through a certain communication medium, thus forming the dynamic behavior of the composed system. This bottom-up representation of the composition, inspired by the specification languages like BPEL [1], relies on the notions of a *local protocol*, which describes the behavior of a particular actor of the composition, and a *communication model*, which characterizes the interaction mechanisms of the composition instance.

## 4.1   Composition of Local Protocols

The local behavior of the participant is given in terms of a local protocol that specifies the states and actions performed by the participant. We distinguish *input actions* $\mathcal{I}$, which represent the reception of message, denoted as $\overleftarrow{\mu}$; *output actions* $\mathcal{O}$, which represent messages sent to other participants, denoted as $\overrightarrow{\mu}$; and *internal actions*, which characterize non-observable operations of the participant, denoted as $\tau$.

**Definition 3 (Local protocol).** *A* local protocol *is a tuple* $\langle S, s_0, \mathcal{A}, T \rangle$, *where*

- $S$ *and* $s_0 \in S$ *are the set of role states and the initial state respectively;*
- $\mathcal{A} = \mathcal{I} \cup \mathcal{O} \cup \{\tau\}$ *is a set of role actions;*
- $T \subseteq S \times \mathcal{A} \times S$ *is a local transition relation.*

The behavior of the composition of local protocols depends on the communication model [4] adopted and used for the description of the message exchanges between partners. Such a communication model is given by a set of communication channels (or queues), and is characterized by the number of the queues, message ordering, bounds etc. The composition of the local projections is therefore parametric with regards to the communication model, and may exhibit different behaviors.

More formally, let us model the interactions with set of $m > 0$ queues with disjoint alphabets $M_j \subseteq M$. A queue $q_j$ may be declared as *bounded*, with the corresponding capacity $0 < b_j < \infty$, or *unbounded*, in which case $b_j = \infty$.

**Definition 4.** *A* communication model *for the composition is a tuple* $\Delta = \langle \mathcal{L}_B, \mathcal{L}_M, \mathcal{L}_O \rangle$, *where* $\mathcal{L}_B = \langle b_1, \ldots, b_m \rangle$, *is a vector of queue bounds,* $\mathcal{L}_M : M \to [1 \ldots m]$ *is a function that associates an operation* $\mu$ *with a queue* $i$, *and* $\mathcal{L}_O : [1 \ldots m] \to \{\top, \bot\}$ *is a function that declares the queue as either ordered or unordered. The alphabet* $M_i$ *of queue* $i$ *is defined as* $M_i = \{\mu \mid \mathcal{L}_M(\mu) = i\}$.

Let $M^*$ be a set of sequences (or strings) of elements from M. Let also $N^M$ be a set of multisets of M, i.e. sets of mappings from M to the set N of natural numbers. Given two elements $w$ and $w'$, we write $w.w'$ to denote string concatenation, if $w, w' \in M^*$, and multiset union, if $w, w' \in N^M$.

We define a queue content as a vector $C = \langle w_1, \ldots, w_m \rangle$, where $w_j \in M_j^*$ and $j^{th}$ queue is ordered, or $w_j \in N^M$ and $j^{th}$ queue is unordered. We extend the operator . to the queue content as follows: $C.\mu = \langle w_1', \ldots, w_m' \rangle$, where $w_j' = w_j.\mu$ if $\alpha \in M_j$, and $w_j' = w_j$ otherwise. We write $|C| \leq \mathcal{L}_B$ to specify that $|q_i| \leq b_i$.

We define the composition of the local protocols as a *composition transition system* (CTS). The definition of the CTS is parametric with respect to the communication model.

**Definition 5 (CTS [4]).** *A* composition transition system *representing the composition of* n *local protocols under a model* $\Delta = \langle \mathcal{L}_B, \mathcal{L}_M, \mathcal{L}_O \rangle$ *is a transition system* $\Sigma_\Delta = \langle \Gamma, \gamma_0, \mathcal{A}, T \rangle$, *where*

- $\Gamma$ is a set of configurations of the form $\gamma = \langle \bar{s}, C \rangle$, and $\gamma_0 = \langle \bar{s}_0, \langle \epsilon, \dots, \epsilon \rangle \rangle$ is an initial configuration;
- $\mathcal{A} = \bigcup_i \mathcal{A}^i$ is a set of actions;
- $\mathcal{T} \subseteq \Gamma \times \mathcal{A} \times \Gamma$ is the global transition relation.
  A transition $(\langle \bar{s}, C \rangle, a, \langle \bar{s}', C' \rangle)$ is in $\mathcal{T}$, if for some $1 \leq i \leq n$, $\bar{s}' = \bar{s}[s_i'/s_i]$, and $(s_i, a, s_i') \in \mathcal{T}^i$, and one of the following holds:
  - $a = \overrightarrow{\mu} \ \wedge \ C' = C.\mu \ \wedge \ |C'| \leq \mathcal{L}_B$;
  - $a = \overleftarrow{\mu} \ \wedge \ C = \mu.C'$;
  - $a = \tau \ \wedge \ C' = C$.

In the following, we say that the channel of a composition have a *bounded growth* if, for each queue $q_i$, either a finite bound $b_i < \infty$ is declared, or there is some constant $K_i$ such that the queue contains at most $K_i$ messages in all reachable states. The composition is *bounded* if it has bounded growth.

We say that the composition is *complete* if all the terminating configurations $\langle \bar{s}, C \rangle$ have empty queue content: $C = \langle \epsilon, \dots, \epsilon \rangle$. We remark that systems that are not complete lose messages: indeed, at the end of the computation there are unconsumed messages in queues.

## 4.2   Behavior of the Local Model

While the emission and the reception of the messages are indistinguishable in the global protocol, this is not the case for the composition of projections. Depending on the communication applied, the messages may be interleaved, reordered, and even ignored. Moreover, the structure of the composition configuration is more complex than that of the global protocol, and depends on the communication model. This is reflected in the way behaviors and conversations are defined. In particular, since the reception of a message does not necessarily follow the emission (the message may be lost), we will define a conversation set in two ways: we denote as $\overrightarrow{\rho}(\pi) = \mu_1, \mu_2, \dots$ the sequence of all the messages emitted on the sequence $\pi$, and as $\overleftarrow{\rho}(\pi)$ the sequence of received messages.

An action $a \in \mathcal{A}$ is *fireable* in $\gamma$, denoted as $\gamma \xrightarrow{a} \gamma'$, if there is a transition $(\gamma, a, \gamma') \in \mathcal{T}$. Let $\omega = \langle \bar{s}_1, C_1 \rangle, a_1, \langle \bar{s}_2, C_2 \rangle, a_2, \dots$ be a (possibly infinite) sequence of configurations and actions. We say that the sequence is fireable from $\langle \bar{s}_1, C_1 \rangle$, written as $\langle \bar{s}_1, C_1 \rangle \xrightarrow{\omega} *$, if $\forall k \geq 1$, $\langle \bar{s}_k, C_k \rangle \xrightarrow{a_k} \langle \bar{s}_{k+1}, C_{k+1} \rangle$. We denote as $\pi(\omega) = \bar{s}_1, a_1, \bar{s}_2, a_2, \dots$ a corresponding sequence of states and actions.

**Definition 6.** *Let* $\Sigma_\Delta = \langle \Gamma, \gamma_0, \mathcal{A}, \mathcal{T} \rangle$ *be a composition of local protocols. Given a sequence* $\omega = \gamma_0, a_0, \gamma_1, a_1$ *such that* $\gamma_0 \xrightarrow{\omega} *$, *a* run *of the composition is a sequence* $\pi(\omega)$. *The* behavior *of the composition is the set of all the runs of the composition:* $\mathrm{B} = \{\pi(\omega) \mid \gamma_0 \xrightarrow{\omega} *\}$. *An* output conversation *(respectively* input conversation*) of the composition is a sequence of messages emitted (resp. received) on some* $\pi \in \mathrm{B}$. *The set of all the output (resp. input) conversations is called the* output conversation set $\overrightarrow{\Omega}$ *(resp. input conversation set* $\overleftarrow{\Omega}$ *).*

## 4.3 Communication Models

The behavior of the composition depends on the communication model. Indeed, the certain ordering should be satisfied for the message to be consumed from the queue, the queue bound should restrict the emission of new messages, etc. One of the key problems for the analysis of the behavior of the protocol is to determine the relations between the behaviors exhibited by different implementations of the communication medium. This requires the introduction of certain relations between communication models, namely *simulation* relations.

**Definition 7.** *We say that a configuration* $\gamma_2 = \langle \bar{s}_2, C_2 \rangle$ *of* $\Sigma_{\Delta_2}$ *simulates a configuration* $\gamma_1 = \langle \bar{s}_1, C_1 \rangle$ *of* $\Sigma_{\Delta_1}$, *written as* $\gamma_1 \preceq \gamma_2$, *iff*

- $\bar{s}_1 = \bar{s}_2$,
- $\forall\, a,\ \forall\, \gamma_1',\ \text{if } \gamma_1 \xrightarrow{a} \gamma_1',\ \text{then } \exists\, \gamma_2',\ s.t.\ \gamma_2 \xrightarrow{a} \gamma_2',\ \text{and } \gamma_1' \preceq \gamma_2'.$

*We write* $\Sigma_{\Delta_1} \preceq \Sigma_{\Delta_2}$ *to denote that* $\gamma_{01} \preceq \gamma_{02}$. *We also write* $\Sigma_{\Delta_1} \approx \Sigma_{\Delta_2}$ *when* $\Sigma_{\Delta_1} \preceq \Sigma_{\Delta_2} \wedge \Sigma_{\Delta_2} \preceq \Sigma_{\Delta_1}$.

**Proposition 1.** $\Sigma_{\Delta_1} \approx \Sigma_{\Delta_2}$ *iff* $\mathrm{B}(\Sigma_{\Delta_1}) = \mathrm{B}(\Sigma_{\Delta_2})$.

When the simulation relation among two communication models $\Delta_1$ and $\Delta_2$ holds for any set of local protocols, we say that $\Delta_2$ is *more general* than $\Delta_1$.

**Definition 8.** *Communication model* $\Delta_2$ *simulates model* $\Delta_1$, *written as* $\Delta_1 \sqsubseteq \Delta_2$, *if for any composition of STSs,* $\Sigma_{\Delta_1} \preceq \Sigma_{\Delta_2}$.

Being reflexive and transitive, this relation forms a partial order on the set of communication models. Below we will show that there is a "most general" model, that is the model $\Delta_{MG}$, such that for any other model $\Delta$ holds $\Delta \sqsubseteq \Delta_{MG}$.

The relation among communication models relies on the structure of the queues. The models differ in two dimensions. First, the relation depends on the queue bounds: the bigger a bound is, the more transitions are enabled. Second, it depends on the distribution of the message alphabets: if the alphabet of each ordered queue in one model is a subset of the alphabet of some ordered queue in another model, then the first model is more general than the other. The following theorem defines a relation between the models with different queue structures.

**Theorem 1.** *Consider two communication models* $\Delta_1 = \langle \mathcal{L}_{1B}, \mathcal{L}_{1M}, \mathcal{L}_{1O} \rangle$ *and* $\Delta_2 = \langle \mathcal{L}_{2B}, \mathcal{L}_{2M}, \mathcal{L}_{2O} \rangle$. *If for each queue* $q_{2i}$ *holds that*

- *if the queue* $q_{2i}$ *is ordered, then there exists an ordered queue* $q_{1j}$, *s.t.* $\mathrm{M}_{2i} \subseteq \mathrm{M}_{1j}$, *and*
- $b_{2i} \geq \sum_{\mathrm{M}_{2i} \cap \mathrm{M}_{1j} \neq \emptyset} b_{1j}$,

*then* $\Delta_1 \sqsubseteq \Delta_2$.

Let us define the *most general* model, that is the model that allows for the largest set of behaviors. In order to respect the assumptions presented above, this model has to allow for potentially unbounded queues, non-blocking emissions, and arbitrary, unordered access to the content of any queue.

**Definition 9.** *The* Most General Communication Model *(MG-model) is a communication model* $\Delta_{MG} = \langle \mathcal{L}_B, \mathcal{L}_M, \mathcal{L}_O \rangle$, *with 1 unordered queue,* $b = \infty$, *and* $\mathcal{L}_M(\alpha_i) = 1$.

It is easy to see that such a model is indeed a generalization of any other communication model w.r.t. the behavior of any composition of STSs.

**Proposition 2 (from [4]).** *For any communication model* $\Delta$, $\Delta \sqsubseteq \Delta_{MG}$.

Whenever a composition under a certain model $\Delta$ simulates the most general composition, we say that this model is *adequate* for the description of the composition scenario.

**Definition 10 (from [4]).** *A communication model* $\Delta$ *is said to be* adequate *for the given composition scenario if* $\Sigma_\Delta \approx \Sigma_{\Delta_{MG}}$.

## 5    Protocol Realizability

A natural question that comes with the specification of the global choreography protocol is the *realizability* of the specification. It consists in deciding whether there is a way to extract the local implementations of the participating roles such that, when composed together, they satisfy the protocol specifications. We refer to these local implementations as *projections*. Sets of such projections will be used as the implementation candidates for the composition.

Intuitively, a behavior of a projection is constructed from those transitions of the global protocol, in which the participant is involved. The internal action $(\mathcal{R}_\tau, \tau)$ is projected onto an internal action of each role $r_i \in \mathcal{R}_\tau$. The interaction action $(r_s, r_d, \mu)$ is projected onto the input action $\overleftarrow{\mu}$ of the role $r_d$, and on the output action $\overrightarrow{\mu}$ of the role $r_s$.

**Definition 11 (Role Projection).** *Given a global protocol* $\langle \mathcal{R}, \mathcal{S}, \bar{s}_0, \mathcal{A}, \mathcal{T} \rangle$, *a projection* on role $r_i$ *is a local protocol* $\langle \mathcal{S}_i, s_{0i}, \mathcal{A}_i, \mathcal{T}_i \rangle$, *where:*

- $\mathcal{S}_i$ *is a set of states, and* $s_{0i}$ *is the initial state of* $r_i$ *respectively;*
- $\mathcal{A}_i = \mathcal{I}_i \cup \mathcal{O}_i \cup \{\tau\}$ *is a set of actions of* $r_i$;
- $\mathcal{T}_i \subseteq \mathcal{S}_i \times \mathcal{A}_i \times \mathcal{S}_i$ *is the transition relation of* $r_i$. *Transition* $(s_i, a_i, s'_i) \in \mathcal{T}_i$, *if* $\exists\, (\bar{s}, a, \bar{s}') \in \mathcal{T}$, *such that one of the following holds:*
    - $a = (r_i, r_j, \mu)$, $a_i = \overrightarrow{\mu} \in \mathcal{O}_i$;
    - $a = (r_j, r_i, \mu)$, $a_i = \overleftarrow{\mu} \in \mathcal{I}_i$;
    - $a = (\mathcal{R}_\tau, \tau)$, $r_i \in \mathcal{R}_\tau$, $a_i = \tau$.

Given the set of all role projections of a global protocol, we can compose them into a CTS according to Definition 5. In the following we denote the composition of role projections under the model $\Delta$ as $\Sigma_\Delta^p$.

This composition enables the analysis of the realizability of the global protocol. In order to perform this analysis, a possibility to compare the behavior of the global protocol with the behavior of the composition of the local projections is needed. This comparison is based on the notion of the behavior expansion that re-defines the behavior of the protocol in terms of the actions of the composition.

**Definition 12 (Behavior Expansion).** *Given a run $\pi$ of the global protocol $P$, the expansion of the run is a sequence $\overline{\pi}$ of states and composition actions obtained as follows:*

- *each interaction transition $(r_i, r_j, \mu)$ is projected onto a sequence of the corresponding send and receive transitions of $r_i$ and $r_j$ respectively;*
- *each internal transition $(\mathcal{R}_\tau, \tau)$ is projected onto a sequence of internal transitions of all roles in $\mathcal{R}_\tau$.*

*The set of all expansions generated by $\mathrm{B}(P)$ is denoted as $\overline{\mathrm{B}}(P)$.*

## 5.1   Synchronous Realizability

An intuitive candidate for realizability is the notion that requires that the composition of the projections behaves exactly as the given global specification regardless the communication model that is applied. We refer to this notion as *synchronous realizability*.

**Definition 13 (Synchronous realizability).** *The global protocol $P$ is synchronously realizable if the behavior expansion of the protocol is equal to the behavior of the composition of the projections under $\Delta_{MG}$: $\overline{\mathrm{B}}(P) = \mathrm{B}(\Sigma^p_{\Delta_{MG}})$.*

The notion of synchronous realizability is closely related to the *synchronizable communication model*. This is the most restricted communication model that can be defined in the local model formalism. In this model there is only one queue of capacity one.

**Definition 14 (Synchronizable communications model).** *The synchronizable communication model is the model $\Delta_1^1 = \langle \mathcal{L}_B, \mathcal{L}_M, \mathcal{L}_O \rangle$, with $\mathcal{L}_B = \langle 1 \rangle$ and $\mathcal{L}_M(\mu) = 1$ for all operations $\mu$.*

The following result immediately follows from the above definitions.

**Proposition 3.** *If the protocol $P$ is synchronously realizable, then the model $\Delta_1^1$ is adequate for the composition of the local projections of $P$.*

Indeed, the synchronous realizability implies that the behavior of the composition under the MG-model is the same as that of the global protocol. Therefore, in any configuration there is at most one message to be received, and from the definition of composition follows that the model $\Delta_1^1$ is also adequate.

It is easy to see that the protocol represented in Fig. 1 is synchronously realizable.

## 5.2   Strong Realizability

The restrictions imposed by the synchronous realizability are often too strong for the implemented system. Indeed, it requires that the order of internal and external actions is respected by the implementation, or that the next emission cannot start before the previous message was received, even if the acting participants are independent.

The notion of *strong realizability* relaxes these constraints. The ordering restrictions concern only the communication actions, and not the internal ones. Intuitively, a protocol is strongly realizable if the set of conversations of the protocol and of the compositions is the same, the composition is bounded, and all the emitted messages are received.

**Definition 15 (Strong realizability).** *Given a protocol $P$ and the composition of the projections under $\Delta_{MG}$, if the composition is bounded and $\Omega(P) = \overrightarrow{\Omega}(\Sigma^p_{\Delta_{MG}}) = \overleftarrow{\Omega}(\Sigma^p_{\Delta_{MG}})$, then the protocol is said to be* strongly synchronizable.

This notion is related to the *globally ordered communication model*.

**Definition 16 (Globally ordered communications model).** *The globally ordered communication model is the model $\Delta_{go} = \langle \mathcal{L}_B, \mathcal{L}_M, \mathcal{L}_O \rangle$, with one ordered queue, such that $\mathcal{L}_B = \langle \infty \rangle$ and $\mathcal{L}_M(\mu) = 1$ for all operations $\mu$.*

**Proposition 4.** *The protocol $P$ is strongly realizable iff $\Delta_{go}$ is adequate for the composition of the projections $\Sigma^p_\Delta$, and the composition is complete and bounded.*

The completeness and adequacy of $\Delta_{go}$ immediately follows from strong realizability of $P$ by the above definitions ($\overrightarrow{\Omega}(\Sigma^p_{\Delta_{MG}}) = \overleftarrow{\Omega}(\Sigma^p_{\Delta_{MG}})$). To see the converse, note that only one participant may send and only one may receive messages at a time (otherwise the reordering would be possible). A sequence of emissions of a participant is projected from the definition of the protocol, and therefore, reflects the sequence of interactions. Thus, $\Omega(P) = \overrightarrow{\Omega}(\Sigma^p_{\Delta_{MG}})$.

While the protocol represented in Fig. 2(a) is not synchronously realizable (the internal activity `prepareToDelivery` may be performed before the shipper receives the `orderDelivery` message), one can see that it satisfies the strong realizability requirements. Indeed, the composition is bounded, all the messages are eventually received, and there are no concurrent message emissions/receptions, which makes the $\Delta_{go}$ adequate for the composition.

## 5.3 Local Realizability

Strong realizability may appear to be too restrictive for a wide class of choreography scenarios. Indeed, it does not allow for concurrent emissions and receptions of messages by independent processes. For instance, if role $A$ interacts with $B$, and then $C$ interacts with $D$, then the global order cannot be preserved by the composition of projections. In many cases, however, this may be irrelevant. Moreover, since the variables are local for each role, the behavior and the information of the local participant is not affected by these reorderings.

We relax the notion of strong realizability by omitting the requirement of conversation equivalence. However, the local behavior of each role should not be affected by possible reorderings of message emissions.

**Definition 17 (Local Realizability).** *The protocol $P$ is* locally realizable *if the composition $\Sigma^p_{\Delta_{MG}}$ is complete, bounded, and for any run $\pi \in B(\Sigma^p_{\Delta_{MG}})$, for any role $r_i$, $\overrightarrow{\pi_i} = \overleftarrow{\pi_i}$, where $\overrightarrow{\pi_i}$ and $\overleftarrow{\pi_i}$ are the sequences of messages sent to and received by the $i^{th}$ participant.*

This property is especially important for monitoring, since it guarantees that the external observed order of messages is locally respected by the receiver.

**Definition 18.** *A* locally ordered communication model *for the composition of $n$ local protocols is a model $\Delta_{lo} = \langle \mathcal{L}_B, \mathcal{L}_M, \mathcal{L}_O \rangle$, with $n$ ordered queues, $b_i = \infty$, and $\forall \alpha$ s.t. $\overleftarrow{\alpha} \in \mathcal{I}^i$, $\mathcal{L}_M(\alpha) = q_i$.*

This communication model, exploited also in [7], requires that messages are queued on a process-by-process way. The following result immediately follows from the definition of the local realizability.

**Proposition 5.** *The protocol $P$ is locally realizable iff $\Delta_{lo}$ is adequate for the composition of the projections $\Sigma^p_\Delta$, and the composition is complete and bounded.*

One can see that the global protocol presented in Fig. 2(b) is locally realizable. While the reordering of messages is possible in the composition (thus violating the strong realizability requirements), the local order of messages is respected.

## 5.4   Weak Realizability

The least restrictive model of realizability further relaxes the ordering constraints, requiring only that the message ordering of the interactions among a pair of the participants is preserved. That is, each participant sending messages to its partner knows that they will be processed and managed in turn. We refer to this notion of realizability as *weak realizability*.

**Definition 19 (Weak realizability).** *The protocol $P$ is* weakly realizable *if the composition $\Sigma^p_{\Delta_{MG}}$ is complete, bounded, and for any run $\pi \in B(\Sigma^p_{\Delta_{MG}})$, for any pair of roles $r_i$ and $r_j$, $\overrightarrow{\pi_{ji}} = \overleftarrow{\pi_{ij}}$, where $\overrightarrow{\pi_{ji}}$ and $\overleftarrow{\pi_{ij}}$ are the sequences of messages sent from $r_j$ to $r_i$ and received by $r_i$ from $r_j$ respectively.*

This definition is related to the *mutually ordered communication model*.

**Definition 20 (Mutually ordered communication model).** *A* mutually ordered asynchronous communication model *is a model $\Delta_{mo} = \langle \mathcal{L}_B, \mathcal{L}_M, \mathcal{L}_O \rangle$, with $n^2 - n$ ordered queues denoted as $q_{i,j}$ $(i \neq j)$ s.t. $b_{i,j} = \infty$, and $\forall \alpha$, $\overleftarrow{\alpha} \in \mathcal{I}^j \wedge \overrightarrow{\alpha} \in \mathcal{O}^j$ iff $\mathcal{L}_M(\alpha) = q_{i,j}$.*

In this model, a pair of queues is defined for each pair of processes, with each queue representing one direction of interaction between these processes. This model, described in [8], provides a natural representation of communicating processes since each process explicitly distinguishes each of its partners. The main feature of this model is that each pair of communicating processes preserves the order of partners' events. In other words, the order of receptions is equivalent for each pair of processes.

**Proposition 6.** *The protocol P is weakly realizable iff $\Delta_{mo}$ is adequate for the composition of the projections $\Sigma_\Delta^p$, and the composition is complete and bounded.*

The global protocol represented in Fig. 2(c) is weakly realizable, while the one in Fig. 2(d) is not. Indeed, the composition of the local projections is incomplete and unbounded, and, moreover, it allows for reorderings of updated quotes.

## 6   Realizability Analysis

The notions of realizability and the respective properties suggest an analysis approach based on the analysis of communication models [4]. It is easy to see that the following hierarchy holds for the models presented above:

$$\Delta_1^1 \sqsubseteq \Delta_{go} \sqsubseteq \Delta_{lo} \sqsubseteq \Delta_{mo} \sqsubseteq \Delta_{MG}$$

Moreover, an analogous hierarchy holds also for the notions of realizability[2]. This allows for the application of the following analysis algorithm.

1. Find a minimal (w.r.t. simulation relation) adequate communication model $\Delta$ for the composition of the local projections of the protocol $P$.
2. Check that the composition is complete and has bounded growth. If this is not the case, the protocol is not realizable.
3. The appropriate level of realizability is determined by the corresponding communication model.

The algorithm for the adequacy check is presented in Fig. 1. We briefly describe its behavior. The reachability tree of the composition is traversed recursively, starting from the initial configuration. In each state the set of enabled transitions is compared with the set of transitions enabled in the corresponding configuration of the composition under the MG-model. If the sets are not equivalent, the current model is not adequate.

Each newly reached configuration is checked for boundedness (the function $isUnbounded(\gamma')$). This is performed by checking whether there exists a loop starting in a configuration with the same state, but with greater queue content. If such a loop exists, the composition is unbounded. The completeness is checked for each terminating state, i.e. a state without fireable transitions.

We remark, that whenever the inadequacy of a certain model is detected (as well as the incompleteness or the unboundedness), the sequence of configurations contained in the search stack represents a counterexample (or a witness), that describes the violation of the analyzed realizability. This counterexample may be used for further analysis of the protocol.

For the sake of simplicity we omitted the definition of variables and the data flow in the global and local models. In [9] we show how the above formalisations and analysis techniques may be extended in order to capture both the

---

[2] Strong realizability, however, requires an additional check that the internal actions are not interleaved with the message receptions. This check may be easily introduced in the presented algorithm.

---

**Algorithm 1.** Composition adequacy check

---

1: $Stack := nil$;     {Stack of configurations}
2: $Visited := nil$;     {Set of all visited configurations}
3: $IS := nil$;     {Set of incomplete configurations}
4: $US := nil$;     {Set of configurations, where unboundedness is detected}

5: $explore(\gamma_0)$;
6: **procedure** explore($\gamma$)
7: $push(\gamma, Stack)$;
8: $Fireable := out(\gamma)$; {fireable transitions}
9: **if** $Fireable \neq out_{MG}(\gamma)$ **then terminate**; {the model is not adequate}
10: **if** $Fireable \neq \emptyset$ **then**
11:     **forall** $trans \in Fireable$ **do**
12:         $\gamma' := trans.target$;
13:         **if** $\gamma' \notin Stack \cup Visited$ **then** {check boundedness}
14:             **if** $isUnbounded(\gamma')$ **then** $US := US \cup \{\gamma'\}$;
15:             **else** $explore(\gamma')$;
16: **else if** $\neg complete(\gamma)$ **then** $IS := IS \cup \{\gamma\}$;
17: $Visited := Visited \cup \{\gamma\}$;
18: $pop(\gamma, Stack)$;
19: **end procedure**

---

control and data in the composition representation. In particular, we show that the boundedness and adequacy results obtained on the data-less model may be propagated to the full model (under certain conditions). Moreover, using the abstraction techniques the representation may be made finite, enabling the model checking techniques as presented in [4].

# 7 Related Work and Conclusions

In this paper we presented a formal framework for the realizability analysis of Web service choreographies. The framework is based on the formalism suitable for modelling a composition both as a global protocol and as a set of interacting local services. For the global protocol we exploit a simple model, which is based on the notion of state transition systems, and allows for the automatic extraction of local projections that can be used as the basis for the service implementations. A composition of local services is formalized using the model of [4]. The key feature of this approach is the ability to specify for the composition a communication mechanism with an arbitrary structure. The most relevant original contribution of this paper is the definition of a hierarchy of notions of choreography realizability, which allows for capturing a wide range of properties of Web service choreographies. We also defined a correspondence between this hierarchy and the hierarchy of communication models presented in [4]. This correspondence allows us to exploit the analysis approach described in [4] for determining the level of realizability of the given global protocol specification.

The problem of the realizability of a global Web service protocol specification has been addressed in [5], while the realizability is defined as the ability of the composition of protocol projections to produce the same set of conversations. Several necessary conditions are formalized in order to enable the protocol realizability analysis. Contrary to our framework, the formalization of [5] is glued to a particular communication mechanism — the synchronous one — thus making the analysis results more restrictive. The framework presented here is also more flexible with respect to a notion of realizability.

The formalization and the analysis of the Web service choreography models are presented also in [6,10,11], while approaches to generate implementation templates from the choreography models are presented in [12,13]. However, the problem of realizability is not covered in these works, and the composition formalization is based on synchronous communications assumptions, which for a large range of scenarios and systems is not realistic.

# References

1. Andrews, T., Curbera, F., Dolakia, H., Goland, J., Klein, J., Leymann, F., Liu, K., Roller, D., Smith, D., Thatte, S., Trickovic, I., Weeravarana, S.: Business Process Execution Language for Web Services (version 1.1) (2003)
2. OMG: Business Process Modeling Language (BPML). (2005) [http://www.bpmi.org].
3. W3C: Web Services Choreography Description Language Version 1.0. (2005) [http://www.w3.org/TR/ws-cdl-10/].
4. Kazhamiakin, R., Pistore, M., Santuari, L.: Analysis of Communication Models in Web Service Compositions. In: Proc. WWW'06. (2006)
5. Fu, X., Bultan, T., Su, J.: Conversation protocols: a formalism for specification and verification of reactive electronic services. Theor. Comput. Sci. **328** (2004) 19–37
6. Busi, N., Gorrieri, R., Guidi, C., Lucchi, R., Zavattaro, G.: Choreography and Orchestration: A Synergic Approach for System Design. In: Proc. ICSOC'05. (2005)
7. Fu, X., Bultan, T., Su, J.: Analysis of Interacting BPEL Web Services. In: Proc. WWW'04. (2004)
8. Brand, D., Zafiropulo, P.: On communicating finite-state machines. J. ACM **30** (1983) 323–342
9. Kazhamiakin, R., Pistore, M.: Static Verification of Control and Data in Web Service Compositions. In: Proc. ICWS '06. (2006)
10. Brogi, A., Canal, C., Pimentel, E., Vallecillo, A.: Formalizing Web Services Choreographies. In: Proc. WS-FM'04. (2004)
11. Foster, H., Uchitel, S., Magee, J., Kramer, J.: Model-Based Analysis of Obligations in Web Service Choreography. In: Proc. AICT-ICIW'06. (2006)
12. Mendling, J., Hafner, M.: From Inter-Organizational Workflows to Process Execution: Generating BPEL from WS-CDL. In: Proc. OTM'05. (2005)
13. Bravetti, M., Guidi, C., Lucchi, R., Zavattaro, G.: Supporting e-commerce systems formalization with choreography languages. In: Proc. SAC '05. (2005)

# Web Cube

I.S.W.B. Prasetya[1], T.E.J. Vos[2,*], and S.D. Swierstra[1]

[1] Dept. of Inf. and Comp. Sciences, Utrecht University, the Netherlands
[2] Instituto Tecnológico de Informática, Valencia, Spain

**Abstract.** This paper introduces a refinement of Misra's Seuss logic, called Web Cube, that provides a model for programming and reasoning over web applications. It features black box composition of web services so that services offered by large systems, such as that of a back-end database, can be treated abstractly and consistently. It inherits the light weight feature of Seuss, which relies on an abstract view towards concurrency control, which leads to a less error-prone style of distributed programming, backed by a clean logic.

## 1 Introduction

Nowadays, sophisticated web applications are built using technologies like PHP, ASP, and servlets. Most are built by directly implementing them over these technologies, resulting in implementations where it is hard to separate implementation details from the core design problems. Debugging, let alone verification, is in general very hard. This is not a good practice. In theory, it is better to first design an application in an abstract-level modelling language. This is the development sequence that we will assume in this paper. At the design level, verifying critical properties is still feasible. Once verified, the design can be implemented. Subsequently, a more practical method, e.g. testing, can be used to validate the consistency between the implementation and the design. Web Cube is a *programming model*, which means it provides useful concepts and structures for constructing models of web applications and specify their critical properties. It also comes with a logic to verify a model against its properties. Web Cube is based on Misra's formalism for distributed and concurrent systems called Seuss [14]. As a modelling language Seuss is quite generic. Web Cube is more concrete than Seuss. It provides concepts which are quite specific for the domain of web applications, so that a Web Cube model can be implemented more directly.

This paper explains Web Cube's concepts and the semantics of its black box logic, which is its strongest feature. We do not at the moment offer a public implementation of Web Cube. There is a prototype, implemented by translating Web Cube source to Web Function library [10] written in the functional language Haskell. It is worth mentioning that alternatively it is often possible to implement a domain specific language by *embedding* it in a general purpose language, e.g. as the embedding of financial contract combinators in Haskell [11]. One could envisage a similar implementation of Web Cube in Haskell or in

---

* This work has been partially supported by the Generalitat Valenciana ref. GV05/261.

Java. An important benefit of embedding is that it gives a first class access to the modelling framework from the same programming language that one uses to write the application itself. This may help encouraging programmers to construct designs.

In Web Cube, a web *application* is modelled by a set of passive Seuss programs called *cubes* whose task is to coordinate a set of *web services* and interface them to users. Figure 1 shows an example of a Web Cube model of a simplified web-based voting application —more will be said at the end of Section 3. As in Seuss, we can specify temporal properties like: a valid vote submitted to the webVote application in Figure 1 *will* eventually be counted, or that the application never silently cancels a valid vote. Web Cube treats services as black boxes. This sacrifices completeness, but allows an application to be verified in isolation! —that is, without using the services' source code. Indeed, abstraction is now forced. But on the other hand, verification is also more feasible. Black box reasoning is however also fundamentally difficult, because parallel composition typically destroys progress properties of a component. Web Cube uses the theory from [18,19] to get a reasonably powerful black box logic while remaining light weight.

**Contribution.** Web Cube proposes a formal programming model for web applications with a Seuss logic support and the black box enhancement from our previous work [18,19]. With respect to Seuss we contribute an extension, namely the notions of web application and service. With respect to [18,19] the novelty here is in showing its application in the domain of web programming.

**Paper Overview.** Section 2 briefly introduces Seuss. Section 3 explains Web Cube's concepts and computation model. The formal machinery is described in Sections 4. Section 5 presents its black box logic. Section 6 discusses related work.

```
application webVote{
 service r = VoteServer ;   -- its contract in in Fig.4

  cube home {
    method home() {
     respond("<form method=post action=<@address.vote@>>
           Enter your vote: <input type=text name=v>
           <input type="submit" value="SUBMIT"> </form>
           <p><a href=<@address.info@>>Click here to get vote info</a>")}
    method vote(v) { r.vote(v) }
    method info() {
      var n = r.info() ;
      respond("<p>Total votes = <@n@>") ;
      if r.open then respond("<p>Open.") else respond("<p>Closed.") }    }}
```

**Fig. 1.** A simple Web Cube application for electronic voting

## 2 Seuss

In Seuss a *box* describes a *reactive* (non-terminating) program. It consists of a set of variables, a set of atomic guarded actions, and a set of methods. The variables define the state of the box. The execution of the box consists of an infinite sequence of steps; at each step an action is non-deterministically, but weakly fair, selected for execution. If the selected action's guard evaluates to true, the action is fully executed, else the effect is just a skip. The methods play a different role. They form the only mechanism for the environment to alter the state of the box. Methods may have parameters, actions can not.

For brevity we will not discuss the 'category' (generic box) [14]. When declaring a variable we omit its type specification. We only consider non-blocking methods (called *total* in [14]). Parameters are passed by value, and a method may return a value.

Figure 2 shows an example of a box called `VoteServer` —for now just consider it to have nothing to do with the `webVote` application in Figure 1. The notation `[]` denotes the empty list. The method `vote` allows the environment to submit a vote to the box. The box continuously executes one of its two actions: `move` and `validate`. The notation $g \rightarrow S$ denotes a guarded (and atomic) action: $g$ is the guard, and $S$ is the action to perform if the guard evaluates to true. The action `move` swaps the entire content of the incoming vote-buffer (`in`) to an internal buffer `tmp` —it can only do so if `tmp` is empty. The full code of `validate` is not displayed; the action takes the votes from `tmp` and if they are valid votes, moves them to `votes`; otherwise they are discarded. The environment can also call the method `info` to inquire after the number of (valid) votes registered so far.

Seuss' key feature is its abstract view towards multiprogramming. To program the control flow it only offers, essentially, parallel composition and guarded actions. It advocates that a programmer should only be concerned with specifying, essentially, the set of concurrent atomic tasks that constitute a system. He *should not be concerned with how to schedule these tasks for optimal performance* —the compiler and the run time system should figure this out. This abstract view leads to a simple logic and clean designs.

Seuss is the evolution of UNITY [4]. With respect to UNITY, Seuss adds methods (which are used to limit interference by the environment of a system) and the ability to structure a system's architecture as a hierarchy of boxes.

```
box VoteServer {
    var    in, votes, tmp = []    ;
           open = True            ;
    method vote(v) { if open then in := insert(v,in) else skip }
           info()  { return length(votes) }
           stop()  { open := False }
    action move     ::  null tmp       -> tmp,in := in,[] ;
           validate ::  not(null tmp) -> ...                      }
```

**Fig. 2.** *An example of a Seuss box*

Seuss logic uses a slightly different set of operators. We will stick to the old UNITY unless and $\mapsto$ (leads-to) to specify temporal properties, which are derived operators in Seuss. We will defer their discussion until Section 4 where we alter their standard definition to deal with 'components'.

## 3  Web Cube

A Web Cube application, or simply *application*, models a server side program that interacts with a client via an HTTP connection. Figure 3-left shows the architecture of a hypothetical Web Cube execution system. Applications (e.g. $A_1$, $A_2$, $B_1$, ... ) may run different machines. We assume a Web Cube aware HTTP server which can direct a client's requests to the correct application, collect the application's reply, and forward it back to the client.

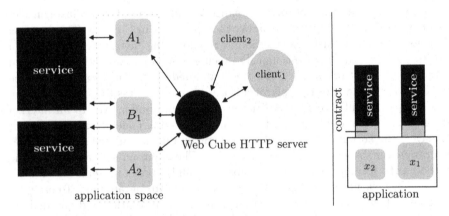

**Fig. 3.** Web Cube architecture

An application $A$ is built, like in Figure 3-right, by composing so-called *cubes* ($x_1$ and $x_2$) and *web services*. A cube $x$ is a 'passive' Seuss box —we will say more on this later— that models a part of $A$ that can interact with a client. A client $E$ interacts by calling $x$'s methods. In practice this will be encoded as HTTP requests; $x$ replies by sending back HTML responses. A web service, or simply *service*, is a black box program described by a contract and can be remotely interacted to (in practice this may happen over a SOAP/HTTP connection) by cubes. We further assume that a service is a state-persistent reactive system. Note that by attaching a contract to $A$ it also becomes a service. A user can use his web browser to enact $A$'s client $E$ and interact with one of its cubes; the browser will display the cube's responses. However, $E$ does not have to be a web browser: it can be another application using $A$ as a service.

The role of a cube is purely for computing the responses to client's requests. It does not have reactive behavior of its own; so, we describe it by a passive Seuss box, which is a box with an empty set of actions. A service on the other hand, may spontaneously execute actions to update its own state. Each client's request may trigger a coordinated computation over the services. For safety reason, the client can only interact with $A$'s cubes; it cannot interact directly with $A$'s services. So, the cubes can also be seen as providing a layer for orchestrating the services. An orchestration language, e.g. [15], can be used in conjunction to Seuss for convenient coding of the orchestration, taking into account the atomicity restriction demanded by Web Cube (Subsection 4.5).

Since a service such as a corporate database is actually a large and complicated system, we will view it as a black box specified by a *contract*. Such a contract includes a Seuss box that abstractly (thus incompletely) specifies how the service behaves as a reactive system. As in *design by contract* [13], some party, e.g. the service owner, is assumed to guarantee the consistency between the service's implementation and its contract.

An application can be deployed as a state-persistent program serving multiple clients. Another scheme, as common in e.g. servlets, is to create a fresh and exclusive instance which lasts for a single session. We are not going to make the distinction in our formal model. With respect to single-session applications, a session is treated to last infinitely long, so the application can be treated in the same way as a persistent application.

**Example.** Figure 1 shows a simple Web Cube application, called `webVote`, which provides an electronic voting service. It consists of a single cube called `home` and a service symbolically called `r` which is linked to the component `VoteServer` from Figure 2. Each application should have a cube called `home` that contains a method `home`. The method is called automatically when an instance of the application is created and so resembles the home-page of the application. For the `webVote` application this will cause the user's browser to show a simple form where the voter can type in his vote, a submit button, and a link to get the voting status.

**HTML Responses.** A cube's method $m$ responds to a client's call by sending back its return value, encoded in HTML. Like in Java servlets, $m$ can also generate responses by calling the `respond` method: it takes a HTML-code which will be sent to the client. The entire response of $m$ to a call consists of the concatenation of strings produced by all the calls to `respond` in $m$, followed by $m$'s HTML-encoded return value. A Web browser client may choose to display both; Web Cube applications acting as clients can only use the return value.

Responses from `respond` are however *ignored* by our Seuss semantics, which makes reasoning simpler. To do so safely we have to require that inlined expressions (below) do *not* have side effects (which is not imposed in servlets).

As in servlets, inlined expressions are allowed, as in: `respond "hello <@ e @>"`; $e$ will be evaluated and its result is inserted in the place where $e$ appears. Inlined expression of the form `address.m` will be substituted by $m$'s URI address, causing $m$ to be called when the user clicks on it.

# 4    Semantics

We have explained the building blocks of a Web Cube application and its execution model. We now give its semantics, operators for specifying properties, and an extension to the Seuss logic for proving properties.

In the sequel $a, b, c$ are actions, $i$ and $j$ are predicates intended to be invariants, $p, q, r$ are predicates, $P, Q, R$ are action systems (explained later), $x, y, z$ are boxes.

## 4.1    Preliminaries

**Selector.** We use tuples to represent composite structures, and selectors to select the various parts. For example, $T = (\mathsf{a} :: U, \mathsf{b} :: V)$ defines a type $T$ consisting of pairs whose elements are of type $U$ and $V$. If $t = (u, v)$ is a value of type $T$, then $t.\mathsf{a} = u$ and $t.\mathsf{b} = v$.

**Actions.** An *action* is an atomic, terminating, and non-deterministic state transition. We model it by a function from the universe of states, denoted by $\mathsf{State}$, to $\mathcal{P}(\mathsf{State})$. Guarded actions are denoted by $g \rightarrow S$, meaning that $S$ will be only executed if $g$ is true, otherwise the action behaves as a skip —the latter implies that in our model $a\ s \neq$ , for any action $a$ and state $s$. If $a$ and $b$ are actions, $a \sqcup b$ is an action that either behaves as $a$ or as $b$. So, $(a \sqcup b)\ s = a\ s \cup b\ s$. If $A$ is a set of actions then $\sqcup A$ denotes $(\sqcup a : a \in A : a)$. If $V$ is a set of variables, skip $V$ is an action that does not change the variables in $V$, but may change variables outside $V$. The notation $\{p\}\ a\ \{q\}$ denotes a Hoare triple over an action $a$ with $p$ and $q$ as pre- and post-condition.

**Predicate Confinement.** State predicates specify a set of program states. A predicate $p$ is *confined* by a set of variables $V$, written $p$ **conf** $V$, if $p$ can only be falsified by actions that manipulate variables in $V$ (it follows that $p$ is confined by its set of free variables). We write $p, q$ **conf** $V$ to abbreviate $p$ **conf** $V$ and $q$ **conf** $V$.

## 4.2    More Preliminaries: Box and Property

The methods of a (Seuss) box $x$ only define the interface with which the environment interacts with $x$. If we strip the methods we obtain the description of the box's own program. This stripped box is called the *action system* and corresponds to a UNITY program ([4], Seuss predecessor). For conciseness we only define properties and parallel composition at the action system level, since this is sufficient for presenting our theorems later. Technically, these notions can be lifted quite naturally to the box and application level. Formally, we will represent box and action system as follows.

$$Box \stackrel{d}{=} (\mathsf{main} :: ActionSys, \mathsf{meths} :: \{Method\}) \tag{1}$$

$$ActionSys \stackrel{d}{=} (\mathsf{acts} :: \{Action\}, \mathsf{init} :: Pred, \mathsf{var} :: \{Var\}) \tag{2}$$

If $P$ is an action system, $P$.init is a predicate specifying $P$'s possible initial states, $P$.var is the set of $P$'s variables. Implicitly, $P$.init has to be confined by $P$.var. We will overload action system's selectors so that they also work on boxes, e.g. $x$.var means $x$.main.var.

A useful property is that of invariant, because it confines the set of states reachable by a reactive program. A predicate $i$ is a *strong invariant* of an action system $P$, denoted by $P \vdash \mathsf{sinv}\ i$, if it holds initially, and is maintained by every action in $P$:

$$P \vdash \mathsf{sinv}\ i \stackrel{d}{=} P.\mathsf{init} \Rightarrow i \ \wedge\ (\forall a : a \in P.\mathsf{acts} : \{i\}\ a\ \{i\}) \tag{3}$$

A predicate $j$ is an *invariant* if there exists a strong invariant $i$ implying $j$. For specifying a broader range of safety properties, Seuss offers the unless operator. Let $p$ and $q$ be state predicates. When $p$ unless $q$ holds in $P$, this means, intuitively, that each action in $P$ will go from *any* state in $p$ to some state in $p \vee q$. Note that the definition quantifies over *all* states. We will deviate from this definition. We parameterize the property with an invariant $(i)$, as in [20], so that the quantification over states can be restricted to those which are actually reachable by $P$. Moreover, we require that $p$ and $q$ to be confined by $P$.var. Although this seems more restrictive, it does not really limit the way in which we usually use the operator. Technically, it makes the property more robust in parallel compositions [16]. Together with the definition of unless we also give the corresponding ensures operator, which specifies progress from $p$ to $q$ by executing a single action:

**Def. 1** : BASIC OPERATORS

1. $P, i \ \vdash\ p\ \mathsf{unless}\ q \stackrel{d}{=} P \ \vdash\ \mathsf{sinv}\ i \ \wedge\ p, q\ \mathbf{conf}\ P.\mathsf{var}$
$\wedge\ (\forall a : a \in P.\mathsf{acts} : \{i \wedge p \wedge \neg q\}\ a\ \{p \vee q\})$

2. $P, i \ \vdash\ p\ \mathsf{ensures}\ q \stackrel{d}{=} P, i \ \vdash\ p\ \mathsf{unless}\ q$
$\wedge\ (\exists a : a \in P.\mathsf{acts} : \{i \wedge p \wedge \neg q\}\ a\ \{q\})$

The general progress operator $\mapsto$ is usually defined as the least transitive and disjunctive closure of ensures. Unfortunately, progress defined in this way is difficult to preserve when subjected to parallel composition —essentially, because we do not put any constraint on the environment. We will return to this issue in Section 4.4.

We only introduce one sort of program composition, namely *parallel composition*. If $P$ and $Q$ are action systems, $P\|Q$ denotes an action system that models the parallel execution of $P$ and $Q$:

$$P\|Q \stackrel{d}{=} (P.\mathsf{acts} \cup Q.\mathsf{acts},\ P.\mathsf{init} \wedge Q.\mathsf{init},\ P.\mathsf{var} \cup Q.\mathsf{var}) \tag{4}$$

If $x$ and $y$ are two boxes, we also write $x\|P$ to denote $x$.main$\|P$ and $x\|y$ to denote $x$.main$\|y$.main.

## 4.3 The Underlying Component Based Approach

Web Cube assumes services to be available as black box entities, also called *components* [25]. A component only reveals partial information about itself in the form of a *contract*. In particular, it does not reveal its full code. The component owner guarantees the consistency of the contract. Obviously a contract that reveals more information allows stronger properties to be inferred from it. However, such a contract is also more constraining, hence making the component less reusable, and the verification of the the component's implementation more costly. Consequently, when writing a contract, a developer will have to consider a reasonable balance.

Essentially the relation between a component $x$ and its contract $c$ is a *refinement/abstraction* relation. That is, $x$ has to refine $c$ (or conversely, $c$ is an abstraction of $x$), usually denoted by $c \sqsubseteq x$. Such a relation preserves properties of interest: a property $\phi$ inferred from the contract $c$ is also a property of the component $x$. In sequential programming refinement traditionally means reduction of non-determinism [2]. Lifted to distributed programming $c \sqsubseteq x$ means that every observable execution trace of $x$ is allowed by $c$. This relation does not however preserve progress properties. There are a number of stronger (more restrictive) alternatives, e.g. Udink's [26] and Vos' [27], that preserve progress; but these are expensive to verify. For Web Cube, we choose a weak notion of refinement, taken from our previous work [18]. It is even weaker than simple reduction of non-determinism, and thus has the advantage that it is less restrictive, and hence easier to verify. Like most refinement relations, it still preserves safety, but surprisingly it also preserves a class of progress properties as we will see below. Although the class is much smaller than for example Vos' [27], we believe it is still quite useful.

We start by defining the refinement at the action level. Let $a$ and $b$ be two actions. Traditionally, $a \sqsubseteq b$ means that $b$ can simulate whatever $a$ can do ([2]). However, this is a bit too restrictive in the context of an action system. Imagine that $a$ is part of an action system $P$, then we can ignore what $b$ does on variables outside $P$.var or what its effect is on the states that are not reachable by $P$. Furthermore, we can also allow $b$ to do nothing, since doing nothing will not break any safety properties of $a$. We capture these issues in our refinement relation in the following formalization. Let $V$ be a set of variables (intended to be $P$.var), and $i$ be a predicate (intended to be an invariant, thus specifying $P$'s reachable states). Action $b$ *weakly refines* action $a$ with respect to $V$ and $i$ is defined as follows:

$$V, i \vdash a \sqsubseteq b$$
$$\overset{d}{=} (\forall p, q : p, q \text{ conf } V : \{i \land p\}\, a \sqcup \text{skip } V\, \{q\} \;\Rightarrow\; \{i \land p\}\, b\, \{q\}) \tag{5}$$

Lifting this definition to the action system level gives us:

**Def. 2** : REFINEMENT/ABSTRACTION
$$i \vdash P \sqsubseteq Q \overset{d}{=} \quad P.\text{var} \subseteq Q.\text{var} \;\land\; (i \land Q.\text{init} \Rightarrow P.\text{init})$$
$$\land \; (\forall b : b \in Q.\text{acts} : P.\text{var}, i \vdash \sqcup P.\text{acts} \sqsubseteq b)$$

So, under the invariance of $i$, $i \vdash P \sqsubseteq Q$ means that every action of $Q$ either does not touch the variables of $P$, or if it does it will not behave worse than some action of $P$. Parallel composition is $\sqsubseteq$-monotonic in both its arguments.

## 4.4    Basic Results on Black Box Composition

Like in [3,26,27] the above refinement relation preserves safety but in general not progress. However, consider the following restricted class of progress properties. Let $B$ be an environment for $P$. We write:

$$P_{\triangleleft}\|B,\ i\ \vdash\ p \mapsto q$$

to express that under the invariance of $i$, the composed system $P\|B$ can progress from $p$ to $q$. Moreover, this progress is *driven by* $P$. That is, the progress is realized even if $B$ does nothing:

**Def. 3** : EXTENDED PROGRESS OPERATORS

1. $P_{\triangleleft}\|B,\ i\ \vdash\ p$ ensures $q\ \stackrel{d}{=}\ P\|B,\ i\ \vdash\ p$ unless $q$
   $\wedge\ (\exists a : a \in P.\text{acts} : \{i \wedge p \wedge \neg q\}\ a\ \{q\})$
2. $P_{\triangleleft}\|B,\ i \vdash p \mapsto q$ is defined such that $(\lambda p, q.\ P_{\triangleleft}\|B,\ i \vdash p \mapsto q)$ is the smallest transitive and disjunctive closure of $(\lambda p, q.\ P_{\triangleleft}\|B,\ i \vdash p$ ensures $q)$.

The result from [18] below states that progress 'driven by $x$' is preserved by weak refinement over $B$:

**Thm. 4** : PRESERVATION OF $\mapsto$

$$\frac{x_{\triangleleft}\|B, i \vdash p \mapsto q\ \wedge\ j \vdash B \sqsubseteq Q\ \wedge\ i \Rightarrow j}{x\|Q, i \vdash p \mapsto q}$$

Note that the same does not hold for weak refinement over $x$.

**Proof:** The formal proof is by induction over $\mapsto$; we refer to [18]. Informally: assume $i$ as an invariant of $x\|Q$. Since $i \Rightarrow j$, $j$ is also an invariant. Since $Q$ refines $B$ under $j$, throughout the computation of $x\|Q$ every action of $Q$ behaves, with respect to variables of $x$ and $Q$, as some action of $B$ or as a skip. Consequently $Q$ cannot destroy any progress in terms of $x_{\triangleleft}\|B$, since this progress is driven by $x$ and cannot be destroyed by any action of $B$.                                  □

The theorem below states that our notion of weak refinement also preserves safety. We refer to [18] for the proof.

**Thm. 5** : PRESERVATION OF UNLESS

$$\frac{x, i \vdash p \text{ unless } q\ \wedge\ j \vdash x \sqsubseteq x'\ \wedge\ i \Rightarrow j}{x', i \vdash p \text{ unless } q}$$

## 4.5    Web Cube Atomicity Restriction

Let $y$ be the environment of a box $x$ in a parallel composition. Seuss allows methods and actions of $y$ to call $x$'s methods. In particular, this allows $y$ to perform multiple method calls to one or more boxes in a single action. Since actions are atomic, this effectively empowers $y$ to force an arbitrary level of atomicity on its accesses to $x$. This is a very powerful feature, but unfortunately it will also allow $y$ to behave more destructively with respect to $x$'s temporal properties. For this reason in Web Cube we will limit the feature, and define a notion of *worst allowed environment* as follows:

$$x.\text{env} \overset{d}{=} (\{\sqcup m \mid m \in x.\text{meth}\}, x.\text{init}, x.\text{var}) \qquad (6)$$

where $\sqcup m$ is an action modeling the disjunction of all possible *single* calls to $m$. So, if $m$ is a 1-arity method, then $\sqcup m = (\sqcup v :: m(v))$.

Now, we define a box $y$ to be a *proper (allowed) environment* of $x$ under an invariant $i$ if it refines the worst allowed environment of $x$. More precisely:

$$y \text{ is a proper environment of } x \text{ (under } i) \overset{d}{=} i \vdash x.\text{env} \sqsubseteq y.\text{main} \sqcup y.\text{env} \qquad (7)$$

Intuitively, every action and method of $x$'s proper environment $y$ can only contain a single call to a state-altering method of $x$. This can be checked statically. The action (method) can however still contain an arbitrary number of calls to $x$'s functional methods (i.e. methods that do not alter the state) and calls to other boxes' methods. The proper environment condition enforces a more deterministic environment, but in return it will behave less destructively with respect to $x$.

### 4.6  Contracts

We will use the following structure to represent contracts:

$$\textit{Contract} = (\text{smodel} :: \textit{Box}, \text{inv} :: \textit{Pred}, \text{progress} :: \{\textit{ProgressSpec}\})$$

If $c$ is a contract, $c.\text{impl}$ denotes a Seuss box which is a component associated with $c$. Let $x = c.\text{impl}$. The methods of $c.\text{smodel}$ specify the visible interface of $x$. The action system of $c.\text{smodel}$ specifies an abstraction over $x$, in the sense of Def. 2. The inv section specifies an invariant. In the progress section we specify the component's critical progress properties. Only progress 'driven by' the component, in the sense of Def. 3, can be specified, so that we can use Thm. 4 to infer its preservation. In practice a component like a database is not written in Seuss. However, as long as its owner can produce the above form of contract, and guarantee it, we can proceed. The relation between $c$ and $c.\text{impl}$ is formalized by:

**Def. 6** : Box-Contract Relation
If $c$ is a contract and $x = c.\text{impl}$, there should exist a predicate $i$ such that:

1. $i$ is a strong invariant of $x\|x.\text{env}$ and it implies $c.\text{inv}$.
2. $c$ and $x$ have a 'compatible' interface. For brevity, here it means that both specify exactly the same set of methods: $c.\text{smodel.meth} = x.\text{meth}$.
3. $c.\text{smodel}$ is a consistent abstraction of $x$, i.e. $i \vdash c.\text{smodel.main} \sqsubseteq x.\text{main}$
4. for every specification $p \mapsto q$ in $c.\text{progress}$ we have $x_\triangleleft\|x.\text{env}, i \vdash p \mapsto q$.

```
contract VoteServer {
  smodel
    var    in, votes  = []    ;
           open       = True  ;
    method vote(v) { if open then in := insert(v,in) else skip } ;
           info()  { return length(votes)) }                     ;
           stop()  { open := False         }                     ;
    action fetch :: in := [] ;
           count :: {var v ;
                       if isValid(v) then votes := insert(v,votes) else skip }

  inv         v in votes ==> isValid(v)

  progress    isValid(v)/\open ; vote(v)  |--> v in votes
}
```

**Fig. 4.** A contract for the component VoteServer (Figure 2)

The invariant $i$ mentioned above is called the *concrete invariant* of $x$, and will be denoted by $x$.concreteInv. This concrete invariant $i$ is partially specified by $c$.inv, since $i \Rightarrow c$.inv. Its full details cannot be inferred from the contract though. The first condition above also implies that $i$.inv is an invariant of $x \| x$.env, though in general it is *not* a *strong* invariant of $x \| x$.env.

The above definition of 'compatible interface' implies $c$.impl.env $= c$.smodel.env So, any environment which is proper according to a contract $c$ is automatically also a proper environment of $c$.impl. Actually, it would be sufficient to require $c$.impl.env $\sqsubseteq c$.smodel.env such that we can weaken the definition of 'compatible interface' and make it more realistic. This, however, is outside the scope of this paper.

Figure 4 shows an example of a contract, that could belong to the component VoteServer in Figure 2. Free variables in the inv and progress sections are assumed to be universally quantified. The contract's action part reveals that VoteServer may from time to time empty the incoming buffer in. It does not, however, specify when exactly this will happen. The contract also says that the server will only fill votes with *valid* votes though it leaves unspecified as to where these votes should come from. Although a very weak one can infer a critical safety property from this abstraction: *no invalid vote will be included in the counting.*

For convenience, we allow methods to be used when specifying state predicates within a temporal specification in the following way. If $p$ is a state predicate and $m(e)$ is a call to a method $m$, the predicate $p; m(e)$ specifies the set of states that result from executing $m(e)$ on states satisfying $p$. So, the progress section in Figure 4 states that after a valid vote is successfully submitted (which only happens if open is true) through a call to the method vote, eventually the vote will be counted by the server (captured by the predicate v in votes). With this property the server guarantees there cannot be any loss of valid votes.

## 4.7 Semantics of Application

We can now give the semantics of a web application. An application consists of cubes and services. The latter are components, so they are represented by their contracts. Formally, we represent an application by this structure:

$$App \overset{d}{=} (\text{svc} :: \{Contract\}, \text{cube} :: \{Box\}) \tag{8}$$

If $C$ is a set of boxes, let $\|C$ denote the parallel composition of all the boxes in $C$. Let $A$ be an application. The Seuss semantics of $A$ is the concrete program induced by $A$, which is just the parallel composition of all its services and cubes:

$$A.\text{impl} \overset{d}{=} (\|c : c \in A.\text{svc} : c.\text{impl}) \| (\| A.\text{cube}) \tag{9}$$

Although this implementation is not visible, we can infer, from the cubes and the contracts, an abstract model for the application:

$$A.\text{model} \overset{d}{=} (\|c : c \in A.\text{svc} : c.\text{smodel}) \| (\| A.\text{cube}) \tag{10}$$

$A.\text{client}$ is $A$'s worst allowed client. It is the one that tries all possible calls to the methods of $A$'s cubes:

$$A.\text{client} \overset{d}{=} (\|x : x \in A.\text{cube} : c.\text{smodel.env}) \tag{11}$$

Note that $A.\text{client}$ is by definition an abstraction of any proper client of $A$.

**Wrapping.** Since semantically, $A.\text{impl}\|client$ is a box, it can be treated as a component by providing a contract. Semantically, it becomes a service. In the implementation this may require some wrapping to make it SOAP-enabled. As a service it can be used to build larger applications.

## 5   Inference

Seuss provides a logic [14] for proving safety and progress properties. Although we have changed the definitions of Seuss temporal operators, it can be proven in a quite standard way that they maintain basic Seuss laws, e.g. using our general proof theory in [17]. We now add important results, namely theorems for inferring properties of an application from the contracts of its services —with just plain Seuss, this is not possible.

Let $A$ be an application. Let $A.\text{inv}$ denote the combined abstract invariant of $A$, which is the conjunction of the invariants specified by the contracts in $A$. Similarly, $A.\text{concreteInv}$ denotes the combined concrete invariant of $A$. The latter cannot be inferred from the contracts. However, we just need to infer that properties inferred from $A$ are consistent with it. Let $client$ be a proper client of $A$ (under $A.\text{inv}$). We have:

**Thm. 7** : INFERRING SAFETY FROM ABSTRACT MODEL

$$\frac{A.\text{model}\|client, \ A.\text{inv} \ \vdash \ p \text{ unless } q}{A.\text{impl}\|client, \ A.\text{concreteInv} \ \vdash \ p \text{ unless } q}$$

**Proof:** the Contract-Box relation (Def. 6) imposed on the services implies that $A$.model is a consistent abstraction of $A$.impl:

$$A.\text{concreteInv} \vdash A.\text{model} \sqsubseteq A.\text{impl} \tag{12}$$

It follows, by Thm. 5, that any **unless** property proven on the abstract model is also a property of the concrete system.                                              $\square$

For inferring progress we have:

**Thm. 8** : Progress by Contract

$$\frac{c \in A.\text{contract} \quad \wedge \quad p \mapsto q \in c.\text{progress}}{A.\text{impl}_{\triangleleft}[\![client, A.\text{concreteInv} \vdash p \mapsto q]\!]}$$

**Proof:** by Def. 6, $c$.progress actually specifies this progress: $c.\text{impl}_{\triangleleft}[\![c.\text{env} \vdash p \mapsto q]\!]$. Imposing the constraint on the atomicity of method calls from Subsection 4.5, makes the rest of the application and the *client* act as a proper environment for $c$. Hence, by Thm. 4 the progress will be preserved in the entire system.      $\square$

Below is the dual of the theorem above, stating that progress solely driven by the *client*, assuming $A$'s abstract model as the environment, will be preserved in the entire system:

**Thm. 9** : Client Progress

$$\frac{client_{\triangleleft}[\![A.\text{model}, A.\text{inv} \vdash p \mapsto q]\!]}{client_{\triangleleft}[\![A.\text{impl}, A.\text{concreteInv} \vdash p \mapsto q]\!]}$$

**Proof:** follows from (12) and Thm. 4.

**Example.** Consider again the example we mentioned in the Introduction: we want a guarantee that a valid vote submitted to the `webVote` application in Figure 1 will eventually be counted. The property is promised by the `VoteServer` service in `webVote`. Now we can use Thm. 8 to conclude that the property will indeed be preserved in the system.

Consider also the property `info()` $\geq N$ **unless** **false**. It is an important safety property, stating that the application will not silently cancel an already counted vote. In order to verify its correctness, Thm. 7 says that we can do so against the *abstract* model of the application. This means isolated verification: we do not need the full code of the services!

We cannot infer everything from a contract, because it is just an abstraction. For example, the component `VoteServer` in Figure 2 will not silently insert a valid-but-fake vote. However, we cannot infer this from the contract in Figure 4.

# 6   Related Work

Formal methods have been used to specify and verify document related properties of web applications. Semantic Web [5] is currently popular as a framework to define the semantics of documents, thus enabling reasoning over them, e.g. simply by using theorem provers. On top of it sophisticated properties can be specified e.g. as [12] that offers a query language, in the spirit of SQL, over documents. Automated verification has also been explored [22,9,1], though we will have to limit ourselves to simple document properties, e.g. the reachability of different parts of a web page from multiple concurrent frames. Web Cube logic focuses on temporal properties over the state maintained by a web application, rather than on document properties —these two aspects are complementary.

A Web Cube is primarily a programming model for constructing a web application. Although it is based on services composition, it is not a dedicated service orchestration language as e.g. BPEL, cl [8], or Orc [15]. Given a Web Cube application $A$, requests from a client are translated to calls to $A$'s cubes' methods. In turn a method may perform a series of calls to multiple services, scripted as a plain Seuss statement. So, orchestration in Web Cube happens at the method level, and is consequently limited by the atomicity constraint over methods. Therefore, the full BPEL concurrency (of orchestration) cannot be mapped to Web Cube's orchestration. Though on the other hand we get a nice back box temporal logic for Web Cube, whereas this would be a problem for BPEL. Orc's [15] type of orchestration matches better to Web Cube. A top level Orc expression is atomic. So in principle it can be used to specify a cube's method. Formalisms like process algebra [6], Petri net [21], or event-based temporal logic [24] have been used to reason over service orchestration. These are more suitable for work-flow oriented style of orchestration (e.g. as in BPEL). In Web Cube calls to services may cause side effect on the services' persistent state. So, Web Cube uses a classical temporal logic which is more suitable to reason over temporal properties over persistent states.

Web Cube assumes a more classical development cycle, where Seuss is used to abstractly describe a web application. Properties are reasoned at this Seuss level. Actual implementation could be obtained by translating Seuss to an implementation language, e.g. Java. Language embedding [11] is also an interesting route to obtain implementation. Others have used refinement to develop an application [23]. Seuss is not a refinement calculus; refinement in Web Cube is used to bind contracts. In *reverse engineering* people attempt to do the opposite direction: to extract models from an existing implementation of a web application, e.g. as in [7,22,9,1]. The models are subsequently subjected to analysis, e.g. verification. Reverse engineering can yield high automation, but defining the procedure to extract the models is not trivial, especially if the programming model used at the model level differs too much from that of the implementation level. This is likely the case with Web Cube, since it tries to be high level, and hence hard to extract from e.g. an arbitrary Java code.

Compared to all the work mentioned above Web Cube is also different because of its component based approach.

# References

1. M. Alpuente, D. Ballis, and M. Falaschi. A rewriting-based framework for web sites verification. In *Proc. 5th Int. W.shop on Rule-based Programming RULE*. Elsevier Science, 2004.
2. R.J. R. Back. *On the Correctness of Refinement Steps in Program Development*. PhD thesis, University of Helsinki, 1978. Also available as report A-1978-5.
3. R.J.R. Back and J. Von Wright. Refinement calculus, part II: Parallel and reactive programs. *Lecture Notes of Computer Science*, 430:67–93, 1989.
4. K.M. Chandy and J. Misra. *Parallel Program Design – A Foundation*. Addison-Wesley Publishing Company, Inc., 1988.
5. M.C. Daconta, L.J. Obrst, and K.T. Smith. *The Semantic Web: A Guide to the Future of XML, Web Services, and Knowledge Management*. 2003.
6. A. Ferrara. Web services: a process algebra approach. In *Proceedings of 2nd International Conference Service-Oriented Computing (ICSOC)*, pages 242–251. ACM, 2004.
7. H. Foster, S. Uchitel, J. Magee, and J. Kramer. LTSA-WS: a tool for model-based verification of web service compositions and choreography. In *Proceeding of the 28th international conference on Software engineering*, pages 771–774. ACM Press, 2006.
8. S. Frolund and K. Govindarajan. cl: A language for formally defining web services interactions. Technical Report HPL-2003-208, Hewlett Packard Laboratories, 2003.
9. M. Haydar. Formal framework for automated analysis and verification of web-based applications. In *Proc. 19th IEEE Int. Conf. on Automated Software Engineering (ASE)*, pages 410–413. IEEE Computer Society, 2004.
10. R. Herk. Web functions, 2005. Master thesis, IICS, Utrecht Univ. No. INF/SCR-2005-014.
11. S. Peyton Jones, J.-M. Eber, and J. Seward. Composing contracts: an adventure in financial engineering. In *Proc. 5th Int. Conf. on Functional Programming*, pages 280–292, 2000.
12. A.O. Mendelzon and T. Milo. Formal models of Web queries. In *Proc. of the 16th ACM Sym. on Principles of Database Systems (PODS)*, pages 134–143, 1997.
13. B. Meyer. Applying design by contract. *IEEE Computer*, 25(10):40–51, 1992.
14. J. Misra. *A Discipline of Multiprogramming*. Springer-Verlag, 2001.
15. J. Misra. A programming model for the orchestration of web services. In *2nd Int. Conf. on Software Engineering and Formal Methods (SEFM'04)*, pages 2–11, 2004.
16. I.S.W.B. Prasetya. *Mechanically Supported Design of Self-stabilizing Algorithms*. PhD thesis, Inst. of Information and Computer Sci., Utrecht University, 1995.
17. I.S.W.B Prasetya, T.E.J. Vos, A. Azurat, and S.D. Swierstra. !UNITY: A HOL theory of general UNITY. In *Emerging Trends Proceedings of 16th Int. Conf. Theorem Proving in Higher Order Logics*, pages 159–176, 2003.
18. I.S.W.B Prasetya, T.E.J. Vos, A. Azurat, and S.D. Swierstra. A unity-based framework towards component based systems. Technical Report UU-CS-2003-043, IICS, Utrecht Univ., 2003.
19. I.S.W.B Prasetya, T.E.J. Vos, A. Azurat, and S.D. Swierstra. A unity-based framework towards component based systems. In *Proc. of 8th Int. Conf. on Principles of Distributed Systems (OPODIS)*, 2004.
20. B.A. Sanders. Eliminating the substitution axiom from UNITY logic. *Formal Aspects of Computing*, 3(2):189–205, 1991.

21. K. Schmidt and C. Stahl. A petri net semantic for BPEL. In *Proc. of 11th Workshop Algorithms and Tools for Petri Nets*, 2004.
22. E. Di Sciascio, F.M. Donini, M. Mongiello, and G. Piscitelli. AnWeb: a system for automatic support to web application verification. In *SEKE '02*, pages 609–616. ACM Press, 2002.
23. G. Di Marzo Serugendo and N. Guelfi. Formal development of java based web parallel applications. In *Proc. of the Hawai Int. Conf. on System Sciences*, 1998.
24. M.P. Singh. Distributed enactment of multiagent workflows: temporal logic for web service composition. In *AAMAS '03: Proceedings of the second international joint conference on Autonomous agents and multiagent systems*, pages 907–914. ACM Press, 2003.
25. C. Szyperski. *Component Software, Beyond Object-Oriented Programming*. Addison-Wesley, 1998.
26. R.T. Udink. *Program Refinement in UNITY-like Environments*. PhD thesis, Inst. of Information and Computer Sci., Utrecht University, 1995.
27. T.E.J. Vos. *UNITY in Diversity: A Stratified Approach to the Verification of Distributed Algorithms*. PhD thesis, Inst. of Information and Computer Sci., Utrecht University, 2000.

# Presence Interaction Management in SIP SOHO Architecture

Zohair Chentouf[1] and Ahmed Khoumsi[2]

[1] Dialexia Communications Inc., Montreal, Canada
czohair@dialexia.com
[2] Université de Sherbrooke, Sherbrooke, Canada
Ahmed.Khoumsi@USherbrooke.ca

**Abstract.** A SOHO (Small Office or Home Office) architecture can be sketched as an architecture that involves an ITSP (Internet Telephony Service Provider) and subscribers. The ITSP offers SIP protocol based telephony and presence services for subscribers. A subscriber can have several presence capable devices that periodically publish the user presence status. The paper defines and proposes a solution to the presence interaction (PI) problem.

**Keywords:** SOHO, Presence interaction (PI) detection and resolution, PI Management Agent (PIMA), PI Management Language (PIML), order relations.

## 1 Introduction

In this article, we consider a particular architecture, called SOHO (Small Office or Home Office), containing an Internet Telephony Service Provider (ITSP) that offers SIP based telephony and presence services for users. Each user can own one or more devices. The devices that are presence capable, periodically publish the user presence status to the ITSP presence server. A *presence interaction* (PI) arises when two or more devices owned by the same user publish contradictory presence status, for example, *available* and *out-for-lunch*.

We propose a multi-agents architecture for managing PI. The detection and resolution procedure is based on order relations. A PI Management Language (PIML) is used to express formally the relevant information for managing PI.

Section 2 introduces the presence service and our proposed architecture. In Section 3, we introduce PI and the approach used for solving them. In Section 4, we propose a Multi-agents approach for managing PI. Section 5 presents PIML that is used to model presence status and resolution policies. And we conclude in Section 6.

## 2 Presence Service and Proposed Architecture

SIP offers an architecture and communication mechanisms for implementing a presence publishing service. The SIP presence architecture [1] encompasses user terminals that publish presence information to a presence server, using the PUBLISH message [2]. Users which publish their presence information are called presentities.

E. Najm et al. (Eds.): FORTE 2006, LNCS 4229, pp. 93–98, 2006.
© IFIP International Federation for Information Processing 2006

The presence server composes the presence information that is published by different terminals that belong to a same presentity in order to produce a single presence document. The users who are interested to be notified about the presence status of a given presentity, subscribe to this service by sending a SUBSCRIBE message to the presence server. Those users are called watchers. Every time his presence status is changed, the presentity publishes the new presence information. The presence server then notifies all the watchers of that presentity about his new presence information by sending a NOTIFY message to every one, including the presence document. In [3], presence information as well as filtering policies are coded in an XML-based language called PIDF. In [4], Schulzrinne proposed RPID that extends PIDF.

We extend the SIP presence architecture by proposing the architecture depicted in Figure 1. The SOHO (Small Office or Home Office) network gathers the devices owned by the same user. The ITSP (Internet Telephony Service Provider) extends the SIP presence server in order to manage the SOHO network.

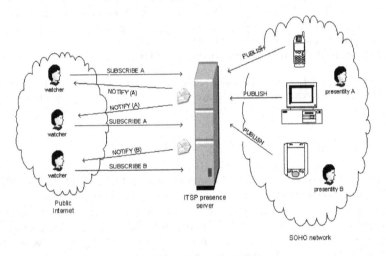

**Fig. 1.** ITSP presence architecture

## 3   Presence Interactions and Solution Approach

For the purpose of the current work, we propose the following eight presence status, which are for example used in [5] and [6]:   Available (1),  Away (2), Busy (3), In-a-meeting (4), Not-available (5), On-the-phone (6), On-vacation (7), Out-for-lunch (8). Notice that the On-the-phone status is special in that it is temporary and not intentional. All the other presence status are intentionally set by the user.

We define the presence interaction (PI) problem as the situation where two or more devices owned by the *same user* report two or more different presence status of the user. This could happen, for example, when a device publishes Out-for-lunch while another publishes On-the-phone. The resolution of a detected PI will consist in keeping one among the conflicting presence status in the manner we will explain. For simplicity, we consider here only PI involving exactly *two* (conflicting) devices.

### 3.1  PI Classification, Order Relations

PI are classified into two categories, denoted OR and RP:

**Obvious Resolution (OR) interactions:** among two conflicting status, the selection of the one to be excluded is obvious. In our case, OR interactions involve the On-the-phone status, because the latter is special in that it is not intentional. All the other presence status are intentionally set by the user. The On-the-phone status should not contradict a user who, for example, receives a call on a device at a period during which he has chosen to appear as Out-for-lunch on another device. The On-the-phone status should be excluded and the other status should appear instead.

**Resolution Policy (RP) interactions:** among two conflicting status, the selection of the one to be excluded needs to conform to a specified policy. The latter is based on the following two types of order relations denoted SOR and DOR:

**Status order relations (SOR):** A SOR is an order relation between status. Let us consider two status $S1$ and $S2$ and a SOR s$or$. If $S1$ sor $S2$, then the policy based on s$or$ consists in excluding $S2$. "is more precise than" is an example of SOR. For example, Away is more precise than Not-available. For our eight presence status identified by 1, 2, ..., 8, the SOR "is more precise than" implies the following pairs (2,5), (3,5), (7,2), (8,2), (4,3), where $(i,j)$ means "$i$ is more precise than $j$".

**Device order relations (DOR):** A DOR is an order relation between devices. Let us consider two devices $D1$ and $D2$ and a DOR $dor$. If $D1$ dor $D2$, then the policy based on $dor$ consists in excluding the status published by $D2$. "is more trustworthy than" is an example of DOR, which can be used by assigning trustworthiness weights to devices. For example, the user can decide to assign more trustworthiness to cell phone than to office phone.

### 3.2  PI Resolution Procedure

PI resolution policies are specified by the SOHO administrator and the end users. We suppose the ITSP provides the suitable interface for the SOHO administrator as well the users in order to specify those policies. The ITSP presence resolution solution is contained in a PIMA (Presence Interaction Management Agent) and is based on the use or SOR and DOR. We consider that for *every user*, we may have a set of SORs $\{sor_1, ..., sor_n\}$ which are ordered by priority, that is, $sor_i$ has priority over $sor_{i+1}$. We also may have a set of DORs $\{dor_1, ..., dor_n\}$ where $dor_i$ has priority over $dor_{i+1}$. We also assume that priorities may be defined between some pairs $(sor_i, dor_j)$.

Some order relations correspond to policies specified by the SOHO administrator and will therefore be called *admin-based order relations*. Other order relations correspond to policies specified by the users (presentities) themselves and will therefore be called *user-based order relations*. For example, the SOR "is more precise than" should be specified by the SOHO administrator, while the DOR "is more trustworthy than" should be specified by the users.

Given two status $S1$ and $S2$ published by devices $D1$ and $D2$, respectively, PIMA solves the interaction $S1$-$S2$ by applying the following resolution procedure:

**Step 1:** *Comparison using SOR, assuming that each $sor_i$ has priority over $sor_{i+1}$*
Check if $S1$ and $S2$ are comparable using $sor_1$, i.e., "$S1\ sor_1\ S2$" or "$S2\ sor_1\ S1$".
If this is the case, the best status wrt $sor_1$ is the solution of Step 1.
If this is not the case, check if $S1$ and $S2$ are comparable by $sor_2$. And so on, we iterate until either we reach a $sor_i$ that permits to compare $S1$ and $S2$, or we reach $sor_n$ without being able to compare $S1$ and $S2$. In the latter case, we say that $S1$ and $S2$ are SOR-incomparable. In the former case, the best status wrt $sor_i$ is the solution of Step 1.

**Step 2:** *Comparison using DOR, assuming that each $dor_i$ has priority over $dor_{i+1}$*
We proceed iteratively as in Step 1, but by comparing devices instead of status. If no $dor_i$ permits to compare $D1$ and $D2$, we say that $D1$ and $D2$ are DOR-incomparable. Otherwise, Step 2 provides a solution $Dv$ ($v = 1, 2$ ).

**Step 3:** we have the following six situations:

**3.a:** Neither Step 1 nor Step 2 provides a solution. In this case, the resolution procedure provides no solution.

**3.b:** Step 1 provides a status $Su$ as a solution and Step 2 provides no solution.
$Su$ is the adopted solution.

**3.c:** Step 2 provides a device $Dv$ as a solution and Step 1 provides no solution.
The status published by $Dv$ is the adopted solution.

**3.d:** Steps 1 and 2 provide compatible solutions, that is, the solution of Step 1 is the status published by the device which is the solution of Step 2.
This status is the adopted solution.

**3.e:** Step 1 and 2 provide incompatible (or contradictory) solutions, that is, the solution of Step 1 *is different from* the status published by the device which is the solution of Step 2. In this case, let $sor_i$ and $dor_j$ be the two order relations providing the solutions of Steps 1 and 2, respectively. Recall that a priority may have been defined between $sor_i$ and $dor_j$.

**3.e.1:** if such a priority has effectively been defined: we select the solution provided by the order relation that has priority over the other.

**3.e.2:** otherwise: the resolution procedure provides no solution.

## 4  Multi-agents Architecture for Managing PI

We propose a multi-agent architecture solution to manage the problem of PI. The agents are called FIMA (Feature Interaction Management Agent) because the proposed solution is aimed to be integrated with a method for managing feature interactions (FI) proposed in [7]. Two types of FIMA are used: several UFIMA (User FIMA) and one NFIMA (Network FIMA) (Fig. 2). A UFIMA is assigned to each device and the NFIMA contains the PIMA and is assigned to the ITSP.

A user has a single interface to manage presence preferences. This interface may be managed by any UFIMA that is located on any device owned by the user. At any time, the user can access the interface in order to set his presence preferences. Those preferences are used to specify the so-called user-based order relations, that is, order relations corresponding to policies specified by the users (presentities). For simplicity, in the following we consider we have a single user-based relation, namely the DOR "is more trustworthy than". The user presence preferences should contain the trustworthiness weighting of all the devices. UFIMA uses the SIP REGISTER message to communicate the weighting information to PIMA (contained in NFIMA), coded in PIML (Figure 2). The general purpose of PIML is to express formally the relevant information for managing PI.

We suppose the registrar server (the server that is responsible of processing REGISTER) located in the same node as the presence server. Otherwise, the registrar has to communicate the received PIML models to the presence server in a suitable manner. Based on this trustworthiness information (coded in PIML) provided by UFIMA, PIMA constructs the DOR "is more trustworthy than" that will be used when executing the resolution procedure for that user.

In the same way, the SOHO administrator has an interface to transmit to PIMA (using REGISTER) necessary information (coded in PIML) for the construction of admin-based order relations, that is, order relations corresponding to policies specified by the SOHO administrator. The SOHO administration interface is managed by any UFIMA that runs on any device owned by the SOHO administrator. For simplicity, in the following we consider we have a single admin-based relation, namely the SOR "is more precise than".

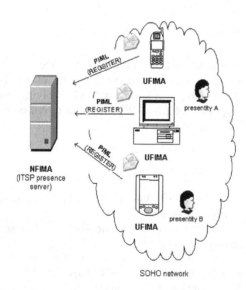

**Fig. 2.** FIMA-SOHO architecture

# 5 Presence Interaction Management Language (PIML)

*Example of PIMLcode using a SOR*

1.  Owner
2.          caller = soho_admin@company.com
3.  SOR: MorePrecise
4.          AWAY, NOTAVAILABLE
5.          BUSY, NOTAVAILABLE

6.              VACATION, AWAY
7.              LUNCH, AWAY
8.              MEETING, BUSY

*Lines 1-2* indicates that soho_admin@company.com is a SIP address that is bound to the SOHO administrator currently used device.

*Line 3*: indicates that the following lines define a SOR called MorePrecise.

*Lines 4-8*: each line S1,S2 means that S1 is more precise than S2.

### *Example PIML code using a DOR*

1.  Owner
2.              caller = user_21@company.com
3.  DOR: MoreTrustworthy
4.              user_21@company.com,  beloxi@company.com
5.              beloxi@company.com,  manager@company.com

*Line 3*: indicates that the following lines define a DOR called MoreTrustworthy.

*Lines 4-5*: each line D1,D2 means that D1 is more trustworthy than S2.


## 6  Conclusion

In this article, we proposed a solution to the presence interaction (PI) problem that arises when two or more devices owned by the same user publish contradictory presence status. For future work, we plan to study PI involving more than two status and to consider other types of relations. We also plan to consider status that can be combined, instead of selecting a single status.


## References

1. Day, M., Aggarwal, S., Mohr, G., Vincent, J.: Instant Messaging/Presence Protocol Requirements. RFC 2779, IETF, February 2000.
2. Niemi, A.: Session Initiation Protocol (SIP) Extension for Event State Publication. RFC 3903, IETF, October 2004.
3. Sugano, H., Fujimoto, S., Klyne, G., Bateman, A., Carr, W., Peterson, J.: Presence Information Data Format (PIDF). RFC 3863, IETF, August 2004.
4. Schulzrinne, H.: RPID: Rich Presence Extensions to the Presence Information Data Format (PIDF). draft-ietf-simple-rpid-10 (work in progress), December 2005.
5. http://www.dialexia.com/pub/products/dial_office.jsp   Accessed on April 2006.
6. http://messenger.msn.com   Accessed on April 2006.
7. Z. Chentouf, S. Cherkaoui, A. Khoumsi, "Service interaction management in SIP user device using Feature Interaction Management Language", NOTERE, June 2004, Saïdia, Morocco.

# Formal Analysis of
# Dynamic, Distributed File-System Access Controls

Avik Chaudhuri[1] and Martín Abadi[1,2]

[1] Computer Science Department, University of California, Santa Cruz
[2] Microsoft Research, Silicon Valley

**Abstract.** We model networked storage systems with distributed, cryptographically enforced file-access control in an applied pi calculus. The calculus contains cryptographic primitives and supports file-system constructs, including access revocation. We establish that the networked storage systems implement simpler, centralized storage specifications with local access-control checks. More specifically, we prove that the former systems preserve safety properties of the latter systems. Focusing on security, we then derive strong secrecy and integrity guarantees for the networked storage systems.

## 1 Introduction

Storage systems are typically governed by access-control policies, and the security of those systems depends on the sound enforcement of the necessary access-control checks. Unfortunately, both the policies and their enforcement can be surprisingly problematic, for several reasons. In particular, the policies may be allowed to change over time, often via interactions with the file-system environment; it is then crucial to prevent unauthorized access-control administration, and to guarantee that authorized access-control administration has correct, prompt effects. Another source of substantial difficulties is distribution. In networked, distributed storage systems, file access is often not directly guarded by access-control checks. Instead, file access is guarded by the inspection of capabilities; these capabilities certify that the relevant access-control checks have been done elsewhere in the past. Yet other difficulties result from the scale and complexity of systems, which present a challenge to consistent administration.

In this paper, we aim to simplify security analyses for storage systems. Specifically, we model network-attached storage (NAS) systems [7,15,11]. We prove that NAS systems are as safe (from the point of view of passing tests [14]) as corresponding centralized storage systems with local access-control enforcement. In other words, reasoning about the safety of the centralized storage systems can be applied for free to the significantly more complicated NAS systems. As important special cases, we derive the preservation of secrecy and integrity guarantees.

The systems that we study include distributed file-system management across a number of access-control servers and disks on the network; they also include dynamic administration of access control. At the same time, we avoid commitments to certain specific choices that particular implementations might make—on file-operation and policy-administration commands, algorithms for file allocation over multi-disk arrays, various scheduling algorithms—so that our results remain simple and apply broadly. We describe those systems and analyze their security properties in an applied pi calculus [3].

E. Najm et al. (Eds.): FORTE 2006, LNCS 4229, pp. 99–114, 2006.

This calculus includes cryptographic primitives and supports file-system constructs. It also enables us to incorporate a basic but sufficient model of time, as needed for dynamic administration.

*Background and Related Work.* Various cryptographic implementations of distributed access control have been proposed as part of the security designs of NAS protocols [6,8,7,15,11,17]. However, the security analyses of these implementations have been at best semi-formal. Some exceptions are the work of Mazières and Shasha on data integrity for untrusted remote storage [10], and Gobioff's security analysis of a NAS protocol using belief logics [7].

In a recent paper [5], we consider a restricted class of NAS systems, with fixed access-control policies and a single network-attached disk interface. We show that those systems are fully abstract with respect to centralized file systems. Full abstraction [12] is a powerful criterion for the security of implementations [1]: it prohibits any leakage of information. It is also fairly fragile, and can be broken by many reasonable implementations in practice. In particular, capability revocation and expiry (more broadly, dynamic administration, as we study it here) give rise to counterexamples to full abstraction that appear impossible to avoid in any reasonable implementation of NAS. We discuss these issues in detail in Section 5. In sum, the systems that we study in this paper are considerably more general and complex than those we consider in our previous work, so much so that we cannot directly extend our previous full-abstraction result. Fortunately, however, we can still obtain strong secrecy and integrity guarantees while retaining the simplicity of our specifications.

We employ a variation of may-tests to observe the behaviour of systems. Proofs based on may-testing for safety and security properties have also been studied elsewhere (*e.g.*, [14,4]). Our treatment of secrecy is also fairly standard (*e.g.*, [4]). On the other hand, our treatment of integrity properties is not. We formalize integrity properties via "warnings". Warnings signal violations that can be detected by monitoring system execution. In this way, our approach to integrity is related to enforceable mechanisms for security policies [16]. Warnings can also indicate the failure of correspondences between events, and hence may be used to verify correspondence assertions (*e.g.*, [9]). On the other hand, it does not seem convenient to use standard correspondence assertions directly in implementation proofs such as ours.

*Outline of the Paper.* In the next section we give an overview of the applied pi calculus that serves as our modeling language. In Section 3, we present a simple storage specification based on a centralized file system with local access-control checks. In Section 4, we show a NAS implementation that features distributed file-system management and cryptographic access-control enforcement. Then, in Section 5, we extract specifications from NAS systems, state our main theorem (safety preservation), and derive some important security consequences. We conclude in Section 6.

## 2   The Applied pi Calculus

We use a polyadic, synchronous, applied pi calculus [13,3] as the underlying language to describe and reason about processes. The syntax is standard. We use the notation $\widetilde{\varphi}$ to mean a sequence $\varphi_1, \ldots, \varphi_k$, where the length $k$ of the sequence is given by $|\widetilde{\varphi}|$.

$$M, N ::= \qquad\qquad\qquad \text{terms}$$

| | |
|---|---|
| $m, n, \ldots$ | name |
| $x, y, \ldots$ | variable |
| $f(\widetilde{M})$ | function application |

The language of terms contains an infinite set of names and an infinite set of variables; further, terms can be built from smaller ones by applying function symbols. Names can be channel names, key names, and so on. Function symbols are drawn from a finite ranked set $\mathcal{F}$, called the signature. This signature is equipped with an equational theory. Informally, the theory provides a set of equations over terms, and we say that $\mathcal{F} \vdash M = N$ for terms $M$ and $N$ if and only if $M = N$ can be derived from those equations.

For our purposes, we assume symbols for shared-key encryption $\{\cdot\}.$ and message authentication $\mathbf{mac}(\cdot, \cdot)$, and list the only equations that involve these symbols below. The first equation allows decryption of an encrypted message with the correct key; the second allows extraction of a message from a message authentication code.

$$\mathbf{decrypt}(\{x\}_y, y) = x \qquad \mathbf{message}(\mathbf{mac}(x, y)) = x$$

We also assume some standard data structures, such as tuples, numerals, and queues, with corresponding functions, such as projection functions $\mathbf{proj}_\ell$. Several function symbols are introduced in Sections 3 and 4. Next we show the language of processes.

$$P, Q ::=\qquad\qquad\qquad \text{processes}$$

| | |
|---|---|
| $\overline{M}\langle \widetilde{N}\rangle.\, P$ | output |
| $M(\widetilde{x}).\, P$ | input |
| $P \mid Q$ | composition |
| $(\nu n)\, P$ | restriction |
| $0$ | nil |
| $!P$ | replication |
| if $M = N$ then $P$ else $Q$ | conditional |

Processes have the following informal semantics.

- The nil process $0$ does nothing.
- The composition process $P \mid Q$ behaves as the processes $P$ and $Q$ in parallel.
- The input process $M(\widetilde{x}).\, P$ can receive any sequence of terms $\widetilde{N}$ on $M$, where $|\widetilde{N}| = |\widetilde{x}|$, then execute $P\{\widetilde{N}/\widetilde{x}\}$. The variables $\widetilde{x}$ are bound in $P$ in $M(\widetilde{x}).\, P$. The notation $\{\widetilde{M}/\widetilde{x}\}$ represents the capture-free substitution of terms $\widetilde{M}$ for variables $\widetilde{x}$. The input blocks if $M$ is not a name at runtime.
- The synchronous output process $\overline{M}\langle \widetilde{N}\rangle.P$ can send the sequence of terms $\widetilde{N}$ on $M$, then execute $P$. The output blocks if $M$ is not a name at runtime; otherwise, it waits for a synchronizing input on $M$.
- The replication process $!P$ behaves as an infinite number of copies of $P$ running in parallel.
- The restriction process $(\nu n)\, P$ creates a new name $n$ bound in $P$, then executes $P$. This construct is used to create fresh, unguessable secrets in the language.
- The conditional process if $M = N$ then $P$ else $Q$ behaves as $P$ if $\mathcal{F} \vdash M = N$, and as $Q$ otherwise.

We elide $\mathcal{F} \vdash$ in the sequel. The notions of free variables and names (fv and fn) are as usual; so are various abbreviations (*e.g.*, $\Pi$ and $\Sigma$ for indexed parallel composition and internal choice, respectively). We call terms or processes closed if they do not contain any free variables. We use a commitment semantics for closed processes [13,4]. Informally, a commitment reflects the ability to do some action, which may be output ($\overline{n}$), input ($n$), or silent ($\tau$). More concretely,

- $P \xrightarrow{\overline{n}} (\nu\tilde{m}) \langle \widetilde{M} \rangle . Q$ means that $P$ can output on name $n$ the terms $\widetilde{M}$ that contain fresh names $\tilde{m}$, and continue as $Q$.
- $P \xrightarrow{n} (\tilde{x}) . Q$ means that $P$ can input terms on $n$, bind them to $\tilde{x}$ in $Q$, and continue as $Q$ instantiated.
- $P \xrightarrow{\tau} Q$ means that $P$ can silently transition to $Q$.

## 3   Specifying a Simple Centralized File System

In this section, we model a simple centralized file system. The model serves as a specification for the significantly more complex distributed file-system implementation of Section 4. We begin with a summary of the main features of the model.

- The file system serves a number of clients who can remotely send their requests over distinguished channels. The requests may be for file operations, or for administrative operations that modify file-operation permissions of other clients.
- Each request is subject to local access-control checks that decide whether the requested operation is permitted. A request that passes these checks is then processed in parallel with other pending requests.
- Any requested modification to existing file-operation permissions takes effect only after a deterministic, finite delay. The delay is used to specify accurate correctness conditions for the expiry-based, distributed access-control mechanism of Section 4.

We present a high-level view of this "ideal" file system, called IFS, by means of a grammar of *control states* (see below). IFS can be coded as a process (in the syntax of the previous section), preserving its exact observable semantics. An IFS control state consists of the following components:

- a pool of threads, where each thread reflects a particular stage in the processing of some pending request to the file system;
- an access-control policy, tagged with a schedule for pending policy updates;
- a storage state (or "disk"); and
- a clock, as required for scheduling modifications to the access-control policy.

| IFS-Th ::= | file-system thread |
| --- | --- |
| $\text{Req}_k(op, n)$ | file-operation request |
| $\text{App}(op, n)$ | approved file operation |
| $\text{Ret}(n, r)$ | return after file operation |
| $\text{PReq}_k(adm, n)$ | administration request |
| $\Delta ::=$ | thread pool |
| $\varnothing$ | empty |

| IFS-Th, $\Delta$ | thread in pool |
|---|---|
| IFS-Control ::= | file-system control state |
| $\Delta : \mathcal{R}^{\mathcal{H}} : \rho : \mathsf{Clk}$ | threads: tagged access policy: disk state: clock |

The threads are of four sorts, explained below: $\mathsf{Req}_k(op, n)$, $\mathsf{App}(op, n)$, $\mathsf{Ret}(n, r)$, and $\mathsf{PReq}_k(adm, n)$. The clock $\mathsf{Clk}$ is a monotonically increasing integer. The storage state $\rho$ reflects the state maintained at the disk (typically file contents; details are left abstract in the model). The access-control policy $\mathcal{R}$ decides which subjects may execute operations on the storage state, and which administrators may make modifications to the policy itself. The schedule $\mathcal{H}$ contains a queue of pending modifications to the policy, with each modification associated with a clock that says when that modification is due.

Let $\mathcal{K}$ be a set of indices that cover both the subjects and the administrators of access control. We assume distinguished sets of channel names $\{\beta_k \mid k \in \mathcal{K}\}$ and $\{\alpha_k \mid k \in \mathcal{K}\}$ on which the file system receives requests for file operations and policy modifications, respectively. A file-operation request consists of a term $op$ that describes the operation (typically, a command with arguments, some of which may be file names) and a channel $n$ for the result. When such a request arrives on $\beta_k$, the file system spawns a new thread of the form $\mathsf{Req}_k(op, n)$. The access-control policy then decides whether $k$ has permission to execute $op$ on the storage state. If not, the thread dies; otherwise, the thread changes state to $\mathsf{App}(op, n)$. The request is then forwarded to the disk, which executes the operation and updates the storage state, obtaining a result $r$. The thread changes state to $\mathsf{Ret}(n, r)$. Later, $r$ is returned on $n$, and the thread terminates successfully.

A policy-modification request consists of a term $adm$ that describes the modification to the policy and a channel $n$ for the acknowledgment. When such a request arrives on $\alpha_k$, the file system spawns a thread of the form $\mathsf{PReq}_k(adm, n)$. Then, if the policy does not allow $k$ to do $adm$, the thread dies; otherwise, the modification is queued to the schedule and an acknowledgment is returned on $n$, and the thread terminates successfully. At each clock tick, policy modifications that are due in the schedule take effect, and the policy and the schedule are updated accordingly.

Operationally, we assume functions **may**, **execute**, **schedule**, and **update** that satisfy the following equations. (We leave abstract the details of the equational theory.)

- **may**$(k, op, \mathcal{R}) = $ **yes** (*resp.* **may**$(k, adm, \mathcal{R}) = $ **yes**) if the policy $\mathcal{R}$ allows $k$ to execute file operation $op$ (*resp.* make policy modification $adm$), and $=$ **no** otherwise.
- **execute**$(op, \rho) = \langle \rho', r \rangle$, where $\rho'$ and $r$ are the storage state and the result, respectively, obtained after executing file operation $op$ on storage state $\rho$.
- **schedule**$(adm, \mathcal{H}, \mathsf{Clk}) = \mathcal{H}'$, where $\mathcal{H}'$ is the schedule after queuing an entry of the form $adm@\mathsf{Clk}'$ (with $\mathsf{Clk}' \geq \mathsf{Clk}$) to schedule $\mathcal{H}$. The clock $\mathsf{Clk}'$, determined by $adm$, $\mathcal{H}$, and $\mathsf{Clk}$, indicates the instant at which $adm$ is due in the new schedule.
- **update**$(\mathcal{R}^{\mathcal{H}}, \mathsf{Clk}) = \mathcal{R}'^{\mathcal{H}'}$, where $\mathcal{R}'$ is the policy after making modifications to policy $\mathcal{R}$ that are due at clock $\mathsf{Clk}$ in schedule $\mathcal{H}$, and $\mathcal{H}'$ is the schedule left.

Further, we assume a function **lifespan** such that **lifespan**$(k, op, \mathcal{H}, \mathsf{Clk}) \geq 0$ for all $k$, $op$, $\mathcal{H}$, and $\mathsf{Clk}$. Informally, if **lifespan**$(k, op, \mathcal{H}, \mathsf{Clk}) = \lambda$ and the file

$$\frac{(Op\ Req)}{\Delta:\mathcal{R}^{\mathcal{H}}:\rho:\mathsf{Clk}\xrightarrow{\beta_k}}{(x,y).\,\mathsf{Req}_k(x,y),\Delta:\mathcal{R}^{\mathcal{H}}:\rho:\mathsf{Clk}}$$

$$\frac{(Op\ Deny)}{\mathbf{may}(k,op,\mathcal{R})=\mathbf{no}}{\mathsf{Req}_k(op,n),\Delta:\mathcal{R}^{\mathcal{H}}:\rho:\mathsf{Clk}\xrightarrow{\tau}\Delta:\mathcal{R}^{\mathcal{H}}:\rho:\mathsf{Clk}}$$

$$\frac{(Op\ Ok)}{\mathbf{may}(k,op,\mathcal{R})=\mathbf{yes}}{\frac{\mathsf{Req}_k(op,n),\Delta:\mathcal{R}^{\mathcal{H}}:\rho:\mathsf{Clk}\xrightarrow{\tau}}{\mathsf{App}(op,n),\Delta:\mathcal{R}^{\mathcal{H}}:\rho:\mathsf{Clk}}}$$

$$\frac{(Op\ Exec)}{\mathbf{execute}(op,\rho)=\langle\rho',r\rangle}{\frac{\mathsf{App}(op,n),\Delta:\mathcal{R}^{\mathcal{H}}:\rho:\mathsf{Clk}\xrightarrow{\tau}}{\mathsf{Ret}(n,r),\Delta:\mathcal{R}^{\mathcal{H}}:\rho':\mathsf{Clk}}}$$

$$\frac{(Op\ Res\ Ret)}{\mathsf{Ret}(n,r),\Delta:\mathcal{R}^{\mathcal{H}}:\rho:\mathsf{Clk}\xrightarrow{\overline{n}}}{\langle r\rangle.\,\Delta:\mathcal{R}^{\mathcal{H}}:\rho:\mathsf{Clk}}$$

$$\frac{(Adm\ Req)}{\Delta:\mathcal{R}^{\mathcal{H}}:\rho:\mathsf{Clk}\xrightarrow{\alpha_k}}{(x,y).\,\mathsf{PReq}_k(x,y),\Delta:\mathcal{R}^{\mathcal{H}}:\rho:\mathsf{Clk}}$$

$$\frac{(Adm\ Deny)}{\mathbf{may}(k,adm,\mathcal{R})=\mathbf{no}}{\frac{\mathsf{PReq}_k(adm,n),\Delta:\mathcal{R}^{\mathcal{H}}:\rho:\mathsf{Clk}\xrightarrow{\tau}}{\Delta:\mathcal{R}^{\mathcal{H}}:\rho:\mathsf{Clk}}}$$

$$\frac{(Adm\ Ok\ Ack)}{\mathbf{may}(k,adm,\mathcal{R})=\mathbf{yes}\quad\mathbf{schedule}(adm,\mathcal{H},\mathsf{Clk})=\mathcal{H}'}{\frac{\mathsf{PReq}_k(adm,n),\Delta:\mathcal{R}^{\mathcal{H}}:\rho:\mathsf{Clk}\xrightarrow{\overline{n}}}{\langle\rangle.\,\Delta:\mathcal{R}^{\mathcal{H}'}:\rho:\mathsf{Clk}}}$$

$$\frac{(Tick)}{\mathbf{update}(\mathcal{R}^{\mathcal{H}},\mathsf{Clk})=\mathcal{R}'^{\mathcal{H}'}}{\Delta:\mathcal{R}^{\mathcal{H}}:\rho:\mathsf{Clk}\xrightarrow{\tau}\Delta:\mathcal{R}'^{\mathcal{H}'}:\rho:\mathsf{Clk}+1}$$

**Fig. 1.** Semantics of a file system with local access control

operation $op$ is allowed to $k$ at $\mathsf{Clk}$, then $op$ cannot be denied to $k$ before $\mathsf{Clk}+\lambda$. Formally, we extend **schedule** to sequences by letting $\mathbf{schedule}(\varnothing,\mathcal{H},\mathsf{Clk})=\mathcal{H}$ and $\mathbf{schedule}(\widetilde{adm'\,adm},\mathcal{H},\mathsf{Clk})=\mathbf{schedule}(\widetilde{adm},\mathbf{schedule}(\widetilde{adm'},\mathcal{H},\mathsf{Clk}),\mathsf{Clk})$; we require that if $\mathbf{lifespan}(k,op,\mathcal{H},\mathsf{Clk})=\lambda$ then there do not exist (possibly empty) sequences of policy-modification commands $\widetilde{adm}_{\mathsf{Clk}},\widetilde{adm}_{\mathsf{Clk}+1},\ldots,\widetilde{adm}_{\mathsf{Clk}+\lambda}$ and policy $\mathcal{R}_{\mathsf{Clk}}$ such that the following hold at once:

- $\mathbf{may}(k,op,\mathcal{R}_{\mathsf{Clk}})=\mathbf{yes}$
- $\mathcal{H}_{\mathsf{Clk}}=\mathcal{H}$
- $\mathcal{H}_{\mathsf{Clk}'}=\mathbf{schedule}(\widetilde{adm}_{\mathsf{Clk}'},\mathcal{H}_{\mathsf{Clk}'},\mathsf{Clk}')$ for each $\mathsf{Clk}'\in\mathsf{Clk}\ldots\mathsf{Clk}+\lambda$
- $\mathcal{R}_{\mathsf{Clk}'+1}^{\mathcal{H}_{\mathsf{Clk}'+1}}=\mathbf{update}(\mathcal{R}_{\mathsf{Clk}'}^{\mathcal{H}_{\mathsf{Clk}'}},\mathsf{Clk}')$ for each $\mathsf{Clk}'\in\mathsf{Clk}\ldots\mathsf{Clk}+\lambda-1$
- $\mathbf{may}(k,op,\mathcal{R}_{\mathsf{Clk}+\lambda})=\mathbf{no}$

For instance, $\mathbf{lifespan}(k,op,\mathcal{H},\mathsf{Clk})$ can return a constant delay $\lambda_c$ for all $k$, $op$, $\mathcal{H}$, and $\mathsf{Clk}$, and $\mathbf{schedule}(adm,\mathcal{H},\mathsf{Clk})$ can return $[\mathcal{H};adm@\mathsf{Clk}+\lambda_c]$ for all $adm$. When $\lambda_c=0$, any requested modification to the policy takes effect at the next clock tick.

The formal semantics of the file system is shown as a commitment relation in Figure 1. The relation describes how the file system spawns threads, how threads evolve, how access control is enforced and administered, how file operations are serviced, and how time goes by, in terms of standard pi-calculus actions.

We assume a set of clients $\{C_k\mid k\in\mathcal{K}\}$ that interact with the file system. We provide macros to request file operations and policy modifications; clients may use these macros, or explicitly send appropriate messages to the file system on the channels $\{\alpha_k,\beta_k\mid k\in\mathcal{K}\}$.

**Definition 1 (Macros for IFS clients).**

**File operation on port** $k$**:** *A file operation may be requested with the macro* $\text{fileop}_k\ op/x;\ P$, *which expands to* $(\nu n)\ \overline{\beta_k}\langle op, n\rangle.\ n(x).\ P$, *where* $n \notin \text{fn}(P)$.

**Administration on port** $k$**:** *A policy modification may be requested with the macro* $\text{admin}_k\ adm;\ P$, *which expands to* $(\nu n)\ \overline{\alpha_k}\langle adm, n\rangle.\ n().\ P$, *where* $n \notin \text{fn}(P)$.

We select a subset of clients whom we call *honest*; these clients may be arbitrary processes, as long as they use macros on their own ports for all interactions with the file system. Further, as a consequence of Definitions 2 and 3 (see below), no other client may send a request to the file system on the port of an honest client.

**Definition 2.** *A set of honest* IFS *clients indexed by* $\mathcal{I} \subseteq \mathcal{K}$ *is a set of closed processes* $\{C_i \mid i \in \mathcal{I}\}$, *so that each* $C_i$ *in the set has the following properties:*

- *all macros in* $C_i$ *are on port* $i$,
- *no name in* $\{\alpha_{i'}, \beta_{i'} \mid i' \in \mathcal{I}\}$ *appears free in* $C_i$ *before expanding macros.*

Let $\mathcal{J} = \mathcal{K} \setminus \mathcal{I}$. We impose no restrictions on the "dishonest" clients $C_j$ ($j \in \mathcal{J}$), except that they may not know the channels $\{\alpha_i, \beta_i \mid i \in \mathcal{I}\}$ initially. In fact, we assume that dishonest clients are part of an arbitrary environment, and as such, leave their code unspecified. The restriction on their initial knowledge is expressed by leaving them outside the initial scope of the channels $\{\alpha_i, \beta_i \mid i \in \mathcal{I}\}$.

**Definition 3.** *An ideal storage system denoted by* $\text{IS}(\mathbb{C}_\mathcal{I}, \mathcal{R}, \rho, \text{Clk})$ *is the closed process* $(\nu_{i\in\mathcal{I}}\ \alpha_i\beta_i)\ (\Pi_{i\in\mathcal{I}}C_i \mid \varnothing : \mathcal{R}^\varnothing : \rho : \text{Clk})$, *where*

- $\mathbb{C}_\mathcal{I} = \{C_i \mid i \in \mathcal{I}\}$ *is a set of honest* IFS *clients indexed by* $\mathcal{I}$,
- $\varnothing : \mathcal{R}^\varnothing : \rho : \text{Clk}$ *is an initial* IFS *control state, and* $\{\alpha_i, \beta_i \mid i \in \mathcal{I}\} \cap \text{fn}(\mathcal{R}, \rho) = \varnothing$.

# 4   An Implementation of Network-Attached Storage

In this section, we model a distributed file system based on network-attached storage (NAS). A typical network-attached file system is distributed over a set of disks that are "attached" to the network, and a set of servers (called managers). The disks directly receive file-operation requests from clients, while the managers maintain file-system metadata and file-access permissions, and serve administrative requests. In simple traditional storage designs, access-control checks and metadata lookups are done for every request to the file system. In NAS, that per-request overhead is amortized, resulting in significant performance gains. Specifically, a client who wishes to request a file operation first contacts one of the managers; the manager does the relevant checks and lookups, and returns a cryptographically signed *capability* to the client. The capability is a certification of access rights for that particular operation, and needs to be obtained only once. The client can then request that operation any number of times at a disk, attaching to its requests the capability issued by the manager. The disk simply verifies the capability before servicing each of those requests. NAS implementations are further optimized by allocating different parts of the file system to different managers and disks. This kind of partitioning distributes load and increases concurrency.

Perhaps the most challenging aspect of NAS's access-control mechanism, and indeed of distributed access controls in general, is the sound enforcement of access revocation. In particular, whenever some permissions are revoked, all previous capabilities that certify those permissions must be invalidated. On the other hand, when issuing a capability, it is impossible to predict when a permission certified by that capability might be revoked in the future. It is possible, in theory, to simulate immediate revocation by communicating with the disks: the disks then maintain a record of revoked permissions and reject all capabilities that certify those permissions. However, this "solution" reduces the performance and distribution benefits of NAS.

A sound, practical solution exists if we allow a deterministic finite delay in revocation. Informally, a capability is marked with an unforgeable timestamp that declares its expiry, beyond which it is always rejected—and any revocation of the permissions certified by that capability takes effect only after the declared expiry. By letting the expiry depend on various parameters, this solution turns out to be quite flexible and effective.

Following the design above, we model a fairly standard network-attached file system, called NAFS. Much as in Section 3, we present the file system using a grammar of control states and a semantics of commitments. A NAFS control state consists of the following components:

- a pool of threads distributed between the managers and the disks;
- the local access-control policy and modification schedule at each manager;
- the local storage state at each disk; and
- a global clock shared between the managers and the disks.

| | |
|---|---|
| NAFS-Th-Server$_a$ ::= | thread at $a^{\text{th}}$ manager |
| $\quad$AReq$_{a.k}(op, c)$ | capability request |
| $\quad$PReq$_{a.k}(adm, n)$ | administration request |
| NAFS-Th-Disk$_b$ ::= | thread at $b^{\text{th}}$ disk |
| $\quad$Req$_b(\kappa, n)$ | authorized file-operation request |
| $\quad$App$_b(op, n)$ | approved file operation |
| $\quad$Ret$(n, r)$ | return after file operation |
| $\ddot{\Delta}$ ::= | distributed thread pool |
| $\quad\varnothing$ | empty |
| $\quad$NAFS-Th-Server$_a$, $\ddot{\Delta}$ | $a^{\text{th}}$-manager thread in pool |
| $\quad$NAFS-Th-Disk$_b$, $\ddot{\Delta}$ | $b^{\text{th}}$-disk thread in pool |
| NAFS-Control ::= | distributed file-system control state |
| $\quad\ddot{\Delta} : \widetilde{\mathcal{R}^{\mathcal{H}}} : \tilde{\rho} : \text{Clk}$ | threads: tagged policies: disk states: clock |

Let $\mathcal{A}$ (*resp.* $\mathcal{B}$) index the set of managers (*resp.* disks) used by the file system. For each $a \in \mathcal{A}$, we assume a distinguished set of names $\{\alpha_{a.k} \mid k \in \mathcal{K}\}$ on which the $a^{\text{th}}$ manager receives requests for policy modifications. A request on $\alpha_{a.k}$ is internally forwarded to the manager $a'$ allocated to serve that request, thereby spawning a thread of the form PReq$_{a'.k}(adm, n)$. This thread is then processed in much the same way as PReq$_k(adm, n)$ in Section 3. At each tick of the shared clock, due modifications to each of the local policies at the managers take effect.

Next, we elaborate on the authorization and execution of file operations. For each $a \in \mathcal{A}$ and $b \in \mathcal{B}$, we assume distinguished sets of names $\{\alpha_{a.k}^{\circ} \mid k \in \mathcal{K}\}$ and

$\{\beta_{b.k} \mid k \in \mathcal{K}\}$ on which the $a^{\text{th}}$ manager and the $b^{\text{th}}$ disk receive requests for authorization and execution of file operations, respectively. An authorization request consists of a term $op$ that describes the file operation and a channel $c$ to receive a capability for that operation. Such a request on $\alpha^{\circ}_{a.k}$ is internally forwarded to the manager $a'$ allocated to serve that request, thereby spawning a thread of the form $\mathsf{AReq}_{a'.k}(op, c)$. If the access-control policy at $a'$ does not allow $k$ to do $op$, the thread dies; otherwise, a capability $\kappa$ is returned on $c$, and the thread terminates successfully. The capability, a term of the form $\mathbf{mac}(\langle op, T, b\rangle, \mathrm{K}_b)$, is a message authentication code whose message contains $op$, an encrypted timestamp $T$, and the disk $b$ responsible for executing $op$. The timestamp $T$, of the form $\{\langle m, \mathsf{Clk}\rangle\}_{\mathrm{K}_b}$, indicates the expiry $\mathsf{Clk}$ of $\kappa$, and additionally contains a unique nonce $m$. (The only purpose of the nonce is to make the timestamp unique.) A secret key $\mathrm{K}_b$ shared between the disk $b$ and the manager is used to encrypt the timestamp and sign the capability. (In concrete implementations, different parts of the key may be used for encryption and signing.) The rationale behind the design of the capability is discussed in Section 5. Intuitively, the capability is unforgeable, and verifiable by the disk $b$; and the timestamp carried by the capability is unique, and unintelligible to any other than the disk $b$.

An execution request consists of a capability $\kappa$ and a return channel $n$. On receiving such a request on $\beta_{b.k}$, the disk $b$ spawns a thread of the form $\mathsf{Req}_b(\kappa, n)$. It then extracts the claimed operation $op$ from $\kappa$ (if possible), checks that $\kappa$ is signed with the key $\mathrm{K}_b$ (thereby verifying the integrity of $\kappa$), and checks that the timestamp decrypts under $\mathrm{K}_b$ to a clock no earlier than the current clock (thereby verifying that $\kappa$ has not expired). If these checks fail, the thread dies; otherwise, the thread changes state to $\mathsf{App}_b(op, n)$. This thread is then processed in much the same way as $\mathsf{App}(op, n)$ in Section 3.

Operationally, we assume a function **manager** (*resp.* **disk**) that allocates file operations and policy modifications to managers (*resp.* file operations to disks). We also assume functions $\mathbf{may}_a$, $\mathbf{execute}_b$, $\mathbf{schedule}_a$, and $\mathbf{update}_a$ for each $a \in \mathcal{A}$ and $b \in \mathcal{B}$, with the same specifications as their analogues in Section 3. Further, we assume a function $\mathbf{expiry}_a$ for each $a \in \mathcal{A}$ with the following property (*cf.* the function **lifespan**, Section 3): if $\mathbf{expiry}_a(k, op, \mathcal{H}, \mathsf{Clk}) = \mathsf{Clk}_e$, then $\mathsf{Clk}_e \geq \mathsf{Clk}$ and there do not exist sequences of policy-modification commands $\widetilde{adm}_{\mathsf{Clk}}, \widetilde{adm}_{\mathsf{Clk}+1}, \ldots, \widetilde{adm}_{\mathsf{Clk}_e}$ and policy $\mathcal{R}_{\mathsf{Clk}}$ such that the following hold at once:

- $\mathbf{manager}(\widetilde{adm}_{\mathsf{Clk}'}) = a$ for each $\mathsf{Clk}' \in \mathsf{Clk} \ldots \mathsf{Clk}_e$
- $\mathbf{may}_a(k, op, \mathcal{R}_{\mathsf{Clk}}) = \mathbf{yes}$
- $\mathcal{H}_{\mathsf{Clk}} = \mathcal{H}$
- $\mathcal{H}_{\mathsf{Clk}'} = \mathbf{schedule}_a(\widetilde{adm}_{\mathsf{Clk}'}, \mathcal{H}_{\mathsf{Clk}'}, \mathsf{Clk}')$ for each $\mathsf{Clk}' \in \mathsf{Clk} \ldots \mathsf{Clk}_e$
- $\mathcal{R}^{\mathcal{H}_{\mathsf{Clk}'+1}}_{\mathsf{Clk}'+1} = \mathbf{update}_a(\mathcal{R}^{\mathcal{H}_{\mathsf{Clk}'}}_{\mathsf{Clk}'}, \mathsf{Clk}')$ for each $\mathsf{Clk}' \in \mathsf{Clk} \ldots \mathsf{Clk}_e - 1$
- $\mathbf{may}_a(k, op, \mathcal{R}_{\mathsf{Clk}_e}) = \mathbf{no}$

In Section 5, we show how the functions $\mathbf{expiry}_a$ and **lifespan** are related: informally, the lifespan of a permission can be defined as the duration between the current clock and the expiry of any capability for that permission.

The formal semantics of NAFS is shown in Figure 2. Next we provide macros for requesting file-operation capabilities and policy modifications at a manager, and authorized file operations at appropriate disks.

---

*At the $a^{th}$ manager:*

**(Auth Req)**

$$\ddot\Delta : \widetilde{\mathcal{R}^\mathcal{H}} : \tilde\rho : \mathsf{Clk} \xrightarrow{\alpha^\circ_{a.k}}$$

$$(op,c).\,\mathsf{AReq}_{a.k}(op,c),\ddot\Delta : \widetilde{\mathcal{R}^\mathcal{H}} : \tilde\rho : \mathsf{Clk}$$

**(Auth Deny)**

$$\mathbf{manager}(op) = a \qquad \mathbf{may}_a(k, op, \mathcal{R}_a) = \mathbf{no}$$

$$\frac{}{\mathsf{AReq}_{a.k}(op,c),\ddot\Delta : \widetilde{\mathcal{R}^\mathcal{H}} : \tilde\rho : \mathsf{Clk} \xrightarrow{\tau}}$$
$$\ddot\Delta : \widetilde{\mathcal{R}^\mathcal{H}} : \tilde\rho : \mathsf{Clk}$$

**(Auth Ok Cap)**

$$\mathbf{manager}(op) = a \qquad \mathbf{may}_a(k, op, \mathcal{R}_a) = \mathbf{yes} \qquad \mathbf{disk}(op) = b$$
$$\{\langle m, \mathbf{expiry}_a(k, op, \mathcal{H}_a, \mathsf{Clk})\rangle\}_{\mathsf{K}_b} = T \text{ for fresh } m \qquad \mathbf{mac}(\langle op, T, b\rangle, \mathsf{K}_b) = \kappa$$

$$\frac{}{\mathsf{AReq}_{a.k}(op,c),\ddot\Delta : \widetilde{\mathcal{R}^\mathcal{H}} : \tilde\rho : \mathsf{Clk} \xrightarrow{\bar{c}} (\nu m)\,\langle \kappa\rangle.\,\ddot\Delta : \widetilde{\mathcal{R}^\mathcal{H}} : \tilde\rho : \mathsf{Clk}}$$

**(Adm Req)**

$$\ddot\Delta : \widetilde{\mathcal{R}^\mathcal{H}} : \tilde\rho : \mathsf{Clk} \xrightarrow{\alpha_{a.k}}$$

$$(adm,n).\,\mathsf{PReq}_{a.k}(adm,n),\ddot\Delta : \widetilde{\mathcal{R}^\mathcal{H}} : \tilde\rho : \mathsf{Clk}$$

**(Adm Deny)**

$$\mathbf{manager}(adm) = a \qquad \mathbf{may}_a(k, adm, \mathcal{R}_a) = \mathbf{no}$$

$$\frac{}{\mathsf{PReq}_{a.k}(adm,n),\ddot\Delta : \widetilde{\mathcal{R}^\mathcal{H}} : \tilde\rho : \mathsf{Clk} \xrightarrow{\tau}}$$
$$\ddot\Delta : \widetilde{\mathcal{R}^\mathcal{H}} : \tilde\rho : \mathsf{Clk}$$

**(Adm Ok Ack)**

$$\mathbf{manager}(adm) = a \qquad \mathbf{may}_a(k, adm, \mathcal{R}_a) = \mathbf{yes}$$
$$\mathbf{schedule}_a(adm, \mathcal{H}_a, \mathsf{Clk}) = \mathcal{H}'_a \qquad \forall a' \neq a : \mathcal{H}'_{a'} = \mathcal{H}_{a'}$$

$$\frac{}{\mathsf{PReq}_{a.k}(adm,n),\ddot\Delta : \widetilde{\mathcal{R}^\mathcal{H}} : \tilde\rho : \mathsf{Clk} \xrightarrow{\bar{n}} \langle\rangle.\,\ddot\Delta : \widetilde{\mathcal{R}^{\mathcal{H}'}} : \tilde\rho : \mathsf{Clk}}$$

*Across managers:*

**(Auth Fwd)**

$$\mathbf{manager}(op) = a' \neq a$$

$$\frac{}{\mathsf{AReq}_{a.k}(op,c),\ddot\Delta : \widetilde{\mathcal{R}^\mathcal{H}} : \tilde\rho : \mathsf{Clk} \xrightarrow{\tau}}$$
$$\mathsf{AReq}_{a'.k}(op,c),\ddot\Delta : \widetilde{\mathcal{R}^\mathcal{H}} : \tilde\rho : \mathsf{Clk}$$

**(Adm Fwd)**

$$\mathbf{manager}(adm) = a' \neq a$$

$$\frac{}{\mathsf{PReq}_{a.k}(adm,n),\ddot\Delta : \widetilde{\mathcal{R}^\mathcal{H}} : \tilde\rho : \mathsf{Clk} \xrightarrow{\tau}}$$
$$\mathsf{PReq}_{a'.k}(adm,n),\ddot\Delta : \widetilde{\mathcal{R}^\mathcal{H}} : \tilde\rho : \mathsf{Clk}$$

**(Tick)**

$$\frac{\forall a : \mathbf{update}_a(\mathcal{R}_a{}^{\mathcal{H}_a}, \mathsf{Clk}) = \mathcal{R}'_a{}^{\mathcal{H}'_a}}{\ddot\Delta : \widetilde{\mathcal{R}^\mathcal{H}} : \tilde\rho : \mathsf{Clk} \xrightarrow{\tau} \ddot\Delta : \widetilde{\mathcal{R}^{\mathcal{H}'}} : \tilde\rho : \mathsf{Clk}+1}$$

*At the $b^{th}$ disk:*

**(Exec Req)**

$$\ddot\Delta : \widetilde{\mathcal{R}^\mathcal{H}} : \tilde\rho : \mathsf{Clk} \xrightarrow{\beta_{b.k}}$$

$$(\kappa,n).\,\mathsf{Req}_b(\kappa,n),\ddot\Delta : \widetilde{\mathcal{R}^\mathcal{H}} : \tilde\rho : \mathsf{Clk}$$

**(Op Ok)**

$$\kappa = \mathbf{mac}(\langle op, T, b\rangle, \mathsf{K}_b)$$
$$\mathbf{decrypt}(T, \mathsf{K}_b) = \langle m, \mathsf{Clk}'\rangle \qquad \mathsf{Clk} \leq \mathsf{Clk}'$$

$$\frac{}{\mathsf{Req}_b(\kappa,n),\ddot\Delta : \widetilde{\mathcal{R}^\mathcal{H}} : \tilde\rho : \mathsf{Clk} \xrightarrow{\tau} \mathsf{App}_b(op,n),\ddot\Delta : \widetilde{\mathcal{R}^\mathcal{H}} : \tilde\rho : \mathsf{Clk}}$$

**(Exec Deny)**

$$\frac{\nexists op, T, m, \mathsf{Clk}' \text{ s.t. } \mathbf{mac}(\langle op, T, b\rangle, \mathsf{K}_b) = \kappa, \mathbf{decrypt}(T, \mathsf{K}_b) = \langle m, \mathsf{Clk}'\rangle, \text{ and } \mathsf{Clk} \leq \mathsf{Clk}'}{\mathsf{Req}_b(\kappa,n),\ddot\Delta : \widetilde{\mathcal{R}^\mathcal{H}} : \tilde\rho : \mathsf{Clk} \xrightarrow{\tau} \ddot\Delta : \widetilde{\mathcal{R}^\mathcal{H}} : \tilde\rho : \mathsf{Clk}}$$

**(Op Exec)**

$$\frac{\mathbf{execute}_b(op, \rho_b) = \langle \rho'_b, r\rangle \qquad \forall b' \neq b : \rho'_{b'} = \rho_{b'}}{\mathsf{App}_b(op,n),\ddot\Delta : \widetilde{\mathcal{R}^\mathcal{H}} : \tilde\rho : \mathsf{Clk} \xrightarrow{\tau} \mathsf{Ret}(n,r),\ddot\Delta : \widetilde{\mathcal{R}^\mathcal{H}} : \tilde\rho' : \mathsf{Clk}}$$

**(Op Res Ret)**

$$\mathsf{Ret}(n,r),\ddot\Delta : \widetilde{\mathcal{R}^\mathcal{H}} : \tilde\rho : \mathsf{Clk} \xrightarrow{\bar{n}}$$

$$\langle r\rangle.\,\ddot\Delta : \widetilde{\mathcal{R}^\mathcal{H}} : \tilde\rho : \mathsf{Clk}$$

**Fig. 2.** Semantics of a network-attached file system with distributed access control

**Definition 4 (Macros for NAFS clients).**

**Authorization on port $k$:** *Authorization may be requested with* $\mathsf{auth}_k\ x$ *for* $op;\ P$, *which expands to* $(\nu c)\ \overline{\alpha^{\circ}_{a.k}}\langle op, c\rangle.\ c(x).\ P$, *for some* $a \in \mathcal{A}$, *and* $c \notin \mathrm{fn}(P)$. *The variable $x$ gets bound to a* capability *at runtime.*

**File operation using $\kappa$ on port $k$:** *An authorized file operation may be requested with* $\mathsf{fileopauth}_k\ \kappa/x;\ P$, *which expands to* $(\nu n)\ \overline{\beta_{b.k}}\langle\kappa, n\rangle.\ n(x).\ P$, *where* $n \notin \mathrm{fn}(P)$, $\mathrm{proj}_3(\mathrm{message}(\kappa)) = b$, *and* $b \in \mathcal{B}$. *(Recall that for a capability $\kappa$ that authorizes $op$, the third component of* $\mathrm{message}(\kappa)$ *is the disk responsible for $op$.)*

**Administration on port $k$:** *Administration may be requested with* $\mathsf{admin}_k\ adm;\ P$, *which expands to* $(\nu n)\ \overline{\alpha_{a.k}}\langle adm, n\rangle.\ n().\ P$, *for some* $a \in \mathcal{A}$, *and* $n \notin \mathrm{fn}(P)$.

As in Section 3, we select a subset of clients whom we call honest; these can be any processes with certain static restrictions on their interactions with the file system. In particular, an honest client uses macros only on its own port for sending requests to the file system; each file-operation request is preceded by a capability request for that operation; a capability that is obtained for a file operation is used only in succeeding execution requests for that operation; and finally, as a consequence of Definitions 5 and 6, no other client may send a request to the file system on the port of an honest client.

**Definition 5.** *A set of honest NAFS clients indexed by $\mathcal{I} \subseteq \mathcal{K}$ is a set of closed processes* $\{\ddot{C}_i \mid i \in \mathcal{I}\}$, *so that each $\ddot{C}_i$ in the set has the following properties:*

- *all macros in $\ddot{C}_i$ are on port $i$,*
- *no name in $\{\alpha^{\circ}_{a.i'}, \alpha_{a.i'}, \beta_{b.i'} \mid i' \in \mathcal{I}, a \in \mathcal{A}, b \in \mathcal{B}\}$ appears free in $\ddot{C}_i$ before expanding macros,*
- *for each subprocess in $\ddot{C}_i$ that is of the form $\mathsf{auth}_i\ \kappa$ for $op;\ P$, the only uses of $\kappa$ in $P$ are in subprocesses of the form $\mathsf{fileopauth}_i\ \kappa/x;\ Q$,*
- *every subprocess $Q$ in $\ddot{C}_i$ that is of the form $\mathsf{fileopauth}_i\ \kappa/x;\ Q$ is contained in some subprocess $\mathsf{auth}_i\ \kappa$ for $op;\ P$, such that no subprocess of $P$ that strictly contains $Q$ binds $\kappa$.*

Dishonest clients $\ddot{C}_j\ (j \in \mathcal{J})$ are, as in Section 3, left unspecified. They form part of an arbitrary environment that does not have the names $\{K_b, \alpha^{\circ}_{a.i}, \alpha_{a.i}, \beta_{b.i} \mid i \in \mathcal{I}, a \in \mathcal{A}, b \in \mathcal{B}\}$ initially.

**Definition 6.** *A NAS system denoted by* $\mathrm{NAS}(\ddot{\mathbb{C}}_{\mathcal{I}}, \widetilde{\mathcal{R}}, \widetilde{\rho}, \mathsf{Clk})$ *is the closed process* $(\nu_{i \in \mathcal{I}, a \in \mathcal{A}, b \in \mathcal{B}}\ \alpha^{\circ}_{a.i}\alpha_{a.i}\beta_{b.i})\ (\Pi_{i \in \mathcal{I}}\ddot{C}_i \mid (\nu_{b \in \mathcal{B}}\ K_b)\ (\varnothing: \widetilde{\mathcal{R}^{\varnothing}}: \widetilde{\rho}: \mathsf{Clk})),\ where$

- $\ddot{\mathbb{C}}_{\mathcal{I}} = \{\ddot{C}_i \mid i \in \mathcal{I}\}$ *is a set of honest NAFS clients indexed by $\mathcal{I}$,*
- $\varnothing: \widetilde{\mathcal{R}^{\varnothing}}: \widetilde{\rho}: \mathsf{Clk}$ *is an initial NAFS control state, and* $\{K_b, \alpha^{\circ}_{a.i}, \alpha_{a.i}, \beta_{b.i} \mid i \in \mathcal{I}, a \in \mathcal{A}, b \in \mathcal{B}\} \cap \mathrm{fn}(\widetilde{\mathcal{R}}, \widetilde{\rho}) = \varnothing.$

# 5 Safety and Other Guarantees for Network-Attached Storage

We now establish that IFS is a sound and adequate abstraction for NAFS. Specifically, we show that network-attached storage systems safely implement their specifications as ideal storage systems; we then derive consequences important for security.

IFS *functions derived from* NAFS *functions*:

$$\frac{\mathbf{manager}(op) = a}{\mathbf{may}(k, op, \widetilde{\mathcal{R}}) = \mathbf{may}_a(k, op, \mathcal{R}_a)} \qquad \frac{\mathbf{manager}(adm) = a}{\mathbf{may}(k, adm, \widetilde{\mathcal{R}}) = \mathbf{may}_a(k, adm, \mathcal{R}_a)}$$

$$\frac{\mathbf{disk}(op) = b \quad \forall b' \neq b : \rho'_{b'} = \rho_{b'} \quad \langle \rho'_b, r \rangle = \mathbf{execute}_b(op, \rho_b)}{\mathbf{execute}(op, \widetilde{\rho}) = \langle \widetilde{\rho'}, r \rangle} \qquad \frac{\mathbf{manager}(adm) = a \quad \forall a' \neq a : \mathcal{H}'_{a'} = \mathcal{H}_{a'} \quad \mathcal{H}'_a = \mathbf{schedule}_a(adm, \mathcal{H}_a, \mathsf{Clk})}{\mathbf{schedule}(adm, \widetilde{\mathcal{H}}, \mathsf{Clk}) = \widetilde{\mathcal{H}'}}$$

$$\frac{\forall a : {\mathcal{R}'_a}^{\mathcal{H}'_a} = \mathbf{update}_a(\mathcal{R}_a{}^{\mathcal{H}_a}, \mathsf{Clk})}{\mathbf{update}(\widetilde{\mathcal{R}}^{\widetilde{\mathcal{H}}}, \mathsf{Clk}) = \widetilde{\mathcal{R}'}^{\widetilde{\mathcal{H}'}}} \qquad \frac{\mathbf{manager}(op) = a}{\mathbf{lifespan}(k, op, \widetilde{\mathcal{H}}, \mathsf{Clk}) = \mathbf{expiry}_a(k, op, \mathcal{H}_a, \mathsf{Clk}) - \mathsf{Clk}}$$

*Honest* IFS-*client code derived from honest* NAFS-*client code*:

$$\lceil 0 \rceil = 0 \qquad \lceil (\nu n) P \rceil = (\nu n) \lceil P \rceil \qquad \lceil u(\widetilde{x}). P \rceil = u(\widetilde{x}). \lceil P \rceil \qquad \lceil \overline{u}\langle \widetilde{M} \rangle. P \rceil = \overline{u}\langle \widetilde{M} \rangle. \lceil P \rceil$$

$$\lceil P | Q \rceil = \lceil P \rceil | \lceil Q \rceil \qquad \lceil !P \rceil = !\lceil P \rceil \qquad \lceil \text{if } M = N \text{ then } P \text{ else } Q \rceil = \text{if } M = N \text{ then } \lceil P \rceil \text{ else } \lceil Q \rceil$$

$$\lceil \mathsf{admin}_i \ adm; \ P \rceil = \mathsf{admin}_i \ adm; \ \lceil P \rceil \qquad \lceil \mathsf{auth}_i \ \kappa \text{ for } op; \ P \rceil = \lceil P \rceil$$

$$\lceil \mathsf{fileopauth}_i \ \kappa/r; \ P \rceil = \mathsf{fileop}_i \ \mathbf{proj}_1(\mathbf{message}(\kappa))/r; \ \lceil P \rceil$$

**Fig. 3.** Abstraction of NAS systems

In our analyses, we assume that systems interact with arbitrary (potentially hostile) environments. We refer to such environments as *attackers*, and model them as arbitrary closed processes. We study the behaviour of systems via *quizzes*. Quizzes are similar to tests, more specifically to may-tests [14], which capture safety properties.

**Definition 7.** *A quiz is of the form* $(E, c, \widetilde{n}, \widetilde{M})$, *where* $E$ *is an attacker,* $c$ *is a name,* $\widetilde{n}$ *is a vector of names, and* $\widetilde{M}$ *is a vector of closed terms, such that* $\widetilde{n} \subseteq \mathtt{fn}(\widetilde{M}) \setminus \mathtt{fn}(E, c)$.

Informally, a quiz provides an attacker that interacts with the system under analysis, and a goal observation, described by a channel, a set of fresh names, and a message that contains the fresh names. The system passes the quiz if it is possible to observe the message on the channel, by letting the system evolve with the attacker. As the following definition suggests, quizzes make finer distinctions than conventional tests, since they can specify the observation of messages that contain names generated during execution.

**Definition 8.** *A closed process* $P$ *passes the quiz* $(E, c, \widetilde{n}, \widetilde{M})$ *iff* $E \mid P \xrightarrow{\tau}{}^* \xrightarrow{\overline{c}} (\nu\widetilde{n}) \langle \widetilde{M} \rangle. Q$ *for some* $Q$.

Intuitively, we intend to show that a NAS system passes a quiz only if its specification passes a similar quiz. Given a NAS system, we "extract" its specification by translating it to an ideal storage system. (The choice of specification is justified by Theorem 2.)

**Definition 9.** *Let* $\mathrm{NAS}(\ddot{\mathbb{C}}_{\mathcal{I}}, \widetilde{\mathcal{R}}, \widetilde{\rho}, \mathsf{Clk})$ *be a network-attached storage system. Then its specification is the ideal storage system* $\varPhi\mathrm{NAS}(\lceil \ddot{\mathbb{C}}_{\mathcal{I}} \rceil, \widetilde{\mathcal{R}}, \widetilde{\rho}, \mathsf{Clk})$, *with* $\lceil \cdot \rceil$ *as defined in Figure 3, and with the* IFS *functions* may, execute, schedule, update, *and* lifespan *derived from their* NAFS *counterparts as shown in Figure 3.*

Next, we map quizzes designed for NAS systems to quizzes that are "at least as potent" on their specifications. Informally, the existence of this map implies that NAFS does not "introduce" any new attacks, *i.e.*, any attack that is possible on NAFS is also possible on IFS. We present the map by showing appropriate translations for attackers and terms.

**Definition 10.** *Let $E$ be an attacker (designed for NAS systems). Then $\Phi E$ is the code*

$$E \mid (\nu_{b\in\mathcal{B}}K_b) \; ( \; \Pi_{\alpha_{a.j}\in\mathtt{fn}(E)}!\alpha_{a.j}(adm, n).\,\overline{\alpha_j}\langle adm, n\rangle$$
$$\mid \Pi_{\beta_{b.j}\in\mathtt{fn}(E)}!\beta_{b.j}(\kappa, n).\,\Sigma_{\beta_{b.j'}\in\mathtt{fn}(E)}\overline{\beta_{j'}}\langle\mathbf{proj}_1(\mathbf{message}(\kappa)), n\rangle$$
$$\mid \Pi_{\alpha^\circ_{a.j}\in\mathtt{fn}(E)}!\alpha^\circ_{a.j}(op, c).\,\Sigma_{b\in\mathcal{B}}(\nu m)\,\overline{c}\langle\mathbf{mac}(\langle op, \{m\}_{K_b}, b\rangle, K_b)\rangle)$$

Informally, $E$ is composed with a "wrapper" that translates between the interfaces of NAFS and IFS. Administrative requests on $\alpha_{a.j}$ are forwarded on $\alpha_j$. A file-operation request on $\beta_{b.j}$, with $\kappa$ as authorization, is first translated by extracting the operation from $\kappa$, and then broadcast on all $\beta_{j'}$. Intuitively, $\kappa$ may be a live, valid capability that was issued in response to an earlier authorization request made on some $\alpha^\circ_{a.j'}$, and a request must now be made on $\beta_{j'}$ to pass the same access-control checks. (This pleasant correspondence is partly due to the properties of **lifespan**.) Finally, authorization requests on $\alpha^\circ_{a.j}$ are "served" by returning fake capability-like terms. Intuitively, these terms are indistinguishable from NAFS capabilities under all possible computations by $E$. To that end, fake secret keys replace the secret NAFS keys $\{K_b \mid b \in \mathcal{B}\}$; the disk $b$ is non-deterministically "guessed" from the finite set $\mathcal{B}$; and an encrypted unique nonce replaces the NAFS timestamp. Notice that the value of the NAFS clock need not be guessed to fake the timestamp, since by design, each NAFS timestamp is unique and unintelligible to $E$.

We now formalize the translation of terms (generated by NAFS and its clients). As indicated above, the translation preserves indistinguishability by attackers, which we show by Proposition 1.

**Definition 11.** *Let $m$ range over names not in $\{K_b \mid b \in \mathcal{B}\}$, and $\mathcal{M}$ range over sequences of terms. We define the judgment $\mathcal{M} \vdash \diamond$ by the following rules:*

$$\varnothing \vdash \diamond \qquad \frac{\mathcal{M} \vdash \diamond}{\mathcal{M}, m \vdash \diamond} \qquad \frac{\mathcal{M} \vdash \diamond \quad f \text{ is a function symbol} \quad \widetilde{M} \subseteq \mathcal{M}}{\mathcal{M}, f(\widetilde{M}) \vdash \diamond}$$

$$\frac{\mathcal{M} \vdash \diamond \qquad \{\langle m, \_\rangle\}_{K_b} \notin \mathcal{M} \qquad op \in \mathcal{M}}{\mathcal{M}, \mathbf{mac}(\langle op, \{\langle m, \mathsf{Clk}\rangle\}_{K_b}, b\rangle, K_b), \{\langle m, \mathsf{Clk}\rangle\}_{K_b} \vdash \diamond}$$

*We say that $\mathcal{M}$ is valid if $\mathcal{M} \vdash \diamond$, and define $\Phi$ on terms in a valid sequence:*

$$\Phi m = m \qquad \Phi f(\widetilde{M}) = f(\widetilde{\Phi M}) \qquad \Phi\{\langle m, \mathsf{Clk}\rangle\}_{K_b} = \{m\}_{K_b}$$
$$\Phi\mathbf{mac}(\langle op, \{\langle m, \mathsf{Clk}\rangle\}_{K_b}, b\rangle, K_b) = \mathbf{mac}(\langle \Phi op, \{m\}_{K_b}, b\rangle, K_b)$$

**Proposition 1.** *Let $M, M'$ belong to a valid sequence. Then $M = M'$ iff $\Phi M = \Phi M'$ (where $=$ is equational, and not merely structural, equality).*

Our main result, which we state next, says that whenever a NAS system passes a quiz, its specification passes a quiz that is meaningfully related to the former:

**Theorem 1 (Implementation soundness).** *Let NAS be a network-attached storage system. If NAS passes some quiz $(E, c, \widetilde{n}, \widetilde{M})$, then $\widetilde{M}$ belong to a valid sequence, and $\Phi$NAS passes the quiz $(\Phi E, c, \widetilde{n}, \widetilde{\Phi M})$.*

The converse of this theorem does not hold, since $\Phi E$ can always return a capability-like term, while NAFS does not if an access check fails. Consequently, full abstraction breaks. In [5], where the outcome of any access check is fixed, we achieve full abstraction by letting the file system return a fake capability whenever an access check fails. (The wrapper can then naïvely translate execution requests, much as in here.) However, it becomes impossible to translate attackers when dynamic administration is allowed (even if we let NAFS return fake capabilities for failed access checks). Intuitively, $\Phi E$ cannot consistently guess the outcome of an access check when translating file-operation requests at runtime—and for any choice of $\Phi E$ given $E$, this problem can be exploited to show a counterexample to full abstraction.

Full abstraction can also be broken by honest clients, with the use of expired capabilities. One can imagine more complex client macros that check for expiry before sending requests. (Such macros require the NAFS clock to be shared with the clients.) Still, the "late" check by NAFS (after receiving the request) cannot be replaced by any appropriate "early" check (before sending the request) without making additional assumptions on the scheduling of communication events over the network.

One might of course wonder if the specifications for NAS systems are "too weak" (thereby passing quizzes by design), so as to make Theorem 1 vacuous. The following standard completeness result ensures that this is not the case.

**Theorem 2 (Specification completeness).** *Let two systems be distinguishable if there exists a quiz passed by one but not the other. Then two ideal storage systems* $IS_1$ *and* $IS_2$ *are distinguishable only if there are distinguishable network-attached storage systems* $NAS_1$ *and* $NAS_2$ *such that* $\Phi NAS_1 = IS_1$ *and* $\Phi NAS_2 = IS_2$.

It follows that every quiz passed by an ideal storage system can be concretized to a quiz passed by some NAS system with that specification.

Several safety properties can be expressed as quiz failures. Next we show two "safety-preservation" theorems that follow as corollaries to Theorem 1. The first one concerns secrecy; the second, integrity. We model the initial knowledge of an attacker with a set of names, as in [2]; let $S$ range over such sets.

**Definition 12.** *Let* $S$ *be a set of names. An attacker* $E$ *is a* $S$-*adversary if* $fn(E) \subseteq S$.

We may then express the hypothesis that a system keeps a term secret by claiming that it fails any quiz whose goal is to observe that term on a channel that is initially known to the attacker.

**Definition 13.** *A closed process* $P$ *keeps the closed term* $M$ *secret from a set of names* $S$ *if* $P$ *does not pass any quiz* $(E, s, \tilde{n}, M)$ *where* $E$ *is an* $S$-*adversary and* $s \in S$.

We now derive preservation of secrecy by NAS implementations. For any $S$ modeling the initial knowledge of a NAS attacker, let $\Phi S$ be an upper bound on $S$, as follows:

$$\Phi S = S \cup \{\alpha_j, \alpha_{j'}^\circ, \beta_{j''} \mid \alpha_{a.j}, \alpha_{a.j'}^\circ, \beta_{b.j''} \in S, a \in \mathcal{A}, b \in \mathcal{B}\}$$

Note that for any $S$-adversary $E$, $\Phi E$ is a $\Phi S$-adversary. Further, note that the inclusion of the name $\alpha_{a.j}$ (*resp.* $\alpha_{a.j'}^\circ$, $\beta_{b.j''}$) in $S$ suggests that $E$ knows how to impersonate the NAFS client $\ddot{C}_j$ for requesting policy modifications (*resp.* capabilities, file operations);

the corresponding inclusion of the name $\alpha_j$ (resp. $\alpha_{j'}^{\circ}$, $\beta_{j''}$) in $\Phi S$ allows the abstract attacker $\Phi E$ to impersonate the IFS client $C_j$. Thus, the following result says that a secret that may be learnt from a NAS system may be also be learnt from its specification with comparable initial knowledge; in other words, a NAS system protects a secret whenever its specification protects the secret.

**Corollary 1 (Secrecy preservation).** *Let* NAS *be a network-attached storage system, S a finite set of names, and M a closed term that belongs to a valid sequence. Then* NAS *keeps M secret from S if* $\Phi$NAS *keeps* $\Phi M$ *secret from* $\Phi S$.

Next we derive preservation of integrity by NAS implementations. In fact, we treat integrity as one of a larger class of safety properties whose violations may be detected by letting a system adequately monitor itself, and we derive preservation of all such properties in NAS. For this purpose, we hypothesize a set of monitoring channels that may be used to communicate warnings between various parts of the system, and to signal violations on detection; we protect such channels from attackers by construction. In particular, clients can use monitoring channels to communicate about begin- and end-events, and to warn whenever an end-event has no corresponding begin-event (thus indicating the failure of a correspondence assertion [9]).

**Definition 14.** *A name n is purely communicative in a closed process P if any occurrence of n in P is in the form* $n(\widetilde{x}). Q$ *or* $\overline{n}\langle\widetilde{M}\rangle. Q$. *Let S be a finite set of names. Then the set of names W monitors a closed process P under S if* $W \cap S = \varnothing$ *and each* $w \in W$ *is purely communicative in P*.

Any message on a monitoring channel may be viewed as a warning.

**Definition 15.** *Let W monitor P under S. Then S causes P to warn on W if for some S-adversary E and* $w \in W$, *P passes a quiz of the form* $(E, w, \widetilde{n}, \widetilde{M})$.

The following result says that whenever an attack causes a warning in a NAS system, an attack with comparable initial knowledge causes that warning in its specification. In other words, since a specification may contain monitoring for integrity violations, a NAS system protects integrity whenever its specification protects integrity.

**Corollary 2 (Integrity preservation).** *Let W monitor an abstracted network-attached storage system* $\Phi$NAS *under* $\Phi S$. *Then S does not cause* NAS *to warn on W if* $\Phi S$ *does not cause* $\Phi$NAS *to warn on W*.

# 6    Conclusion

In this paper we study networked storage systems with distributed access control. In particular, we relate those systems to simpler centralized storage systems with local access control. Viewing the latter systems as specifications of the former ones, we establish the preservation of safety properties of the specifications in the implementations. We derive the preservation of standard secrecy and integrity properties as corollaries. We expect that such results will be helpful in reasoning about the correctness and the security of larger systems (which may, for example, include non-trivial clients that rely on file storage). In that context, our results imply that we can do proofs using the simpler centralized storage systems instead of the networked storage systems. In our current work, we are developing proof techniques that leverage this simplification.

**Acknowledgments.** We thank Cédric Fournet and Ricardo Corin for helpful comments. This work was partly supported by the National Science Foundation under Grants CCR-0204162, CCR-0208800, and CCF-0524078, and by Livermore National Laboratory, Los Alamos National Laboratory, and Sandia National Laboratory under Contract B554869.

# References

1. M. Abadi. Protection in programming-language translations. In *ICALP'98: International Colloquium on Automata, Languages and Programming*, pages 868–883. Springer-Verlag, 1998.
2. M. Abadi and B. Blanchet. Analyzing security protocols with secrecy types and logic programs. *Journal of the ACM*, 52(1):102–146, 2005.
3. M. Abadi and C. Fournet. Mobile values, new names, and secure communication. In *POPL'01: Principles of Programming Languages*, pages 104–115. ACM, 2001.
4. M. Abadi and A. D. Gordon. A calculus for cryptographic protocols: The spi calculus. *Information and Computation*, 148(1):1–70, 1999.
5. A. Chaudhuri and M. Abadi. Formal security analysis of basic network-attached storage. In *FMSE'05: Formal Methods in Security Engineering*, pages 43–52. ACM, 2005.
6. G. A. Gibson, D. P. Nagle, K. Amiri, F. W. Chang, E. Feinberg, H. G. C. Lee, B. Ozceri, E. Riedel, and D. Rochberg. A case for network-attached secure disks. Technical Report CMU–CS-96-142, Carnegie Mellon University, 1996.
7. H. Gobioff. *Security for a High Performance Commodity Storage Subsystem*. PhD thesis, Carnegie Mellon University, 1999.
8. H. Gobioff, G. Gibson, and J. Tygar. Security for network-attached storage devices. Technical Report CMU-CS-97-185, Carnegie Mellon University, 1997.
9. A. D. Gordon and A. Jeffrey. Typing correspondence assertions for communication protocols. *Theoritical Computer Science*, 300(1-3):379–409, 2003.
10. D. Mazières and D. Shasha. Building secure file systems out of byzantine storage. In *PODC'02: Principles of Distributed Computing*, pages 108–117. ACM, 2002.
11. E. L. Miller, D. D. E. Long, W. E. Freeman, and B. Reed. Strong security for network-attached storage. In *FAST'02: File and Storage Technologies*, pages 1–13. USENIX, 2002.
12. R. Milner. Fully abstract models of typed lambda-calculi. *Theoretical Computer Science*, 4(1):1–22, 1977.
13. R. Milner. The polyadic pi-calculus: a tutorial. In *Logic and Algebra of Specification*, pages 203–246. Springer-Verlag, 1993.
14. R. D. Nicola and M. C. B. Hennessy. Testing equivalences for processes. *Theoretical Computer Science*, 34(1–2):83–133, 1984.
15. B. C. Reed, E. G. Chron, R. C. Burns, and D. D. E. Long. Authenticating network-attached storage. *IEEE Micro*, 20(1):49–57, 2000.
16. F. B. Schneider. Enforceable security policies. *ACM Transactions on Information and System Security*, 3(1):30–50, 2000.
17. Y. Zhu and Y. Hu. SNARE: A strong security scheme for network-attached storage. In *SRDS'03: Symposium on Reliable Distributed Systems*, pages 250–259. IEEE, 2003.

# Analysing the MUTE Anonymous File-Sharing System Using the Pi-Calculus

Tom Chothia

CWI, Kruislaan 413, 1098 SJ, Amsterdam, The Netherlands

**Abstract.** This paper gives details of a formal analysis of the MUTE system for anonymous file-sharing. We build pi-calculus models of a node that is innocent of sharing files, a node that is guilty of file-sharing and of the network environment. We then test to see if an attacker can distinguish between a connection to a guilty node and a connection to an innocent node. A *weak bi-simulation* between every guilty network and an innocent network would be required to show possible innocence. We find that such a bi-simulation cannot exist. The point at which the bi-simulation fails leads directly to a previously undiscovered attack on MUTE. We describe a fix for the MUTE system that involves using authentication keys as the nodes' pseudo identities and give details of its addition to the MUTE system.

## 1 Introduction

MUTE is one of the most popular anonymous peer-to-peer file-sharing systems. Peers, or nodes, using MUTE will connect to a small number of other, known nodes; only the direct neighbours of a node know its IP address. Communication with remote nodes is provided by sending messages hop-to-hop across this overlay network. Routing messages in this way allows MUTE to trade efficient routing for anonymity. There is no way to find the IP address of a remote node, and direct neighbours can achieve a level of anonymity by claiming that they are just forwarding requests and files for other nodes. Every node picks a random pseudo ID that it uses to identify itself. There is a danger that an attacker may be able to link the pseudo ID and the IP address of it direct neighbours, and thus find out which files the neighbours are requesting and offering.

We analyse MUTE by building pi-calculus processes that model a node that is guilty of sharing files, a node that is innocent of sharing files (but does forward messages) and a third pi-calculus process that models the rest of the network. These processes are connected by channels, which can be bound by the pi-calculus new operator or left free to give the attacker access. We use the pi-calculus because it is expressive enough to define an accurate model of MUTE, while still being simple enough to analyse by hand or with automatic tools. There is also a large body of theoretical and implementational work to support analysis in the pi-calculus. We do not make an explicit model of the attacker, rather we aim to show that for every network in which the attacker connects to a guilty node, there is another network in which the attacker connects to an innocent

E. Najm et al. (Eds.): FORTE 2006, LNCS 4229, pp. 115–130, 2006.

node, and that the two networks are indistinguishable. For this we use *weak bi-simulation*, which holds between pi-calculus processes if and only if all observable inputs and outputs of a system are the same. We show that the environment can provide "cover" for a guilty node by showing that for every guilty node $G$ and environment $E$ there is an innocent node $I$ and another environment $E'$ such that $G \mid E$ is weakly bi-similar to $I \mid E'$. In general, weak bi-simulation is necessary, but not sufficient, to show anonymity because it says nothing about how likely the actions of the two processes are. However, once a weak bi-simulation is shown to hold, we can prove that the guilty nodes have "possible innocence" [RR98] by showing that, assuming a fair scheduler, the matching actions in the weak bi-simulation occur with a non-negligible probability.

The contributions of this paper are the formal model of the MUTE system, the description of an attack on MUTE, found by analysing this model, and a fix for the attack. We note that this attack was only found while testing the model, the model was not built with this attack in mind, and while the checking of the model was performed by hand, it is a mechanical procedure that does not require any special insight. Furthermore, MUTE has an active development community that, in over two years of development, had not found this serious fault, as had a number of academic papers that tried to examine or extent MUTE [ALRV05, BASM04, KKK05].

There are a number of other anonymous peer-to-peer file-sharing systems [Ant03, was03] and theoretical designs [BASM04, SGRE04], for more information we direct readers to our previous survey paper [CC05]. Also related are anonymous publishing systems such as Freenet [CSWH01] or Free Haven [DFM00], which hide the original author of a file rather than the up loader, and the Tor middleware [DMS04]. Bhargava and Palamidessi [BP05] model the dinning cryptographers protocol in the probabilistic pi-calculus [HP00]. They propose a new notion of anonymity that makes a careful distinction between non-deterministic and probabilistic actions. In other work Deng, Palamidessi and Pang [DPP05] define "weak probabilistic anonymity" and use PRISM [KNP02] to show that it holds for the dinning cryptographers protocol. Chatzikokolakis and Palamidessi further explore the definition of "probable innocence" [CP05]. Garcia et al. [GHPvR05] develop a formal framework for proving anonymity based on epistemic logic, Schnider and Sidiropoulos [SS96] use CSP to check anonymity and Kremer and Ryan analyse a voting protocol in the applied pi-calculus [KR05]. Their approaches do not take into account the probability of observing actions.

In the next section we describe the MUTE system, then in Section 3 we review the pi-calculus. We carry out our analysis of MUTE in Section 4, with one sub-section on the pi-calculus model and another showing why we cannot get a bi-simulation. We discuss how this break down in bi-simulation can be turned into a real attack on a MUTE network in Section 5, and how MUTE can be fixed in Section 6. Finally, Section 7 concludes and suggests further work. Readers who are only interested in the attack and the fix may skip ahead to sections 5 and 6.

# 2   The Ants Protocol and the MUTE System

The MUTE system [Roh06] is based on the Ant Colony Optimisation algorithm (Ants Protocol) [DD99, GSB02]. This protocol is in turn based on the way ants use pheromones when looking for food [BDG92] and was not originally designed to keep users anonymous, rather it was designed for networks in which nodes do not have fixed positions or well-known identities. In this setting, each node has a pseudo identity that can be used to send messages to a node but does not give any information about its true identity (i.e., the node's IP address).

In order to search the network, a node broadcasts a search message with its own pseudo ID, a unique message identifier and a time-to-live counter. The search message is sent to all of the node's neighbours, which in turn send the message to all of their neighbours until the time-to-live counter runs out. Upon receiving a message a node first checks the message identity and discards any repeated messages, it then records the connection on which the message was received and the pseudo ID of the sender, in this way each node dynamically builds and maintains a routing table for all the pseudo identities it sees. To send a message to a particular pseudo ID a node sends a message with the pseudo ID as a "to ID". If a node has that pseudo ID in its routing table, it forwards the message along the most common connection. Otherwise, it forwards the message to all its neighbours. Some random rerouting can be added to allow nodes to discover new best routes, in case the network architecture has changed.

MUTE implements the Ants protocol with a non-deterministic time-to-live counter, as well as a host of other features designed to make the system efficient and user friendly. The kinds of attacker that MUTE defends against are nodes in the system that wish to link the IP address of their direct neighbours with a pseudo ID. Attackers may make as many connections to a node as they like but we do not let an attacker monitor the whole network or even all of the connections going into or out of a node; without the possibility of an unmonitored connection to an honest node the target loses all anonymity. A complete summary of a piece of software of the size of MUTE is beyond the scope of this paper, we highlight a few key features and refer the interested reader to the MUTE developer web-page for more information.

MUTE uses a complex three phase "Utility Counter" to control how far a search message travels. The first phase is equivalent to the searcher picking a time-to-live value from a long-tail distribution, which is then counted down to zero before moving to the second phase. The aim of this phase is to stop an attacker from being able to tell if their neighbour originated a search message. Once this first phase is finished the counter moves to the second phase, which is a standard time-to-live counter that counts up to 35 in increments of 7. This means that the message is forwarded for a further 5 hops. The values of 35 and 7 are used to be compatible with an older version of MUTE that used a more fine-grained, but less anonymous, version of the counter.

The third phase of the utility counter is a non-deterministic forwarding. Each node decides when it starts up how many nodes it is going to forward phase-3 messages to. A node will drop a phase-3 message with probability 3/4, and

Process $P, Q ::= 0$                                           The stopped process
    |   rec $a(x); P$                  Input of $x$ on channel $a$
    |   send $a(b)$                    Output of $b$ on channel $a$
    |   new $a; P$                     New name declaration
    |   $P \mid Q$                      $P$ running in parallel with $Q$
    |   repeat$\{ P \}$                 An infinite number of $P$s
    |   if $(condition)$ then $\{ P \}$ Run $P$, if $a = b$
    |   $\prod_{j \in \{a_1,\ldots,a_n\}} P(x)$    $P(x)$ in parallel for all $j$

**Fig. 1.** The Pi-calculus Syntax

forward the message to $n$ neighbours with probability $1/(3 \times 2^n)$. The aim of this last phase is to quickly end the search and to stop an attacker from being able to send a search message that it knows will not be forwarded to any other nodes. There must always be a chance of forwarding more copies of a search message to stop a number of attackers that are connected to the same node knowing when they have received all of the forwarded copies of a search.

All of the probabilistic choices made by a MUTE node (such as the value of the phase-1 counter or how many nodes phase-3 messages are forwarded to) are fixed when the node first starts up. This protects against statistical attacks by ensuring that the repetition of the same action yields no new information to the attacker.

MUTE's routing table stores information for the last one hundred different IDs it has seen. For each ID the routing table stores the last fifty connections over which a message from this ID was received. When either list is full the oldest entries are dropped. When a node needs to forward a message to a particular ID it randomly chooses one of the stored connections for that ID and forwards the message along that connection. If the node does not have an entry for the destination ID it sends the message to all of its neighbours.

## 3    The Pi-Calculus

We use the asynchronous pi-calculus [HT91, Mil93] to build a formal model of the MUTE system. The pi-calculus can be thought of as a small concurrent language that is simple enough to be formally analysed while still expressive enough to capture the key elements of a system. The syntax of our version of the pi-calculus is shown in Figure 1. It is an asynchronous, late version of the calculus that includes conditional branching. We also include a product term that effectively defines families of processes. To express some of the details of the MUTE protocol, we extend the set of names to include tuples and natural numbers. Process terms are identified by a *structural congruence* "$\equiv$". The semantics of the calculus is shown in Figure 2. The labels on the arrows indicate the kind of reduction that is taking place, either an input $a$, an output $\bar{a}$ or an internal action $\tau$. Output actions may carry new name declarations along with them, indicated by the $\nu$ label. The side conditions on some of the rules ensure

$$\text{send } a(b) \xrightarrow{\bar{a}\langle b\rangle} 0 \qquad\qquad \text{rec } a(x); P \xrightarrow{a(x)} P$$

$$\frac{P \equiv P' \quad P' \to Q' \quad Q' \equiv Q}{P \to Q} \qquad \frac{P \xrightarrow{\nu\bar{c}.\bar{a}\langle b\rangle} P'}{\text{new } c'; P \xrightarrow{\nu c',\bar{c}.\bar{a}\langle b\rangle P'} P'}$$

$$\frac{P \xrightarrow{a(x)} P' \quad Q \xrightarrow{\nu\bar{c}.\bar{a}\langle b\rangle} Q'}{P \mid Q \xrightarrow{\tau} \text{new } \bar{c}; (P[b/x] \mid Q)} \quad \bar{c} \cap fn(P) = \emptyset$$

$$\frac{P \xrightarrow{\alpha} P'}{P \mid Q \xrightarrow{\alpha} P' \mid Q} \quad bn(\alpha) \cap fn(P) = \emptyset$$

$$\frac{P \xrightarrow{\alpha} P'}{\text{new } a.P \xrightarrow{\alpha} \text{new } a.P'} \quad a \notin \alpha$$

**Fig. 2.** Pi-calculus Semantics

than the new name declaration does not accidentally capture other names. We further define $\xRightarrow{\alpha}$ to be any number of internal ($\tau$) actions followed by an $\alpha$ action and then another sequence of internal actions.

The first piece of syntax stop represents a stopped process, all processes must end with this term although we usually do not write it. The send $a(b)$ operation broadcasts the name $b$ over channel $a$. The receive operation receives a name and substitutes it into the continuing process. The new operation creates a new communication channel. The repeat operator can perform recursion by spinning off an arbitrary number of copies of a process, $!P \equiv P \mid !P$. The bar $\mid$ represents two processes running in parallel and the match operation, if (condition) then $\{P\}$, executes $P$ if and only if the condition holds. The product term defines the parallel composition of any number of processes $\prod_{j\in\{a_1,\ldots,a_n\}} P(x) \equiv P[a_1/x] \mid P[a_2/x] \mid \ldots \mid P[a_n/x]$. We will drop the set of names from this operator when their meaning is clear.

The semantic rules of the calculus allow two processes to communicate:

$$\text{send } a(b) \mid \text{rec } a(x); P \xrightarrow{\tau} P[b/x]$$

Here, the name $b$ has been sent over the channel $a$ and substituted for $x$ in $P$. The $\tau$ on top of the arrow indicates that a communication has taken place. $bn$ is defined as the names that are bound by a new operator and $fn$ are the free names, i.e., those that are not bound. The side conditions on the reduction rules stop names from becoming accidentally bound by a new operator. One of the most important aspects of the pi-calculus is that new names are both new and unguessable, for instance the process new $a$; rec $a(x); P$ can never receive a communication on the channel $a$, no matter what the surrounding processes might try. For more information on the pi-calculus we refer the reader to one of the many survey papers [Par01].

# 4    Analysing MUTE in the Pi-Calculus

Our formal model of MUTE comes in three pieces. We make a process that models an innocent node "$I$", which forwards messages and searches for files and another process that models a guilty node "$G$", which will also return a response to a request. A third kind of process "$E$", models the rest of the environment. These processes are parameterised on the communication channels that run between them. We can bind these channels with a new operator to hide them from the attacker or leave them free to allow the attacker access. The parameters also specify the probabilistic choices a node makes when it starts up, such as the value of the phase-1 counter. The behaviour of a parameterised node is non-deterministic, as oppose to probabilistic, i.e., the choice of which actions happen is due to chance occurrences that cannot be meaningfully assign a probability inside our framework, such as how often a user will search for a file.

Weak bi-simulation is often used as an equality relation between processes. Two processes are weakly bi-similar if every visible action of one process can be matched by the other process and the resulting processes are also weakly bi-similar:

**Definition 1 (Weakly bi-similar).** *Processes $P$ and $Q$ are weakly bi-similar if there exists an equivalence relation $\approx$ such that $P \approx Q$ and for all $P_1$ and $Q_1$ such that $P_1 \approx Q_1$, if $P_1 \overset{\alpha}{\Rightarrow} P_1'$ then:*

- *if $\alpha$ is an output or an internal action there exists a process $Q_1'$ such that $Q_1 \overset{\alpha}{\Rightarrow} Q_1'$ and $P_1' \approx Q_1'$.*
- *if $\alpha$ is an input action, i.e., $\alpha = a(x)$, then for all names $b$, there exists a process $Q_1'$ such that $Q_1 \overset{\alpha}{\Rightarrow} Q_1'$ and $P_1'[b/x] \approx Q_1'[b/x]$.*

A pi-calculus process cannot distinguish between two other pi-calculus processes that are weakly bi-similar. So for any possible pi-calculus process *Attacker* that models an attempt to break the anonymity of a node: if the two processes *A_is_Guilty* and *A_is_Innocent* are bi-similar then we know that the processes *A_is_Guilty* | *Attacker* and *A_is_Innocent* | *Attacker* are also bi-similar, so no pi-calculus attacker can discern if $A$ is guilty.

We would like to show that a network in which the attacker can connect to a guilty node on channels $c_1, \ldots, c_i$ and to the environment on channels $c_1', \ldots, c_j'$:

$$\text{new } c_{i+1}, .., c_k; (\ G(c_1, .., c_i, c_{i+1}, .., c_k) \mid E(c_{i+1}, .., c_k, c_1'', \ldots, c_j'))$$

is weakly bi-similar to a network in which an attacker can connect to an innocent node and a slightly different environment:

$$\text{new } c_{i+1}, .., c_k; (\ I(c_1, .., c_i, c_{i+1}, .., c_k) \mid E'(c_{i+1}, .., c_k, c_1'', \ldots, c_j'))$$

where $c_1, \ldots, c_i$ are the private communication channels between the nodes and the environment, and $c_{i+1}, .., c_k$ are channels that the attacker can use to communicate with $I$ and $G$. In the next sub-section we give the process terms for $I, G$ and $E$ and in the following sub-section we show that there can be no bi-simulation between guilty and innocent networks.

## 4.1   A Model of MUTE in the Pi-Calculus

We make a number of abstractions while building our model; the aim of these simplifications is to make the model small enough to check without losing its overall correctness. These abstractions include the following:

(1) No actual files are transferred and no search keywords are used. Instead we use a "search" message that is responded to with a "reply" message.
(2) We parameterise our nodes on a fixed time-to-live value for the phase-1 counter. This value is reduced by one each hop. The counter goes to phase-2 when this value reaches zero.
(3) We simplify the nodes routing table: when forwarding a message to a particular ID the node picks any connection over which it has previously received a message from that ID. The pi-calculus does not include a concept of random access memory, so to represent storing an ID and a connection we send a pair $(id, connection)$ on a particular name. When we want to read from memory we receive on the same channel and test the $id$, if it matches the ID of the node we are looking for we use the connection otherwise we look for another packet. This can be thought of as using a buffered communication channel to store values.
(4) We assume that a node always knows the "to ID" of any reply message it sees. A more realistic model would have to test for this and send the reply message to all of the node's neighbours if the "to ID" is unknown.
(5) We do not use message IDs and do not drop repeated messages. We also allow a node to send a message back over the connection on which it was received, returning the message to its sender. This does not give an attacker any extra power because there is no way to limit an attacker to just one connection.
(6) In closely packed networks a node may send a request over one connection and receive the same request back over another. To simplify our model we assume that these kinds of communications do not happen.

Point 6 removes details that may reveal some information to the attacker, exactly what will depend on the arrangement of the network, we leave a fuller investigation as further work.

The results of these simplifications are that the channels pass messages with four fields:

Message format = (kind of message, the "to ID", the "from ID",
phase of the counter, value of the counter)

A message kind may be a "*search*" or a "*reply*" to a search. The from and to IDs are the pseudo IDs of the originator of the message and its final destination (not the IDs of the nodes that the message is being past between on the current hop). Search messages are broadcast to the network and so do not use the "to ID" field, in this case we will write "none" as the "to ID".

The processes are parameterised on the communication channels they will use to talk to the environment and the attacker. To stop a node communicating with

$I(connections, forward, ttl)$
$\quad \equiv$ new $my\_id, memory; I_{ID}(my\_id, connections, forward, ttl, memory)$

$I_{ID}(my\_id, \langle \ \langle c_1^i, c_1^o \rangle, .., \langle c_n^i, c_n^o \rangle \ \rangle, \langle \ \langle c_{for\_1}^i, c_{for\_1}^o \rangle, .., \langle c_{for\_p}^i, c_{for\_p}^o \rangle \ \rangle, ttl, memory)$
$\quad \equiv \Pi_j$ repeat $\{$ rec $c_j^i(kind, to\_id, from\_id, phase, counter);$
$\qquad\qquad\qquad$ send $memory(from\_id, c_j^o)$
$\qquad\qquad\qquad | $ if $(kind = search)$ then $\{ \ FORWARDMESSAGE \ \}$
$\qquad\qquad\qquad | $ if $(kind = reply)$ then $\{ \ REPLY \ \}$
$\qquad\qquad \}$
$\qquad | $ repeat $\{ \ \Pi_l$ send $c_l^o(search, none, my\_id, 1, ttl)\}$

$FORWARDMESSAGE \equiv$
$\quad$ if $(phase = 1$ and $counter > 1)$ then
$\qquad\qquad \{\Pi_k$ send $c_k^o(kind, to\_id, from\_id, 1, counter - 1)\}$
$\quad | $ if $(phase = 1$ and $counter = 1)$ then
$\qquad\qquad \{\Pi_k$ send $c_k^o(kind, to\_id, from\_id, 2, 0)\}$
$\quad | $ if $(phase = 2$ and $counter < 35)$ then
$\qquad\qquad \{\Pi_k$ send $c_k^o(kind, to\_id, from\_id, 2, counter + 7)\}$
$\quad | $ if $(phase = 2$ and $counter \geq 35)$ then
$\qquad\qquad \{\Pi_k$ send $c_{for\_k}^o(search, to\_id, from\_id, 3, 0)\}$
$\quad | $ if $(phase = 3)$ then $\{\Pi_k$ send $c_{for\_k}^o(search, to\_id, from\_id, 3, 0)\} \ \}$

$REPLY \equiv$ if $(to\_id = my\_id)$ then $\{stop\}$
$\qquad\qquad | $ if $(to\_id \neq my\_id)$ then
$\qquad\qquad \{$ new $loop;$ send $loop;$
$\qquad\qquad\quad$ repeat$\{$ rec $loop;$ rec $memory(x, channel); ($send $memory(x, channel)$
$\qquad\qquad\qquad\qquad | $ if $(x \neq to\_id)$ then $\{$send $loop\}$
$\qquad\qquad\qquad\qquad | $ if $(x = to\_id)$ then
$\qquad\qquad\qquad\qquad\qquad \{$send $channel(kind, to\_id, from\_id, phase, counter)\} \ ) \ \}$

**Fig. 3.** An Innocent Node

itself we represent communication streams as a pair $c_j = \langle c_j^i, c_j^o \rangle$. The node will use the $c_j^i$ channel for input and the $c_j^o$ channel for output. In order not to clutter our process terms, we will write "new $c_j$" for "new $c_j^i, c_j^o$".

The process term for the innocent node is given in Figure 3. The node's parameters are defined as follows:

$\quad I($ a tuple of connections to other nodes,
$\qquad$ a tuple of the connections on which the node will forward phase 3 messages,
$\qquad$ the initial time-to-live value used for phase-1 when generating a search message)

We define $I$ in terms of another process $I_{ID}$ that also states the node's ID and the channel name it uses for memory. The $I_{ID}$ process listens repeatedly, for a message on any of its input channels. When it receives a message it stores the message's "from ID" and the channel on which the message was received by sending them on the memory channel. The node then tests the message's

$G(connections, forward, ttl)$
    $\equiv$ new $my\_id, memory; G_{ID}(my\_id, connections, forward, ttl, memory)$

$G_{ID}(my\_id, \langle\, \langle c_1^i, c_1^o \rangle, .., \langle c_n^i, c_n^o \rangle\, \rangle, \langle c_{for}^i, c_{for}^o \rangle, ttl, memory) \equiv$
    $\Pi_j$ repeat{rec $c_j^i(kind, to\_id, from\_id, phase, counter)$;
            send $memory(from\_id, c_i^o)$
        | if$(kind = search)$ then
            {new $loop$; send $loop$;
                repeat{rec $loop$; rec $memory(x, channel)$; (send $memory(x, channel)$
                    | if $(x \neq from\_id)$ then {send $loop$}
                    | if $(x = from\_id)$ then
                            {send $channel(reply, from\_id, my\_id, none, none)$} ) }
                | $FORWARDMESSAGE$ }
            | if $(kind = reply)$ then { $REPLY$ } }
        | repeat { $\Pi_l$ send $c_i^o(search, none, my\_id, 1, ttl)$}

**Fig. 4.** A Guilty Node

kind to see if it is a search message or a reply message. If the message is a
search message the utility counter is tested and altered, and the message is
forwarded.

If the message received by the node is a reply message then the node checks
to see if the message is addressed to itself. If it is then this thread of the process
stops and the node continues to listen on its connections (this test and stop
has no functionality and is included for clarity). If the reply is addressed to
another node then the process looks up the "to ID" in its memory and forwards
the message. The last line of the $I_{ID}$ process allows the node to send search
messages to any of its neighbours.

The process term for a guilty node is given in Figure 4. This process works
in the same way as the innocent node except that, after receiving any search
message, the node looks up the "from ID" and returns a reply.

Figure 5 contains a pi-calculus model of the environment which has one connection to a node. The process $E(c, n, j)$ models an environment that communicates over the channel $c$ and includes $n$ individual nodes that may search for
files, out of which $j$ nodes will reply to requests for files. The parameters of the
$E_{ID}$ process include the IDs of its nodes and meta-functions that map each ID
to a utility counter value. There is not a true structural equivalence between
$E$ and $E_{ID}$ because the meta-functions are not really part of the calculus, but
rather a device that allows us to define a family of processes.

In Figure 6 we expand this to the environment with $m$ connections by over-
loading $E$ and $E_{ID}$. This process uses a tuple of values for each of the single
values in the one connection environment. For $i$, ranging from 1 to $m$, the process
uses the channel $c_i$ over which $n_i$ individual nodes may search for files. These
nodes use the IDs $id\_i_1, \ldots, id\_i_{n_i}$ and the first $j_i$ of these will reply to requests
for files.

$E(c, n, j) \cong$ new $id_1, \ldots, id_n; E_{ID}(c, \langle id_1, \ldots, id_n \rangle, j, f_p, f_c)$

$E_{ID}(\langle c^i, c^o \rangle, \langle id_1, \ldots, id_n \rangle, j, f_p, f_c)$
    $\equiv$ repeat$\{$rec $c^i(kind, to\_id, from\_id, phase, counter)$;
        if$(kind = search)$ then
            $\{\Pi_{i \in \{1, \ldots, j\}}$ send $channel(reply, from\_id, id_j, 0, 0); \} \}$
    $\mid \Pi_i$ repeat $\{$ send $c^o(search, none, id_i, f_p(id_j), f_c(id_j)) \}$

**Fig. 5.** The Environment with one connection

$E_{ID}(\langle \langle c_1^i, c_1^o \rangle, \ldots, \langle c_m^i, c_m^o \rangle \rangle, \langle n_1, \ldots, n_m \rangle, \langle j_1, \ldots, j_m \rangle)$
    $\cong$new $(id\_1_1, \ldots, id\_1_{n_1}), (id\_2_1, \ldots, id\_2_{n_2}), \ldots, (id\_m_1, \ldots, id\_m_{n_m})$;
    $E_{ID}(\langle \langle c_1^i, c_1^o \rangle, \ldots, \langle c_m^i, c_m^o \rangle \rangle, \langle j_1, \ldots, j_m \rangle,$
        $\langle \langle id\_1_1, \ldots, id\_1_{n_1} \rangle, \langle id\_2_1, \ldots, id\_2_{n_2} \rangle, \ldots, \langle id\_m_1, \ldots, id\_m_{n_m} \rangle \rangle,$
        $\langle f_1^p, \ldots, f_m^p \rangle, \langle f_1^c, \ldots, f_m^c \rangle )$
$E_{ID}(\ldots) \equiv \Pi_{k \in \{1, \ldots, m\}}$repeat$\{$rec $c_k^i(kind, to\_id, from\_id, phase, counter)$;
        if$i(knd = search)$ then
            $\{\Pi_{i \in \{1, \ldots, j_k\}}$ send $channel(reply, from\_id, id\_k_j, 0, 0); \} \}$
    $\mid \Pi_{k \in \{1, \ldots, m\}} \Pi_{i \in \{1, \ldots, n_k\}}$repeat$\{$send $c_k^o(search, none, id\_k_i, f_m^p(id\_k_i), f_m^c(id\_k_i))\}$

**Fig. 6.** The Environment with $m$ connections

## 4.2  No Bi-Simulations Between Guilty and Innocent Nodes

The environment should provide "cover" for guilty nodes. As an example, consider the case in which a guilty node has one connection to the attacker and one connection to the environment:

$$\text{new } c_2; G(\langle c_1, c_2 \rangle, \langle c_2 \rangle, m) \mid E(c_2, n, j)$$

The only communication channel in this process that is not new is the $c_1$ channel, therefore this is the only channel that the attacker may use to communicate with the process. The guilty node will reply to a search request sent on $c_1$, and so expose its own ID. The environment will do likewise and expose its IDs along with their utility counter values:

$\qquad$ new $c_2; G(\langle c_1, c_2 \rangle, \langle c_2 \rangle, m) \mid E(c_2, n, j)$
$\cong$ new $c_2; G(\langle c_1, c_2 \rangle, \langle c_2 \rangle, m) \mid$ new $id_1, \ldots, id_n; E(c_2, \langle id_1, \ldots, id_n \rangle, j, f_p, f_c)$
$\overset{\vec{\alpha}}{\Rightarrow}$ new $c_2, mem; G_{ID}(g\_id, \langle c_1, c_2 \rangle, \langle c_2 \rangle, m, mem) \mid$ send $mem(id_1, c_2) \ldots$
$\qquad \mid$ send $mem(id_j, c_2) \mid$ new $id_{j+1}, \ldots, id_n; E(c_2, \langle id_1, \ldots, id_n \rangle, j, f_p, f_c) )$

where the $\vec{\alpha}$ actions are the search input from the attacker followed by some permutation of the responses on channel $c_1$.

The anonymity should come from the fact that the same observations may come from an innocent node and an environment that provides one more response with a phase-1 utility counter set to one higher than $m$. We can verify that this innocent network can perform the same $\vec{\alpha}$ actions as the guilty network:

new $c_2$; $I(\langle c_1, c_2 \rangle, \langle c_2 \rangle, m) \mid E(c_2, n, j + 1)$

$\cong$ new $c_2$; $I(\langle c_1, c_2 \rangle, \langle c_2 \rangle, m) \mid$ new $id_1, \ldots, id_n$; $E(c_2, \langle id_1, \ldots, id_n \rangle, (j + 1), f_p', f_c')$

$\overset{\bar{\alpha}}{\Rightarrow}$ new $c_2, mem, i\_id$; $I_{ID}(i\_id, \langle c_1, c_2 \rangle, \langle c_2 \rangle, m, mem) \mid$ send $mem(id_1, c_2) \ldots$

$\mid$ send $mem(id_{j+1}, c_2) \mid$ new $id_{j+2}, \ldots, id_n$; $E(c_2, \langle id_1, \ldots, id_n \rangle, j + 1, f_p', f_c')$ )

where $f_p'(id_{j+1} = 1), f_c'(id_{n+1}) = m + 1$. So, in order to be able to show some level of anonymity, we would like to show the following bi-simulation:

$$\text{new } c_2; G(\langle c_1, c_2 \rangle, \langle c_2 \rangle, m) \mid E(c_2, n, j)$$
$$\approx \text{new } c_2; I(\langle c_1, c_2 \rangle, \langle c_2 \rangle, m) \mid E(c_2, n, j + 1)$$

where $j < n$, i.e., there are both innocent and guilty nodes in the environment.

Upon examination we find that relations of this kind do not hold. Let us start with $P_G$ and $P_I$ as follows:

$$P_G \equiv \text{new } c_2; (\ G(\langle c_1, c_2 \rangle, \langle c_2 \rangle, m) \mid E(c_2, n, j)\ )$$
$$P_I \equiv \text{new } c_2; (\ I(\langle c_1, c_2 \rangle, \langle c_2 \rangle, m) \mid E(c_2, n, j + 1)\ )$$

We follow a fixed method to check the bi-similarity of two processes. We enumerate all of the inputs, outputs and internal actions that a process can perform and then look for matching actions in the other process. We then test each pair of resulting processes for bi-similarity. Most possible actions will not produce interesting reactions, for instance any node will discard messages that do not use "search" or "reply" as its kind. Ultimately the processes may loop around to processes that we already consider bi-similar, in which case we proceed to check the other processes. If we find processes that do not match we backtrack and see if there were any other possible matchings of actions that would have worked. If processes are to complicated to effectively check by hand they can be checked with automated tools such as the Mobility Workbench [VM94] or Level 0/1 [Tiu04].

One of the first actions that we must check for $P_G$ and $P_I$ is the input of a well-formed search message. In response both processes return equivalent reply messages. In the $P_G$ network these include the reply from the guilty note. The innocent network can match these outputs with replies from the environment. At this point the IDs are public and the node has recorded the IDs from the environment:

$P_G \overset{\bar{\alpha}_1}{\Rightarrow}$ new $c_2, mem$; ( $G_{ID}(n\_id, \langle c_1, c_2 \rangle, \langle c_2 \rangle, m, mem) \mid$ send $mem(id_1, c_2) \ldots$

$\mid$ send $mem, (id_j, c_2) \mid E(c_2, \langle id_1, \ldots, id_n \rangle, j, f_p', f_c')$ )

$P_I \overset{\bar{\alpha}_1}{\Rightarrow}$ new $c_2, mem$; ( $I_{ID}(n\_id, \langle c_1, c_2 \rangle, \langle c_2 \rangle, m, mem) \mid$ send $mem(id_1, c_2) \ldots$

$\mid$ send $mem(id_{j+1}, c_2) \mid E(c_2, \langle id_1, \ldots, id_n \rangle, j + 1, f_p', f_c')$ )

The free names that are available to the attacker in $P_G$ now include $id_1, \ldots, id_j$ and $n\_id$ and in $P_I$ they include $id_1, \ldots, id_j, id_{j+1}$. As these are all new names the attacker cannot distinguish between these two sets ... yet.

We must now check to see if the two processes behave in the same way when they receive inputs that use the names that have just been outputted. For the guilty network one message that must be checked is send $c_1(search, none, n\_id,$ $1, 7)$, i.e., a search message with the guilty node's ID as the "from ID". As $n\_id$ is just one of a set of free names this action can be matched by the innocent network with a similar message using an ID from the environment, $id_k$ say, resulting in the processes:

$$P_G \stackrel{\vec{\alpha_3}}{\Rightarrow} \text{ new } c_2, mem; G_{ID}(n\_id, \langle c_1, c_2 \rangle, \langle c_2 \rangle, m, mem)$$
$$| \text{ send } mem(n\_id, c_1) \mid \text{ send } mem(id_1, c_2) \mid \ldots$$
$$| \text{ send } mem(id_j, c_2) \mid E(c_2, \langle id_1, .., id_n \rangle, j, f'_p, f'_c) )$$
$$P_I \stackrel{\vec{\alpha_3}}{\Rightarrow} \text{ new } c_2, mem; I_{ID}(n\_id, \langle c_1, c_2 \rangle, \langle c_2 \rangle, m, mem)$$
$$| \text{ send } mem(id_k, c_1) \mid \text{ send } mem(id_1, c_2) \mid \ldots$$
$$| \text{ send } mem(id_{j+1}, c_2) \mid E(c_2, \langle id_1, .., id_n \rangle, j + 1, f'_p, f'_c) )$$

For $P_G$ and $P_I$ to be bi-similar these processes must be bi-similar. Both of them can indeed perform the same inputs and outputs. Including the input of a reply message address to the ID that has just been used for the search message, i.e., send $c_1(reply, n\_id, a_{id}, 0, 0)$ for $P_G$ and send $c_1(reply, id_k, a_{id}, 0, 0)$ for $P_I$ The innocent node looks up the ID, it may find the $c_1$ connection and return the request on $c_1$ as output. The guilty node, on the other hand, recognises its own ID and accepts the message. It cannot perform the same output as the innocent node and therefore $P_G$ and $P_I$ cannot be bi-similar.

If we examine the actions that lead to these un-similar processes we can see that the attacker tried to "steal" one of the IDs that it has seen as a "from ID" of a reply to its message. The attacker can then use this process to test IDs to see which one belongs to its neighbour because, out of all the IDs in all the reply messages that an attacker may see, the guilty node's ID is the only one that cannot be stolen.

## 5     Description of the Attack on MUTE

The difference between the processes in the pi-calculus model was that the innocent node might be able to perform an action, whereas the guilty node could not. To build a real attack out of this we must force the innocent node to perform the action so the guilty node will stand out. The idea behind the real attack is that the attacker can "steal" an ID by sending fake messages using the target ID as the "from ID". If it sends enough messages then its neighbouring nodes will forward messages addressed to the target ID over their connection with the attacker. One exception to this is if the ID the attacker is trying to steal belongs to the neighbour, as the neighbour will never forward messages addressed to itself. Therefore the attacker can use this method of stealing IDs to test any IDs it sees, if the ID cannot be stolen then the ID belongs to the neighbour.

We saw in Section 2 that MUTE looks at the last fifty messages when deciding where to route a message. Only IDs that are seen on search messages with phase-1 counters are possibilities for the neighbours ID and only search messages with phase-3 counters can be dropped. Therefore, if the attacker sees some messages with a phase-1 counter and others reach the neighbour with a phase-3 counter and are dropped, we know that the messages that are dropped must be slower and so they will not affect the routing table. This means that if the attacker can send fifty messages with the target ID to its neighbour, without any messages with that ID coming from the neighbour, then the attacker will receive any messages send to that ID via the target node, unless the ID belongs to the target node. There is still a small possibility that the neighbour is receiving or forwarding a file from the real owner of the ID, in which case the large number of messages that the neighbour is receiving might mean the attacker fails to steal an address that does not belong to the target node. To avoid this possibility the attack can be repeated at regular intervals.

The attack on MUTE would run as follows:

1. The attacker makes two connections to the target node, monitors these connections and selects the "from ID" with the highest time-to-live counter.
2. The attacker forms new search messages using the selected ID as the "from ID" and repeatedly sends them to the neighbour until it has sent fifty messages without receiving any messages from the ID it is trying to steal.
3. The attacker then sends a reply message addressed to the selected ID along its other connection with the target node. If the message is not sent back to the attacker then it is likely that the target ID belongs to the neighbour.
4. These steps can be repeated at regular intervals to discount the possibility that the neighbour is receiving or forwarding a file from the target ID.
5. If the attacker receives the message back then the selected ID does not belong to the target node, so the attacker must select another ID and start again.
6. If the neighbour still does not bounce the message back to the attacker then, with a high degree of probability, the attacker has found the neighbour's ID and the attacker can then find out what files the neighbour is offering.

## 6    Fixing MUTE

This attack is made possible by the Ants Protocol's adaptive routing system and the fact that nodes will never forward messages addressed to themselves. Key to the success of the attack is the attacker's ability to corrupt its neighbour's routing table in a known way. This in turn is only possible because the attacker can fake messages with another node's ID.

We can solve this problem by stopping the attacker from being able to forge messages. This can be done by having all nodes start by generating an authentication and signature key, from any suitably secure public key encryption scheme. The nodes can then use the authentication keys as their IDs. This authentication key would be used in exactly the same way as the node's ID. However, each node would also sign the message ID. When any node receives a message, it can check the signed message ID using the "from ID". As the attacker cannot correctly sign the message ID it can no longer forge messages. Such a scheme also benefits from a fair degree of backward compatibility. Older nodes need not be aware that the ID is also an authentication key. The checking is also optional; nodes may choose to only check messages it they spot suspicious activity.

The level of popularity enjoyed by any system that offers anonymity to the user will be partly based on the level of trust potential users place in these claims. To maintain a level of trust in the MUTE system it is important to implement this fix before the flaw is widely known. With this in mind we sent an early copy of this paper to the lead programmer on the MUTE project. They were happy to accept the results of the formal analysis and agreed to implement the fix suggested above. To remain compatible with earlier versions of the client the pseudo IDs could not be longer than 160-bits, which is too short for a RSA public key. We briefly considered using an elliptic curve digital signature algorithm that would allow for public keys of this length, but the use of less well known cryptographic algorithms proved unpopular.

The final solution was to use a SHA1 hash of a 1024-bit RSA authentication key as the pseudo ID and include the authentication key in the message header, along with the signed message ID. This would require changing the message header from random a "From ID" and "Message ID" to a 1024-bit RSA authentication key, the SHA1 hash of that key as the "From ID", along with the signed message ID. It was also found that nodes would only store message IDs for a few hours so to avoid replay attacks a counter based timestamp was included in the signature of the message. This solutions was added to the 0.5 release of MUTE; the C++ source code for the implementation is available at http://mute-net.cvs.sourceforge.net/mute-net.

## 7   Conclusion and Further Work

We have modelled the MUTE system in the pi-calculus and we have shown that it is not possible to have a bi-simulation between every network in which the attacker connects to a guilty node and a network in which the attacker connects to an innocent node. The point at which this bi-simulation fails leads to an attack against the MUTE system. The attack, which involves "stealing" the name of another node, is a serious problem that compromises the anonymity of any node that neighbours an attacker. We suggested a fix for this attack based on using an authentication key as the node's pseudo ID.

Our general methodology was to try to show that the environment could provide cover for any guilty node. In particular that for all parameters $p_g, p_e$ there exists some other parameters $p_i, p'_e$ such that:

$$\text{Guilty node}(p_g) \mid \text{Environment } (p_e) \approx \text{Innocent node } (p_i) \mid \text{Environment } (p'_e)$$

We hope that this method can be used to prove the anonymity of other systems in which the environment provides cover for guilty nodes.

As further work we hope to be able to prove that some form of the Ants protocol does provide anonymity. If we do not allow inputs to our model that use IDs that have been observed as outputs we can show for every guilty network there is a bi-similar innocent network. However a true correctness result will require a more realistic model of the environment. We would expect a node not to be anonymous when connected to some small, pathological environments. So it would be necessary to find out what kind of environments provide adequate cover for a node.

## Acknowledgement

We would like to thank the Comète Team at the École Polytechnique for many useful discussions about anonymity, and especially Jun Pang for comments on an early draft of this paper. We would also like to thank Jason Rohrer, who is responsible for creating MUTE and who implemented the fix described in this paper.

## References

[ALRV05]   Andres Aristizabal, Hugo Lopez, Camilo Rueda, and Frank D. Valencia. Formally reasoning about security issues in p2p protocols: A case study. In *Third Taiwanese-French Conference on Information Technology*, 2005.

[Ant03]   Ants p2p, http://antsp2p.sourceforge.net/, 2003.

[BASM04]   Steve Bono, Christopher A, Soghoian, and Fabian Monrose. Mantis: A high-performance, anonymity preserving, p2p network, 2004. Johns Hopkins University Information Security Institute Technical Report TR-2004-01-B-ISI-JHU.

[BDG92]   R. Beckers, J. L. Deneubourg, and S. Goss. Trails and u-turns in the selection of the shortest path by the ant lasius niger. *Journal of Theoretical Biology*, 159:397–415, 1992.

[BP05]   Mohit Bhargava and Catuscia Palamidessi. Probabilistic anonymity. In *CONCUR, LNCS 3653*, pages 171–185, 2005.

[CC05]   Tom Chothia and Konstantinos Chatzikokolakis. A survey of anonymous peer-to-peer file-sharing. In *EUC Workshops, LNCS*, pages 744–755, 2005.

[CP05]   Konstantinos Chatzikokolakis and Catuscia Palamidessi. Probable innocence revisited. In *Formal Aspects in Security and Trust, LNCS 3866*, pages 142–157, 2005.

[CSWH01]   Ian Clarke, Oskar Sandberg, Brandon Wiley, and Theodore W. Hong. Freenet: A distributed anonymous information storage and retrieval system. *LNCS*, 2009:46+, 2001.

[DD99]   Marco Dorigo and Gianni Di Caro. The ant colony optimization meta-heuristic. In David Corne, Marco Dorigo, and Fred Glover, editors, *New Ideas in Optimization*, pages 11–32. McGraw-Hill, London, 1999.

[DFM00]   Roger Dingledine, Michael J. Freedman, and David Molnar. The free haven project: Distributed anonymous storage service. In *Proceedings of the Workshop on Design Issues in Anonymity and Unobservability*, July 2000.

[DMS04]   R. Dingledine, N. Mathewson, and P. Syverson. Tor: The second-generation onion router. In *Proceedings of the 13th USENIX Security Symposium*, 2004.

[DPP05]    Y. Deng, C. Palamidessi, and J. Pang. Weak probabilistic anonymity. In *Proc. 3rd International Workshop on Security Issues in Concurrency (SecCo'05)*, 2005.

[GHPvR05]  Flavio D. Garcia, Ichiro Hasuo, Wolter Pieters, and Peter van Rossum. Provable anonymity. In *Proceedings of the 3rd ACM Workshop on Formal Methods in Security Engineering (FMSE05)*, 2005.

[GSB02]    Mesut Gunes, Udo Sorges, and Imed Bouazzi. Ara – the ant-colony based routing algorithm for manets. In *Proceedings of the International Workshop on Ad Hoc Networking (IWAHN 2002)*, Vancouver, August 2002.

[HP00]     Oltea Mihaela Herescu and Catuscia Palamidessi. Probabilistic asynchronous pi-calculus. In *Foundations of Software Science and Computation Structure*, pages 146–160, 2000.

[HT91]     Kohei Honda and Mario Tokoro. An object calculus for asynchronous communication. In *European Conference on Object-Oriented Programming*, LNCS, pages 133–147, 1991.

[KKK05]    Byung Ryong Kim, Ki Chang Kim, and Yoo Sung Kim. Securing anonymity in p2p network. In *sOc-EUSAI '05: Proceedings of the joint conference on Smart objects and ambient intelligence*. ACM Press, 2005.

[KNP02]    M. Kwiatkowska, G. Norman, and D. Parker. Prism: Probabilistic symbolic model checker. In *Proc. 12th International Conference on Modelling Techniques and Tools for Computer Performance Evaluation (TOOLS'02)*, volume LNCS 2324, pages 200–204, 2002.

[KR05]     Steve Kremer and Mark D. Ryan. Analysis of an electronic voting protocol in the applied pi-calculus. In *Proceedings of the 14th European Symposium on Programming (ESOP'05)*, LNCS, pages 186–200, 2005.

[Mil93]    Robin Milner. The polyadic $\pi$-calculus: A tutorial. In *Logic and Algebra of Specification*, volume 94 of *Computer and Systems Sciences*, pages 203–246. 1993.

[Par01]    Joachim Parrow. *Handbook of Process Algebra*, chapter An Introduction to the pi-calculus. Elsevier, 2001.

[Roh06]    Jason Rohrer. Mute technical details. http://mute-net.sourceforge.net/technicalDetails.shtml, 2006.

[RR98]     M. Reiter and A. Rubin. Crowds: anonymity for web transactions. *ACM Transactions on Information and System Security*, 1(1):66–92, 1998.

[SGRE04]   Emin Gun Sirer, Sharad Goel, Mark Robson, and Doan Engin. Eluding carnivores: File sharing with strong anonymity, 2004. Cornell Univ. Tech. Rep.

[SS96]     Steve Schneider and Abraham Sidiropoulos. CSP and anonymity. In *ESORICS*, pages 198–218, 1996.

[Tiu04]    Alwen Tiu. Level 0/1 prover: A tutorial. Avilable online at: http://www.lix.polytechnique.fr/~tiu/lincproject/, 2004.

[VM94]     Björn Victor and Faron Moller. The Mobility Workbench — a tool for the $\pi$-calculus. In *CAV'94: Computer Aided Verification*, LNCS 818, pages 428–440, 1994.

[was03]    Waste, http://waste.sourceforge.net/, 2003.

# Towards Fine-Grained Automated Verification of Publish-Subscribe Architectures

Luciano Baresi, Carlo Ghezzi, and Luca Mottola

Dipartimento di Elettronica ed Informazione—Politecnico di Milano
{baresi, ghezzi, mottola}@elet.polimi.it

**Abstract.** The design and validation of distributed applications built on top of Publish-Subscribe infrastructures remain an open problem. Previous efforts adopted finite automata to specify the components' behavior, and model checking to verify global properties. However, existing proposals are far from being applicable in real contexts, as strong simplifications are needed on the underlying Publish-Subscribe infrastructure to make automatic verification feasible.

To face this challenge, we propose a novel approach that embeds the asynchronous communication mechanisms of Publish-Subscribe infrastructures *within* the model checker. This way, Publish-Subscribe primitives become available to the specification of application components as additional, domain-specific, constructs of the modeling language. With this approach, one can develop a fine-grained model of the Publish-Subscribe infrastructure without incurring in state space explosion problems, thus enabling the automated verification of application components on top of realistic communication infrastructures.

## 1 Introduction

The Publish-Subscribe interaction paradigm is rapidly emerging as an appealing solution to the needs of applications designed for highly-dynamic environments. Using this paradigm, application components *subscribe* to event patterns and get *notified* when other components *publish* events matching their subscriptions. Its asynchronous, implicit and multi-point communication style is particularly amenable to those scenarios where application components can be added or removed unpredictably, and the communication must be decoupled both in time and in space [1]. Because of this flexibility, Publish-Subscribe infrastructures have been developed for a wide range of application scenarios, from wide-area notification services to wireless sensor networks.

However, the high degree of decoupling brings also several drawbacks. In particular, verifying how a federation of independently-written software components interconnected in such a loosely-coupled manner is often difficult because of the absence of a precise specification of the behavior of the communication infrastructure. Model checking has been proposed as a possible solution, but existing works do not propose a precise characterisation of the different guarantees the underlying Publish-Subscribe infrastructure can provide. For instance, different message delivery policies, reliability guarantees or concurrency models can easily change the final outcome of the verification effort.

The wide spectrum of deployment scenarios, and the consequent vast range of available systems, makes the aforementioned characterization non-trivial. In addition,

E. Najm et al. (Eds.): FORTE 2006, LNCS 4229, pp. 131–135, 2006.
© IFIP International Federation for Information Processing 2006

modeling these features using the primitives of existing model checkers inevitably results in state space explosion problems, thus ultimately hindering the verification effort.

In this paper we argue that a fine-grained Publish-Subscribe model requires a different approach to the problem. We propose to augment an existing model-checker with domain-specific constructs able to expose Publish-Subscribe primitives as constructs of the modeling language. This way, the mechanisms needed to implement the Publish-Subscribe interaction style can be embedded *within* the model-checker, and one can achieve a fine-grained characterization of the different guarantees of the Publish-Subscribe system without incurring in state space explosion problems.

The rest of the paper is structured as follows. Section 2 briefly surveys the existing approaches, and highlights how they miss important characteristics of existing Publish-Subscribe infrastructures. Section 3 proposes our solution and reports on some initial results demonstrating how our approach better scales to complex systems than existing ones. Finally, Section 4 concludes the paper with an outlook on our current and future research plans.

## 2   Modeling Publish-Subscribe Systems

The identification of the different guarantees provided by Publish-Subscribe infrastructures is a challenging task. This becomes even harder when we consider those characteristics that would impact the verification of applications running on top. To this end, Table 1 summarizes a set of QoS dimensions provided by existing Publish-Subscribe infrastructures that could affect the outcome of the verification process. We claim that the majority of available systems can be precisely classified along these different dimensions. However, existing proposals for automated verification of Publish-Subscribe infrastructures fail to capture many of these different characteristics.

The work in [2, 3] is limited to the CORBA Communication Model (CCM) as middleware. Similarly, [4] concentrates on the addition of a Publish-Subscribe notification service to an existing groupware protocol. On the other hand, the work in [5] develops a compositional reasoning based on an assume-guarantee methodology. The technique is shown to be applicable to particular instances of Publish-Subscribe middleware. In all these cases, the proposed solution addresses just a very narrow scenario, i.e., a particular instance of Publish-Subscribe system.

Garlan et al. [6] provide a set of pluggable modules that allow a modeler to choose one possible instance out of a set of possible choices. However, the available models are far from fully capturing the different characteristics of existing Publish-Subscribe systems. For instance, application components cannot change their interests (i.e., subscriptions) at run-time, and the event dispatching policy is only characterized in terms of delivery policy (*asynchronous, synchronous, immediate* or *delayed*). The approach is improved in [7] by adding more expressive events, dynamic delivery policies and dynamic event-method bindings. However, this proposal only deals with the specification of different delivery policies depending on the state of the overall model, and still does not capture finer-grained guarantees such as real-time constraints.

Finally, the work in [8] characterizes the Publish-Subscribe infrastructure in terms of reliability, event delivery order (the same as publications, the same as publications

**Table 1.** Publish-Subscribe QoS dimensions

| QoS Class | Possible Choices | Description |
|---|---|---|
| *Message Reliability* | Absent | Notifications can be lost. |
| | Present | Notifications are guaranteed to eventually arrive at the interested subscribers. |
| *Message Ordering* | None | Notifications are delivered in random order. |
| | Pair-wise FIFO | Notifications are delivered to a given subscriber in FIFO order with respect to publish operations from the same publisher. |
| | System-wide FIFO | Notifications are delivered to subscribers in the same order as publish operations, regardless of the component that published the message. |
| | Causal Order | Causally related notifications are delivered according to the causality chain among them. |
| | Total Order | All components subscribed to the same events are notified in the same order (which is not necessarily the order in which these events are published). |
| *Filtering* | Precise | Notifications are only delivered for subscribed events. |
| | Approximate | Components can be notified on events for which they are not subscribed (false positives), or miss events in which they are interested. (Notice how approximate filtering is deterministic, while reliability problems are in general unpredictable.) |
| *Real-Time Guarantees* | None | Notifications are delivered without time guarantees. |
| | Soft RT | On the average, notification are delivered in $T$ time units after the publish operation. |
| | Hard RT | Notifications are guaranteed to be delivered within $T$ time units after the publish operation. |
| *Subscription Propagation Delay* | Absent | Subscriptions are immediately active and deliver event notifications. |
| | Present | Subscriptions start to deliver event notifications after a random time. |
| *Repliable Messages* | Absent | Subscriptions set up to convey replies travel independently of the original notification. If subscriptions are delayed, the deliver of the reply is not guaranteed. |
| | Present | Subscriptions used to convey replies travel with the originating message. Therefore, they are guaranteed to be active at the time the reply is published. |
| *Message Priorities* | Absent | All notifications are treated in the same way. |
| | Present | Notifications are delivered according to specific priorities, no mechanism is used to prevent starvation of messages. |
| | Present w/ Queue Scrunching | Notifications are delivered according to specific priorities, queue scrunching dynamically raises the priority of messages that waited too long in their original priority queue. This way, each message is eventually delivered. |
| *Queue Drop Policy* | None | Queues are of infinite length. |
| | Tail Drop | Given queues of length $L$, messages exceeding this threshold are dropped upon arrival. |
| | Priority Drop | Given queues of length $L$, messages are dropped starting from lower priority messages up to higher priority messages. |

but only referring to the same publisher, or none), and subscription propagation delay. Still, it does not consider several of the dimensions listed in Table 1.

## 3  Our Proposal

The definition of all the mechanisms described in Table 1 is clearly unfeasible if one keeps the traditional approach of expressing both the application components and the communication infrastructure in terms of the primitives of the model checker. Based on this, we propose a novel approach to augment an existing model checker with Publish-Subscribe-style constructs. This way, we build the communication infrastructure *inside* the model checker, thus avoiding the aforementioned performance problems.

Our approach leverages off the simplicity of the Publish-Subscribe APIs (composed of the basic operations `publish(Event)` and `subscribe(EventPattern)`), and makes them available as additional constructs of the input language of the model

**Table 2.** Comparing our approach with [8]

| Scenario | Bogor with embedded Publish-Subscribe | | SPIN - Promela | |
|---|---|---|---|---|
| | Memory | Time | Memory | Time |
| Causal2Publish | 32.8 Mb | 103 sec | 298.3 Mb | >15 min |
| Causal5Publish | 45.6 Mb | 132 sec | 589.6 Mb | >1 hour |
| Causal7Publish | 52.3 Mb | 158 sec | OutOfMemory | NotConcluded |
| Causal10Publish | 61.1 Mb | 189 sec | OutOfMemory | NotConcluded |
| Priorities2Publish | 18.3 Mb | 47 sec | 192 Mb | >10 min |
| Priorities5Publish | 26.9 Mb | 103 sec | 471.2 Mb | >30 min |
| Priorities7Publish | 37.9 Mb | 134 sec | OutOfMemory | NotConcluded |
| Priorities10Publish | 49.1 Mb | 163 sec | OutOfMemory | NotConcluded |

checker. [1] Before performing the actual verification, the user binds this general Publish-Subscribe API to a particular combination of the different guarantees highlighted in Table 1, thus "instantiating" a particular communication infrastructure on top of which the application model is run.

To implement our approach, we are currently embedding a Publish-Subscribe communication mechanisms —with the various guarantees highlighted in Table 1— within the model checker Bogor [9]. Its open architecture makes it easy to add domain-specific mechanisms to the model checker. To check our additions, we devised a wide range of test cases. Every test is represented by a set of Bogor processes expressed in BIR (Bogor Intermediate Language), which make use of the aforementioned Publish-Subscribe API as any other BIR construct.

The solution we propose impacts on two orthogonal aspects. Firstly, it enables automated verification of application components on top of realistic communication infrastructures. This way, the gap between the system model in the early design phases and the actual implementation can be narrowed down, and potential problems caught in advance. Secondly, it eases the translation of the behavior of application components —usually expressed in a given specification formalism— into the input language of the model checker, since the application components and the model checker rely on the same communication primitives.

### 3.1 Early Results

To substantiate our claims, we report some initial results we gathered by comparing our approach with the solution in [8], which uses SPIN and Promela. We designed a set of possible interactions among five different processes with the only goal of making processes coordinate by exchanging messages. We characterized the different scenarios by means of the number of publish operations to be performed —on a per-process basis— during each run of the test application. On the average, half of the processes are subscribed to published events and receive the corresponding notifications. The properties we are interested in are simple assertions, whose only goal is to make sure that messages are delivered according to the chosen policy (i.e., in causal order or according to the respective priorities). In a sense, these assertions verify that the implemented mechanisms are semantically correct.

---

[1] Notice how the Publish-Subscribe APIs we consider explicitly deal with subscriptions to general patterns of events, therefore overcoming the limitations of existing proposals (e.g., [6]).

Table 2 illustrates the performance of the two approaches, both in terms of memory consumption and time needed to complete the verification process. The experiments were executed on a Pentium 4 with 1 Gb RAM. Our approach outperforms the one based on SPIN in all cases. When the number of publish operations increases, our solution allows the verification effort to terminate where SPIN would run out of memory. This clearly highlights how the requirement of realistically modeling the communication infrastructure cannot be addressed by using only the primitives provided by conventional model checkers.

## 4  Conclusions and Future Work

This paper presents a novel approach to the automated verification of applications built on top of fine-grained and realistic models of Publish-Subscribe architectures. We argue that such a level of detail cannot be achieved by means of conventional model checkers. Our proposal flips the problem and augments the input language of an existing model checker with the primitives of Publish-Subscribe communication infrastructures. The first results summarized in this paper are encouraging and motivate further work.

We plan to conclude the implementation in Bogor of the different guarantees illustrated in Table 1, and further evaluate the effectiveness of our approach with meaningful test cases. However, our ultimate objective is the development of a tool to enable automated verification of applications built on top of Publish-Subscribe systems.

## References

1. Eugster, P.T., Felber, P.A., Guerraoui, R., Kermarrec, A.M.:   The many faces of publish/subscribe. ACM Comput. Surv. **35** (2003)
2. Deng, X., Dwyer, M.B., Hatcliff, J., Jung, G.: Model-checking middleware-based event-driven real-time embedded software. In: Proc. of the $1^{st}$ Int. Symposium on Formal Methods for Components and Objects. (2002)
3. Hatcliff, J., Deng, X., Dwyer, M.B., Jung, G., Ranganath, V.: Cadena: an integrated development, analysis, and verification environment for component-based systems. In: Proc. of the $25^{th}$ Int. Conf. on Software Engineering (ICSE03). (2003)
4. Beek, M.H., Massink, M., Latella, D., Gnesi, S., Forghieri, A., Sebastianis, M.: A case study on the automated verification of groupware protocols. In: Proc. of the $27^{th}$ Int. Conf. on Software engineering (ICSE05). (2005)
5. Caporuscio, M., Inverardi, P., Pelliccione, P.: Compositional verification of middleware-based software architecture descriptions. In: Proc. of the $19^{th}$ Int. Conf. on Software engineering (ICSE04). (2004)
6. Garlan, D., Khersonsky, S.: Model checking implicit-invocation systems. In: Proc. of the $10^{th}$ Int. Workshop on Software Specification and Design. (2000)
7. Bradbury, J.S., Dingel, J.: Evaluating and improving the automatic analysis of implicit invocation systems. In: Proc. of the $9^{th}$ European software engineering Conf. (2003)
8. Zanolin, L., Ghezzi, C., Baresi, L.:  An approach to model and validate publish/subscribe architectures. In: Proc. of the SAVCBS'03 Workshop. (2003)
9. Robby, Dwyer, M.B., Hatcliff, J.: Bogor: an extensible and highly-modular software model checking framework. In: Proc. of the $9^{th}$ European software engineering Conf. (2003)

# A LOTOS Framework for Middleware Specification

Nelson Souto Rosa and Paulo Roberto Freire Cunha

Universidade Federal de Pernambuco, Centro de Informática
Recife, Pernambuco
{nsr, prfc}@cin.ufpe.br

**Abstract.** This paper presents a LOTOS framework for the specification of middleware systems. The framework consists of a library of basic middleware components and some guidelines on how to compose them. The components of the framework facilitate the formal specification of different middleware systems.

## 1 Introduction

Middleware specifications are not trivial to be understood, as the middleware itself is usually very complex [4]. Firstly, middleware systems have to hide the complexity of underlying network mechanisms from the application. Secondly, the number of services provided by the middleware is increasing, e.g., the CORBA specification contains fourteen services. Finally, in addition to hide communication mechanisms, the middleware also have to hide fails, mobility, changes in the network traffic conditions and so on. On the point of view of application developers, they very often do not know how the middleware really works. On the point of view of middleware developers, the complexity places many challenges that include how to integrate services in a single product [6] or how to satisfy new requirements of emerging applications [Blair 98].

Formal description techniques have been used together middleware in the RM-ODP, in which the trader service is formally specified in E-LOTOS. The Z notation and High Level Petri Nests have been adopted for specifying CORBA services [2][3], the Naming service [5], and the Security service [1]. Most recently, Rosa [8] adopted software architecture principles for structuring LOTOS specifications of middleware systems. Despite the adoption of formal techniques, they focus on specific aspects of middleware systems, i.e., they address either a specific service or a specific middleware model.

The main objective of this paper is to propose a framework that helps to formally describe middleware behaviour in LOTOS by providing a set of basic abstractions. These abstractions are generic in the sense that may be combined in different ways in order to specify several middleware systems. Main in our approach is the fact that the abstractions are defined and organised according to their role in relation to the message request. Hence, instead of adopting the traditional approach of organising middleware systems in layers [9], the proposed abstractions are defined considering their role in the message request. For example, the abstractions are grouped into classes related to storage, communication, dispatching, and mapping of message requests. A

E. Najm et al. (Eds.): FORTE 2006, LNCS 4229, pp. 136–142, 2006.

message request is any message that an application (e.g., client, server, sender, transmitter) sends to another application.

This paper is organised as follows: Section 2 presents a general overview of proposed framework. Section 3 presents how the proposed framework may be used to specify client-server and message-oriented middleware systems. Finally, last section presents an evaluation of the research until now and some future work.

## 2 LOTOS Specifications of Middleware Components

As mentioned before, the proposed framework consists of a set of abstractions that addresses a number of common functionalities of middleware systems. The framework also defines how these abstractions work together to formalise different middleware models. For example, the abstractions may be combined to produce the specification of a message-oriented middleware, whilst they also may be combined to define a procedural middleware (client-server applications) or a tuple space based middleware.

The whole framework is "message-centric" in the sense that basic elements of the framework are grouped according to how they act on the message. Figure 1 shows a general overview of the proposed approach in which the message is intercepted by both middleware elements on the transmitter and receiver sides. It is worth observing that the message may be either a request in which the transmitter ask for the execution of a task on the receiver side or a simple information between loosely-coupled applications.

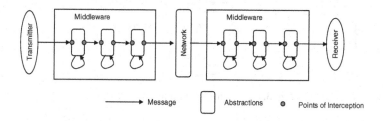

Fig. 1. Message-centric approach

The abstractions of the framework are categorised into four classes: mappers (e.g., stub and skeletons), multiplexers (e.g., dispatcher), communication (e.g., communication channel), and storage (e.g., queue and topic). Whatever the class of the middleware element, it intercepts the message, processes it and forwards the message to the next element. The next element may be a local or remote one. Only communication elements may forward the message to a remote element, i.e., an element only accessible through the network. A non-communication element may need to communicate with a remote element to carry out its task, but it does not send the message itself to a remote element. For example, a transaction service may need to obtain a remote lock before pass the request to the next element of the middleware.

## 2.1 Basic Abstractions

Mapper elements typically represent remote objects, serve as input points of the middleware, their basic function is to (un)marshal application data (arguments and results) into a common packet-level (e.g., GIIOP request), and are usually found in middleware systems that support request/reply applications in heterogeneous environments. Additionally, non-conventional mappers may also compress data. The specification of a typical mapper, named Stub, is defined as shown in Figure 2.

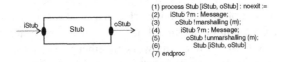

```
(1) process Stub [iStub, oStub] : noexit :=
(2)     iStub ?m : Message;
(3)         oStub !marshalling (m);
(4)         iStub ?m : Message;
(5)         oStub !unmarshalling (m);
(6)         Stub [iStub, oStub]
(7) endproc
```

**Fig. 2.** Mapper Element

In this specification, the Stub receives a message sent by the transmitter and intercepted by the middleware (2), marshals it (3), passes it to the next element (4), and then waits for the reply from the receiver. The reply is also intercepted by the middleware and passed to the Stub (4) that takes responsibility of unmarshalling the reply (5).

Communication elements get a message and communicate it to a remote element. They act as an interface between the middleware and the operating system. The structure of a communication element, named Channel, is shown in Figure 3.

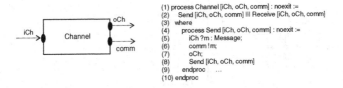

```
(1) process Channel [iCh, oCh, comm] : noexit :=
(2)     Send [iCh, oCh, comm] ||| Receive [iCh, oCh, comm]
(3)     where
(4)         process Send [iCh, oCh, comm] : noexit :=
(5)             iCh ?m : Message;
(6)             comm !m;
(7)             oCh;
(8)             Send [iCh, oCh, comm]
(9)         endproc    ...
(10) endproc
```

**Fig. 3.** Communication Element

In a similar way to Stub, the input (iCh) and output (oCh) ports serves as interception points of the element. However, communication elements have an additional port, named comm, used to communicate the message to a remote element. Additionally, the Channel is composed by Send and Receive processes that are responsible to send and receive messages, respectively. In this case, the Channel receives the message intercepted by the middleware (5) and then communicates it to a remote element (6).Dispatchers get the request and forward it to the right object (service). The destination object is defined by inspecting the message, in which the destination has been set during the binding. In practical terms, the dispatcher acts as a multiplexer inside the middleware. The general structure of a Dispatcher is depicted in Figure 4. The dispatcher receives a message (2) and inspects it, through the function multiplexer, to define the destination object (3).

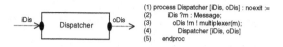

```
(1) process Dispatcher [iDis, oDis] : noexit :=
(2)         iDis ?m : Message;
(3)             oDis !m ! multiplexer(m);
(4)             Dispatcher [iDis, oDis]
(5)     endproc
```

**Fig. 4.** Dispatcher Element

Finally, storage elements express the need of some middleware systems of store the message prior it to be sent, e.g., for asynchronous communication or to keep a copy of the message for recovery reasons. The general structure of a Storage element is shown in Figure 5.

```
(1) process Storage [iSto, oSto] (q: Queue): noexit :=      process Queue [enq, fst, empt, deq] (q : Queue) : noexit :=
(2)      hide enq, fst, empt, deq in                        enq ?n : Nat;
(3)          Manager [iSto, oSto, enq, fst, empt, deq]         Queue [enq, fst, empt, deq] (enqueue (q, n))
(4)          I[enq, fst, empt, deq]I                        [] fst !first (q);
(5)          Queue [enq, fst, empt, deq] (q)                   Queue [enq, fst, empt, deq] (q)
(6)      where                                             [] deq;
(7)          ...                                              Queue [enq, fst, empt, deq] (dequeue (q))
(8) endproc                                                endproc
```

**Fig. 5.** Storage Element

In this particular element, the storage element (left side) is modelled as a Queue that is administered by the Manager. It is worth observing that with minor changes to the storage element, it may be defined as a buffer or a file.

## 2.2  Putting the Basic Abstractions Together

By using the basic abstractions defined in the previous section, middleware systems may be specified by composing them according to the desired distribution model. The general structure of any middleware specified according to the framework is defined as follows:

```
specification TemplateMiddleware [invC,terC,invS,terS,comm] : noexit
  ...
behaviour
  (Transmitter[invC,terC]|[invC,terC]|LocalMiddleware[invC,terC, comm])
  |[comm]|
  RemoteMiddleware [invS,terS,comm] |[invS,terS]| Receiver[invS,terS])
  ...
endspec
```

where a Transmitter sends a message to the Receiver through the middleware, which is made up of a local (LocalMidleware) and remote middleware (RemoteMidleware) that communicates through the port comm (e.g., it may abstract the whole network). Whatever the middleware model, its internal structure is defined as follows (except for the number of components):

```
process Middleware [invC, terC, comm] : noexit :=
  hide iC1, oC1, iC2, oC2 in
      ((C1 [iC1,oC1]  |||  C2  [iC2,oC2,comm])
       |[iC1, oC1, iC2, oC2]|
       Interceptor [invC,terC,iC1,oC1,iC2,oC2])
  where ...
endproc
```

The middleware is composed of a set of components (e.g., C1 and C2), depending on its complexity. The composition is expressed in the process Interceptor. As our approach is message-centric, each component "intercepts" the request in the port iCN (iC refers to "input port of component CN" that represents the point where the request enters in the component). Next, the request is processed inside the component and then passed to the next component through the port oCN (oC refers to the "output port of component N" that represents the point where the request exits the component) according to the constraints imposed by the process Interceptor.

## 3  Adopting the Framework Elements

In order to illustrate how the elements introduced in the previous session may be used to facilitate the middleware specification, we present the specification of a simple middleware that has a similar structure as CORBA and a message-oriented middleware (MOM).

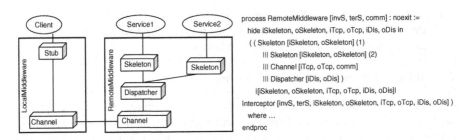

**Fig. 6.** Client-Server Middleware

Figure 6 presents a client-server middleware where the local middleware is a composition of a stub and channels elements. On the server side (remote), the middleware is more complex, as it is composed by a communication element (Channel), a dispatcher (Dispatcher) that forwards the request to the proper skeleton, and some skeletons (Skeleton). It is worth observing that additional middleware elements are easily added to the middleware just including them in the parallel composition (|||) and changing the Interceptor element.

A MOM is characterised by the use of a buffer to the asynchronous communication and it is widely adopted to communicate loosely coupled applications. Figure 6 shows a simple MOM specified by using the basic abstractions defined in Section 2.

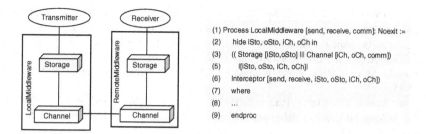

(1) Process LocalMiddleware [send, receive, comm]: Noexit :=
(2)    hide iSto, oSto, iCh, oCh in
(3)    (( Storage [iSto,oSto] ||| Channel [iCh, oCh, comm])
(5)       |[iSto, oSto, iCh, oCh]|
(6)    Interceptor [send, receive, iSto, oSto, iCh, oCh])
(7)    where
(8)    ...
(9)    endproc

**Fig. 7.** Message-Oriented Middleware

This MOM has two elements, namely `Channel` and `Storage`. The abstraction `Channel` is similar to Figure 6, whilst `Storage` is defined as presented in Section 2. MOMs that execute on the transmitter side are usually similar to one on the receiver (remote) side.

## 4  Conclusion and Future Work

This paper has presented a framework useful to formalise middleware behaviour based on LOTOS. The framework consists of a set of common elements usually found in the development of middleware systems. The framework is now being defined, but it is possible to observe that a formalisation approach centred on the message request instead of middleware layer facilitates the treatment of middleware complexity: simple abstractions are highly reusable (see abstraction `Channel` in Section 3) and easier to find specification errors and verify desired behaviour properties; and the way of composing middleware abstractions considering the order they intercept the message request enormously facilitate the composition of middleware abstractions.

We are now extending the proposed set of abstractions including more sophisticated communication and concurrent elements. Meanwhile, it is also planned to include the specification of middleware services in such way that composition constraints may also consider middleware service composition.

## References

[1] Basin, David, Rittinger, Frank and Viganò, Luca (2002) "A Formal Analysis of the CORBA Security Service", In: Lecture Notes in Computer Science, No. 2272, pp. 330-349.

[2] Bastide, Rèmi, Palanque, Philippe, Sy, Ousmane and Navarre, David (2000) "Formal Specification of CORBA Services: Experience and Lessons Learned", In: OOPSLA'00, p. 105-117.

[3] Bastide, Rèmi, Sy, Ousmane, Navarre, David and Palanque, Philippe (2000) "A Formal Specification of the CORBA Event Service", In: FMOODS'00, p. 371-396.

[4] Campbell, Andrew T., Coulson, Geoff and Kounavis, Michael E. (1999) "Managing Complexity: Middleware Explained", IT Professional, IEEE Computer Society, Vol 1(5), pp. 22-28, October.

[5] Kreuz, Detlef (1998) "Formal Specification of CORBA Services using Object-Z", In: Second IEEE International Conference on Formal Engineering Methods, pp., December.

[6] Venkatasubramanian, Nalini (2002) "Safe Composability of Middleware Services", Communications of the ACM, Vol 45(6), pp. 49-52, June.

[7] Vinoski, Steve, (2002) "Where is Middleware?", IEEE Internet Computing, Vol. 6(2), pp. 83-85.

[8] Rosa, Nelson and Cunha, Paulo (2004) "A Software Architecture-Based Approach for Formalising Middleware Behaviour", Electronic Notes in Theoretical Computer Science, Vol. 108, pp. 39–51.

[9] Schmidt, Douglas and Buschmann, Frank (2003) "Patterns, Frameworks, and Middleware: Their Synergistic Relationships", Proceedings of the 25th international conference on Software Engineering, pp. 694-704.

# Automatic Synthesis of Assumptions
# for Compositional Model Checking[*]

Bernd Finkbeiner[1], Sven Schewe[1], and Matthias Brill[2]

[1] Universität des Saarlandes
66123 Saarbrücken, Germany
{finkbeiner, schewe}@cs.uni-sb.de
[2] Carl von Ossietzky Universität
26121 Oldenburg, Germany
matthias.brill@informatik.uni-oldenburg.de

**Abstract.** We present a new technique for automatically synthesizing the assumptions needed in compositional model checking. The compositional approach reduces the proof that a property is satisfied by the parallel composition of two processes to the simpler argument that the property is guaranteed by one process provided that the other process satisfies an assumption $A$. Finding $A$ manually is a difficult task that requires detailed insight into how the processes cooperate to satisfy the property. Previous methods to construct $A$ automatically were based on the learning algorithm $L^*$, which represents $A$ as a deterministic automaton and therefore has exponential worst-case complexity. Our new technique instead represents $A$ as an equivalence relation on the states, which allows for a quasi-linear construction. The model checker can therefore apply compositional reasoning without risking an exponential penalty for computing $A$.

## 1 Introduction

Compositional model checking is a divide-and-conquer approach to verification that splits the correctness proof of a concurrent system into arguments over its individual processes. Compositional reasoning [12,4,11,15,20,23] is always advisable when one tries to analyze a complex program; for model checking, which automatically verifies a system by traversing its state space, compositionality is particularly helpful, because the number of states grows exponentially with the number of processes.

In order to check that a property $P$ holds for the parallel composition $M \| N$ of two processes $M$ and $N$, the compositional approach introduces an assumption $A$ such that $P$ holds for $M \| N$ if and only if $P$ holds for $M \| A$. Because the assumption $A$ is an abstraction of the implementation $N$, neglecting details not relevant for the property $P$, $A$ can be much simpler than $N$. Recently,

---

[*] This work was partly supported by the German Research Foundation (DFG) as part of the Transregional Collaborative Research Center "Automatic Verification and Analysis of Complex Systems" (SFB/TR 14 AVACS).

E. Najm et al. (Eds.): FORTE 2006, LNCS 4229, pp. 143–158, 2006.

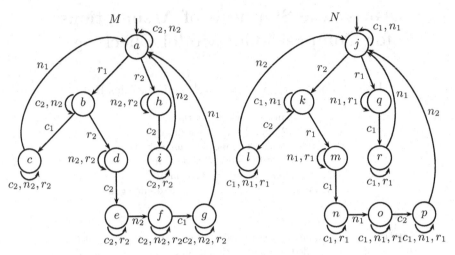

**Fig. 1.** Mutual exclusion protocol with two processes. Each process can request access to a critical resource $(r_1, r_2)$, obtain the resource $(c_1, c_2)$, and release it $(n_1, n_2)$.

there has been a lot of interest in finding $A$ automatically. There are at least three application scenarios for such a synthesis procedure. The first and most obvious scenario is to use $A$ as program documentation, to be used during system optimization and maintenance: a modification to process $N$ is safe as long as $A$ is still valid. In a second scenario, the model checker provides $A$ as a *certificate* (cf. [18]) for the validity of $P$: once $A$ is known, *revalidating* the proof, possibly using a different model checker, is simple. The third and most ambitious scenario is to compute and use $A$ during the *same* model checking run, accelerating the verification by compositional reasoning.

An interesting candidate for $A$ is the *weakest* environment assumption under which process $M$ guarantees $P$ [8]. The weakest assumption is independent of $N$ and therefore only needs to be computed once if $M$ is used in different environments. However, because the weakest assumption must account for all possible environment behaviors, it usually has a large state space.

Several researchers have therefore investigated a different construction based on the $L^*$ algorithm, a *learning* technique for deterministic automata [6,2,1]. In this setting, a candidate assumption $A'$, represented as a deterministic automaton, is evaluated against both $N$ and $P$ by model checking. As long as either $A'$ rejects some computation of $N$ or $M \| A'$ accepts a computation that violates $P$, $A'$ is refined to eliminate the particular counter example. The advantage of this approach is that it takes $M$ into account and therefore produces assumptions that are much smaller than the weakest assumption. However, it is a less general technique: it will only yield an assumption if $M \| N$ actually satisfies $P$ (and is therefore a compositional *proof* technique rather than a compositional *verification* technique). Furthermore, the structure of the deterministic automaton does not correspond to the structure of the (possibly nondeterministic) process $N$ and is therefore usually not a good form of documentation. Also, learning (and

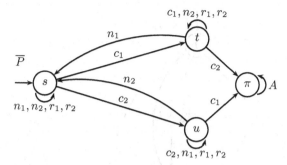

**Fig. 2.** Error LTS for the mutual exclusion property. Mutual exclusion forbids a second access to the critical resource by $c_2$ after a first access by $c_1$ has occurred that has not yet been released by $n_1$, and, symmetrically, an access by $c_1$ after an access by $c_2$ before the next $n_2$. In these cases, the property reaches the error state $\pi$.

storing) a deterministic automaton is expensive. Experience with the LTSA tool [6] suggests that the cost of computing the assumption in this way is several orders of magnitude higher than verifying the property by simple non-compositional model checking. In the worst case, the size of $A$ (and therefore also the cost of the learning process) is exponential in the size of $N$.

In this paper, we argue that the synthesis of the assumption should not be significantly more expensive than solving the verification problem itself. We present a new approach to finding $A$, where, rather than synthesizing a deterministic automaton, we compute in linear time an *equivalence relation* $\sim$ on the states of $N$. The assumption $A$ is the quotient of $N$ with respect to $\sim$.

This reduction technique resembles the methods for process minimization used in compositional reachability analysis [21,22,10,3], which reduce a partially composed system to an observationally equivalent process. However, our equivalence relation is different: rather than preserving the entire observational behavior of a process, we only preserve the reachability of an error. Since this is a much coarser equivalence, the resulting quotient is much smaller.

Consider the mutual exclusion protocol in Figure 1. Each of the two processes can request access to a critical resource with the action $r_1$ (for process $M$) or $r_2$ (for process $N$), then obtain the resource with $c_1$ or $c_2$, and finally release the resource with $n_1$ or $n_2$. The protocol satisfies the mutual exclusion property, which forbids the $c_2$ action to occur after $c_1$ has happened and before the next $n_1$ has happened, and, symmetrically, the $c_1$ action to occur after a $c_2$ and before the next $n_2$. Mutual exclusion can be proven by *model checking*, i.e., by composing $M\|N$ with the error system for the mutual exclusion property, shown in Figure 2, and showing that the error state $\pi$ is unreachable.

Compositional model checking considers the composition $M\|A$ instead of the full system $M\|N$. In our approach, the assumption $A$ is the quotient of $N$ with respect to an equivalence relation on the states of $N$ that merges two states into a single equivalence class if they either both lead to an error in $M\|N$ or both

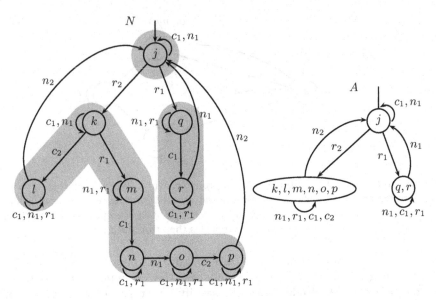

**Fig. 3.** Assumption $A = N/\sim$ for the compositional proof of mutual exclusion, defined by the equivalence relation $\sim$ on the states of LTS $N$. The equivalence classes of $\sim$ are shown in grey.

avoid the error in $M\|N$. Figure 3 shows the equivalence relation for the example. There are three equivalence classes: state $j$, states $q, r$, and states $k, l, m, n, o, p$. The quotient $A = N/\sim$ (where each equivalence class is a state, and there is an edge from one equivalence class to another if there is an edge from one of the members of the first class to a member of the second class) thus has only three states.

Like the weakest assumption, the quotient $A$ can be used as an assumption both in proving *and* in disproving the property $P$. The full system $M\|N$ satisfies $P$ if and only if the composition $M\|A$ satisfies $P$. Our algorithm for constructing the equivalence relation takes $O(|M|\cdot|N|\cdot\log|N|\cdot|P|)$ time, exceeding the cost of standard model checking only by a logarithmic factor. The generated assumption $A$ is related to the process $N$ by a simple homomorphism. Our construction is therefore a good solution for the first application scenario (documentation) as well as for the second scenario (certification).

Can we furthermore use the construction of $A$ in the third scenario, to accelerate the model checking process by compositional reasoning? For this purpose, the complexity of the basic construction is too expensive. We give a modified construction that runs in $O(|\mathcal{M}| \cdot |N| \cdot \log|N| \cdot |P|)$ time, where $\mathcal{M}$ is an *abstraction* of $M$. The abstraction is computed in an automatic *abstraction refinement loop* that, starting with the trivial abstraction, incrementally increases the size of the abstraction. The loop can be interrupted after any number of iterations, yielding a sound (but not necessarily minimal) assumption. The algorithm terminates when the assumption cannot be reduced any further.

## 2    Labeled Transition Systems

We use *labeled transition systems* (LTS) to describe the behavior of processes. A labeled transition system $M = \langle V, E, v_0, A \rangle$ is given as a set $V$ of states with a designated initial state $v_0 \in V$, a finite alphabet $A$ of actions, and a set $E \subseteq V \times A \times V$ of edges.

A sequence $\vec{a} = a_1 a_2 a_3 \ldots a_n \in A^*$ of actions in the alphabet of an LTS $M$ is called a *run* of $M$ if there is a sequence $\vec{v} = v_0 v_1 v_2 \ldots v_n \in V^+$, starting in the initial state $v_0$, such that $(v_{i-1}, a_i, v_i) \in E$ is an edge of $M$ for all $i = \{1, \ldots, n\}$. $\vec{v}$ is called a *state trace* of $\vec{a}$. The set of runs of an LTS is called its *language*.

A system generally consists of multiple processes. The LTS of each process restricts the possible behavior of the system: a sequence $\vec{a}$ of actions is a run of the system iff it is a run of all processes.

**Composition.**    The *composition* $M\|N$ of two LTS $M = \langle V_1, E_1, v_0^1, A \rangle$ and $N = \langle V_2, E_2, v_0^2, A \rangle$ is the LTS $\langle V, E, v_0, A \rangle$ with

- $V' = V_1 \times V_2$ and $v_0 = (v_0^1, v_0^2)$,
- $((v_1, v_2), a, (v_1', v_2')) \in E'$
  $\Leftrightarrow (v_1, a, v_1') \in E_1 \wedge (v_2, a, v_2') \in E_2$,
- $V \subseteq V'$ is the set of *reachable* states of $V'$, and
- $E = E' \cap V \times A \times V$ is the set of reachable transitions.

**Specification.**    An LTS $M = \langle V, E, v_0, A \rangle$ is called *deterministic* if, for all states $v \in V$ of $M$ and all actions $a \in A$ of the alphabet of $M$ at most one edge with label $a$ exits ($|E \cap \{v\} \times \{a\} \times V| \leq 1$). A deterministic LTS $P$ is called a *property*.

An LTS $S$ *satisfies* $P$, denoted by $S \models P$, iff the language of $S$ is contained in the language of $P$. For a (deterministic) property $P = \langle V, E, v_0, A \rangle$, the LTS $\overline{P} = \langle V \cup \{\pi\}, E_\pi, v_0, A \rangle$ with $E_\pi = E \cup \{\pi\} \times A \times \{\pi\} \cup \{(v, a, \pi) \mid v \in V, a \in A$ and $\{v\} \times \{a\} \times V \cap E = \emptyset\}$ is called the *error LTS* of $P$.

The error state $\pi$ is treated specially in the composition $S\|\overline{P}$ of a process $S$ and an error LTS. For $S = \langle V_1, E_1, v_0^1, A \rangle$ and $P = \langle V_2, E_2, v_0^2, A \rangle$, $S\|\overline{P}$ is the LTS $\langle V, E, v_0, A \rangle$ with

- $V' = (V_1 \times V_2) \cup \{\pi\}$ and $v_0 = (v_0^1, v_0^2)$,
- $((v_1, v_2), a, (v_1', v_2')) \in E'$
  $\Leftrightarrow (v_1, a, v_1') \in E_1 \wedge (v_2, a, v_2') \in E_2$,
- $(\pi, a, v) \in E' \Leftrightarrow v = \pi$,
- $((v_1, v_2), a, \pi) \in E' \Leftrightarrow \{v_1\} \times \{a\} \times V_1 \cap E_1 \neq \emptyset$ and
  $\{v_2\} \times \{a\} \times V_2 \cap E_2 = \emptyset$,
- $V \subseteq V'$ is the set of *reachable* states of $V'$, and
- $E = E' \cap V \times A \times V$ is the set or reachable transitions.

**Model checking.**    The verification problem is to decide for a given system $S$ and a property $P$ if $S \models P$. The verification problem can be solved by *model checking*, which checks if the error state $\pi$ is reachable in the composition $S\|\overline{P}$. If $S = M\|N$ consists of two processes, the cost of model checking is in time and space $O(|M| \cdot |N| \cdot |P|)$.

**Abstraction.** Abstraction is a general verification technique, in which the behavior of a given process is approximated over a smaller state space. In this paper, we consider *homomorphic abstractions*, as introduced by Clarke, Grumberg, and Long [5]. An LTS $A = \langle V', E', v'_0, A \rangle$ is a (homomorphic) *abstraction* of an LTS $N = \langle V, E, v_0, A \rangle$ if there exists a total and surjective function $h : A \to A'$, such that $h(v_0) = v'_0$, and for all edges $(v, a, v')$ in $E$ there is an edge $(h(v), a, h(v'))$ in $E'$.

In the following, we identify the homomorphism $h$ with the induced equivalence $v \approx v' \equiv h(v) = h(v')$ on the states. The canonic abstraction defined by an equivalence relation $\approx$ is the quotient LTS with respect to $\approx$. We denote the equivalence class of a state $n$ with respect to $\approx$ by $[n]_\approx$, or, if $\approx$ is clear from the context, by $[n]$. Let $V/\approx = \{[v] \mid v \in V\}$ denote the set of equivalence classes of a set $V$ of states. The *quotient* of the LTS $N = \langle V, E, v_0, A \rangle$ with respect to $\approx$ is the LTS $N/\approx = \langle V/\approx, E', [v_0], A \rangle$, where $([v], a, [v']) \in E'$ iff there are two states $w \in [v]$ and $w' \in [v']$ such that $([v], a, [v']) \in E$.

**Compositional verification.** Our approach is based on the following compositional verification rule [19,2]:

$$\frac{(1)\ M\|A \models P \qquad (2)\ \ N\ \ \models A}{M\|N \models P}$$

To prove that a two-process system $M\|N$ satisfies a property $P$, the rule replaces, in premise (1), the process $N$ by the *assumption* $A$, which, according to premise (2), must be chosen such that its language contains the language of $N$. In our setting, $A = N/\approx$ is the quotient of $N$ with respect to an equivalence relation $\approx$ on the states of $N$. Since the language of an LTS is always contained in the language of its quotient, we obtain the following simplified rule:

$$\frac{M\|N/\approx \models P}{M\|N\ \ \models P}$$

For an arbitrary equivalence relation $\approx$, the rule is sound but not necessarily invertible: the language of $M\|N$ may be a proper subset of the language of $M\|N/\approx$. In order to use the assumption both for proving and for disproving properties, we are interested in equivalences $\sim$ such that $M\|N/\sim \models P$ iff $M\|N \models P$. In the following sections, we present methods to construct such equivalences.

## 3   Forward Equivalence

We call two states $n_1$ and $n_2$ of $N$ *forward-equivalent* if merging them does not make additional states in $M\|N\|\overline{P}$ reachable. For example, in Figure 3, the states $m, n, o,$ and $p$ are forward equivalent.

Let $m_0, n_0,$ and $p_0$ be the initial states of $M, N,$ and $P$, respectively. The *forward equivalence relation* $\sim_F$ is defined as follows.

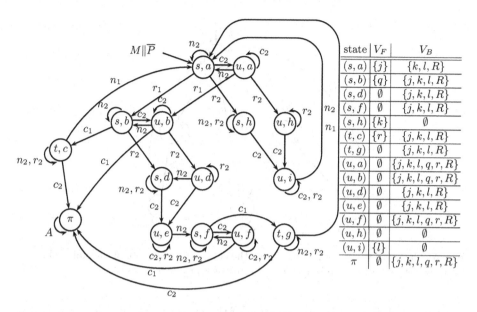

The table shown in the figure:

| state | $V_F$ | $V_B$ |
|---|---|---|
| $(s,a)$ | $\{j\}$ | $\{k,l,R\}$ |
| $(s,b)$ | $\{q\}$ | $\{j,k,l,R\}$ |
| $(s,d)$ | $\emptyset$ | $\{j,k,l,R\}$ |
| $(s,f)$ | $\emptyset$ | $\{j,k,l,R\}$ |
| $(s,h)$ | $\{k\}$ | $\emptyset$ |
| $(t,c)$ | $\{r\}$ | $\{j,k,l,R\}$ |
| $(t,g)$ | $\emptyset$ | $\{j,k,l,R\}$ |
| $(u,a)$ | $\emptyset$ | $\{j,k,l,q,r,R\}$ |
| $(u,b)$ | $\emptyset$ | $\{j,k,l,q,r,R\}$ |
| $(u,d)$ | $\emptyset$ | $\{j,k,l,R\}$ |
| $(u,e)$ | $\emptyset$ | $\{j,k,l,R\}$ |
| $(u,f)$ | $\emptyset$ | $\{j,k,l,q,r,R\}$ |
| $(u,h)$ | $\emptyset$ | $\emptyset$ |
| $(u,i)$ | $\{l\}$ | $\emptyset$ |
| $\pi$ | $\emptyset$ | $\{j,k,l,q,r,R\}$ |

**Fig. 4.** Labeling of $M\|\overline{P}$ in the computation of the forward and backward equivalences in the mutual exclusion example. The labeling with $V_F$, obtained during the forward traversal and shown in the second column, indicate that states $m$, $n$, $o$, and $p$ of $N$ are forward equivalent and can be merged into a single equivalence class $R$ (cf. Figure 5). The labeling with $V_B$, obtained during the backward traversal and shown in the third column, indicates that states $q$ and $r$, and states $k$, $l$ and $R$ of $N_F$ are backward equivalent. Merging these states yields the assumption shown in Figure 3.

Two states $n_1$ and $n_2$ of $N$ are forward equivalent, $n_1 \sim_F n_2$, iff, for all states $m$ of $M$ and all states $p$ of $P$, there is a path from $v_0 = (m_0, n_0, p_0)$ to the $(m, n_1, p)$ if and only if there is a path from $v_0$ to $(m, n_2, p)$.

The forward equivalence relation yields an invertible verification rule: $M\|N/\sim_F \models P$ iff $M\|N \models P$.

We compute $\sim_F$ in two steps. In the first step, we decorate the states of $Q = M\|\overline{P}$ with sets $V_F$ of states of $N$ such that the label of a state $q$ of $Q$ contains a state $n$ of $N$ iff there is a path from $v_0$ to $(n, q)$ in $N\|Q$. In the second step, we extract the equivalence relation from the labels: for two states $n_1$ and $n_2$ of $N$, $n_1 \sim_F n_2$ iff for every label $V_F$ on some state of $Q$, $n_1$ is in $V_F$ if and only if $n_2$ is in $V_F$.

The labeling process is carried out as a fixed point computation, beginning with $\{n_0\}$ as the label on $(m_0, p_0)$ and the empty set on all other states. If there is an edge with action $a$ from a state $(m, p)$ labeled with set $V_F$ to a state $(m', p')$, then every state $n$ of $N$ that has an incoming edge with action $a$ from some state in $V_F$ is added to the label of $(m', p')$. By traversing the graph forward in a breadth-first manner, it suffices to consider each edge in $M\|\overline{P}$ at most once. The fixed point is therefore reached after at most $|M| \cdot |N| \cdot |P|$ steps. Let $N_F$ be the quotient of $N$ with respect to $\sim_F$.

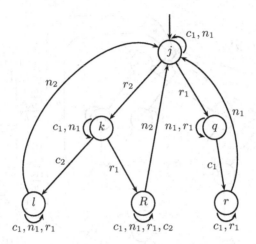

**Fig. 5.** The quotient $N_F$ of process $N$ for the compositional proof of mutual exclusion. States $m$, $n$, $o$, and $p$ have been merged into the equivalence class $R$.

Figure 4 illustrates the computation of the forward equivalence on the states of process $N$ from the mutual exclusion example. The second column shows the result $V_F$ of the forward labeling process. States $m$, $n$, $o$ and $p$ are forward-equivalent, since they are not contained in the label of any state of $M\|\overline{P}$. Figure 5 shows the resulting quotient $N_F$.

A careful analysis shows that $N_F$ can be constructed in $O(\log|N_F| \cdot |M| \cdot |N| \cdot |P|)$ time. We fix an arbitrary order $<_{M\|\overline{P}}$ on the states $V_{M\|\overline{P}}$ of $M\|\overline{P}$, and defer a linear pre-order $\preceq_N$ on the states $V_N$ of $N$, such that two states $v, v' \in V_N$ are identified iff they are forward equivalent ($\simeq_N \equiv \sim_F$). Let $dec : V_{M\|\overline{P}} \to 2^{V_N}$ be the function that maps each state of $M\|\overline{P}$ to the set of states it is decorated with. We define $\prec_N = \{(v, v') \in V_N{}^2 \mid \exists w \in V_{M\|\overline{P}}.v \notin dec(w) \ni v' \wedge \forall w' <_{M\|\overline{P}} w. v \in dec(w) \leftrightarrow v' \in dec(w)\}$ and $\simeq_N = \{(v, v') \in V_N{}^2 \mid \forall w \in V_{M\|\overline{P}}.v \in dec(w) \leftrightarrow v' \in dec(w)\}$.

We can therefore construct the quotients by sorting the states of $V_N$ with respect to $\preceq_N$, using AVL-trees. Concurrently to the sorting, we immediately merge equivalent states. The nodes of the AVL-tree is therefore bound by the number $|N_F|$ of quotients. Since comparing two elements of $V_N$ can be performed in time $O(M)$, $N_F$ can be constructed in time $O(\log|N_F| \cdot |M| \cdot |N| \cdot |P|)$.

## 4   Backward Equivalence

We call two states $n_1$ and $n_2$ of $N_F$ (cf. Figure 5) *backward-equivalent* if merging them neither introduces nor removes an error path in $M\|N$. In the example of Figure 3, the states $k, l, R$ and the states $q, r$ are backward equivalent.

Two states $n_1$ and $n_2$ of $N_F$ are *backward equivalent*, $n_1 \sim_B n_2$, iff, for all states $m$ of $M$ and all states $p$ of $P$, there is a path from $(m, n_1, p)$ to the error state $\pi$ if and only if there is a path from $(m, n_2, p)$ to $\pi$.

Combining the backward equivalence relation with the forward equivalence relation, we again obtain an invertible verification rule:

$$M \| N_F / \sim_B \models P \quad \text{iff} \quad M \| N_F \models P \quad \text{iff} \quad M \| N \models P.$$

The construction of $\sim_B$ is based on a labeling of the state graph of $Q = M \| \overline{P}$ with sets $V_B$ of states of $N_F$ such that the label of a state $q$ of $Q$ contains a state $n$ of $N_F$ iff there is a path from $(n, q)$ to $\pi$ in $N_F \| Q$. We extract the equivalence relation from the labels as follows: for two states $n_1$ and $n_2$ of $N_F$, $n_1 \sim n_2$ iff for every label $V$ on some state of $Q$, $n_1$ is in $V$ if and only if $n_2$ is in $V$.

The labeling process is carried out as a fixed point computation beginning with the entire state set of $N$ as the label on the error state $\pi$ and the empty set on all other states. If there is an edge with action $a$ between a state $(m, p)$ and a state $(m', p')$ labeled with set $V$, then every state $n$ of $N$ that has an edge with action $a$ to some state in $V$ is added to the label of $(m, p)$. By following the edges backwards from the error states in a breadth-first manner, it suffices to consider each edge in $M \| \overline{P}$ at most once. The fixed point is therefore again reached after at most $|M| \cdot |N| \cdot |P|$ steps. The assumption $A$ is defined by the composition $\sim \; := \; \sim_B \circ \sim_F$ of the two equivalence relations: for two states $n_1$, $n_2$ of $N$, $n_1 \sim n_2$ iff $[n_1]_{\sim_F} \sim_B [n_2]_{\sim_F}$.

For the mutual exclusion example, the result $V_B$ of the backward labeling is shown in the third column of the table in Figure 4. States $k$, $l$ and $R$, and states $q$ and $r$ occur in the label of the same states of $M \| \overline{P}$. Consequently, they are backward-equivalent, and $\sim_B$ reduces the forward quotient $N_F$ to the assumption LTS depicted in Figure 3.

## 5    Assumptions from Abstractions

Traversing the state space of $M \| \overline{P}$, as in the constructions of the previous sections, is not feasible if $M$ is large, for example because it is again composed from multiple processes. In this section, we modify the algorithms to work on an *abstraction* of $M$. We assume that the abstraction is defined by a given equivalence relation $\approx$. This equivalence relation is used to construct a modal transition system, which in turn is used to compute upper and lower bounds for the labels $V_F$ (or $V_B$) of the states of $M \| \overline{P}$. We present an algorithm for computing $\approx$ in Section 6.

Replacing $M$ with an abstraction $\mathcal{M}$ introduces the possibility that two states of $N$ both lead to an error when composed with $\mathcal{M}$, but only one of them leads to an error when composed with $M$. The algorithm must therefore distinguish situations that *may* lead to an error (i.e., the error is reached in the composition with $\mathcal{M}$ but not necessarily in $M$) from situations that *must* lead to an error (both in composition with $\mathcal{M}$ and in composition with $M$). Merging two states of $N$ is safe in two cases: (1) if they *both must* lead to an error and (2) if *neither* of them *may* lead to an error. We formalize this idea using modal transition systems. (The concept of modal transition systems has recently been successfully applied in model checking for single processes [7,14,9].)

A *modal transition system* (MTS) [17,16] is a tuple $\mathcal{M}=\langle V, E_{must}, E_{may}, v_0, A\rangle$ such that $\mathcal{M}_{must} = \langle V, E_{must}, v_0, A\rangle$ and $\mathcal{M}_{may} = \langle V, E_{may}, v_0, A\rangle$ are labeled transition systems and $E_{must} \subseteq E_{may}$.

An abstraction, given as an equivalence $\approx$ on the states of a labeled transition system $M = \langle V, E, v_0, A\rangle$, defines a modal transition system $\mathcal{M} = \langle V/\approx, E_{must}, E_{may}, [v_0], A\rangle$, where there is a *may* edge $([v], a, [v']) \in E_{may}$ iff *there is a state $w \in [v]$ and a state $w' \in [v']$ such that $(w, a, w') \in E$.*

An intuitive symmetric definition for the must edges $E_{must}$, which can be applied both for the computation of forward and backward equivalence classes, would be $E_{must}=\{([v], a, [v']) \in E_{may} \,|\, \forall w \in [v] \,\forall w' \in [v']. \,(w, a, w') \in E\}$. Stronger results can be obtained by using different sets of must edges for forward and backward analysis:

- For the computation of *forward* equivalence classes, an edge $([v], a, [v']) \in E_{must}$ is a must edge iff for all states $w' \in [v']$ there is a state $w \in [v]$ such that $(w, a, w') \in E$.
- For the computation of *backward* equivalence classes, an edge $([v], a, [v']) \in E_{must}$ is a must edge iff for all states $w \in [v]$ there is a state $w' \in [v']$ such that $(w, a, w') \in E$.

We extend the composition operator to modal transition systems. The *composition* $\mathcal{M}\|N$ of an MTS $\mathcal{M} = \langle V_1, E_1^{must}, E_1^{may}, v_0^1, A\rangle$ and an LTS $N = \langle V_2, E_2, v_0^2, A\rangle$ is constructed such that $(\mathcal{M}\|N)_{must} = \mathcal{M}_{must}\|N$ and $(\mathcal{M}\|N)_{may} = \mathcal{M}_{may}\|N$.

We construct the assumption $A$ for the model checking problem $M\|N \models P$ again as an equivalence $\simeq := \simeq_B \circ \simeq_F$ on the states of $N$. Let $\mathcal{M}$ be the MTS defined by an abstraction of $M$, and let $m_0$, $n_0$, and $p_0$ be the initial states of $\mathcal{M}$, $N$, and $P$, respectively. The forward equivalence relation $\simeq_F$ is defined as follows: for two states $n_1$ and $n_2$ of $N$,

> $n_1 \simeq_F n_2$ iff for all states $m$ of $\mathcal{M}$ and all states $p$ of $P$, one of the following two conditions holds: (1) there is a path from $(m_0, n_0, p_0)$ to $(m, n_1, p)$ *and* a path from $(m_0, n_0, p_0)$ to $(m, n_2, p)$ in $\mathcal{M}_{must}\|N\|\overline{P}$, or (2) there is *no* path from $(m_0, n_0, p_0)$ to $(m, n_1, p)$ *and* there is *no* path from $(m_0, n_0, p_0)$ to $(m, n_2, p)$ in $\mathcal{M}_{may}\|N\|\overline{P}$.

To compute $\simeq_F$, we apply the fixed point construction from Section 3 twice: once on the graph $\mathcal{M}_{must}\|\overline{P}$, labeling each state with a subset $V_{lower}$ of the states of $N$, and once on the graph $\mathcal{M}_{may}\|\overline{P}$, labeling each node with a subset $V_{upper}$ of the states of $N$. If a state $[s]$ of $\mathcal{M}_{must}\|\overline{P}$ is labeled with $(V_{lower}, V_{upper})$ then all states $t \in [s]$ of $M\|\overline{P}$ are labeled with a *subset* $V_F \subseteq V_{upper}$ of $V_{upper}$ (using the method suggested in Section 3). Likewise, if $\approx$ does not identify the initial state with any other state $([(m_0, p_0)] = \{(m_0, p_0)\})$, all states $t \in [s]$ of $M\|\overline{P}$ are labeled with a *superset* $V_F \supseteq V_{lower}$ of $V_{lower}$. These upper and lower

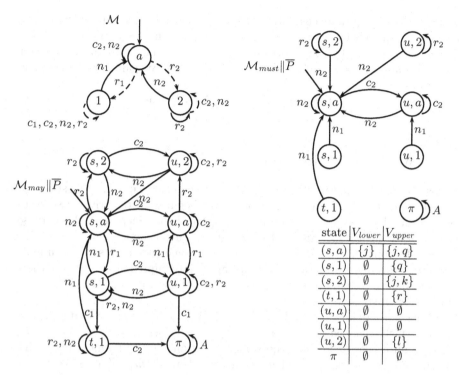

**Fig. 6.** Computation of the forward equivalence in the mutual exclusion example, based on an abstraction $\mathcal{M}$ of process $M$. The MTS $\mathcal{M}$ is the result of merging states $b, c, d, e, f$ and $g$ of $M$ into equivalence class 1 and states $h$ and $i$ into equivalence class 2. States $m$, $n$, $o$, and $p$ of $N$ are forward-equivalent because they occur in none of the $V_{upper}$ labels. Merging these states results in the quotient $N_F$ shown in Figure 5.

bounds on the labeling of the single states of $M\|\overline{P}$ allow for the definition of an equivalence relation $\simeq_F$: For two states $n_1$ and $n_2$ of $N$, $n_1 \simeq_F n_2$ iff for every pair of labels $V_{lower}$ and $V_{upper}$ on some state, either $n_1$ is in $V_{lower}$ and $n_2$ is in $V_{lower}$, or $n_1$ is in $V \smallsetminus V_{upper}$ and $n_2$ is in $V \smallsetminus V_{upper}$. Let $N_F$ be the quotient of $N$ with respect to $\simeq_F$.

Figure 6 illustrates the computation of $\simeq_F$ for the mutual exclusion example. The MTS $\mathcal{M}$ is the result of merging states $b, c, d, e, f$ and $g$ of $M$ into equivalence class 1 and merging states $h$ and $i$ into equivalence class 2. States $m$, $n$, $o$, and $p$ of $N$ are forward-equivalent because they occur in none of the $V_{upper}$ labels. Merging these states results in the quotient $N_F$ shown in Figure 5.

To compute $N_F$, we proceed in two steps. In a first step, we compute those states $V_N^1 \subseteq V_N$ of $N$, which are in $V_{upper}$ but not in $V_{lower}$ for some state of $M\|\overline{P}$. Since these states always form a quotient of their own, they can be excluded from further consideration. The construction of $N_F$ is then completed by construction quotients for the states in $V_N \smallsetminus V_N^1$ using the sorting approach suggested in the previous section. The overall construction again takes $O(\log |N_F| \cdot |M| \cdot |N| \cdot |P|)$ time.

The backward equivalence relation $\simeq_B$ can be defined and computed analog to the forward equivalence relation $\simeq_F$. Since the equivalences $\sim_F$ and $\sim_B$ obtained without abstraction (by the algorithms in Sections 3 and 4) are always coarser than the equivalences $\simeq_F$ and $\simeq_B$ obtained using $\mathcal{M}$, we again obtain invertible proof rules:

$$M\|N/\simeq_F \models P \quad \text{iff} \quad M\|N \models P, \quad \text{and}$$
$$M\|N_F/\simeq_B \models P \quad \text{iff} \quad M\|N_F \models P.$$

## 6   Abstraction Refinement

In this section, we give a construction for the equivalence $\approx$ on the states of $M$ needed in the algorithms in Section 5. We begin with the trivial two-state abstraction (that merges all non-initial states) and then incrementally increase the size of the abstraction in an abstraction refinement loop.

Since the constructions in Section 5 produce some (not necessarily minimal) assumption for any abstraction, the loop can be interrupted at any time. Otherwise, the loop terminates as soon as the upper and lower bounds $(V_{lower}, V_{upper})$ coincide for all states of $M\|\overline{P}$.

As long as there is some state labeled with $(V_{lower}, V_{upper})$ such that $V_{lower} \neq V_{upper}$, we pick a *may* edge $(s, a, s')$ of $\mathcal{M}_{may}\|\overline{P}$ that does not occur in $\mathcal{M}_{must}\|\overline{P}$.

To obtain a coarser forward equivalence relation $\simeq_F$, we refine $\approx$ by distinguishing any two states $m_1$ and $m_2$ represented by $s'$ $(m_1', m_2' \in [s']_M$, where $[s]_M = [m]$ for $s = ([m], p)$ and $[\pi]_M = V_M)$ if there is an edge $(m_1, a, m_1')$ in $M$ with $m_1 \in [s]_M$, but no edge $(m_2, a, m_2')$ with $m_2 \in [s]_M$. I.e., the equivalence relation $\approx$ is refined into the new equivalence $\approx_{(s,a,s')}$, with

$$\approx_{(s,a,s')} = \approx \setminus \{(m_1, m_2) \in [s']_M^2 \mid (\exists m \in [s]_M . (m, a, m_1) \in E_M)$$
$$\leftrightarrow (\exists m \in [s]_M . (m, a, m_2) \in E_M)\}.$$

Note that the previously computed upper and lower bounds remain valid after the refinement of $\approx$. We preserve and use this information: The previous values of $V_{lower}$ can be used as a starting point for the fixed point construction of the new $V_{lower}$. Since a split can introduce new may edges, this method does not only accelerate the computation of the fixed point, but also provides sharper lower bounds. The refinement loop is guaranteed to terminate: in the worst case, the number of refinement steps is equal to the size of $M$. How fast the loop terminates depends on the choice of the *may* edges to refine on.

We avoid the explicit computation of the upper bounds $V_{upper}$ by choosing an edge $(s, a, s')$ such that

- $s$ and $s'$ were labeled during the forward traversal with $V_{lower}$ and $V_{lower}'$, respectively, and
- $V_{lower} \times \{a\} \times V_N \setminus V_{lower}'$ is not disjoint from the edges of $N$.

The second condition avoids the choice of edges that cause no difference in the labeling of $s'$. If there are multiple such edges, we pick one where the distance from the initial state to $s$ is minimal in $\mathcal{M}_{must}\|\overline{P}$.

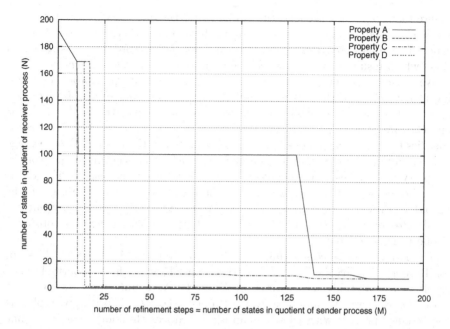

**Fig. 7.** Experimental data from the *sliding window protocol* benchmark. Property A expresses that the protocol does not invent messages, Property B and C express that the *sender* process and the receiver process, respectively, do not invent messages, and Property D expresses (incorrectly) that no messages are delivered. The figure shows the number of states in the quotient of the *receiver* process ($N$) after a given number of refinement steps. Since each refinement step introduces a new state in the abstraction of the *sender* process ($M$), the number of refinement steps is equal to the number of states in the quotient of $M$.

The refinement step for the backward equivalence $\simeq_B$ can be defined analogously.

## 7    Experimental Results

We have implemented the algorithms of this paper in a small prototype tool, which is intended as a front-end to the model checker SPIN [13]. Our tool reads a two-process system written in (a subset of) Promela and produces a modified system, where the second process is replaced by the assumption LTS. The tool applies the abstraction refinement algorithm and switches every ten steps between computing the forward and computing the backward equivalence. The process can be interrupted after an arbitrary number of refinement steps and terminates once the upper and lower bounds for the labels coincide in both constructions.

Figure 7 shows experimental data from the verification of the classic *sliding window protocol* benchmark. In the sliding window protocol, the *sender* (process $M$) transmits messages over an unreliable channel to the *receiver* (process $N$). To ensure that no packets are lost, the sender stores the messages in a sliding buffer until acknowledgments are received. In our benchmark, there are three different types of messages (*red, white,* and *blue*) and the buffer stores two messages at a time, which results in 192 states each for the *sender* and the *receiver*.

We consider four properties: Property A expresses that the protocol does not invent messages ("if there is no *white* message in the input of the *sender*, then there will be no *white* message in the output of the receiver"). Properties B and C express the same condition locally for the two processes, i.e., Property B specifies that the *sender* does not invent messages ("if there is no *white* message in the input of the *sender*, then there will be no *white* message on the network"), Property C specifies that the *receiver* does not invent messages ("if there is no *white* message on the network, then there will be no *white* message in the output"). Property D expresses that the receiver never produces any output. While Properties A, B, and C are satisfied by the sliding window protocol, Property D is violated.

The refinement process terminates after 169 steps for Property A, 18 steps for Property B, 168 steps for Property C, and 15 steps for Property D. The resulting assumption has 8 states for Property A, 1 state for Property B, 8 states for Property C, and 1 state for Property D. Not surprisingly, replacing the *receiver* process with these assumptions reduces the model checking time (Property A: 4s instead of 19s, Property B: 3s instead of 19s, Property C: 4s instead of 18s, Property D: 3s instead of 18s, on an Athlon XP 2600+ with 2GB RAM).

If the purpose of computing the assumption is to improve the time and memory performance of a *single* model checking run, it appears to be beneficial to interrupt the refinement process early. Figure 7 shows the number of states in the quotient of $N$ that is reached when the refinement process is interrupted after a certain number of steps. A significant drop in the number of states in the assumption occurs already very early on, when only a small percentage of the states of $M$ have been considered.

# 8    Conclusions and Future Work

Compositionality and abstraction are generally considered the two key methods in avoiding the state-space explosion problem. The combination of the two methods in our assumption synthesis algorithm adds a new twist to classic abstraction refinement: rather than starting with a coarse abstraction of process $N$, which would need to be corrected through a successive elimination of spurious counter examples, we start with an abstraction of its environment ($M$), which always (at any point in the refinement cycle) allows us to produce an assumption that is free of spurious counter examples.

Our approach has several advantages. First, and perhaps most important, the resulting assumption is *acceptance preserving*. The result of model checking is the same if we use the assumption or the original process. Second, while using the assumption may significantly accelerate the model checking, there is no penalty in the form of increased complexity as introduced by the intermediate state explosion problem [10,8] or by using deterministic automata [6,2,1,8]. In the worst case, the generated assumption is as large as the process itself. Even this, however, is unlikely to occur for well-designed software architectures.

A third advantage of our approach is that the generated assumptions have applications beyond classic model checking. They are well-suited as certificates. Using an arbitrary assumption automaton $A$ for $N$, the language containment check is PSPACE-hard in the size of $N$ and EXPSPACE-hard in the size of $A$. Since our method generates a homomorphic abstraction of $N$, language containment can be checked in linear time. For similar reasons, the generated abstraction is useful both in the documentation of a process and in the maintenance phase.

In future work, we intend to expand on our prototype tool implementation. In particular, the application to larger systems needs good heuristics for the refinement of the modal LTSs. An interesting open question is the extension of our method to obtain assumptions for more than one process. It is always possible to replace one process after another by a homomorphic abstraction, but more experience is needed to determine the sequence in which the processes should be considered and to decide whether it is worthwhile to alternate between the processes during the refinement cycle.

# References

1. Rajeev Alur, Pavol Cerny, P. Madhusudan, and Wonhong Nam. Synthesis of interface specifications for Java classes. In *Proc. POPL*, pages 98–109, New York, NY, USA, 2005. ACM Press.
2. Rajeev Alur, P. Madhusudan, and Wonhong Nam. Symbolic compositional verification by learning assumptions. In *Proc. CAV*, volume 3576 of *LNCS*, pages 548–562, 2005.
3. Shing Chi Cheung and Jeff Kramer. Context constraints for compositional reachability analysis. *ACM Trans. Softw. Eng. Methodol.*, 5(4):334–377, 1996.
4. E. Clarke, D. Long, and K. McMillan. Compositional model checking. In *Proc. LICS*, pages 353–362, 1989.
5. Edmund M. Clarke, Orna Grumberg, and David E. Long. Model checking and abstraction. In $19^{th}$ *ACM Symp. Princ. of Prog. Lang.*, pages 343–354, 1992.
6. Jamieson M. Cobleigh, Dimitra Giannakopoulou, and Corina S. Păsăreanu. Learning assumptions for compositional verification. In *Proc. TACAS*, pages 331–346, 2003.
7. Luca de Alfaro, Patrice Godefroid, and Radha Jagadeesan. Three-valued abstractions of games: Uncertainty, but with precision. In *Proc. LICS*, pages 170–179, 2004.
8. Dimitra Giannakopoulou, Corina S. Păsăreanu, and Howard Barringer. Assumption generation for software component verification. In *Proc. ASE*, pages 3–12, Washington, DC, USA, 2002. IEEE Computer Society.
9. Patrice Godefroid, Michael Huth, and Radha Jagadeesan. Abstraction-based model checking using modal transition systems. In *Proc. CONCUR*, pages 426–440. Springer-Verlag, 2001.

10. Susanne Graf, B. Steffen, and G. Lüttgen. Compositional minimization of finite state systems using interface specifications. *Formal Aspects of Computation*, 8, September 1996.
11. Orna Grumberg and David E. Long. Model checking and modular verification. *ACM Transactions on Programming Languages and Systems*, 16(3):843–871, May 1994.
12. Thomas A. Henzinger, Shaz Qadeer, and Sriram K. Rajamani. You assume, we guarantee: Methodology and case studies. In *Proc. CAV*, pages 440–451, 1998.
13. G.J. Holzmann. *The Spin Model Checker, Primer and Reference Manual*. Addison-Wesley, Reading, Massachusetts, 2003.
14. Michael Huth, Radha Jagadeesan, and David Schmidt. Modal transition systems: A foundation for three-valued program analysis. In *Proc. European Symposium on Programming*, pages 155–169. Springer-Verlag, 2001.
15. Cliff B. Jones. Specification and design of (parallel) programs. In *IFIP Congress*, pages 321–332, 1983.
16. Kim G. Larsen. Modal specifications. In *Proc. Automatic Verification Methods for Finite State Systems*. Springer-Verlag, 1989.
17. Kim G. Larsen and Bent Thomsen. A modal process logic. In *Proc. LICS*, pages 203–210. IEEE Computer Society Press, 1988.
18. Kedar S. Namjoshi. Certifying model checkers. In *Proc. CAV*, pages 2–13. Springer-Verlag, 2001.
19. Kedar S. Namjoshi and Richard J. Trefler. On the completeness of compositional reasoning. In *Proc. CAV*, pages 139–153. Springer-Verlag, 2000.
20. A. Pnueli. In transition from global to modular temporal reasoning about programs. In *Logics and models of concurrent systems*, pages 123–144. Springer-Verlag, 1985.
21. Krishan. K. Sabnani, Aleta M. Lapone, and M. Ümit Uyar. An algorithmic procedure for checking safety properties of protocols. *IEEE Trans. Commun.*, 37(9):940–948, September 1989.
22. Kuo-Chung Tai and Pramod V. Koppol. An incremental approach to reachability analysis of distributed programs. In *Proc. IWSSD*, pages 141–150, Los Alamitos, CA, USA, 1993. IEEE Computer Society Press.
23. Qiwen Xu, Willem P. de Roever, and Jifeng He. The rely-guarantee method for verifying shared variable concurrent programs. *Formal Aspects of Computing*, 9(2):149–174, 1997.

# Refined Interfaces for Compositional Verification

Frédéric Lang

INRIA Rhône-Alpes / VASY
655 avenue de l'Europe, 38 334 St Ismier Cedex, France
Phone: +33 (0)4 76 61 55 11; Fax: +33 (0)4 76 61 52 52
Frederic.Lang@inria.fr

**Abstract.** The compositional verification approach of Graf & Steffen aims at avoiding state space explosion for individual processes of a concurrent system. It relies on interfaces that express the behavioural constraints imposed on each process by synchronization with the other processes, thus preventing the exploration of states and transitions that would not be reachable in the global state space. Krimm & Mounier, and Cheung & Kramer proposed two techniques to generate such interfaces automatically. In this paper, we propose a refined interface generation technique, in which the interface of a process is derived automatically from the examination of (a subset of) concurrent processes. This technique is applicable to formalisms in which concurrent processes are composed either using synchronization vectors or process algebra parallel composition operators (including those of CCS, CSP, μCRL, LOTOS, and E-LOTOS), for which we developed a tool. Several experiments indicate state space reductions by more than two orders of magnitude for the largest processes.

## 1 Introduction

*Enumerative verification* is a popular technique that consists in exploring and checking reachable states and transitions of a concurrent system. It is confronted with the *state explosion* problem, which occurs when the number of states grows exponentially as the number of concurrent processes increases. To avoid or reduce state explosion, various approaches have been proposed, among which symbolic verification, on-the-fly verification, partial order reductions, symmetries, data-flow analysis, and compositional verification. This paper deals with the latter approach, which assumes that the concurrent system under study can be expressed as a collection of communicating sequential processes, the behaviours of which are modeled as finite state machines or LTSs (*Labelled Transition Systems*). The sequential processes are composed in parallel, either in a flat or hierarchical manner.

In its simplest forms [10,28,32,38,33,34,36,31], compositional verification (also called incremental reduction [32], incremental reachability analysis [33,34], compositional state space generation [36], or inductive compression [31]) consists in replacing each sequential process by an *abstraction*, simpler than the original process but still preserving the properties to be verified on the whole system.

E. Najm et al. (Eds.): FORTE 2006, LNCS 4229, pp. 159–174, 2006.
© IFIP International Federation for Information Processing 2006

Quite often, abstracting a process is done by minimizing its corresponding LTS modulo an appropriate equivalence or preorder relation (e.g., a bisimulation relation, such as strong, branching, or observational equivalence). If the system has a hierarchical structure, minimization can also be applied at every intermediate level in the hierarchy. Although this simple form of compositional verification has been applied successfully to some complex systems (e.g., [11,5] in the case of the LOTOS language [22]), it may be counter-productive in some other cases: generating the LTS of each process separately may lead to state explosion, whereas the generation of the whole system of concurrent processes might succeed if processes constrain each other when composed in parallel. Indeed, there may be many states of a process that, although useful in a general environment, are useless (i.e., never explored) in a particular environment.

This issue has been addressed by enhanced compositional verification approaches [19,7,37,8,9,18,26,6,16], which permit the generation of the LTS of an individual process by taking into account *interface constraints* (also known as *environment constraints* or *context constraints*). These constraints express the behavioural restrictions imposed on the considered process by synchronization with its neighbour processes. Taking into account the environment of a process permits local elimination of states and transitions unreachable in the LTS of the whole system.

In general, interface constraints are expressed in the form of an LTS simply called *interface*. There exist two approaches to restrict the behaviour of a process w.r.t. an interface. In the first one, the process is composed in parallel with the interface, which must have been transformed beforehand so that the composition does not affect the global behaviour of the system (a property known as *context transparency*) [6,7,8,9]. This approach is supported in the framework of CSP by the TRACTA tool [16]. In the second approach, the process is constrained using a specific *semi-composition* operator [19,18,26], which cuts the process states and transitions that cannot be reached when considering the traces of the interface as the only possible interactions between the process and its environment. This approach is supported in the framework of LOTOS by the PROJECTOR [26] and SVL [12] tools of CADP (*Construction and Analysis of Distributed Processes*) [13] and was used in the verification of an industrial protocol [35].

Interfaces can be either written by the user (and possibly checked automatically [26]), or generated automatically. Although automated generation has the neat advantage to relieve users from the burden of calculating appropriate constraints, existing automated interface generation techniques undergo two main limitations: first, they are specific to a given composition operator and thus not directly applicable in the framework of concurrent languages featuring different and/or more general operators; second, as already observed in [7], they may fail to capture effective interface constraints due to deficiencies in their analysis of synchronizations between processes[1].

In this paper, we propose to generate interfaces automatically using a new technique that relies on a translation of the system into an intermediate

---

[1] See in particular Examples 2 and 3, Section 3 of this paper.

concurrent model, named *network of* LTSs, which describes the synchronization between processes in a flat manner. This intermediate representation permits the derivation of effective interface constraints imposed on a given process by a set of its neighbour processes automatically, independently of the hierarchy of processes and of the nature of the composition operators. This permits combination of constraints induced by distant processes, and improvement of the accuracy of interfaces by exploiting more precisely the synchronizations between processes. For this reason, we qualify as *refined* the interfaces generated using this technique.

As regards practical aspects, we implemented refined interface generation in the EXP.OPEN 2.0 tool for on-the-fly verification of networks of LTSs [27] of CADP. Interfaces can be generated automatically from systems made of LTSs composed using operators taken from several languages (CCS [29], CSP [4], $\mu$CRL [21], LOTOS [22], the E-LOTOS international standard [24], and general concurrent specification formalisms). In the framework of LOTOS specifications, the SVL scripting language was also extended to facilitate the combined use of the various CADP tools involved to use refined interfaces in a compositional verification task. For behavioural restriction, we rely on PROJECTOR and its semicomposition operator, which is general enough to be applicable in the framework of the above concurrent languages, although originally designed for LOTOS.

Using a flat intermediate concurrent model such as networks of LTSs is not new, as most model-checkers start by flattening the process hierarchy, for instance generating an intermediate Petri net [14] in the case of LOTOS, *Linear Process Equations* in the case of $\mu$CRL [20], or using a *supercombinator*-based compilation mechanism called *supercompilation* [17] in the case of CSP. The model we use in this paper is close to MEC *synchronization vectors* [1] and FC2 *synchronization networks* [3]. The originality of our work resides in both the treatment we make on the intermediate model to generate interfaces, and the effective use of this model to handle many different operators in a compositional verification setting.

This paper focuses on communication by *rendez-vous* between processes which run asynchronously (i.e., at independent speeds). It naturally generalizes to communication through bounded buffers if buffers are represented as finite processes communicating by *rendez-vous* with the rest of the system[2]. The current approach can be used to constrain such buffers in the same way as any process. Approaches to constrain processes communicating through buffers that are not bounded *a priori* (i.e., the bound of each buffer, if any, is not known statically but determined at execution time) have been proposed [25] but are out of the scope of this paper.

The paper is organized as follows: Section 2 presents the technical background. Section 3 recalls semi-composition and discusses the limitations of existing interface generation methods. Section 4 defines refined interface generation, which

---

[2] See http://www.inrialpes.fr/vasy/cadp/case-studies which references more than 80 case studies in various application domains, many of which use bounded buffers.

improves over existing interface generation methods. Section 5 describes the implementation of refined interface generation in CADP. Section 6 presents some experimental results. Section 7 finally concludes.

## 2   Technical Background

**Definition 1 (Vectors).** A *vector* of *length* $n$ over a set $S$ is an element of $S^n$, written $t$ or $(t_1, \ldots, t_n)$. For $i \in 1..n$, $t[i]$ denotes the $i$th element $t_i$ of $t$, and $t[i \leftarrow t'_i]$ represents a copy of $t$ where $t[i]$ is replaced by $t'_i$. Given $t \in S$, we write $t^n$ the vector of length $n$ such that $(\forall i \in 1..n)\ t^n[i] = t$. Given $I \subseteq 1..n$, the *projection* $t_{\downarrow I}$ is defined by: $t_{\downarrow I} = (t[k_1], \ldots, t[k_m])$ where $\{k_i \mid i \in 1..m\} = I$ and $(\forall i < j)\ k_i < k_j$.

**Definition 2 (Labelled Transition System).** Let $\mathcal{A}$ be a set of symbols called *observable actions*, and $\tau \notin \mathcal{A}$ the *unobservable action*. Given $A \subseteq \mathcal{A}$, we write $A_\tau$ the set $A \cup \{\tau\}$. An LTS is a quadruple $S = (Q, A, T, q_0)$, where $Q$ is the set of *states*, $A \subseteq \mathcal{A}$ — also written $act(S)$ — is the set of *observable actions*, $T \subseteq Q \times A_\tau \times Q$ is the *transition relation*, and $q_0 \in Q$ is the *initial state*. As usual, we may write $q_1 \xrightarrow{a}_T q_2$ (or $q_1 \xrightarrow{a} q_2$ when $T$ is clear from the context) instead of $(q_1, a, q_2) \in T$. A *trace* of $S$ is a sequence of actions $a_1 \ldots a_{n \geq 0} \in (A_\tau)^n$, such that $(\exists q_1, \ldots, q_n \in Q)\ (\forall i \in 0..n-1)\ q_i \xrightarrow{a_{i+1}}_T q_{i+1}$ (note that the sequence starts in the initial state $q_0$ of $S$). An *observable trace* is a trace in which all occurrences of $\tau$ have been removed. We write $\mathcal{L}(S)$ the set of observable traces of $S$. An action $a \in A$ is *reachable* if there is a trace containing $a$. A state $q \in Q$ is *reachable* if there exists a trace such that $q_n = q$. A transition $(q_1, a, q_2) \in T$ is *reachable* if $q_1$ is reachable. Two LTSs $S_1, S_2$ are *equal*, written $S_1 = S_2$, if and only if they have the same initial states and reachable transitions.

## 3   Semi-composition

Semi-composition [26] (implemented in the PROJECTOR tool of CADP) permits restriction of the behaviour of a process *on-the-fly* by taking into account interface constraints, usually derived from its environment. Since semi-composition was designed in the framework of LOTOS, its definition is tightly related to the following LOTOS-like parallel composition and hiding operators.

**Definition 3 (Parallel Composition, Hiding).** Let $S_i = (Q_i, A_i, T_i, q_{0i})$ $(i = 1, 2)$ be two LTSs, and $A \subseteq \mathcal{A}$. The *parallel composition* "$S_1 \parallel_A S_2$" models the concurrent execution of $S_1$ and $S_2$ with forced synchronization on $A$. It is defined as the LTS $(Q, A_1 \cup A_2, T, (q_{01}, q_{02}))$, where $Q$ and $T$ are the smallest sets satisfying both $(q_{01}, q_{02}) \in Q$ and the following properties:

$$\frac{(q_1, q_2) \in Q,\ q_1 \xrightarrow{a}_{T_1} q'_1,\ q_2 \xrightarrow{a}_{T_2} q'_2,\ a \in A}{(q'_1, q'_2) \in Q,\ (q_1, q_2) \xrightarrow{a}_T (q'_1, q'_2)}$$

$$\frac{(q_1, q_2) \in Q,\ q_1 \xrightarrow{a}_{T_1} q'_1,\ a \notin A}{(q'_1, q_2) \in Q,\ (q_1, q_2) \xrightarrow{a}_T (q'_1, q_2)} \qquad \frac{(q_1, q_2) \in Q,\ q_2 \xrightarrow{a}_{T_1} q'_2,\ a \notin A}{(q_1, q'_2) \in Q,\ (q_1, q_2) \xrightarrow{a}_T (q_1, q'_2)}$$

Note that, by construction, the states belonging to $Q$ are reachable. A state $p$ of $S_1$ (respectively $S_2$) is said *reachable* in $S_1 \parallel_A S_2$ if there is a state $(p, q)$ (resp. $(q, p)$) in $S_1 \parallel_A S_2$. Similarly, a transition $p \xrightarrow{a} p'$ of $S_1$ (respectively $S_2$) is said *reachable* in $S_1 \parallel_A S_2$ if there is a transition $(p, q) \xrightarrow{a} (p', q')$ (resp. $(q, p) \xrightarrow{a} (q', p')$) in $S_1 \parallel_A S_2$. The expression "hide $A$ in $S_1$" denotes the LTS $(Q_1, A_1 \setminus A, T_1', q_{01})$, where $T_1'$ is defined as follows:

$$\frac{q \xrightarrow{a}_{T_1} q', \; a \in A}{q \xrightarrow{\tau}_{T_1'} q'} \qquad \frac{q \xrightarrow{a}_{T_1} q', \; a \notin A}{q \xrightarrow{a}_{T_1'} q'}$$

Semi-composition takes as input two LTSs $S_1$, $S_2$ and a set of actions $A$, and returns the LTS which contains exactly the states and transitions of $S_1$ that are reachable in $S_1 \parallel_A S_2$.

**Definition 4 (Semi-Composition).** Let $S_i = (Q_i, A_i, T_i, q_{0i})$ $(i = 1, 2)$ be two LTSs, $A \subseteq \mathcal{A}$, and $(Q', A', T', q_0') = S_1 \parallel_A S_2$. The *semi-composition of $S_1$ and $S_2$*, written "$S_1 \parallel\!\!\!|_A S_2$", is the LTS $(Q, A_1, T, q_{01})$, where $Q = \{p \mid (p, q) \in Q'\}$ and $T = T_1 \cap \{(p_1, a, p_2) \mid (p_1, q_1) \xrightarrow{a}_{T'} (p_2, q_2)\}$. $A$ is called the *synchronization set* and the pair $(A, S_2)$ is called the *interface*[3]. We say that an action $a \in A_1$ is *controlled* by the interface $(A, S_2)$ if $a \in A$.

*Example 1.* The following holds:

State $q_3$ and transitions $q_2 \xrightarrow{d} q_2, q_2 \xrightarrow{a} q_3$, and $q_3 \xrightarrow{c} q_2$ do not belong to $S_3$ because they are not reachable in $S_1 \parallel_{\{a,c,d\}} S_2$.

Three properties of semi-composition are essential to ensure its practicability:

- Semi-composition is a state space reduction, since the sets of states and transitions of $S_1 \parallel\!\!\!|_A S_2$ are by definition subsets of $S_1$. The worst case is when $\mathcal{L}(\text{hide } (\mathcal{A} \setminus A) \text{ in } S_1) \subseteq \mathcal{L}(\text{hide } (\mathcal{A} \setminus A) \text{ in } S_2)$, yielding $S_1 \parallel\!\!\!|_A S_2 = S_1$.
- $(S_1 \parallel\!\!\!|_A S_2) \parallel_A S_2 = S_1 \parallel_A S_2$. Therefore semi-composition can be used to reduce $S_1$ given its environment $S_2$ by removing the unreachable states and transitions, without losing any temporal property of the system $S_1 \parallel_A S_2$. Note that, unlike Cheung & Kramer's approach, which requires that the interface be context transparent — and thus be transformed into a deterministic LTS using a well-known but expensive algorithm — no restriction is made here on the shape of $S_2$.

---

[3] This definition of semi-composition is simpler but equivalent to that given in [26].

- $S_1 \parallel_A S_2 = S_1 \parallel_A S_2'$ if $\mathcal{L}(\text{hide } (\mathcal{A} \setminus A) \text{ in } S_2) = \mathcal{L}(\text{hide } (\mathcal{A} \setminus A) \text{ in } S_2')$. Therefore, reductions of the interface can be achieved by first hiding uncontrolled actions and then minimizing the LTS modulo a relation preserving observable traces (e.g., *safety equivalence* [2]), which permits reduction of the number of states to explore while calculating semi-composition. Safety minimization is less expensive than determinization and, unlike determinization which can induce a dramatic growth of the LTS, yields an LTS that contains fewer states than the input. Minimization of the interface is not mandatory but important to reduce the cost of semi-composition, the complexity of which is the same as parallel composition, hence sensitive to the size of its operands.

In practice, the equation $S_1 \parallel_A S_2 = (S_1 \parallel_A S_2) \parallel_A S_2$ is not sufficient to compute interfaces in the case of systems consisting of more than two LTSs: it may happen that $S_2$ does not constrain $S_1$ but that a more distant LTS in the environment of $S_1$ does. Krimm & Mounier proposed a method to compute an exact interface in the framework of more general systems of communicating LTSs built upon parallel composition and action hiding. Given two LTSs $S_1$ and $S_2$ in such a system, this method permits to synthesize a synchronization set $A$ such that $S_1$ can be replaced by $S_1 \parallel_A S_2$ without changing the global LTS of the system. It is defined inductively, based on the following semi-composition laws:

$$S_1 \parallel_A S_2 = (S_1 \parallel_A S_2) \parallel_A S_2 \qquad (1)$$

$$(S_1 \parallel_{A_1} S_3) \parallel_{A_2} S_2 = ((S_1 \parallel_B S_2) \parallel_{A_1} S_3) \parallel_{A_2} S_2 \qquad (2)$$
$$\text{where } B = A_2 \cap (A_1 \cup (act(S_1) \setminus act(S_3)))$$

$$(\text{hide } A_1 \text{ in } S_1) \parallel_{A_2} S_2 = (\text{hide } A_1 \text{ in } (S_1 \parallel_{A_2 \setminus A_1} S_2)) \parallel_{A_2} S_2 \qquad (3)$$

Unfortunately, the interface $(A, S_2)$ built using Krimm & Mounier's method generally does not give the best account of environment constraints, as illustrated by the following two examples.

*Example 2.* Let $E = S_1 \parallel_{\{a,b,d\}} (S_2 \parallel_{\{c,d\}} S_3)$ with $S_1, S_2$, and $S_3$ as follows:

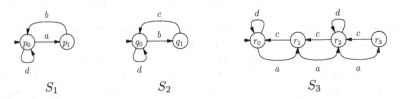

According to the semi-composition laws, $S_3$ can be replaced in $E$ either by $S_3 \parallel_{\{a,d\}} S_1$, or by $S_3 \parallel_{\{c,d\}} S_2$, but both expressions result in $S_3$ itself. Yet, one can see that actions $a$ and $c$ are executed with some alternation in $E$, due to the mandatory synchronization on $b$ between $S_1$ and $S_2$. As a consequence, state $r_3$ is not reachable in $E$. To capture such a constraint, it should be possible to build an interface that takes simultaneously into account the constraints induced by both $S_1$ and $S_2$, even though there is no sub-expression of $E$ containing $S_1$ and $S_2$ only. This is not possible with Krimm & Mounier's method[4].

*Example 3.* Let $E = S_1 \parallel_{\{a,b\}} (S_2 \parallel_{\{a\}} S_3)$ with $S_1, S_2$, and $S_3$ as follows:

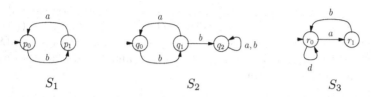

$$S_1 \qquad\qquad S_2 \qquad\qquad S_3$$

According to the semi-composition laws, $S_2$ can be replaced by $S_2 \parallel_{\{a\}} S_1$, but this expression yields $S_2$ itself. Yet, it is clear from $S_1$ and the synchronizations in $E$ that state $q_2$ of $S_2$ is unreachable in $E$, as two successive $b$ actions cannot be fired without an $a$ in between. A better interface should permit to take into account the environment constraints due to synchronizations on $b$, even though every $b$ of $S_1$ does not necessarily synchronize with a $b$ of $S_2$. Unfortunately, this is not possible using the Krimm & Mounier's method[5].

In the sequel, we propose to generate interface constraints automatically in a way that palliates these limitations.

## 4   Refined Interface Generation

*Refined interface generation* is a new method that permits the computation of an interface capturing the constraints imposed on a given process $P$ in a concurrent system by one or several processes of its environment. This interface can then be semi-composed with $P$ on-the-fly, so as to restrict $P$'s behaviour.

As regards the model of concurrency on which we establish our results, we use the following network model named "*network of* LTSs", in which the composition hierarchy is completely flattened. The network of LTSs model is more general than the parallel composition operator defined in the previous section, and the parallel composition, renaming, hiding and cutting operators from many process algebras can be translated into networks of LTSs [27]. Networks of LTSs thus make our work non-specific to a particular process algebra and permit an easier way of reasoning about the synchronization structure of systems.

**Definition 5 (Network of LTSs).** Let $\bullet \notin \mathcal{A}_\tau$ be a special symbol denoting that a particular LTS has no role in a given synchronization. A *synchronization rule* is a pair $(t, a)$, where $t$ is a vector over $\mathcal{A}_\tau \cup \{\bullet\}$ (called a *synchronization vector*) and $a \in \mathcal{A}_\tau$. The components $t$ and $a$ are called respectively the left- and

---

[4] This limitation holds similarly for Cheung & Kramer's method, as mentioned in [7].

[5] Cheung & Kramer do not provide a solution to this issue as their method relies on a CSP-like parallel composition operator whose semantics states that synchronization on $b$ is mandatory between all processes containing $b$ in their action set.

right-hand sides of the synchronization rule. A *network of* LTSs (or simply *network*) $N$ of *dimension* $n > 0$ is a pair $(\boldsymbol{S}, V)$ where $\boldsymbol{S}$ is a vector of LTSs of length $n$ and $V$ is a set of synchronization rules, whose left-hand sides are all of length $n$. Each left-hand side $\boldsymbol{t}$ expresses a synchronization constraint on $\boldsymbol{S}$, all components $\boldsymbol{S}[i]$ where $\boldsymbol{t}[i] \neq \bullet$ having to take a transition labeled respectively $\boldsymbol{t}[i]$ altogether so that a transition labeled with the corresponding right-hand side $a$ be generated in the product. More formally, let $\boldsymbol{S}[i] = (Q_i, A_i, T_i, q_{0i})$ $(i \in 1..n)$. To $N = (\boldsymbol{S}, V)$ corresponds an LTS $(Q, A, T, \boldsymbol{q_0})$, written $sem(N)$ or $sem(\boldsymbol{S}, V)$, such that $A = \{a \mid (\boldsymbol{t}, a) \in V\}$, $\boldsymbol{q_0} = (q_{01}, \ldots, q_{0n})$, and $Q$ and $T$ are the smallest sets satisfying both $\boldsymbol{q_0} \in Q$ and:

$$\frac{\boldsymbol{q} \in Q, \ (\boldsymbol{t}, a) \in V, \ (\forall i \in 1..n) \ (\boldsymbol{t}[i] = \bullet \wedge \boldsymbol{q'}[i] = \boldsymbol{q}[i]) \vee \boldsymbol{q}[i] \xrightarrow{\boldsymbol{t}[i]}_{T_i} \boldsymbol{q'}[i]}{\boldsymbol{q'} \in Q, \ (\boldsymbol{q}, a, \boldsymbol{q'}) \in T}$$

Note that, by construction, the states that belong to $Q$ are reachable. Synchronization rules must obey the following *admissibility* properties, which forbid cutting, synchronizations and renaming of $\tau$ transitions and therefore ensure that safety equivalence and stronger relations (e.g., observational, branching, and strong equivalences) are congruences for networks of LTS [27]:

$$((\exists i \in 1..n) \ \tau \text{ is reachable in } \boldsymbol{S}[i]) \implies (\exists (\boldsymbol{t}, \tau) \in V) \ \boldsymbol{t}[i] = \tau$$
$$(\forall (\boldsymbol{t}, a) \in V) \ ((\exists i \in 1..n) \ \boldsymbol{t}[i] = \tau) \implies (a = \tau \wedge (\forall j \in 1..n \setminus \{i\}) \ \boldsymbol{t}[j] = \bullet)$$

*Example 4.* Systems of communicating LTSs built upon various operators can be translated into networks of LTSs. As an example, given $S_1$ and $S_2$, the parallel composition $(S_1 \parallel_A S_2)$ can be translated into $((S_1, S_2), V_{sync} \cup V_{async})$, where:

$$V_{sync} = \{((a, a), a) \mid a \in act(S_1) \cap act(S_2) \cap A\}$$
$$V_{async} = \{((a, \bullet), a) \mid a \in act(S_1)_\tau \setminus A\} \cup \{((\bullet, a), a) \mid a \in act(S_2)_\tau \setminus A\}$$

Given a network $N = (\boldsymbol{S}, V)$ and an LTS $\boldsymbol{S}[k]$ in this network, we address the problem of computing automatically an interface of the form $(\mathcal{A}, C)$ that will permit reduction of $\boldsymbol{S}[k]$ by taking into account its interactions with a subset $\{\boldsymbol{S}[i] \mid i \in I\}$ $(k \notin I)$ of LTSs in its environment. The goal is to permit the replacement of LTS $\boldsymbol{S}[k]$ by LTS $\boldsymbol{S}[k] \parallel_{\mathcal{A}} C$ in $N$ without affecting the LTS of the global system. To this aim, we define the following refined interface generation procedure, whose inputs are $N$, $k$, and $I$. The refined interface generated consists of a product of the LTSs $\boldsymbol{S}[i]$ $(i \in I)$, synchronized by synchronization rules derived systematically from the synchronization rules of $N$, each rule $(\boldsymbol{t}, a)$ being transformed into a rule $(\boldsymbol{t}_{\downarrow I}, \boldsymbol{t}[k])$ if $\boldsymbol{t}[k] \neq \bullet$, or $(\boldsymbol{t}_{\downarrow I}, \tau)$ otherwise. Therefore, whenever a transition $q \xrightarrow{a} q'$ can be fired in $sem(N)$ using a synchronization rule $(\boldsymbol{t}, a)$ with $\boldsymbol{t}[k] \neq \bullet$, then the participating transition $q[k] \xrightarrow{\boldsymbol{t}[k]} q'[k]$ of $\boldsymbol{S}[k]$ is also a transition of $\boldsymbol{S}[k] \parallel_{\mathcal{A}} C$. Conversely, transitions of $\boldsymbol{S}[k]$ that cannot participate in any mandatory synchronization with $C$ (i.e., the $\boldsymbol{S}[i]$'s) are eliminated by the semi-composition $\boldsymbol{S}[k] \parallel_{\mathcal{A}} C$.

**Definition 6 (Refined Interface Generation).** Let $\varphi : A_\tau \cup \{\bullet\} \to A_\tau$, defined by $\varphi(\bullet) = \tau$ and $(\forall a \in A_\tau) \ \varphi(a) = a$. Let $N = (\boldsymbol{S}, V)$ be a network of dimension $n$, $I$ a set of indices such that $\emptyset \subset I \subset 1..n$, and $k$ an index such that $k \in 1..n \setminus I$. The *refined interface* of $S[k]$ capturing constraints induced by $\{S[i] \mid i \in I\}$, written $refint(N, k, I)$, is the interface $(\mathcal{A}, sem(S_{\downarrow I}, V'))$, where $V' = \{(t_{\downarrow I}, \varphi(t[k])) \mid (t, a) \in V\}$.

*Example 5.* Consider the network $N$ displayed on the left below, with arbitrary LTss $S_1, \ldots, S_4$. The refined interface of $S_1$ capturing constraints induced by $S_3$ and $S_4$, written $refint(N, 1, \{3, 4\})$, is the LTS corresponding to the network displayed on the right below. Note the projection on $S_3$ and $S_4$, and observe that the right-hand sides of synchronization rules in the result are the elements of column $S_1$, where $\bullet$ is renamed into $\tau$.

$$refint\left(\left(\begin{pmatrix} (S_1, S_2, S_3, S_4), \\ \left\{ \begin{array}{l} ((a_1, a_2, a_3, a_4),\ a), \\ ((\ \bullet,\ b_2, b_3,\ \bullet),\ b), \\ ((\ c_1,\ c_2,\ \bullet,\ \bullet),\ c) \end{array} \right\} \end{pmatrix}\right), 1, \{3, 4\}\right) = sem\left(\begin{pmatrix} (S_3, S_4), \\ \left\{ \begin{array}{l} ((a_3, a_4),\ a_1), \\ ((\ b_3,\ \bullet),\ \tau), \\ ((\ \bullet,\ \bullet),\ c_1) \end{array} \right\} \end{pmatrix}\right)$$

The following theorem states that, in an arbitrary network $N$, any interface $refint(N, k, I)$ can be used to restrict $S[k]$ using semi-composition because the LTS of $N$ and the LTS of $N$ in which $S[k]$ is replaced by its restriction are equal.

**Theorem 1.** *Let $N = (S, V)$ be a network of dimension $n$, $I$ such that $\emptyset \subset I \subset 1..n$, $k \in 1..n \setminus I$, and $(A, C) = refint(N, k, I)$. If $S' = S\big[k \leftarrow (S[k] \,\|_A\, C)\big]$ then $sem(S, V) = sem(S', V)$.*

*Proof.* Since $S[k] \,\|_A\, C$ is a sub-LTS of $S[k]$ by definition of semi-composition, it follows that $sem(S', V)$ is a sub-LTS of $sem(S, V)$. We show that, conversely, $sem(S, V)$ is a sub-LTS of $sem(S', V)$. To this aim, we consider an arbitrary state $q$ reachable in $sem(S, V)$. In a first step we assume that $q_{\downarrow I}$ is reachable in $C$, $(q[k], q_{\downarrow I})$ is reachable in $S[k] \,\|_A\, C$, $q[k]$ is reachable in $S'[k]$, $q$ is reachable in $sem(S', V)$ and given a transition $q \xrightarrow{a} q'$ of $sem(S, V)$ induced by a vector $(t, a)$, we show simultaneously that (1) $q'_{\downarrow I}$ is reachable in $C$, (2) $(q'[k], q'_{\downarrow I})$ is reachable in $S[k] \,\|_A\, C$, which implies that $q'[k]$ is reachable in $S'[k]$, and (3) $q \xrightarrow{a} q'$ is a transition of $sem(S', V)$, which implies that $q'$ is reachable in $sem(S', V)$. We consider two cases:

- If $t[k] = \bullet$ then by definition $q[k] = q'[k]$ and property (3) is obvious. In addition, by definition of *refint*, the transition $q_{\downarrow I} \xrightarrow{\tau} q'_{\downarrow I}$ belongs to $C$, which implies properties (1) and (2).

- If $t[k] \neq \bullet$ then by hypothesis $q[k] \xrightarrow{t[k]} q'[k]$ belongs to $S[k]$ and $q_{\downarrow I} \xrightarrow{t[k]} q'_{\downarrow I}$ belongs to $C$ by definition of *refint*, which implies property (1). Therefore, $(q[k], q_{\downarrow I}) \xrightarrow{t[k]} (q'[k], q'_{\downarrow I})$ belongs to $S[k] \,\|_A\, C$, which implies property (2). By definition of semi-composition, $q[k] \xrightarrow{t[k]} q'[k]$ belongs to $S'[k]$, which implies property (3).

In a second step, given $q_0$ the initial state of $sem(S, V)$, we observe that $q_{0\downarrow I}$, $(q_0[k], q_{0\downarrow I})$, $q_0[k]$, and $q_0$ are the initial states of, respectively, C, $S[k] \,\|_A\, C$,

$S'[k]$, and $sem(S',V)$. Given a state $q$ reachable in $sem(S,V)$, an induction using properties (1), (2), and (3) shows that $q_{\downarrow I}$, $(q[k],q_{\downarrow I})$, $q[k]$, and $q$ are reachable in, respectively, $C$, $S[k] \parallel_{\mathcal{A}} C$, $S'[k]$, and $sem(S',V)$. Therefore, every transition of $sem(S,V)$ is also a transition of $sem(S',V)$, which implies that $sem(S,V)$ and $sem(S',V)$ are equal.                      □

The following examples show that refined interfaces solve the issues raised in Examples 2 and 3 of Section 3.

*Example 6 (back to Example 2 page 164).* Expression $E = S_1 \parallel_{\{a,b,d\}} (S_2 \parallel_{\{c,d\}} S_3)$ defined in Example 2 can be translated into the network $N$ displayed below. $S_3$ may be restricted using a refined interface $(\mathcal{A}, sem(N')) = refint(N,3,\{1,2\})$ that takes simultaneously both $S_1$ and $S_2$ into account, where $N'$ and $sem(N')$ are displayed below. $S_3 \parallel_{\mathcal{A}} sem(N')$, also displayed below, reduces $S_3$ by eliminating the unreachable state $r_3$ and transitions $r_2 \xrightarrow{a} r_3, r_3 \xrightarrow{c} r_2$, and $r_2 \xrightarrow{d} r_2$.

$$N = \left( \begin{array}{c} (S_1, S_2, S_3), \\ \left\{ \begin{array}{c} ((\ a, \ \bullet, \ a), a), \\ ((\ b, \ b, \ \bullet), b), \\ ((\ \bullet, \ c, \ c), c), \\ ((\ d, \ d, \ d), d) \end{array} \right\} \end{array} \right) \qquad N' = \left( \begin{array}{c} (S_1, S_2), \\ \left\{ \begin{array}{c} ((\ a, \ \bullet), a), \\ ((\ b, \ b), \tau), \\ ((\ \bullet, \ c), c), \\ ((\ d, \ d), d) \end{array} \right\} \end{array} \right)$$

sem(N')

$S_3 \parallel_{\mathcal{A}} sem(N')$

*Example 7 (back to Example 3 page 165).* Expression $E = S_1 \parallel_{\{a,b\}} (S_2 \parallel_{\{a\}} S_3)$ defined in Example 3 can be translated into the network $N$ displayed below. $S_2$ may be restricted using a refined interface $(\mathcal{A}, sem(N')) = refint(N,2,\{1\})$ that takes $S_1$ into account, where $N'$ and $sem(N')$ are displayed below. In practice, $sem(N')$ can be minimized modulo safety equivalence, yielding an LTS with 2 states and 3 transitions. $S_2 \parallel_{\mathcal{A}} sem(N')$ is isomorphic to $S_1$.

$$N = \left( \begin{array}{c} (S_1, S_2, S_3), \\ \left\{ \begin{array}{c} ((\ a, \ a, \ a), a), \\ ((\ b, \ b, \ \bullet), b), \\ ((\ b, \ \bullet, \ b), b), \\ ((\ \bullet, \ \bullet, \ d), d) \end{array} \right\} \end{array} \right) \qquad N' = \left( \begin{array}{c} (S_1), \\ \left\{ \begin{array}{c} ((\ a\ ), a), \\ ((\ b\ ), b), \\ ((\ b\ ), \tau), \\ ((\ \bullet\ ), \tau) \end{array} \right\} \end{array} \right)$$

sem(N')

This example shows that without using more LTSs from the environment of $S_2$ than in Example 3, but simply by taking a better account of the synchronization structure of the system, the *refint* operation permits refinement of the interface with respect to that obtained using equation (2), turning the set of observable traces of the interface from $a^*$ with $b$ uncontrolled in Example 3 to $a^* + b + (ba^+)^*$ in the current example. The latter set of traces does not contain any trace with two consecutive $b$'s, thus disabling the transition $q_1 \xrightarrow{b} q_2$ in $S_2$ and making state $q_2$ and transitions $q_2 \xrightarrow{a} q_2$, $q_2 \xrightarrow{b} q_2$ also unreachable.

The *refint* operation may create synchronization rules of the form $(\bullet^n, a)$, which induce a self-looping transition labelled $a$ in each state of the interface (see for instance the last synchronization rule of the right-hand side network in Example 5 and the last synchronization rule of network $N'$ in Example 7, which induces the $\tau$-loops in states $p_0$ and $p_1$). Some of these synchronization rules can be eliminated as follows:

- Every synchronization rule of the form $(\bullet^n, \tau)$ can merely be removed. Indeed, for all $S$ and $V$, $\mathcal{L}(sem(S, V \cup (\bullet^n, \tau))) = \mathcal{L}(sem(S, V))$.
- Every synchronization rule of the form $(\bullet^n, a)$ where $a \neq \tau$ can be removed if the set of synchronization rules does not contain another rule with the same action $a$ as right-hand side. Indeed, for all $S$, $S'$, $A$, and $V$ in which $a$ does not occur as a right-hand side, $S' \parallel_A sem(S, V \cup (\bullet^n, a)) = S' \parallel_{A \setminus a} sem(S, V)$. Eliminating this rule transforms the synchronization set of the interface from $A$ into $A \setminus a$.

Algorithmically, refined interface generation has the same complexity as the synchronization product of the LTSs taken into account in the environment. In practice, the cost of computing the interface can be reduced by minimizing the individual LTSs participating in the interface modulo safety equivalence, which is correct due to the above mentioned congruence property of safety equivalence. In addition, well-known partial order reductions preserving observable traces can be used to further reduce interfaces on-the-fly during their construction.

So far, refined interface generation required that each (high-level) process of the concurrent system under verification was replaced by its LTS, which apparently contradicts the claim that refined interfaces can be used to restrict processes on-the-fly. However, it is clear from Definition 6 that the states and transitions of LTS $S[k]$ (corresponding to the process to restrict) are not needed for interface generation. In practice, only the observable actions of $S[k]$ are needed to compute the synchronization rules of the network from higher level operators as in Example 4. To do so, $S[k]$ can be replaced by an abstraction consisting of an arbitrary (and much smaller) LTS containing the same set of actions. In fact, the method remains correct if the abstraction contains a superset of $S[k]$'s actions, although the reduction obtained on $S[k]$ by semi-composition generally increases while the set of actions of the abstraction gets closer to the exact set of actions of $S[k]$.

In practice, users must provide such an abstraction "by hand", which is not hard as it suffices to examine the gates (or channels) occurring in the process specification and the types of their data, and to enumerate actions of this type appropriately. If the abstraction provided by the user lacks some action of $S[k]$, then the generated interface might be wrong, but this is detected automatically during the compositional verification task as explained in [26]. Calculating this abstraction automatically from source code or from an internal representation of processes would not present any difficulty.

# 5   Implementation in the CADP Toolbox

Our method was implemented in CADP (*Construction and Analysis of Distributed Processes*) [13], a popular toolbox for protocol engineering. Refined interface generation is implemented as an option (**-interface**) of the EXP.OPEN 2.0 tool [27] for on-the-fly verification of products of communicating LTSs, which can be combined using the following operators:

- standard parallel composition, action cutting, action hiding, and action renaming from CCS, CSP, LOTOS, and $\mu$CRL;
- networks of LTSs and generalized parallel composition from E-LOTOS, which includes $n$-ary parallel composition, "$n$ among $m$" parallel composition, and parallel composition with synchronization interfaces [15];
- generalized forms of action hiding, action renaming, and transition cutting, where actions can be defined using regular expressions.

EXP.OPEN 2.0 also implements several partial order reductions, one of which can be used to partially reduce the interface on-the-fly while preserving its observable traces (**-weaktrace** option).

To simplify the use of refined interfaces in the more specific framework of LOTOS descriptions, we have also extended the SVL scripting language [12] with a new operator, named "**refined abstraction**", which can be used in the context of any parallel composition expression. As an example, given a LOTOS file `"file.lotos"` defining the system "(P | [A, C] | Q) | [A, B] | R", where P, Q, and R are LOTOS processes, one may write the following SVL script:

```
% DEFAULT_LOTOS_FILE="file.lotos"
"file.bcg" = root leaf strong reduction of
((refined abstraction Q, R using "act.bcg" of P) |[A, C]| Q) |[A, B]| R
```

This script computes the LTS corresponding to the system by first restricting P on-the-fly w.r.t. the constraints induced by Q and R, using the LTS `"act.bcg"` as the abstraction of P. To this aim, Q and R are first minimized modulo safety equivalence and an interface generated automatically using EXP.OPEN 2.0. Once the LTSs corresponding to processes P (restricted using the refined interface), Q, and R have been generated, the "`root leaf strong reduction`" operation minimizes them modulo strong bisimulation, and then minimizes their product once they have been composed in parallel. The result is stored in `"file.bcg"`.

# 6   Applications

We applied refined interfaces to three case studies. The first one is a LOTOS description written by J. Romijn [30] of the HAVi (*Home Audio-Video*) asynchronous leader election protocol[6], which consists of seven concurrent processes named BUSRESET, DCM1, DCM2, CMM1, CMM2, MS1, and MS2. Given a LOTOS process ABS_DCM1 containing the actions of DCM1, we made the following experiments:

---

[6] See `ftp://ftp.inrialpes.fr/pub/vasy/demos/demo_27`

| Exp. | Interface | | | | DCM1 | | Total time | Max memory |
| | generated | | minimized (safety) | | generated | | | |
| | states | trans. | states | trans. | states | trans. | | |
|---|---|---|---|---|---|---|---|---|
| E1 | 0 | 0 | 0 | 0 | **404,477** | **3,025,842** | 99.9 s | 54 Mb |
| E2 | 3,904 | 42,697 | 3 | 37 | **365,923** | **2,514,848** | 182.1 s | 46 Mb |
| E3 | 704 | 7,145 | 4 | 45 | **17,199** | **73,130** | 12.1 s | 5.9 Mb |
| E4 | 2,328 | 14,158 | 52 | 613 | **645** | **2,020** | 10.7 s | 8.5 Mb |

**Fig. 1.** LTS sizes, computation time and memory consumption for experiments E1-E4

E1 Generation of DCM1 without interface.

E2 Generation of DCM1 using an interface consisting of the LTS of the sub-system including CMM1, CMM2, MS1, and MS2, and of a synchronization set computed as defined by Krimm & Mounier's semi-composition laws.

E3 Generation of DCM1 using a refined interface capturing the constraints induced by CMM1, CMM2, MS1, and MS2.

E4 Same as E3, capturing also the constraints induced by BUSRESET and DCM2.

The table in Figure 1 shows for each experiment E1 to E4 the size of the interface before and after safety minimization, the size of DCM1 restricted by the interface (if any), the total computation time, and the peak memory consumption. It shows that refined interfaces permit state space reductions by more than two orders of magnitude (from $404,477$ states reachable in a general environment down to 645 states reachable in an environment that takes an account of all processes — experiment E4), while globally reducing verification time by a factor of almost 10 and peak memory consumption by a factor of up to 9.

Experiments E2 and E3 take an account of the same processes to restrict DCM1, the difference being that E2 uses Krimm & Mounier's method and E3 the *refint* operation to compute the interface. Figure 1 thus shows that *refint* yields an LTS with more than 20 times fewer states and 35 times fewer transitions than Krimm & Mounier's method, while the execution time and peak memory consumption are reduced by factors of 15 and 8 respectively. Note that Krimm & Mounier's method does not permit the computation of an interface that takes an account of all processes in a way analogous to E4, because the processes in the environment of DCM1 belong to different sub-expressions.

Second, we considered an ODP (*Open Distributed Processing*) trader [23], an E-LOTOS model of which was presented in [15][7]. An ODP trader is an agent that registers services that can be provided by distant servers, receives service requests from distant clients, and provides to the requesting clients the address of a server that can furnish the requested service. The client and server are then able to exchange the service directly without communicating with the trader anymore. Note that the trader is a central component in the ODP model in the sense that the ability of two agents to communicate is initiated by the trader. Such central components generally have large state spaces, especially in compositional verification settings where their LTS have to be generated outside of any context.

---

[7] See ftp://ftp.inrialpes.fr/pub/vasy/demos/demo_37

In our experiment, the components (trader, clients and services) are described in LOTOS and the synchronization structure describing their interactions in EXP.OPEN 2.0 using the "*n* among *m*" E-LOTOS parallel composition operator to model the dynamicity of object exchanges. In this example, the ODP trader executes in an environment consisting of 4 objects and 5 services. A refined interface is generated automatically from this environment to restrict the LTS corresponding to the trader, which is thus limited to 256 states instead of 1 million otherwise.

At last, we studied a standard cache coherency protocol for multiprocessor architectures, which consists of a remote directory process and several agent processes accessing the directory concurrently[8]. In a configuration with 5 agents, refined interface generation has allowed us to reduce the size of the LTS corresponding to the remote directory from 1 million states and 40 million transitions downto less than 60 states. This method has allowed us to generate easily the LTS corresponding to larger configurations, which could not be generated using other methods.

# 7   Conclusion

Compositional verification in which the behaviours of concurrent processes are restricted using interface constraints is an effective method to avoid the state explosion that may occur when the state space of a process is generated out of its environment. This paper alleviates the lack of efficient methods to synthesize constraints automatically, by proposing a method based on the analysis of the synchronizations between concurrent processes.

Compared to prior work [7,9,26,6], our method performs a finer analysis of synchronization constraints: our implementation in the EXP.OPEN 2.0 tool of CADP exhibits more than two orders of magnitude better state space reductions on an industrial case study studied by Romijn [30]. Moreover, it provides a systematic way of using the semi-composition operator of Krimm & Mounier [26] (which is implemented in the PROJECTOR tool of CADP) in the framework of languages whose composition operators are not limited to LOTOS parallel composition and hiding; indeed, both synchronization vectors and a large number of parallel composition operators are supported, including those of CCS, CSP, LOTOS, $\mu$CRL, and E-LOTOS. Alternatively, we believe that we can also use parallel composition instead of semi-composition as advocated by Cheung & Kramer [7,9,6]; indeed the interfaces generated for semi-composition can be transformed into "context-transparent" interfaces using the algorithm given in [7].

**Acknowledgements.** The author thanks the anonymous referees, and Hubert Garavel, Radu Mateescu, Gwen Salaün, and Wendelin Serwe from the VASY team at INRIA Rhône-Alpes for useful comments on this paper and on earlier versions of this paper.

---

[8] See ftp://ftp.inrialpes.fr/pub/vasy/demos/demo_28

# References

1. A. Arnold. MEC: A System for Constructing and Analysing Transition Systems. In *Proc. of the 1st Workshop on Automatic Verification Methods for Finite State Systems*, LNCS vol. 407, 1989.
2. A. Bouajjani, J.-C. Fernandez, S. Graf, C. Rodríguez, and J. Sifakis. Safety for Branching Time Semantics. In *Proc. of 18th ICALP*. 1991.
3. A. Bouali, A. Ressouche, V. Roy, and R. de Simone. The Fc2Tools set: a Toolset for the Verification of Concurrent Systems. In *Proc. of CAV'96*, LNCS vol. 1102, 1996.
4. S. D. Brookes, C. A. R. Hoare, and A. W. Roscoe. A Theory of Communicating Sequential Processes. *Journal of the ACM*, 31(3):560–599, 1984.
5. G. Chehaibar, H. Garavel, L. Mounier, N. Tawbi, and F. Zulian. Specification and Verification of the PowerScale Bus Arbitration Protocol: An Industrial Experiment with LOTOS. In *Proc. of FORTE/PSTV'96*. IFIP, Chapman & Hall, 1996. Full version available as INRIA Research Report RR-2958.
6. K. H. Cheung. *Compositional Analysis of Complex Distributed Systems*. PhD thesis, Hong Kong University of Science and Technology, 1998.
7. S. C. Cheung and J. Kramer. Enhancing Compositional Reachability Analysis with Context Constraints. In *Proc. of the 1st ACM SIGSOFT International Symposium on the Foundations of Software Engineering*. ACM Press, 1993.
8. S. C. Cheung and J. Kramer. Compositional Reachability Analysis of Finite-State Distributed Systems with User-Specified Constraints. In *Proc. of the 3rd ACM SIGSOFT International Symposium on the Foundations of Software Engineering*. ACM Press, 1995.
9. S. C. Cheung and J. Kramer. Context Constraints for Compositional Reachability. *ACM Transactions on Software Engineering Methodology*, 5(4):334–377, 1996.
10. J.-C. Fernandez. *ALDEBARAN : un système de vérification par réduction de processus communicants*. PhD thesis, Université Joseph Fourier (Grenoble), 1988.
11. J.-C. Fernandez, H. Garavel, L. Mounier, A. Rasse, C. Rodríguez, and J. Sifakis. A Toolbox for the Verification of LOTOS Programs. In *Proc. of ICSE*. ACM, 1992.
12. H. Garavel and F. Lang. SVL: a Scripting Language for Compositional Verification. In *Proc. of FORTE'2001*. IFIP, Kluwer Academic Publishers, 2001. Full version available as INRIA Research Report RR-4223.
13. H. Garavel, F. Lang, and R. Mateescu. An Overview of CADP 2001. *European Association for Software Science and Technology Newsletter*, 4:13–24, 2002. Also available as INRIA Technical Report RT-0254 (2001).
14. H. Garavel and J. Sifakis. Compilation and Verification of LOTOS Specifications. In *Proc. of PSTV'90*. IFIP, North-Holland, 1990.
15. H. Garavel and M. Sighireanu. A Graphical Parallel Composition Operator for Process Algebras. In *Proc. of FORTE/PSTV'99*. IFIP, Kluwer, 1999.
16. D. Giannakopoulou. *Model Checking for Concurrent Software Architectures*. PhD thesis, Imperial College, University of London, 1999.
17. M. Goldsmith. Operational Semantics for Fun and Profit. In *Proc. of the Symposium on the Occasion of 25 Years of CSP*, LNCS vol. 3525, 2005.
18. S. Graf, B. Steffen, and G. Lüttgen. Compositional Minimisation of Finite State Systems using Interface Specifications. *Formal Aspects of Computation*, 8(5):607–616, 1996.
19. S. Graf and B. Steffen. Compositional Minimization of Finite State Systems. In *Proc. of the 2nd Workshop on Computer-Aided Verification*, LNCS vol. 531, 1990.

20. J. F. Groote and M. Reniers. *Algebraic Process Verification*. In *Handbook of Process Algebra*, chapter 17. North-Holland, 2001.

21. J.F. Groote and A. Ponse. Syntax and semantics of $\mu$-CRL. In *Proc. of Algebra of Communicating Processes*, Workshops in Computing, 1995.

22. ISO/IEC. LOTOS — A Formal Description Technique Based on the Temporal Ordering of Observational Behaviour. International Standard 8807, International Organization for Standardization — Information Processing Systems — Open Systems Interconnection, Genève, 1989.

23. ISO/IEC. Open Distributed Processing – Reference Model. International Standard 10746, International Organization for Standardization — Information Processing Systems, Genève, 1995.

24. ISO/IEC. Enhancements to LOTOS (E-LOTOS). International Standard 15437:2001, International Organization for Standardization — Information Technology, Genève, 2001.

25. J.-P. Krimm. *Application des ordres partiels à la génération compositionnelle de systèmes asynchrones*. PhD thesis, Université Joseph Fourier, Grenoble, 2000.

26. J.-P. Krimm and L. Mounier. Compositional State Space Generation from LOTOS Programs. In *Proc. of TACAS'97*, LNCS vol. 1217, 1997.

27. F. Lang. EXP.OPEN 2.0: A Flexible Tool Integrating Partial Order, Compositional, and On-the-fly Verification Methods. In *Proc. of IFM'2005*, LNCS vol. 3771, 2005. Full version available as INRIA Research Report RR-5673.

28. J. Malhotra, S. A. Smolka, A. Giacalone, and R. Shapiro. A Tool for Hierarchical Design and Simulation of Concurrent Systems. In *Proc. of the BCS-FACS Workshop on Specification and Verification of Concurrent Systems*, 1988. British Computer Society.

29. R. Milner. *Communication and Concurrency*. Prentice-Hall, 1989.

30. J. Romijn. Model Checking the HAVi Leader Election Protocol. Technical Report SEN-R9915, CWI, Amsterdam, The Netherlands, 1999.

31. A.W. Roscoe. *The Theory and Practice of Concurrency*. Prentice Hall, 1998.

32. K. K. Sabnani, A. M. Lapone, and M. U. Uyar. An Algorithmic Procedure for Checking Safety Properties of Protocols. *IEEE Transactions on Communications*, 37(9):940–948, 1989.

33. K. C. Tai and V. Koppol. Hierarchy-Based Incremental Reachability Analysis of Communication Protocols. In *Proc. of the IEEE International Conference on Network Protocols*. IEEE Press, 1993.

34. K. C. Tai and V. Koppol. An Incremental Approach to Reachability Analysis of Distributed Programs. In *Proc. of the 7th International Workshop on Software Specification and Design*. IEEE Press, 1993.

35. F. Tronel, F. Lang, and H. Garavel. Compositional Verification Using CADP of the ScalAgent Deployment Protocol for Software Components. In *Proc. of FMOODS'2003*, LNCS vol. 2884, 2003. Full version available as INRIA Research Report RR-5012.

36. A. Valmari. Compositional State Space Generation. In *Proc. of Advances in Petri Nets*, LNCS vol. 674, 1993.

37. W. J. Yeh. *Controlling State Explosion in Reachability Analysis*. PhD thesis, Software Engineering Research Center Laboratory, Purdue University, 1993. Technical Report SERC-TR-147-P.

38. W. J. Yeh and M. Young. Compositional Reachability Analysis Using Process Algebra. In *Proc. of the ACM SIGSOFT Symposium on Testing, Analysis, and Verification*. ACM Press, 1991.

# On Distributed Program Specification and Synthesis in Architectures with Cycles

Julien Bernet and David Janin

LaBRI, Université de Bordeaux I,
351, cours de la libération,
F-33 405, Talence Cedex, France
{bernet, janin}@labri.fr

**Abstract.** In this paper, we consider discrete distributed synthesis problems, as defined by Pnueli and Rosner [17], on possibly cyclic architectures with zero-delay semantics and global specifications.

We describe a uniform (and complete) translation of these problems into distributed games problems. We prove the correctness of this translation and we also obtain, in this setting, a characterization of distributed architectures with decidable synthesis problems.

It shall be noted that, as opposed to former approaches, zero-delay semantics requires a specific treatment for modeling instantaneous value propagation. Moreover, cyclic dependencies with zero-delay semantics involve equations with potentially many solutions. Accordingly, several variants of the distributed synthesis problem are proposed and studied.

## Introduction

Automatic or semi-automatic synthesis of programs from specifications has been for long a challenging research goal in formal methods.

In the context of distributed discrete events systems, Pnueli and Rosner gave one of the first abstract definitions of this problem, proved its general undecidability, and characterized a decidable class of problems: distributed synthesis on the pipeline architecture [17].

Since then, distributed program synthesis has received a lot of attention: in the framework defined by Pnueli and Rosner [5,10,11,12], in control theory [2,13,1,4,20], or in the framework of true concurrency [7,6]. Many variations of this problem have been considered and solved: cyclic or acyclic architectures, from synchronous to asynchronous communications, interleaved or true concurrent models, with or without zero-delay semantics, with point to point or broadcast communication channels.

From a theoretical point of view, solving a distributed synthesis problem - where programs to be synthesized only have local knowledge of the global state of the system - amounts to solving a multiplayer game with partial information. This general problem has been defined and studied already in [16,19].

More recently, a regain of interest for distributed synthesis has led to a specialized version of multiplayer games, *distributed games*, that aims at defining a

E. Najm et al. (Eds.): FORTE 2006, LNCS 4229, pp. 175–190, 2006.

common framework where distributed synthesis problems can be encoded and solved [14]. In particular, these games have been equipped with various automata based tools [3] that help in this process.

## Objective of This Work

In this paper, we first aim at illustrating the relevance of this unifying approach by giving a clear, uniform and complete reduction of distributed synthesis problems into distributed games. As a subgoal, we expect this reduction to be efficient, both in the sense that decidable cases are strictly preserved, and in the sense that the complexity of solving these problems does not increase through the reduction.

In order to do so, we study the distributed synthesis problem in the case of architectures with cycles, zero-delay semantics and branching time global specifications; this case has not been considered so far. It occurs that zero-delay semantics require a specific treatment for modeling instantaneous value propagation. Moreover, cyclic dependencies with zero-delay semantics involve equations with potentially many solutions. Accordingly, several variants of the distributed synthesis problem are proposed and studied.

The relevance of studying cyclic architecture with zero-delay semantics first comes from digital circuits design as illustrated, for instance, by the classical R/S flip flop [8]. In this setting, one may consider extensions of Hardware Description Languages such as VHDL [9] with modules for automatic program synthesis. Studying zero-delay semantics also makes sense at the application level.

Investigating furthermore the relevance of this approach in various application fields like telecommunication or web services, distributed database or parallel scientific computing, etc..., is however not the purpose of this paper. Following Pnueli and Rosner original works and motivations [17], we stick to a level of abstraction that is application independent.

There is little doubt that application of automatic distributed synthesis still requires a lot more research efforts for exhibiting both richer decidable frameworks and more tractable solutions.

## Organization of the Paper

A model of zero-delay synchronous behaviors is presented in the first section. On architecture with cycles, it is shown that global behaviors may not be uniquely defined by sets of local behaviors. Accordingly, three variants of the distributed synthesis problem are defined: the angelic, the strict and the demonic variant.

The notion of hierarchical architectures is defined and studied in the second section. It is equivalent to a similar notion defined in [5]. Our main result is then stated: the angelic and strict variant of the distributed synthesis problem with arbitrary MSO specification are decidable if and only if the underlying architecture is hierarchical.

A proof of this theorem is given in the fourth part. More precisely, after briefly reviewing the definition of distributed games, we prove that both variants of the distributed synthesis problem can be encoded into distributed games that are decidable when the underlying architecture is hierarchical.

Some open problems are presented as a conclusion.

**Notations**

A word on an alphabet $A$ is a partial function $w : \omega \to A$ with downward-closed domain, i.e. $w(i)$ is the $i+1$th letter of word $w$. When $dom(w)$ is finite, we say $w$ is a finite word, otherwise $w$ is an infinite word. The length $|w|$ of a word $w$ is the cardinality of its domain. The set of finite words (resp. finite non empty words) over alphabet $A$ is written $A^*$ (resp. $A^+$), the set of infinite words is written $A^\omega$, the set of finite or infinite words is written $A^\infty$. The empty word is written $\varepsilon$. The concatenation of a word $u \in A^*$ and a word $v \in A^\infty$ is written $u.v$.

Given alphabet $B$, a $B$-labeled $A$-tree is a partial function $t : A^* \to B$ with prefix-closed domain.

Given two sets $A$ and $B$, we write $\pi_A$ (resp. $\pi_B$) for the left (resp. right) projection from $A \times B$ to $A$ (resp. from $A \times B$ to $B$). These notations are extended to any subset of $A \times B$ and words on $A \times B$. Given $P \subseteq A \times B$, (resp. $w \in (A \times B)^\infty$), we may also write $P[1]$ for $\pi_A(P)$ and $P[2]$ for $\pi_B(P)$ (resp. $w[1]$ for $\pi_A(w)$ and $w[2]$ for $\pi_B(w)$). These notations are generalized to larger products.

# 1    Distributed Program Synthesis with Zero-Delay Semantics

In this section, we rephrase Pnueli and Rosner's distributed synthesis problem for zero-delay semantics and arbitrary - possibly cyclic - architectures. In this context, behavior semantics and architecture structures are studied and interrelated one with the other.

## 1.1    Models of Behaviors

Programs considered in this paper produce a sequence of output events from a sequence of input events. We assume moreover that programs are *synchronous* and *zero-delay*: no output event is produced prior to any input event and every input event produces one and only one output event.

**Definition 1.** *A synchronous zero-delay behavior with input alphabet $A$ and output alphabet $B$ is a mapping $f : A^* \to B^*$ such that there exists a mapping $k_f : A^* \to (A \to B)$, called the kernel of $f$ such that $f(\varepsilon) = \varepsilon$ and, for every $u \in A^*$ and $a \in A$, $f(u.a) = f(u).k_f(u)(a)$.*

*In the remainder of the text, a synchronous zero-delay behavior $f : A^* \to B^*$ is simply called a sequential function and, for every $u \in A^*$, $k_f(u) : A \to B$ is called the one-step behavior of function $f$ after input $u$.*

A *sequential function* $f : A^* \to B^*$ has finite memory *when its kernel* $k_f :$
$A^* \to (A \to B)$ *is eventually periodic, i.e. there are some integers m and n*
*such that, for every* $u \in A^*$ *with* $|u| > m$, *for every* $v \in A^*$ *with* $|v| = n$,
$k_f(u.v) = k_f(u)$.

One can easily check that each sequential function has a unique kernel and,
conversely, each mapping $k : A^* \to (A \to B)$ is the kernel of a unique sequential function. Specifying or synthesizing sequential functions thus amounts
to specifying and synthesizing their kernels. Moreover, since kernels are infinite
$A \to B$-labeled $A$-trees, Monadic Second Order Logic (MSO) - or any of its
sub logics such as LTL, CTL or the mu-calculus - is available for specification
purposes and the related infinite tree-automata theory [18] can be applied for
synthesis algorithms.

   Another interesting characteristic of this notion of kernel, especially for distributed synthesis, is the good behavior of kernels w.r.t. function composition
since, in some sense, it commutes with it. More precisely, writing $f; g$ for the
composition $g \circ f$, for all sequential functions $f : A^* \to B^*$ and $g : B^* \to C^*$ and
for every input sequence $u \in A^*$, one has $k_{f;g}(u) = k_f(u); k_g(f(u))$.

   In other words, the one-step behavior of the sequential composition of function
$f$ with function $g$ after some time is just the sequential composition of the one-
step behaviors of $f$ with the next step behavior of $g$ after the same amount of
time.

**Remark.** In the setting defined by Pnueli an Rosner [17] and considered in
subsequent works [5,14,10], a sequential behavior $f : A^* \to B^*$ is generated by
a $A$-branching $B$-labeled $A$-tree $h_f : A^* \to B$ (with irrelevant root value) by
$f(\varepsilon) = \varepsilon$ and for every $u \in A^*$ and $a \in A$, $f(u.a) = f(u).h_f(u.a)$. In this model,
for every $u \in A^+$, $h_f(u) \in B$ is the last output produced after input sequence $u$.

   It shall be clear that these two approaches are equivalent in the sense that
they both define the same sequential functions. However, dealing with the latter
definition is much harder when composing functions. In fact, for all sequential
functions $f : A^* \to B^*$ and $g : B^* \to C^*$ and for every input sequence $u \in A^*$,
one has $h_{f;g}(u) = h_g(f(u))$. This difficulty entails for instance, in the approach
presented in [14], an *asynchronous* encoding of *synchronous* distributed synthesis
problems into distributed games. This somehow artificial asynchronism is not
necessary as shown in the present paper.

**Remark.** A sequential function is, by definition, zero-delay. Still, we can provide
a semantical definition of a one-delay behavior. A sequential function $f : A^* \to$
$B^*$ is *one delayed* when, for every $u \in A^*$, every $a_1$ and $a_2 \in A$, $f(u.a_1) =$
$f(u.a_2)$, i.e. the output event produced after a given input event only depends
on the previous input events.

   Observe that one-delay sequential functions have a very simple characterization in terms of their functional kernel. In fact, a sequential function $f : A^* \to B^*$
is one-delay if and only if, for every $u \in A^*$, the one-step behavior $k_f(u)$ is a
constant function.

## 1.2  Distributed Architectures

Our definition of distributed architecture is adapted from Pnueli and Rosner's definition [17] allowing single write/multiple read channels as in [5].

**Definition 2.** *A* distributed architecture $\mathcal{H}$ *is defined as a tuple*

$$\mathcal{H} = \langle I, S, r, \{A_c\}_{c \in I \cup S} \rangle,$$

*with a finite set $I$ of (global) input channels, a disjoint finite set $S$ of process sites (identified with output channels), a mapping $r : S \rightarrow \mathcal{P}(I \cup S)$ that maps every process $p \in S$ to the set of channels $r(p)$ where process $p$ read input values, and, for every channel $c \in I \cup S$, the finite alphabet $A_c$ of possible events on channel $c$.*

*We always assume that alphabets are pairwise disjoint. We also always assume that $I \subseteq \bigcup\{r(p) : p \in S\}$, i.e. any input is read by at least one process.*

*As a notation, we write $A$ for the alphabet of all possible channel events at a given time, i.e. $A = \Pi_{c \in I \cup S}$. For every set of channels $X \subseteq I \cup S$, we write $A_X$ for the product alphabet $\Pi_{c \in X} A_c$. In particular, $A_{r(p)}$ is the input alphabet of process $p$ on the bigger channel formed by all channels of $r(p)$.*

*Given any sequence $w \in A^+$ of channel input/output events in the architecture $\mathcal{H}$, we write $in(w)$ for the corresponding sequence of events $\pi_{A_I}(w)$ on architecture input channels and we write $out(w)$ for the corresponding sequence of events $\pi_{A_S}(w)$ on architecture output channels. Similarly, for every process $p \in S$, we also write $in_p(w)$ for the corresponding sequence of events $\pi_{A_{r(p)}}(w)$ on process $p$ input channels, and $out_p(w)$ for the corresponding sequence of events $\pi_{A_p}(w)$ on process $p$ output -.*

*As a particular case, when $r(p) = \emptyset$, we define $A_{r(p)}$ to be a singleton alphabet, say $A_{r(p)} = \{1\}$, with, in this case, $in_p(w) = 1^{|w|}$. The intuition behind this case is that, with no input channels, a process still receives time clicks.*

**Remark.** Two processes that read on the same set of channels (and thus share the same information) can be seen as a single process that writes on two distinct channels.

## 1.3  Distributed Behaviors

In presence of loops, giving zero-delay semantics to a distributed architecture is a priori non-trivial. Following Pnueli and Rosner [17], the intuitive idea would be to define distributed behavior of an architecture as the global behavior resulting from the composition of local sequential behaviors (one per process).

However, with zero-delay semantics, loops may create cyclic dependencies between the values of the output channels, i.e. systems of equations that may have several solutions. Zero, one or more global behaviors may be compatible with a given set of local behaviors. Consider for instance the system drawn below, where the left-hand process (resp. right-hand process) writes at each time the logical OR (resp. AND) of the last values it reads on its two inputs. Suppose now that the value of $x$ is 0 (in short $x = 0$) and that $y = 1$. Then, one can either have $a = 0$ and $b = 0$, or $a = 1$ and $b = 1$ ; hence there are several global behaviors corresponding to this set of local behaviors.

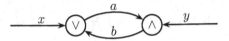

Thus the notion of distributed realization of a global behavior defined by Pnueli and Rosner [17] is no longer functional.

**Definition 3.** *Let $\mathcal{H} = \langle I, S, r, \{A_c\}_{c \in I \cup S}\rangle$ be a distributed architecture. A global behavior $f : A_I^* \to A_S^*$ of architecture $\mathcal{H}$ is realizable by a set of local behaviors $f_p : A_{r(p)}^* \to A_p^*$, one per process $p \in S$, when the following condition is satisfied:*

*for every global input/output $u \in A^*$ with $out(w) = f(in(w))$, for every $p \in S$, one has $out_p(w) = f_p(in_p(w))$.*

*The set of local behaviors $\{f_p\}_{p \in S}$ is incoherent (resp. ambiguous) when it realizes no (resp. more than one) global behavior.*

In order to solve distributed synthesis problem, we need a more local definition of realizable behavior.

**Definition 4 (One-step realizability).** *A global one-step behavior $k : A_I \to A_S$ is one-step realized by a set of local one-step behaviors $k_p : A_{r(p)} \to A_p$, one per process $p \in S$, when the following condition is satisfied:*

*for every global input/output events $a \in A$, such that $out(a) = k(in(a))$, one has, for every process $p \in S$, $out_p(a) = k_p(out_p(a))$.*

*A set of local one-step behavior $\{k_p\}_{p \in S}$ is called incoherent (resp. ambiguous) when it realizes no (resp. more than one) global one-step behavior.*

**Remark.** From this definition, one may be tempted to (re)define realizable global behaviors as sequential functions $f : A_I^* \to A_S^*$ such that, for every $u \in A_I^*$, the one-step global behavior $k_f(u)$ has a one-step realization.

Unfortunately, such a definition would be wrong as it would miss the fact that, for every process $p$, after any sequence of global input/output $w \in A^*$ with $out(w) = f(in(w))$, the one-step behavior of every process $p$ can only depend on the input sequence $in_p(w)$ actually read by process $p$.

Both definitions of one-step and general realizability are still related as follows:

**Lemma 1.** *A global behavior $f : A_I^* \to A_S^*$ of architecture $\mathcal{H}$ is realizable by a set of local behaviors $f_p : A_{r(p)}^* \to A_p^*$, one per process $p \in S$, if and only if, for every global input/output sequence of events $w \in A^*$ with $out(w) = f(in(w))$, the set of one-step local behaviors $\{k_{f_p}(in_p(w))\}_{p \in S}$ realizes the global one-step behavior $k_f(in(w))$.*

*Proof.* For any $w \in A^*$, for any $v \in A$ with $f(in(w.v)) = out(w.v)$, for any process $p \in S$, one has $f_p(in_p(w.v)) = out_p(w.v)$, thus :

$$k_{f_p}(in_p(w))(in_p(v)) = out_p(w).out_p(v)$$

Since $f_p(in_p(w))=out_p(w)$, it is clear that the global one-step behavior $k_f(in(w))$ is realized by the set of local one-step behaviors $\{k_{f_p}(in_p(w))\}_{p \in S}$. The converse is clearly true.    □

**Remark.** Observe that, on *acyclic* architecture, a set of *zero-delay* local behaviors is always coherent and non ambiguous. Observe also that, on *arbitrary* architecture, a set of *one-delay* local behaviors is also always coherent and non ambiguous.

### 1.4   Distributed Synthesis Problems

The distributed synthesis problem is the following: given a specification of an expected global behavior find a distributed realization of it, *i.e.* a set of local behaviors, one for each process site, such that the corresponding global behaviors meet the specification.

With arbitrary zero-delay local behaviors several cases are possible. This leads us to consider three possible semantics for the synthesis problem.

**Definition 5 (Distributed synthesis problem).** *Given an architecture* $\mathcal{H} = \langle I, S, r, \{A_c\}_{c \in I \cup S}\rangle$, *given a specification* $\varphi$ *of sequential functions with input alphabet* $A_I$ *and output alphabet* $A_S$, *the angelic, strict or, resp. demonic distributed synthesis problem for* $\langle \mathcal{H}, \varphi\rangle$ *is to find a set of finite memory local sequential behavior* $\{f_p\}_{p \in S}$ *such that :*

- *angelic case: there is at least one function* $f$ *realized by* $\{f_p\}_{p \in S}$ *such that* $f \models \varphi$,
- *strict case: there is a unique function* $f$ *realized by* $\{f_p\}_{p \in S}$ *and, moreover,* $f \models \varphi$,
- *or, demonic case: the set of local behaviors* $\{f_p\}_{p \in S}$ *is coherent and for every function* $f$ *realized by* $\{f_p\}_{p \in S}$, *one has* $f \models \varphi$.

**Remark.** The intuition behind these definitions is the following. In the angelic case, the programmer has the opportunity to add extra (hopefully limited) control channels in the architecture that allow control over the choice of the global behavior to be realized. In the strict case, these extra control channels described above are no longer needed: the architecture and the global specification are permissive enough to allow their (implicit) encoding within the architecture itself. Last, in the demonic case, extra control is just not available.

Observe that a distributed synthesis problem that has a solution with strict semantics also has a solution with demonic semantics. The main issues about these three semantics is the decidability problem.

It occurs that, as shown in the next section, both angelic and strict distributed synthesis problem are, as in the one-delay or the acyclic case, decidable on architectures called hierarchical. The demonic case remains an intriguing open problem.

# 2    Distributed Synthesis on Hierarchical Architectures

We review here the notion of knowledge of a process in an architecture. This leads to define hierarchical architecture and to state our main result in the angelic and strict case.

## 2.1    Process Knowledge

A similar notion is defined by Finkbeiner and Schewe in [5]. Both lead to equivalent notions of hierarchical architectures on the class of architecture common to both approaches. However, since this notion is somehow subtle and for the sake of completeness, we give here our own definition and related intuition.

**Definition 6.** *Given architecture $\mathcal{H}$ as above, for every process $p \in S$, we define the knowledge of process $p$ to be the greatest set of channels $K_p \subseteq I \cup S$ such that:*

> *for all $q \in K_p$, either $q \in I$ and $q \in r(p)$, or $q \in S$ with $q \neq p$ and $r(q) \subseteq K_p$.*

*The knowledge relation $\preceq_{\mathcal{H}}$ is then defined on $S$ to be the relation defined by $p \preceq_{\mathcal{H}} q$ when $q \in K_p$, meaning, informally, that process $p$ potentially knows more than process $q$.*

One can check that the knowledge relation $\preceq_{\mathcal{H}}$ is a preorder, i.e. it is reflexive and transitive. In the sequel, we write $\simeq_{\mathcal{H}}$ for the induced equivalence relation, i.e. $p \simeq_{\mathcal{H}} q$ when $p \preceq_{\mathcal{H}} q$ and $q \preceq_{\mathcal{H}} p$.

At every moment in an running distributed architecture, the *immediate knowledge* of a process $p$ is just the sequence of inputs it is receiving on channels of $r(p)$ and the sequence of outputs it is producing on channel $p$. The intended meaning of the knowledge relation is to capture a notion of *deducible knowledge* process $p$ may have from its own immediate knowledge.

The following lemma gives a semantical characterization of the knowledge relation defined above:

**Lemma 2.** *For every process $p$, $K_p$ is the set of channels $q$ such that, for every $k : A_I \rightarrow A_S$ that is one-step realizable, for every $a_1$ and $a_2 \in A$, such that $out(a_1) = k(in(a_1))$ and $out(a_2) = k(in(a_2))$, if $in_p(a_1) = in_p(a_2)$ then $in_q(a_1) = in_q(a_2)$.*

*Proof.* The full proof is omitted here due to space restrictions. Essentially, it suffices to remark that each process site $q$ that is not in $K_p$ is such that there exists an input channel $x \notin r(p)$ and a path from $x$ to $q$ that avoids $p$. Using the fact that there is a one-step realization of $k$, one can show that $in_p(a_1) = in_p(a_2)$ and $in_q(a_1) \neq in_q(a_2)$ if and only if $q$ satisfies this path condition.    $\square$

## 2.2   Hierarchical Architectures

We (re)define here the notion of hierarchical architectures that is induced by the notion of process knowledge.

**Definition 7.** *An architecture is called* hierarchical *when the knowledge relation is total, i.e. for every $p$ and $q \in S$, either $p \preceq_{\mathcal{H}} q$ or $q \preceq_{\mathcal{H}} p$. Equivalently, an architecture is hierarchical when the quotient set $S/ \simeq_{\mathcal{H}}$ is linearly ordered by the relation $\preceq_{\mathcal{H}}$.*

It shall be clear that, on architectures that are common to both definitions, the definition presented here and the one of Finkbeiner and Schewe [5] are the same.

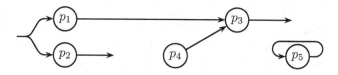

In the above example, one has $p_1 \simeq p_2 \preceq p_3 \preceq p_4 \simeq p_5$ : it is therefore hierarchical.

## 2.3   Main Result

**Theorem 1.** *The angelic or strict distributed synthesis problem for architecture $\mathcal{H}$ is decidable with arbitrary global MSO specification $\varphi$ if and only if the architecture $\mathcal{H}$ is hierarchical.*

*Proof.* In section 3, both angelic and demonic distributed synthesis problem on hierarchical architectures are encoded into pipeline distributed games (in the sense of [14,3]) that are thus decidable.

Conversely, any non hierarchical architecture contains an undecidable pattern (in the sense of [11]) or an information fork (in the sense of [5]) hence it is undecidable (even with one-delay semantics). □

Since the one-delay semantics is a particular case of (say strict) zero-delay semantics (the one-delay assumption can be encoded into the global specification) this result generalizes previous result for distributed synthesis problems on architecture with global specification.

## 3   Game Encodings of Distributed Synthesis Problems

In this section, we show that (strict or angelic) distributed synthesis problems can be encoded into distributed games. On hierarchical architecture one gets pipeline games. Since these games are decidable, this induces a decision procedure for the distributed synthesis problem for hierarchical architectures (for both strict and angelic semantics). .

## 3.1 Distributed Games

Distributed games [14] are a special kind of multiplayer games with partial information [15] extended to infinite plays. In short, two-player games are played on a bipartite graph, in which each position belongs to either the first player (called the Process) or to the second player (called the Environment). Distributed games are an extension of two-player games, where $n$ Process players play together against one Environment player.

**Definition 8 (Game arenas).** *A one-Process (or two players) game arena is a tuple $\mathcal{G} = \langle P, E, T, s \rangle$ where $P$ is a set of Process position, $E$ is a set of Environment position, $T \subseteq P \times E \cup E \times P$ is a set of possible transition moves, and $s \in P \cup E$ is an initial position.*

*Given $n$ one-Process game arenas $\mathcal{G}_i = \langle P_i, E_i, T_i, s_i \rangle$ for $i \in [1, n]$, a synchronous distributed game arena $\mathcal{G}$ built from the local game arenas $\mathcal{G}_1, \ldots, \mathcal{G}_n$, is a game arena $\mathcal{G} = \langle P, E, T, s \rangle$ with $P = \prod_i P_i$, $E = \prod_i E_i$ and $s = (s_1, \ldots, s_n)$, and such that the set of moves $T$ satisfies the following conditions: for every $u \in P$ and $v \in E$:*

- *Process team: $(u, v) \in T$ if and only if for every $i \in [1, n]$, $(u[i], v[i]) \in T_i$,*
- *Environment: if $(v, u) \in T$ then for every $i \in [1, n]$, $(v[i], u[i]) \in T_i$.*

**Remark.** Observe that there is a unique distributed game arena built from the local arenas $\mathcal{G}_1, \ldots, \mathcal{G}_n$ with maximal set of Environment moves. This arena, written $\mathcal{G}_1 \otimes \cdots \otimes \mathcal{G}_n$, is called the free synchronous product of the arenas $\mathcal{G}_1, \ldots, \mathcal{G}_n$.

Observe that any other distributed arena $\mathcal{G}$ built from the same local arenas can just be seen as a subgame of the free product obtained by possibly disallowing some Environment moves. It follows that, in the sequel, we will use the notation $\mathcal{G} \subseteq \mathcal{G}_1 \otimes \cdots \otimes \mathcal{G}_n$ to denote this fact.

**Remark.** In [14] or in [3], a more general notion of distributed with *asynchronous* moves is defined. For the study presented here, the additional expressiveness gained with asynchronism is not used in this paper. Since we are essentially establishing lower bounds result, this fact makes our result even stronger.

**Definition 9.** *Given a two player game arena $\mathcal{G} = \langle P, E, T, s \rangle$, a strategy for the Process player (resp. a strategy for the Environment player) is a mapping $\sigma : P^+ \to E$ (resp. a mapping $\tau : E^+ \to P$).*

*From the initial position $s \in E + T$, the play induced by strategies $\sigma$ and $\tau$ from position $s$, written $\sigma * \tau$ is defined to be the maximal word $w \in (P + E)^\infty$ such that $w(0) = s$ and for every $i \in dom(w)$ with $i > 0$, $(w(i - 1), w(i)) \in T$ and, given $w' = w(0) \cdots w(i - 1)$, if $w(i - 1) \in P$ then $w(i) = \sigma \circ \pi_P(w')$ and if $w(i - 1) \in E$ then $w(i) = \tau \circ \pi_E(w')$.*

*Strategy $\sigma$ for Process is non blocking when, for every counter strategy $\tau$, if $\sigma * \tau$ is finite then it ends in an Environment position.*

*Given an $n$-process game arena $\mathcal{G} \subseteq \mathcal{G}_1 \otimes \cdots \otimes \mathcal{G}_n$, a Process strategy $\sigma : P^+ \to E$ is a distributed strategy where there is a set of local process strategies $\{\sigma_i :$*

$P_i^+ \to E\}_{i \in [1,n]}$ *such that, for every word* $w \in P^+$, $\sigma(w) = (\sigma_1 \circ \pi_{P_1}(w), \cdots, \sigma_n \circ \pi_{P_n}(w))$.

*In other words, a Process strategy is distributed when every local Process player only plays following its own local view of the global play.*

Until now, we didn't specify how to win in such a game. For any play $w$ that ends in a position without successor, the convention we use is to declare that $w$ is won by the Processes (resp. by the Environment) if and only if the last position of $w$ belongs to $E$ (resp. to $P$). This corresponds to the idea that whenever a player may not make a game move anymore, it looses the play.

Since loops are allowed in the game arena, a Process strategy may also induce infinite plays. A *winning condition* for a distributed arena $\mathcal{G} = \langle P, E, T, s \rangle$ should therefore be defined as a set *Acc* of infinite plays won by the Process, *i.e.* infinite words from $(P+E)^\omega$. In order to describe such a set in a finite way, one can either use some decidable logic over infinite words (either monadic second order logic MSO, or one of its specializations, such as $\mu$-calculus or LTL). In the scope of this paper, however, we do not want to be specific about the formalism chosen for the specification; therefore we simply assume that *Acc* is an $\omega$-regular language (equivalently a language definable in MSO).

**Definition 10 (Distributed games and winning strategies).** *A distributed game is a tuple* $\mathcal{G} = \langle P, E, T, s, Acc \rangle$ *where* $\langle P, E, T, s \rangle$ *is a distributed arena, and* $Acc \subseteq (P+E)^\omega$ *is an $\omega$-regular winning condition.*

*A distributed Process strategy* $\sigma$ *in game* $\mathcal{G}$ *is a winning strategy when it is non blocking and for any strategy* $\tau$ *for the Environment, if the play* $\sigma * \tau$ *(from initial position s) is infinite then it belongs to Acc.*

*Observe that a distributed game arena can just be seen as a distributed game with infinitary winning condition* $Acc = (P+E)^\omega$. *In this case, winning strategies and non blocking strategies are the same.*

## 3.2 Distributed Games for the Strict Case

We prove here that unambiguous realizable behaviors can be encoded as distributed non blocking strategies in distributed arenas.

**Definition 11.** *Let* $\mathcal{H} = \langle I, S, r, \{A_c\}_{c \in I \cup S} \rangle$ *with* $S = \{1, \ldots, n\}$ *a $n$-process distributed architecture. We define the $n$-process strict distributed arena* $\mathcal{G}_\mathcal{H}^S = \langle P, E, T, s \rangle$ *from a free synchronous product arena* $\mathcal{G}_1 \otimes \cdots \otimes \mathcal{G}_n$ *of the game arenas* $\mathcal{G}_i$ *as follows.*

*For every* $p \in \{1, \cdots, n\}$, *the game arena* $\mathcal{G}_p = \langle P_p, E_p, T_p, s_p \rangle$ *is defined by taking*

1. $P_p = \{*_p, \perp_p\} \cup A_{r(p)}$
2. $E_p = (A_{r(p)} \to A_p)$,
3. $T_p$ *is the union of the sets* $(P_p - \{\perp_p\}) \times E_p$ *and* $E_p \times (P_p - \{*_p\})$,
4. *and* $s_p = *_p$,

*The intended meaning of this game arena is that, at every step, Process p chooses a one-step local behavior (in $A_{r(p)} \rightarrow A_p$) and Environment answers by choosing one local direction.*

*The distributed arena $\mathcal{G}^S_{\mathcal{H}}$ is then defined from the free product by restricting Environment global moves as follows: from an Environment distributed position $e = (k_p)_{p \in [1,n]}$,*

1. *Environment checks that the set of one-step local behaviors $\{k_p\}_{p \in [1,n]}$ is an unambiguous one-step realization of a global one-step behavior $k_e$,*
2. *if so, Environment chooses a global input event $a = (a_c)_{c \in I}$, compute the corresponding global output event $(a_c)_{c \in S} = k_e(a)$, and distribute back to processes their corresponding local inputs, i.e. Environment moves to Process distributed position $(b_p)_{p \in [1,n]}$ with $b_p = (a_c)_{c \in r(p)}$, otherwise Environment moves to the final position $(\perp_1, \perp_2, \cdots, \perp_n)$.*

Unambiguous distributed behaviors of architecture $\mathcal{H}$ are encoded as non blocking distributed strategies in the distributed arena $\mathcal{G}^S_{\mathcal{H}}$ as follows. Every process $p \in S$ defines, step by step, in game $\mathcal{G}_p$, the local behavior process $p$ will have in architecture $\mathcal{H}$. The environment player checks that these choices are compatible one with another in such a way that the resulting global behavior is well defined (and thus has a coherent and unambiguous distributed realization).

**Theorem 2.** *A distributed strategy $\sigma = \sigma_1 \otimes \cdots \otimes \sigma_n$ is non blocking in the game arena $\mathcal{G}^S_{\mathcal{H}}$ if and only if the set $\{f_{\sigma_p}\}_{p \in S}$ of the behaviors defined on local games $\mathcal{G}_1, \ldots, \mathcal{G}_n$ by strategies $\sigma_1, \ldots, \sigma_n$ is the distributed realization of an unambiguously realizable sequential function $f_\sigma : A^*_I \rightarrow A^*_S$.*

*In particular, a strategy $\sigma$ is finite memory if and only if the sequential function $f_\sigma$ is finitely generated (i.e. it has a finite memory kernel).*

*Proof.* Let $\sigma : P^* \rightarrow E$ be a non blocking distributed strategy for the process team with $\sigma = \sigma_1 \otimes \cdots \otimes \sigma_n$.

By definition, from every coherent and unambiguous $e \in E$ there is a unique mapping $k_e : A_I \rightarrow A_S$ locally realized by $e$. Moreover, for every input value $a \in A_I$, there is one and only one position $p_{e,a} \in P$ where environment player can move to and, moreover, value $a$ can be read in values stored in $p_{e,a}$ hence all positions $\{p_{e,a}\}_{a \in A_I}$ are distinct one from the other.

It follows that there is a unique mapping $h_\sigma : A^*_I \rightarrow P^+$ such that $h_\sigma(\varepsilon) = (*_1, \cdots, *_n)$ and, for every $u \in A^*_I$, for every $a \in A_I$, given $e = \sigma(h_\sigma(u))$, one has $h(u.a) = h_\sigma(u).p_{e,a}$.

We define then the mapping $k_\sigma : A^*_I \rightarrow (A_I \rightarrow A_S)$, the *functional kernel* of the sequential function induced by strategy $\sigma$, by taking, for every $u \in A_I$, $k_\sigma(u) = k_e$ with $e = \sigma(h_\sigma(u))$.

By construction, $k_\sigma$ is the functional kernel of an unambiguously realizable behavior $f_\sigma$ of architecture $\mathcal{H}$. In fact, for every $u \in A^*_I$, the environment position $\sigma(h_\sigma(u))$ is the local realization of $k_\sigma(u)$ since it is a coherent and unambiguous position hence Lemma 1 applies.

Conversely, let $f : A^*_I \rightarrow A^*_S$ be a distributed architecture behavior realized by a coherent and unambiguous set of local process behaviors $\{f_p\}_{p \in S}$. Given, for every $p \in S$ a non blocking strategy $\sigma_p$ in game $\mathcal{G}_p$ that corresponds to behavior $f_p$, it is not hard to see that the distributed strategy $\sigma_f = \sigma_1 \otimes \cdots \otimes \sigma_n$ is non blocking in the distributed arena $\mathcal{G}_\mathcal{H}$.    □

### 3.3    Distributed Games for the Angelic Case

We prove here that coherent realizable behaviors can be encoded as non blocking distributed strategies in distributed arenas.

**Definition 12.** *Again, let* $\mathcal{H} = \langle I, S, r, \{A_c\}_{c \in I \cup S} \rangle$ *with* $S = \{1, \ldots, n\}$ *an* $n$-*process distributed architecture. We define the* $n + 1$-*process angelic distributed arena* $\mathcal{G}_\mathcal{H}^A = \langle P, E, T, s \rangle$ *from a free synchronous product arena* $\mathcal{G}_0 \otimes \mathcal{G}_1 \otimes \cdots \otimes \mathcal{G}_n$ *as follows.*

*For every* $p \in \{1, \cdots, n\}$, *the game arena* $\mathcal{G}_p = \langle P_p, E_p, T_p, s_p \rangle$ *is defined as in the strict case (see Definition 12) and the game arena* $\mathcal{G}_0 = \langle P_0, E_0, T_0, s_0 \rangle$ *is defined as follows:*

1. $P_0 = \{*_0, \perp_0\} \cup A_I$
2. $E_0 = (A_I \to A_S)$,
3. $T_0$ *is defined to be the union of the sets* $(P_0 - \{\perp_0\}) \times E_0$ *and* $E_0 \times (P_0 - \{*_0\})$,
4. *and* $s_0 = *_0$.

*The intended meaning of this game arena is that, at every step, Process 0 chooses a one-step global behavior and Environment answers by choosing one global input.*

*The distributed arena* $\mathcal{G}_\mathcal{H}^A$ *is then defined from the free product by restricting Environment global moves as follows: from an Environment distributed position* $e = (k_p)_{p \in [0,n]}$,

1. *Environment checks that the set of one-step local behaviors* $\{k_p\}_{p \in [1,n]}$ *is a one-step realization of the global one-step behavior* $k_0$,
2. *if so, Environment chooses a global input event* $a = (a_c)_{c \in I}$, *compute the corresponding global output event* $(a_c)_{c \in S} = k_e(a)$, *and distributes back to processes their corresponding local inputs, i.e. Environment moves to Process position* $(b_p)_{p \in [0,n]}$ *with* $b_p = (a_c)_{c \in r(p)}$ *when* $p \in [1,n]$ *and* $b_p = a$ *when* $p = 0$, *otherwise Environment moves to the final position* $(\perp_0, \perp_1, \perp_2, \cdots, \perp_n)$.

Coherent distributed behaviors of architecture $\mathcal{H}$ are encoded as non blocking distributed strategies in the distributed game $\mathcal{G}_\mathcal{H}$ as follows. Every process $p \in S$ defines, step by step, in game $\mathcal{G}_p$, the local behavior process $p$ will have in architecture $\mathcal{H}$, and process 0 defines, step by step, the intended global realizable behavior. The environment player checks that these choices are compatible one with the other in such a way that the chosen global behavior defined by player 0 is realizable by the coherent (though possibly ambiguous) set of local behaviors that are built by the other players.

**Theorem 3.** *A distributed strategy* $\sigma = \sigma_0 \otimes \sigma_1 \otimes \cdots \otimes \sigma_n$ *is non blocking in game* $\mathcal{G}_\mathcal{H}^A$ *if and only if the set* $\{f_{\sigma_p}\}_{p \in [1,n]}$ *of the local behaviors defined on local* games $\mathcal{G}_1, \ldots, \mathcal{G}_n$ by strategies $\sigma_1, \ldots, \sigma_n$ is a distributed realization of the global behavior $f_{\sigma_0} : A_I^* \to A_S^*$ defined on local game $\mathcal{G}_0$.

In particular, strategy $\sigma$ is finite memory if and only if the sequential function $f_{\sigma_0}$ is finitely generated (i.e. it has a finite memory kernel).

*Proof.* The argument are essentially the same as in the proof of Theorem 2.  □

### 3.4   Distributed Synthesis Problem in Distributed Games

Now we show that any $n$-process strict distributed synthesis problem on hierarchical architecture can be encoded into a $n$-process pipeline distributed game.

The first step is to prove that:

**Lemma 3.** *If architecture $\mathcal{H}$ is hierarchical then both distributed games $\mathcal{G}_{\mathcal{H}}^S$ and $\mathcal{G}_{\mathcal{H}}^A$ are pipeline game arenas in the sense of [14,3].*

*Proof.* This follows immediately from the definition of hierarchical architecture (see section 2.2), Lemma 2 and Definitions 11 or Definition 12. In fact, Environment always transmit local inputs to Process players. It follows that any linearization of the knowledge order on processes will give an order that process the game is a pipeline game [14].

In the angelic case, Process 0 knows the global input and the global behavior. It follows that he also knows every other process inputs. It is thus already a leader (see [14,3]) and can be added as the least element in this total order.  □

It follows:

**Theorem 4.** *For every hierarchical architecture $\mathcal{H} = \langle I, S, r, \{A_c\}_{c \in I \cup S} \rangle$ with $n$ Process players and every MSO specification $\varphi$ of (kernel of) sequential function from $A_I^*$ to $A_S^*$ there is an $n + 1$-process for the strict case (resp. $n + 2$-process for the angelic case) decidable distributed game $\mathcal{G}_{\langle \mathcal{H}, \varphi \rangle}^S$ (resp. $\mathcal{G}_{\langle \mathcal{H}, \varphi \rangle}^A$) such that there is an unambiguously realizable (resp. realizable) behavior for $\mathcal{H}$ that satisfies specification $\varphi$ if and only if there is a (finite memory) distributed winning strategy for the process team in game $\mathcal{G}_{\langle \mathcal{H}, \varphi \rangle}^S$ (resp. $\mathcal{G}_{\langle \mathcal{H}, \varphi \rangle}^A$).*

*Proof.* First, one can easily translate the global specification $\varphi$ to a global strategy specification $\psi$ that is satisfied only by global strategies that encode global behaviors that satisfy $\varphi$. Then the result immediately follows from Theorem 2, Theorem 3, Lemma 3 and the fact that, as described in [3], pipeline games with such external conditions are decidable.  □

## 4   Conclusion

We have shown that strict and angelic distributed synthesis problem are decidable on hierarchical architectures with zero-delay semantics.

The demonic case remain, so far, an open problem. For proving decidability, one may try to adapt the above proof to this case by letting Environment (instead of player 0 in the angelic case) choose any behaviors realized by the local behaviors built by Processes. But this would break the pipeline structure of the resulting game so this approach would be non conclusive.

On the other side, for proving undecidability in the presence of a cycle in the architecture, one may try to force - by means of the external specification - some subset of processes to choose coherent, but ambiguous, local behaviors that would induce equations with multiple solutions. Then, following demonic semantics, Environment could pick arbitrary values among these solutions, creating thus another arbitrary input in the architecture that could behave such as a typical undecidable architecture. But this approach is inconclusive too since we do not know, so far, how to force in a global specification such a kind of set of ambiguous local behaviors.

Less directly related with our proposal, one may observe that, in the case of non hierarchical architecture, with the notable exception of local specifications[12], hardly any restriction on the global specification have been established for increasing the class of decidable distributed synthesis problems. This is certainly a open research direction that could be followed. The notion of process knowledge could be tuned to take into account the global specification. Distributed games, where both architecture and specification have been merged, could serve as a tool to achieve new results in this direction.

Even more distant from our present work, but still related, one can also observe that asynchronous behaviors, with fairness assumption that guarantees only finitely many output events are produced after every single input event, can be encoded by extending the notion of kernels to mapping from $A^*$ to $A \to B^*$. Though the resulting vertex labeling would be on an infinite alphabet, the distributed game techniques that are used here could be extended to this case.

## Acknowledgment

We are grateful to anonymous referees. Their comments strongly helped us revising former versions of this work. We would also like to thank Dietmar Berwanger for his suggestions for the final version of this paper.

## References

1. L. de Alfaro, T. A. Henzinger, and F. Y. C. Mang. The control of synchronous systems, part II. In *CONCUR*, volume 2154 of *LNCS*, pages 566–582, 2001.
2. A. Arnold, A. Vincent, and I. Walukiewicz. Games for synthesis of controlers with partial observation. *Theoretical Comp. Science*, 303(1):7–34, 2003.
3. J. Bernet and D. Janin. Tree automata and discrete distributed games. In *Foundation of Computing Theory*, volume 3623 of *LNCS*, pages 540–551. Springer-Verlag, 2005.
4. C. G. Cassandras and S. Lafortune. *Introduction to Discrete Event Systems*. Kluwer Academic Publishers, 1999.
5. B. Finkbeiner and S. Schewe. Uniform distributed synthesis. In *IEEE Symp. on Logic in Computer Science (LICS)*, pages 321–330, 2005.

6. P. Gastin, B. Lerman, and M. Zeitoun. Causal memory distributed games are decidable for series-parallel systems. In *Proceedings of FSTTCS'04*, LNCS. Springer-Verlag, 2004. To appear.
7. P. Gastin, B. Lerman, and M. Zeitoun. Distributed games and distributed control for asynchronous systems. In *Proceedings of LATIN'04*, volume 2976 of *LNCS*, pages 455–465. Springer-Verlag, 2004.
8. J. L. Hennessy and D. A. Patterson. *Computer organization and design (2nd ed.): the hardware/software interface.* Morgan Kaufmann Publishers Inc., San Francisco, CA, USA, 1998.
9. IEEE Std 1076-1993. *IEEE Standard VHDL*, 1993.
10. O. Kupferman and M. Y. Vardi. Synthesizing distributed systems. In *IEEE Symp. on Logic in Computer Science (LICS)*, pages 389–398, 2001.
11. P. Madhusudan. *Control and Synthesis of Open Reactive Systems*. PhD thesis, University of Madras, 2001.
12. P. Madhusudan and P.S. Thiagarajan. Distributed control and synthesis for local specifications. In *Int. Call. on Aut. and Lang. and Programming (ICALP)*, volume 2076 of *LNCS*. Springer-Verlag, 2001.
13. P. Madhusudan and P.S. Thiagarajan. A decidable class of asynchrnous distributed controlers. In *CONCUR'02*, volume 2421 of *LNCS*, pages 145–160. Springer-Verlag, 2002.
14. S. Mohalik and I. Walukiewicz. Distributed games. In *Found. of Soft. tech and Theor. Comp. Science*, volume 2914 of *LNCS*, pages 338–351. Springer-Verlag, 2003.
15. G.L. Peterson and J.H. Reif. Multiple-person alternation. In *20th Annual IEEE Symposium on Foundations of Computer Sciences*, pages 348–363, october 1979.
16. G.L. Peterson, J.H. Reif, and S. Azhar. Decision algorithms for multiplayer non-cooperative games of incomplete information. *Computers and Mathematics with Applications*, 43:179–206, january 2002.
17. A. Pnueli and R. Rosner. Distributed reactive systems are hard to synthesize. In *IEEE Symposium on Foundations of Computer Science*, pages 746–757, 1990.
18. M. O. Rabin. Decidability of second order theories and automata on infinite trees. *Trans. Amer. Math. Soc.*, 141:1–35, 1969.
19. J.H. Reif. Universal games of incomplete information. In *11th Annual ACM Symposium on Theory of Computing*, pages 288–308, 1979.
20. K. Rudie and W.M. Wonham. Think globally, act locally: Decentralized supervisory control. *IEEE Transactions on Automatic Control*, 37(11):1692–1708, November 1992.

# Generalizing the Submodule Construction Techniques for Extended State Machine Models

Bassel Daou and Gregor v. Bochmann

School of Information Technology and Engineering (SITE), University of Ottawa
bdaou@site.uottawa.ca, bochmann@site.uottawa.ca

**Abstract.** In previous research we extended the submodule construction techniques to cover a more expressive and compact behavioral model that handles data through parameterized interactions, state variables, and simple transition guards. The model was based on extended Input/Output Automata, and the algorithm on the Chaos concept. In this paper we generalize these extensions and improve the submodule construction techniques and algorithms. The generalizations include regular transition guards including equality and inequality, negation, conjunction and disjunction of predicates. The algorithm is improved by utilizing the concept of generic transitions (non refined transitions) that are refined as needed instead of considering all possible refinements of the Chaos. The algorithm selects needed refinements through dataflow relations bridging which involves forward propagation of definitions and backward propagation of usages. The new approach provides a more intuitive explanation of the submodule construction algorithm, gives justification for the number of variables in the new module and results in a much smaller and compact solution.

## 1 Introduction

Submodule construction, also called equation solving or factorization, considers the following situation: An overall system is to be constructed which consists of several components. It is assumed that the specification S of the desired behavior of the system is given, as well as a specification of the behavior of all the components, except one. The process of submodule construction has the objective to find a specification for the latter component X such that when joined with all other components , referred to as the Context C, together provide a behavior consistent with the behavior specification S. If the modeling paradigm for the behavior specifications is sufficiently limited, e.g. finite state models, an algorithm for submodule construction can be defined [MeBo83, Parr89, LaXi90, JoLa91, LeQi90, PeYe98, DrBo99, CDFM01]. Submodule construction finds application in the synthesis of controllers for discrete event systems [BrWo94], for communication gateway design and protocol conversion [KeHa93, KNM97, TBD97].

Service Oriented Architecture (SOA) is an area of possible application for submodule construction. The submodule construction techniques may be used in Services synthesis and implementation. However, these techniques need to be developed to fit SOA requirements, such as data manipulation and handling nonfinite state models.

E. Najm et al. (Eds.): FORTE 2006, LNCS 4229, pp. 191–195, 2006.
© IFIP International Federation for Information Processing 2006

In this paper we report the continuation of work published in FORTE 2005 [DaBo05] where we extended the submodule construction techniques that has been limited in the past to finite state models. In this work we ease the restrictions that were applied to these extensions and we modify the solution approach and parts of the algorithm to fit the new model and to provide a smaller, more compact and more intuitive solution.

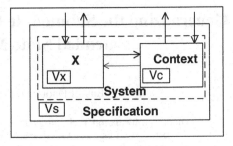

**Fig. 1.** Submodule Construction: General Architecture

## 2  Model Extensions

In the previous model [DaBo05], data manipulation and value passing were achieved by extending finite automata models with parameterized interactions, local variables, simple transition guards and variable assignments. Transition guards were limited to the conjunction of equality predicates between variables and transition parameters. In this paper we eliminate this restriction so that guards can include disjunction and negation as well as inequality predicates between variables and parameters. Moreover, in the previous model, variables were only assigned parameter values; in the new model we ease this restriction to allow assignment of variables between one another.

## 3  New Solution Approach

Our previous algorithm followed the general steps of the submodule construction algorithm for finite state machines. It starts with a general superset of behaviors, called Chaos, it then removes unwanted behaviors through composition, hiding, determinization and bad or uncontrollable state removal. These steps were adapted for the extended specification paradigm. During the construction of a deterministic model, the effect of hidden guards and hidden variables was taken care of through state splitting transformations based on previously collected information about variable configurations. In the new approach we continue to use the same general outline of the algorithm, however, we use the duality concept to obtain a superset of the wanted behavior before hiding, instead of using Chaos machine concept.

We define the dual of a given behavior G as the most general matching behavior G' that when joined with G will never generate an output that is not specified among inputs accepted by G. Besides, G' always accepts as input any matching output of G.

G' puts no restrictions on inputs that are not generated by G. In our model G' is obtained from G by labeling inputs as outputs and outputs as inputs. So G' has a set of variables V' matching the set of variables V of G.

Thus, as shown in figure 2 the superset of behaviors that is used in the new submodule construction algorithm will be the dual of C joined with the dual of S, *(C.S')'*, which is in general a much smaller set of behaviors than the Chaos machine. This approach provides the following benefits:

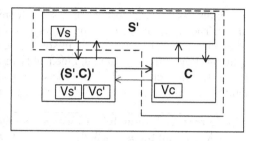

**Fig. 2.** Dual Based Approach for Submodule Construction

1. A better explanation for the number of variables needed for describing the most general behavior of the new module (in fact, a copy of the variables in S and in C suffice).
2. A smaller representation of the most general behavior for the new module which results from the fact that a single mapping of new module variables to the variables of S and C can be used, instead of having a solution with all possible permutations of variable mappings. Each variable of the new module is mapped to its original variable in either C or S.

The other aspect of our new approach is the use of the concept of generic "unrefined" transitions instead of using "interaction chaos" and the means of selecting only refinements that contribute to the solution. In our previous algorithm all possible refinements were explicitly considered, which though theoretically possible, becomes very unpractical for rather simple submodule construction problems. We need to note that in the behavior superset only transitions that are executed by the new module can be refined since we have full control over the new module. And thus two types of refinements are possible. These are: conditions on what the new module sends or receives, and options of where the new module stores received values.

Traditionally to overcome the effect of hiding in the case of finite label transition systems, transition closure and determinization were enough. However, when variables enter the picture as in our model we need to do something more, we basically need to make sure that variables are used properly, that is variables use the right values as defined in the specifications. We are especially interested in dataflow relations that cross machine borders. The Chaos solution explicitly generates all possible refinements and consequently all possible dataflow associations, however, not all these dataflow relations are needed or at least need to be identified, we only need to find all possible dataflow relations that simulate specification dataflow relations.

Thus the idea behind our approach is to perform dataflow analysis on the general behavior in order to identify the needed refinements. Accordingly, parameter value storage refinements are identified using forward propagation of definitions dataflow analysis. Meanwhile, conditions on received and sent data refinements are identified using backward propagation of usage dataflow analysis.

# 4 Algorithm Modifications

The new algorithm manipulates guards using the disjunctive normal form (disjunction of conjuncts). So, a transition can be viewed as a group of transitions where each transition has a guard formed of a single conjunct of the original transition's conjuncts. The algorithm handles the conjuncts collectively when possible and separately when situation demands such as in some cases of the backward state and transition splitting. Regarding negation and inequality their effect is limited to the conformance predicate which checks whether a transition guard is enabled for a given matching relations which we represent using a variable partition.

| Alogrithm 1. Submodule Construction Algorithm Steps [DaBo05]: | Algorithm 2. New Submodule Construction Algorithm Steps: |
|---|---|
| Given C, S:, $\sum$X Alphabet | Given C, S:, $\sum_X$ Alphabet |
| 1. G1:=Chaos($\sum$X , \|S.V\|+\|C.V\|).(S'. C) | 1. G0:= (S.C)'.(S'.C) |
| 2. R := ComputePartitions(G1) | 2. G1 = AddRefinements(G0) |
| 3. G2 := Split(G1, $\sum$X , R,) | 3. R := ComputePartitions(G1) |
| 4. G3:= Hide(G2, ($\sum$C U $\sum$S )-$\sum$X, S.V U C.V) | 4. G2 = Split(G1, $\sum_X$ , R,) |
| 5. G4:= Determinize(G3) | 5. G3 :=Hide(G2, ($\sum$C U $\sum$S ) - $\sum$X , S.V U C.V) |
| 6. X:=RemoveUncontrollableBehavior(G4) | 6. G4 := Determinize(G3) |
| | 7. X := RemoveUncontrollableBehavior(G4) |
| 7. Return X | 8. Return X |

In the following we provide a high level outline of the new algorithm step "AddRefinements" sub-algorithm focusing on refinements added due to specification context definition and corresponding new module usage.

| Algorithm 3. AddRefinements (G) |
|---|
| • CX = { (t1, t2, c1, s1) \| t1 is a transition where the definition of C variable c1 simulates definition of specification variable s1 and t2 is the transition where the corresponding usage of s1 takes place in X } |
| • Done = { } //represent handled define-use associations. |
| • Loop While not ( CX = {}) |
|     ▪ Remove (t1, t2, c1, s1) from CX |
|     ▪ Done := Done U {(t1, t2,c1, s1)} |
|     ▪ CX := CX U ( { (t3, t2, c3, s1) \| t3 is a transition where c1 is used to define c3 such as c3:=c4} – Done) |
|     ▪ For each t in {t \| t has an output interaction sent from C to X,  where a parameter p of t takes c1 value} |
|         ▪ If t already has an assigning s1 to a parameter p2 other than p |
|             • Replicate t3 replace s1:= p2 with s1 = p |
|         ▪ Else Add s1:=p to t3 |

The algorithm is guaranteed to stop since the possible dataflow relations existing are finite and the algorithm does not handle dataflow relation that has been already handled.

## 5   Conclusion and Future Work

This paper continues the work done on extending submodule construction techniques for finite state machines to more expressive behavioral models. We have eased the restriction on the model mainly allowing conjunction, disjunction, explicit negation and state variables equality predicates in state transition guards. We have presented a new solution approach that improves the practicality and efficiency of the algorithm, justifies the number of variables used in the new module, and results in a smaller solution by considering a standard mapping of new module variables to context and specification variables. We have provided an outline of the new algorithm that is based on dataflow analysis mainly backward propagation of criteria and forward propagation of definitions. This work will be the basis for adding more extensions to the behavioral model, such as considering functions and general predicates over variables which we are currently considering.

# References

[BrWo94]   B. A. Brandin, and W.M. Wonham. Supervisory Control of Timed Discrete Event Systems. IEEE Transactions on Automatic Control, Vol. 39, No. 2, pp. 329-342, 1994.

[CDFM01]   V. Carchiolo, N. De Francesco, A. Fantechi, G. Mangioni, "ESA: an approach to Systems Design by Equation Solving". FMICS'2001, Paris, France, July 2001.

[DaBo05]   B. Daou and G.V. Bochmann. Submodule Construction for Extended State machine Models. FORTE 05,pp. 396-410, 2005.

[DrBo99]   J. Drissi, and G.V. Bochmann. Submodule Construction for Systems of I/O Automata. Tech. Rep. no. 1133, DIRO, University of Montreal, 1999.

[JoLa91]   B. Jonsson, K.G. Larsen. On the complexity of equation solving in behavior expression algebra. TAPSOFT'91, vol. 1, LNCS 493, pp. 381-396, 1991.

[KeHa93]   S.G. Kelekar, G. W. Hart. Synthesis of Protocols and Protocol Converters Using the Submodule Construction Approach. PSTV93, pp. 307-322, 1993.

[KNM97]   R. Kumar, S. Nelvagal, and S. I. Marcus. A Discrete Event Systems Approach for Protocol Conversion. Discrete Event Dynamical Systems: Theory and Applications, Vol. 7, No. 3, pp. 295-315, 1997.

[LaXi90]   K. Larsen, L. Xinxin.   Equation solving using modal transition systems. LICS'90, 1990.

[LeQi90]   P. Lewis and H. Qin. Factorization of finite state machines under observational equivalence. LNCS 458, Springer, 1990.

[MeBo83]   P. Merlin, and G. v. Bochmann. On The Construction of Submodule Specifications and Communication Protocols, ACM Trans. On Programming Languages and Systems. Vol. 5, No. 1, pp. 1-25, 1983

[PeYe98]   A. Petrenko and N. Yevtushenko. Solving Asynchronous Equations. FORTE'98, (1998), 231-247.

[Parr89]   J. Parrow. Submodule Construction as Equation Solving in CCS. Theoretical Computer Science, Vol. 68, 1989.

[TBD97]   Z. Tao, G. v. Bochmann and R. Dssouli. A Formal Method For Synthesizing Optimized Protocol Converters And Its Application To Mobile Data Networks. Mobile Networks & Applications, Vol.2, No. 3, pp. 259-69, 1997.

# Decidable Extensions of Hennessy-Milner Logic⋆

Radu Mardare[1] and Corrado Priami[1,2]

[1] University of Trento, Italy
[2] Microsoft Research - University of Trento
Center for Computational and Systems Biology, Trento, Italy

**Abstract.** We propose a new class of logics for specifying and model-checking properties of distributed systems - Dynamic Epistemic Spatial Logics. They have been designed as extensions of Hennessy-Milner logic with spatial operators (inspired by Cardelli-Gordon-Caires spatial logic) and epistemic operators (inspired by dynamic-epistemic logics). Our logics focus on observers, agents placed in different locations of the system having access to some subsystems. Treating them as epistemic agents, we develop completely axiomatized and decidable logics that express the information flow between them in a dynamic and distributed environment. The knowledge of an epistemic agent, is understood as the information, locally available to our observer, about the overall-global system.

## 1 Introduction

The development of computer networks came with new paradigms of computation. The concept of *monolithic computational systems* (one-agent system) was replaced by the *concurrent distributed computing systems* (multi-agent systems), representing programs or processors running in parallel and organized in networks of subsystems. They interact, collaborate, communicate and interrupt each other. Underlying this new paradigm is the assumption that each such part has its own identity, as a subsystem. We shall associate to a subsystem an *agent*.

The agents are needed for discriminating between the events of the systems behavior. If we wish to identify a particular event, we have little choice but to identify the agents involved. Hence the agents might be understood as (associated with) separate and independently observable units of behavior and computation. They evolve in a given environment, following some primitive rules, their evolution influencing the structure of the whole (multi-agent) system. The main feature of the agents is their ability to communicate, that is to exchange information inside their environment.

Such a multi-agent system reflects interactive, concurrent and distributed behaviors and computations of agents, thus is extremely complex. The success in dealing with this complexity depends on the mathematical model we choose to abstract the system. Further we focus on two major paradigms.

---

⋆ Work partially supported by EU-IST project 016004 SENSORIA.

E. Najm et al. (Eds.): FORTE 2006, LNCS 4229, pp. 196–211, 2006.

## 1.1    The Agent Is Nothing More But Its Behavior

Process Algebra [1] abstracts the agents of the system on the level of their behavior and using some algebraic calculi and operational semantics describes the evolution of the whole system. Further, as the behavior of a concurrent system is a succession of affine states in (possibly branching) time, it was considered the possibility of applying modal (especially temporal) logics for specifying properties of the processes that modelled distributed systems.

In studying security problems, for example, we may want to be able to specify systems composed by agents that deal with fresh or secret resources. We may want to express properties such as *"the agent has the key"*, *"eventually the agent crosses the firewall"* or *"there is always at most one agent here able to decrypt the message"*.

Hennessy-Milner logic [2] is one of the first modal logics that proposes some dynamic operators, indexed by CCS actions, $\langle \alpha \rangle \phi$ to capture the weakest precondition of a program w.r.t. a given post-specification $\phi$. The idea was further developed in combination with temporal operators [3] and applied to other process calculi [4,5,6]. All these logics are characterized by their *extensional nature* - they distinguish processes up to their behavior.

The specific applications of mobile computing call for an increased degree of expressiveness for specifying and reasoning about locations, resources, independence, distribution, connectivity or freshness. Thus, *Spatial logics* [7,8] propose, in addition to the modal-temporal operators, some modal-spatial operators such as the *parallel operator* $\phi | \psi$ (meaning that the current system can be split into a parallel composition of two subsystems, one satisfying $\phi$ and the other satisfying $\psi$), and its adjoint - the *guarantee operator* $\phi \triangleright \psi$, or *ambient-location operators*[1] such as $n[\phi]$ (meaning that the current system can be described as a box $n[P]$ containing a subsystem $P$ that satisfies $\phi$), etc. A formula in a spatial logic describes a property of a particular part of the system at a particular time. These spatial modalities have an *intensional flavor*, the properties they express being invariant only for simple spatial rearrangements of the system.

Still most of the spatial logics face with decidability problems: it was proved that the basic spatial operators, in combination with temporal operators, generate undecidable logics [11,12,13] even against a finite piece of CCS[14].

## An Agent Is Defined by Its "Knowledge"

The other paradigm of modelling multi-agent systems is inspired by epistemic logics: reasoning about systems in terms of *knowledge of the agents* [15]. The knowledge of an agent is understood as the sum of actions the agent (subsystem) may take as a function of its local state in a given environment. Thus the agent "knows" its *protocol* in a given system, its knowledge consists in the information related to evolution of this subsystem in an unknown environment.

---

[1] These operators are characteristic for Ambient Logic [8], a special spatial logic developed for Ambient Calculus [9,10].

*Epistemic logics* [15] formalize, in a direct manner, notions of knowledge, possessed by an agent, or a group of agents, using modalities like $K_A\phi$ (*A knows* $\phi$), or $Ck\phi$ (*all the agents knows* $\phi$, *i.e.* $\phi$ *is a common knowledge*). These logics supports Kripke-model based semantics, each basic modality being associated with a binary *accessibility relation* in these models. Thus for each epistemic agent $A$ we devise an accessibility relation $\xrightarrow{A}$, called *indistinguishability relation for* $A$, expressing the agent's uncertainty about the current state. The states $s'$ such that $s \xrightarrow{A} s'$ are the *epistemic alternatives* of $s$ to agent $A$: if the current state of the whole system is $s$, $A$ thinks that any of the alternatives $s'$ may be the current state (as it does not have enough information to distinguish them). These logics have been extensively studied and applied to model complex communication-based multi-agent systems.

By mixing dynamic [16] and epistemic [15] formalisms have been developed Dynamic Epistemic Logics [17,18,19]. These logics combine a rich expressivity with low complexity ensuring decidability and complete axiomatizations.

## Our Approach

The two paradigms of modelling concurrent distributed systems presented before were developed in parallel, but to our knowledge, there has been no unified paradigm. We propose such a paradigm in this paper, used for constructing a new logic for concurrency completely axiomatized and decidable that combines the features of spatial logics with the epistemic logics thus obtaining a special type of dynamic epistemic logic equipped with spatial operators. We call it Dynamic Epistemic Spatial Logic. While the dynamic and spatial features allow to express complex spatial/temporal properties, the epistemic operators denote the knowledge state of the agents. Thus we can express, for a security protocol, that Alice knows the key $k$, but she also knows that Bob knows that she knows this key. The hierarchic epistemic statements are relevant for expressing and validating complex security protocols [20,17].

Formally, we extend Hennessy-Milner logic with the parallel operator and epistemic operators. In our logics the epistemic agents are named by the processes they are related with. Thus $K_P\phi$ means *the agent related with $P$ knows* $\phi$ and it holds iff $\phi$ is satisfied by any process having $P$ as subprocess. The intuition is that the agent related with $P$ can see only $P$. So, it cannot differentiate between the global states $P$, $P|Q$ or $P|R$ of the whole system, as in all these states it sees only $P$. Thus its knowledge rests on the properties $\phi$ that are satisfied by each of these states (processes).

We prove that Dynamic Epistemic Spatial Logic is decidable and we develop sound-complete Hilbert-style axiomatic systems, against process semantics based on a fragment of CCS [14], for two differently expressive such logics.

Concluding, the novelty of our logic with respect to the classical spatial logics is the use of the epistemic operators for expressing global properties while ensuring decidability. The epistemic operators allow to refer directly to agents of our system by mean of their knowledge. By combining the partial knowledge of the agents we can specify complex properties of distributed multi-agent systems.

## Outline of the Paper

The paper is organized as follows. In section 2 we introduce and study a small finite fragment of CCS on which we will focus for the rest of the paper[2]. Some new concepts will be introduced and used further, such as structural bisimulation and pruning processes and sets of processes. Starting with section 3 we define our logics. Two such systems will be introduced $\mathcal{L}_{DS}$ and its extension $\mathcal{L}_{DES}$. For both we will prove the bounded finite model property and develop sound complete Hilbert-style axiomatic systems against the chosen semantics. Eventually we end the paper with some concluding remarks.

For the proofs of the theorems presented in this paper, and for additional results the reader is referred to [21] for Dynamic Epistemic Spatial Logic and to [22] for Dynamic Spatial Logic. Some extensions of these logics have been presented in [23]

## 2  Processes and Contexts

In this section, focusing on the fragment of CCS introduced in definition 1, we develop some concepts on which we will base the further constructs.

**Definition 1 (Processes).** *Consider the fragment of CCS generated by the next syntax, where $\mathbb{A}$ is a denumerable set of actions and $\alpha \in \mathbb{A}$:*

$$P ::= 0 \mid \alpha.P \mid P|P$$

*Hereafter this calculus[3] is the object of our paper. We will use $\alpha, \beta$ to range over $\mathbb{A}$ and we will denote by $\mathfrak{P}$ the class of processes. As standard, we consider defined over $\mathfrak{P}$ a structural congruence, Table 1, and a labelled transition system, Table 2.*

**Table 1.** The axioms the structural congruence

$$P|0 \equiv P \qquad P|Q \equiv Q|P \qquad P|(Q|R) \equiv (P|Q)|R$$

**Table 2.** The transition system

$$\frac{}{\alpha.P \xrightarrow{\alpha} P} \qquad \frac{P \equiv Q \quad P \xrightarrow{\alpha} P'}{Q \xrightarrow{\alpha} P'} \qquad \frac{P \xrightarrow{\alpha} P'}{P|Q \xrightarrow{\alpha} P'|Q}$$

**Assumption [Representativeness modulo structural congruence]:** As the structural congruence is the ultimate level of expressivity we want for our logic, hereafter we will speak about processes up to structural congruence.

---

[2] This calculus provides a semantics against which the classical spatial logic is undecidable [11].

[3] We can, additionally, consider an involution on $\mathbb{A}$ that associate to each action $\alpha \in \mathbb{A}$ an action $\overline{\alpha} \in \mathbb{A}$, as usual in CCS, and also consider the silent action $\tau$. But all these represent just syntactic sugar, irrelevant from the point of view of the logic we discuss.

**Definition 2.** *We call a process $P$ guarded iff $P \equiv \alpha.Q$ for $\alpha \in \mathbb{A}$. We introduce the notation $P^k \stackrel{def}{=} \underbrace{P|...|P}_{k}$, and convey to denote $P^0 \equiv 0$.*

We extend the operators from processes to sets of processes.

**Definition 3.** *For any sets of processes $M, N \subset \mathfrak{P}$ and any $\alpha \in \mathbb{A}$ we define:*
$$\alpha.M \stackrel{def}{=} \{\alpha.P \mid P \in M\} \qquad\qquad M|N \stackrel{def}{=} \{P|Q \mid P \in M, Q \in N\}$$
*As we speak about processes up to structural congruence, the parallel operator on sets of processes will be commutative, associative and will have $\{0\}$ as null.*

Now we define the *contexts*. The intuition is that a *context* $\mathcal{M}$ is a (possibly infinite) set of processes that contains, in a maximal manner, any process representing a possible state of our system or of a subsystem of our system. Hence if a process belongs to a context then any process obtained by pruning its syntactic tree should belong to the context, as it might represent a possible state of a. For the same reason, the context should be also closed to transitions. $\pi(P)$ denotes the set of all processes obtained by pruning the syntactic tree of $P$.

**Definition 4 (Pruning the syntactic tree).** *For $P \in \mathfrak{P}$ define[4] $\pi(P) \subset \mathfrak{P}$:*

1. $\pi(0) \stackrel{def}{=} \{0\}$     2. $\pi(\alpha.P) \stackrel{def}{=} \{0\} \cup \alpha.\pi(P)$     3. $\pi(P|Q) \stackrel{def}{=} \pi(P)|\pi(Q)$

*We extend the definition of $\pi$ to sets of processes $M \subset \mathfrak{P}$ by $\pi(M) \stackrel{def}{=} \bigcup_{P \in M} \pi(P)$.*

**Definition 5 (Context).** *A context is a nonempty set $\mathcal{M} \subseteq \mathfrak{P}$ such that:*
1. *if $P \in \mathcal{M}$ and $P \longrightarrow P'$ then $P' \in \mathcal{M}$*     2. *if $P \in \mathcal{M}$ then $\pi(P) \subset \mathcal{M}$*

## 2.1 Size of a Process

Further we define the *size of a process*, following a similar idea developed in [24] for sizes of trees. The intuition is that the process has a *height* given by the vertical size of its syntactic tree, and a *width* equal to the maximum number of bisimilar subprocesses that can be found in a node of the syntactic tree.

**Definition 6 (Size of a process).** *We define, inductively, the* size $(h, w)$ *(h stays for height and w for width) of a process $P$, denoted by $[\![P]\!]$:*

1. $[\![0]\!] \stackrel{def}{=} (0,0)$   2. $[\![P]\!] \stackrel{def}{=} (h, w)$ *iff*
    - $P = (\alpha_1.Q_1)^{k_1} | (\alpha_2.Q_2)^{k_2} |...| (\alpha_j.Q_j)^{k_j}, [\![Q_i]\!] = (h_i, w_i), i \in 1..j$
    - $h = 1 + max(h_1, ..., h_k), \ w = max(k_1, ..., k_j, w_1, ..., w_j)$

*We convey to write $(h_1, w_1) \leq (h_2, w_2)$ for $h_1 \leq h_2$ and $w_1 \leq w_2$ and $(h_1, w_1) < (h_2, w_2)$ for $h_1 < h_2$ and $w_1 < w_2$.*

**Definition 7 (Size of a set of processes).** *Let $M \subset \mathfrak{P}$. We write $[\![M]\!] = (h, w)$ iff $(h, w) = max\{[\![P]\!] \mid P \in M\}$[5].*

---

[4] We consider also $\pi(P)$ defined up to structural congruence.

[5] Observe that not all the sets of processes have a size, as for an infinite one it might be not possible to have the maximum required.

*Example 1.* We show the size for some processes:

1. $[\![0]\!] = (0,0)$
2. $[\![\alpha.0]\!] = (1,1)$
3. $[\![\alpha.0|\beta.0]\!] = (1,1)$
4. $[\![\alpha.0|\alpha.0]\!] = (1,2)$
5. $[\![\alpha.\alpha.0]\!] = [\![\alpha.\beta.0]\!] = (2,1)$
6. $[\![\alpha.(\beta.0|\beta.0)]\!] = (2,2)$

## 2.2 Substitutions

For the future constructs is also useful to introduce the substitutions of actions in a process.

**Definition 8 (The set of actions of a process).** *We define* $Act(P) \subset \mathbb{A}$ *by:*

1.$Act(0) \stackrel{def}{=} \emptyset$   2.$Act(\alpha.P) \stackrel{def}{=} \{\alpha\} \cup Act(P)$   3.$Act(P|Q) \stackrel{def}{=} Act(P) \cup Act(Q)$

*For a set* $M \subset \mathfrak{P}$ *of processes we define* $Act(M) \stackrel{def}{=} \bigcup_{P \in M} Act(P).$

**Definition 9 (Action substitution).** *We call* action substitution *any function* $\sigma : \mathbb{A} \longrightarrow \mathbb{A}$. *We syntactically extend it, from actions to processes, by:*

1. $\sigma(0) \stackrel{def}{=} 0$     2. $\sigma(P|Q) \stackrel{def}{=} \sigma(P)|\sigma(Q)$     3. $\sigma(\alpha.P) \stackrel{def}{=} \sigma(\alpha).\sigma(P)$

*For* $M \subset \mathfrak{P}$ *let* $\sigma(M) \stackrel{def}{=} \{\sigma(P) \mid P \in M\}$. *We also use notation* $M^\sigma$, $P^\sigma$ *for* $\sigma(M)$ *and* $\sigma(P)$. *The set of actions of* $\sigma$, $act(\sigma)$, *is defined as*

$$act(\sigma) \stackrel{def}{=} \{\alpha, \beta \in \mathbb{A} \mid \alpha \neq \beta,\ \sigma(\alpha) = \beta\}$$

## 2.3 Structural Bisimulation

The *structural bisimulation* is a congruence on processes (then extended to contexts) defined as an approximation of the structural congruence bound by two sizes: the *height* (the depth of the syntactic tree) and the *weight* (the maximum number of bisimilar subprocesses that can be found in a node of the syntactic tree) of a process. A conceptually similar congruence was proposed in [24] for analyzing trees of location for the static ambient calculus.

The structural bisimulation analyzes the behavior of a process focusing on a boundary $(h, w)$ of its syntactic tree. The intuition is that $P \approx_h^w Q$ ($P$ and $Q$ are structurally bisimilar on size $(h, w)$) iff when we consider for both processes their syntactic trees up to the depth $h$ only (we prune them on the height $h$) and we ignore the presence of more than $w$ parallel bisimilar subprocesses in any node of the syntactic trees (we prune the trees on weight $w$), we obtain identical syntactic trees.

**Definition 10 (Structural bisimulation).** *For* $P, Q \in \mathfrak{P}$ *we define* $P \approx_h^w Q$ *by:*

$P \approx_0^w Q$ *always*

$P \approx_{h+1}^w Q$ *iff for any* $i \in 1..w$ *and any* $\alpha \in \mathbb{A}$ *we have*

- *if* $P \equiv \alpha.P_1|...|\alpha.P_i|P'$ *then* $Q \equiv \alpha.Q_1|...|\alpha.Q_i|Q'$ *with* $P_j \approx_h^w Q_j$, *for* $j = 1..i$

- *if* $Q \equiv \alpha.Q_1|...|\alpha.Q_i|Q'$ *then* $P \equiv \alpha.P_1|...|\alpha.P_i|P'$ *with* $Q_j \approx_h^w P_j$, *for* $j = 1..i$

**Theorem 1 (Congruence).** $\approx_h^w$ *is a congruence on processes.*

We extend the definitions of structural bisimulation from processes to contexts.

**Definition 11 (Structural bisimulation over contexts).** *Let $\mathcal{M}, \mathcal{N}$ be two contexts. We write $\mathcal{M} \approx_h^w \mathcal{N}$ iff*

    *1. for any $P \in \mathcal{M}$ there is a $Q \in \mathcal{N}$ with $P \approx_h^w Q$*

    *2. for any $Q \in \mathcal{N}$ there is a $P \in \mathcal{M}$ with $P \approx_h^w Q$*

*We convey to write $(\mathcal{M}, P) \approx_h^w (\mathcal{N}, Q)$ for the case when $P \in \mathcal{M}$, $Q \in \mathcal{N}$, $P \approx_h^w Q$ and $\mathcal{M} \approx_h^w \mathcal{N}$.*

*Example 2.* Consider the processes $R \equiv \alpha.(\beta.0|\beta.0|\beta.0)|\alpha.\beta.0$ and $S \equiv \alpha.(\beta.0|\beta.0)|\alpha.\beta.\alpha.0$. We can verify the requirements of the definition 10 and decide that $R \approx_2^2 S$. But $R \not\approx_3^2 S$ because on the depth 2 $R$ has an action $\alpha$ (in figure 1 marked with a dashed arrow) while $S$ does not have it (because the height of $S$ is only 2). Also $R \not\approx_2^3 S$ because $R$ contains only 2 (bisimilar) copies of $\beta.0$ while $S$ contains 3 (the extra one is marked with a dashed arrow). Hence, for any weight bigger than 2 this feature will show the two processes as different. But if we remain on depth 1 we have $R \approx_1^3 S$, as on this deep the two processes have the same number of bisimilar subprocesses, i.e. any of them can perform $\alpha$ in two ways giving, further, processes in the relation $\approx_0^3$. Indeed $R \equiv \alpha R'|\alpha R''$, where $R' \equiv \beta.0|\beta.0|\beta.0$ and $R'' \equiv \beta.0$ and $S \equiv \alpha.S'|\alpha.S''$, where $S' \equiv \beta.0|\beta.0$ and $S'' \equiv \beta.\alpha.0$. By definition, $R' \approx_0^3 S'$ and $R'' \approx_0^3 S''$.

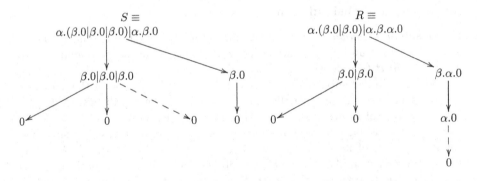

**Fig. 1.** Syntactic trees

## 2.4 Pruning Processes and Contexts

We introduce an effective method to construct, given a process $P$, a minimal process $Q$ that has an established size $(h, w)$ and is structurally bisimilar to $P$ on this size. Because the construction is based on pruning the syntactic tree of $P$ on a given size, we call this method *bound pruning*, and we refer to $Q$ as *the pruned of $P$ on the size $(h, w)$.*

**Theorem 2 (Bound pruning theorem).** *For any process $P \in \mathfrak{P}$ and any $(h, w)$ exists a process $Q \in \mathfrak{P}$ with $P \approx_h^w Q$ and $[\![Q]\!] \leq (h, w)$.*

*Proof.* We describe the construction[6] of $Q$ by induction on $h$.

**For** $h = 0$: we just take $Q \equiv 0$, because $P \approx_0^w Q$ and $\llbracket 0 \rrbracket = (0,0)$.

**For** $h + 1$: suppose that $P \equiv \alpha_1.P_1|...|\alpha_n.P_n$.

Let $P_i'$ be the result of pruning $P_i$ by $(h, w)$ (we use the inductive step of construction) and $P' \equiv \alpha_1.P_1'|...|\alpha_n.P_n'$. As for any $i = 1..n$ we have $P_i \approx_h^w P_i'$ (by the inductive hypothesis), we obtain, using theorem 1, that $\alpha_i.P_i \approx_{h+1}^w \alpha_i.P_i'$ and further $P \approx_{h+1}^w P'$.

Consider the canonical representation of $P' \equiv (\beta_1.Q_1)^{k_1}|...|(\beta_m.Q_m)^{k_m}$.

Let $l_i = min(k_i, w)$ for $i = 1..m$. Then we define $Q \equiv (\beta_1.Q_1)^{l_1}|...|(\beta_m.Q_m)^{l_m}$.

Obviously $Q \approx_{h+1}^w P'$ and as $P \approx_{h+1}^w P'$, we obtain $P \approx_{h+1}^w Q$. By construction, $\llbracket Q \rrbracket \leq (h+1, w)$.

**Definition 12 (Bound pruning processes).** *For a process $P$ and for a tuple $(h, w)$ we denote by $P_{(h,w)}$ the process obtained by pruning $P$ to the size $(h, w)$ by the method described in the proof of theorem 2.*

*Example 3.* Consider the process $P \equiv \alpha.(\ \beta.(\gamma.0|\gamma.0|\gamma.0)\ |\ \beta.\gamma.0\ )\ |\ \alpha.\beta.\gamma.0$

Observe that $\llbracket P \rrbracket = (3,3)$, hence $P_{(3,3)} \equiv P$. For constructing $P_{(3,2)}$ we have to prune the syntactic tree of $P$ such that to not exist, in any node, more than two bisimilar branches. Hence $P_{(3,2)} = \alpha.(\ \beta.(\gamma.0|\gamma.0)\ |\ \beta.\gamma.0)\ |\ \alpha.\beta.\gamma.0$

If we want to prune $P$ on the size $(3, 1)$, we have to prune its syntactic tree such that, in any node, there are no bisimilar branches. The result is $P_{(3,1)} = \alpha.\beta.\gamma.0$.

For pruning $P$ on the size $(2, 2)$, we have to prune all the nodes on depth 2 and in the new tree we have to let, in any node, a maximum of two bisimilar branches. As a result of these modifications, we obtain $P_{(2,2)} = \alpha.(\beta.0|\beta.0)\ |\ \alpha.\beta.0$. Going further we obtain the smaller processes $P_{(0,0)} = 0$, $P_{(1,1)} = \alpha.0$, $P_{(1,2)} = \alpha.0|\alpha.0$, $P_{(2,1)} = \alpha.\beta.0$.

Further we define the bound pruning of a context $\mathcal{M}$ as the context generated by the set of pruned processes of $\mathcal{M}$.

**Definition 13 (Bound pruning contexts).** *We say that the set $M \subset \mathfrak{P}$ is a system of generators for the context $\mathcal{M}$ if $\mathcal{M}$ is the smallest context that contains $M$. We denote this by $\overline{M} = \mathcal{M}$. For any context $\mathcal{M}$ and any $(h, w)$ we define*
$$\mathcal{M}_{(h,w)} \stackrel{def}{=} \overline{\{P_{(h,w)} \mid P \in \mathcal{M}\}}.$$

**Theorem 3.** *For any context $\mathcal{M}$, any $P \in \mathcal{M}$, and any size $(h, w)$ we have $(\mathcal{M}, P) \approx_w^h (\mathcal{M}_{(h,w)}, P_{(h,w)})$.*

**Definition 14.** *Let $A \subset \mathbb{A}$. Consider the sets:*

$$\mathfrak{P}_{(h,w)}^A \stackrel{def}{=} \{P \in \mathfrak{P} \mid Act(P) \subseteq A,\ \llbracket P \rrbracket \leq (h,w)\}$$

$$\mathfrak{M}_{(h,w)}^A \stackrel{def}{=} \{\overline{M} \subset \mathfrak{P} \mid Act(M) \subseteq A,\ \llbracket M \rrbracket \leq (h,w)\}$$

---

[6] This construction is not necessarily unique.

**Theorem 4.** *If $A \subset \mathbb{A}$ is a finite set of actions, then the following hold:*

1. $\mathfrak{P}^A_{(h,w)}$ *is finite*   2. *any* $\mathcal{M} \in \mathfrak{M}^A_{(h,w)}$ *is a finite context*   3. $\mathfrak{M}^A_{(h,w)}$ *is finite.*

**Theorem 5 (Bound pruning theorem).** *Let* $\mathcal{M}$ *be a context. Then for any* $(h,w)$ *there is a context* $\mathcal{N} \in \mathfrak{M}^{Act(\mathcal{M})}_{(h,w)}$ *such that* $\mathcal{M} \approx^w_h \mathcal{N}$. *Moreover,* $\mathcal{N} = \mathcal{M}_{(h,w)}$ *has this property.*

# 3   Logics for Specifying Distributed Systems

In this section we introduce Dynamic Spatial Logic, $\mathcal{L}_{DS}$, as an extension of Hennessy-Milner logic with the parallel operator and Dynamic Epistemic Spatial Logic, $\mathcal{L}_{DES}$, which extends $\mathcal{L}_{DS}$ with the epistemic operators. The intuition is to define the knowledge of the process $P$ in the context $\mathcal{M}$ as the common properties of the processes in $\mathcal{M}$ that contain $P$ as subprocess. Hence the knowledge implies a kind of universal quantifier over $\mathcal{M}$.

The satisfiability relations will evaluate a formula to a process in a context.

For our logics, we propose Hilbert-style axiomatic systems proved to be sound and complete with respect to process semantics. $\mathcal{L}_{DS}$ and $\mathcal{L}_{DES}$ satisfy the bond finite model property against the process semantics that entails the decidability for satisfiability, validity and model checking for both logics.

## 3.1   Syntax

**Definition 15 (Languages).** *We define the language of Dynamic Spatial Logic, $\mathcal{F}_{DS}$, and the language of Dynamic Epistemic Spatial Logic, $\mathcal{F}_{DES}$, for $\alpha \in \mathbb{A}$:*

$$\phi := 0 \mid \top \mid \neg\phi \mid \phi \wedge \phi \mid \phi|\phi \mid \langle\alpha\rangle\phi \qquad\qquad (\mathcal{F}_{DS})$$
$$\phi := 0 \mid \top \mid \neg\phi \mid \phi \wedge \phi \mid \phi|\phi \mid \langle\alpha\rangle\phi \mid K_Q\phi \quad (\mathcal{F}_{DES})$$

**Definition 16 (Derived operators).** *In addition we have derived operators:*

1. $\bot \stackrel{def}{=} \neg\top$

2. $\phi \vee \psi \stackrel{def}{=} \neg((\neg\phi) \wedge (\neg\psi))$

3. $\phi \to \psi \stackrel{def}{=} (\neg\phi) \vee \psi$

4. $[\alpha]\phi \stackrel{def}{=} \neg(\langle\alpha\rangle(\neg\phi))$

5. $1 \stackrel{def}{=} \neg((\neg 0) \mid (\neg 0))$

6. $\langle!\alpha\rangle\psi \stackrel{def}{=} (\langle\alpha\rangle\psi) \wedge 1$

7. $\widetilde{K}_Q\phi \stackrel{def}{=} \neg K_Q\neg\phi$

We could also introduce, for each action $\alpha$, a derived operator[7] $\langle\alpha, \overline{\alpha}\rangle$ to express communication by $\alpha$, supposing that we have defined an involution $co : \mathbb{A} \longrightarrow \mathbb{A}$ which associates to each action $\alpha$ its co-action $\overline{\alpha}$:

$$\langle\alpha, \overline{\alpha}\rangle\phi \stackrel{def}{=} \bigvee_{\phi \leftrightarrow \phi_1|\phi_2} \langle\alpha\rangle\phi_1|\langle\overline{\alpha}\rangle\phi_2$$

---

[7] The disjunction is considered up to logically-equivalent decompositions $\phi \leftrightarrow \phi_1|\phi_2$ that ensures the use of a finitary formula.

## 3.2    Process Semantics

A formula of $\mathcal{F}_{DS}$, or of $\mathcal{F}_{DES}$, will be evaluated to processes in a given context, by mean of a satisfaction relation $\mathcal{M}, P \models \phi$.

**Definition 17 (Models and satisfaction).** *A model of $\mathcal{L}_{DS}$ or of $\mathcal{L}_{DES}$ is a context $\mathcal{M}$ for which we define the satisfaction relation, for $P \in \mathcal{M}$, as follows:*

$\mathcal{M}, P \models \top$ *always*
$\mathcal{M}, P \models 0$ *iff $P \equiv 0$*
$\mathcal{M}, P \models \neg\phi$ *iff $\mathcal{M}, P \not\models \phi$*
$\mathcal{M}, P \models \phi \wedge \psi$ *iff $\mathcal{M}, P \models \phi$ and $\mathcal{M}, P \models \psi$*
$\mathcal{M}, P \models \phi|\psi$ *iff $P \equiv Q|R$ and $\mathcal{M}, Q \models \phi$, $\mathcal{M}, R \models \psi$*
$\mathcal{M}, P \models \langle\alpha\rangle\phi$ *iff there exists a transition $P \overset{\alpha}{\longrightarrow} P'$ and $\mathcal{M}, P' \models \phi$*
$\mathcal{M}, P \models K_Q\phi$ *iff $P \equiv Q|R$ and $\forall Q|R' \in \mathcal{M}$ we have $\mathcal{M}, Q|R' \models \phi$*

Then the semantics of the derived operators will be:

$\mathcal{M}, P \models [\alpha]\phi$ iff for any $P' \in \mathcal{M}$ such that $P \overset{\alpha}{\longrightarrow} P'$ (if any), $\mathcal{M}, P' \models \phi$
$\mathcal{M}, P \models 1$ iff $P \equiv 0$ or $P \equiv \alpha.Q$ ($P$ is null or guarded)
$\mathcal{M}, P \models \langle!\alpha\rangle\phi$ iff $P \equiv \alpha.Q$ and $\mathcal{M}, Q \models \phi$
$\mathcal{M}, P \models \tilde{K}_Q\phi$ iff either $P \not\equiv Q|R$, or it exists $Q|S \in \mathcal{M}$ such that $\mathcal{M}, Q|S \models \phi$

Remark the interesting semantics of the operators $K_0$ and $\tilde{K}_0$ that allow to encode, in syntax, the validity and the satisfiability w.r.t. a context:

$\mathcal{M}, P \models K_0\phi$ iff for any $Q \in \mathcal{M}$ we have $\mathcal{M}, Q \models \phi$
$\mathcal{M}, P \models \tilde{K}_0\phi$ iff it exists a process $Q \in \mathcal{M}$ such that $\mathcal{M}, Q \models \phi$

## 3.3    Characteristic Formulas

In this subsection we use the peculiarities of the dynamic and epistemic operators to define characteristic formulas for processes and for finite contexts. Such formulas will be useful in providing appropriate axiomatic systems for our logics and, eventually, for proving the completeness.

**Definition 18 (Characteristic formulas for processes).** *In $\mathcal{F}_{DS}$ we define a class of formulas $(c_P)_{P\in\mathfrak{P}}$, indexed by ($\equiv$-equivalence classes of) processes, by:*

$$1.\ c_0 \overset{def}{=} 0 \qquad 2.\ c_{P|Q} \overset{def}{=} c_P|c_Q \qquad 3.\ c_{\alpha.P} \overset{def}{=} \langle!\alpha\rangle c_P$$

**Theorem 6.** $\mathcal{M}, P \models c_Q$ iff $P \equiv Q$.

As $\mathcal{F}_{DES}$ is an extension of $\mathcal{F}_{DS}$, $(c_P)_{P\in\mathfrak{P}}$ characterize processes also in $\mathcal{F}_{DES}$. Specific for $\mathcal{F}_{DES}$ only is the possibility to exploit the semantics of the operators $K_0$ and $\tilde{K}_0$, as they can describe validity and satisfiability w.r.t a model, in defining characteristic formulas for finite contexts.

**Definition 19 (Characteristic formulas for contexts).** *In $\mathcal{F}_{DES}$, if $\mathcal{M}$ is a finite context, we can define its characteristic formula by:*

$$c_{\mathcal{M}} = K_0(\bigvee_{Q \in \mathcal{M}} c_Q) \wedge (\bigwedge_{Q \in \mathcal{M}} \tilde{K}_0 c_Q)$$

Suppose that $\mathcal{N}, P \models c_{\mathcal{M}}$. Then the first conjunct $K_0(\bigvee_{Q \in \mathcal{M}} c_Q)$ tells us that $\bigvee_{Q \in \mathcal{M}} c_Q$ is a validity in $\mathcal{N}$, hence each element of $\mathcal{N}$ is an element of $\mathcal{M}$, $\mathcal{N} \subseteq \mathcal{M}$. The second conjunct tells us that for each $Q \in \mathcal{M}$, $\mathcal{N}, P \models \tilde{K}_0 c_Q$. By the semantics of $\tilde{K}_0$ this means that it exists a process $P' \in \mathcal{N}$ such that $\mathcal{N}, P' \models c_Q$, i.e. $P' \equiv Q$. As the processes are identified up to structural congruence, $\mathcal{M} \subseteq \mathcal{N}$. Hence $\mathcal{M} = \mathcal{N}$.

**Theorem 7.** *If $\mathcal{M}$ is a finite context and $P \in \mathcal{M}$ then $\mathcal{M}, P \models c_{\mathcal{N}}$ iff $\mathcal{N} = \mathcal{M}$.*

## 3.4 Bound Finite Model Property and Decidability

Now we prove the finite model property for Dynamic Epistemic Spatial Logic that will entail the decidability against the process semantics. As a consequence, we obtain decidability for Dynamic Spatial Logic (being less expressive). Anticipating, we define a size for formulas $\phi$; then we prove that if $\mathcal{M}, P \models \phi$ then substituting, by $\sigma$, all the actions in $\mathcal{M}$ (and implicitly in $P$) that are not in the syntax of $\phi$ (as indexes of dynamic or epistemic operators) by a fixed action with the same property, and then pruning $\mathcal{M}^\sigma$ and $P^\sigma$ to the size of $\phi$ we will obtain a couple $(\mathcal{N}, Q)$ such that $\mathcal{N}, Q \models \phi$. The fixed action of substitution can be chosen as the successor[8] of the maximum action of $\phi$, which is unique. Hence $\mathcal{N} \in \mathfrak{M}_{(h,w)}^A$ where $(h, w)$ is the size of $\phi$ and $A$ is the set of actions of $\phi$ augmented with the successor of its maximum, thus $A$ is finite. But then theorem 4 ensures that the set of pairs $(\mathcal{N}, Q)$, with this property, is finite.

**Definition 20 (Size of a formula).** *We define the sizes of a formula, $(\!|\phi|\!)$ (height and width), inductively on $\mathcal{F}_{DES}$, by:*

1. $(\!|0|\!) = (\!|\top|\!) \stackrel{def}{=} (0,0)$      2. $(\!|\neg\phi|\!) \stackrel{def}{=} (\!|\phi|\!)$

*and supposing that $(\!|\phi|\!) = (h, w)$, $(\!|\psi|\!) = (h', w')$ and $[\![R]\!] = (h_R, w_R)$, further:*

3. $(\!|\phi|\psi|\!) \stackrel{def}{=} (max(h, h'), w + w')$      4. $(\!|\phi \wedge \psi|\!) \stackrel{def}{=} (max(h, h'), max(w, w'))$

5. $(\!|\langle\alpha\rangle\phi|\!) \stackrel{def}{=} (1+h, 1+w)$      6. $(\!|K_R\phi|\!) \stackrel{def}{=} (1+max(h, h_R), 1+max(w, w_R))$

The next theorem states that $\phi$ is *"sensitive"* via satisfaction only up to size $(\!|\phi|\!)$. In other words, the relation $\mathcal{M}, P \models \phi$ is conserved by substituting the couple $(M, P)$ with any other couple $(N, P)$ structurally bisimilar to it at the size $(\!|\phi|\!)$.

**Theorem 8.** *If $(\!|\phi|\!) = (h, w)$, $\mathcal{M}, P \models \phi$ and $(\mathcal{M}, P) \approx_h^w (\mathcal{N}, Q)$ then $\mathcal{N}, Q \models \phi$.*

---

[8] We consider defined, on the class of actions $\mathbb{A}$, a lexicographical order.

Using this theorem, we conclude that if a process, in a context, satisfies $\phi$ then by pruning the process and the context on the size $(\!|\phi|\!)$, we still have satisfiability for $\phi$. Indeed the theorems 2 and 3 prove that if $(\!|\phi|\!) = (h, w)$ then $(\mathcal{M}, P) \approx_w^h (\mathcal{M}_{(\!|\phi|\!)}, P_{(\!|\phi|\!)})$. Hence $\mathcal{M}, P \models \phi$ implies $\mathcal{M}_{(\!|\phi|\!)}, P_{(\!|\phi|\!)} \models \phi$.

**Definition 21 (The set of actions of a formula).** *We define the set of actions of a formula $\phi$, $act(\phi) \subset \mathbb{A}$, inductively by:*

1. $act(0) \overset{def}{=} \emptyset$

2. $act(\top) \overset{def}{=} \emptyset$

3. $act(\phi \wedge \psi) = act(\phi|\psi) \overset{def}{=} act(\phi) \cup act(\psi)$

4. $act(\neg\phi) = act(\phi)$

5. $act(K_R\phi) \overset{def}{=} Act(R) \cup act(\phi)$

6. $act(\langle\alpha\rangle\phi) \overset{def}{=} \{\alpha\} \cup act(\phi)$

The next result states that a formula $\phi$ does not reflect properties that involve more then the actions in its syntax. Thus if $\mathcal{M}, P \models \phi$ then any substitution $\sigma$ having the elements of $act(\phi)$ as fix points preserves the satisfaction relation.

**Theorem 9.** *If $\mathcal{M}, P \models \phi$ and $act(\sigma) \bigcap act(\phi) = \emptyset$ then $\mathcal{M}^\sigma, P^\sigma \models \phi$.*

Suppose that on $\mathbb{A}$ we have a lexicographical order $\ll$. So, for a finite set $A \subset \mathbb{A}$ we can identify a maximal element that is unique. Hence the successor of this element is unique as well. We convey to denote by $A_+$ the set obtained by adding to $A$ the successor of its maximal element. Moreover, for a context $\mathcal{N} \ni P$, for a size $(h, w)$ and for a finite set of actions $A \subset \mathbb{A}$ we denote by $\mathcal{N}_{(h,w)}^A$ (and by $P_{(h,w)}^A$ respectively) the context (respectively the process) obtained by substituting all the actions $\alpha \in Act(\mathcal{N}) \setminus A$ ($\alpha \in Act(P) \setminus A$ respectively) by the successor of the maximum element of $A$ and then pruning the context (the process) obtained to size $(h, w)$.

**Theorem 10 (Bound finite model property).**

*If $\mathcal{M}, P \models \phi$ then $\exists \mathcal{N} \in \mathfrak{M}_{(\!|\phi|\!)}^{act(\phi)+}$ and $Q \in \mathcal{N}$ such that $\mathcal{N}, Q \models \phi$.*

*Moreover $\mathcal{N} = \mathcal{M}_{(\!|\phi|\!)}^{act(\phi)}$ and $Q = P_{(\!|\phi|\!)}^{act(\phi)}$ fulfill the requirements of the theorem.*

Because $act(\phi)$ is finite implying $act(\phi)_+$ finite, we apply theorem 4 ensuring that $\mathfrak{M}_{(\!|\phi|\!)}^{act(\phi)+}$ is finite and any context $\mathcal{M} \in \mathfrak{M}_{(\!|\phi|\!)}^{act(\phi)+}$ is finite as well. Thus we obtain the bound finite model property for our logic. A consequence of theorem 10 is the decidability for satisfiability, validity and model checking against the process semantics.

**Theorem 11 (Decidability of $\mathcal{L}_{DES}$).** *For $\mathcal{L}_{DES}$ validity, satisfiability and model checking are decidable against the process semantics.*

**Corollary 1 (Decidability of $\mathcal{L}_{DS}$).** *For $\mathcal{L}_{DS}$ validity, satisfiability and model checking are decidable against the process semantics.*

## 3.5  Axiomatic Systems

In Table 3 we propose a Hilbert-style axiomatic system for $\mathcal{L}_{DS}$. We assume the axioms and the rules of propositional logic. In addition we will have a set of spatial axioms and rules, and a set of dynamic axioms and rules.

Concerning the axioms and rules we make two observations. The disjunction involved in Axiom S6 is finitary, as we considered the processes up to structural congruence level. Also the disjunction involved in Rule DR4 has a finite number of terms, as a consequence of the finite model property.

**Table 3.** The axiomatic system of $\mathcal{L}_{DS}$

**Spatial axioms**

S1: $\vdash \top \mid \bot \rightarrow \bot$

S2: $\vdash (\phi \mid \psi) \mid \rho \rightarrow \phi \mid (\psi \mid \rho)$

S3: $\vdash \phi \mid 0 \leftrightarrow \phi$

S4: $\vdash \phi \mid (\psi \vee \rho) \rightarrow (\phi \mid \psi) \vee (\phi \mid \rho)$

S5: $\vdash \phi \mid \psi \rightarrow \psi \mid \phi$

S6: $\vdash (c_P \wedge \phi \mid \psi) \rightarrow \bigvee_{P \equiv Q \mid R} (c_Q \wedge \phi) \mid (c_R \wedge \psi)$

**Spatial rules**

SR1: $\vdash \phi \rightarrow \psi$ then $\vdash \phi \mid \rho \rightarrow \psi \mid \rho$

**Dynamic axioms**

D7: $\vdash \langle \alpha \rangle \phi \mid \psi \rightarrow \langle \alpha \rangle (\phi \mid \psi)$

D8: $\vdash [\alpha](\phi \rightarrow \psi) \rightarrow ([\alpha]\phi \rightarrow [\alpha]\psi)$

D9: $\vdash 0 \rightarrow [\alpha]\bot$

D10: For $\alpha_i \neq \beta$, $\vdash \langle !\alpha_1 \rangle \top \mid ... \mid \langle !\alpha_n \rangle \top \rightarrow [\beta]\bot$

D11: $\vdash \langle !\alpha \rangle \phi \rightarrow [\alpha]\phi$

**Dynamic rules**

DR2: $\vdash \phi$ then $\vdash [\alpha]\phi$

DR4: $\vdash \bigvee_{P \in \mathfrak{P}_{(\phi)}^{act(\phi)+}} c_P \rightarrow \phi$ then $\vdash \phi$

DR3: If $\vdash \phi_1 \rightarrow [\alpha]\phi_1'$ and $\vdash \phi_2 \rightarrow [\alpha]\phi_2'$ then $\vdash \phi_1 \mid \phi_2 \rightarrow [\alpha](\phi_1' \mid \phi_2 \vee \phi_1 \mid \phi_2')$

The axiomatic system for $\mathcal{L}_{DES}$ is just an extension of the axiomatic system of $\mathcal{L}_{DS}$ with the set of epistemic axioms and rules presented in Table 4. Observe that Rule DR4 has been replaced by Rule DR'4, as this logic is sensitive to contexts (due to universal quantifier involved by the semantics of the epistemic operator).

For the epistemic axioms and rules we point on their similarities with the classic axioms of knowledge. Thus Axiom E12 is the classical (K)-axiom stating that our epistemic operator is a normal one, while Axiom E13 is just the necessity axiom, for the epistemic operator. Also Axiom E14 is well known in epistemic logics. It states that our epistemic agents satisfy *the positive introspection property*: if $P$ knows $\phi$ then it knows that it knows $\phi$. Axiom E15 states a variant of the *negative introspection*, saying that if an agent $P$ is active and if it doesn't know $\phi$, then it knows that it doesn't know $\phi$. These axioms are present in all the epistemic logics [15]. Axiom E16 is also interesting as it states the equivalence between *to be active* and *to know* for our epistemic agents.

**Table 4.** The axiomatic system $\mathcal{L}_{DES}^{\mathfrak{S}}$

**Dynamic rule**

DR'4: $\vdash \bigvee_{\mathcal{M} \in \mathfrak{M}_{(\phi)}^{act(\phi)_+}} c_{\mathcal{M}} \to \phi$ then $\vdash \phi$

**Epistemic axioms**

E12: $\vdash K_Q\phi \wedge K_Q(\phi \to \psi) \to K_Q\psi$

E13: $\vdash K_Q\phi \to \phi$

E14: $\vdash K_Q\phi \to K_Q K_Q\phi$

E15: $\vdash K_Q\top \to (\neg K_Q\phi \to K_Q\neg K_Q\phi)$

E16: If $P \in \mathfrak{S}$ then $\vdash K_P\top \leftrightarrow c_P|\top$

E17: $\vdash K_Q\phi \leftrightarrow (K_Q\top \wedge K_0(K_Q\top \to \phi))$

E18: $\vdash K_0\phi \wedge \psi|\rho \to (K_0\phi \wedge \psi)|(K_0\phi \wedge \rho)$

E19: $\vdash K_0\phi \to [\alpha]K_0\phi$

E20: $\vdash K_0\phi \to (K_Q\top \to K_Q K_0\phi)$

**Epistemic rules**

ER5: $\vdash \phi$ then $\vdash K_Q\top \to K_Q\phi$

ER6: If $\mathcal{M} \ni P$ is a finite context and $\vdash c_{\mathcal{M}} \wedge c_P \to K_0\phi$ then $\vdash c_{\mathcal{M}} \to \phi$

### 3.6 Soundness and Completeness

The choice of the axioms is motivated by the soundness theorem.

**Theorem 12 (Soundness).** *The systems $\mathcal{L}_{DS}$ and $\mathcal{L}_{DES}$ are sound w.r.t. process semantics.*

Hence everything expressed by our axioms and rules about the process semantics is correct and, in conclusion, using our system, we can derive only theorems that can be meaningfully interpreted in CCS.

Further we state the completeness of $\mathcal{L}_{DS}$ and of $\mathcal{L}_{DES}$ with respect to process semantics. The intuition is that, because $c_P$ is a characteristic formulas, we should have an equivalence between $\mathcal{M}, P \models \phi$ and $\vdash c_P \to \phi$ for $\mathcal{L}_{DS}$, and between $\mathcal{M}, P \models \phi$ and $\vdash c_{\mathcal{M}} \wedge c_P \to \phi$ for $\mathcal{L}_{DES}$ (when $\mathcal{M}$ is a finite context). Using this intuition we proved the completeness theorem. Observe that $\mathcal{L}_{DS}$ logic is not sensitive to contexts, while $\mathcal{L}_{DES}$ is, because of the universal quantifier involved in the semantics of the epistemic operator.

**Theorem 13 (Completeness).** *The $\mathcal{L}_{DS}$ and $\mathcal{L}_{DES}$ are complete with respect to process semantics.*

The completeness ensures that everything that can be derived in the semantics can be proved as theorem. In this way we have the possibility to syntactically verify (prove) properties of distributed systems.

## 4 Concluding Remarks

In this paper we developed two decidable and complete axiomatized logics for specifying and model-checking concurrent distributed systems: Dynamic Spatial Logic - $\mathcal{L}_{DS}$ and Dynamic Epistemic Spatial Logic - $\mathcal{L}_{DES}$. They extend Hennessy-Milner logic with the parallel operator and respectively with epistemic operators. The lasts operators are meant to express global properties over contexts. We propose these operators as alternative to the guarantee operator of the classical spatial logics, in order to obtaining a logic adequately expressive and decidable.

$\mathcal{L}_{DES}$ is less expressive than the classic spatial logic. Using the guarantee operator and the characteristic formulas, we can express our epistemic operators in classic spatial logic, while guarantee operator cannot be expressed by using our logic: $K_Q \phi \overset{def}{=} c_Q | \top \wedge (\neg(c_Q | \top \rightarrow \phi) \triangleright \bot)$.

Validity and satisfiability in a model can be syntactically expressed in $\mathcal{L}_{DES}$. Combining this feature with the possibility to characterize processes and finite contexts, we may argue on utility of this logic.

In the context of decidability, our sound and complete Hilbert-style axiomatic systems provide powerful tools for making predictions on the evolution of the concurrent distributed systems. Knowing the current state or a sub-state of a system, we can characterize it syntactically. And because any other state can be characterized, we can project any prediction-like problem in syntax and verify its satisfiability. Hence if the system we considered can reach the state we check, we will obtain that the formula is satisfiable and this method will provide also a minimal model.

The axioms and rules considered are very similar to the classical axioms and rules in epistemic logic, and some derivable theorems state meaningful properties of epistemic agents. All these relates our logic with the classical epistemic/doxastic logics and focus the specifications on external observers as epistemic agents. This interpretation is consistent with the spirit of process algebras.

Further researches are to be considered such as adding other operators in logics to fit with more complex process calculi. Challenging will be also the perspective of considering recursion in semantics.

**Acknowledgements.** We thank to Alexandru Baltag for contributing with valuable comments, since the beginning, on the construction of this logic. Thanks also to Luca Cardelli for comments and related discussions. The name *structural bisimulation* was suggested to us by Gordon Plotkin.

# References

1. Bergstra, J.A.: Handbook of Process Algebra. Elsevier Science Inc., New York, NY, USA (2001)
2. Hennessy, M., Milner, R.: Algebraic laws for nondeterminism and concurrency. JACM **vol: 32(1)** (1985) 137–161
3. Stirling, C.: Modal and temporal properties of processes. Springer-Verlag New York, Inc., New York, NY, USA (2001)
4. Milner, R., Parrow, J., Walker, D.: Modal logics for mobile processes. Theoretical Computer Science **vol:114** (1993) 149–171
5. Dam, M.: Proof systems for $\pi$-calculus. (In de Queiroz, editor, Logic for Concurrency and Synchronisation, Studies in Logic and Computation. Oxford University Press. To appear)

6. Dam, M.:   Model checking mobile processes.   Information and Computation **vol:129(1)** (1996) 35–51
7. Caires, L., Cardelli, L.: A spatial logic for concurrency (part i). Information and Computation **Vol: 186/2** (November 2003) 194–235
8. Cardelli, L., Gordon, A.D.: Ambient logic. To appear in Mathematical Structures in Computer Science (2003)
9. Cardelli, L., Gordon, A.D.: Anytime, anywhere: Modal logics for mobile ambients. (2000) 365–377
10. Cardelli, L., Gordon, A.D.: Mobile ambients. In: Foundations of Software Science and Computation Structures: First International Conference, FOSSACS '98, Springer-Verlag, Berlin Germany (1998)
11. Caires, L., Lozes, E.: Elimination of quantifiers and decidability in spatial logics for concurrency. Volume vol:3170. (2004)
12. Charatonik, W., Talbot, J.M.: The decidability of model checking mobile ambients. Volume 2142 of Lecture Notes in Computer Science. (2001) 339–354
13. Charatonik, W., Gordon, A.D., Talbot, J.M.: Finite-control mobile ambients. In: ESOP '02: Proceedings of the 11th European Symposium on Programming Languages and Systems, Springer-Verlag (2002) 295–313
14. Milner, R.: A Calculus of Communicating Systems. Springer-Verlag New York, Inc. (1982)
15. Fagin, R., Halpern, J.Y., Moses, Y., Vardi, M.Y.: Reasoning about Knowledge. MIT Press (1995)
16. Harel, D., Kozen, D., Tiuryn, J.: Dynamic Logic. MIT Press (2000)
17. Baltag, A., Moss, L.S.: Logics for epistemic programs. In: Synthese: J. Symons, J. Hintikka. (Eds.), Knowledge, Rationality and Action, Springer **139 (2)** (2004) 165–224
18. J. Gerbrandy, W.G.: Reasoning about information change. Journal of Logic, Language and Information **6** (1997) 146–169
19. van Benthem, J.F.A.K.: Games in dynamic epistemic logic. Bulletin of Economic Research, Los Altos **53(4)** (2001) 219–248
20. Syverson, P., Cervesato, I.: The logic of authentication protocols. In: Riccardo Focardi, Roberto Gorrieri (Eds.): Foundations of Security Analysis and Design, Springer **LNCS 2117** (2001)
21. Mardare, R., Priami, C.: Dynamic epistemic spatial logics. Technical Report, 03/2006, Microsoft Research Center for Computational and Systems Biology, Trento, Italy (2006)
22. Mardare, R., Priami, C.: A decidable extension of hennessy-milner logic with spatial operators. Technical Report DIT-06-009, Informatica e Telecomunicationi, University of Trento (2006)
23. Mardare, R.: Logical analysis of complex systems: Dynamic epistemic spatial logics. PhD. thesis, DIT, University of Trento, Italy, available from http://www.dit.unitn.it/~mardare/publications.htm (March 2006)
24. Calcagno, C., Cardelli, L., Gordon, A.D.: Deciding validity in a spatial logic for trees. (2003) 62–73

# Symbolic Verification of Communicating Systems with Probabilistic Message Losses: Liveness and Fairness*

C. Baier[1], N. Bertrand[2], and Ph. Schnoebelen[2]

[1] Universität Bonn, Institut für Informatik I, Germany
[2] LSV, ENS de Cachan & CNRS, France

**Abstract.** NPLCS's are a new model for nondeterministic channel systems where unreliable communication is modeled by probabilistic message losses. We show that, for ω-regular linear-time properties and finite-memory schedulers, qualitative model-checking is decidable. The techniques extend smoothly to questions where fairness restrictions are imposed on the schedulers. The symbolic procedure underlying our decidability proofs has been implemented and used to study a simple protocol handling two-way transfers in an unreliable setting.

## 1 Introduction

*Channel systems* [15] are systems of finite-state components that communicate via asynchronous unbounded fifo channels. *Lossy* channel systems [17,6], shortly LCS's, are a special class of channel systems where messages can be lost while they are in transit. They are a natural model for fault-tolerant protocols where communication is not supposed to be reliable (see example in Fig. 1 below). Additionally, the lossiness assumption makes termination and safety properties decidable [22,17,6,4,20,8] while reliable, i.e., non-lossy, systems are Turing-powerful.

LCS's are a convenient model for verifying safety properties of asynchronous protocols, and this can be automated [4]. However, they are not adequate for verifying liveness and progress properties: firstly these properties are undecidable for LCS's [5], and secondly the model itself is too pessimistic when liveness is considered. Indeed, to ensure any kind of progress, one must assume that at least some messages will not be lost. This is classically obtained via fairness assumptions on message losses [18] but fairness assumptions in LCS's make decidability even more elusive [5,21].

*Probabilistic LCS's*, shortly PLCS's, are LCS's where message losses are seen as faults having a *probabilistic* behavior [27,10,31,1,29,2,7]. Thanks to its probabilistic framework, this model automatically fulfills strong fairness conditions on the message losses. Additionally it allows one to state so-called *qualitative* questions, whether a linear-time property will be satisfied *"with probability 1"*, that are decidable. However, PLCS's are not a realistic model for protocols because they consider that the choices between different actions are made probabilistically rather than nondeterministically. When modeling communication protocols, *nondeterminism* is an essential feature. It

---

* The first author is supported by the DFG-NWO project VOSS II and the DFG-project PROB-POR. The last two authors were supported by the ACI Sécurité & Informatique project Persée.

is used to model the interleaved behavior of distributed components, to model an unknown environment, to delay implementation choices at early stages of the design, and to abstract away from complex control structures at later stages.

This prompted us to introduce NPLCS's, i.e., channel systems where message losses are probabilistic and actions are nondeterministic [13,14]. These systems give rise to infinite-state Markov decision processes, and are a more faithful model for analyzing protocols. The drawback is that they raise very difficult verification problems.

**Qualitative Verification for NPLCS's.** Our early results in [14] rely on the assumption that idling was always a possible choice. This simplifies the analysis considerably, but is an overkill: a necessary ingredient for most liveness properties of a compound system is the inherent liveness of the components, which disappears if they can idle.

We developed new techniques and removed the idling limitation in [9] where we show that decidability can be maintained if we restrict our attention to *finite-memory* schedulers (strategies for the nondeterministic choices). This seems like a mild restriction, and we adopt it in this paper since we aim for automatic verification.

**Our Contributions.** In this paper we extend the preliminary work from [9] in three directions: (1) We allow linear-time formulas referring to the contents of the channels rather than just the control locations. We did not consider this extension earlier because we lacked the techniques for proving the convergence of fixpoint computations. However, the extension is required in practical applications where fairness properties have to express that "a rule is firable," which depends on channel contents for read actions. (2) We develop symbolic representations and algorithms for sets of NPLCS configurations. These algorithms have been implemented in a prototype tool that we use to analyze a simple communication protocol. (3) We consider qualitative verification with quantification over *fair* schedulers, i.e., schedulers that generate fair runs almost surely.

**Outline of the Paper.** Section 2 recalls the necessary technical background for nondeterministic probabilistic channel systems, and section 3 introduces the new symbolic framework we use for handling sets of configurations. We present our decidability results in sections 4 (for finite-memory schedulers) and 5 (for fair schedulers). Finally we apply our algorithms on Pachl's protocol in section 6. All proofs omitted in this extended abstract can be found in the complete version available on the web.

## 2 Nondeterministic Probabilistic Channel Systems

We assume the reader has some familiarity with the verification of Markov decision processes, or MDPs, (otherwise see [11]) and refer to [9] for complete definitions regarding our framework. Here we recall the main definitions and notations without motivating or illustrating all of them.

**Lossy Channel Systems.** A lossy channel system (a LCS) is a tuple $\mathcal{L} = (Q, C, M, \Delta)$ of a finite set $Q = \{p, q, \ldots\}$ of control *locations*, a finite set $C = \{c, \ldots\}$ of *channels*, a finite *message alphabet* $M = \{m, \ldots\}$ and a finite set $\Delta = \{\delta, \ldots\}$ of *transition rules*. Each rule has the form $q \xrightarrow{op} p$ where *op* is an *operation* of the form *c!m* (sending message $m$ along channel $c$), $c?m$ (receiving message $m$ from channel $c$), or $\sqrt{}$ (an internal action with no communication). For example, the protocol displayed in Fig 1, is naturally modeled as a LCS: building the asynchronous product of the two processes $P_L$ and $P_R$ yields a bona fide LCS with two channels and a five-message alphabet $M = \{a_0, a_1, d_0, d_1, eod\}$.

**Operational Semantics.** A *configuration* of $L$ as above is a pair $s = (q, w)$ of a location and a channel valuation $w : C \to M^*$ associating with any channel its current content (a sequence of messages). $M^{*C}$, or $M^*$ when $|C| = 1$, denotes the set of all channel valuations, and Conf the set of all configurations. $\varepsilon$ denotes both the empty word and the empty channel valuation. The size $|s|$ of a configuration is the total number of messages in $s$. The rules of $L$ give rise to transitions between configurations in the obvious way [9]. We write $\Delta(s)$ for the set of rules $\delta \in \Delta$ that are enabled in configuration $s$.

We write $s \xrightarrow{\delta}_{\text{perf}} s'$ when $s'$ is obtained by firing $\delta$ in $s$. The "perf" subscript stresses the fact that the step is perfect, i.e., no messages are lost. However, in lossy systems, arbitrary messages can be lost. This is formalized with the help of the subword ordering: we write $\mu \sqsubseteq \mu'$ when $\mu$ is a subword of $\mu'$, i.e., $\mu$ can be obtained by removing (any number of) messages from $\mu'$, and we extend this to configurations, writing $(q, w) \sqsubseteq (q', w')$ when $q = q'$ and $w(c) \sqsubseteq w'(c)$ for all $c \in C$. As a consequence of Higman's Lemma, $\sqsubseteq$ is a well-quasi-order (a *wqo*) between configurations of $L$. Now, we define *lossy steps* by letting $s \xrightarrow{\delta} s'' \stackrel{\text{def}}{\Leftrightarrow}$ there is a perfect step $s \xrightarrow{\delta}_{\text{perf}} s'$ such that $s'' \sqsubseteq s'$. This gives rise to a labeled transition system $LTS_L \stackrel{\text{def}}{=} (\text{Conf}, \Delta, \to)$. Here the set $\Delta$ of transition rules serves as action alphabet. In the following we assume that for any location $q \in Q$, $\Delta$ contains at least one rule $q \xrightarrow{op} p$ where $op$ is not a receive operation. This hypothesis ensures that $LTS_L$ has no deadlock configuration and makes the theory smoother. It is no real loss of generality as demonstrated in [2, § 8.3].

**An Example.** Pachl's protocol [22] handles two-way communications over lossy channels and is our case study for our algorithms. It consists of two identical processes, $P_{L(eft)}$ and $P_{R(ight)}$, that exchange data over lossy channels using an acknowledgment mechanism based on the alternating bit protocol. See Fig 1 below. The actual contents of the data messages is abstracted away, and we just use $d_0, d_1 \in M$ to record the alternating control bit. Messages $a_0, a_1 \in M$ are the corresponding acknowledgments. The protocol starts in configuration $(L0, R4)$ where $P_L$ is the sender and $P_R$ the receiver. At any time (provided its last data message has been acknowledged) the sender may signal the end of its data sequence with the $eod \in M$ control message and then the two processes swap their sending and receiving roles. Note that $eod$ does not need to carry a control bit, and that its correct reception is not acknowledged. In section 6 we explain how such a two-process protocol is modeled as an LCS, and give some outcomes of our automated analysis.

**From LCS's to NPLCS's.** A NPLCS $\mathcal{N} = (L, \tau)$ is a LCS $L$ further equipped with a *fault rate* $\tau \in (0, 1)$ that specifies the probability that a given message stored in one of the message queues is lost during a step [13, 14]. The operational semantics of NPLCS's has the form of an infinite-state Markov decision process $MDP_{\mathcal{N}} \stackrel{\text{def}}{=} (\text{Conf}, \Delta, \mathbf{P}_{\mathcal{N}})$. The

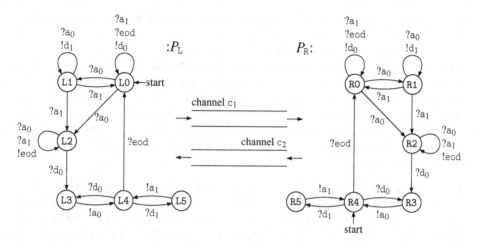

**Fig. 1.** Pachl's communication protocol, from [22]

stepwise probabilistic behavior is formalized by a three-dimensional transition proba-bility matrix $\mathbf{P}_{\mathcal{N}} : \mathrm{Conf} \times \Delta \times \mathrm{Conf} \to [0,1]$. For a given configuration $s$ and an enabled rule $\delta \in \Delta(s)$, $\mathbf{P}_{\mathcal{N}}(s, \delta, \cdot)$ is a distribution over Conf, while $\mathbf{P}_{\mathcal{N}}(s, \delta, \cdot) = 0$ for any tran-sition rule $\delta$ that is not enabled in $s$. The intuitive meaning of $\mathbf{P}_{\mathcal{N}}(s, \delta, t) = \lambda > 0$ is that with probability $\lambda$, the system moves from configuration $s$ to configuration $t$ when $\delta$ is the chosen transition rule in $s$.

For lack of space, this extended abstract omits the technically heavy but quite natural definition of $\mathbf{P}_{\mathcal{N}}$, and only lists its two essential properties:

1. the labeled transition system underlying $MDP_{(L,\pi)}$ is exactly $LTS_L$.
2. the set $Q_\varepsilon = \{(q, \varepsilon) \mid q \in Q\}$ of configurations where the channels are empty is an *attractor*, i.e., from any starting configuration, $Q_\varepsilon$ will eventually be visited with probability 1 [2,7].

**Schedulers and Probability Measure.** The nondeterminism in an MDP is resolved by a *scheduler*, also often called "adversary", "policy" or "strategy". Here a "scheduler" is a *history-dependent deterministic scheduler* in the classification of [28]. Formally, a scheduler for $\mathcal{N}$ is a mapping $\mathcal{U}$ that assigns to any finite path $\pi$ in $\mathcal{N}$ a transition rule $\delta \in \Delta$ that is enabled in the last state of $\pi$. The given path $\pi$ specifies the history of the system, and $\mathcal{U}(\pi)$ is the rule that $\mathcal{U}$ chooses to fire next. A scheduler $\mathcal{U}$ only gives rise to certain paths: we say $\pi = s_0 \xrightarrow{\delta_1} s_1 \xrightarrow{\delta_2} \cdots$ is *compatible with* $\mathcal{U}$ or, shortly, is a $\mathcal{U}$-*path*, if $\mathbf{P}_{\mathcal{N}}(s_{i-1}, \delta_i, s_i) > 0$ for all $i \geq 1$, where $\delta_{i+1} = \mathcal{U}(s_0 \xrightarrow{\delta_1} \cdots \xrightarrow{\delta_i} s_i)$ is the rule chosen by $\mathcal{U}$ at step $i$ along $\pi$. In practice, it is only relevant to define how $\mathcal{U}$ evaluates on finite $\mathcal{U}$-paths.

A *finite-memory*, or fm-, scheduler $\mathcal{U} = (U, D, \eta, u_0)$ is specified via a finite set $U$ of *modes*, a *starting mode* $u_0 \in U$, a *decision rule* $D : U \times \mathrm{Conf} \to \Delta$ choosing the next rule $D(u, s) \in \Delta(s)$ based on the current mode and the current configuration, and a *next-mode function* $\eta : U \times \mathrm{Conf} \to U$ specifying the mode-changes of $\mathcal{U}$. The modes are used to store some relevant information about the history. An fm-scheduler $\mathcal{U}$ is *memoryless* if it has a single mode: then $\mathcal{U}$ is not history-dependent and can be specified more simply as a mapping $\mathcal{U} : \mathsf{Conf} \to \Delta$.

Now, given an NPLCS $\mathcal{N}$, a starting configuration $s = s_0$ and a scheduler $\mathcal{U}$, the behavior of $\mathcal{N}$ under $\mathcal{U}$ can be formalized by an infinite-state Markov chain $MC_{\mathcal{U}}$. For arbitrary schedulers, the states of $MC_{\mathcal{U}}$ are finite paths in $\mathcal{N}$, while for fm-schedulers it is possible to consider pairs $(u, s)$ of a mode of $\mathcal{U}$ and a configuration of $\mathcal{N}$. One may now apply the standard machinery for Markov chains and define (for fixed starting configuration $s$) a sigma-field on the set of infinite paths starting in $s$ and a probability measure on it, see, e.g., [28,23,11]. We shall write $\Pr_{\mathcal{U}}(s \models \ldots)$ to denote the standard probability measure in $MC_{\mathcal{U}}$ with starting state $s$.

**LTL/CTL-notation.** We use simple LTL and CTL formulas to denote properties of respectively paths and configurations in $MDP_L$. Here configurations and locations serve as atomic propositions: for example $\Box \Diamond s$ (resp. $\Box \Diamond q$) means that $s \in \mathsf{Conf}$ (resp. $q \in Q$) is visited infinitely many times, and $q$ Until $s$ means that the control location remains $q$ until configuration $s$ is eventually reached. These notations extend to sets and, for $T \subseteq \mathsf{Conf}$ and $P \subseteq Q$, $\Box \Diamond T$ and $\Box \Diamond P$ have the obvious meaning. For $P \subseteq Q$, $P_\varepsilon$ is the set $\{(p, \varepsilon) \mid p \in P\}$ so that $\Diamond Q_\varepsilon$ means that eventually a configuration with empty channels is reached. It is well-known that for any scheduler $\mathcal{U}$, the set of paths starting in some configuration $s$ and satisfying an LTL formula, or an $\omega$-regular property, $\varphi$ is measurable [32,16]. We write $\Pr_{\mathcal{U}}(s \models \varphi)$ for this measure.

**Reachability Analysis.** For a set $A \subseteq \mathsf{Conf}$ and a rule $\delta \in \Delta$, we let $Pre[\delta](A) \overset{\text{def}}{=} \{s \mid \exists t \in A, s \overset{\delta}{\to} t\}$ denote the set of configurations from which $A$ can be reached in one step with rule $\delta$. $Pre(A) \overset{\text{def}}{=} \bigcup_{\delta \in \Delta} Pre[\delta](A)$ contains all *one-step predecessors*, and $Pre^*(A) \overset{\text{def}}{=} A \cup Pre(A) \cup Pre(Pre(A)) \cup \cdots$ all *iterated predecessors*. The successor sets $Post[\delta](A)$, $Post(A)$, and $Post^*(A)$ are defined analogously. Recall that reachability between configurations of LCS's is decidable [6,30], which is also implied by Theorem 3.2 below.

**Constrained Reachability.** We sometimes need to reach a set $A$ using only rules that cannot get us out of some set $T \subseteq \mathsf{Conf}$. Formally, for $T, A \subseteq \mathsf{Conf}$, we define

$$\widehat{Pre}_T(A) \overset{\text{def}}{=} \{s \in \mathsf{Conf} \mid \exists \delta \in \Delta(s) \text{ s.t. } Post[\delta](s) \cap A \neq \emptyset \text{ and } Post[\delta](s) \subseteq T\}.$$

In other words, $s$ is in $\widehat{Pre}_T(A)$ if there is a rule $\delta$ that may take $s$ to some state in $A$ but that cannot take it outside $T$. The set of iterated $T$-*constrained* predecessors is

$$\widehat{Pre}_T^*(A) \overset{\text{def}}{=} A \cup \widehat{Pre}_T(A) \cup \widehat{Pre}_T(\widehat{Pre}_T(A)) \cup \cdots$$

## 3  Symbolic Representations for Sets of Configurations

Symbolic model-checking relies on symbolic objects representing sets of configurations, and algorithmic methods for handling these objects meaningfully.

In this section, we present a symbolic framework for NPLCS's based on *differences of prefixed upward-closures*. This extends previous techniques from [4,3,20] in that it permits dealing with set differences and checking which is the first message in a channel. For simplicity in the presentation, *we assume that the NPLCS under consideration only has a single channel.* We also omit most of the algorithmic details pertaining to data structures, normal forms, canonization, ..., that are present in our prototype implementation (see section 6).

Recall that a set $T \subseteq \mathsf{Conf}$ is *upward-closed* (resp., *downward-closed*) if for all $s \in T$, and for all $s' \sqsupseteq s$ (resp., $s' \sqsubseteq s$), $s' \in T$. For $T \subseteq \mathsf{Conf}$, we let $\uparrow T \stackrel{\mathrm{def}}{=} \{s \in \mathsf{Conf} | \exists s' \in T \wedge s' \sqsubseteq s\}$ denote the *upward-closure* of $T$, and $\downarrow T \stackrel{\mathrm{def}}{=} \{s \in \mathsf{Conf} | \exists s' \in T \wedge s \sqsubseteq s'\}$ denote the *downward-closure* of $T$. For singleton sets we write shortly $\uparrow t$ and $\downarrow t$ rather than $\uparrow \{t\}$ and $\downarrow \{t\}$.

Our symbolic sets are defined with the following abstract grammar:

| | | |
|---:|:---|:---|
| prefix: | $\alpha := \varepsilon \mid m$ | $m \in \mathsf{M}$ |
| prefixed closure: | $\theta := \alpha{\uparrow}u$ | $u \in \mathsf{M}^*$ |
| sum of prefixed closures: | $\sigma := \theta_1 + \cdots + \theta_n$ | $n \geq 0$ |
| simple symbolic set: | $\rho := \langle q, \theta - \sigma \rangle$ | $q \in Q$ is a location |
| symbolic set: | $\gamma := \rho_1 + \cdots + \rho_n$ | $n \geq 0$ |

Prefixed (upward-)closures and their sums denote subsets of $\mathsf{M}^*$ defined with $[\![\alpha{\uparrow}u]\!] \stackrel{\mathrm{def}}{=} \{\alpha v \mid u \sqsubseteq v\}$ and $[\![\theta_1 + \cdots + \theta_n]\!] \stackrel{\mathrm{def}}{=} [\![\theta_1]\!] \cup \cdots \cup [\![\theta_n]\!]$. Symbolic sets denote subsets of $\mathsf{Conf}$ defined with $[\![\langle q, \theta - (\theta_1 + \cdots + \theta_n)\rangle]\!] \stackrel{\mathrm{def}}{=} \{\langle q, v\rangle \in \mathsf{Conf} \mid v \in [\![\theta]\!] \smallsetminus ([\![\theta_1]\!] \cup \cdots \cup [\![\theta_n]\!])\}$. A *region* is any subset of $\mathsf{Conf}$ that can be denoted by a symbolic set. It is a *control region* if can be written under the form $\sum_i \langle q_i, \varepsilon{\uparrow}\varepsilon\rangle$, where channel contents are unrestricted.

We abuse notation and write $\emptyset$ to denote both empty (i.e., with $n = 0$) sums of prefixed closures and empty symbolic sets. We also sometimes write $\uparrow v$ for $\varepsilon{\uparrow}v$, $\theta - \theta_1 - \cdots - \theta_n$ for $\theta - (\theta_1 + \cdots + \theta_n)$, and $\theta$ for $\theta - \emptyset$. We write $\gamma \equiv \gamma'$ when $[\![\gamma]\!] = [\![\gamma']\!]$, i.e., when $\gamma$ and $\gamma'$ denote the same region.

**Theorem 3.1 (Effective symbolic computation: basics).**

**Boolean closure:** *Regions are closed under union, intersection, and complementation. Moreover, there exist algorithms that given symbolic sets $\gamma_1$ and $\gamma_2$ return terms denoted $\gamma_1 \sqcup \gamma_2$, $\gamma_1 \sqcap \gamma_2$ and $\neg\gamma$ such that $[\![\gamma_1 \sqcup \gamma_2]\!] = [\![\gamma_1]\!] \cup [\![\gamma_2]\!]$, $[\![\gamma_1 \sqcap \gamma_2]\!] = [\![\gamma_1]\!] \cap [\![\gamma_2]\!]$ and $[\![\neg\gamma]\!] = \mathsf{Conf} \smallsetminus [\![\gamma]\!]$.*

**Upward closure:** *Regions are closed under upward closure. Moreover, there exists an algorithm that given a symbolic set $\gamma$ returns a term denoted $\uparrow\gamma$ such that $[\![\uparrow\gamma]\!] = \uparrow[\![\gamma]\!]$.*

**Vacuity:** *It is decidable whether $[\![\gamma]\!] = \emptyset$ given a region $\gamma$.*

**One-step predecessors:** *Regions are closed under the $Pre(\_)$ and $\widehat{Pre}_{-}(\_)$ operations. Moreover, there exist algorithms that given symbolic sets $\gamma$ and $\gamma'$ return terms denoted $Pre(\gamma)$ and $\widehat{Pre}_{\gamma'}(\gamma)$, and such that $[\![Pre(\gamma)]\!] = Pre([\![\gamma]\!])$ and $[\![\widehat{Pre}_{\gamma'}(\gamma)]\!] = \widehat{Pre}_{[\![\gamma']\!]}([\![\gamma]\!])$.*

Theorem 3.1 provides the basic ingredients necessary for symbolic model-checking of LCS's. These ingredients can then be used for computing sets defined as fixpoints.

For example, using standard $\mu$-calculus notation, a symbolic set denoting $Pre^*(\llbracket\gamma\rrbracket)$ would be defined as $\mu X.\gamma \sqcup Pre(X)$. In [8] we show how a symbolic representation for sets defined by such fixpoint expressions can be computed effectively (when some guardedness condition holds).

**Theorem 3.2 (Effective symbolic computation: fixpoints).**

**Iterated (constrained) predecessors:** *Regions are closed under the $Pre^*(\_)$ and the $\widehat{Pre}^*(\_)$ operations. Moreover, there exist algorithms that given symbolic sets $\gamma$ and $\gamma'$ return terms denoted $Pre^*(\gamma)$ and $\widehat{Pre}^*_{\gamma'}(\gamma)$, and such that $\llbracket Pre^*(\gamma)\rrbracket = Pre^*(\llbracket\gamma\rrbracket)$ and $\llbracket\widehat{Pre}^*_{\gamma'}(\gamma)\rrbracket = \widehat{Pre}^*_{\llbracket\gamma'\rrbracket}(\llbracket\gamma\rrbracket)$.*

**Safe sets (see section 4):** *For any region $\gamma$, the set $\nu X.(\gamma \sqcap \widehat{Pre}_X(\mathsf{Conf}))$ is a region, and a term for it can be computed effectively.*

**Promising sets (see section 4):** *For any region $\gamma$, the set $\nu X.\widehat{Pre}^*_X(\gamma)$ is a region, and a term for it can be computed effectively.*

**∃CTL:** *The set of configurations satisfying an ∃CTL formula (i.e., a CTL formula where only the modalities "$\exists(\_$ Until $\_)$" and "$\exists$Next$\_$" are allowed) is a region when the atomic propositions are themselves regions. Moreover, a symbolic set for that region can be obtained algorithmically from the ∃CTL formula.*

## 4   Verifying Safety and Liveness Properties for NPLCS's

This section considers various types of safety and liveness properties where regions serve as atoms, and presents algorithms for checking the existence of a fm-scheduler $\mathcal{U}$ such that $\Pr_{\mathcal{U}}(s \models \varphi)$ is $> 0$, $= 1$, $< 1$ or $= 0$.

We start with reachability properties $\Diamond A$ and invariants $\Box A$ for some region $A$.

For eventually properties with the satisfaction criteria "with positive probability", decidability relies on the computation of iterative predecessors in (non-probabilistic) lossy channel systems:

**Theorem 4.1.** *Let $s \in \mathsf{Conf}$ and $A \subseteq \mathsf{Conf}$. There exists a scheduler $\mathcal{U}$ with $\Pr_{\mathcal{U}}(s \models \Diamond A) > 0$ iff $\Pr_{\mathcal{U}}(s \models \Diamond A) > 0$ for some memoryless scheduler $\mathcal{U}$ iff $s \in Pre^*(A)$.*

For other satisfaction criteria, or for other properties, we have to develop more ad-hoc characterizations of the sets of configurations where the qualitative properties hold.

For invariants $\Box A$, we introduce the concept of safe sets:

**Definition 4.2 (Safe sets).** *Let $A, T \subseteq \mathsf{Conf}$. $T$ is called safe for $A$ if $T \subseteq A$ and for all $s \in T$, there exists a transition rule $\delta$ enabled in $s$ such that $Post[\delta](s) \subseteq T$.*

Since the union of safe sets is safe, the largest safe set for $A$, denoted $Safe(A)$, exists.

There exists a simple fixpoint characterization for $Safe(A)$ (here and in the sequel, we use the standard $\mu/\nu$-notations for fixpoints).

**Lemma 4.3.** *For any $A \subseteq \mathsf{Conf}$, $Safe(A) = \nu X.A \cap \widehat{Pre}_X(\mathsf{Conf})$.*

Thus, if $A$ is a region, $Safe(A)$ is a region too, and a symbolic representation can be computed effectively (Theorem 3.2). This is the key for verifying invariants:

**Theorem 4.4 (Safe sets and invariants).** *Let $A \subseteq$ Conf and $s \in$ Conf.*

(a)  $s \in Safe(A)$
     iff *there exists a scheduler $\mathcal{U}$ such that* $\mathrm{Pr}_{\mathcal{U}}(s \models \Box A) = 1$
     iff *there exists a memoryless scheduler $\mathcal{U}$ such that* $\mathrm{Pr}_{\mathcal{U}}(s \models \Box A) = 1$.
(b)  $s \models \exists(A \text{ Until } Safe(A))$
     iff *there exists a scheduler $\mathcal{U}$ such that* $\mathrm{Pr}_{\mathcal{U}}(s \models \Box A) > 0$
     iff *there exists a memoryless scheduler $\mathcal{U}$ such that* $\mathrm{Pr}_{\mathcal{U}}(s \models \Box A) > 0$.

The corollary is that, for a region $A$, we can compute a symbolic representation for the set of all configurations where $\mathrm{Pr}_{\mathcal{U}}(s \models \Box A) > 0$ or $= 1$ for some scheduler $\mathcal{U}$.

**Definition 4.5 (Promising sets).** *Let $A, T \subseteq$ Conf. $T$ is called* promising *for $A$ if for all $s \in T$ there exists a path $s = s_0 \xrightarrow{\delta_1} s_1 \xrightarrow{\delta_2} \cdots \xrightarrow{\delta_m} s_m$ with $m \geq 0$ such that $s_m \in A$ and for all $1 \leq i \leq m$, $Post[\delta_i](s_{i-1}) \subseteq T$.*

As for safe sets, the largest promising set for $A$ exists: we denote it $Prom(A)$.

**Lemma 4.6.** *For any $A \subseteq$ Conf, $Prom(A) = \nu X.\widehat{Pre}_X^*(A)$.*

Thus, if $A$ is a region, $Prom(A)$ is a region too, and a symbolic representation can be computed effectively (Theorem 3.2).

**Theorem 4.7 (Promising sets and almost sure reachability).** *Let $s \in$ Conf and $A \subseteq$ Conf. $s \in Prom(A)$ iff $\mathrm{Pr}_{\mathcal{U}}(s \models \Diamond A) = 1$ for some scheduler $\mathcal{U}$ iff $\mathrm{Pr}_{\mathcal{U}}(s \models \Diamond A) = 1$ for some memoryless scheduler $\mathcal{U}$.*

The corollary is that, for a region $A$, we can compute the set of all configurations $s$ such that $\mathrm{Pr}_{\mathcal{U}}(s \models \Diamond A) > 0$ or $= 1$ for some $\mathcal{U}$.

We now consider repeated reachability and persistence properties. The question whether a repeated reachability property $\Box \Diamond A$ holds under some scheduler with positive probability is undecidable when ranging over the full class of schedulers, but is decidable for the class of fm-schedulers. This was shown in [14,9] for the case where $A$ is a set of locations (*i.e.* a control region). We now show that the decidability even holds if $A$ is a region. More precisely, we show that if $A$ is a region and $\varphi \in \{\Box \Diamond A, \Diamond \Box A\}$, then the set of configurations $s$ where $\mathrm{Pr}_{\mathcal{U}}(s \models \varphi) > 0$ or $= 1$ for some fm-scheduler is a region.

For $A \subseteq$ Conf let $Prom^{\geq 1}(A)$ denote the largest set $T$ of configurations such that for all $t \in T$ there exists a finite path $s = s_0 \xrightarrow{\delta_1} s_1 \xrightarrow{\delta_2} \cdots \xrightarrow{\delta_m} s_m$ with $m \geq 1$, $s_m \in A$ and $Post[\delta_i](s_{i-1}) \subseteq T$ for all $1 \leq i \leq m$. Note that the definition of $Prom^{\geq 1}(A)$ is different from $Prom(A)$ since the paths must have length at least 1. We then have $Prom^{\geq 1}(A) = \nu X.\widehat{Pre}_X^+(A)$, and, if $A$ is a region then so is $Prom^{\geq 1}(A)$. Thus, the following theorem provides the decidability of repeated reachability and persistence properties:

**Theorem 4.8 (Repeated reachability and persistence).** *Let $s \in$ Conf and $A \subseteq$ Conf.*

(a) $s \in Prom^{\geq 1}(A)$ *iff* $\Pr_{\mathcal{U}}(s \models \Box\Diamond A) = 1$ *for some scheduler $\mathcal{U}$*
    *iff* $\Pr_{\mathcal{U}}(s \models \Box\Diamond A) = 1$ *for some memoryless scheduler $\mathcal{U}$.*

(b) $s \in Pre^*(Prom^{\geq 1}(A))$ *iff* $\Pr_{\mathcal{U}}(s \models \Box\Diamond A) > 0$ *for some fm-scheduler $\mathcal{U}$*
    *iff* $\Pr_{\mathcal{U}}(s \models \Box\Diamond A) > 0$ *for some memoryless scheduler $\mathcal{U}$.*

(c) $s \in Prom(Safe(A))$ *iff* $\Pr_{\mathcal{U}}(s \models \Diamond\Box A) = 1$ *for some scheduler $\mathcal{U}$*
    *iff* $\Pr_{\mathcal{U}}(s \models \Diamond\Box A) = 1$ *for some memoryless scheduler $\mathcal{U}$.*

(d) $s \in Pre^*(Safe(A))$ *iff* $\Pr_{\mathcal{U}}(s \models \Diamond\Box A) > 0$ *for some scheduler $\mathcal{U}$*
    *iff* $\Pr_{\mathcal{U}}(s \models \Diamond\Box A) > 0$ *for some memoryless scheduler $\mathcal{U}$.*

We now consider the Streett formula $\varphi_S = \bigwedge_{1 \leq i \leq n} \Box\Diamond A_i \to \Box\Diamond B_i$ where $A_1, \ldots, A_n$ and $B_1, \ldots, B_n$ are regions. Here again we only consider fm-schedulers since the problem is undecidable for the full class of schedulers [9].

For $A, B \subseteq$ Conf, let $Prom_A^{\geq 1}(B)$ be the largest subset $T$ of $A$ such that for all $t \in T$ there exists a path $t = s_0 \xrightarrow{\delta_1} \cdots \xrightarrow{\delta_m} s_m$ with $m > 0$, $s_m \in B$ and $Post[\delta_i](s_{i-1}) \subseteq T$ for all $1 \leq i \leq m$. We have $Prom_A^{\geq 1}(B) = \nu X. \widehat{Pre}_X^+(B) \cap A$ and if $A, B$ are regions then so is $Prom_A^{\geq 1}(B)$. In addition, $s \in Prom_A^{\geq 1}(B)$ iff $\Pr_{\mathcal{U}}(s \models \Box\Diamond B \wedge \Box A) = 1$ for some fm-scheduler $\mathcal{U}$.

The above is useful to show decidability of the questions whether $\Pr_{\mathcal{U}}(s \models \varphi_S) < 1$ or $= 0$ for some fm-scheduler $\mathcal{U}$. For this, we use the fact that $\Pr_{\mathcal{U}}(s \models \varphi_S) < 1$ iff $\Pr_{\mathcal{U}}(s \models \Box\Diamond A_i \to \Box\Diamond B_i) < 1$ for some $i$ iff $\Pr_{\mathcal{U}}(s \models \Box\Diamond A_i \wedge \Diamond\Box\neg B_i) > 0$ for some $i$.

**Theorem 4.9 (Streett property, probability less than 1).** *There exists a fm-scheduler $\mathcal{U}$ with $\Pr_{\mathcal{U}}(s \models \Box\Diamond A \wedge \Diamond\Box\neg B) > 0$ iff there exists a memoryless scheduler $\mathcal{U}$ with $\Pr_{\mathcal{U}}(s \models \Box\Diamond A \wedge \Diamond\Box\neg B) > 0$ iff $s \in Pre^*(Prom_{\neg B}^{\geq 1}(A))$. In particular, $\Pr_{\mathcal{U}}(s \models \varphi_S) < 1$ for some fm-scheduler $\mathcal{U}$ iff $s \in \bigcup_{1 \leq i \leq n} Pre^*(Prom_{\neg B_i}^{\geq 1}(A_i))$.*

Let $T_i$ be the set of all configurations $t \in$ Conf such that $\Pr_{\mathcal{W}}(s \models \Box\Diamond A_i \wedge \Diamond\Box\neg B_i) = 1$ for some fm-scheduler $\mathcal{W}$. Note that $T_i = Pre^*(Prom_{\neg B_i}^{\geq 1}(A_i))$ is a region. Thus, $T_S = T_1 \cup T_2 \cup \cdots \cup T_n$ is a region too. This and the following theorem yields the decidability of the question whether $\Pr_{\mathcal{U}}(s \models \varphi_S) = 0$ for some scheduler $\mathcal{U}$.

**Theorem 4.10 (Streett property, zero probability).** *There exists a fm-scheduler $\mathcal{U}$ such that $\Pr_{\mathcal{U}}(s \models \varphi_S) = 0$ if and only if $s \in Prom(T_S)$.*

We next consider the satisfaction criterion "with positive probability". The treatment of the special case of a single strong fairness formula $\Box\Diamond A \to \Box\Diamond B \equiv \Diamond\Box\neg A \vee \Box\Diamond B$ is obvious as we have: There exists a finite-memory (resp. memoryless) scheduler $\mathcal{U}$ such that $\Pr_{\mathcal{U}}(s \models \Box\Diamond A \to \Box\Diamond B) > 0$ iff at least one of the following conditions holds: (i) there exists a fm-scheduler $V$ such that $\Pr_V(s \models \Diamond\Box\neg A) > 0$ or (ii) there exists a fm-scheduler $\mathcal{W}$ such that $\Pr_{\mathcal{W}}(s \models \Box\Diamond B) > 0$. We now extend this observation to the general case (several Streett properties). For $I \subseteq \{1, \ldots, n\}$, let $A_I$ denote the set of configurations $s$ such that there exists a finite-memory scheduler satisfying $\Pr_{\mathcal{U}}(s \models \bigwedge_{i \in I} \Box\Diamond B_i \wedge \bigwedge_{i \notin I} \Box\neg A_i) = 1$ and let $A$ be the union of all $A_I$'s, i.e., $A = \bigcup_{I \subseteq \{1,\ldots,n\}} A_I$. Then, the sets $A_I$ and $A$ are regions. Thus, the algorithmic treatment of Streett properties the satisfaction criteria "positive probability" and "almost surely" relies on the following theorem:

**Theorem 4.11 (Streett properties, positive probability and almost surely).**

*(a) There exists a fm-scheduler $\mathcal{U}$ such that $\mathrm{Pr}_{\mathcal{U}}(s \models \varphi_S) > 0$ iff $s \in Pre^*(A)$.*
*(b) There exists a fm-scheduler $\mathcal{U}$ such that $\mathrm{Pr}_{\mathcal{U}}(s \models \varphi_S) = 1$ iff $s \in Prom(A)$.*

We conclude with the following main theorem gathering all previous results:

**Theorem 4.12 (Qualitative model-checking).** *For any NPLCS $\mathcal{N}$ and Streett property $\varphi = \bigwedge_i \Box \Diamond A_i \to \Box \Diamond B_i$ where the $A_i$'s and $B_i$'s are regions, the set of all configurations $s$ s.t. for all fm-schedulers $\mathcal{U}$ $\mathrm{Pr}_{\mathcal{U}}(s \models \varphi)$ satisfies a qualitative constraint "$= 1$", or "$< 1$", or "$= 0$", or "$> 0$", is a region that can be computed effectively.*

With the techniques of [9, § 7], Theorem 4.12 extends to all $\omega$-regulars properties

# 5   Verification Under Fair Finite-Memory Schedulers

We now address the problem of verifying qualitative linear time properties under fairness assumptions. Following the approaches of [19,32,12], we consider here a notion of *scheduler-fairness* which rules out some schedulers that generate unfair paths with positive probability. This notion of scheduler-fairness has to be contrasted with extreme- and alpha-fairness introduced in [24,25,26] which require a "fair" resolution of probabilistic choices and serve as verification techniques rather than fairness assumptions about the nondeterministic choices.

A scheduler $\mathcal{U}$ is called *fair* if it generates almost surely fair paths, according to some appropriate fairness constraints for paths. We deal here with *strong fairness* for selected sets of transition rules. I.e., we assume a set $\mathcal{F} = \{f_0, \dots, f_{k-1}\}$ where $f_i \subseteq \Delta$ and require strong fairness for all $f_i$'s. (The latter means whenever some transition rule in $f_i$ is enabled infinitely often then some transition rule in $f_i$ will fire infinitely often.) For instance, process fairness for $k$ processes $P_0, \dots, P_{k-1}$ can be modelled by $\mathcal{F} = \{f_0, \dots, f_{k-1}\}$ where $f_i$ is the set of transition rules describing $P_i$'s actions.

A set $f \subseteq \Delta$ is called enabled in configuration $s$ if there is a transition rule $\delta \in f$ that is enabled in $s$, i.e., if $\Delta(s) \cap f \neq \emptyset$. If $F$ is a subset of $\mathcal{F}$ and $s \in \mathrm{Conf}$ then $F$ is called enabled in $s$ if some $f \in F$ is enabled in $s$, i.e., if $\exists f \in F.f \cap \Delta(s) \neq \emptyset$. We write $\mathrm{Enabl}(F)$ to denote the set of configurations $s \in \mathrm{Conf}$ where $F$ is enabled.

**Definition 5.1 (Fair paths, fair schedulers).** *Let $\mathcal{F} \in 2^{2^\Delta}$ be a (finite) set consisting of subsets of $\Delta$. An infinite path $s_0 \xrightarrow{\delta_1} s_1 \xrightarrow{\delta_2} \cdots$ is called $\mathcal{F}$-fair iff for all $f \in \mathcal{F}$ either $\delta_j \in f$ for infinitely many $j$ or there is some $i \geq 0$ such that $f$ is not enabled in the configurations $s_j$ for all $j \geq i$. Scheduler $\mathcal{U}$ is called $\mathcal{F}$-fair (or briefly fair) if for each starting state $s$, almost all $\mathcal{U}$-paths are $\mathcal{F}$-fair.*

We first consider *reachability* properties $\Diamond A$ and show that fairness assumptions are irrelevant for the satisfaction criteria "with positive probability" and "almost surely". This follows from the fact that from the moment on where a configuration in $A$ has been entered one can continue in an arbitrary, but $\mathcal{F}$-fair way. Thus:

$$\exists \mathcal{V} \; \mathcal{F}\text{-fair s.t. } \mathrm{Pr}_{\mathcal{V}}(s \models \Diamond A) > 0 \quad \text{iff} \quad \exists \mathcal{U} \text{ s.t. } \mathrm{Pr}_{\mathcal{U}}(s \models \Diamond A) > 0$$
$$\exists \mathcal{V} \; \mathcal{F}\text{-fair s.t. } \mathrm{Pr}_{\mathcal{V}}(s \models \Diamond A) = 1 \quad \text{iff} \quad \exists \mathcal{U} \text{ s.t. } \mathrm{Pr}_{\mathcal{U}}(s \models \Diamond A) = 1$$

By the results of section 4, given an NPLCS $\mathcal{N}$, starting configuration $s$ and region $A$, the questions whether there exists a $\mathcal{F}$-fair scheduler $\mathcal{U}$ such that $\Pr_{\mathcal{U}}(s \models \Diamond A) > 0$ or $= 1$ are decidable.

The treatment of *invariant* properties $\Box A$ under fairness constraints relies on generalizations of the concept of safe and promising sets. For $A, B \subseteq$ Conf, $Prom_A(B)$ denotes the largest set $T \subseteq A \cup B$ such that for all $t \in T$ there exists a path $t = s_0 \xrightarrow{\delta_1} \cdots \xrightarrow{\delta_m} s_m$ with $m \geq 0$, $s_m \in B$ and $Post[\delta_i](s_{i-1}) \subseteq T$ for all $1 \leq i \leq m$. The fixed-point definition of $Prom_A(B)$ would be $\nu X.\widehat{Pre}_X^*(B) \cap (A \cup B)$.

For $\mathcal{F} \subseteq 2^\Delta$ and $A \subseteq$ Conf, let $Safe_{\mathcal{F}}(A) = \bigcup_{F \subseteq \mathcal{F}} Safe[F](A)$ where $Safe[F](A)$ is defined as follows. If $F$ is a nonempty subset of $\mathcal{F}$ then $Safe[F](A)$ denotes the largest set $T \subseteq A \setminus \text{Enabl}(\mathcal{F} \setminus F)$ such that for all $t \in T$ and $f \in F$ there is a path $s_0 \xrightarrow{\delta_1} \cdots \xrightarrow{\delta_m} s_m$ with $t = s_0$, $m \geq 1$, $\delta_m \in f$ and $Post[\delta_i](s_{i-1}) \subseteq T$ for all $1 \leq i \leq m$. Moreover, $Safe_{\mathcal{F}}[\emptyset](A) = Safe(A \setminus \text{Enabl}(\mathcal{F}))$.

Since $\text{Enabl}(\mathcal{F} \setminus F)$ can be expressed by $Pre[\mathcal{F} \setminus F](\text{Conf})$, we get the following mu-calculus terms for $Safe[\emptyset](A)$ and $Safe[F](A)$:

- $Safe[\emptyset](A) = \nu X.(A \setminus Pre[\mathcal{F}](\text{Conf})) \cap \widehat{Pre}_X(\text{Conf})$, and
- $Safe[F](A) = \nu X.(A \setminus Pre[\mathcal{F} \setminus F](\text{Conf})) \cap \bigcap_{f \in F} \widehat{Pre}_X^*(\widehat{Pre}_X[f](\text{Conf}))$.

**Theorem 5.2 (Fair invariants).** *Let $A \subseteq$ Conf and $s \in$ Conf.*

(a) *There is a $\mathcal{F}$-fair fm-scheduler $\mathcal{V}$ s.t. $\Pr_{\mathcal{V}}(s \models \Box A) > 0$ iff $s \models \exists (A \text{ Until } Safe_{\mathcal{F}}(A))$.*

(b) *There is a $\mathcal{F}$-fair fm-scheduler $\mathcal{V}$ s.t. $\Pr_{\mathcal{V}}(s \models \Box A) = 1$ iff $s \in Prom_A(Safe_{\mathcal{F}}(A))$.*

Observe that, for a region $\gamma$, $Safe_{\mathcal{F}}(\llbracket \gamma \rrbracket)$ and $Prom_A(Safe_{\mathcal{F}}(\llbracket \gamma \rrbracket))$ are regions that can be built effectively (based on the same reasoning that we use for Theorem 3.2). Thus, Theorem 5.2 yields the decidability of the questions whether for a given NPLCS, region $A$ and configuration $s$, there exists a $\mathcal{F}$-fair fm-scheduler $\mathcal{U}$ such that $\Pr_{\mathcal{U}}(s \models \Box A) > 0$ or $= 1$.

In the sequel, for $A \subseteq$ Conf, we denote by $T_{\Box A}^{\mathcal{F}}$ the set of all configurations $s$ such that $\Pr_{\mathcal{U}}(s \models \Box A) = 1$ for some $\mathcal{F}$-fair fm-scheduler $\mathcal{U}$.

We now come to *repeated reachability* $\Box \Diamond A$ and *persistence* $\Diamond \Box A$ properties under fairness constraints. For $A \subseteq$ Conf, we define $T_{\Box \Diamond A}^{\mathcal{F}} = \bigcup_{F \subseteq \mathcal{F}} T_F$ where $T_F$ is the largest subset of Conf $\setminus \text{Enabl}(\mathcal{F} \setminus F)$ such that for all $t \in T_F$:

- there is a finite path $s_0 \xrightarrow{\delta_1} \cdots \xrightarrow{\delta_m} s_m$ with $m \geq 1$, $t = s_0$, $s_m \in A$ and $Post[\delta_i](s_{i-1}) \subseteq T_F$ for all $1 \leq i \leq m$,

- for each $f \in F$ there is a finite path $s_0 \xrightarrow{\delta_1} \cdots \xrightarrow{\delta_m} s_m$ with $t = s_0$, $m \geq 1$, $\delta_m \in f$ and $Post[\delta_i](s_{i-1}) \subseteq T_F$ for all $1 \leq i \leq m$.

**Theorem 5.3 (Fair repeated reachability and persistence).** *Let $A \subseteq$ Conf and $s \in$ Conf.*

(a) *There exists a $\mathcal{F}$-fair fm-scheduler $\mathcal{U}$ with $\Pr_{\mathcal{U}}(s \models \Box \Diamond A) = 1$ iff $s \in Prom(T_{\Box \Diamond A}^{\mathcal{F}})$.*

(b) *There exists a $\mathcal{F}$-fair fm-scheduler $\mathcal{U}$ with $\Pr_{\mathcal{U}}(s \models \Box \Diamond A) > 0$ iff $s \in Pre^*(T_{\Box \Diamond A}^{\mathcal{F}})$.*

*(c)  There exists a $\mathcal{F}$-fair fm-scheduler $\mathcal{U}$ with $\Pr_{\mathcal{U}}(s \models \Diamond \Box A) = 1$ iff $s \in Prom(T_{\Box A}^{\mathcal{F}})$.*
*(d)  There exists a $\mathcal{F}$-fair fm-scheduler $\mathcal{U}$ with $\Pr_{\mathcal{U}}(s \models \Diamond \Box A) > 0$ iff $s \in Pre^*(T_{\Box A}^{\mathcal{F}})$.*

With similar arguments as for $Prom(A)$, the sets of configuration $T_{\Box \Diamond A}^{\mathcal{F}}$ and $T_{\Box A}^{\mathcal{F}} = Prom_A(Safe_{\mathcal{F}}(A))$ are regions whenever $A$ is a region. This entails the decidability of the questions whether given region $A$, there exists a $\mathcal{F}$-fair fm-scheduler $\mathcal{U}$ such that $\Pr_{\mathcal{U}}(s \models \varphi) = 1$ or $> 0$ where $\varphi = \Box \Diamond A$ or $\Diamond \Box A$.

We next consider *linear time* properties, formalized by LTL formulas $\varphi$ where regions serve as atomic propositions. The idea is to encode the fairness constraints in the model (the NPLCS) by a Streett property

$$fair = \bigwedge_{f \in \mathcal{F}} (\Box \Diamond A_f \rightarrow \Box \Diamond B_f)$$

(with regions $A_f, B_f \subseteq Conf$) that will be considered in conjunction with $\varphi$. We modify the given LCS $L = (Q, C, M, \Delta)$ and construct a new LCS $L' = (Q', C, M, \Delta')$ as follows. We introduce new locations $q_F$ for all subsets $F$ of $\mathcal{F}$ and $q \in Q$, i.e., we deal with $Q' = \{q_F : q \in Q, F \subseteq \mathcal{F}\}$. $\Delta'$ is the smallest set of transition rules such that $p_G \xrightarrow{op} q_F \in \Delta'$ if $p \xrightarrow{op} q \in \Delta$, $G \subseteq \mathcal{F}$ and $F = \{f \in \mathcal{F} : p \xrightarrow{op} q \in f\}$. For $f \in \mathcal{F}$, $B_f$ is the set of configurations $\langle q_F, w \rangle$ in $L'$ such that $f \in F$, while $A_f$ denotes the set of all configurations $\langle q_F, w \rangle$ of $L'$ where $f$ is enabled in the configuration $\langle q, w \rangle$ of $L$. We finally transform the given formula $\varphi$ into $\varphi'$ by replacing any region $C$ of $L$ that appears as an atom in $\varphi$ with the region $C' = \{\langle q_F, w \rangle : \langle q, w \rangle \in C, F \subseteq \mathcal{F}\}$. For instance, if $\varphi = \Box \Diamond (q \wedge (c \neq \varepsilon))$ then $\varphi' = \Box \Diamond ((q \vee \bigvee_{F \subseteq \mathcal{F}} q_F) \wedge (c \neq \varepsilon))$.

In the sequel, let $\mathcal{N} = (L, \tau)$ be the NPLCS that we want to verify against $\varphi$ and let $\mathcal{N}' = (L', \tau)$ the associated modified NPLCS. Obviously, for each fm-scheduler $\mathcal{U}$ for $\mathcal{N}$ there is a "corresponding" fm-scheduler $\mathcal{U}'$ for $\mathcal{N}'$, and vice versa. Corresponding means that $\mathcal{U}'$ behaves as $\mathcal{U}$ for the current configuration $\langle q, w \rangle$ with $q \in Q$. If the current configuration of $\mathcal{U}'$ is $\langle q_F, w \rangle$ then $\mathcal{U}'$ behaves as $\mathcal{U}$ for $\langle q, w \rangle$. Then, $\Pr_{\mathcal{U}}(s \models \varphi) = \Pr_{\mathcal{U}'}(s \models \varphi')$ for all configurations $s$ in $\mathcal{N}$. Here, each configuration $s = \langle q, w \rangle$ of $\mathcal{N}$ is identified with the configuration $\langle q_0, w \rangle$ in $\mathcal{N}'$. Moreover, $\mathcal{U}$ is $\mathcal{F}$-fair iff $\Pr_{\mathcal{U}'}(s \models fair) = 1$. This yields part (a) of the following lemma. Part (b) follows from the fact that $\Pr_{\mathcal{U}}(s \models \varphi) = 1 - \Pr_{\mathcal{U}}(s \models \neg \varphi)$ for each scheduler $\mathcal{U}$.

**Lemma 5.4.** *Let $s$ be a configuration in $\mathcal{N}$ (and $\mathcal{N}'$) and $\varphi$ an LTL formula. Then:*

*(a)  There exists a $\mathcal{F}$-fair fm-scheduler $\mathcal{U}$ for $\mathcal{N}$ such that $\Pr_{\mathcal{U}}(s \models \varphi) = 1$ if and only if there exists a fm-scheduler $\mathcal{U}'$ for $\mathcal{N}'$ such that $\Pr_{\mathcal{U}'}(s \models fair \wedge \varphi') = 1$.*
*(b)  There exists a $\mathcal{F}$-fair fm-scheduler $\mathcal{U}$ for $\mathcal{N}$ such that $\Pr_{\mathcal{U}}(s \models \varphi) = 0$ if and only if there exists a fm-scheduler $\mathcal{V}$ for $\mathcal{N}'$ such that $\Pr_{\mathcal{V}}(s \models fair \wedge \neg \varphi') = 1$.*
*(c)  There exists a $\mathcal{F}$-fair fm-scheduler $\mathcal{U}$ for $\mathcal{N}$ such that $\Pr_{\mathcal{U}}(s \models \varphi) > 0$ if and only if there exists a fm-scheduler $\mathcal{V}$ for $\mathcal{N}'$ such that $\Pr_{\mathcal{V}}(s \models fair \wedge \varphi') > 0$.*
*(d)  There exists a $\mathcal{F}$-fair fm-scheduler $\mathcal{U}$ for $\mathcal{N}$ such that $\Pr_{\mathcal{U}}(s \models \varphi) < 1$ if and only if there exists a fm-scheduler $\mathcal{V}$ for $\mathcal{N}'$ such that $\Pr_{\mathcal{V}}(s \models fair \wedge \neg \varphi') > 0$.*

Lemma 5.4 even holds for arbitrary $\omega$-regular properties. It provides a reduction from the verification problem for qualitative LTL formulas in NPLCS's and fair fm-schedulers to the same problem for the full class of fm-schedulers. Thus, all decidability results that have been established for NPLCS's and qualitative verification problems for the class of fm-schedulers (see 4) also hold when fairness assumptions are made.

## 6    Automatic Verification of Pachl's Protocol

Fig. 1 directly translates into a LCS $\mathcal{L}_{\text{Pachl}}$ when the asynchronous product of $P_L$ and $P_R$ is considered. $\mathcal{L}_{\text{Pachl}}$ has $6 \times 6 = 36$ control locations and $(18 + 18) \times 6 = 216$ transition rules. In order to reason about notions like "a rule $\delta$ has been fired", that are ubiquitous in fairness hypothesis, our tool adds an history variable recording the last fired rule (actually, only its action label). This would further multiply the number of states and of transitions by 20, but not all pairs (location,last action) are meaningful so that the final model can be stripped down to 144 locations and 948 rules. In all our results below we do not use the names of these 144 locations, but rather project them to the more readable underlying 36 locations.

### 6.1    Safety Analysis

Pachl [22] computed manually the set $Post^*(\text{Init})$ of all configurations reachable in $\mathcal{L}_{\text{Pachl}}$ from the initial empty configuration $\text{Init} = (\text{L0}, \text{R4}, \varepsilon, \varepsilon)$, and such forward computations can sometimes be done automatically with the techniques described in [4] (although termination of the forward-reachability computations cannot be guaranteed in general). These computations show that the protocol does indeed preserve the integrity of communication in the sense that no confusion between data messages is introduced by losses.

Our calculus for regions is geared towards backward computation, where termination is guaranteed. Our implementation can compute automatically the set of deadlock configurations:

$$\text{Dead} \stackrel{\text{def}}{=} \text{Conf} \smallsetminus Pre(\text{Conf}) = \langle \text{L4}, \text{R4}, \varepsilon, \varepsilon \rangle.$$

Hopefully, $\text{Dead}$ is not reachable from $\text{Init}$. We can compute the set $Pre^*(\text{Dead})$ of all unsafe configurations, that can end up in a deadlock. Intersecting with $\uparrow\text{Init}$, we obtain the set of unsafe starting channel contents:

$Pre^*(\text{Dead}) \sqcap \uparrow\text{Init} =$
$$\langle \text{L0}, \text{R4}, \uparrow\varepsilon, \uparrow a_0 d_0 \rangle + \langle \text{L0}, \text{R4}, \uparrow eod\, a_0, \uparrow a_0 \rangle + \langle \text{L0}, \text{R4}, \uparrow d_0 eod\, a_0, \uparrow\varepsilon \rangle.$$

Thus eventual deadlock is possible from location $(\text{L0}, \text{R4})$ if the channels initially contain the appropriately unsafe contents.

### 6.2    Liveness Analysis

We now come to what is the main motivation of our work: proving progress under fairness hypothesis. In this case study, the problem we address is in general to compute the set of all configurations satisfying some $\mathrm{Pr}_{\mathcal{U}}(s \models \Box \Diamond A) = 1$ for all schedulers $\mathcal{U}$ satisfying some fairness conditions $\mathcal{F}$. Following equivalences of section 5, this is related to the computation of $T^{\mathcal{F}}_{\Box \Diamond A}$. More precisely: $\{s | \forall \mathcal{U} \mathcal{F}\text{-fair } \mathrm{Pr}_{\mathcal{U}}(s \models \Box \Diamond A) = 1\} = \mathrm{Conf} \setminus Pre^*(T^{\mathcal{F}}_{\Box \Diamond A})$.

When computing $T^{\mathcal{F}}_{\Box \Diamond A}$, all subsets of $\mathcal{F}$ have to be considered and this induces a combinatorial explosion for large $\mathcal{F}$. Since we did not yet develop and implement heuristics to overcome this difficulty, we only checked examples considering "small" $\mathcal{F}$ sets (meaning a number of fairness sets, each of which can be a large set of rules) in this preliminary study. For example, we considered "strong process fairness" $\mathcal{F}_{\mathrm{process}} = \{F_{\mathrm{left}}, F_{\mathrm{right}}\}$ (with obvious meaning for the sets of transitions $F_{\mathrm{left}}, F_{\mathrm{right}}$), or "strong fairness for reading" $\mathcal{F}_{\mathrm{read}} = \{F_{\mathrm{read}}\}$.

Regarding the target set $A$, we consider questions whether a given transition (in $P_{\mathrm{L}}$ or $P_{\mathrm{R}}$) is fired infinitely often (using the history variable), or whether a process changes control states infinitely often, etc. Observe that a conjunction of "$\mathrm{Pr}_{\mathcal{U}}(s \models \Box \Diamond A_i) = 1$" gives $\mathrm{Pr}_{\mathcal{U}}(s \models \bigwedge_i \Box \Diamond A_i) = 1$, so that we can check formulas like $\bigwedge_i \Box \Diamond \mathrm{Li} \wedge \bigwedge_i \Box \Diamond \mathrm{Ri}$, expressing progress in communication between the two processes.

In the three following cases :

- $\mathcal{F} = \mathcal{F}_{\mathrm{read}}$ and $A = After_{\mathrm{left}}$
- $\mathcal{F} = \mathcal{F}_{\mathrm{read}}$ and $A = After_{\mathrm{left-move}}$
- $\mathcal{F} = \{F_{\mathrm{read}}, F_{\mathrm{right-read}}\}$ and $A = After_{\mathrm{left}}$

our prototype model checker yields that $\mathrm{Init} \in \mathrm{Conf} \setminus Pre^*(T^{\mathcal{F}}_{\Box \Diamond A})$. This means that, in all three cases, starting from $\mathrm{Init}$, the set of configurations $A$ will be visited infinitely often almost surely, under all $\mathcal{F}$-fair schedulers.

# 7  Conclusion

We introduced NPLCS's, a model for nondeterministic channel systems where messages are lost probabilistically, and showed the decidability of qualitative verification question of the form "does $\varphi$ holds with probability 1 for all $\mathcal{F}$-fair finite-memory schedulers?" where $\varphi$ is an $\omega$-regular linear-time property and $\mathcal{F}$ a strong fairness condition.

When atomic propositions can refer to the contents of channels, which is required when one wants to express fairness and firability of rules, our decidability results rest upon a new notion of symbolic regions based on "prefixed upward-closures". These symbolic methods can be implemented rather directly and we used them to analyze simple systems.

These results are the outcome of a research project that started in [13,14] with the first early definition of NPLCS's and was continued in [9] where the key notions for reducing to constrained reachability questions have been first identified in a simplified framework. Further developments will focus on incorporating algorithmic ideas from symbolic verification (normal forms, caches, sharing, ...) in our naive prototype verifier, turning it into a more solid analysis tool.

# References

1. P. A. Abdulla, C. Baier, S. Purushothaman Iyer, and B. Jonsson. Simulating perfect channels with probabilistic lossy channels. *Information and Computation*, 197(1–2):22–40, 2005.
2. P. A. Abdulla, N. Bertrand, A. Rabinovich, and Ph Schnoebelen. Verification of probabilistic systems with faulty communication. *Information and Computation*, 202(2):141–165, 2005.
3. P. A. Abdulla, A. Bouajjani, and J. d'Orso. Deciding monotonic games. In *Proc. 17th Int. Workshop Computer Science Logic (CSL 2003) and 8th Kurt Gödel Coll. (KGL 2003), Vienna, Austria, Aug. 2003*, volume 2803 of *Lecture Notes in Computer Science*, pages 1–14. Springer, 2003.
4. P. A. Abdulla, A. Collomb-Annichini, A. Bouajjani, and B. Jonsson. Using forward reachability analysis for verification of lossy channel systems. *Formal Methods in System Design*, 25(1):39–65, 2004.
5. P. A. Abdulla and B. Jonsson. Undecidable verification problems for programs with unreliable channels. *Information and Computation*, 130(1):71–90, 1996.
6. P. A. Abdulla and B. Jonsson. Verifying programs with unreliable channels. *Information and Computation*, 127(2):91–101, 1996.
7. C. Baier, N. Bertrand, and Ph. Schnoebelen. A note on the attractor-property of infinite-state Markov chains. *Information Processing Letters*, 97(2):58–63, 2006.
8. C. Baier, N. Bertrand, and Ph. Schnoebelen. On computing fixpoints in well-structured regular model checking, with applications to lossy channel systems. RR cs.CS/0606091, Computing Research Repository, June 2006. Visible at http://arxiv.org/abs/cs.CS/0606091.
9. C. Baier, N. Bertrand, and Ph. Schnoebelen. Verifying nondeterministic probabilistic channel systems against ω-regular linear-time properties. RR cs.LO/0511023, Computing Research Repository, April 2006. To be published in *ACM Trans. Computational Logic*, visible at http://arxiv.org/abs/cs.LO/0511023.
10. C. Baier and B. Engelen. Establishing qualitative properties for probabilistic lossy channel systems: An algorithmic approach. In *Proc. 5th Int. AMAST Workshop Formal Methods for Real-Time and Probabilistic Systems (ARTS '99), Bamberg, Germany, May 1999*, volume 1601 of *Lecture Notes in Computer Science*, pages 34–52. Springer, 1999.
11. C. Baier, B. R. Haverkort, H. Hermanns, J.-P. Katoen, and M. Siegle, editors. *Validation of Stochastic Systems – A Guide to Current Research*, volume 2925 of *Lecture Notes in Computer Science*. Springer, 2004.
12. C. Baier and M. Kwiatkowska. Model checking for a probabilistic branching time logic with fairness. *Distributed Computing*, 11(3):125–155, 1998.
13. N. Bertrand and Ph. Schnoebelen. Model checking lossy channels systems is probably decidable. In *Proc. 6th Int. Conf. Foundations of Software Science and Computation Structures (FOSSACS 2003), Warsaw, Poland, Apr. 2003*, volume 2620 of *Lecture Notes in Computer Science*, pages 120–135. Springer, 2003.
14. N. Bertrand and Ph. Schnoebelen. Verifying nondeterministic channel systems with probabilistic message losses. In Ramesh Bharadwaj, editor, *Proc. 3rd Int. Workshop on Automated Verification of Infinite-State Systems (AVIS 2004), Barcelona, Spain, Apr. 2004*, 2004.
15. D. Brand and P. Zafiropulo. On communicating finite-state machines. *Journal of the ACM*, 30(2):323–342, 1983.
16. C. Courcoubetis and M. Yannakakis. The complexity of probabilistic verification. *Journal of the ACM*, 42(4):857–907, 1995.
17. A. Finkel. Decidability of the termination problem for completely specificied protocols. *Distributed Computing*, 7(3):129–135, 1994.
18. B. Hailpern and S. Owicki. Verifying network protocols using temporal logic. In *Proc. NBS/IEEE Symposium on Trends and Applications 1980: Computer Network Protocols, Gaithersburg, MD, May 1980*, pages 18–28. IEEE Comp. Soc. Press, 1980.

19. S. Hart, M. Sharir, and A. Pnueli. Termination of probabilistic concurrent programs. *ACM Transactions on Programming Languages and Systems*, 5(3):356–380, 1983.
20. A. Kučera and Ph. Schnoebelen. A general approach to comparing infinite-state systems with their finite-state specifications. *Theoretical Computer Science*, 2006. To appear.
21. B. Masson and Ph. Schnoebelen. On verifying fair lossy channel systems. In *Proc. 27th Int. Symp. Math. Found. Comp. Sci. (MFCS 2002), Warsaw, Poland, Aug. 2002*, volume 2420 of *Lecture Notes in Computer Science*, pages 543–555. Springer, 2002.
22. J. K. Pachl. Protocol description and analysis based on a state transition model with channel expressions. In *Proc. 7th IFIP WG6.1 Int. Workshop on Protocol Specification, Testing, and Verification (PSTV '87), Zurich, Switzerland, May 1987*, pages 207–219. North-Holland, 1987.
23. P. Panangaden. Measure and probability for concurrency theorists. *Theoretical Computer Science*, 253(2):287–309, 2001.
24. A. Pnueli. On the extremely fair treatment of probabilistic algorithms. In *Proc. 15th ACM Symp. Theory of Computing (STOC '83), Boston, MA, Apr. 1983*, pages 278–290. ACM Press, 1983.
25. A. Pnueli and L. D. Zuck. Verification of multiprocess probabilistic protocols. *Distributed Computing*, 1(1):53–72, 1986.
26. A. Pnueli and L. D. Zuck. Probabilistic verification. *Information and Computation*, 103(1):1–29, 1993.
27. S. Purushothaman Iyer and M. Narasimha. Probabilistic lossy channel systems. In *Proc. 7th Int. Joint Conf. Theory and Practice of Software Development (TAPSOFT '97), Lille, France, Apr. 1997*, volume 1214 of *Lecture Notes in Computer Science*, pages 667–681. Springer, 1997.
28. M. L. Puterman. *Markov decision processes: discrete stochastic dynamic programming*. John Wiley & Sons, 1994.
29. A. Rabinovich. Quantitative analysis of probabilistic lossy channel systems. In *Proc. 30th Int. Coll. Automata, Languages, and Programming (ICALP 2003), Eindhoven, NL, July 2003*, volume 2719 of *Lecture Notes in Computer Science*, pages 1008–1021. Springer, 2003.
30. Ph. Schnoebelen. Verifying lossy channel systems has nonprimitive recursive complexity. *Information Processing Letters*, 83(5):251–261, 2002.
31. Ph. Schnoebelen. The verification of probabilistic lossy channel systems. In Baier et al. [11], pages 445–465.
32. M. Y. Vardi. Automatic verification of probabilistic concurrent finite-state programs. In *Proc. 26th IEEE Symp. Foundations of Computer Science (FOCS '85), Portland, OR, USA, Oct. 1985*, pages 327–338. IEEE Comp. Soc. Press, 1985.

# A New Approach for Concurrent Program Slicing

Pierre Rousseau

CEDRIC - CNAM Paris
292, rue St Martin, 75003 Paris
rousseau@cnam.fr
http://quasar.cnam.fr

**Abstract.** Regarding the progress made in model analysis, more complex models, and consequently more complex programs can now be analyzed. However, this remains a difficult task in particular for concurrent programs which induce a lot of combinatory. Another way to reduce this complexity is to use program decomposition. Program decomposition technics extract a part of a given program while preserving the behavior of the original program w.r.t. a specified property.

QUASAR analyzes concurrent Ada programs, using program slicing as decomposition technic. The program slicer is built using the ASIS tools, that provides syntactic and semantic informations on an Ada source code. These informations can be considered as the "semantic and syntactic graph" mapping an Ada program. This allows to save building the graphs used by traditional program slicing technics and thus to design a simpler and more evolutive algorithm.

This paper presents YASNOST, the program slicer used by QUASAR, describes the method used to slice concurrent Ada programs and illustrates with two significant examples how concurrent programs analysis can take advantage of program slicing for reducing the analyzed program complexity.

## 1 Introduction

This paper presents a program slicer which doesn't need to build static dependence graphs before slicing a given concurrent program. It records dynamically these dependences when it traverses the syntactic and semantic graph generated by the program compiler. This traversal relies on the standard ASIS tool available for Ada programs. This slicer is part of the QUASAR project developed by our research team.

QUASAR [EKPPR03] is an automatic program analysis tool which aims to formally validate properties of concurrent Ada programs. It generates a formal model from a source code and validates a specified property on the generated model.

The main difficulty of this method is the possible combinatory explosion induced by the process execution interleaving when constructing the reachable state space. To face this problem, QUASAR uses various technics at each step of its analysis process :

1. **program decomposition:** at first, QUASAR uses program slicing in order to reduce the program size while preserving its behavior w.r.t the studied property. The reduced program will help to generate a smaller and simpler state space.
2. **model generation:** this step can be seen as the heart of the QUASAR tool. It translates an Ada program into a corresponding colored Petri Net. The model

E. Najm et al. (Eds.): FORTE 2006, LNCS 4229, pp. 228–242, 2006.

construction aims to stay as close as possible of the source code formalism and to produce models trying to limit as much as possible the combinatory of the Ada program [EKPPR03, EKPP⁺05].

3. **model-checking:** at this step, QUASAR uses the model-checker HELENA [Eva05] to verify the property on the colored Petri Net generated at the second step. This tool combines different structural technics and model-checking optimizations in order to deal better with huge state space.

The first step is the most important as it addresses the program at its source.This paper presents YASNOST the Ada program slicer which carries out the program slicing step of QUASAR analysis process.

The concepts and methodology founding QUASAR have been experimented with the Ada language for several concomitant advantages. Ada presents today the most complete and powerful concurrency features. Ada concurrency semantic is well and precisely defined. Ada is currently used for practical and critical applications which need validation. Concurrency analysis methods performed for Ada programs can be used for other languages. For instance, using QUASAR and simulating some Java programs in Ada, we have shown some weakness of Java concurrency semantics [EKPPR06].

## 2  Program Slicing

Program slicing was first introduced by M. Weiser in [Wei84] and most of the slicing definitions and technics are reviewed in [Tip95] and [XQZ⁺05]. This part of the paper presents the essential definitions used in the whole paper and legitimates the kind of program slicing carried out by YASNOST.

The principle of program slicing is to observe a particular behavior of a program from a specified point of view. The point of view is specified as a *slicing criterion* commonly defined by a couple $\langle n, V \rangle$, with $n$ a statement of the original program and $V$ a set of variables.

The result of the program slicing operation is called a *slice* and can be a set of statements (*non-executable slicing*) or a reduced compilable and executable program (*executable slicing*). This slice must preserve all the behavior of the original program w.r.t. the slicing criterion (ie, at statement n, the values of the variables of the set V have to be computed in the same way in the original program and in the slice). Obtaining a minimal slice is undecidable, however precise slices can be obtained using existing technics.

The slice is obtained by collecting all the parts of a program that may have an effect on the values of a set of variables V at a defined statement n (this is *backward slicing*) or may be affected by the values of the set (this is *forward slicing*).

The kind of program slicing introduced by Weiser is called *static program slicing*. It means that all possible values of program input are considered, thus that all possible executions of the original program have to be considered. The other kind of program slicing is *dynamic program slicing* which considers a particular set of input program values and studies a particular set of executions of the program corresponding to the program execution for these program input values.

YASNOST carries out a static executable backward program slicing. Static because QUASAR validates properties holding for all possible executions of a program; executable for some technical reasons (QUASAR second step process uses computable Ada programs); and backward slicing has been chosen because most of the studied properties validated by QUASAR deal with reachable states of the original program, and thus the slicing criterion definition is closer to the kind of properties analyzed by QUASAR than with forward slicing.

```
 1  procedure Robot is                 1  procedure Robot is
 2                                      2
 3      Nails : Natural := 0;           3      Nails : Natural := 0;
 4      Start : Natural := 0;           4      Start : Natural := 0;
 5      Total : Natural := 0;           5      Total : Natural := 0;
 6      Used  : Natural := 0;           6
 7                                      7
 8  begin                              8  begin
 9      Get (Start);                    9      Get (Start);
10      Total := Nails + Start;        10      Total := Total + Start;
11      Nails := Total;                11      Nails := Total;
12      while Nails > 0 loop           12      while Nails > 0 loop
13          Nails := Nails - 1;        13          Nails := Nails - 1;
14          Used  := Used + 1;         14
15      end loop;                      15      end loop;
16      if Used = 0 then               16
17          Put ("Nothing_done");      17
18      end if;                        18
19      Put (Nails);                   19      Put (Nails);
20  end Robot;                         20  end Robot;
```

**Fig. 1.** Slicing of program Robot with ⟨19, {*Nails*}⟩ as slicing criterion

Figure 1 shows an example of static executable backward program slicing. The program on the left is the original program, and the program on the right is one of its slice observed through the slicing criterion ⟨19, *Nails*⟩. It means that we want to know the statements which have an effect on the value of the variable Nails at line 19. The elements related to the variable Used are irrelevant to the value of the variable Nails at line 19, thus they do not belong to the slice.

In order to achieve program slicing YASNOST has to be able to define which statements can have an effect on the variables values of the slicing criterion. Weiser had defined two kinds of dependences for sequential program slicing:

- **The control dependence** represents the link between a statement and another statement of which it can control the execution. The most trivial example is the if-then-else statement that controls the execution of the statements of its both branches.
- **The data dependence** represents the link between a statement referencing (reading the value of) a variable and the statements defining (modifying) it. For instance, in Figure 1, the statements of line 11 (referencing the variable Total) is data dependent on the statement of line 10 (defining Total).

  This dependence is *transitive*. The modifying statements may reference variables which are also modified in previous statements, and thus these statements have to be included into the slice because the values of the variables that they modify transitively impact the firstly referenced variable. For instance, as already explained, the statement of line 11 is data dependent on the statement of the line 10. The line 10 references the variable `Start`, defined at line 9. Thus the statement of line 11 is by transitivity data dependent on the statement defining the variable Start (line 9).

# 3   Concurrent Program Slicing

QUASAR analyzes concurrent Ada programs, thus YASNOST has to slice concurrent programs, and to deal with concurrency specific problems described in [Che93, NR00, Kri03], such as dependences introduced by the synchronization between tasks or the non transitivity of the data dependence relation.

To illustrate this last issue considers the following examples (Figure 2).

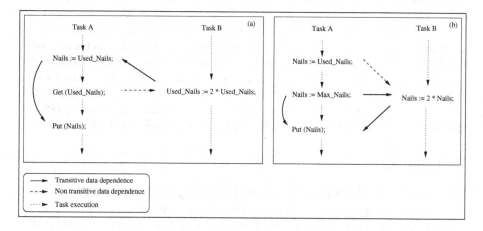

**Fig. 2.** Examples of imprecise data dependences sequences

In Figure 2 (a), if the data dependence is considered as transitive, the following sequence may be built:

```
{
  Get (Used_Nails);
  Used_Nails := 2 * Used_Nails;
  Nails := Used_Nails;
  Put (Nails);
}.
```

Indeed `Put (Nails)` depends on `Nails := Used_Nails` which depends on `Used_Nails := 2 * Used_Nails` which depends on `Get (Used_Nails)`.

However this sequence can't be executed by the program or else it would mean that `Get (Used_Nails)` could be executed before `Nails := Used_Nails` what is impossible.

In the second example (Figure 2 (b)), a variable is modified twice in a task and read and modified in a single statement in another task. In all possible executions, the value of the variable `Nails` is never dependant of the statement `Nails := Used Nails` because the variable `Nails` is always defined by `Nails := Max Nails`. For instance the data dependence relation may take into account this useless sequence:

```
{
  Nails := Used_Nails;
  Nails := Max_Nails;
  Nails := 2 * Nails;
  Put (Nails);
}
```

In both cases, considering the dependence relation as transitive leads to take into account sequences of statements that are impossible (first case) or useless (second case). So the resulting slice will contain statements that do not affect the slicing criterion and thus is imprecise.

Previous works [CX01, Kri03] are all based on an augmentation of the dependence graph approach. These graphs are complex and contain all possible dependences relation between all the program statements. YASNOST, the QUASAR slicer, relies on another concurrent program slicing approach which is based on ASIS, an Ada tool which allows to inspect the syntactic tree of an Ada program by using the semantic links existing between its elements. Instead of building a static dependence graph, YASNOST records dependences "on the fly" which naturally avoid to build useless dependences.

## 4   YASNOST

At the moment, YASNOST supports the basic Ada language (assignment, conditioned statements, ...), subprograms and the part of the language related to concurrency (tasks, protected object, rendez-vous, ...). Pointers and dynamic structures are not yet supported except the dynamic task allocation. Unstructured control flow such as `exit` statements are supported but exceptions and jumps are not. However, non supported parts of the language can be wholly included into the slice.

### 4.1   Tree Manipulator: ASIS

ASIS (Ada Semantic Interfaces Specification [ISO95]) is an interface between an Ada environment and tools requiring static information about the syntax and the semantic of an Ada program.

ASIS provides two ways for obtaining information about an Ada source code. First, there is an iterator allowing traversing the syntactic tree of an Ada program with a depth-first left-hand method. The second tool is a set of queries that allows the user to navigate in the syntactic tree following semantical dependences between its nodes. The tree associated with the ASIS queries can be view as a "syntactic and semantic" graph.

Figure 3 shows an example of ASIS graph used to get information about a source code. The plain lines represent the syntactic tree of the Ada program of Figure 1 (original program on the left). The dashed line represents an ASIS query linking an identifier

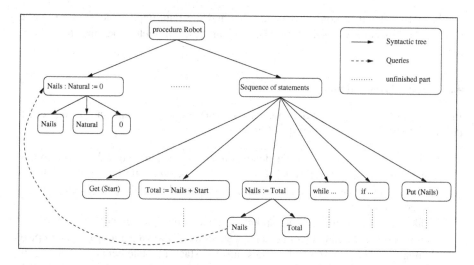

**Fig. 3.** Part of an ASIS graph of program of Figure 1

(Nails) to its declaration (Nails : Natural := 0). Note that the ASIS syntactic tree has been simplified for the sake of simplicity.

The first way to use this interface is to implement already known program slicing algorithms, as done in [SC03]. A second way is to deduce the dependence graph from ASIS syntactic tree. YASNOST uses the ASIS tools in a third way : build dependences "on the fly" with the ASIS queries.

### 4.2   Algorithm

The algorithm used by YASNOST aims to separate as much as possible the search of the different kind of dependences. YASNOST uses a stack in which are pushed the elements (nodes of the syntactic tree) of which YASNOST needs to check the dependences and thus that have to be kept. The following algorithm is carried out:

1. Push statement of the slicing criterion into the stack. With YASNOST, the user can use annotations to specify some statements to keep in the slice. These statements are also pushed into the stack at this step.
2. Push instantied tasks into the stack. At this step, each task declaration and allocation is kept. This step is done traversing the syntactic tree and collecting every task declarations and every statements allocating dynamically a task.
3. Looking for dependences. This step is repeated as long as the stack is not empty
   (a) Pop the first element of the stack and add it to the list of the kept nodes.
   (b) Push control dependent statements into the stack.
   (c) Push data dependent statements into the stack
   (d) Push all declarations related to the popped element into the stack. This step is carried out in order to have an executable slice.
4. Create the executable slice with the list of kept nodes.

The parts related to control dependences and the data dependences, in particular when data dependences have to be checked through parameters passing, have to be detailed.

### 4.3   Control Dependences

In order to collect the control dependences YASNOST uses the weak and strong dependences defined by Cheng [Che93] as follow:

- Strong control dependence is the dependence explained in section 2. ASIS provides a query giving the father node of any node of the syntactic tree. Every father is pushed into the stack. By this way all elements enclosing the popped element are pushed into the stack.
- Weak control dependence corresponds to statements that depend on the termination of another statement (for instance a statement following a loop). If the popped element is a body, YASNOST pushes into the stack all statements related to concurrency and all statements that may not terminate or that may terminate another statement:
  - loops the termination of which cannot be statically evaluated.
  - the calls to protected sub-program (in Ada protected objects are Hoare monitor constructs [Hoa74] with function, procedure and guarded entries).
  - rendez-vous statements.
  - some unstructured control flow statement are also kept at this step. For instance, `exit` statements included in a kept loop. Jump statements such goto are not yet supported by YASNOST.

### 4.4   Data Dependences

In order to find data dependences, YASNOST follows the algorithm described Figure 4. This algorithm uses two lists:

- `Read` : a list of variables for which YASNOST searches statements modifying them.
- `Writers` : the list of elements modifying at least a variable from `Read`. ASIS provides a set of queries allowing to retrieve all statements that contains an identifier corresponding to a given declaration. Statements which belong to the same task are sorted by their textual position (line and column numbers).

YASNOST also uses a transitivity graph for all the variables of the slicing criterion. These graphs are built using sequences of transitive data dependences between the program statements. These graphs are built on the fly. If a data dependence between two statements would lead to only build paths in the transitivity graph such the ones described in section 3, the data dependence is not transitive and thus the statement from the `Writers` set is not added to the slice.

In order to realize this, YASNOST has to be able to know when a statement can be executed before another. The precedence between statements which belong to the same task is checked as follow:

- if two statements are in the same body, the precedence is determined by the textual position (line and column number). If both statements belong to the same loop, they are considered as mutual predecessors.
- if they don't belong to the same body, it means that they are in different subprograms, then, the precedence between the calls (and between both statements) are checked.

If the statement `Writer` has to be added to the slice, then the modified variable is removed from the `Read` set and from the slicing criterion set. Thus for any other elements of the set Writers, YASNOST has to check again if it modifies an element which still belongs to the `Read` set. This is done to avoid to include in the slice old and useless variable value modification.

Statements which belong to different tasks are considered as mutual predecessors. In this case, the transitivity only is checked.

```
Read ← Read_By (Current_Element) & Variables (Slicing_Criterion);
Writers ← Modifying (Read)
for reverse Writer of Writers loop
    if Same_Task (Writer, Current_Element) then – transitivity holds
        if Modify (Writer, Read) and
            Precedence (Writer, Current_Element) – check precedence
        then
            Push (Writer, Stack);
            Remove (Modified_Variables (Writer), Read);
            Remove (Modified_Variables (Writer), Slicing_Criterion);
            Add (Writer, Current_Element, Transitivity_List);
        end if;
    else – precedence holds
        if Transitive (Writer, Transitivity_List) then – check transitivity
            Push (Writer, Stack);
            Add (Current_Element, Transitivity_List);
        end if;
    end if;
end loop;
```

**Fig. 4.** Part of algorithm to find data dependences

## 4.5    Inter-procedural Slicing Issues

When slicing an inter-procedural program, YASNOST has to deal with parameter passing, and to retrieve the parameters of which the final values computed by the subprograms (the parameters modifications or the return value of the sub-program) depend.

As YASNOST produces executable slices, all calls to a procedure have to be written with all effective parameters corresponding to all formal parameters used by the declaration of the called sub-program.

This could lead to build imprecise slice. For instance, consider the procedure `Proc` of Figure 5, which is sliced in order to know the value of the variable `Arg4` at line 28. All the parameters of the procedure `Proc` have to be added to the slice. But only two of them are useful at the call at line 21 ; the others are also in the slice because of the call at line 26. Thus, at the procedure call at line 21, without information linking the modified parameters to the parameters used to modify them, lines 19 and 20 would be added to the slice as `Arg1` and `Arg2` are referenced by this last call. This would be imprecise since line 21 is in the slice because this statement is needed to evaluate the condition of the if statement at line 23 which uses only the values of Arg1 and Arg3. The value of Arg4 is newly defined at line 22 so the value of Arg4 computed at line 21 (the call) is not relevant to the final value of Arg4. And then Arg1 which is used to compute the value of Arg4 through the call should not be considered and the statement defining it at line 19 should not belong to the slice.

```
1  procedure Example is               1  procedure Example is
2     procedure Proc                   2     procedure Proc
3        (In1  :  in       Integer;    3        (In1  :  in       Integer;
4         In2  :  in       Integer;    4         In2  :  in       Integer;
5         Out1  :      out Integer;    5         Out1  :      out Integer;
6         Out2  :      out Integer)    6         Out2  :      out Integer)
7     is                               7     is
8     begin                            8     begin
9        Out1 := In1;                  9        Out1 := In1;
10       Out2 := In2;                  10       Out2 := In2;
11    end Proc;                        11    end Proc;
12                                     12
13    Arg1 : Integer := 0;             13    Arg1 : Integer := 0;
14    Arg2 : Integer := 0;             14    Arg2 : Integer := 0;
15    Arg3 : Integer := 0;             15    Arg3 : Integer := 0;
16    Arg4 : Integer := 0;             16    Arg4 : Integer := 0;
17                                     17
18 begin                              18 begin
19    Arg1 := 1;                       19    Arg1 := 1;
20    Arg2 := 2;                       20
21    Proc (Arg1, Arg2, Arg3, Arg4);   21    Proc (Arg1, Arg2, Arg3, Arg4);
22    Arg4 := 4;                       22    Arg4 := 4;
23    if Arg3 > Arg1 then              23    if Arg3 > Arg1 then
24       Arg2 := 6;                    24       Arg2 := 6;
25       Arg1 := 7;                    25
26       Proc (Arg1, Arg2, Arg3, Arg4);26       Proc (Arg1, Arg2, Arg3, Arg4);
27    end if;                          27    end if;
28    Put (Arg4);                      28    Put (Arg4);
29 end;                               29 end;
```

**Fig. 5.** Example of inter-procedural slicing

In [HRB90], to slice sequential inter-procedural programs, the authors use summary arcs in their dependence graph in order to know for every call which parameter have an effect on the results produced by the sub-program. But, as pointed Krinke, due to the non-transitivity of the data dependencie, these arcs can't be used to slice concurrent programs using dependence graphs. It is shown Figure 6. If all the dependences were considered transitive then the statement Used_Nails := Used_Nails + 1 would have to be included into the slice because Nails := Unused_Nails is considered as transitively dependent of statement Unused_Nails := Total_Nails - Used_Nails. Then the summary arc would link the variable Nails with the variable Used_Nails and thus, the call to Update_Nails (Used Nails, Nails) would be considered as referencing the Used_Nails variable. This would build an imprecise slice, since in concurrent programs, data dependence is not transitive and thus the value of the parameter Used Nails has no effect on the final value of Nails.

However as YASNOST builds only transitive data dependency sequences, and thus builds a transitivity graph where there is always at least one path from a statement to

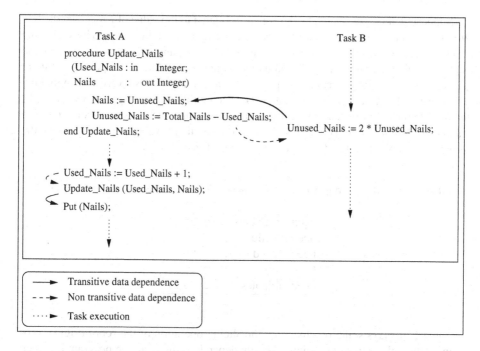

**Fig. 6.** Exemple of precise slice for inter-procedural concurrent program

another one which belongs to a transitive data dependence sequence of statements, it can build these summary arcs also in a concurrent context. As shown Figure 6, only the plain arrows are considered as transitive data dependences, the dashed ones are not considered and thus are not added to the slice.

# 5   Examples

## 5.1   The Robot Example

The example presented Figure 7 is a simple robot which plants nails. This program uses three tasks : the main program, the task managing the right arm and the task managing the left arm. It shows how program slicing reduces a program size and thus helps to debug it.

The main program starts by asking how many times the nails box should be filled when empty, then just surveys that the nail box always contains at least one nail. If not, it calls the right arm to fill the mailbox. When the max number of filling has been reached, the program stops. The left arm places the nail to plant (if there is at least one nail in the box) and then asks the right arm to hit the nail with the hammer. The right arm waits orders and either fills the nail box or hits a nail with a hammer when asked.

Even if this source code is simple, it may be difficult to understand its behavior and then to find bugs.

Suppose that one wants to check properties related to the value of Nails at the line 90 (the last statement of the main procedure). So the slice will be obtained by slicing the original program with the slicing criterion ⟨90, {Nails}⟩, and will allow to focus on the statements that may have an effect on the variable Nails. The sliced program is more clear. Before the model-checking step one bug can already be discovered when looking at the use of the variable Nails : at line 71, when it fills the box, right arm removes 10 nails from the count instead of adding them to the count. Afterwards model-checking can be used to find more subtle mistakes, or to formally prove some property about the program variables taking advantage of the reduced size of the slice.

**Table 1.** Part of the report generated by YASNOST after slicing the program of the Figure 7

| | | |
|---|---|---|
| sliced statements | :: | 16 (55%) |
| sliced functions | :: | - |
| sliced procedures | :: | 6 (86%) |
| sliced entries | :: | 0 (0%) |
| sliced variables | :: | 2 (33%) |

Table 1 displays some results about the slicing operation of the robot original program. Although the result of slicing largely depends on the way the program has been written, this table shows that more than 50%of the program statements have been sliced. Assuming that the sliced procedures could be much more complex than a simple output, the sliced statements ratio could be widely larger without increasing the computation time which is instantaneous to slice this program.

## 5.2   The Client-Server Example

The second example (Figure 8) shows a more subtle possible use of slicing operation. YASNOST slices concurrent programs in order to make easier the model-checking step of QUASAR. The size of the generated model and, in most cases, the size of the state space, are intuitively related to the size of the studied program.

But for concurrent programs, the size of the state space is more related to the combinatory induced by the indeterminism of concurrency than to the size of the program. Our second example shows that even when the original program is not significantly reduced, the slicing operation may be useful by removing a lot of combinatory from the original program.

This example (Figure ⟨64, ∅⟩) is a simple client-server architecture where the server dynamically allocates a task for every client accessing its services. Here presence of deadlock is checked ; thus the slicing criterion ⟨64, ∅⟩ is used (last statement, no variables).

As recorded Table 2, the reduction obtained by program slicing operation is small, but, when checking presence of deadlocks, QUASAR use shows that the two lines removed from the original program were generating a lot of combinatory that led to the state space explosion.

**Table 2.** Part of the report generated by YASNOST after slicing the program of the Figure 8

| | |
|---|---|
| sliced statements | :: 2 (18%) |
| sliced functions | :: - |
| sliced procedures | :: 0  (0%) |
| sliced entries | :: 0  (0%) |
| sliced variables | :: 1 (17%) |

Here the slicing operation didn't remove a lot of statements (although the statements computed by the procedure Get_Value could be much more complicated as it is supposed to compute the requested service offered by the server) but removed a lot of complexity of the program as shown in Table 3 in a instantaneous time which as to be compared to the time needed to compute the nodes of the state space (which is naturally long).

**Table 3.** State space generated by HELENA for the model of the program of Figure 8

| Clients | Running tasks | Reachable states | Reachable states with slicing |
|---|---|---|---|
| 1 | 4 | 247 | 221 |
| 2 | 6 | 9 499 | 5 939 |
| 3 | 8 | 735 767 | 239 723 |
| 4 | 10 | - | 12 847 017 |

## 6   Related Works

A slicer for Ada programs already exists, Adaslicer [SC03], but it operates only on sequential programs. Few other tools have been designed for slicing concurrent Java and C ANSI programs [DCH+99, Kri03, Zha99]. Only [Kri03] builds slices which take into account the non-transitivity of data dependence in a concurrent context and demonstrates that the slices are more precise and more quickly computed.

These approaches use augmentation of the dependence graphs and build all the dependences between all the program statements. Thus they will have better execution times than YASNOST when computing a lot of slices for a given program, but will be slower for a unique slice since they have to build the complete dependence graphs while YASNOST records dependences only w.r.t. the statements which already belong to the slice. As YASNOST is the first step of QUASAR which carries out a formal analysis by model-checking, building all possible slices of a program is not necessary.

## 7   Conclusions and Further Works

This paper has shown how static analysis can greatly help formal analysis to deal with large and complex programs by removing useless statements regarding the property to check and also by removing a lot of complexity from these programs. Other static

```
1  with Ada.Text_IO;        use Ada.Text_IO;
2  with Ada.Integer_Text_IO; use Ada.Integer_Text_IO;
3
4  procedure Robot is
5
6    Used_Nails : Natural := 0;
7    Nails      : Natural := 0;
8
9    task type Left_Arms;
10   Left_Arm : Left_Arms;
11
12   task type Right_Arms is
13     entry Hit_Nail;
14     entry Fill_Nails_Box;
15   end Right_Arms;
16   Right_Arm : Right_Arms;
17
18   task body Left_Arms is
19     procedure Take_Nail is
20     begin
21       Put_Line ("Left_arm_took_a_nail");
22     end Take_Nail;
23
24     procedure Set_Nail is
25     begin
26       Put_Line ("Left_arm_set_the_nail");
27     end Set_Nail;
28   begin
29     loop
30       if Nails > 0 then
31         Take_Nail;
32         Nails := Nails - 1;
33         Set_Nail;
34         Right_Arm.Hit_Nail;
35       end if;
36     end loop;
37   end Left_Arms;
38
39   task body Right_Arms is
40     procedure Take_Hammer is
41     begin
42       Put_Line ("Right_arm_took_the_hammer");
43     end Take_Hammer;
44
45     procedure Hit_Nail_3_Times is
46     begin
47       Put_Line ("Right_arm_hit_to_the_nail");
48     end Hit_Nail_3_Times;
49
50     procedure Taking_Nails_From_Reserve is
51     begin
52       Put_Line ("Right_arm_took_nails_from_the_reserve");
53     end Taking_Nails_From_Reserve;
54
55     procedure Put_Nails_In_Box is
56     begin
57       Put_Line ("Right_arm_fill_the_nails_box");
58     end Put_Nails_In_Box;
59   begin
60     loop
61       select
62         accept Hit_Nail do
63           Take_Hammer;
64           Hit_Nail_3_Times;
65           Used_Nails := Used_Nails + 1;
66         end Hit_Nail;
67       or
68         accept Fill_Nails_Box do
69           Taking_Nails_From_Reserve;
70           Put_Nails_In_Box;
71           Nails := Nails - 10;
72         end Fill_Nails_Box;
73       end select;
74     end loop;
75   end Right_Arms;
76
77   Filling : Natural := 0;
78   U_Check : Natural := 0;
79
80 begin
81   Get (Filling);
82   while Filling > 0 loop
83     if Nails < 1 then
84       Right_Arm.Fill_Nails_Box;
85       Filling := Filling - 1;
86     else
87       U_Check := U_Check + 1;
88     end if;
89   end loop;
90   Put (Nails);
91 end Robot;
```

```
1
2
3
4  procedure Robot is
5
6
7    Nails      : Natural:=0;
8
9    task type Left_Arms;
10   Left_Arm : Left_Arms;
11
12   task type Right_Arms is
13     entry Hit_Nail;
14     entry Fill_Nails_Box;
15   end;
16   Right_Arm : Right_Arms;
17
18   task body Left_Arms is
19
20
21
22
23
24
25
26
27
28   begin
29     loop
30       if Nails > 0 then
31
32         Nails := Nails - 1;
33
34         Right_Arm.Hit_Nail;
35       end if;
36     end loop;
37   end;
38
39   task body Right_Arms is
40
41
42
43
44
45
46
47
48
49
50
51
52
53
54
55
56
57
58
59   begin
60     loop
61       select
62         accept Hit_Nail do
63
64
65           null;
66         end;
67       or
68         accept Fill_Nails_Box do
69
70
71           Nails := Nails - 10;
72         end;
73       end select;
74     end loop;
75   end;
76
77   Filling : Natural:=0;
78
79
80 begin
81
82   while Filling > 0 loop
83     if Nails < 1 then
84       Right_Arm.Fill_Nails_Box;
85       Filling := Filling - 1;
86
87
88     end if;
89   end loop;
90
91 end;
```

**Fig. 7.** Slicing of Robot program with ⟨90, {*Nails*}⟩ as slicing criterion

analysis approach could be used such as settling variable limits in order to limit at the very most the size of types used and thus help to reduce the size of the state space.

The slicing algorithm carried out by YASNOST is more adapted than previous ones to be a first step of a complete formal analysis process, such the one performed by QUASAR, saving time and resources for the long and complex model-checking step

```
 1  procedure Server is                                        1  procedure Server is
 2                                                             2
 3      Max_Client : Integer := 5;                             3      Max_Client : Integer:=5;
 4                                                             4
 5      protected type Datas is                                5      protected type Datas is
 6          procedure Get_Value (Value : out Integer);         6          procedure Get_Value
 7      private                                                7      private
 8          Data_Value : Integer := 0;                         8
 9      end Datas;                                             9      end;
10                                                            10
11      protected body Datas is                               11      protected body Datas is
12          procedure Get_Value (Value : out Integer) is      12          procedure Get_Value              is
13          begin                                             13          begin
14              Data_Value := Data_Value + 1;                 14
15              Value := Data_Value;                          15              null;
16          end Get_Value;                                    16          end;
17      end Datas;                                            17      end;
18                                                            18
19      Data : Datas;                                         19      Data : Datas;
20                                                            20
21      task type Thread is                                   21      task type Thread is
22          entry Get_Value (Param : out Integer);            22          entry Get_Value
23      end Thread;                                           23      end;
24      type Access_Thread is access Thread;                  24      type Access_Thread is access Thread;
25                                                            25
26      task body Thread is                                   26      task body Thread is
27      begin                                                 27      begin
28          accept Get_Value (Param : out Integer) do         28          accept Get_Value                 do
29              Data. Get_Value (Param);                      29              Data. Get_Value     ;
30          end Get_Value;                                    30          end;
31      end Thread;                                           31      end;
32                                                            32
33      task type Task_Server is                              33      task type Task_Server is
34          entry Get_Thread (Id : out Access_Thread);        34          entry Get_Thread (Id : out Access_Thread);
35      end Task_Server;                                      35      end;
36                                                            36
37      task body Task_Server is                              37      task body Task_Server is
38      begin                                                 38      begin
39          for I in 1..Max_Client loop                       39          for I in 1..Max_Client loop
40              accept Get_Thread (Id : out Access_Thread) do 40              accept Get_Thread (Id : out Access_Thread) do
41                  Id := new Thread;                         41                  Id := new Thread;
42              end Get_Thread;                               42              end;
43          end loop;                                         43          end loop;
44      end Task_Server;                                      44      end;
45                                                            45
46      The_Task_Server : Task_Server;                        46      The_Task_Server : Task_Server       ;
47                                                            47
48      task type Client;                                     48      task type Client;
49      type Access_Client is access Client;                  49      type Access_Client is access Client;
50                                                            50
51      task body Client is                                   51      task body Client is
52          Id    : Access_Thread;                            52          Id    : Access_Thread;
53          Value : Integer;                                  53
54      begin                                                 54      begin
55          The_Task_Server. Get_Thread (Id);                 55          The_Task_Server. Get_Thread (Id);
56          Id. Get_Value (Value);                            56          Id. Get_Value       ;
57      end Client;                                           57      end;
58                                                            58
59      A_Client : Access_Client;                             59      A_Client : Access_Client;
60  begin                                                     60  begin
61      for I in 1..Max_Client loop                           61      for I in 1..Max_Client loop
62          A_Client := new Client;                           62          A_Client := new Client;
63      end loop;                                             63      end loop;
64  end Server;                                               64  end;
```

**Fig. 8.** Client-Server example $\langle 64, \emptyset \rangle$ as slicing criterion

which follows the slicing step. Programs written in other programming languages could be sliced using the technics presented in this paper, however the semantic and syntactic information on the tree representation of the program as provided by ASIS (such as the query linking the node of an identifier and the node of its declaration) has to be obtained.

# References

[Che93]    Jingde Cheng. Slicing concurrent programs - a graph-theoretical approach. In *Proceedings of the First International Workshop on Automated and Algorithmic Debugging*, pages 223–240. Springer-Verlag, 1993.

[CX01]     Zhenqiang Chen and Baowen Xu. Slicing concurrent java programs. *SIGPLAN Not.*, 36(4):41–47, 2001.

[DCH⁺99]    Matthew B. Dwyer, James C. Corbett, John Hatcliff, Stefan Sokolowski, and Hongjun Zheng. Slicing multi-threaded java programs: A case study. Technical Report 99-7, KSU, 1999.

[EKPP⁺05]   Sami Evangelista, Claude Kaiser, Jean François Pradat-Peyre, Christophe Pajault, and Pierre Rousseau. Dynamic tasks verification with QUASAR. In *International Conference on Reliable Software Technologies (Ada-Europe)*, volume 3555, page 91. Springer-Verlag, June 2005.

[EKPPR03]   Sami Evangelista, Claude Kaiser, Jean François Pradat-Peyre, and Pierre Rousseau. Quasar, a new tool for concurrent ada program analysis. In *International Conference on Reliable Software Technologies (Ada-Europe)*, volume 2655, pages 168–181. Springer-Verlag, June 2003.

[EKPPR06]   Sami Evangelista, Claude Kaiser, Jean François Pradat-Peyre, and Pierre Rousseau. Comparing Java, C# and Ada monitors queuing policies : a case study and its ada refinement. In *Ada Letters*. ACM Press, 2006.

[Eva05]     Sami Evangelista. High level petri nets analysis with helena. In *26th International Conference on Applications and Theory of Petri Nets 2005, ICATPN 2005*, volume 3536, page 455. Springer-Verlag, 2005.

[Hoa74]     C. A. R. Hoare. Monitors: an operating system structuring concept. *Commun. ACM*, 17(10):549–557, 1974.

[HRB90]     Susan Horwitz, Thomas Reps, and David Binkley. Interprocedural slicing using dependence graphs. *ACM Trans. Program. Lang. Syst.*, 12(1):26–60, 1990.

[ISO95]     ISO/IEC-15291. Ada semantic interface specification. 1995.

[Kri03]     Jens Krinke. Context-sensitive slicing of concurrent programs. In *Proceedings of the 9th European software engineering conference held jointly with 10th ACM SIGSOFT international symposium on Foundations of software engineering*, pages 178–187. ACM Press, 2003.

[NR00]      Mangala Gowri Nanda and S. Ramesh. Slicing concurrent programs. In *Proceedings of the International Symposium on Software Testing and Analysis*, pages 180–190. ACM Press, 2000.

[SC03]      Ricky E. Sward and A.T. Chamillard. Adaslicer: an ada program slicer. In *Proceedings of the 2003 annual international conference on Ada*, pages 10–16. ACM Press, 2003.

[Tip95]     F. Tip. A survey of program slicing techniques. *Journal of programming languages*, 3:121–189, 1995.

[Wei84]     M. Weiser. Program slicing. *IEEE Transactions on Software Engineering*, 10(4):352–357, 1984.

[XQZ⁺05]    Baowen Xu, Ju Qian, Xiaofang Zhang, Zhongqiang Wu, and Lin Chen. A brief survey of program slicing. *SIGSOFT Softw. Eng. Notes*, 30(2):1–36, 2005.

[Zha99]     Jianjun Zhao. Slicing concurrent java programs. In *IWPC '99: Proceedings of the 7th International Workshop on Program Comprehension*, page 126. IEEE Computer Society, 1999.

# Reducing Software Architecture Models Complexity: A Slicing and Abstraction Approach

Daniela Colangelo[1], Daniele Compare[1],
Paola Inverardi[2], and Patrizio Pelliccione[2]

[1] Selex Communications, L'Aquila, Italy
{daniela.colangelo, daniele.compare}@selex-comms.com
[2] University of L'Aquila, Computer Science Department
Via Vetoio, 67010 L'Aquila, Italy
{inverard, pellicci}@di.univaq.it

**Abstract.** Software architectures (SA) represents a critical design level for software systems. Architectural choices need to be analyzed and verified to achieve a better software quality while reducing the time and cost of production. Model-checking is one of the most promising verification techniques, however its use for very large systems is not always possible due to the *state explosion problem*. In this paper we propose an approach that *slices* and *abstracts* the SA of a system in order to reduce the model complexity without compromising the verification validity. This approach exploits the characteristics of the SA model and the structure of the property of interest. It is applied to an industrial telecommunication system of the Selex Communications company.

## 1 Introduction

Recently, Software Architectures (SA) [1,2] have been largely accepted as a well suited tool to achieve better software quality while reducing time and cost of production. SA provide both a high-level behavioral abstraction of components and of their interactions (connectors) and, a description of the static structure of the system. The aim of SA descriptions is twofold: on one side they force the designer to separate architectural concerns from other design ones, thus abstracting away many details. On the other side, they allow for analysis and verification of architectural choices, both behavioral and quantitative, in order to obtain better software quality in an increasingly shorter time-to-market development scenario [3].

Formal Architectural Description Languages (ADL) have been employed to specify SA in a formal and rigorous way. They are the basis for many methods and tools for analysis and verification of software architectures, both behavioral and quantitative [3]. One of the most promising verification technique is model-checking since is fully automated and its use requires no supervision or formal methods expertise. Due to these reasons, in recent years model checking has gained popularity and it is increasingly used also in industrial contexts [4,5]. However the application of model checking techniques is still prevented by the

E. Najm et al. (Eds.): FORTE 2006, LNCS 4229, pp. 243–258, 2006.
© IFIP International Federation for Information Processing 2006

*state explosion problem.* As remarked by Gerald Holzmann in [6] no paper has been published on reachability analysis techniques without a serious discussion of this problem. State explosion occurs either in systems composed of (not too) many interacting components, or in systems where data structures assume many different values. The number of global states easily becomes enormous and intractable. To solve this problem, many methods have been developed by exploiting different approaches [7]. They can be logically classified into two disjoint sets [8]. The first set, that we call *Internal Methods*, considers algorithms and techniques used internally to the model checker in order to efficiently represent transition relations between concurrent processes, such as *Binary Decision Diagrams* [9] (used for synchronous processes) and *Partial Order Reduction* [10] techniques (used for asynchronous processes). The second set, that we call *External Methods* includes techniques that operate on the input of the model checker (models), and can be used in conjunction with Internal Methods. In this set there are *Abstraction* [11], *Symmetry* [12], *Compositional Reasoning* [13,14,8], and *Slicing* [15,16].

In this paper we propose an *architectural slicing* and *abstraction* approach which exploits the characteristic of the SA model and the structure of the property of interest for reducing the model complexity without compromising the verification validity. *Program slicing* [17] is a technique which attempts to decompose the system by extracting elements that are related to a particular computation. It is defined for conventional programming languages and therefore it is based on the basic elements of a program, i.e. variables and statements. *Architectural slicing* is the result of applying the slicing idea to SA [18,19]. Thus the basic elements on which is based the *Architectural slicing* are components, connectors, ports, roles, and messages exchanged between components. An architectural slicing can be considered a subset of the behaviour of a software architecture with the attempt to isolate its parts that are involved in the slicing criterion. In the approach that we are proposing the slicing criterion is the property we want to check on the SA. Thanks to the architectural slicing we are able to extract the parts of the system that play a role on the behavior implied by the property of interested.

Our approach makes use of TeStor [20], an algorithm that, taking in input state machines and scenarios expressed in terms of Property Sequence Charts (PSC) [21,22], generates test sequences in the form of scenarios. TeStor generates all traces containing the messages expressed in the input PSC and in the same order defined in the PSC by suitably abstracting with respect to message repetitions and loops. In this way it generates a final number of traces. Thus, given in input the state machines defining the behavior of the components composing the system and the property of interest (expressed in PSC notation), TeStor identifies all dependencies in the state machines and can be used as basis for the architectural slicing. In this work, we propose to extend TeStor in order to colorize the states of the components state machines that are involved on the considered property. When this step is done we can cut off from the SA the states that are not colored, thus obtaining a reduced and sliced SA.

After the slicing is performed some *architectural abstraction* criteria can be furtherly used to abstract parts of the system that are implied by the property, but that are not directly involved in its formulation. Finally, the reduced system model can be model checked by using the CHARMY [23,24] tool. The efficacy of this approach strictly depends on the characteristic of the SA. However it can be completely automatized and for some systems offers a good reduction, as in the industrial case study presented in Section 5. Through the case study, we show how the traditional approach fails with the used hardware resources, and, contrariwise, how the system can be successfully verified following this approach.

After an analysis of related work in Section 2, in Section 3 we introduce the notions and the instruments required to understand the approach. The approach is detailed in Section 4, and put in practice in Section 5, by presenting an industrial case study is presented. Finally, in Section 6 we present conclusion and future work.

## 2  Related Work

Program slicing was firstly introduced in [25] and later extended in other works [26,27]. For the sake of brevity, we report here only relevant works at the software architecture level.

In [19] the authors propose a dependence analysis technique called chaining to support software architectures testing maintenance and so on. Links in chaining reflect the dependence relationships that are in the architecture description. The relationships are been both structural and behavioral and based on components ports. A similar approach is proposed in [16] where is proposed a dependence analysis based on three different kinds of analysis based respectively on: relationships between a component and a connector; relationships between a connector and a component; and relationships inside a connector or a component. In this work and in [18] the author suggests to use the system dependence net to slice architectural descriptions written in the ACME ADL, and in the WRIGHT ADL respectively. This method produces a reduced textual architectural description just containing the ADL code lines associated with a particular slicing criterion. The works [19] and [16] are very similar in the main goal; however [19] does not focus on the description of the components themselves, but rather on the more abstract nature of the components and the connections. Our work builds on these prior works and it is based on a well detailed description of the component itself. Contrary to these works that give an abstract description of the components, by introducing only a dependence relationship between two different ports of a component or between two different roles of a connector, our work is based on a component description in terms of state machines that give a detailed description of the component behavior.

The works introduced above present static slice and dependence analysis techniques. In [15] authors propose a dynamic slicing, determined according to the input at run time. This kind of technique gives a slice that is smaller in size than the static one, and helps to isolate a specific execution path. Our work, although is not performed at run time, is strongly related to this work. In fact we are interested in identifying the execution paths that are implied by the property that we want to verify on the system. This property is represented, as already explained, as a PSC diagram and represents the slicing criterion in our approach. The slicing criterion of the approach presented in [15] contains the event to be observed, in addition our slicing criterion contains a set of events to be observed and temporal relationships between them.

# 3    Background

## 3.1    Charmy: A Tool for SA Designing and Model-Checking

CHARMY [23,24] is a project whose goal is to easy the application of model-checking techniques to validate the SA conformance to certain properties. In CHARMY the SA is specified through state diagrams used to describe how architectural components behave. Starting from the SA description CHARMY synthesizes, through a suitable translation into Promela (the specification language of the SPIN [5] model checker) an actual SA complete model that can be executed and verified in SPIN. This model can be validated with respect to a set of properties, e.g., deadlock, correctness of properties, starvation, etc., expressed in Linear-time Temporal Logic (LTL) [28] or in its Büchi Automata representation [29]. CHARMY allows users to describe temporal properties by using an extension of UML 2.0 sequence diagrams, called Property Sequence Charts (PSC) [21,22], that are successively translated into a temporal property representation for SPIN. The model checker SPIN, is a widely distributed software package that supports the formal verification of concurrent systems permitting to analyze their logical consistency by on-the-fly checks, i.e., without the need of constructing a global state graph, thus reducing the complexity of the check. It is the core engine of CHARMY and it is not directly accessible by a CHARMY user.

The state machine-based formalism used by CHARMY is an extended subset of UML state diagrams: labels on arcs uniquely identify the architectural communication channels, and a channel allows the communication only between a pair of components. The labels are structured as follows: '['$guard$']'$event$'('$parameter\_list$')' '/'$op_1$';'$op_2$';'$\cdots$';'$op_n$ where $guard$ is a boolean condition that denotes the transition activation, an $event$ can be a message sent or received (denoted by an exclamation mark "!" or a question mark "?", respectively), or an internal operation ($\tau$) (i.e., an event that does not require synchronization between state machines). Both sent and received messages are performed over defined channels $ch$, i.e., connectors. An event can have several parameters as defined in the parameters list. $op_1, op_2, \cdots, op_n$ are the operations performed when the transition fires.

## 3.2    Property Sequence Charts (PSC)

PSC [21,22] is a diagrammatic formalism for specifying temporal properties in a user-friendly fashion. It is a scenario-based visual language that is an extended graphical notation of a subset of UML2.0 Sequence Diagrams. PSC can express a useful set of both *liveness* and *safety* properties in terms of messages exchanged among the components forming a system. Finally, an algorithm, called PSC2BA, translates PSC into Büchi automata.

PSC uses a UML notation, stereotyped so that: (i) each rectangular box represents an architectural component, (ii) each arrow defines a communication line (a channel) between two components. Between a pair of messages we can select if other messages can occur (loose relation) or not (strict relation). Message constraints are introduced to define a set of messages that must never occur in between the message containing the constraint and its predecessor or successor. Messages are typed as *regular messages* (optional messages), *required messages* (mandatory messages) and *fail messages* (messages representing a fault).

An example of PSC is in Figure 4.

### 3.3 TEst Sequence generaTOR (TeStor)

TeStor [20] is an algorithm, which, taking in input state machines and scenarios, generates test sequences in the form of scenarios. The algorithm is based on the idea that scenarios are usually incomplete specifications and represent important and expected system interactions. Such incomplete specifications may be "completed" by recovering, from state machines, the missing information. The output of the algorithm is a set of sequence diagrams (outSD) containing the sequence of messages expressed by the input sequence diagram (inSD), enhanced and completed with information gathered by the components' state machines.

TeStor, focussing on the first (not visited) message $m$ in the selected inSD, and looking inside each state machine, searches a trace which permits to reach $m$, starting from the current state of the state machine. When such trace is found, TeStor recursively moves to the next (not visited) message $m'$ in inSD, and checks a trace which permits to reach $m'$ starting from the current state. At the end of this process, TeStor tries to merge together the different trace portions in a set of traces (the set outSD) which move from the initial state and covers any message in the inSD.

For more information on the TeStor algorithm, please refer to [20].

## 4    The Approach

Our proposal makes use of TeStor, the algorithm introduced in Section 3.3, which aims to extract test sequences from a SA specification (given in terms of state machines) following the trail suggested by a PSC property. We propose to use an extension of TeStor, called DepCol, which, instead of returning a set of sequences, colors the state machines highlighting the parts of the SA model that are required to correctly verifying the property of interest. After this step is done the abstraction step can be performed. The idea is to compact, if and when is possible, some states of a component in only one abstract state. Since the transition from one state to another is made when a message is exchanged between a couple of components, this step is not trivial. When a final reduced SA model is obtained, cutting off the parts of the system that can be removed and suitably abstracting the system, CHARMY can be used. CHARMY and TESTOR use the same representation for state machines. Since the notation used in CHARMY for expressing the property is PSC, the integration between this approach and CHARMY is straightforward. In the following we detail the approach step by step. Note that the whole approach can be fully automatized.

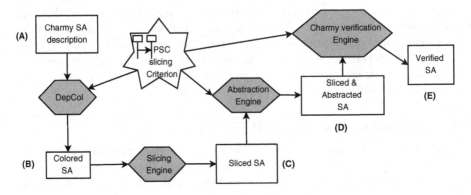

**Fig. 1.** The Approach

Figure 1 summarizes the approach: **(A)** we start from a CHARMY SA description, i.e. a SA described in terms of components and connectors with communicating state machines used to represent components and connectors behaviors. The PSC property is our slicing criterion. **(B)** DEPCOL, the extension of TESTOR that we propose, gets in input the CHARMY SA and the slicing criterion and returns a colored SA. **(C)** The colored SA contains information about the parts of the system that are necessary and the parts of the system that can be cut off. Thus, the slicing engine gets in input the colored SA, cuts off the unnecessary parts and returns a sliced SA. **(D)** The sliced SA is the input of the abstraction engine that returns a sliced and abstracted SA. **(E)** Finally, CHARMY can be used to check, through model checking techniques, if the reduced SA satisfies the property we want to verify, expressed as a PSC.

Section 4.1 explains the steps **(A)**, **(B)**, and **(C)**, while Section 4.2 details the step **(D)**. The step **(E)** is the standard use of CHARMY and it is explained in Section 3.1.

## 4.1   Architectural Slicing

The inputs of this step are the state machines representing the components behavior and the property of interest expressed as a PSC diagram.

Based on TESTOR we define the new algorithm that we call DEPCOL. This algorithm colors the parts of the state machines that are required for the SA verification. Let $M$ be the set of messages that are $arrowMSGs$ or $intraMSGs$ of the considered PSC. Each start or target state of a $m \in M$ in at least one sequence generated by TeStor is colored. This modification of TeStor is very easy. Unfortunately it is not enough. In fact the DepCol state machines (the same used by Charmy) make use also of variables to synchronize and store the state machines computation state. These variables can be *local* to a state machine but can be also *shared* among different state machines. Thus, let $v_l$ be a *local* variable contained in a transition that has a colored target state. For each occurrence of $v_l$ in the same state machine, if it is contained in a transition that has a non colored target state $s$, then each path leading from the initial state to $s$ is colored. Analogously, for each *shared* variable $v_s$ contained in a transition that has a target colored state, every occurrence of $v_s$ in each state machine is identified. Also in this case, if $v_s$ is contained in a transition that has a non colored target state $s$, each path from the initial state of the component containing $v_s$ leading $s$ is colored.

While coloring the paths, new messages can be considered (messages that have both start state and target state as colored states). Since messages have a component sender and a component receiver, new parts of the state machines require to be colored. Doing this step new messages could be considered, and then the whole coloring process must be iterated. It is important to note that only one state machine at a time is considered while coloring, thus we do not have problems of states explosion.

At the end of this step we have the state machine colored. The following properties hold:

- each state playing a role in the property is colored;
- each state that is non colored does not play a role in the property;
- is not possible to have a non colored state in the middle of a path that starts with the initial state of a state machine and that ends with a colored state. This is assured by construction, since we start from a state and we color each state traversed in reaching the initial state.

Thus, for each state machine, every message that has a start state or a target state not colored is cut off. For each state machine, every state not colored is cut off. Note that, it is impossible with the cut to generate two or more not connected parts of a state machine.

## 4.2  Architectural Abstraction

The idea of this step is to reduce the complexity of the model by abstracting parts of the state machines without compromising the validity of the verification. In the following we refer to the state machine formalism used by Charmy and shortly described in Section 3.1. We introduce the following two abstraction rules:

R1: For each state machine that has only one state, each sent message $m \notin M$ could be deleted. In order to do it we have to analyze each reception of $m$ (on other state machines). Let $s_0$ be the start state and $s_1$ be the target state of the message $m$ $(s_0 - ?m \rightarrow s_1)$. If $outdegree(s_0) == 1$[1] then for

---

[1] *Outdegree($s$)* is the number of messages that have $s$ as start state.

each message $m'$ that has $s_0$ as target state, $s_1$ becomes the new target state of $m'$ and the state $s_0$ can be deleted.

If $m$ has a guard, the guard is preserved while $m$ can be deleted. If $m$ has an operation $op$, and $s_0$ is the initial state of the state machine, then $op$ is preserved and $m$ is deleted; otherwise if $s_0$ is not the initial state of the state machine, then $op$ is added to the operations of each message that has $s_0$ as target state. A state machine with only one state without messages can be deleted. The same rule applies for received messages.

R2: Let $SM_1$ be a state machine, for each pair of consecutive exchanged messages[2], $s_1 - m_1 \rightarrow s_2$ and $s_2 - m_2 \rightarrow s_3$ and with $m_1, m_2 \notin M$, if $m_1$ and $m_2$ are always exchanged consecutively and in the same order in any other state machine $SM_2$, $s'_1 - m_1 \rightarrow s'_2$, and $s'_2 - m_2 \rightarrow s'_3$, then they can be abstracted and $s_1$ and $s_3$ collapse in the same state inheriting all entering and exiting messages. The same holds for $s'_1$ and $s'_3$. Note that not necessary $s_1$ ($s'_1$), $s_2$ ($s'_2$), and $s_3$ ($s'_3$) must be different states.

This rule can be applied iff $m_1$ or $m_2$ are self transitions or the states $s_2$ and $s'_2$ have *degree* (i.e. the number of entering and exiting messages) equals to 2, i.e. $s_2$ ($s'_2$) has only one entering message, $m_1$ ($m'_1$) and only one exiting message $m_2$ ($m'_2$). In fact, we cannot abstract if the states $s_2$ or $s'_2$ are involved in other paths.

These two rules are applied until it is not possible to further abstract the system.

The algorithm operates separately on each state machine without requiring they parallel composition.

## 5   The Integrated Environment for Communication on Ship (IECS) Case Study

The Integrated Environment for Communication on Ship (IECS), a project developed by Selex Communications, operates in a naval communication environment. IECS provides heterogeneous services on board of the ship.

The purpose of the system is to fulfill the following main functionalities: *i)* provide voice, data and video communication modes; *ii)* prepare, elaborate, memorize, recovery and distribution of operative messages; *iii)* configuration of radio frequency, variable power control and modulation for transmission and reception over radio channel; *iv)* remote control and monitoring of the system for detection of equipment failures in the transmission/reception radio chain and for the management of system elements; *v)* data distribution service; *vi)* implement communication security techniques to the required level of evaluation and certification. The SA is composed of the IECS Management System (IECS-MS), CTS, and EQUIPMENT components as highlighted in Figure 2.

---

[2] Note that here we do not consider send and receive of messages because the rule is independent of the operations. Thus, if $SM_1$ sends $m_1$, $SM_2$ has to receive it in order to apply this rule and viceversa.

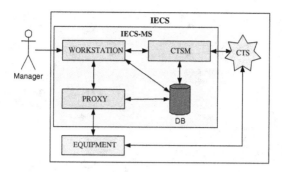

**Fig. 2.** IECS Software Configuration

In the following we focus on the IECS-MS, the more critical component since it coordinates different heterogeneous subsystems, both software and hardware. Indeed, it controls the IECS system providing both internal and external communications. The IECS-MS complexity and heterogeneity need the definition of a precise software architecture to express its coordination structure. The system involves several operational consoles that manage the heterogenous system equipment including the ATM based Communication Transfer System (CTS) through Proxy computers. For this reason the high level design is based on a manager-agent architecture that is summarized in Figure 2, where the Workstation (WS) component represents the management entity while the Proxy and the Communication Transfer System Manager (CTSM) components represent the interface to control the managed equipment and the CTS, respectively.

The functionalities of interest of the IECS-MS are: *i)* service activation; *ii)* service deactivation; *iii)* service reconfiguration; *iv)* equipment configuration; *v)* control equipment status; *vi)* fault CTS. A *service*, in this context, denotes a unit base of planning and the implementation of a logic channel of communication through the resources of communications on the ship. All the above described functionalities are "atomics", since it is not possible to execute two different functionalities at the same time on the system.

In this paper we focus on the *Service Activation* functionality for showing how we reduced the complexity of the SA for the verification of properties.

**Service Activation Functionality:** The Manager actor requests a service activation to the Workstation component that updates the information of the service that the Manager wants to activate on the DB component. If the CTSM is online, then the Workstation proceeds in parallel to create the chain of communication and configures the parameters of the equipments involved in the service. The DB component is finally updated.

## 5.1   IECS Case Study: System Modeling and Verification

In the previous sections we defined the static SA of the IECS-MS system. Now we extract from the specification, the state machines that describe the

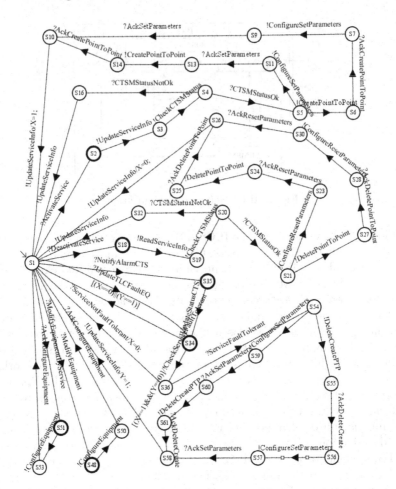

**Fig. 3.** Workstation internal behavior

internal behavior of the system components and the PSC scenarios that define the properties that the system has to satisfy.

Figure 3 shows the state machine for the WS component. This component has only one thread of execution. The actual size of the system does not permit to report in the paper details about the whole system. For this reason in the following we illustrate our approach only on significant excerpts of the system in order to give an idea of the modeling technique and of the analysis of the process followed.

The WS component coordinates and manages all the functionalities of the system. The access to each functionality is obtained through the reception of a message from the other components (e.g. USER, CTSM and Equipment); the reception of this message leads to a state that is the entry state of the functionality, represented in Figure 3 as a bold state. For example, when WS receives the message *Activate Service* it goes in the state *S2* to entry the path that manages the *service activation* functionality.

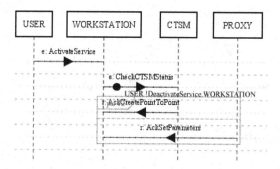

**Fig. 4.** Property: Service Activated

Furthermore, in the state machine is represented the "atomicity" of the functionalities of the system that are managed by the WS component. Every time a new functionality is required, if WS is ready for satisfying the request (i.e. a request can be satisfied only when previously requested functionalities are accomplished), this component goes from state *S1* to the path that manages this functionality. Finally, in the state machines are introduced two variables, one *shared*, X, for storing the service activation, and one *local*, Y, for storing the reconfiguration of the service in case of a fault of the CTS or Equipment components.

In order to check that the system correctly implements these functionalities, we define some properties that the SA should satisfy. The properties are modeled as PSC scenarios. Due to space reasons, in this paper we focus only on one property, that we use to show the approach. Figure 4 reports the considered property that concerns the service activation. The property is composed of two *regular messages* (the precondition of the property) that realize the service activation request. When the precondition is satisfied, if the USER does not deactivate the service (the constraint of the second message) the service must be activated (the last two *required* messages of the scenario).

When state machines and the PSC diagrams are modeled in CHARMY, the runnable Promela prototype of the system and the Büchi Automata of the property can be automatically generated. Through the use of the SPIN model checker we verified that the SA of our system is deadlock free, does not contain invalid end states, and does not contain unreachable parts (the standard verification of SPIN). The check is performed by using a PC with 3 Gb of RAM and with 4 processors of 1 Ghz. The size of the model is the following: $States = 1.27e + 08$ $Transitions = 6.15646e + 08$ $Memory = 2037.528Mb$.

Unlikely, when we tried to verify the properties of interest, we run into the *state explosion problem*. Thus, the next step is to apply the approach presented in Section 4 trying to reduce the complexity of the system.

**Slice and Abstraction Applied to the Case Study.** From the CHARMY SA description and the property *Service Activated* is now possible to obtain a colored SA, through the use of the algorithm DEPCOL. This colored SA, represented in Figure 5, highlights all paths required by the property.

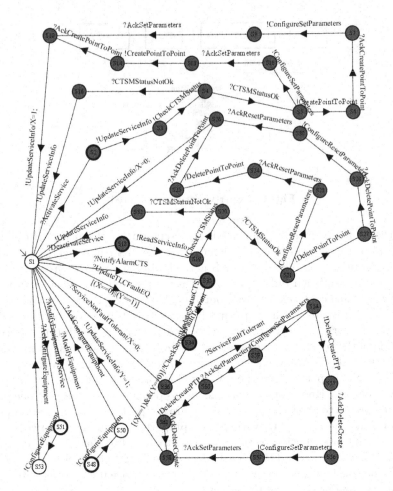

**Fig. 5.** Colored SA on WS state machines

The path that starts with the state $S2$ identifies the functionality *Service Activation* that is useful for the property we want verify. Instead, the message *DeactivateService* conducts to the path that manages the functionality *Service Deactivation*, while the messages *NotifyAlarmCTS* or *UpdateTLCFaultEQ* represent the entry in the path that manages the *Service Reconfiguration* when there is a fault in the components CTS or Equipment, respectively. The last two path are colored since they contain operations with *shared* and *local* variables. The states not colored in Figure 5 are then deleted to obtain the sliced SA.

Then, we proceed with the abstraction on the sliced SA, following the rules of abstraction presented in Section 4.2. Thanks to the first rule, in the case study we can delete all the state machines with only one state and containing messages that do not belong to the property. In the case study we deleted one *Thread* with only one state of the component DB, and consequently we deleted the relative

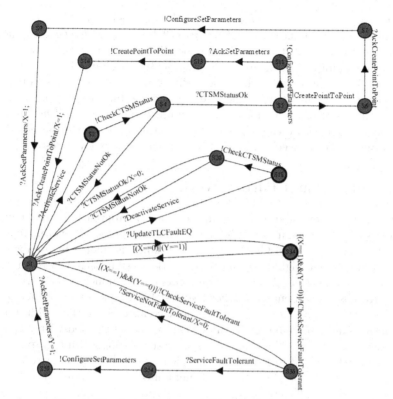

**Fig. 6.** Sliced and abstracted SA on WS state machines

send messages on the other components, e.g. considering the WS components, all the *UpdateServiceInfo* and *ReadServiceInfo* messages are deleted (refer to Figure 6).

Furthermore, still considering the WS component, the send message *UpdateServiceInfo* contains some operations; so, when the message is deleted the

**Table 1.** Resources used for verification of the properties

| Property | System | Depth | Memory (Mb) | States | Transitions |
|---|---|---|---|---|---|
| Activate | full | > 8766 | > 3034.084 | > 1.51433e + 08 | > 1.20706e + 09 |
| Service | reduced | 108.829 | 239.614 | 1.6719e + 007 | 2.8475e + 006 |
| Deactivate | full | > 8766 | > 3034.084 | > 1.51433e + 08 | > 1.07926e + 09 |
| Service | reduced | 9253 | 186.264 | 2.11009e + 006 | 1.18284e + 007 |
| Reconfiguration | full | > 8802 | > 3034.084 | > 1.51433e + 08 | > 1.50446e + 09 |
| Service | reduced | 2619 | 153.598 | 1.65737e + 006 | 9.73146e + 006 |
| Modify | full | > 8678 | > 3034.084 | > 1.51433e + 08 | > 9.32346e + 08 |
| Equipment | reduced | 265 | 34.302 | 741 | 2063 |
| Modify Equipment | full | > 8678 | > 3034.084 | > 1.51433e + 08 | > 9.32346e + 08 |
| by Service | reduced | 471 | 34.302 | 741 | 2063 |

operations are added to the messages that happen before it. The second rule allows us to delete the message *DeleteCreatePtP* and *AckDeleteCreate*. The approach is iterated until it is not further possible to abstract the system. The obtained model for the WS component is presented in Figure 6.

In Table 1 we report the result of the verification for all properties, comparing the resources used for verifying the reduced and the full model. Since for each property the result of the verification of the full model was *out of memory*, the information reported are the last result before the error. As can be noted, the verifications of the reduced SA are obtained by using very lower resources.

## 6   Conclusion and Future Work

In this paper we presented a slicing and abstraction approach for reducing the complexity of a SA description. The approach is composed of several steps: the SA description, in terms of CHARMY state machines, is colored by an algorithm called DEPCOL that highlights the parts of the system that are required for the property verification. A slicing engine cuts off the unnecessary parts of the system. An abstraction engine further reduces the complexity of the model abstracting parts of the state machines without compromising the validity of the verification. Thus, the reduced SA model can be model checked with respect to the property of interest. The property of interest is expressed in a graphical formalism called PSC and it represents the slicing and abstraction criterion. The approach has been applied on a Selex Communications company case study in order to validate its efficacy.

On the future work side we plan to fully automatize the approach and to try to use it in other case studies. It is also planned to investigate other abstraction and slicing rules that could further reduce the system SA. For instance the abstraction rule R1, presented in Section 4.2, can be successfully instantiated for internal messages.

## Acknowledgements

This work is partially supported by the PLASTIC project: Providing Lightweight and Adaptable Service Technology for pervasive Information and Communication. Sixth Framework Programme. http://www.ist-plastic.org.

## References

1. Bass, L., Clements, P., Kazman, R.: Software Architecture in Practice. Addison-Wesley, Massachusetts (1998)
2. Perry, D.E., Wolf, A.L.: Foundations for the study of software architecture. In: SIGSOFT Software Engineering Notes. Volume 17. (1992) 40–52
3. Bernardo, M., Inverardi, P.: Formal Methods for Software Architectures, Tutorial book on Software Architectures and Formal Methods. SFM-03:SA Lectures, LNCS 2804 (2003)

4. Compare, D., Inverardi, P., Pelliccione, P., Sebastiani, A.: Integrating model-checking architectural analysis and validation in a real software life-cycle. In: the 12th International Formal Methods Europe Symposium (FME 2003). number 2805 in LNCS, Springer (2003)
5. Holzmann, G.J.: The SPIN Model Checker: Primer and Reference Manual. Addison Wesley (2003)
6. Holzmann, G.J.: The logic of bugs. In: FSE 2002, Foundations of Software Engineering, Charleston, SC, USA (2002)
7. Clarke, E.M., Grumberg, O., Peled, D.A.: Model Checking. The MIT Press (2001)
8. Caporuscio, M., Inverardi, P., Pelliccione, P.: Compositional verification of middleware-based software architecture descriptions. In: Proceedings of the International Conference on Software Engineering (ICSE 2004), Edimburgh (2004.)
9. Bryant, R.E.: Graph-based algorithms for boolean function manipulation. IEEE Transaction on Computers **C-35**(8) (1986) 677–691
10. Katz, S., Peled, D.: An efficient verification method for parallel and distributed programs. In: Workshop on Linear Time, Branching Time and Partial Order Logics and Models for Concurrency. Volume 354 of LNCS., Springer (1988) 489–507
11. Frantz, F.K.: A taxonomy of model abstraction techniques. In: WSC '95: Proceedings of the 27th conference on Winter simulation, New York, NY, USA, ACM Press (1995) 1413–1420
12. Emerson, F.A., Sistla, A.P.: Symmetry and Model Checking. Formal Methods in System Design: An International Journal **9**(1/2) (1996) 105–131
13. Francez, N.: The Analysis of Cyclic Programs. PhD thesis, The Weizmann Institute of Science (1976)
14. Pnueli, A.: In transition from global to modular temporal reasoning about programs. Logics and Models of Concurrent Systems, sub-series F: Computer and System Science (1985) 123–144 Springer-Verlag.
15. Kim, T., Song, Y.T., Chung, L., Huynh, D.T.: Software architecture analysis: A dynamic slicing approach. Journal of Computer & Information Science (2) (2000) 91–103
16. Zhao, J.: Using dependence analysis to support software architecture understanding. in M. Li (Ed.), New Technologies on Computer Software, International Academic Publishers (1997) 135–142
17. Tip, F.: A survey of program slicing techniques. Journal of programming languages **3** (1995) 121–189
18. Zhao, J.: Applying slicing technique to software architectures. In: Proceedings of 4th IEEE International Conference on Engineering of Complex Computer Systems. (1998) 87–98
19. Stafford, J.A., Wolf, A.L.: Architecture-level dependence analysis for software systems. International Journal of Software Engineering and Knowledge Engineering **11**(4) (2001) 431–451
20. Pelliccione, P., Muccini, H., Bucchiarone, A., Facchini, F.: Deriving Test Sequences from Model-based Specifications. In: Proc. Eighth International SIGSOFT Symposium on Component-based Software Engineering (CBSE 2005). Lecture Notes in Computer Science, LNCS 3489, St. Louis, Missouri (USA) (2005) 267–282
21. Autili, M., Inverardi, P., Pelliccione, P.: A scenario based notation for specifying temporal properties. In: 5th International Workshop on Scenarios and State Machines: Models, Algorithms and Tools (SCESM'06). (Shanghai, China, May 27, 2006.)
22. PSC home page: http://www.di.univaq.it/psc2ba: (2005)

23. Charmy Project: Charmy web site. http://www.di.univaq.it/charmy (2004)

24. Inverardi, P., Muccini, H., Pelliccione, P.: Charmy: an extensible tool for architectural analysis. In: ESEC/FSE-13: Proceedings of the 10th European software engineering conference held jointly with 13th ACM SIGSOFT international symposium on Foundations of software engineering, New York, NY, USA, ACM Press (2005) 111–114

25. Weiser, M.: Program slicing. In: ICSE '81: Proceedings of the 5th international conference on Software engineering, Piscataway, NJ, USA, IEEE Press (1981) 439–449

26. Agrawal, H., Horgan, J.R.: Dynamic program slicing. In: Proceedings of the ACM SIGPLAN '90 Conference on Programming Language Design and Implementation. Volume 25., White Plains, NY (1990) 246–256

27. Korel, B., Laski, J.: Dynamic slicing of computer programs. J. Syst. Softw. **13**(3) (1990) 187–195

28. Manna, Z., Pnueli, A.: The temporal logic of reactive and concurrent systems. Springer-Verlag New York, Inc. (1992)

29. Buchi, R.: On a decision method in restricted second order arithmetic. In Press, S.U., ed.: Proc. of the Int. Congress of Logic, Methodology and Philosophy of Science. (1960) 1–11

# Branching Time Semantics for UML 2.0 Sequence Diagrams

Youcef Hammal

LSI, Département d'Informatique, Faculté d'Electronique & Informatique
Université des Sciences et de la Technologie Houari Boumediene
BP 32, El-Alia 16111, Bab-Ezzouar, Algiers, Algeria
yhammal@wissal.dz

**Abstract.** This paper presents formal definitions for UML Sequences Diagrams based on branching time semantics and partial orders in a denotational style. The obtained graphs are close to lattices and specify faithfully the intended behaviors rather than trace based semantics. We also define few generalized algebraic operations on graphs so that it makes it easy to provide formal definitions in a compositional manner to interaction operators. Next we extend our formalism with logical clocks and time formulas over values of these clocks to express timing constraints of complex systems. We present also some algorithms to extract time annotations that adorn sequence diagrams and transform them into timing constraints in our timed graphs. Obviously, this approach alleviates more the hard task of consistency checking between UML diagrams, specifically interaction diagrams with regards to state diagrams. Timeliness and performance analysis of timed graphs related to sequence diagrams could take advantages of works on model checking of timed automata.

## 1 Introduction

Scenarios-based specifications have become increasingly accepted as a means of requirements elicitation for concurrent systems such as telecommunications software. Indeed scenarios describe in an intuitive and visual way how system components and users interact in order to provide system level functionality. They are also used during the more detailed design phase where the precise inter-process communication must be specified according to formal protocols [3, 4, 7, 10, 12, 8].

The Unified Modeling language (UML [8]) which is an OMG standard and multiparadigm language for description of various aspects of complex systems, adopted early this kind of visual and flexible notations for expressing the interactions between system components and their relationships, including the messages that may be dispatched among them. More precisely, UML contains 3 kinds of these interactions diagrams: sequence diagrams, communication diagrams and timing diagrams [8].

Recently, many established features of MSC (Message Sequence Charts) [5] have been integrated into the version 2.0 of UML [8], namely the interaction operators among fragments and the adoption of partial order among interaction events rather than the related messages.

Each interaction fragment alone is a partial view of the system behavior but when combined all together by means of the new interaction operators, interactions provide relatively a whole system description.

E. Najm et al. (Eds.): FORTE 2006, LNCS 4229, pp. 259–274, 2006.

However in spite of the expressiveness and precise syntactic aspects of UML notations, their semantics remain described in natural language with sometimes OCL formulas. Accordingly, to use automated tools for analysis, simulation and verification of parts of produced UML models, UML diagrams should be given a precise and formal semantics by means of rigorous mathematical formalisms [12, 4].

In this context, this paper presents a new formal approach to defining branching time semantics for UML Sequences Diagrams in denotational style. Our approach deals with the partial order and yields lattice-like graphs that specify faithfully the intended behaviors by recording both traces of all interaction components together with branching bifurcations. We provide our mathematical structure with few generalized algebraic operations making it easy to give formal definitions of interaction operators in a compositional manner. Next we extend our formalism with logical clocks and time formulas over these clocks to express timing constraints of complex systems. Some given algorithms show how to extract time annotations of sequence diagrams and transform them into timing constraints in our timed graphs.

Obviously, this approach alleviates more the hard task of consistency checking between UML diagrams, specifically interaction diagrams with regards to state diagrams. Timeliness and performance analysis of timed graphs related to sequence diagrams could take advantage of works on model checking of timed automata [1].

The paper is structured as follows: The next section shows the basic features of UML Sequences Diagrams (DS) and in section 3 we present our formal model and its algebraic operations. Then in section 4, the semantics of DS are given in compositional style by combining the denotations of interaction fragments using our algebraic operations and section 5 presents a temporal enhancement of our graphs with logical clocks and temporal formulas and then we give the method to extract into our timed graphs the timing constraints from time annotations on sequence diagrams. Finally last sections compare related work with ours and give concluding remarks.

## 2   Interactions and Sequences Diagrams

The notation for an interaction in a sequence diagram is a solid-outline rectangle of which upper left corner contains a pentagon. Inside this pentagon, the keyword **sd** is written followed by the interaction name and parameters [8].

In a sequence diagram (Fig.1), participants (components, objects ...) that participate in the interaction are located at the top of the diagram across the horizontal axis. From each component shown using a rectangle, a lifeline is drawn to the bottom and the dispatching of every message is depicted by a horizontal arc going from the sender component to the receiver one. These messages are ordered from top to bottom so that the control flow over time is shown in a clear manner. Each message is defined by two events: message emission and message reception and events situated on the same lifeline are ordered from top to down [8].

Accordingly a message defines a particular communication among communicating entities. This communication can be "raising a signal", "invoking an operation", "creating" or "destroying an instance". The message specifies not only the kind of communication but also the sender and the receiver. The various kinds of communication involved in distributed systems are considered in UML sequence diagrams. Hence messages may be either synchronous or asynchronous [8].

Basic interaction fragment only represents finite behaviors without branching (when executing a sequence diagram, the only branching is due to interleaving of concurrent events), but these can be composed to obtain more complete descriptions. Basic interaction fragments can be composed in a composite interaction fragment called combined interaction or combined fragment using a set of operators called interaction operators. The unary operators are OPT, LOOP, BREAK and NEG. The others have more than one operand, such as ALT, PAR, and SEQ. Recurrently the combined fragments can be combined themselves together until obtaining a more complete diagram sequence [8] (see fig.1).

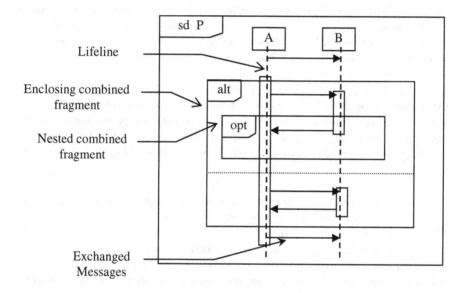

**Fig. 1.** Sequence Diagram.

The notation for a combined fragment in a sequence diagram is a solid-outline rectangle. The operator is in a pentagon at the upper left corner of the rectangle.

The operands of a combined fragment are shown by tiling the graph region of the combined fragment using dashed horizontal lines to divide it into regions corresponding to the operands.

Finally interactions in sequence diagrams are considered as collections of events instead of ordered collections of messages as in UML 1.x. These stimuli are partially ordered based on which execution thread they belong to. Within each thread the stimuli are sent in a sequential order while stimuli of different threads may be sent in parallel or in an arbitrary order.

**Notations.** Let $\Sigma$ be a vocabulary of symbols. $\Sigma^*$ is the set of all finite words over $\Sigma$ including the empty word $\varepsilon$. Let $w \in \Sigma^*$, $|w|$ denotes the length of w and $w(n)$ denotes the $n^{th}$ symbol of w. If u, v $\in \Sigma^*$, u.v denotes the concatenation of u and v.

# 3  Formal Model for Interaction Behavior

We present below the mathematical model used for the definition of the branching time semantics of sequence diagrams. This model is a *lattice-like* graph which records faithfully from sequences diagrams the intended traces of events together with the choices possibilities. Moreover it preserves the partial order among events in such a way that structure may contain diamond-shaped parts.

$G = <O, \Sigma, <_\Sigma, S, s_0, T>$ where :

- O is the set of participants involved in an interaction.
- $\Sigma$ is the set of events occurrences. Note that $\Sigma$ contains an unobservable event $\tau \neq \varepsilon$ modeling change of control flow. This event $\tau$ may be also adorned with a guard.
- $<_\Sigma \subset \Sigma \times \Sigma$, is a set of pairs of events occurrences where each one represents a binary relation between two occurrences to describe that one event must occur before the other in a valid trace. This mechanism provides a partial order on events occurrences so that the set of possible sequences is more restricted.
- $S = \{s_k : O \to \Sigma^*, k \in \aleph \}$

    $= \{s_k : o_i \to w \in \Sigma^* / \forall n \leq |w|, \forall m \leq n : (w(n) , w(m)) \notin <_\Sigma \}$

Every mapping $s_k$ from S assigns to each participant some word (trace of events occurrences) at some point k of its evolution such that the binary relation $<_\Sigma$ among events remains preserved. Hence, these mappings constitute the nodes of the graph.

- $s_0 \in S$ represents the initial node where no event is recorded. $\forall o_i \in O, s_0(o_i) = \varepsilon$.
- $T : S \times \Sigma \to S$

    $(s_i, e) \to s_j$

Each transition records any occurring event different from $\tau$ onto the trace of the relating object. For more convenience, we write $s_i$ |----e-----$s_j$.

If $e = \tau$ then $\forall o \in O: s_j(o) = s_i(o)$

If $e \neq \tau$ then there exits exactly one object o where:

$e \in$ lifeline(o) $\wedge s_j(o)=s_i(o).e \wedge \forall o' \in O, \forall e' \in s_i(o') : (e,e') \notin <_\Sigma$.

(e should never occur if it precedes any other recorded event via the partial order)

$\forall o' \neq o: s_j(o') = s_i(o')$   ($s_j$ does not record e onto o' trace if o' ≠ lifeline (e)).

We prefer call final nodes leaf nodes rather than acceptance nodes because sequence diagrams are only some pieces of the expected behavior. So any recorded trace is only a prefix of some whole traces we can only compute from State Diagrams.

Below we define two binary and one unary algebraic operations on these kinds of graphs. These operations are generalized making it possible to define the formal semantics of interaction operators on interaction fragments in a compositional style.

## 3.1  Choice Operation

This operation achieves an adjunct of graphs. Choice is made between them via internal $\tau$-actions. Let $G_1$, $G_2$ be two graphs where:

$G_1 = <O^1, \Sigma^1, <_\Sigma^1, S^1, s_0^1, T^1>, \quad G_2 = <O^2, \Sigma^2, <_\Sigma^2, S^2, s_0^2, T^2>$ Such that $O^1 = O^2$

$G_1 \oplus G_2 = <O, \Sigma, <_\Sigma, S, s_0, T>$ where :

- $O = O^1 = O^2$.          - $\Sigma = \Sigma^1 \cup \Sigma^2$.          - $<_\Sigma = <_\Sigma^1 \cup <_\Sigma^2$

- $S = S^1 \cup S^2 \cup \{s_0\}$ where $s_0 \in S$ is new initial node.
- $T = T^1 \cup T^2 \cup T'$ where    $T' = \{s_0 \mathbin{\text{---}}\tau\text{---} s_0^1, s_0 \mathbin{\text{---}}\tau\text{---} s_0^2\}$

## 3.2 Parameterized Cartesian Product

This product achieves merging of all pairs of traces from the two graphs but in such a way the partial order among events remain preserved. Whenever we try concatenate two traces, we should check that none of events occurrences of the second trace is ordered before an event from the previous trace.

Let $G_1$, $G_2$ be two graphs where:

$$G_1 = <O^1, \Sigma^1, <_\Sigma^1, S^1, s_0^1, T^1> , \quad G_2 = <O^2, \Sigma^2, <_\Sigma^2, S^2, s_0^2, T^2>$$

$G_1 \otimes_{\text{Prior}} G_2 = <O, \Sigma, <_\Sigma, S, s_0, T>$ where :

- $O = O^1 \cup O^2$.    - $\Sigma = \Sigma^1 \cup \Sigma^2$    - $<_\Sigma = <_\Sigma^1 \cup <_\Sigma^2 \cup$ Prior

Prior $\subseteq (\Sigma^1 x \Sigma^2) \cup (\Sigma^2 x \Sigma^1)$ is a subset of new particular order relations among events.

- $S = \text{PRUNE}(\ (S^1 \otimes S^2) \cup (S^2 \otimes S^1)\ )$.

$$s_k \in S : o \rightarrow s_k(o) = \begin{cases} s_i^1(o) \otimes s_j^2(o) & \text{where } s_i^1 \in S^1 \text{ and } s_j^2 \in S^2 \\ s_i^2(o) \otimes s_j^1(o) & \text{where } s_i^2 \in S^2 \text{ and } s_j^1 \in S^1 \end{cases}$$

$$s_i^1(o) \otimes s_j^2(o) = \begin{cases} s_i^1(o).s_j^2(o) \text{ such that } o \in O^1 \cap O^2 \wedge \forall e \in s_i^1(o), \forall e' \in s_j^2(o): (e',e) \notin <_\Sigma \\ s_i^1(o) \text{ if } o \notin O^2 \\ \varepsilon \text{ otherwise.} \end{cases}$$

$$s_i^2(o) \otimes s_j^1(o) = \begin{cases} s_i^2(o).s_j^1(o) \text{ such that } o \in O^1 \cap O^2 \wedge \forall e \in s_i^2(o), \forall e' \in s_j^1(o): (e',e) \notin <_\Sigma \\ s_i^2(o) \text{ if } o \notin O^1 \\ \varepsilon \text{ otherwise.} \end{cases}$$

The function PRUNE removes all unreachable nodes from the initial node through T.

- $s_0 = s_0^1 \otimes s_0^2 = s_0^2 \otimes s_0^1$ (hence $\forall o \in O: s_0(o) = \varepsilon$ ).

- $T : S \times \Sigma \rightarrow S$

$T = \{ (s_k, e, s_{k'}) / s_k = s_i^1 \otimes s_j^2, s_{k'} = s_m^1 \otimes s_n^2, \exists o \in O: (s_i^1(o), e, s_m^1(o)) \in T^1 \vee (s_j^2(o), e, s_n^2(o)) \in T^2 \}$
$\cup \{ (s_k, e, s_{k'}) / s_k = s_i^2 \otimes s_j^1, s_{k'} = s_m^2 \otimes s_n^1, \exists o \in O: (s_i^2(o), e, s_m^2(o)) \in T^2 \vee (s_j^1(o), e, s_n^1(o)) \in T^1 \}$

## 3.3 Star Operation

This operation adds to the graph new $\tau$-transitions outgoing from leaf nodes to the initial node. Furthermore it adds a new empty node $s_\varepsilon$ connected to the initial node by a $\tau$-transition (see figure 2). Let $G_1$ be the starting graph $G_1 = <O^1, \Sigma^1, <_\Sigma^1, S^1, s_0^1, T^1>$

STAR $(G) = <O, \Sigma, <_\Sigma, S, s_0, T>$ where :

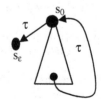

- $O = O^1$,    $\Sigma = \Sigma^1$,    $<_\Sigma = <_\Sigma^1$,    $S = S' \cup S''$
- $S' = \{ s_k : O \rightarrow \Sigma^*, k \in \aleph \}$ where for all k we have :

$$s_k : o \rightarrow s_k(o) = \begin{cases} (s_k^1(o))^+ & \text{if } s_k \in \text{LEAF}(S^1) \\ s_k^1(o) & \text{otherwise.} \end{cases}$$

- $S'' = \{ s_\varepsilon : O \rightarrow \{\varepsilon\} \}$

The sole node $s_\varepsilon$ records empty traces for all objects.    **Fig. 2.** Star operation

- $s_0 = s_0^1$.
- $T = T^1 \cup T' \cup T'' / T' = \{\forall s_F \in \text{LEAF}(S^1): s_F \vdash\!\text{-}\text{-}\tau\text{-}\text{-}\text{-} s_0^1\}$ where
  $\text{LEAF}(S) = \{s \in S / \text{NOT} (\exists s' \in S, e \in \Sigma : s \vdash\!\text{-}\text{-}e\text{-}\text{-}\text{-} s')\}$
  $T'' = \{ s_0^1 \vdash\!\text{-}\text{-}\tau\text{-}\text{-}\text{-} s_\varepsilon\}$

**Property.** The two operations $\otimes$ and $\oplus$ on graphs are associative.

**Lemma 1.** let G be the graph $<O, \Sigma, <_\Sigma, S, s_0, T>$
$\forall s_k \in S, \forall o \in O: u = s_k(o) \Rightarrow (\forall i, j \in \aleph : i, j \leq |u| \wedge (u(i), u(j)) \in <_\Sigma) \Rightarrow i < j$.

**Proof.** Definitions of S and T compel event occurrences concerned by $<_\Sigma$ to occur in a way so that the partial order remains preserved. The other events may appear in any order in the sequence.

**Definition 1.** Let u and w be two sequences from $s_k(o)$ $(o \in O, s_k \in S)$
u and w are equivalent (we write $u \approx w$) if and only if $\forall a \in \Sigma: a \in u \Leftrightarrow a \in w$.
The precedence relation is preserved for ordered events in both u and w.

**Definition 2.** Let $s_i$ and $s_j$ be two nodes from S
$s_i$ and $s_j$ are equivalent (we write $s_i \approx s_j$) if and only if $\forall o \in O: s_i(o) \approx s_j(o)$.

**Definition 3.** Let G be a graph = $<O, \Sigma, <_\Sigma, S, s_0, T>$. A reduced graph (automaton) may be obtained from the graph G by reducing the equivalent nodes into equivalence class of nodes as follows: $G = <O, \Sigma, <_\Sigma, S', s_0, T'>$
  $S' = \{[s_k] / s_k \in S\}$ where $[s_k] = \{s_i \in S / s_i \approx s_k\}$.
  $T' = \{ [s_k] \vdash\!\text{-}\text{-}\text{-}e\text{-}\text{-}\text{-}\text{-}\text{-}\text{-}[s_{k'}] / \exists s_i \in [s_k], \exists s_j \in [s_{k'}], \exists (s_i \vdash\!\text{-}\text{-}\text{-}\text{-}e\text{-}\text{-}\text{-}\text{-}\text{-}s_j) \in T\}$

*Remark1.* On the other hand side, we can unfold our graph (namely cycles and diamond shapes) in order to obtain the equivalent transition system.

### 3.4 Handling of Synchronous Messages

Although the subset "Prior" is used particularly to handle specific features of interaction operators used among combined fragments (as explained later), we can also use it to handle synchronous messages when assembling jointly many lifelines in one interaction fragment or when combining many sequence diagrams by means of interaction operators. We have only to add into the partial order subset "Prior" other general orderings with regards to send and receive events of those specific messages.

Let M be the set of synchronous messages between two combined fragments $SD_i$ and $SD_j$ (which could be only lifelines of participants).

"Prior" is then increased with the set $\cup_{m \in M}(\text{Prior}_m)$ where :

$$\text{Prior}_m = \{(m!, e) \quad / m! \in \Sigma_j \wedge \exists e \in \Sigma_i : (m?, e) \in <_{\Sigma i}\}$$
$$\cup \{(m?, e') / m? \in \Sigma_i \wedge \exists e' \in \Sigma_j: (m!, e') \in <_{\Sigma j}\}$$

This means that once the send event (m!) occurs the executing thread will stop until the receive event (m?) occurs on the other lifeline thanks to its precedence level against the successive events of the send event. Similarly, if we observe first a receive event on the second participant lifeline, the related thread should stop until the send event occurs on the first participant. Note that only related threads to these events should synchronize and other concurrent threads could continue performing parallel activities and generating others events.

# 4 Formal Semantics of Interaction Fragments and Operators

## 4.1 Lifeline of a Participant

We associate to each interaction fragment X a related graph denoted $|[X]|$.

Let P be a participant in some interaction. Its graph is $|[P]|=<O,\Sigma, <_\Sigma, S, s_0, T>$ where:

- $O = \{P\}$ is a singleton set consisting in the only one participant P.
- $\Sigma = \{ e / \exists m: e = Receive(m) \wedge Receiver(m)=P \vee e = Send(m) \wedge Sender(m)=P\}$
- $<_\Sigma = \{(e,e') \in \Sigma x \Sigma /$ the event occurrence e occurs before e' on the lifeline(P)$\}$

Frequently the order on a same lifeline is total i.e. if we take two event occurrences e, e' on the same lifeline then $e<e'$ or $e'<e$. But if the lifeline of P contains a coregion area then the order of event occurrences on this part is insignificant.

- $S = \{s_k : O \rightarrow \Sigma^*, k \in \aleph \}$
    $= \{s_k : P \rightarrow w / \forall n \leq |w|, \forall m \leq n : (w(n), w(m)) \notin <_\Sigma \}$
- $s_0(P) = \varepsilon.$
- $T = \{(s_i, e, s_j) / s_j(P) = s_i(P).e \wedge e \in \Sigma\}$

Thus each transition yields a new trace onto the target node by adding its labeling event occurrence to the previous trace recorded in the source node of the transition.

In the following example (fig.3), we use notational shorthand called "coregion area" for combined fragments where the order of events occurrences on the lifeline is insignificant.

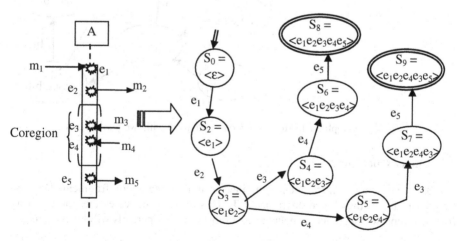

**Fig. 3.** The graph related to a life-line of one participant ($s_6 \approx s_7$. $s_8 \approx s_9$).e1 = m1?, e2 = m2!, e3=m3?, e4 = m4?, e5=m5!

## 4.2  Basic Interaction Fragment

Recall that a basic interaction fragment is a piece of an interaction which involves many participants without using any interaction operator.

Let DS be a basic interaction between two participants $P_1$ and $P_2$. Herein $O^1 \cap O^2 = \emptyset$. The graph related to DS is obtained by a parallel merge of the graphs relating to the participants lifelines with respect to the partial order between send and receive events.

$|[DS]| = |[P1]| \otimes_{Prior} |[P2]|$  where :

Prior = $\{ (e,e') \in (\Sigma^1 x \Sigma^2) \cup (\Sigma^2 x \Sigma^1)$ / $\exists$ message m : e=send(m) $\wedge$ e'=receive(m) $\}$

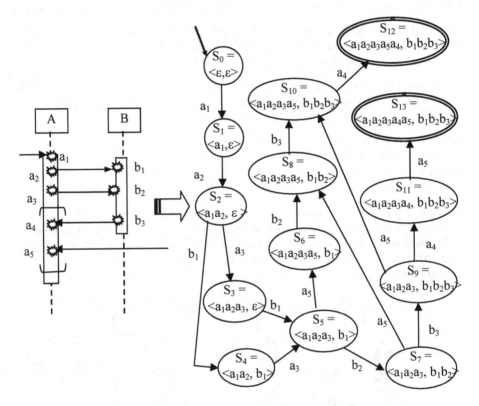

**Fig. 4.** the graph related to an interaction fragment with two participants

## 4.3  Choice Operator ALT

Let DS be an interaction fragment combined from two interaction fragments $DS_1$ and $DS_2$ by means of the choice operator **ALT**. This operator indicates that the resulting fragment represent a choice of behavior. At most one the operands will be chosen.

Formally, $|[DS_1 \text{ ALT } DS_2]| = |[DS_1]| \oplus |[DS_2]|$ (see fig.5)

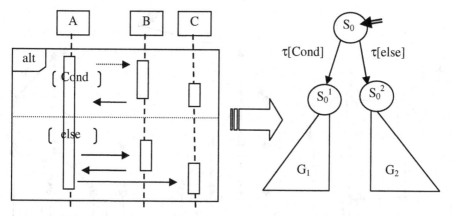

**Fig. 5.** The graph related to an interaction fragment with ALT operator

## 4.4  Operator BREAK

Even though **BREAK** is a unary operator which operand is a nested fragment in an enclosing interaction fragment, this operator can reduce to an interaction operation **ALT** between the nested fragment and the remainder of the enclosing interaction fragment.

## 4.5  Operator OPT

Let DS' be a new interaction fragment obtained by applying the operator **OPT** on another interaction fragment DS. The operator **OPT** designates that the resulting fragment represents a choice of behavior where either the sole operand happens or nothing happens. Formally, this means:

$$|[\text{ DS'}]|=|[\textbf{OPT}(\text{DS})]| = |[\text{DS } \textbf{ALT } \text{DS}_\varnothing]| = |[\text{DS}]| \oplus |[\text{DS}_\varnothing]|$$

The empty interaction fragment $\text{DS}_\varnothing$ is mapped into an empty graph as follows:

$|[\text{DS}_\varnothing]| = \langle O,\varnothing,\varnothing,\{s_0\}, s_0, \varnothing\rangle$ where O is the same collection of participants in DS and $s_0: O\rightarrow\{\varepsilon\}$ associates to each participant in O an empty sequence of events.

## 4.6  Operator PAR

Let DS be interaction fragment combined from two interaction fragments $\text{DS}_1$ and $\text{DS}_2$ by means of the parallel operator PAR. We realize here an interleaving between all sequences occurring in diagrams (fig.6) without adding further orderings.

$$|[\text{DS}_1 \textbf{ PAR } \text{DS}_2]|= |[\text{DS}_1]| \otimes_{\text{Prior}} |[\text{DS}_2]| \text{ where Prior} = \varnothing.$$

## 4.7  Operator of Strict Sequencing

Let DS be an interaction fragment combined from two interaction fragments $\text{DS}_1$ and $\text{DS}_2$ by means of the strict sequencing operator **SEQs**.

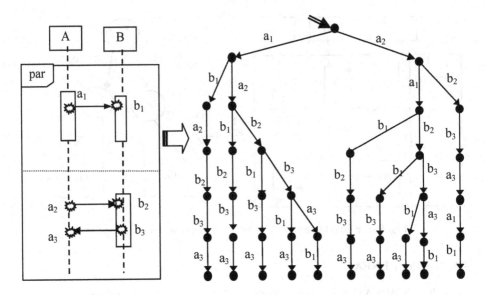

**Fig. 6.** The graph related to an interaction fragment with PAR operator

Similarly to sequential composition in process algebra, the semantics of strict sequencing defines a strict ordering of the operands on the first level. So the former operand should first be carried out entirely. After that only the second one is executed. Therefore all events occurrences of the first interaction fragment are granted more priority over those of the second one.

$$|[DS_1 \ \textbf{SEQs} \ DS_2]| = |[DS_1]| \otimes_{Prior} |[DS_2]| \text{ where Prior} = \Sigma^1 \times \Sigma^2.$$

Herein we carry out concatenations between paths belonging respectively to the two diagrams $DS_1$ and $DS_2$ such that events occurrences from the first diagram always occur before those of the second diagram.

### 4.8 Operator of Weak Sequencing

Let DS be an interaction fragment combined from two interaction fragments $DS_1$ and $DS_2$ by means of the weak sequencing operator **SEQw**.
The weak sequencing expresses three properties [8]:

- The ordering of events occurrences within each of the operands are maintained in the result.
- Occurrence specifications on different lifelines from different operands may come in any order.
- Occurrence specifications on the same lifeline from different operands are ordered such that an event occurrence of the 1st operand comes before that of the 2nd one.

Hence the weak sequencing reduces to a parallel merge between events occurrences on different lifelines but restricted by strict sequencings among events occurrences belonging to same lifelines (thanks to Prior set of added precedence relations). Formally, $|[DS_1 \; \textbf{SEQw} \; DS_2]| = |[DS_1]| \otimes_{Prior} |[DS_2]|$

where Prior=$\{(e,e') \in \Sigma^1 x \Sigma^2 \; / \; e,e'$ belong both to the same lifeline(o)$\}$.

### 4.9  Operator LOOP

Let DS be a combined fragment from an interaction fragment $DS_1$ by means of the loop operator **LOOP** parameterized by a guard G given as un integer $\in \{min \; ..max\}$.

The loop operator would be repeated a given number of times as long as the guard is fulfilled. $|[LOOP(G, DS)]| = (|[(DS \; \textbf{SEQs} \; LOOP(G-1, DS)]|$

However this solution does not pay attention when iterating to the evaluation event of the loop guard. So we have to add $\tau$-transitions to record this internal choice.

$|[\textbf{LOOP}(G, DS)]| = (|[(DS \; \textbf{SEQs} \; DS_\tau) \; \textbf{SEQs} \; \textbf{LOOP}(G-1, DS)]|$

The graph of $\tau$-interaction fragment $DS_\tau$ is: $|[DS_\tau]| = <O, \{\tau\}, \varnothing, \{s_0, s_1\}, s_0, \{s_0|--\tau---s_1\}>$

When the number of iterations is undefined (max = $\infty$), the correct solution consists in using the star operation on traces with adorning loop transitions with $\tau$ which models guard evaluation (see fig. 2). So the related graph should be.

$|[\textbf{LOOP}(G,DS)]| = STAR (|[ DS]|)$

*Remark2.* we prefer use strict sequencing rather than weak one to avoid a pathological case of divergence in loop combination when using asynchronous communication

*Remark3.* All above rules can be used to handle the operator **NEG** in order to build the graph containing invalid traces of events with recording all branching choices.

## 5   Extraction of Timing Information

The sequence diagram in figure 7 shows how time and timing notations may be applied to describe time observation and timing constraints [8]. The "User" sends a message "Code" and its duration is measured. The "ACSystem" will send two messages back to the "User". "CardOut" is constrained to last between 0 and 13 time units. Furthermore the interval between sending of Code and the reception of "OK" is constrained to last between d and 3*d where d is the measured duration of the "Code" signal. We also notice the observation of the time point t at the sending of "OK" and how this is used to constrain the time point of the reception of "CardOut".

Our approach consists in extracting time formulas over logical clocks from the time annotations in sequence diagrams. Then we adorn related nodes and transitions in our graph by these timing conditions in a similar way to timed automata [1].

**Definition 4 (timing constraint).** Let H be a finite set of clocks ranging over $\Re > 0$ (set of non negative real numbers). The set $\Psi(H)$ of timing constraints on H is defined by the following syntax:    $\psi ::= true \mid x \langle\langle c \mid x - y \langle\langle c \mid not \; \psi \mid \psi \wedge \psi$

where x, y $\in$ H, c $\in \Re$ (Integers) and $\langle\langle \in \{<, \le\}$.

Other assertions such as, x>3, 2≤x<y+5, $\psi \vee \psi'$ can be defined as abbreviations.

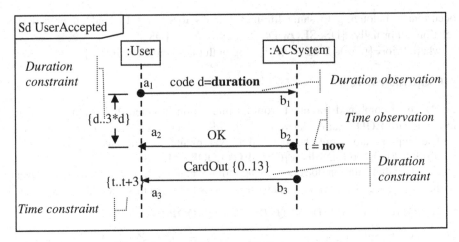

**Fig. 7.** Sequence Diagram with timing concepts

### 5.1 Enhancing Graphs with Timing Constrains

We add two mappings δ1, δ2 as follows:

$$\delta_1 : S \rightarrow \Psi(H)$$
$$\delta_2 : T \rightarrow 2^H,$$

**Fig. 8.** Timed graphs

The first mapping $\delta_1$ assigns to each node a condition called activity *condition* which may be *true*. The second mapping $\delta_2$ associates with each transition a set of clocks initializations which may be empty.

The behavior of the new timed graph becomes as follows:

The control could stay in a node $s_i$ (Fig.8) while the constraint $\delta_1(s)$ is fulfilled but once $\delta_1(s)$ becomes false we should leave $s_i$ by execution of an instantaneous event occurrence e (an event occurs with no duration [8]). It's obvious that the control could stay indefinitely in $s_j$ (Fig.8) if its activity condition is *true*.

When a transition t occurs, all clocks ($h_i \in \delta_2(t)$) are reset to zero. So these clocks start measuring time progress since this point but may be used later at different instants.

### 5.2 Extracting Time Constrains from Sequence Diagrams

Time observations, timing constraints are related to points on the lifelines of the sequence diagram. These points are the instances at which send or receive events occur. Likewise, duration observations or constraints are related to messages, each one of them is related to two events on the same lifeline or on two different lifelines.

The main idea of our approach to handling time constraint is to generate a logical clock "h" at any related time observation point "t". Any outgoing arc from this point will be adorned with initialization of the clock h making it possible to count time progress from this starting point.

For a time constraint of the form "t+a...t+b", we search out in our graph the set of nodes of which outgoing transitions are labeled with the event related to this constraint. Every such a node should receive a timing constraint of the form a≤h≤b.

**Algorithm** Extract_time & Duration_constraints
  **Input**  SD : Sequence Diagram;  G : Graph
  **Output** G' : a timed graph.

```
H := ∅;
For each s∈S do δ1(s) = true;

For each time observation "t" at an event occurrence e
Do {
        Generate a new clock h;   H := H ∪ {h};
        // h measures time progress since the observation point
        Find out the set A of transitions labeled with e;
        For each t∈A do δ2(t) = δ2(t) ∪(h,0);

        For each time constraint c of the form {a...b} on event
        occurrence e';
        Do {
            Find out the set N of nodes which outgoing transi-
            tions are labeled with e';
            For each s∈N do δ1(s) = δ1(s) ∧ h≥a ∧ h ≤b;
        }
}
```

Likewise, for handling duration constraint, we generate two logical clocks; "$h_1$" at start point and "$h_2$" at final point related to duration observation "d". Any outgoing arc from these points will be tagged with initializations of related clocks so that the difference between their values ($h_1$-$h_2$) gives later the duration between the two events.

For any duration constraint of the form "a(d)..b(d)" between two events e and e', we add in a similar way a clock $h_3$ related to the first event e for counting the time progress since this first point. Next we search out in our graph the set of nodes of which outgoing transitions are labeled with the second event e'. Every such a node should then receive a timing constraint of the form $a(h_1-h_2) \leq h_3 \leq b(h_1-h_2)$.

```
For each duration observation d on a message m
Do {
        Let e be the event occurrence related to sending (m);
        Let e' be the event occurrence related to receiving (m);
        Generate two new clocks h1 and h2;   H := H ∪ {h1, h2};
        // h1 starts at the sending moment of m.
        Search out the set A of transitions labeled with e;
        For each t∈A do δ2(t) = δ2(t) ∪(h1,0) ;
        // h2 starts at the receiving moment of m.
        Find out the set B of transitions labeled with e';
        For each t∈A do δ2(t) = δ2(t) ∪(h2,0);

        For each duration constraint c of the form {a(d)...b(d)}
        between two events (e",e"') or on a message m'
        Do {
```

```
        Let e" be the first event occurrence or the sending
        event of m';
        Let e"' be the second event occurrence or the re-
        ceiving event of m';
        Generate a new clock h₃;    H := H ∪ {h₃};
        // h₃ measures time since the occurrence of e"
        Find out the set A of transitions labeled with e";
        For each t∈A do δ₂(t) = δ₂(t) ∪(h₃,0) ;
        Find out the set N of nodes which outgoing transi-
        tions are labeled with e"'
        For each s∈N do δ₁(s)=δ₁(s)∧ h₃≥a(h₁-h₂)∧ h₃≤b(h₁-
        h₂);
        }
   }
```

```
For each duration constraint c of the form {a...b} between
two events occurrences (e,e') or on a message m
Do {
        Let e be the first event occurrence or the sending event
        of m;
        Let e' be the second event occurrence or the receiving
        event of m;
        Generate a new clock h;    H := H ∪ {h};
        Find out the set A of transitions labeled with e;
        For each t∈A do δ₂(t) = δ₂(t) ∪(h,0) ;
        Find out the set N of nodes which outgoing transitions
        are labeled with e'
        For each s∈N do δ₁(s) = δ₁(s) ∧ h≥a ∧ h ≤b;
   }
```

At last we notice that the above approach can be also extended in straight way to handle other possible cases of time constraints.

The timed graph related to the diagram of fig.7 is the following:

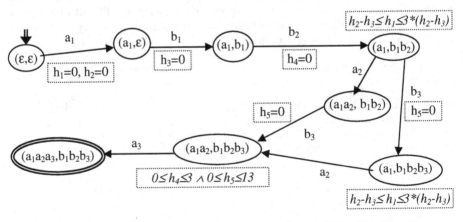

**Fig. 9.** The timed graph related to the sequence diagram depicted by figure 7

# 6  Related Work

Because of the widespread use of interaction diagrams in complex systems, many efforts have been made to give them formal meanings in order to allow systematic tool support during design, implementation and validation phases.

Besides the textual semantics given in UML specification document [8], many approaches [4], [10] present formal semantics of sequence diagrams (SD) where the runs are widely defined in terms of pairs of valid and invalid traces and do not record information about choice opportunities and coordination actions. Hence contrary to our approach, these linear time semantics are not enough faithful to allow complete consistencies checking over UML dynamic diagrams particularly in concurrent systems. Moreover, timing constraints are not handled within these models.

On the other hand side, some papers attempt to synthesize high level diagrams (StateCharts [12] [3], Petri nets [2]) from SD or MSC. However in our opinion as are assembly languages for high level programming ones, the sequence diagrams are less structured description languages in spite of the recent improvements. Furthermore the built high level models seem too unfolded or flattened and their high level syntactic constructs are not suitably used and may generate some inconsistencies with regards to the original sequence diagrams [12]. In this later work, the authors try to retrieve state diagrams of objects involved in interactions described by means of relatively simple sequence diagrams. The approach consists in deriving flat automata of some object from its lifelines in all interaction fragments and then combines them by means of simple interaction operators (choice, strict sequencing and loop). The other operators are discarded as the parallel operator so that the resulting automaton is flat and unfolded (without orthogonality) and may generate some irregular behaviors because of the removal of coordination information when extracting partial views.

An interesting work [3] considers good and bad interactions of reactive systems as safety and liveness properties that are described in terms of Büchi automata allowing refinement. SD traces become only prefixes of accepted infinite sequences and the various combinations between automata are not specified with regard to SD operators.

Another paper [7] uses process algebra terms to characterize the traces of scenario based specification that are defined by a causal ordering. It proves a canonical solution for correcting race conditions within the system behavior by weakening the causal relationship.

Note that many papers were proposed to overcome shortcomings of UML 1.x specification that relies on the ordering of messages instead of related actions. Hence authors of [2] and [9] proposed a formal semantics to the interaction diagrams of UML 1.x by the generation of an order relation that schedules the message emissions and receptions and can be automatically translated into a flattened Petri net or automata. Similarly, [6] presented a methodology to convert UML 1.x SD to a context-free grammar and applied parsing theory to locate non-determinism behavior. Additional information is discussed to attain deterministic behaviors for embedded systems modeling. Also, the approach of [11] proposes a formal semantics of UML 1.x sequence diagrams in terms of ordered hierarchical tree structure that represents the hierarchical relations among the messages (method invocations).

However, the new specification of UML 2.0 [8] adopts an ordering over events occurrences corresponding to sending and receiving of messages. Also high level features of MSC [5] have been included in UML interactions allowing description of more complex behaviors. Moreover all the above works do not pay attention to time annotations on sequence diagrams.

# 7  Conclusion

In this paper, we have given a formal semantics for UML 2 sequence diagrams by using a faithfully branching time structure rather than traces. This model (a lattice-like graph) records both traces of all interaction components together with branching bifurcations and can be directly unfolded into a transition system capturing the intended behavior. The graphs related to interaction fragments are equipped with few generalized algebraic operations which help us define the formal semantics of all interaction operations in compositional manner. Moreover, we have proposed a method to extract time properties of UML interactions into time constraints we add to our graph in order to achieve timeliness and performance analysis.

Hence resulting graphs modeling valid and invalid behaviors would be compared to the state diagram to achieve semantically and temporal consistencies checking.

# References

1. R. Alur, D. Dill.  A theory of timed automata. Theorical Computer Science. 126 (1994) 183-235.
2. J. Cardoso, C. Sibertin-Blanc. An operational semantics for UML interaction: sequencing of actions and local control. European Journal of Automatised Systems. APII-JESA 36 P.1015-1028 (ISBN 2-7462-0573-4), Hermés-Lavoisier 2002.
3. R. Grosu and S.A. Smolka. Safety-Liveness Semantics for UML 2.0 sequence diagrams. In Proc. of ACSD'05, the 5th International Conference on Application of Concurrency to System Design, Saint-Malo, France. June 2005.
4. Ø. Haugen, K.E. Husa, R.K. Runde, K. Stølen. STAIRES towards formal design with sequence diagrams. Software & System Modeling, online first: 1-13, 2005.
5. ITU-T. Z.120. Message sequence charts (MSC), November 1999.
6. E. Latronico and P. Koopman, Representing Embeded System Sequence Diagrams as a Formal Language. In Proc. of UML'2001 Conference, Toronto Ontario, 3-5 Oct.2001.
7. B. Mitchell. Inherent Causal Orderings of Partial Order Scenarios.  In proc. of International Colloquium on Theorical Aspects of Computing, Guiyang, China, (LNCS 3407) PP 114-129. September 2004.
8. OMG. Unified Modeling Language: Superstructure version 2.0, Final Adopted Specification. Object Management Group, 2004 Available from http:// www.omg.org.
9. C. Sibertin-Blanc, O. Tahir and J. Cardoso. Interpretation of UML sequence diagrams as causality flows. In Proc. of ISSADS'2005, (LNCS 3563), pp. 126-140. 2005.
10. H. Störrle. Trace semantics of interactions in UML 2 .0. Technical Report TR 0403, University of Munich, Germany. 09/2004.
11. Xiaosham Li , Zhiming-Liu and He Jifeng. A formal semantics of UML sequence Diagram. In Proc. of Australian Software Engineering Conference 2004, Australia. April 2004.
12. T. Ziadi, L. Hélouët, J-M. Jézéquel. Revisiting statechart synthesis with an Algebraic Approach. In proc. of International conference on Software Engineering (ICSE'04). 2004.

# Formalizing Collaboration Goal Sequences for Service Choreography

Humberto Nicolás Castejón and Rolv Bræk

NTNU, Department of Telematics, N-7491 Trondheim, Norway
{humberto.castejon, rolv.braek}@item.ntnu.no

**Abstract.** Methods for service specification should be simple and intuitive. At the same time they should be precise and allow early validation and detection of inconsistencies. UML 2.0 collaborations enable a systematic and structured way to provide overview of distributed services, and decompose cross-cutting service behaviour into features and interfaces by means of collaboration-uses. To fully take advantage of the possibilities thus opened, a way to compose (i.e. choreograph) the joint collaboration behaviour is needed. So-called collaboration goal sequences have been introduced for this purpose. They describe the behavioural composition of collaboration-uses (modeling interface behaviour and features) within a composite collaboration. In this paper we propose a formal semantics for collaboration goal sequences by means of hierarchical coloured Petri-nets (HCPNs). We then show how tools available for HCPNs can be used to automatically analyse goal sequences in order to detect implied scenarios.

## 1 Introduction

Many authors have identified the cross-cutting nature of distributed services (e.g. [8,5]) i.e. that services in the general case, involve several collaborating components playing different roles, that each may participate in several services. For service engineering, this implies a need to specify services in terms of their roles and cross-cutting service behaviour, then to specify the detailed behaviour of each service role and, finally, to compose the behaviour of service roles into complete, coordinated and correct component behaviours. UML 2.0 collaborations [7] provide language concepts and mechanisms that partially support this and are therefore very promising from a service engineering point of view. Being both structural and behavioural classifiers in UML 2.0, collaborations can be used to define a service as a structure of roles with associated cross-cutting behaviour defined using e.g. sequence diagrams. Detailed role behaviour can be defined using e.g. state machines. UML collaborations can be bound to specific contexts (e.g. larger collaborations) by means of collaboration-uses. This feature enables a compositional and incremental specification of services.

As an example consider a simple transport service (inspired by a case study from [12]) in which one vehicle transports one passenger at a time between two terminals. Figure 1a depicts this service as a UML 2.0 collaboration. This collaboration identifies three roles, namely $P$ (Passenger), $T$ (Terminal) and $V$

E. Najm et al. (Eds.): FORTE 2006, LNCS 4229, pp. 275–291, 2006.

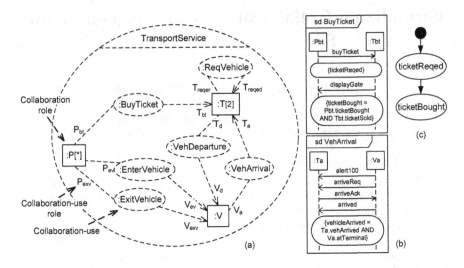

**Fig. 1.** (a) Transport service as a UML 2.0 collaboration; (b) Sequence diagrams for *BuyTicket* and *VehArrival* sub-collaborations; (c) Service-goal tree for *BuyTicket*

(Vehicle); as well as seven sub-collaborations representing interfaces and features of the service. These sub-collaborations are specified as UML collaboration-uses, whose roles are bound to the *TransportService*'s roles (e.g. *BuyTicket*'s role $T_{bt}$ is bound to *TransportService*'s role $T$). Bound roles are classified as either *initiating* (i.e. takes the initiative to start the collaboration) or *offered* (i.e. accepts the initiative), indicated by an arrow head with offered roles. For the sake of clarity, in the following we will refer to $P$, $T$ and $V$ as service-roles, and to $T_{bt}, T_d$ and the like as sub-roles (of $T$, $P$ or $V$). The *TransportService*'s sub-collaborations have been identified from the following service requirements. In order to travel, a passenger must buy a ticket at one of the terminals (collaboration-use *BuyTicket*). When this happens, if the vehicle is waiting at the terminal, the departure gate is indicated, and the passenger can enter the vehicle (*EnterVehicle*). The terminal then dispatches the vehicle (*VehDeparture*) and, after arriving at the second terminal (*VehArrival*), the passenger disembarks (*ExitVehicle*). If the vehicle is not at the terminal where the passenger buys the ticket, that terminal requests the vehicle from the other terminal (*ReqVehicle*), which dispatches the vehicle towards the requesting terminal. When the vehicle arrives, the departure gate is displayed and the service continues as explained before. In order to support validation and composition, service-goals [9] are associated with each of the identified sub-collaborations. These goals are expressed in terms of predicates over properties of the collaborations. Two types of service-goals can be described: event-goals, denoting desired events; and state-goals, which are properties of global collaboration states that we wish to reach, and which entail combinations of role goals. The ordered sequence of goals for an individual collaboration can be described with a *service-goal tree*, which is a directed graph with an initial node, zero or more intermediary nodes representing event-goals, and one or more leaf nodes representing state-goals. Figure 1c shows the service-goal tree for *Buy-Ticket*, with an event-goal (i.e. *ticketReqed*) and a state-goal (i.e. *ticketBought*). Goal trees describe the behaviour of elementary collaborations at a high-level of abstraction, since the interactions are not detailed. These interactions can be specified in sequence diagrams annotated with goal information (by means of continuations), such as the ones presented for *BuyTicket* and *VehArrival* in Fig. 1b.

What remains in Fig. 1 is to specify the overall cross-cutting behaviour of the *TransportService* collaboration, that is, how its sub-collaborations interact. This kind of behaviour will be distributed among the collaboration roles and is traditionally referred to as a *choreography* in SOA. *Collaboration goal sequences* have been proposed by Sanders [9,11], and extended in [2], to describe the choreography of collaborations. They capture the liveness aspects of composite service collaborations by describing the execution order of their sub-collaborations, and by showing the interactions between these sub-collaborations in terms of goal achievement (hence the name collaboration *goal* sequences). While *service-goal trees* describe the sequence of goals for individual collaborations, *collaboration goal sequences* specify the sequence of goals for their composition. The information provided by the goal trees and the goal sequence should therefore be consistent. In the following we will assume this is the case.

In this paper, we present the formal syntax of goal sequences and provide semantics to them by means of hierarchical coloured Petri-nets (HCPNs) [4] (see Sect. 2). We also show how a general purpose tool for HCPNs (i.e. CPN Tools [3]) can be used to analyse goal sequences for the detection of implied scenarios (see Sect. 3). These scenarios are a direct consequence of concurrency and correspond to service behaviour that has not been explicitly described in the specification of the service, but that will be present in any implementation of it [1]. The proposed detection approach avoids a global analysis of the service specification, limiting thus the effect of the state-explosion problem. We end with related work and some discussion in Sects. 4 and 5.

## 2   Collaboration Goal Sequences

Collaboration goal sequences complement UML collaborations for the specification of services by describing the execution dependencies that exist between the sub-collaborations (i.e. features) of the service. As an example, Fig. 2 depicts the goal sequence for the *TransportService* collaboration. The actual meaning of this diagram will become clear in the following, when we explain the syntax and semantics of goal sequences.

### 2.1   Syntax for Goal Sequences

The goal sequences presented here are inspired by UML activity diagrams. Conceptually, they show an ordering of service phases for a service collaboration $C$. Each of these phases corresponds to an activity (i.e. round-cornered rectangle)

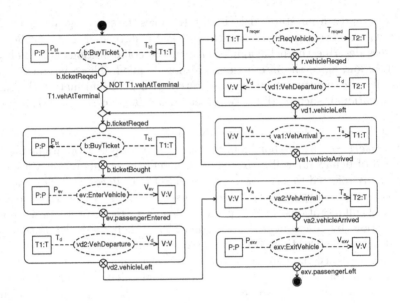

**Fig. 2.** Goal sequence for the *TransportService* collaboration

in the goal sequence. In each phase or activity, a specific sub-collaboration of $C$ is active (so-called activity's *active collaboration*). This is represented by adorning the activity with a collaboration-use, whose roles are bound to instances of $C$'s roles. For example, in Fig. 2, the *BuyTicket* collaboration is active in the first activity. This is expressed by adorning that activity with a *b:BuyTicket* collaboration-use, whose roles (i.e. $P_{bt}$ and $T_{bt}$) are bound to instances of *TransportService*'s roles (i.e. *P:P* and *T1:T*). The arrow in the binding identifies the offered role. In a goal sequence, the same sub-collaboration may be active in several activities. In some cases these activities represent different phases of that sub-collaboration, while in other cases they represent different occurrences of the sub-collaboration. In the former cases activities are annotated with the same collaboration-use, such as the two first activities to the left in Fig. 2. They represent different phases of *BuyTicket* (i.e. before and after requesting the ticket) and are therefore annotated with the same collaboration-use (i.e. *b:BuyTicket*). In the latter cases, activities are annotated with distinct collaboration-uses, as for instance *va1:VehArrival* and *va2:VehArrival* in Fig. 2.

Each activity has one or more exit-points, and may or may not have one entry-point. Both entry- and exit-points represent execution points at which an activity's active collaboration interact with other collaborations. They are labeled with predicates describing goals of the active collaboration. Exit-points can be of two different types. An empty-circle ($\bigcirc$) is used for *suspension* exit-points. They are annotated with event-goals, and correspond to execution points of an active collaboration where the latter can be (or must be) suspended for another collaboration to be started (or resumed). In Fig. 2 a suspension exit-point is used in the first activity. The activity's active collaboration (i.e. *b:BuyTicket*) will therefore be suspended when the *ticketRequed* event-goal of *BuyTicket* holds. A crossed-circle ($\otimes$) is used for *end-of-execution* exit-points. They are annotated with state-goals, and represent the end of execution of an active collaboration. Entry-points are drawn as empty circles and annotated with event-goals. They represent the execution point at which a previously suspended active collaboration is to be resumed. When an activity does not have an entry-point, its active collaboration starts execution from its initial state.

Edges (i.e. directed connections between activities) and control-flow nodes (i.e. decision, merge, fork, join, initial and final nodes) are respectively used to allow and coordinate the flow of control among activities. An activity can only have one incoming edge, so multiple incoming edges must be AND- or OR-joined.

According to the concrete syntax just described, the formal syntax of goal sequences can be defined as:

**Definition 1 (collaboration goal sequence).** *A collaboration goal sequence, for a collaboration $C$, is a tuple $GS = (N, E, g_d, \ m_{\text{exp-a}}, R_{\text{GS}}, AC, m_{\text{a-ac}}, m_{\text{enp-a}}, l_{\text{ep-pred}}, exp_{\text{type}})$ where*

(i) *$N$ is a set of nodes. It is partitioned into an initial node ($n_0$) and sub-sets of activities ($N_A$), entry-points ($N_{\text{EnP}}$), exit-points ($N_{\text{ExP}}$), control flow nodes ($N_{\text{FLOW}}$) and final nodes ($N_{\text{FI}}$). In turn, $N_{\text{FLOW}}$ is partitioned into decision ($N_D$), merge ($N_M$), fork ($N_F$) and join ($N_J$) nodes.*

(ii) *$E \subseteq (N_{\text{ExP}} \cup N_{\text{FLOW}} \cup \{n_0\}) \times (N_A \cup N_{\text{EnP}} \cup N_{\text{FI}} \cup N_{\text{FLOW}})$ is a set of directed edges between nodes.*

(iii) *$g_d$ is a guard function for decision nodes' outgoing edges. It is defined from $\{(s, t) \in E \mid s \epsilon N_D\}$ into boolean expressions.*

(iv) *$R_{\text{GS}} = \{(id, type) : type \in R_C\}$ is a set of role instances, with $R_C$ being the set of roles of collaboration $C$.*

(v) *$AC = \{(id, type, B)\}$ is a set of active collaborations, that is, a collaboration-use representing a specific occurrence of one of $C$'s sub-collaborations. For each $ac \in AC$, $id$ is the name of the collaboration-use; type is the name of the collaboration that actually describes the collaboration-use (i.e. one of $C$'s sub-collaborations); and $B \subseteq R_{\text{type}} \times R_{\text{GS}}$ is a set of role bindings, where $R_{\text{type}}$ is the set of roles of the sub-collaboration named type.*

(vi) *$m_{\text{a-ac}} : N_A \rightarrow AC \times CL$ is a non-injective function that maps active collaborations to activities and classifies the active collaboration's roles as initiating or offered roles within the context of the mapping (i.e. for the given activity). More formally, $CL$ is a set of binary relations, such that if $m_{\text{a-ac}}(n_a) = (ac, cl)$, then $cl = \{(r, typ) : r$ is a role of the collaboration with name ac.type and $typ \in \{INIT, OFF\}\}$.*

(vii) *$m_{\text{enp-a}} : N_{\text{EnP}} \rightarrow N_A$ and $m_{\text{exp-a}} : N_{\text{ExP}} \rightarrow N_A$ are functions mapping entry- and exit-points to activities.*

(viii) *$l_{\text{ep-pred}} : (N_{\text{EnP}} \cup N_{\text{ExP}}) \rightarrow P$ is an injective function labeling each entry and exit-point of an activity with a state predicate of the activity's active collaboration.*

(ix) *$exp_{\text{type}} : N_{\text{ExP}} \rightarrow \{END, SUSPENSION\}$ is a function that classifies exit-points either as end-of-execution or as suspension ones.*

## 2.2  Semantics for Goal Sequences

Goal sequences are given a token-game semantics. Intuitively, when an activity receives an input token, its active collaboration is enabled. If the token is directly received from an edge (i.e. not via an entry-point), the active collaboration can begin execution from its initial state. Otherwise, if the token is received through an entry-point, the active collaboration can resume execution from the state represented by the event-goal labeling the entry-point. The active collaboration in reality begins or resumes its execution when one of its roles takes the appropriate initiative. Thereafter, it evolves until an interaction point with other collaborations is eventually reached. That is, the active collaboration runs until the predicate of one of its activity's exit-points holds. When this happens, the control token is passed on to the next activity or control node. According to this semantics, the intended behaviour of the *TransportService* collaboration, as specified by its goal sequence (Fig. 2), closely reflects the requirements. Initially the *BuyTicket* collaboration is started and thereafter suspended after the ticket is requested. At that point, a check is performed to determine if the vehicle is at the terminal (i.e. at *T1*). If the result is positive, *BuyTicket* is finished and *EnterVehicle* is enabled, followed by *VehDeparture*, *VehArrival* and *ExitVehicle*. If the vehicle was not at *T1*, this role initiates *ReqVehicle* to request the vehicle from *T2*. *VehDeparture* is then executed, followed by *VehArrival*, which allows *BuyTicket* to be resumed. Thereafter the service progresses as explained before.

Formal semantics for goal sequences is provided by mapping them into hierarchical coloured Petri-nets (HCPNs). The selection of HCPNs as the semantic domain has been mainly motivated by two facts. First, Petri-nets in general, and HCPNs in particular, have been extensively studied, and quite a number of quality tools exist that support and automate their analysis. Second, the mapping of goal sequences into HCPNs is rather intuitive, as will become clear later on. Due to space limitations we will assume that the reader is familiar with traditional Petri-nets and will only give a short introduction to (H)CPNs.

Coloured Petri-nets (CPNs) [4] extend traditional Petri-nets by associating a *colour* or data type with each token. In this way, tokens are distinguishable from each other, unlike in traditional Petri-nets. Places has also an associated data type (or *colour domain*) determining the kind of tokens they can contain. Transitions can modify the type and value of their output tokens. In addition, they can have an associated guard stating conditions over its input tokens, that must be satisfied for the transition to become enabled.

**Definition 2 (CPN).** *A non-hierarchical CPN is a tuple $CPN = (\Sigma, P, T, A, N, C, G, E, I)$ [4] where $\Sigma$ is a finite set of non-empty types, $P$ is a finite set of places, $T$ is a finite set of transitions, $A$ is a finite set of arcs, $N : A \rightarrow (P \times T) \cup (T \times P)$ is a node function, $C : P \rightarrow \Sigma$ is a colour function, $G$ is a guard function mapping boolean guards to transitions, $E$ is an arc expression function labeling arcs, and $I$ is an initialisation function for places.*

In a hierarchical CPN it is possible to define *substitution transitions*, which can be decomposed into so-called *subpages* (i.e. subnets). Each subpage has a number of places called *port places*, through which the subpage communicates with its surroundings. The relationship between a substitution transition and its subpage is specified by describing a *port assignment*, which couples the port places of the subpage with the surrounding places, or so-called *socket places*, of the substitution transition. Port and socket places can be classified as input (i.e. accept tokens), output (i.e. deliver tokens) or I/O (i.e. both accept and deliver tokens) places.

**Definition 3 (HCPN).** *A hierarchical CPN is a tuple $HCPN = (S, SN, SA, PN, PT, PA, FS, FT, PP)$ where $S$ is a finite set of pages (i.e. subnets), $SN$ is a set of substitution transitions, $SA : SN \rightarrow S$ is a page assignment function, $PN$ is a set of port nodes, $PT : PN \rightarrow \{in, out, i/o, general\}$ is a port type function, $PA$ is a port assignment function mapping, for a given substitution transition, its sockets with its subnet's ports, $FS$ is a finite set of fusion sets, $FT$ is a fusion type function, and $PP$ is a multi-set of prime pages [4].*

**Informal Mapping.** The main idea behind the mapping of goal sequences to HCPNs is to map the collaboration-uses of a goal sequence to substitution transitions, and decompose them into subnets describing the behaviour of those collaboration-uses.

Given a goal sequence describing the behaviour of a collaboration $C$ (composed of a set of sub-collaborations), we map each collaboration-use of the goal sequence into a substitution transition. This means that several activities may be mapped into the same substitution transition, if they are annotated with the same collaboration-use (e.g. the two activities annotated with *b:BuyTicket* in Fig. 2 are mapped to the same substitution transition). The mapping of activities and their collaboration-uses is illustrated in Fig. 3b. Note that entry-points, as well as *suspension* exit-points of an activity are mapped into I/O socket places of the corresponding substitution transition, while *end-of-execution* exit-points are mapped into output socket places. Therefore, socket places represent event- and state-goals (i.e. the goals labeling the entry- and exit-points). In addition, an input socket is added, representing the starting point of the collaboration, as well as an *id* I/O socket, which is used to uniquely identify the specific collaboration-use the substitution transition represents. The colours used for socket places are CTRL_ST and CTRL_STxDEP, which are two custom defined data-types. CTRL_ST represents $C$'s global state, and is composed of the individual states of $C$'s sub-collaborations. CTRL_STxDEP is a Cartesian product of CTRL_ST and DEP. The latter is an enumeration with two values: depUnres (for dependency unresolved) and depResolved (for dependency resolved). The CTRL_STxDEP type is used to cope with suspend-resume dependencies, which require sub-collaborations to give away the control token while in the middle of execution (i.e. at *suspension* exit-points in the goal sequence). To enforce this behaviour, all tokens leaving I/O socket places (except the *id* one) must be marked with depUnres, while all arriving tokens must be marked with depResolved.

The initial node, as well as the final and merge nodes of the goal sequence are mapped into places, while join and fork nodes are mapped into normal

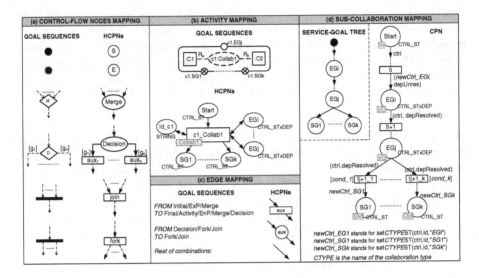

**Fig. 3.** Mapping of goal sequence elements to HCPN elements

transitions. The mapping of a decision node yields a place interconnected to as many transitions as the node has outgoing edges. The guards of these edges are then assigned to the transitions. Edges become net arcs, possibly with auxiliary transitions or places so as to respect the bipartite nature of Petri nets. All these mappings are summarized in Figs. 3a and 3c.

The translation of activities, edges and control-flow nodes, we have just explained, yields the main net of the final HCPN. For the mapping to be complete, we need to describe the decomposition of substitution transitions into subnets. These subnets will describe the behaviour of the goal sequence's collaboration-uses that the substitution transitions represent. As the collaboration-uses of the goal sequence (e.g. *va1:VehArrival* in Fig. 2) are occurrences of the sub-collaborations of *C* (e.g. *VehArrival* in Fig. 1a), the subnets will describe the behaviour of those sub-collaborations. Several substitution transitions may be assigned the same subnet, if they represent collaboration-uses of the same type (i.e. occurrences of the same sub-collaboration of *C*).

We are not interested on subnets describing detailed behaviour, but rather aim at high-level, abstract behaviour descriptions. Service goal trees (*SGTs*) provide such descriptions, so we use them as input for the mapping of sub-collaborations into subnets (see Fig. 3d). The *SGT* nodes are translated into net places, and the *SGT* arcs into net arcs plus an auxiliary transition. Places are characterized as port places: the *Start* place becomes an input port, places representing event-goals (*EG*) become I/O (i.e. bidirectional) ports, and those representing state-goals (*SG*) become output ports. Then, when coupling the subnet's ports with the sockets of a substitution transition, those ports and sockets representing the same goal are interconnected. The *Start* place, as well as those places representing state-goals are typed with the CTRL_ST colour, while the CTRL_STxDEP colour is used for places representing event-goals. Custom defined functions are used to modify the state of the collaboration (represented by CTRL_ST) as the control token travels form the *Start* input port to the output port(s). At each point in time the value of the token reflects the place the token has reached, thus reflecting the event-/state-goal that has been achieved. In addition, all tokens arriving at an I/O port are marked with depUnres, while all tokens leaving an I/O port are marked with depResolved. This ensures that the control token leaves the net at I/O ports, in order to satisfy suspend-resume dependencies.

All transitions of the subnet will be unguarded, except possibly those leading to output ports (i.e. places representing state-goals). If several transitions lead to different output ports from the same place, as illustrated in Fig. 3d, guards may be imposed on those transitions if a deterministic choice is wanted. These guards would determine the conditions to achieve each of the goals. They can be constructed from the information provided by the goal sequence, since the latter describes the relationships between sub-collaboration goals (i.e. it tells us the goal that a sub-collaboration must achieve in order for another sub-collaboration to achieve its own goal). The process to determine these guards is explained in the next section.

Figure 4a partially shows the HCPN resulting from the mapping of the *TransportService*'s goal sequence. Each one of the collaboration-uses in Fig. 2 has been mapped to a substitution transition. Note that the two activities referring to *b:BuyTicket* correspond now to a single substitution transition (i.e. *b_BuyTicket*). This substitution transition has one I/O socket (i.e. *b_ticketReqed*) representing both the suspension exit-point of the first activity and the entry-point of the second activity to the left in Fig. 2. Figure 4b depicts the subnet describing the behaviour of *BuyTicket*. This is the subnet assigned to the *b_BuyTicket* substitution transition, and closely resembles the service-goal tree in Fig. 1c.

**Formal Semantics.** For the mapping of goal sequences, we define two semantic functions: $[\![\_]\!]_{\text{CPN}}$, which maps elementary sub-collaborations into non-hierarchical CPNs; and $[\![\_]\!]_{\text{HCPN}}$, which maps collaboration goal sequences into HCPNs. $[\![\_]\!]_{\text{CPN}}$ takes a service-goal tree and a collaboration goal sequence, and returns a *CPN* representing the collaboration whose goals are described by the service-goal tree. A service-goal tree is defined as:

**Definition 4 (Service-goal tree).** *A service-goal tree is a directed graph $SGT = (cId, GN, GA)$ where: $cId$ is the name of the collaboration whose goals $SGT$ describes; $GN = \{start\} \cup EG \cup SG$ is a set of nodes, with start being the initial node, $EG$ being a set of intermediary nodes representing event-goals, and $SG$ being a set of final nodes representing sate-goals; and $GA \subseteq N \times N$ is a set of directed arcs between nodes, such that $\forall(s,t) \in GA : [s \notin SG \land t \neq start]$.*

According to the mapping explained in the previous section, and given $SGT = (cId, GN, GA)$ and $GS = (N, E, g_{\text{d}}, m_{\text{exp−a}}, R_{\text{GS}}, AC, m_{\text{a−ac}}, m_{\text{enp−a}}, l_{\text{ep−pred}}, exp_{\text{type}})$, we define $[\![SGT, GS]\!]_{\text{CPN}} = (\Sigma, P, T, A, N, C, G, E, I)$, where:

$$\Sigma = \{CTRL\_ST,\ CTRL\_ST \times DEP,\ STRING\}$$

$$P = GN \cup \{Id\} \qquad T = \{t_{ga} : ga \in GA\}$$

$$A = \{sourceTOt_{ga}, t_{ga}TOtarget : ga = (source, target) \in GA\}$$
$$\cup \{IdTOt_{ga}, t_{ga}TOId : Id \in P, ga \in GA\}$$

$$N(a) = (source, target),\ \text{if } a \text{ is in the form } sourceTOtarget$$

$$C(p) = \begin{cases} CTRL\_ST, & \text{if } p \in SG \cup \{start\} \\ CTRL\_ST \times DEP, & \text{if } p \in EG \\ STRING, & \text{if } p = Id \end{cases}$$

$$E(a) = \begin{cases} ctrl, & \text{if } (a = s\_t_{ga}) \wedge (s = start) \\ (setCTYPEnST(ctrl,id,\text{"tgn"}),depUnres), & \text{if } (a = t_{ga}\_t) \wedge (t \in EG) \\ (ctrl,depResolved), & \text{if } (a = s\_t_{ga}) \wedge (s \in EG) \\ setCTYPEnST(ctrl,id,\text{"t"}), & \text{if } (a = t_{ga}\_t) \wedge (t \in SG) \\ iId, & \text{if } [(a = s\_t_{ga}) \wedge (s = Id)] \vee [(a = t_{ga}\_t) \wedge (t = Id)] \end{cases}$$

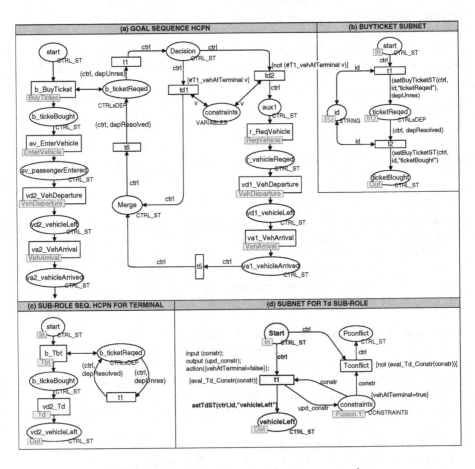

**Fig. 4.** Nets for the *TransportService* case study

No initial marking ($I$) is defined for the resulting CPN. The guard function $G$ assigns *true* to all transitions of the CPN, except possibly to those leading to places $p \in SG$. To describe how the guards are assigned to those transitions, let us consider the example net in Fig. 3d. To determine the set of conditions $cond\_i$, we just need to search for entry-points in the goal sequence that are labeled with $EG_j$. For each entry-point, if its associated activity $A$ has several exit-points, then the conditions are set to *true* (i.e. representing a non-deterministic choice). Otherwise, if the state-goal labeling $A$'s exit-point is $SG_n$, then $cond\_n$ is set to the value of the goal labeling the exit-point of the activity immediately preceding $A$. Note that $cond\_n$ may actually be a boolean expression of goals, if several activities lead to $A$ through a control flow node.

As a convention, in the following we will use the notation $T.E$, meaning element $E$ of tuple $T$, in order to access the elements of a tuple. We can now define $[\![\_]\!]_{\mathrm{HCPN}}$, which takes a goal sequence $GS = (N, exp_{type}, m_{enp-a}, m_{exp-a}, R_{\mathrm{GS}}, AC, m_{a-ac}, l_{ep-pred}, E, g_d)$ and a set of service-goal trees $\{SGT_{ac} = (cId, GN, GA), SGT_{ac}.cId = ac.type, ac \in GS.AC\}$ (i.e. one for each sub-collaboration referred to by $GS$), and returns a $HCPN = (S, SN, SA, PN, PT, PA, FS, FT, PP)$. We start by introducing the set of subnets ($S_{\mathrm{AC}}$), the set of transitions due to the mapping of decision nodes and edges ($T_{\mathrm{D}}$ and $T_{\mathrm{edges}}$), the set of places due to the mapping of arcs ($P_{\mathrm{edges}}$), the set of arcs connecting $id$ places to substitution transitions ($A_{\mathrm{Id}}$), and the set of arcs connecting the *constraint* place to transitions generated by decision nodes ($A_{\mathrm{constr}}$) as:

$$S_{\mathrm{AC}} = \{[\![(SGT_{ac}, GS)]\!]_{CPN} : SGT_{ac}.cId = ac.type, ac \in AC\}$$
$$T_{\mathrm{D}} = \{t_d : d \in N_{\mathrm{D}}, (d, \_) \in E\}$$
$$T_{\mathrm{edges}} = \{t_{(es,et)} : (es, et) \in E, es \in \{n_0\} \cup N_{\mathrm{M}} \cup N_{\mathrm{ExP}},$$
$$et \in N_{\mathrm{FI}} \cup N_{\mathrm{A}} \cup N_{\mathrm{EnP}} \cup N_{\mathrm{M}} \cup N_{\mathrm{D}}\}$$
$$P_{\mathrm{edges}} = \{p_{(es,et)} : es \in T_{\mathrm{D}} \cup N_F \cup N_J, et \in N_F \cup N_J, (es, et) \in E\}$$
$$A_{\mathrm{Id}} = \{ac.id\_IdTOac.id\_ac.type, ac.id\_ac.typeTOac.id\_Id : ac \in AC\}$$
$$A_{\mathrm{constr}} = \{constrTOt_d, t_dTOconstr : constr \in P, t_d \in T_{\mathrm{D}}\}$$

Now we define the main net ($s_{\mathrm{main}}$) describing the interconnection of substitution transitions (representing collaboration uses of the goal sequence). This net is a $CPN = (\Sigma, P, T, A, N, C, G, E, I)$ described as:

$$\Sigma = \{CTRL\_ST, CTRL\_ST \times DEP, STRING, VARIABLES\}$$
$$P = \{n_0\} \cup N_{FI} \cup N_D \cup N_M \cup \{constr\} \cup \{ac.id\_Id : ac \in AC\}$$
$$\cup \{ac.id\_p_{s_{ac}} : p_{s_{ac}} \in P_{s_{ac}}, s_{ac} \in S_{AC}\} \cup P_{\mathrm{edges}}$$
$$T = \{ac.id\_ac.type : ac \in AC\} \cup T_D \cup T_{\mathrm{edges}}$$
$$A = A_{Id} \cup A_{\mathrm{constr}} \cup \{esTOt_{(es,et)}, t_{(es,et)}TOet : t_{(es,et)} \in T_{\mathrm{edges}}\}$$
$$\cup \{esTOp_{(es,et)}, p_{(es,et)}TOet : p_{(es,et)} \in P_{\mathrm{edges}}\}$$
$$\cup \{esTOet : (es, et) \in E, t_{(es,et)} \notin T_{\mathrm{edges}}, p_{(es,et)} \notin P_{\mathrm{edges}}\}$$

$$N(a) = (source, target), \text{ if } a \text{ is in the form } sourceTOtarget$$

$$C(p) = \begin{cases} CTRL\_ST, & \text{if } p \in \{n_0\} \cup N_{FI} \cup N_D \cup N_M \cup P_{arcs} \\ STRING, & \text{if } p \text{ is in the form } ac.id\_Id \\ VARIABLES, & \text{if } p = constr \\ C(p'), & \text{if } p \text{ is a socket connected to port } p' \end{cases}$$

$$E(a) = \begin{cases} (ctrl, depUnres), & \text{if } a = sourceTOtarget \\ & \text{and } source \text{ is a socket connected to an i/o port} \\ (ctrl, depResolved), & \text{if } a = sourceTOtarget \\ & \text{and } target \text{ is a socket connected to an i/o port} \\ varbl, & \text{if } a \in A_{constr} \\ id, & \text{if } a \in A_{Id} \\ ctrl, & \text{otherwise} \end{cases}$$

$$G(t) = \begin{cases} g_D(e), & \text{if } t = t_d \in T_D, e = (d, \_) \in E, d \in N_D \\ true, & \text{otherwise} \end{cases}$$

The initialisation function $(I)$ of $s_{\text{main}}$ assigns to the starting place (i.e. $p = n_0$) a token of type CTRL_ST. This token describes the initial state of the composite collaboration described by $GS$, where all state predicates representing the goals of the collaboration are set to *false*.

Finally, we define $[\![GS, \{SGT_{ac}\}]\!]_{\text{HCPN}} = (S, SN, SA, PN, PT, PA, FS, FT, PP)$, where:

$$S = \{s_{\text{main}}\} \cup S_{\text{AC}} \qquad SN = \{ac.id\_ac.type : ac \in AC\}$$

$$PN = \bigcup_{s_{ac} \in S_{AC}} P_{s_{ac}} \qquad FS = \emptyset \qquad PP = \{s_{\text{main}}\}$$

$$SA(t) = s_{ac}, \text{ if } t = ac.id\_ac.type, ac \in AC, s_{ac} \in S_{AC}$$

$$PT(p) = \begin{cases} in, & \text{if } p = start \\ out, & \text{if } p \in GT_{ac}.SG \\ i/o, & \text{if } p \in GT_{ac}.EG \cup \{Id\} \end{cases} , \forall p \in P_{s_{ac}}, \forall s_{ac} = [\![(SGT_{ac}, GS)]\!]_{\text{CPN}} \in S_{AC}$$

$$PA(t) = (ac.id\_p, p), \forall p \in PN, \forall ac.id\_p \in P_{s_{main}}$$

# 3   Detection of Implied Scenarios

A goal sequence describes the intended behaviour of a service from a global perspective, and can be used to synthesize state-machines for the service-roles. The actual service behaviour is performed by the components playing those roles. Since components only have a local view of the service, unexpected interactions may arise. These are the so-called implied scenarios [1], which correspond to service behaviour that has not been explicitly specified, but follows implicitly, and will be present in any implementation of the service. An implied scenario may capture some overlooked positive behaviour, but it may also represent undesired behaviour. Detecting implied scenarios is therefore important.

In the context of the collaboration-based service specification approach treated here, an implied scenario may arise due to the existence of multiple initiatives, from the service-roles, to engage in sub-collaborations. In the collaboration goal sequence these initiatives are ordered in some desired sequence. However, this ordering may not be guaranteed at runtime due to the independence between the initiatives of different service-roles. Therefore, all possible orderings should be analyzed in order to determine if undesired behaviours may arise. Fortunately, this can be done without performing a global analysis of the service collaboration. It suffices to analyse, separately, the sub-role sequences that each service-role may execute. These sub-role sequences can be obtained from the collaboration goal sequence. For example, the following sub-role sequence: $V_{ev} \to V_d \to V_a \to V_{exv}$; can be extracted from the goal sequence in Fig. 2 for the $V$ service-role.

Separate sub-role sequences are extracted for each (instance of a) service-role (e.g. $T1{:}T$, $T2{:}T$, ...). This can be done by invoking the $VISIT$ algorithm (see Algorithm 1), with $i = 0$ and $n = n_0$, for each service-role ($rType$), and for each instance of that role ($rIns$). This algorithm traverses the goal sequence's graph ($GSG$) with a depth-first search method, looking for occurrences of $rIns$. While traversing the $GSG$ forwards, the algorithm creates a role-sequence graph ($RSG$) that includes only those activities (and their associated entry-/exit-points) *related* to $rIns$. $RSGs$ have the same syntax and semantics as $GSGs$. If a fork node is found, the algorithm adds it to the $RSG$ and continues the search through one of the fork's outgoing edges. When a decision node is found, one of its outgoing edges is also chosen to continue the search, but the decision node is not added to the $RSG$ (since at runtime only one of the branches can be executed). Instead, different $RSGs$ will be generated for each of the decision's branches (e.g. in our case study two $RSGs$ are generated for $T1{:}T$, one for $vehAtTerminal$ and other for $NOT\ vehAtTerminal$). In order to know the decision node's branch a $RSG$ corresponds to, the branch's guard is saved in a dedicated table ($decisions$). Once a final node is found, a sub-role sequence has been obtained. From there, a copy of the $RSG$ is done and the algorithm begins the backtracking phase. During this phase the previously added nodes are removed from the $RSG$ until a decision or fork node with unvisited edges is found. If this happens, one of the unvisited edges is selected and the $GSG$ is again traversed forwards (so new nodes are added to the $RSG$). Otherwise, if the initial node is reached during backtracking, the extraction process ends. Note that if fork (resp. join) nodes where found while traversing the $GSG$, the generated $RGSs$ describe a path through only one of the outgoing (resp. incoming) edges of these nodes. The individual $RGSs$ sharing fork (resp. join) nodes must therefore be merged at the end. To help in this process, each time a fork (resp. join) node is found, information about the traversed edge is saved in a dedicated table ($forks$; resp. $joins$). Note also that loops are traversed only once (i.e. only one iteration is performed). This is achieved by annotating in a table ($visited$) the number of times each node is visited. With this restriction we avoid infinite role sequences, while we ensure that all possible non-repetitive sequences of sub-roles are considered.

Once the sub-role sequences have been obtained, their analysis can start. For each service-role, its sub-role sequences are first analysed individually, and thereafter their interactions are studied. In the individual analysis, we look for any

**Algorithm 1.** VISIT($GSG,n,rIns,RSG[rIns,i]$)

// All variables except $adjNodes$ and $nextN$ are global
// All elements of the $visited$ array are initialized to 0 before first call to VISIT
$visited[n]++;\ adjNodes[n] = GETADJACENTNODES(n, GSG)$
**while** $adjNodes[n] \neq \emptyset$ **do**
  $nextN = adjNodes[n].pop()$
  **if** $visited[nextN] < 2$ **then**
    **if** $((n \in N_{\mathrm{EnP}}) \vee (n \in N_{\mathrm{ExP}}) \vee (n \in N_{\mathrm{A}})) \wedge RELATED(n, rIns)$ **then**
      $ADDTOGRAPH(n, RSG[rIns,i])$
    **else if** $(n \in N_{\mathrm{F}}) \vee (n \in N_{\mathrm{J}})$ **then**
      $ADDTOGRAPH(n, RSG[rIns,i])$ and update $forks[rIns,i]/joins[rIns,i]$
    **else if** $n \in N_D$ **then** update $decisions[rIns,i]$
    **else if** $n = n_0$ **then** $ADDTOGRAPH(n, RSG[rIns,i])$
    **end if**
    $VISIT(GSG, nextN, rIns, RSG[rIns,i])$
**end while** //There are no (more) adjacent nodes
$visited[n] = visited[n] - 1$
**if** $n \in N_{FI}$ **then** //Final node
  $ADDTOGRAPH(n, RSG[rIns,i]);\ RSG[rIns, i+1] = RSG[rIns,i];\ i++$
**end if**
$REMOVEFROMGRAPH(n, RSG[rIns,i])$ //Backtracking

set of two or more consecutive offered sub-roles (i.e. offered sub-roles connected by edges and/or join/fork nodes) that the sequence may contain. Consecutive offered sub-roles may represent a conflict, if they are played in collaborations with different parties, and these collaborations maintain some kind of dependency (e.g. one of them should not finish before the other does). In that case, the dependency might be violated, since the initiatives to start the collaborations are taken by different parties. In the *TransportService* example this happens for the $V$ service-role. According to their sub-role sequences, $V_{ev}$ is to be played in *EnterVehicle* before $V_d$ in *VehDeparture* (see Fig. 2). However there is no way for $T$, which takes the initiative in *VehDeparture*, to know if *Passenger (P)* has taken the initiative to start *EnterVehicle*, and when this has finished (i.e. the condition *ev.passEntered* is not visible for *Terminal*). Thus $T$ may request $V$ to play $V_d$ before $P$ has requested it to play $V_{ev}$.

After the individual analysis, we study how the sub-role sequences of a single service-role interact with each other, if executed concurrently. Intuitively, we first constrain the execution of sub-roles by imposing pre- and post-conditions, and then build the cross-product of the sub-role sequences to detect constraint conflicts. For that purpose, sub-role sequences are semantically mapped into HCPNs. This mapping follows the same guidelines as the goal sequence mapping detailed in Sect. 2.2, the only difference being substitution transitions labeled with sub-role names, rather than with active collaboration names. As an example, consider Fig. 4c, which depicts the HCPN for the sub-role sequence obtained when the *TransportService*'s goal sequence is projected onto $T1:T$ and *T1.vehAtTerminal* is *true*. Figure 4d presents the subnet representing role $T_d$ (part in boldface).

The execution constraints (i.e pre- and post-conditions) to be imposed on sub-roles follow from the requirements and the service domain. For example, in our case study we can further restrict the execution of role $T_d$ (from *VehDeparture*) by setting *VehAtTerminal* and *NOT VehAtTerminal* as part of $T_d$'s pre- and post-condition, respectively. In our HCPN model constraints are represented as boolean tokens that reside in a place shared by all the sub-role sequence nets. Since HCPNs do not allow guards to be imposed on substitution transitions (which, remember, represent sub-roles), the pre-condition for the execution of a sub-role is instead specified as a guard on the first transition of the subnet describing the sub-role behaviour. If the guard is satisfied, the transition fires and it updates the value of the constraints according to the post-condition. This is illustrated in Fig. 4d for the $T_d$ sub-role, where the result of calling function *eval_Td_Constr(constr)* has been imposed as guard of transition *t1*. This function processes the value of the *constr* token, which represents the constraints, and returns *true* if *VehAtTerminal* is *true*. The value of *VehAtTerminal* is updated when *t1* fires, by its code segment. Note that in addition to the *constraints* place, a *Tconflict* transition and a *Pconflict* place have been added to the subnet of $T_d$. Note also that *Tconflict* can only be fired when *t1* can not, that is, when *VehAtTerminal* is *false*. In such a case, *Tconflict* "steals" the tokens from the *Start* and *constraints* places forcing a dead-marking to be reached. This behaviour reflects our desire of a (potential) conflict to be reported if a sub-role cannot be immediately executed when it receives the control token, because its pre-condition is not satisfied.

At the end, the sub-role sequences are composed in parallel and the reachability graph of the resulting net is constructed and analysed in search of dead-markings, which would represent potential conflicts. In order to test our analysis method, we used CPN Tools [3] to analyse an extended version of the *Transport-Service* (with a control center for mediation between the terminals). A reachability graph with 37 nodes and 58 arcs was generated for the analysis of the sub-role sequences of the *Terminal* (T) service-role. This analysis revealed two implied scenarios: a passenger may miss the vehicle after buying the ticket, if the vehicle is dispatched following a request from the control center; or the vehicle may depart with the passenger before a control center's request has been completely processed. A reachability graph of similar size was generated for the *Vehicle* (V) service-role. As a comparison, the detection method by Uchitel et al. [12], which is of exponential complexity with the number of service-roles, needs to build a safety property for the same case study of 4414 states, if heuristics are used. Although no formal conclusions can be obtained from this comparison, we believe the results show the potential of our approach.

## 4   Related Work

Service-oriented specification has been addressed in several works. Rößler et al. [8] suggested collaboration based design with a tighter integration between interaction and state diagram models, and created a specific language, CoSDL, to define collaborations. CoSDL is inspired by SDL, so it fails at providing the cross-cutting service composition offered by UML collaborations and goal sequences. Krüger et al. [5] propose an approach to service engineering that has many commonalities with our own. They consider, as we do, services as collaborations between roles played by components, and use a combination of Use Cases and an extended MSC language to describe them. Liveness is expressed by means of the operators provided by their MSC language, while service structure and role binding are described with, so-called, role and deployment domain models. In our approach UML collaboration diagrams are used to provide a unified way of describing service structure and role bindings, and to provide a framework for expressing liveness with goal sequences. Goal sequences provide interesting opportunities for analysis, as we have discussed.

The concept of implied scenarios was first introduced by Alur et al. in [1], where they presented an algorithm to detect this kind of scenarios from MSC specifications. This work was later extended by Uchitel et al. [12], who proposed an approach for the incremental specification (using both MSCs and HMSCs) of systems, driven by the detection of implied scenarios. The main drawback of Uchitel et al.'s work is, however, the state explosion problem (although they limit it by applying heuristics). Munccini has proposed an approach for the detection of implied scenarios based on the analysis of HMSCs [6]. His work builds over a previous work of Uchitel et al., and avoids the state explosion problem. Our method also limits the state explosion problem and it is applicable to UML collaboration-based specifications, while Munccini's approach applies to HMSC-based specifications.

## 5    Discussion and Conclusions

UML 2.0 collaborations provide very useful structuring mechanisms for specifying cross-cutting service behaviours. They enable: (a) an attractive structured overview; (b) structural decomposition into features, by means of collaboration-uses; (c) re-usability; and (d) definition of semantic interfaces for dynamic discovery, binding and compatibility checks [10]. Still, a proper way to describe the choreography or joint behaviour of the sub-collaborations of a composite collaboration is needed. Collaboration goal sequences can be used to fill this gap. They help to understand and document the relationships and execution dependencies between sub-collaborations, in terms of their goals. Moreover, they can be analysed in order to detect inconsistencies and implied scenarios at an early stage of service specification.

Formal semantics for goal sequences based on hierarchical coloured Petri-nets has been presented here that allows their automated analysis using general purpose tools available for HCPNs. The detection of implied scenarios is done in two phases. First, sub-role sequences are extracted from the goal sequence and individually analysed. Then the cross-product of the sub-role sequences of each service-role is built to examine how they interact. The proposed analysis suffers little from the state explosion problem since the sub-role sequences of each service-role are analysed separately, so the complexity is linear with the number of service-roles. In addition, the analysis is done at a high-level of abstraction (i.e. with role sequences and not message sequences). The proposed implied scenario detection approach demonstrates, in addition, that we have much to gain from the explicit description of features dependencies, and from the analysis and understanding of concurrency on interfaces.

Although we can use HCPN-tools for the analysis of goal sequences, their mapping into HCPNs is still performed manually. Thus, a short-term objective is to provide tool support for the mapping, so the whole process can be automatized. Another interesting issue we plan to work on is how to address the elimination of the implied scenarios. One possibility might be to specify negative goal sequences (as the the negative scenarios in [12]).

## Acknowledgements

We would like to thank Gregor von Bochmann, Cyril Carrez and the anonymous reviewers for their valuable comments on this work.

## References

1. Alur, R., Etessami, K., Yannakakis, M.: Inference of message sequence charts. In: 22nd Intl. Conf. on Software Engineering (ICSE'00). (2000) 304–313
2. Castejón, H.N., Bræk, R.: A collaboration-based approach to service specification and detection of implied scenarios. In: ICSE's 5th Intl. Workshop on Scenarios and State Machines: models, algorithms and tools (SCESM'06), ACM Press (2006)
3. CPN Group: CPN Tools Manual. Technical report, Univ. of Aarhus, Denmark (2005) available at http://wiki.daimi.au.dk/cpntools/cpntools.wiki.
4. Jensen, K.: Coloured Petri Nets. Basic Concepts, Analysis Methods and Practical Use. Volume 1. Springer-Verlag (1997)
5. Krüger, I.H., Gupta, D., Mathew, R., Moorthy, P., Phillips, W., Rittmann, S., Ahluwalia, J.: Towards a process and tool-chain for service-oriented automotive software engineering. In: ICSE'04 Workshop on Software Engineering for Automotive Systems (SEAS). (2004)
6. Muccini, H.: Detecting implied scenarios analyzing non-local branching choices. In: 6th Intl. Conf. of Fundamental Approaches to Software Engineering (FASE'03). LNCS 2621. (2003) 372–386
7. Object Management Group: UML 2.0 Superstructure Specification. (2005)
8. Rößler, F., Geppert, B., Gotzhein, R.: Collaboration-based design of SDL systems. In: 10th SDL Forum. LNCS 2078 (2001) 72–89
9. Sanders, R.T., Bræk, R.: Modeling peer-to-peer service goals in UML. In: 2nd IEEE Intl. Conf. on Software Engineering and Formal Methods (SEFM'04). (2004)
10. Sanders, R.T., Bræk, R., von Bochmann, G., Amyot, D.: Service discovery and component reuse with semantic interfaces. In: 12th SDL Forum. LNCS 3530 (2005)
11. Sanders, R.T., Castejón, H.N., Kraemer, F.A., Bræk, R.: Using UML 2.0 collaborations for compositional service specification. In: ACM/IEEE 8th Intl. Conf. on Model Driven Engineering Languages and Systems (MoDELS). LNCS 3713 (2005)
12. Uchitel, S., Kramer, J., Magee, J.: Incremental elaboration of scenario-based specifications and behavior models using implied scenarios. ACM TOSEM **13** (2004)

# Composition of Use Cases Using Synchronization and Model Checking

R. Mizouni[1], A. Salah[2], S. Kolahi[3], and R. Dssouli[1]

[1] Electrical and Computer Engineering Department, Concordia University
{mizouni, dssouli}@encs.concordia.ca
[2] Computer Science Department, UQAM University
aziz.salah@uqam.ca
[3] Computer Science Department, Concordia University
s_kolahi@cs.concordia.ca

**Abstract.** Capturing the behavior of a system by use cases have been intensively investigated in the last decade. The challenge is to find both the adequate model that fits the needs of the analyst and a formal composition mechanism which helps the generation of the expected behavior. In this paper, we propose a formal approach for specifying and composing use cases based on assignments. Those assignments are used to express new use cases. An assignment provides the join points and the composition operators that will be taken into account during the composition. These join points are, in fact, determined through a model checking step. They represent states where a property defined by the analyst holds. In order to evaluate these assignments, we define a composition mechanism based on the well known concept of synchronized product.

**Keywords:** Use cases, model checking, composition operators, synchronized product.

## 1 Introduction

Capturing the system behaviors within use cases has gained a lot of interest during the last decade. Use cases represent a partial behavior of the system, which helps the requirement elicitation process. However, composing use cases in order to generate the system specification is a challenging task. Its complexity lies within the formality of the model representing use cases, the detection of states on which the composition is performed, and the level of automation of the composition.

Defining interactions among use cases is another challenge for the analyst which may be specified explicitly using composition operators, namely sequential concatenation, iteration, alternative and etc. After the composition according to specified operator semantics, the obtained behavior may not meet the analyst's intended point of view because of possible unexpected interactions. Retrieving unexpected interactions is a hard task which makes the incremental construction of the specification a helpful means for getting the right system behavior.

E. Najm et al. (Eds.): FORTE 2006, LNCS 4229, pp. 292–306, 2006.

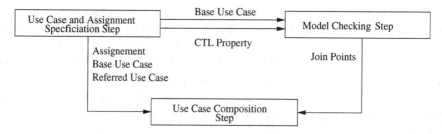

**Fig. 1.** Approach Overview

Furthermore, in order to explicitly specify the interactions, the analyst has to choose the states where to compose use cases, called *join points*. This choice again is a hard task that requires deep understanding of the characteristics of each state within the use case. The usage of temporal property for determining these composition join points helps the process of generating the system specification, especially when the size of use cases increases.

This paper addresses a formal, automated and incremental approach for use case composition using *assignments*. The approach consists of three steps, as shown in Fig. 1: use cases and assignments specification step, a model checking step, and a composition step. First, the analyst provides a set of use cases and a set of assignments. For each assignment, a new use case that represents the evaluation of this assignment is generated. Each assignment uses two use cases: the base use case and the referred use case. The base use case is the one where the new behavior will be added while the referred use case represents the additional behavior to be weaved within the base use case. Moreover, the assignment includes a composition operator and a CTL [1] property which is used to identify the join points. The states of the base use case where the property holds are determined by a model checker, and then, selected as joint points. The composition will be performed on these states respecting the semantics of the composition operator of the assignment. These semantics are achieved by means of the composition based on the synchronization product of two use cases on common labels, as we will show later. The use case that results from the composition represents the evaluation of the assignment.

The paper is structured as follows. In Section 2, we give an overview of the notation we are using in the paper, and in Section 3, we present the definition of assignments. In Section 4, we describe our approach for composing use cases and synthesizing the system automaton. By an example of an invoicing system, Section 5 shows the applicability of our approach to distributed use cases. Discussion of related works is given in Section 6. Finally, we draw our conclusions and discussions on future works in Section 7.

## 2 Preliminaries

A use case is used to describe a functional behavior of the system regarding a certain concern. The behavior represented as a use case is composed of sequences of actions.

A finite state automaton model is used to express the behavior of a use case because of its expressiveness power and its formality level. A finite state automaton (FSA) is defined as a 5-tuple $(S, s^0, S^f, L, E)$, where $S$ is the set of states, $s^0 \in S$ is the initial state, $S_f \subseteq S$ is the set of final states, $L$ is the set of labels, and $E \subseteq S \times L \times S$ is the set of transitions. For a transition $(s, l, s') \in E$, we write $s \xrightarrow{l} s' \in E$. A clone of a use case is an automaton generated from the use case, with having the same structure and same set of behaviors, but different edge labeling. Next, we present the formal definition of a clone of a use case FSA.

### Definition 1 (Clone of a use case)
A clone of use case FSA $A=(S, s^0, S^f, L, E)$ respecting a renaming function *Rename*: $L \rightarrow L'$ is a use case FSA $A'=(S, s^0, S^f, L', E')$ such that:

$$\forall e = (s_1, l, s_2) \in E, \exists e' \in E' \text{ such that } e' = (s_1, Rename(l), s_2)$$

The clone of a use case is obtained by renaming its different labels using a renaming function.

We will use synchronization for composing FSAs. We present our definition of synchronized product which is based on synchronization at common labels.

### Definition 2 (Synchronized product on common labels)
Let $A_i = (S_i, s^0_i, S^f_i, L_i, E_i)$ for n FSAs. We define the synchronized product of $A_i$ $i=1..n$ in their common labels as the connected component containing the state ( $s^0_1$, ...,$s^0_n$) of the FSA $(S, s^0, S^f, L, E)$ where $S \subseteq S_1 \times ... \times S_n$, $s^0 = ( s^0_1, ..., s^0_n)$, $S^f \subseteq (S^f_1 \times ... \times S_n)$ $\cup (S_1 \times S^f_2 \times ... \times S_n) \cup ... \cup (S_1 \times S_2 \times ... \times S^f_n)$, $L \subseteq (L_1 \cup L_2 \cup ... \cup L_n)$, and $E$ is the set of transition defined by the inference rules :

$$\frac{(s_i \xrightarrow{l} s_i' \in E_i), (l \notin L_j, 1 \leq j \neq i \leq n)}{(s_1, s_2, .., s_i, .., s_n) \xrightarrow{l} (s_1, s_2, .., s_i', .., s_n) \in E} \tag{1}$$

$$\frac{((s_i \xrightarrow{l} s_i' \in E_k), k \in J) \text{ where } J = \{j / l \in (\underset{1 \leq j \neq i \leq n}{\cap} L_j)\}}{((s_1, ..., s_n) \xrightarrow{l} (s_1'', ..., s_n'') \in E), (s_i'' = s_i' \text{ if } (i \in J)), (s_i'' = s_i \text{ if } (i \notin J))} \tag{2}$$

Rule (1) states that when a label belongs to a unique FSA, then only this FSA fires the transition. Rule (2) shows that when a label belong to more than one FSA, then all these FSAs synchronize in order to fire the transition at the same moment.

After specifying the use cases to compose, the analyst has to describe properties. We use the *Computation Tree Logic* (CTL) formalism for its expressiveness to describe both safety and liveness properties of the system in the states. Given a CTL formula $\varphi$ and a state s, $s \models \varphi$ whenever $\varphi$ is true in s.

### Definition 3 (Join Point Set)
Let $A = (S, s^0, S^f, L, E)$ a use case FSA. Join point Set J of a CTL formula $\varphi$ in A is a set of states S such that $J=\{s \in S / s \models \varphi\}$.

This set defines the states where the composition will be performed.

# 3  Assignment Specification

## 3.1  Use Case Composition Operators

The analyst can specify different operators to model interactions between use cases. The `Include` composition operator specifies that the base use case has to include the behavior of the referred use case during the execution flow in the join point. After the execution of the referred use case, the base use case would resume from the join point. The `Extend_with` composition operator specifies that the behavior of the base use case *may* include the behavior of the referred use case. Again After the execution of the referred use case, the base use case would be resumed from the join point. Finally, the `Interrupt_with` composition operator specifies that the flow of execution of the base use case may be interrupted by the referred use case. In this case, unlike the previous operators, base use case would not be resumed after the execution of the referred one. We are presenting our approach in the case of these three which are the most known operators. However, our approach is not limited to them and the same process can be applied in order to consider other operators such as sequential concatenation.

## 3.2  Assignment Description

Assignments are used to specify the composition information between two use cases. These assignments are equations used to create new use case FSAs from the existing ones with respect to the semantics of the composition operators. They follow the syntax:

$$\text{Z: = Composition\_Operator (X, Y) Where } \varphi$$

`Where` Z represents the FSA that will be generated from the evaluation of the assignment, X is the base use case and Y is the referred one. `Composition_Operator` represents one of the three specified composition operators, `Include`, `Extend_with`, and `Interrupt_with`. Finally, `Where` $\varphi$ defines the set of join points where the composition will be performed. As said previously, it is defined by the set of states where the property $\varphi$ holds.

It is important to note that the composition is performed on states rather than transitions. Contrarily to a transition based composition, a state based composition results in all edges related to that state being affected by the assignment. Furthermore, unlike other approaches such as aspect-oriented approaches, there is no need for the qualifiers *Before* and *After* defined with the join point where the composition is done. In our case, the two expressions "*Before s*" and "*After s*" lead to bisimilar FSAs .

# 4  Use Case Composition Approach

## 4.1  Join Point Generation

After the definition of the assignment by the analyst, the property as well as the base use case is sent for model checking. As stated before, this property is used to find the set of states on which the composition should be performed. Since model checkers return only true or false with a counterexample, for each state of the base use case starting from the initial one, we run the model checker as if it was the initial state of the base use case. If it returns true then the property holds in that state, if it returns a counter example, then the property does not hold in that state and is not a member of our joint point set. The resulting set would act as the place where the composition should be done.

As a result of the model checking step, the join point set could be empty or not. In case of empty set, the base use case will never verify such property and no new use case can be generated from the evaluation of the assignment. Therefore a revision of either the property or the use cases is needed. On the other hand, when the resulting join point set contains more than one state, the composition of the two use cases should be done in all these states. For that purpose, two approaches can be considered. The first one is to do the composition in an incremental manner. This means that we compose first the two use cases in one state. Then, the resulting use case from the first iteration is used for composition in another state and so on until all the join points are considered. This approach brings the problem of state traceability since the resulting states from the first iteration are no more the states present in the base use case and hence they can not be traced. Moreover the convergence of the approach has to be proved since the synchronized product may duplicate states in the resulting use case. The second solution consists of generating FSAs that takes into account the semantics of the assignment on the different states where the property holds and then applying synchronization on all of them in order to derive the new use case. We present this solution in the next section.

### 4.2  Composition Approach

After retaining the join point set, base and referred use cases have to be composed. From behavioral point of view, the traces of the referred use cases are inserted within the trace of the base use case in all the states of the join point set with respect to the semantics of the operator. In order to achieve this composition, we propose to synthesize a set of FSAs from the use case FSA, which we call *builders*. Each builder reflects the semantics of the composition operator in a join point. Builders would synchronize in order to generate the intended new use case. They are generated automatically from use cases with respect to specific synthesis rules as we will show next. Fig. 2 shows the composition approach. After determining the set of join points, a set of referred use case clones has to be generated by labeling renaming. Next, builders are generated and then composed, resulting in a synchronized product from which we extract an intermediate use case FSA. Finally, we generate the new use case by recovering the original labeling of the referred use case. This new use case is added to the originally specified set of use cases and may be used for describing new assignments. In the next section, we present the formal details of each of these steps.

### 4.2.1  Clone Synthesis

As mentioned in Definition 1, clones of a use case are generated using a renaming function for relabeling the alphabet of the original use case. In fact, for each join point $s \in J$, a clone of the referred use case has to be generated. This is for two reasons: (1) to differentiate it during the synchronization and hence avoid deadlock caused by common labels (2) to synchronize with the base use case builder generated for composition in state s.

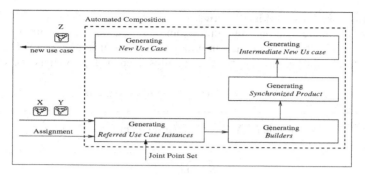

**Fig. 2.** Composition Approach

In order to automate the synthesis of the clone FSA, we define a renaming function that modifies the labeling of the FSA. It uses the joint point state where the clone will be considered for composition. Let $A_1 = (S_1, s^0_1, S^f_1, L_1, E_1)$ and $A_2 = (S_2, s^0_2, S^f_2, L_2, E_2)$ two use case FSAs such that $A_1$ is the base use case and $A_2$ is the referred one. Let $\varphi$ be the property specified in the assignment and $J$ the set of join points retained from the model checking phase. The renaming function for state $s \in J$ is:

$$f_s : L_2 \cup \{begin, end\} \rightarrow L^s_2 \cup \{begin_s, end_s\} \, such \, that :$$
$$\forall l \in L_2, f_s(l) = l_s$$
$$f_s(begin) = begin_s$$
$$f_s(end) = end_s$$

The labels *begin* and *end* are put during the generation of builders. They are used for synchronization in order to indicate where the referred use case has to be inserted in the base use case. The generated clone of FSA $A_2$ with the renaming function $f_s$ is the FSA $A^s_{2_{clone}} = (S_2, s^0_2, S^f_2, L^s_2, E^s_2)$.

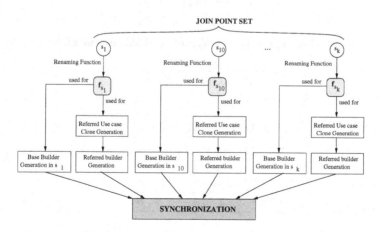

**Fig. 3.** Synthesis of base and referred builders

### 4.2.2  Base Use Case Builders Synthesis

When there is more than one state in the join point set, we end up with a set of base builders, each of them constructed in order to show the insertion of a corresponding referred builder in the join point state, as illustrated in Fig. 3. It is the renaming

**Table 1.** Synthesis Rules of Base builders

| Include (X,Y) Where $\varphi$ ($\varphi$ holds in the state s) |
|---|

$$\frac{S}{Q = S \cup \{q,q'\}} \tag{3}$$

$$\frac{S^f}{Q^f = S^f} \tag{4}$$

$$\frac{(x \xrightarrow{a} x' \in E),((x' \neq s))}{x \xrightarrow{a} x' \in T} \tag{5}$$

$$\frac{(x \xrightarrow{a} x' \in E),(x' = s)}{(x \xrightarrow{a} q \in T) \in T,(q \xrightarrow{f_s(begin)} q') \in T,(q' \xrightarrow{f_s(end)} x_1) \in T} \tag{6}$$

| Extend_with(X,Y) Where $\varphi$ ($\varphi$ holds in the state s) |
|---|

$$\frac{S}{Q = S \cup \{q,q'\}} \tag{7}$$

$$\frac{S^f}{Q^f = S^f} \tag{8}$$

$$\frac{(x \xrightarrow{a} x' \in E),(x \neq s)}{x \xrightarrow{a} x' \in T} \tag{9}$$

$$\frac{(x = s)}{(x \xrightarrow{f_s(begin)} q) \in T,(q \xrightarrow{f_s(end)} q') \in T} \tag{10}$$

$$\frac{(x \xrightarrow{a} x' \in E),(x = s)}{(s \xrightarrow{a} x' \in T),(q' \xrightarrow{a} x' \in T)} \tag{11}$$

| Interrupt_with(X,Y)Where $\varphi$($\varphi$ holds in state s) |
|---|

$$\frac{S}{Q = S \cup \{q,q'\}} \tag{12}$$

$$\frac{S^f}{Q^f = S^f \cup \{q'\}} \tag{13}$$

$$\frac{(x \xrightarrow{a} x' \in E)}{x \xrightarrow{a} x' \in T} \tag{14}$$

$$\frac{(x = s)}{(x \xrightarrow{f_s(begin)} q) \in T,(q \xrightarrow{f_s(end)} q') \in T} \tag{15}$$

function $f_s$ which is building this link. In fact, for each state in the set of join points, a clone of the referred use case is created using $f_s$ and a base builder is synthesized to show the insertion of referred use case in the state $s$.

For each $s \in J$, we construct a base builder from the use case $A_1$ with respect to the renaming function $f_s$. The synthesized base builder is an FSA $A_1^s = (Q, q^0, Q^f, L \cup \{f_s(begin), f_s(end)\}, T)$ that reflects the semantics of the composition operator as well as the join point $s$. The labels of the base use case are not renamed in the base builder, only two labels $f_s$ *(begin)* and $f_s(end)$) are added which serve as the common label indicating the start and the end of the insertion of the referred use case within the base one. The two builders will synchronize on these labels. We present the set of synthesis rules of the FSA $A_1^s$ in Table 1 for each of the composition operators we defined. These rules are defined for a unique join point $s$.

Let's consider the case of an Extend_with composition in the state $s$. The synthesis of the base builder follows the rules (7-11). Rule (7) defines the set of the states of the builder FSA while Rule (8) defines the set of its final states. Rule (9) shows that the labeling of all the transitions that are not outgoing from $s$ are labeled with the same label $a$. Rule (10) demonstrates that from the state $s$ new added transitions labeled with $f_s(begin)$ and $f_s(end)$ synchronize with the builder of referred use case clone. Finally, Rule (12) shows that all the outgoing transitions of $s$ are duplicated in order to handle resuming of the base use case after the insertion of the referred use case clone. Fig. 4 (d) gives an example of such a base builder.

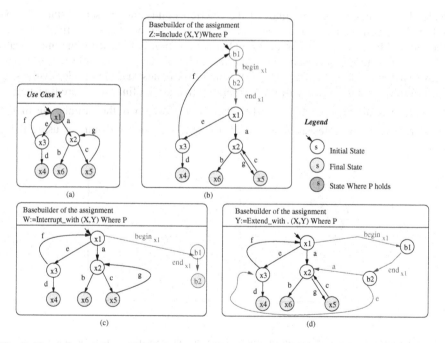

**Fig. 4.** Examples of Base Builder of an assignment : (a) base use case (b) synthesized base builder with include operator in state $x_1$ (c) synthesized base builder with Interrupt_with operator in state $x_1$ (d) synthesized base builder with Extend_with operator in state $x_1$

### 4.2.3 Synthesis of Referred Builders

The synthesis of the referred builder is independent of the operator and the states in the join points set. Each referred builder is synthesized from clones of the referred use case using the following rules. Let $A^s_{2_{clone}} = (S_2, s^0_2, S^f_2, L^s_2, E^s_2)$ the FSA of the referred use case clone synthesized from $A_2$ *with* the renaming function $f_s$.

The referred builder of $A^s_2$ with the same renaming $f_s$ is a use case FSA $A^s_2 = (Q, q^0, Q^f, L^s_2 \cup \{f_s(begin), f_s(end)\}, T)$ such that:

$$\frac{S}{(Q = S \cup \{q\})} \tag{16}$$

$$\frac{S}{(Q^f = \{q\})} \tag{17}$$

$$\frac{s^0}{q \xrightarrow{f_s(begin)} s^0 \in T} \tag{18}$$

$$\frac{s \xrightarrow{a} s' \in E}{s \xrightarrow{a} s' \in T} \tag{19}$$

$$\frac{s \in S^f}{s \xrightarrow{f_s(end)} q \in T} \tag{20}$$

Rule (16) defines the set of states of the referred builder as the set of states of the referred use case with an additional state $q$. Rule (17) defines the set of final states of the referred builder. According to Rule (18), a transition is fired from the initial state of the builder to the corresponding state of the initial state of the referred use case. This transition is labeled with $f_s(begin)$. Rule (19) implies that the builder evolves as the referred use case. Finally, Rule (20) reflects that all the final states are transited to the unique final state of $A^s_2$ with the label $f_s(end)$, which is the initial state of the builder. Fig. 5 illustrates an example of a synthesized referred builder using these rules.

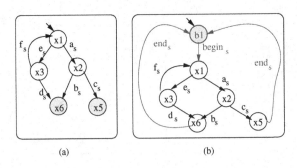

(a)                                    (b)

**Fig. 5.** Example of referred builder (a) referred use case clone with a renaming function $f_s$ (b) its referred builder synthesized using rules (16-20)

### 4.2.4  Intermediate Use Case Generation

When builders are generated, their composition is achieved within their synchronized product on common labels (using Definition 2). During this synchronization, the referred builders will never synchronize since they have different edges labeling. In addition, referred and base builders synchronize only on $f_s(begin)$ and $f_s(end)$, $s \in J$. Hence, we verify that $L_1 \cap (\bigcup_{s \in J} L_2^s) = \varnothing$. This verification does not constraint the approach. In fact, if the intersection is not the empty set, a simple renaming for the common labels can be made and then recovered after the synchronization.

The resulting automaton still does not represent the intermediate use case since some of its transitions are labeled by $f_s(begin)$ and $f_s(end)$, $s \in J$. These transitions are treated as $\varepsilon$-transition and removed using the $\varepsilon$-transition removal algorithm in [2]. They were needed only for the generation of the synchronized product of the builders reflecting the semantics of the composition operator in the join points. After this step, the synthesized FSA represents the intermediate use case. It is illustrated in step (4) in Fig. 6.

### 4.2.5  Labeling and Final States Recovery

Let $A_1 = (S_1, s^0{}_1, S^f{}_1, L_1, E_1)$ be the base use case and $\{A_{2_{clone}}^s, s \in J\}$ the set of the referred use case clones where $J$ is the set of join points. Let $C = (Q, q^0, Q^f, L_1 \cup (\bigcup_{s \in J} L_2^s), T)$ the generated intermediate use case. We call it intermediate since it still holds the renaming of labels used to generate the different clones of the referred use case. Therefore, we have to restore the original labeling to gain the final use case. For this purpose, we define a renaming function $g$ such that:

$$g : L_1 \cup (\bigcup_{s \in J} L_2^s) \to L_1 \cup L_2 \ where:$$

$$\begin{cases} \forall l \in L_1, g(l) = l \\ \forall l \in L_s, s \in J, g(f_s(l)) = l \end{cases}$$

The label restoration of the intermediate use case results in the new use case as shown in step(5) of Fig. 6. By determining the set of final states, the final use case would be achieved. The set of final states $S^f$ of the newly generated use case $D = (S, s^0, S^f, L_1 \cup L_2, E)$ is defined with respect to the composition operator specified between $A_1$ and $A_2$. In the case of Include and Extend_with composition operators, the set of final states of the new use case represents all the states labeled by one of the final state of the base use case.

$$\frac{((s_1, s_2, ..., s_n) \in S), (s_i \in S_1^f)}{(s_1, s_2, ..., s_n) \in S^f} \tag{21}$$

However, in the case of Interrupt_with composition operator, the set of final states of the new use case represents the union of all the states that are labeled by one of the final states of the base use case or the referred use case. This stems from the fact that the Interrupt_with operator does not let resumption of the base use case after the execution. Therefore the set of the final states in this case follow the rule (22) as well as the rule (21):

$$\frac{((s_1, s_2, ..., s_n) \in S), (s_i \in S_2^f)}{(s_1, s_2, ..., s_n) \in S^f}$$

(22)

It is important to mention that unlike the approach in [3] , our approach does not introduce any non-determinism. In fact, if the use cases specified are deterministic, the generated use cases from assignments would be also deterministic. An example of the overall process of the composition is shown in Fig. 6.

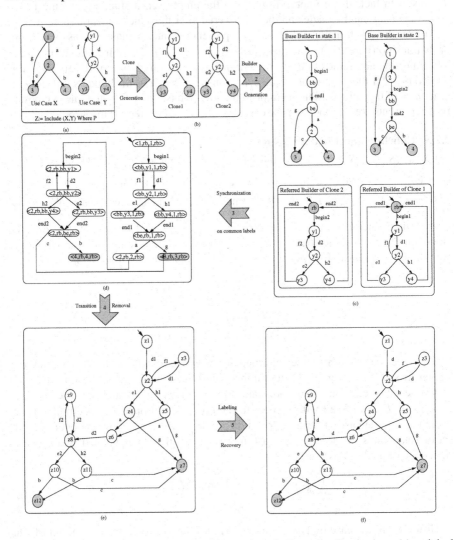

**Fig. 6.** Example of Use Case Composition using Assignment Expression: (a) original specification: use case X and Y and the assignment Z (b) clones of the referred use case (c) builders of the use case X in state 1 and state 2 as well as the referred builders of the clones of Y (d) Synchronized product of base and referred builders (e) the intermediate use case (f) the generated use case Z

# 5  Application on Distributed Use Cases

Distributed use cases are those where the communication between the different entities is described. In order to show the applicability of our approach on the distributed systems, we choose the specification of a distributed Invoice Ordering System.

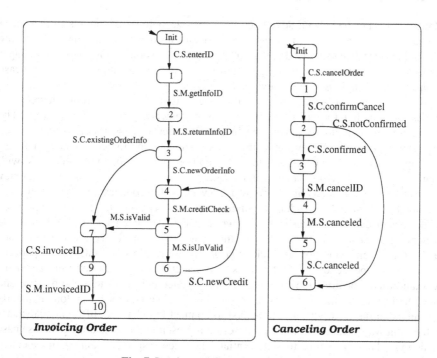

**Fig. 7.** Invoice and Cancel order use cases

In order to let our use case model handle the description of distributed use cases, we represent the labeling of the FSA in the form of $(O_1.O_2.m)$ where $O_1$ and $O_2$ are the communicating objects, and m is the message sent from the object $O_1$ to the object $O_2$ [4]. We present in Fig. 7 two use cases of the invoice ordering system specification. Three objects are communicating in the system: the customer (C), the system (S), and the resource manager (M). Let's build a new use case, *Ordering*, where it shows that the costumer is authorized to cancel its ordering if the order is not yet invoiced. The assignment is:

```
Ordering: = Interrupt_with (Invoicing, Canceling) Where
        (AG(orderID) ∧ AG((!invoiced) U (invoiced))
```

The CTL property states that the customer may cancel his order from the time of receiving the confirmation of his order ID (new or existing) and before invoicing his order. According to this assignment, the set of states that verify the property is {3,4,5,6,7}. The use case *Canceling order* will be composed with the

`Interrupt_With` semantics in those states. We note that after the composition of use cases, it is possible to decompose the obtained FSA to communicating FSAs per object. This could be done with the projection of the behavior on the objects, as presented in our previous work [4].

# 6 Related Work and Discussions

Many approaches have been developed to synthesize state-based models from a set of use cases [5-11]. State-based models are basically needed to verify and validate the user requirements in order to detect design problems as soon as possible. In this paper we tackled the issue of automatic generation of system automaton based on use case composition through assignment evaluation.

The emerged notations to specify use cases have different degrees of expressiveness and formality. Glinz [12] uses statecharts to model scenarios. The integration of scenarios is performed in a way to retrieve the relationship between scenarios by keeping their internal structure unchanged, and to detect inconsistencies. The approach proposed carries only the composition of disjoint scenarios with elementary constructors (sequential, alternative, iteration and concurrency constructor). As an extension of this work, Ryser [13] introduces a new kind of chart and notation to model dependencies among scenarios. The advantage of this approach is the fact of capturing clearly these inter-scenarios dependencies. Yet, this work is presenting a notation rather than a methodology that can clarify the dependencies between different scenarios. Bordeleau *et al.* [14] have proposed integration patterns for scenario dependencies. UCMs are used to detect dependencies between scenarios. A state-based specification per use case is generated for each component and integrated to reflect the scenarios dependencies. The whole process is done manually and relies on the creativity of the analyst to connect together the different statecharts in the right way. Araujo *et al.* [15] focuses on representing aspects during the use case modeling. They propose to differentiate between aspectual and non-aspectual scenarios. Similar to our approach, the integration is done on the state machine level. The relationships between use cases are defined through an interaction pattern and defined in term of roles. In our case, we propose composition operators to generate new use cases that integrate the behaviors of the original ones.

During the composition of use cases into transition-based system, the challenge is to identify states at the scenario level that serve as join points between use cases. There are two kinds of state characterization: trace-based [5-7, 16], and variable (or label) state-based characterization [8, 9, 17 ]. In this paper, we propose to detect these states using a model checking approach. The state where the composition has to be made verifies a certain property of the use case. This helps considerably the analyst since he has no more the arduous task to detect the right state.

Our approach differs substantially from the earlier presented work in some points. During the process of generating the specification, the analyst has the opportunity to define assignments in an incremental manner. Hence the order in which these assignments are specified has a direct impact on the resulting use cases. In fact, the states that will be generated from the model checking system will differ with different orders in presenting the assignments. Consequently, having different combinations of defining assignments and then choosing the proper order may ease the process of obtaining the expected behavior. In addition, we kept the model as rich as possible by having use cases described as FSAs without complicating the composition procedure. Having well-established synthesis rules for each composition operator and a composition based on the well known concept of synchronized product makes the composition automated, formal and straightforward.

# 7  Conclusion

In this paper, we presented an approach for composing use cases based on the notion of assignments. Each assignment includes a base use case, a referred use case, a composition operator, and a CTL property which is used to identify the states on which the composition will be done, called joint points. The CTL property and the base use case are sent to a model checking tool in order to determine the joint points, where to perform the composition. The composition approach consists of three steps. First, clones of the referred use case are generated using a renaming function. Then, proper builders that reflect the semantics of the composition operator and the join pints are synthesized and their synchronized product on common labels is generated. Finally the obtained automaton is processed through a relabeling function in order to recover the original labeling. The obtained FSA represents the behavior of the base and the referred use cases, merged on the states which hold the specified property with respect to the semantics of the composition operator.

Our approach is fully automated because of the synthesis rules for constructing builders and the synchronization mechanism used for composition. It also has the advantage of providing a helpful support for the analyst, especially when join points are not clearly evident, which may be the case proceeding with the composition. In fact, the size of the use case automaton grows significantly after the composition, adding to the complexity of specifying join points manually. Furthermore, an optional validation by the analyst after the selection of the join points may be envisaged. The expansion and enrichment of the model as well as the composition approach is seen as a part of future work. A tool supporting and visualizing the composition approach is under construction.

# References

[1]  E. M. Clarke, J. O. Grumberg, and D. A. Peled, *Model Checking*: MIT Press, 1999.
[2]  J. E. Hopcroft, R. Motwani, and J. D. Ullman, *Introduction to Automata Theory, Languages, and Computation* second edition ed: Addison Wesley 2000.
[3]  R. Mizouni, A. Salah, R. Dssouli, and S. Kolahi, "Role of Variables and Interactions in Use Case Composition," presented at New Technologies for Distributed Systems (NOTERE'06), Toulouse, France, 2006.
[4]  A. Salah, R. Mizouni, R. Dssouli, and B. Parreaux, "Formal Composition of Distributed Scenario," presented at FORTE : International Conference on Formal Techniques for Networked and Distributed Systems, Spain, 2004.
[5]  D. Harel and H. Kugler, "Synthesizing State-Based Object Systems from LSC Specifications," *Int. J. of Foundations of Computer Science*, vol. 13, pp. 5-51, 2002.
[6]  K. Koskimies and E. Mäkinen, "Automatic Synthesis of State Machines from Trace Diagrams," *Software-Practice and Experience*, vol. 24, pp. 643-658, 1994.

[7]  E. Mäkinen and T. Systä, "MAS – An Interactive Synthesizer to Support Behavioral Modeling in UML," presented at ICSE 2001, Toronto, Canada, 2001.

[8]  R. Dssouli, S. Some, J. Vaucher, and A. Salah, "Service creation environment based on scenarios," *Information and Software Technology*, vol. 41, pp. 697-713, 1999.

[9]  S. Uchitel, J. Kramer, and J. Magee, "Synthesis of behavioral models from scenarios," *IEEE Transactions on Software Engineering*, vol. 29, pp. 99-115, 2003.

[10] J. S. Jon Whittle, "Generating statechart designs from scenarios.," presented at the 22nd International Conference on Software Engineering, 2000.

[11] D. Amyot, W. D. Cho, X. He, and Y. He, "Generating Scenarios from Use Case Map Specifications," presented at Third International Conference on Quality Software (QSIC'03), Dallas, November 2003.

[12] M. Glinz, "An integrated formal model of scenarios based on statecharts," presented at Proceedings of the~Fifth~European Software Engineering Conference, 1995.

[13] J. Ryser and M. Glinz, "Dependency Charts as a Means to Model Inter-Scenario

[14] Dependencies," presented at In G. Engels, A. Oberweis and A. Zündorf (eds.): Modellierung 2001. GI-Workshop, volume P-1, Bad Lippspringe, Germany, 2001.

[15] F. Bordeleau and J. P. Corriveau, "On the Importance of Inter-Scenario Relationships in Hierarchical State Machine Design," presented at In Proceedings of Fundamental Approaches to Software Engineering (FASE'2001), held as part of the Joint European Conferences on Theory and Practice of Software ETAPS'2001., Genova, Italy, 2001.

[16] J. W. J Araújo, D-K Kim, "Modeling and Composing Scenario-Based Requirements with Aspects " presented at the 12th IEEE International Requirements Engineering Conference (RE'04), Kyoto, Japan, 2004.

[17] I. Krüger, R. Grosu, P. Scholz, and M. Broy, "From MSCs to Statecharts," presented at Distributed and Parallel Embedded Systems, 1998.

[18] A. Salah, R. Dssouli, and G. Lapalme, "Compiling real-time scenarios into a Timed Automaton," presented at FORTE : International Conference on Formal Techniques for Networked and Distributed Systems, 2001.

# PN Standardisation: A Survey

L. Hillah[1], F. Kordon[1], L. Petrucci[2], and N. Trèves[3]

[1] Université P. & M. Curie - Paris 6, CNRS UMR 7606 - LIP6/MoVe
4, place Jussieu, F-75252 Paris CEDEX 05, France
Fabrice.Kordon@lip6.fr, Lom-Messan.Hillah@lip6.fr
[2] LIPN, CNRS UMR 7030, Université Paris XIII
99, avenue Jean-Baptiste Clément
F-93430 Villetaneuse, France
Laure.Petrucci@lipn.univ-paris13.fr
[3] Cedric, CNAM
292, rue St Martin
F-75141 Paris Cedex 03, France
treves@cnam.fr

**Abstract.** Petri Nets formalism requires standardisation to facilitate
the work of researchers in this field and to enable the data exchange
between different Petri Nets tools through a common format. Following
this, a three-part International Standard (ISO/IEC 15909) has been developed. Part 1 is devoted to terms and definitions for Place/Transition
Nets and High-Level Petri Nets. It is now completed (published as a standard) but will include an addendum on Symmetric Nets. Part 2 aims at
providing a transfer format for High-level Petri Nets, called PNML, based
on XML. Work on part 3 which deals with extensions has not started yet.
In this paper the first two parts of the standard are presented. Then, to
support part 2, an implementation of PNML, through an API framework
to be integrated into Petri Net tools, is proposed. It allows for the translation of any Petri Net, designed by a given tool in a dedicated format,
into PNML.

## 1 The Challenge of PN Standardisation

Petri Nets [4,8,26,28] are a mathematically defined formalism and may thus
be used to provide unambiguous specifications and descriptions of applications.
They are especially dedicated to specify and design discrete event systems and
this technique is particularly suited to parallel and distributed systems development as it supports concurrency. The technique allows for specification of
systems at a level which is independent of the implementation choices (i.e., by
software, hardware — electronic and/or mechanical — or humans, or a combination of these) and has been widely used to describe telecommunication systems,
protocols, microprocessor architectures,... since their invention in 1962. They
also constitute an executable technique, allowing specification prototypes to be
developed to test ideas at the earliest and cheapest opportunity. Specifications
written in the technique may be subject to analysis methods to prove properties about the specifications, before implementation commences, thus saving on

E. Najm et al. (Eds.): FORTE 2006, LNCS 4229, pp. 307–322, 2006.
© IFIP International Federation for Information Processing 2006

testing and maintenance time and providing a high confidence in the quality of the product to be developed. However these analysis methods are efficient only if they are supported by tools: for example, CPN-AMI [25], GreatSPN [9], PEP [13], CPNtool [22], automate the analysis process.

A problem with Petri nets is the explosion of the huge number of elements when described in their graphical form, for specification of complex systems. High-level Petri Nets [17] were developed to overcome this problem by introducing higher-level concepts, such as the use of complex structured data carried by tokens, and using algebraic expressions to annotate net elements. The use of high-level concepts within this Petri net framework is analogous to the use of those in high-level programming languages (as opposed to assembly languages). In the Petri nets community the term High-level net is generally used to refer to nets using such concepts.

Two of the early forms of high-level nets are Predicate-Transition Nets [12] and Coloured Petri Nets [16], first introduced in 1979 and further developed during the 1980s. Most of nowadays high-level nets build on these. They also use some of the notions developed for Algebraic Petri Nets [29], first introduced in the mid-1980s.

Furthermore, there are many different variants of Petri nets. Extensions of the technique, including time, stochastic features, capacities, and hierarchies as well as special Petri net types exist in the literature (see [2,8]...).

Standardisation of the technique has been seen as an opportunity to obtain a better organisation of the work in the Petri Net community. It has several issues:

- to enable the stakeholder — researchers, as well as engineers using Petri nets — to use the same terminology;
- to develop future extensions on a stable common basis, e.g., P/T nets or High-level nets;
- to provide a reference implementation that will facilitate the data exchange between different Petri nets tools through a common format.

The purpose of this paper is to present the PN standard, referenced under ISO/IEC 15909, as well as related work. First, the standard, which is organised in three different parts, is described. Then the current status of the work is given, followed by an implementation which is expected to prove very useful for the PN community.

## 2    The Structure of the Standard

The PN standard has been designed into three independent parts in order to enable flexibility of the standardisation process.

Part 1 [15] provides the mathematical definitions of High-level Petri Nets, called the semantic model, the graphical form of the technique, known as High-level Petri Net Graphs (HLPNGs), and its mapping to the semantic model. Part 1 also introduces some common notational conventions for HLPNGs.

Part 2 [18] [19] of this international standard defines a transfer format in order to support the exchange of High-level Petri Nets among different tools. This format is called the Petri Net Markup Language (PNML). Since there are many different versions of Petri nets in addition to High-level Petri Nets, this standard defines the core concepts of all Petri Net types along with an XML syntax, which can be used for exchanging any kind of Petri Net. Based on this PNML core model, part 2 also aims at defining the transfer syntax for the two versions of Petri Nets that are already defined in part 1 of this International Standard, Place/Transition Nets and High-level Petri Nets.

An addendum to Part 1 [20] of this standard introduces Symmetric Nets, formerly known as Well-Formed nets [6], as a subclass of High-level Petri Nets, which uses a restricted set of algebraic operators and allows for good analysis possibilities.

Part 3 is devoted to the standardisation of Petri nets extensions, including hierarchies, time and stochastic features. These extensions will be built upon extensions of the core model. They require a stable version of the core model to be available. This is not the current situation at this stage. Hence, only parts 1 and 2 are presented below.

The standardisation process is quite long and relatively complex. A standard must be built in order to be stable enough to be used by the people involved. It is developed within a schedule which should not exceed three years and is subject to revision every five years. More information on the rules can be found at [10].

Part 1 obtained the status of International Standard in december 2004. The addendum has been proposed by France and has currently the level of Working Draft (stage 20.60 in the ISO nomenclature).

At this level, the possibility is offered to the community to contribute. When the standard has reached the step forward, the Committee Draft level, it gains restricted aceess, with rights reserved to ISO experts only.

Part 2 has today the same status as the addendum.

Work on part 3 has not started yet, as it requires a stable version of the PNML core model to be available. As a consequence, the work on this part will start as soon as PNML is standardised.

## 2.1   Part 1

The first part of ISO/IEC 15909 was published as an International Standard (IS) in december 2004. It provides a comprehensive documentation of the terminology, the semantical model and the graphical notations for High-level Petri nets. It also describes different conformance levels. Finally, a tutorial example given in annex illustrates the different concepts in the standard.

A *glossary* introduces the different terms to be used in the Petri net context. They thus have a precise meaning, which is explained in natural language in the glossary and further detailled later using mathematical notations. The document is thus self-contained and avoids any ambiguity.

The *semantic model for High-level Petri nets* is defined, using precise mathematical notations. All basic elements required to work with High-level Petri nets are thus introduced: *high-level Petri net*, *marking*, *enabling* of transition modes, and *transition rule*.

These mathematically defined concepts are then reintroduced using natural language and explanations, and related to the *graphical notations* which are more commonly used in practice. Hence, the graphics representing the nets are defined.

This graphical presentation is further formalised as a *High-level Petri Net Graph*. It also has a semantics. It can be viewed as a graph oriented perspective for the high-level Petri net semantic model.

An important issue in standards design is the conformance level. Indeed, other work or tools can be compliant with the standard as a whole, or just part of it. This latter case may be sufficient for some particular purposes. Different conformance levels are thus defined, both for Petri nets and High-level Petri nets, depending on whether the graphical notation is taken into account.

Extensive mathematical notations are defined as normative in an annex. Another normative annex defines net classes. Up to now it only comprises *Place/Transitions nets* (i.e. Petri nets). Another class definition for *Symmetric nets* (formerly known as Well-Formed nets) is currently in the process of being an addendum to part 1 of the standard.

## 2.2    Part 2

The objective of part 2 is to define an interchange format for Petri nets called PNML (Petri Net Markup Language) [3]. This interchange format relies on XML technology.

However, designing an interchange format in the context of this standard is a difficult task since part 3 will introduce more Petri net types. It is obvious that an exchange format only suitable for the Petri net types defined in part 1 is not appropriate. This problem was already outlined in a preliminary study in 2000 that was classifying tools according to the type of supported Petri nets [1].

Moreover, tools usually introduce small variations in Petri nets and create their own "dialect". These variations are mainly due to syntactical aspects, to some graphical facilities or the way "actions" are added to the specifications. Actions are a way to provide help to the system designer, for example by making available instructions to ease animation of the specification, or add breakpoints.

So, to cope with all these goals, PNML must be able to:

1. allow to introduce smoothly new information associated with new Petri nets types or, by restriction, allow to hide some information from an inherited Petri net class.
2. support data aside of the standard, to let tools supporting non-standard extensions of another tool be able to handle it.

We provide hereafter some details about these two points. The next section will provide information about the way we handle them appropriately in the standard by using model engineering techniques implemented using EMF [11] technology from Eclipse.

*Handling a hierarchy of Petri net types.* Our first problem is related to the adjunction of new Petri net types in part 3 of the standard. Let us consider the small hierarchy expressed in figure 1. *P/T nets* are the root class since they only define the basics of Petri nets. Then, they can be extended to *Symmetric nets* proposed to be an addendum to part 1 [20]. Since Symmetric nets are a restriction on the color functions and types allowed in a *High-level net*, there is another trivial relation to them.

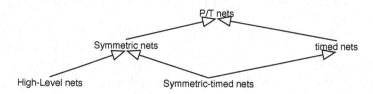

**Fig. 1.** Example of Petri net types hierarchy

Let us now consider another set of features in Petri nets: time management. So, *timed nets* can be derived from P/T nets by adding the time information to transitions as in [2]. We can also consider that *Symmetric-timed nets* inherit from both timed nets and symmetric nets.

The interchange standard must be flexible enough so as to allow any conversion from one of these representations to any other one without loosing information when the tools do handle them. It is crucial that the standard is able to handle a hierarchy of Petri net types.

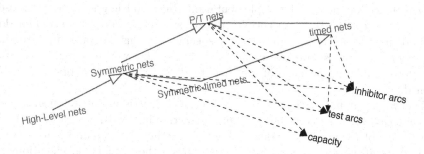

**Fig. 2.** Connections of the Petri net hierarchy to "local variations"

*Handling small variations in Petri net types.* Our second problem is to deal with local variations within a Petri net type such as inhibitor arcs, capacity in places or any other tool specific information (such as graphical specificities). This is illustrated in figure 2. We consider there variations such as inhibitor and test arcs, as well as capacity places. Such variations can be operated for several types of Petri nets. In our figure, we consider they are all relevant for Symmetric nets and for P/T nets. Only inhibitor and test arcs are also considered for timed nets.

Once again, the standard must be able to cope with such variations at various levels in the Petri net types hierarchy. It is important to normalize as many variations as possible to have them compatible all over the Petri net hierarchy.

# 3    Current Implementation of Part 2

The second part of the standard defines a universal transfer format (PNML) for exchanging Petri net models among Petri net tools. Hence, its primary purpose is to enable *interoperability*.

In this section, we first of all highlight how PNML design is being carried out through the specification work on the standard. Then, we introduce the incentives for the first implementation of a translation software framework to back the standard, using model engineering techniques.

## 3.1    PNML Design

The adopted methodology to design PNML is structured in two main steps:

1. the *abstract syntax* definition through Petri net types definition with meta-models;
2. the *concrete syntax* definition by mapping the abstract syntax onto PNML schema.

During the first step, main Petri net types are defined using *metamodeling techniques*. It means that we describe the concepts and rules structuring these types and their meaning, at a high level of abstraction, independently from any technological choice for their future implementation. Metamodeling is always purpose- or business-oriented. It is an activity during which experts of a particular domain define the precise semantics of the specific concerns they are interested in. For example, business process modelers might design a workflow metamodel for a supply chain, the purpose of which is to discover where synergies could be gained.

Following our motivations stated in section 2.2, it is important, using such techniques, to reach a sufficient level of abstraction in PNML design. Indeed, we should be able, when further developing the standard (Part 3 and maintenance updates of all parts), to easily refine and extend the primary specifications to define new types or variants of Petri nets. Therefore, it would be useless to fall at first in a too low level of specifications, from which no valuable abstraction could be made to improve the standard.

Three main Petri net types are defined. They are described using the Unified Modeling Language (UML) class diagrams. They are:

1. The *Core model*. It is the most fundamental one, depicted by fig. 3. Core concepts of Petri nets can be found in this basic type: nodes, connectors, basic labels (e.g., names) and graphical information associated with these objects. It provides the foundation for further definition of new Petri net types.

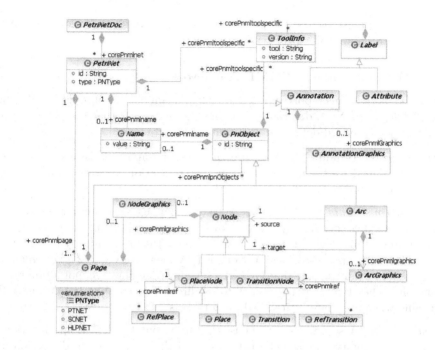

**Fig. 3.** PNML Core model

2. *P/T Systems metamodel.* It essentially defines new labels for this type of Petri nets and relies on the Core model for the central concepts. It is thus built upon extensions of the Core model.

3. *High-level Petri Nets metamodel.* Its design is in progress. New labels and high-level functions are being defined, while relying on the concepts provided by the Core model and P/T Systems type. As a consequence, it is also built on extensions of P/T Systems.

An important aspect of this first stage is to state semantic constraints on the metamodels. This may be achieved using the Object Constraint Language (OCL) [24]. For instance, in P/T Systems, two connected nodes must not be of the same kind (i.e., no place-place or transition-transition arc is permitted).

During the second step, PNML schema is defined to match the specifications carried out by the metamodels. Technical details set apart, each relevant element of the metamodels is mapped onto a PNML tag.

PNML schema technology is currently *RELAX NG*-based, which is "being developed as an International Standard ISO/IEC 19757-2" [7]. RELAX-NG is XML schema-like, more flexible and maintenance-friendly for the standard designers than XML schema. However, coming to High-level Petri Nets type, using this technology to directly define a notation to express high-level labels and functions does not seem appropriate. Consequently, MathML [31] is being investigated since it seems to offer the complete set of annotations that could be used to define high-level labels and functions. We are taking a particular care in extracting the most accurate subset of MathML features since it allows for great flexibility and powerful expressivity.

## 3.2   The First Impact: PNML Framework

From the motivations reported in section 2.2 and emphasized through the design methodology of PNML described in section 3.1, it is clear that the *extensibility* issue for the standard definition is of central importance.

**Motivations.** In addition, there are three other important issues we should cope with that drive the implementation of a translation software framework to support the standard.

*Semantic constraints.* The Petri Net Markup Language should carry the syntax of Petri net types specified by the standard. However, capturing the semantics is also an important issue. Moreover, how to ensure that it is enforced? Semantic constraints are expressed in the metamodels by means of OCL [24] statements. But it is important to note that OCL is a specification language, not a programming one. Therefore, it is not meant to be directly executable. It takes its full meaning when associated with UML annotations.

*Compatibility.* A second important issue pointed out by PNML specifications is the compatibility among Petri net types and their variants (cf. discussion in section 2.2 related to Petri net types hierarchy). Since all variants of the main types may not be specified by the standard, how to continuously ensure the interoperability and thus the exchange of Petri net models ?

Another related issue is the compatibility between PNML successive versions. For example, at least a top-level *Page* is mandatory in the current version under development, unlike the previous one.

*Automation and integration in Petri nets tools.* Since PNML is XML-based, it is error-prone to manual editing. Therefore, it obviously needs an application to perform this task.

To ensure that 1) all issues we pointed out are equally dealt with, and 2) to favor an up-to-date compatibility with the standard along with 3) an easy integration of its implementation into Petri net tools, we have developed a model-based translation framework to back the standard.

In the following, we describe this framework, called *PNML Framework*, and its use.

## 4   PNML Framework

To make the standard applicable and provide a reference implementation to Petri net tools developers, we have developed PNML Framework. Its first release was published in March 2006 [21].

In this section, we first present this tool and the benefits it offers to tools developers. Then we describe its features and give an overview of its use. Eventually we conclude by sketching further work. Open issues are discussed in section 5.

## 4.1   Goals of PNML Framework

The primary aim is to provide efficient and standard compliant import and export features of PNML models for Petri net tools. Figure 4 illustrates how PNML Framework could make the standard interoperability goal achievable. It shows two tools, *A* and *B*, exchanging a Petri net model via the standard transfer format, using the framework. More details about the operations involved are given in sections 4.2 and 4.3. PNML Framework is designed using model engineering techniques and, more precisely, EMF (Eclipse Modeling Framework) [5] technology.

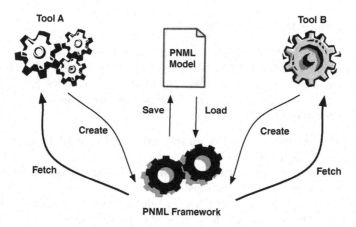

**Fig. 4.** Interoperability using PNML Framework

PNML Framework is a generated set of comprehensive and easy to use tailored API to import and export Petri net models designed according to the standard specifications. It is intended to be used as a library, therefore it can be easily integrated into Petri net tools. Tools developers are considered as the primary users of PNML Framework.

Thanks to this framework, tools developers would rather focus on their applications core development instead of coping with how to stay up-to-date and compliant with the standard. Furthermore, they would not have to deal with ensuring continuous compatibility with other tools and many Petri net types and variants.

Moreover, PNML Framework's flexibility enables them to export and import appropriate elements of Petri net models, according to their needs. For example, after having loaded (this term is explained in the following sections) a high-level net into the framework, one can only fetch the P/T net associated structure.

*How is it generated?* The API is generated from the standard metamodels using EMF's tools.

First, metamodels from the standard are implemented in EMF's ecore modeling language [5]. In its modeling approach, EMF can be seen as an optimized implementation of OMG's Essential Meta Object Facility (EMOF) [23] specification but with some differences, due to the experience gained from at least five years of development and wide use.

After having designed the metamodels using ecore, code is then generated so as to enable manipulation of model instances of these metamodels. To meet PNML specific requirements we have extended the Java Emitter Templates [27] code generation tool integrated in EMF. Consequently, the generated code is completely tailored to PNML. PNML Framework is thus extensible to include any Petri net type since its implementation is model-driven and follows the requirements expressed in the previous sections.

## 4.2   Features of PNML Framework

The design of PNML Framework is model-driven. It is supported by EMF, which is a mature model-driven application development framework. It implements Petri net types metamodels defined in the standard. It handles PNML models which are instances of these metamodels. From the framework's point of view the representation of a PNML model is twofold:

- it is a Petri net model which is an instance of a Petri net type metamodel; in that case it is handled in memory;
- it is a Petri net model written in PNML (XML-based) syntax in a PNML document. In that case it is an instance of PNML schema. A PNML document can contain one or more PNML models. PNML schema is the RELAX NG-based XML schema which is mapped onto Petri net types metamodels. It describes the concrete syntax of PNML models.

As a benefit of using model engineering techniques, PNML Framework offers two well-defined principal features in the context of PNML models:

- **export**: PNML models are *created* as instances of Petri net types metamodels and *saved* in PNML syntax;
- **import**: PNML models are *loaded* from PNML documents and created as instances of Petri net types metamodels in the framework. Their elements are *fetched* by the framework's user (tool developer).

These features are offered through the API which is structured in four sections:

1. **Create.** This section entitles tools developers to translate user-defined Petri net models represented in their proprietary format into PNML models as instances of Petri net types metamodels.
2. **Save.** It is used to save created PNML models into PNML syntax in PNML documents. Tools developers are offered a single method in this section to trigger that operation.
3. **Load.** PNML models are read by parsing PNML documents and loaded into the framework by using the *Create* section. Here again, a single method is provided in this section to perform the transfer.
4. **Fetch.** It is used to retrieve elements of PNML models that have been loaded.

In addition to these features, we have implemented rules to enforce semantic constraints on PNML metamodels that are expressed by means of OCL [24] statements in the standard. Therefore, users should not have to cope with how to integrate these constraints since the framework natively implements them.

### 4.3   Using PNML Framework

Figure 5 describes typical interactions between a tool developer's application core program and PNML Framework. In this figure, the four sections of the API label the interactions. *My model* represents a Petri net model in a proprietary format. *My Program* is the tool developer's core program which drives the model translation from the proprietary format into PNML syntax. It uses PNML Framework as a library to perform this task.

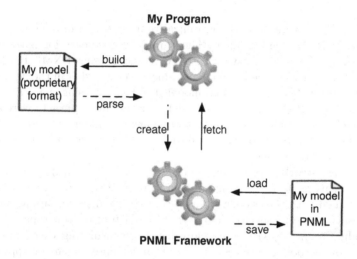

**Fig. 5.** Overview of tools developers' use of PNML Framework

To export a Petri net model represented in a proprietary format or handled in any application into PNML, a tool developer may first be entitled to *parse* it. Then, using the predefined *create* API, the corresponding PNML model can be created in the framework. Eventually the model will be *saved* in PNML syntax.

To import a Petri net model represented in PNML syntax (*My model in PNML* in fig. 5), the framework first *loads* that model. Then, using the predefined *fetch* API, tools developers can retrieve its elements and *build* the corresponding model represented in their proprietary formats or perform another task.

Let us show an example of a P/T model exchanged between a proprietary format and PNML, using PNML Framework. In this example, we focus on the export feature from the proprietary format into PNML. That format, called CAMI, is used in our CASE environment, CPN-AMI [25]. We have developed an application, named PNML Converter, which uses PNML Framework *create* and *save* API to perform the export.

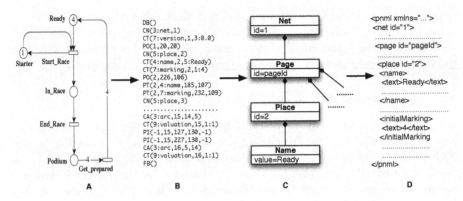

**Fig. 6.** An example of model transformation from CAMI to PNML

In fig. 6, P/T model $A$ is the graphical representation of a Petri net model created in CPN-AMI environment. The graphical representation is transformed into model $B$, the syntax of which is CAMI. Then using PNML Framework's *create* API, it is transformed into a model instance (called $C$ in the figure) of the standard-defined P/T Systems metamodel [18]. Finally, using the *save* API, it is transformed into PNML syntax, as model $D$. Subsequently, there were actually three model transformations. The first two ones are under the responsibility of the tool designer, the role of whom we took in this example. PNML Framework is in charge of the last one.

PNML Framework is packaged as a Java library. It provides command-line invocation features to ease its integration in tools. For instance, once *My Program* packaged with the framework as a complete translation application, that application becomes a service for the considered tool. It will then be invoked by providing a simple API to develop driver encapsulating users' invocations caught through tools interfaces. We have implemented such an approach for CPN-AMI [25] and it was successful.

### 4.4   Current Work

Presently, P/T Systems are supported by the framework. The core model is of course implemented. But since we do not consider it is a concrete Petri net type suitable for exchange among Petri nets experts, we do not offer the possibility to export and import it explicitly by the framework. Indeed, as explained before, the core model is intended to set a strong basis for the definitions of concrete Petri net types.

In further developments of this framework, we are implementing Symmetric Nets. Symmetric Nets are annotated with higher-level labels and functions. Those labels are being defined using MathML, as stated in section 3.1. In the next section we discuss related issues to this work.

We are also planning to develop an advanced version of PNML Framework, which will generate specific APIs for local variations on Petri net types, not specified by the standard. This will help tools developers with very specific needs to exchange their models, provided that they share the newly generated APIs. The normal version of the framework which is fully standard compliant will simply discard these particular local variations. The use of this advanced version requires deep knowledge of metamodeling and code generation techniques using EMF's powerful features.

## 5  Open Issues for Future Work

As mentionned in the previous section, high-level labels and functions are defined using MathML. However, since MathML is very expressive, there are often different equivalent ways to define the same function. Consequently, it is prone to break the interoperability and compatibility objectives through the non-unification of the semantics, if MathML is used "as is". Moreover, in exchanging automatically processed PNML higher-level models, we cannot expect a meaningful interoperability to take place. Let us recall that metamodels should always carry as much as possible a precise semantics for a specific purpose. To make high-level labels and functions use both unambiguous and fully understandable, we should define the metamodel that carries their semantics for higher-levels of Petri nets (Symmetric Nets, High-level Petri Nets). This is of utmost importance since part 3 of the standard will introduce new types of Petri nets.

Our approach to tackle this issue relies on an unambiguous schema of a subset of predefined labels and functions expressed in MathML to be defined in the standard. This schema would be mapped as a concrete syntax to the corresponding high-level annotations metamodel for higher-level Petri nets. This schema corresponds to a normalised way to define abstract syntax trees for complex labels (independent from any technology implementing the syntax). This approach is consistent with the methodology adopted for the definition of the second part of the standard, described in section 3.1. To ensure interoperability and compliance with the standard, tools developers must enforce the use of this predefined subset. Therefore we propose to ease the application of this requirement by integrating its implementation in a future version of PNML Framework.

It is of interest to experiment first this strategy to Symmetric Nets: this type of Petri nets only allows for a restricted set of algebraic operators and no user-defined function.

High-level Petri nets allow for a larger set of algebraic operators than Symmetric Nets, but the user can also define his/her own functions. This last point may lead to ambiguous representation of these functions if no normalised action (such as strict structuration of MathML expressions) is considered. This is also a challenge, when we consider that part 3 of the standard will introduce new types of Petri nets.

## 6  Conclusion

A survey of the standardisation work on Petri nets, known as ISO/IEC-15909, is presented in this paper. The standard is structured into three parts.

Part 1 is now an International Standard. Part 2 is currently under development. It provides the abstract definitions of significant Petri net types and their concrete syntax. This syntax is intended to be a universal transfer format to enable interoperability among Petri net tools. A wide adoption of the standard among Petri net experts can thus be reached. It is called Petri Net Markup Language (PNML). Part 3 will rely on definitions carried out by part 2. It will define new types and variants of Petri nets. When a stable version of part 2 is reached, the work on part 3 will start.

We are also experimenting an implementation of part 2 in PNML Framework. PNML Framework primary purpose is to make the standard applicable. Therefore it puts the interoperability goal into action. It offers Petri nets tools a flexible way to remain up-to-date and comply with the standard while dealing with extensibility, compatibility and semantic issues. To cope with such issues, we are using model engineering techniques to sustain PNML Framework development. In [14], we set the rationale for this approach.

The first release of PNML Framework was published in March 2006 [21]. It is implemented in Java, to achieve the cross-platform objective expressed in PNML earliest requirements. We provided in this release a tool developer's guide and a tutorial. We also provided an application example of conversion using GraphViz [30] *dot* format, to ease the full understanding of PNML Framework's capabilities:

- efficient model-driven import and export tool for PNML models,
- standalone execution (outside Eclipse);
- easy integration in Petri net tools.

We are currently enhancing PNML Framework with a new type defined in the standard: Symmetric Nets. This will assess the consistency of our approach in PNML Framework design. Symmetric Nets are a first step towards the support of High-level Petri Nets in the standard. We also take into account the Petri net community feedback.

It is of interest to set up a prototype implementation project from part 2 of the standard in PNML Framework. It contributes to establish a meaningful assessment of the standard implementation and use in the context of tools design.

## Acknowledgements

We would like to thank ISO/IEC 15909 editors, especially Jonathan Billington and Ekkart Kindler, for the insightful discussions that helped us enhancing this paper.

## References

1. R. Bastide, D. Buchs, M. Buffo, and F. Kordon adn O. Sy. characteristics of currently used petri nets. Technical report, Univ. P. & M. Curie, available at http://www-src.lip6.fr/homepages/Fabrice.Kordon/PN_STD_WWW/Qresult.html, 2000.
2. Bernard Berthomieu and Michel Diaz. Modeling and verification of time dependent systems using time petri nets. *IEEE Trans. Software Eng.*, 17(3):259–273, 1991.

3. J. Billington, S. Christensen, K. van Hee, E. Kindler, O. Kummer, L. Petrucci, R. Post, C. Stehno, and M. Weber. The Petri Net Markup Language: Concepts, technology and tools. In *Proc. 24th Int. Conf. Application and Theory of Petri Nets (ICATPN'2003), Eindhoven, The Netherlands, June 2003*, volume 2679 of *Lecture Notes in Computer Science*, pages 483–505. Springer, 2003.

4. Brauer, W., Reisig, W., and Rozenberg, G., editors. *Petri Nets: Central Models and Their Properties.*, volume 254. Springer-Verlag Lecture Notes in Computer Science: Advances in Petri Nets 1986, Part I, Proceedings of an Advanced Course, Bad Honnef, September 1986, 1987.

5. F. Budinsky, D. Steinberg, E. Merks, R. Ellersick, and T.J. Grose. *Eclipse Modeling Framework.* The Eclipse Series. Addison-Wesley Professional, August 2003.

6. G. Chiola, C. Dutheillet, G. Franceschinis, and S. Haddad. On Well-Formed Coloured Nets and their symbolic reachability graph. In G. Rozenberg and K. Jensen, editors, *LNCS : High Level Petri Nets. Theory and Application.* Springer Verlag, June 1991.

7. J. Clark. *RELAX NG Home Page.* OASIS, http://www.relaxng.org/, 2003.

8. M. Diaz. *Vérification et mise en oeuvre des réseaux de Petri.* Hermes Sciences - Lavoisier, 2003.

9. GreatSPN: GRaphical Editor, Analyzer for Timed, and Stochastic Petri Nets. url: http://www.di.unito.it/~greatspn/.

10. International Organization for Standardization. *International harmonized stage codes.* ISO, http://www.iso.org/iso/en/widepages/stagetable.html#95.

11. Eclipse Foundation. *Eclipse Modeling Framework.* http://www.eclipse.org/emf/.

12. H. J. Genrich. Predicate/transition nets. In Brauer, W., Reisig, W., and Rozenberg, G., editors, *Lecture Notes in Computer Science: Petri Nets: Central Models and Their Properties, Advances in Petri Nets 1986, Part I, Proceedings of an Advanced Course, Bad Honnef, September 1986*, volume 254, pages 207–247. Springer-Verlag, 1987. NewsletterInfo: 27.

13. Parallel Systems Group. *Programming Environment based on Petri Nets.* University of Oldenburg, http://theoretica.informatik.uni-oldenburg.de/~pep/.

14. L. Hillah, F.Kordon, L. Petrucci, and N. Trèves. Model engineering on petri nets for iso/iec 15909-2: Api framework for petri net types metamodels. *Petri Net Newsletter*, (69):22–40, October 2005.

15. ISO/IEC. Software and Systems Engineering - High-level Petri Nets, Part 1: Concepts, Definitions and Graphical Notation, International Standard ISO/IEC 15909, December 2004.

16. K. Jensen. Coloured petri nets - basic concepts, analysis methods and practical use, vol. 3: Practical use. *EATCS Monographs on Theoretical Computer Science*, 1997.

17. Jensen, K. and Rozenberg, G., editors. *High-Level Petri Nets.* Berlin, Germany: Springer-Verlag, 1991. NewsletterInfo: 39.

18. E. Kindler. Software and Systems Engineering - High-level Petri Nets. Part2: Transfert Format. Working Draft for the International Standard ISO/IEC 15909 Part 2 - Version 0.9.0, June 2005.

19. E. Kindler. The petri net markup language and iso/iec 15909-2: Concepts, status, and future directions. In *Entwurf komplexer Automatisierungssysteme*, To appear.

20. F. Kordon and L. Petrucci. Proposal for an addendum to ISO/IEC 15909-1, document reference MAL-12. NWI For the Malaga Meeting, November 2004.

21. Modeling and Verification Department. *PNML Framework.* LIP6, http://www.lip6.fr/pnml.

22. University of Aarhus. *Computer Tool for Coloured Petri Nets - CPNTool.* http://wiki.daimi.au.dk/cpntools/cpntools.wiki.
23. OMG. *MetaObjectFacility 2.0 Core Specification, document no:omg/2003-10-04.* OMG, October 2003.
24. OMG. *OCL 2.0 Specification - Version 2.0 ptc/2005-06-06.* OMG, June 2005.
25. The CPN-AMI Home page. url : http://www.lip6.fr/cpn-ami.
26. J. Peterson. *Petri Net Theory and the Modeling of Systems.* Englewood Cliffs, New Jersey: Prentice Hall, Inc., 1981.
27. Remko Popma. *Introduction to JET.* Azzurri Ltd., http://eclipse.org/emf/docs.php?doc=tutorials/jet1/jet_tutorial1.html, 2005.
28. W. Reisig. *Petri Nets.*, volume 4. Springer-Verlag EATCS Monographs on Theoretical Computer Science, original edition, 1985. NewsletterInfo: 19 translation of the German: "W. Reisig, Petrinetze. (1982)".
29. W. Reisig. Petri nets and algebraic specifications. *Theoretical Computer Science*, 80:1–34, 1991. NewsletterInfo: 38,39.
30. AT&T Research. *GraphViz.* http://www.graphviz.org/.
31. W3C. *MathML 2.0, W3C Math Home.* W3C, http://www.w3.org/Math/.

# Resource Allocation Systems: Some Complexity Results on the S$^4$PR Class

Juan-Pablo López-Grao[1] and José-Manuel Colom[2]

[1] Dpt. of Computer Science and Systems Engineering (DIIS)
[2] Aragonese Engineering Research Institute (I3A)
University of Zaragoza, Spain
{jpablo, jm}@unizar.es

**Abstract.** In recent times, Petri nets have consolidated as a powerful formalism for the analysis and treatment of deadlocks in Resource Allocation Systems (RAS). In particular, the methodological framework yielded by the S$^4$PR class has raised considerable interest on the grounds of a well-balanced compromise between modelling flexibility and the provision of sound and effective correction techniques. These are strengthened by the advantages of the abstraction process, which allows the effective application of these techniques to diverse application domains. Most of the works on this class focus on providing tools and algorithms for dealing with the so-called resource allocation problem. This paper takes a different approach to provide an insight into the inherent computational complexity of the problem, from the perspective of optimality in either prevention, avoidance or detection of deadlocks. In particular, we will prove that most of the problems involved fall within the category of NP or co-NP-complete problems.

## 1   Introduction

A Resource Allocation System (RAS) is, in rough words, a discrete event system in which a finite set of concurrent processes share a finite set of resources. This is strongly connected to the resource allocation problem, which consists in meeting the demand of resources by the set of processes, eventually accomplishing certain goals. From the qualitative standpoint, the objective is often dealing with the set of potential system deadlocks: the focus of this paper.

A RAS is in a deadlock state if a set of processes are indefinitely waiting for a set of resources that are already held by the same set of processes. Coffman defined in [1] four necessary conditions for the existence of a deadlock, but a general characterization remains elusive, leaving place for a wide family of works which study different subclasses of RAS, often providing solutions over abstract models that allow their application on different domains.

The strategies for handling deadlocks are categorized in three groups. Deadlock prevention techniques consist in constructing a system such that, by definition, no deadlock is reachable. Deadlock avoidance techniques ensure that a deadlock is not reachable by deciding on-line if a resource allocation request is granted or not, based on the current system state information (e.g., the banker's

E. Najm et al. (Eds.): FORTE 2006, LNCS 4229, pp. 323–338, 2006.
© IFIP International Federation for Information Processing 2006

algorithm [2]). Finally, deadlock detection techniques act 'a posteriori', allowing the deadlock situation to occur and subsequently resolve it.

Among formal models, Petri nets [3] has proven to be a fruitful tool for the modelling, analysis and synthesis of RAS ([4,5,6,7]). In particular, the $S^4PR$ class [8] ($S^3PGR^2$ in [7]) has attracted significant attention since it deals with a very general class of Sequential RAS (S-RAS, i.e., RAS in which the processes are sequential), while exist efficient characterizations for deadlock states, i.e. states from which a given transition cannot be fired anymore. Despite that most of those works stress the application on Flexible Manufacturing Systems, the fact that we employ a purely systemic approach enables applying this Petri net models, as well as their well-known analysis and synthesis techniques, to very different application domains, such as distributed systems or communication protocols.

The $S^4PR$ class is capable to model systems in which the processes are allowed to decide between alternative execution paths all along their execution, provided there are no internal iterations. Besides, several resources of several types can be reserved at the same time, and they can be acquired and released at any execution state. Note that we assume that the resources are used in a conservative way by every process (i.e. the resources are *serially reusable*).

This work investigates the computational complexity on providing optimal solutions for the problems of deadlock prevention, avoidance and detection for S-RAS supported by the $S^4PR$ class. Some previous works have successfully studied computational issues on S-RAS, although they differ from this both in the type of systems and the problems subject to analysis. In [2] the problem of deciding whether a resource allocation is safe is studied, and proved NP-complete for S-RAS with multi-resource requests and processes without routing decisions. In this model, resources that are freed in intermediary states are immediately required back. Additionally, some restrictions on this problem are presented, which are proved polynomial. In [9], it is proved that optimal deadlock avoidance is NP-complete for a subclass of S-RAS in which no alternative paths per process are allowed. Finally, in [10] the same problem is proven NP-complete for a class of S-RAS in which alternative paths are allowed, but only one resource type is used in each stage, which is again a subclass of our model.

In section 2, we provide a motivating example that hopefully will enlighten the scope of the $S^4PR$ class. The class is also formally introduced, along with some basic results that are used in section 3. Section 3 is divided in four parts. First, we introduce the computational complexity of characterizing non-liveness for a marked $S^4PR$ with an acceptable initial marking. Second, the results are extended to the case in which any arbitrary reachable marking is considered. This is strongly related to optimal deadlock prevention. Third, we state the computational complexity in determining the markings that are doomed to deadlock, which is the key to optimal deadlock avoidance and detection in this context. And four, the computational complexity in determining spurious markings is revealed, which severely affects the efficiency of structural techniques for this type of models. Finally, section 4 summarizes the conclusions of the paper.

## 2    The S⁴PR Class

### 2.1    A Motivating Example

Suppose we are considering the installment of an on-line, on-demand video streaming service business on the Internet. In order to provide a reasonably good service, certain Quality of Service (QoS) requirements must be formally established and satisfied, for every requested transmission. These QoS specs obviously depend on a wide range of parameters such as the client type, her/his maximum supported bandwidth, the format and resolution of the requested video, etc.

To provide the service, we own a pool of video servers. These video servers are connected to a mesh network of router nodes. Some of these nodes act as gateways to the Internet. We will assume that multicast video streams will disseminate from the gateways onwards, so as to not increase our internal traffic. Figure 1 depicts the system structure (on the left, the video servers; on the right, the gateways; in the middle, the intermediate routers).

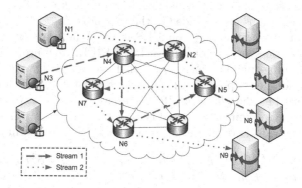

**Fig. 1.** Our video streaming system, simultaneously transmitting two video streams

A video stream is composed of a set of fixed-size packets that must be transmitted from the sender (video server) to the receiver (client). When a receiver requests a video stream to one of the servers, a virtual circuit is constructed. All the packets of the video stream will travel through the same virtual circuit. Besides, each node of the circuit assumes its own minimum resource requirements (CPU, storage, bandwidth) for processing and transmitting each packet of the stream. These requirements will be based on the QoS specs for the transmission.

Both (circuit and resource requirements) can be determined and established through a signaling protocol in a similar vein to RSVP [11,12]. In order to maximize our system productivity and reduce costs, however, we want to 'relax' the resource reservation strategy. Hence once a packet is effectively transmitted from a node to the next one, the required resources are freed, and must be reacquired for the next packet. Doing so, nodes can accept and manage a higher amount of concurrent streams minimizing resource idling. As a drawback, when the traffic is high and resources are overused, some jittering could appear since some packets could be idle in intermediate nodes, waiting for the release of some required resources. In the worst case, a circular wait for resources could appear, and the system would reach a deadlock.

Such a kind of systems can be effectively modellized and studied via the $S^4$PR class. Figure 2 models the system of figure 1. The different constructive elements in the model will be presented in the next subsection. In the example, the system has reached a deadlock. The existing analysis and synthesis techniques will allow us to handle deadlocks. In particular, we will be able to apply prevention (e.g. disallow a pre-established circuit if there might be a potential deadlock situation), avoidance (e.g. retain temporarily packets if they lead to deadlock situations) or detection and correction techniques (e.g. abort a video stream to free resources and unlock the system). In the following, we will study the computational complexity of the optimal approach for these three strategies.

## 2.2   Formal Definition of the Class

From now on, we assume the reader has some basic knowledge on Petri nets. Some useful definitions are provided in the appendix A.

As it was already pointed out, the $S^4$PR is a P/T net class aimed to the modelling, analysis and synthesis of S-RAS. In an $S^4$PR, each process is a strongly connected state machine in which no internal cycles are allowed throughout its execution. Besides, each process has an initial local state in which no resource is used, represented by the *idle place*. Resources are modelled as tokens within the *resource places*, and their usage by every process is conservative, which imposes restrictions on the form of the set of p-semiflows. In formal terms:

**Definition 1.** *[13] Let $I_\mathcal{N}$ be a finite set of indices. An $S^4PR$ is a connected generalized pure P/T net $\mathcal{N} = \langle P, T, C \rangle$ where:*

1. $P = P_0 \cup P_S \cup P_R$ *is a partition such that:*
   (a) *[idle places]* $P_0 = \bigcup_{i \in I_\mathcal{N}} \{p_{0_i}\}$.
   (b) *[process places]* $P_S = \bigcup_{i \in I_\mathcal{N}} P_{S_i}$, *where*
      $\forall i \in I_\mathcal{N}, P_{S_i} \neq \emptyset$, *and* $\forall i, j \in I_\mathcal{N}, i \neq j, P_{S_i} \cap P_{S_j} = \emptyset$.
   (c) *[resource places]* $P_R = \{r_1, r_2, r_3, ..., r_n\}, n > 0$.
2. $T = \bigcup_{i \in I_\mathcal{N}} T_i$, *where* $\forall i \in I_\mathcal{N}, T_i \neq \emptyset$, *and* $\forall i, j \in I_\mathcal{N}, i \neq j, T_i \cap T_j = \emptyset$.
3. *For each $i \in I_\mathcal{N}$ the subnet generated by $\{p_{0_i}\} \cup P_{S_i}, T_i$ is a strongly connected state machine such that every cycle contains $p_{0_i}$.*
4. *For each $r \in P_R$ there exists a unique minimal p-semiflow $Y_r \in \mathbb{N}^{|P|}$ such that $\{r\} = \|Y_r\| \cap P_R, P_0 \cap \|Y_r\| = \emptyset, P_S \cap \|Y_r\| \neq \emptyset$, and $Y_r[r] = 1$.*
5. $P_S = \bigcup_{r \in P_R} (\|Y_r\| \setminus \{r\})$.

Meanwhile, we call *process net* [13] to the subnet generated by $\{p_{0_i}\} \cup P_{S_i} \cup P_{R_i}$ and $T_i$, where $i \in I_\mathcal{N}$ and $P_{R_i} = \{r \in P_R \mid (\|Y_r\| \cap P_{S_i} \neq \emptyset)\}$.

In the case of figures 1 and 2, each video stream is modelled as a concurrent sequential process. Resources associated to each node Ni are modellized using the places labelled R-Ni. Note that there could be several resource places per router

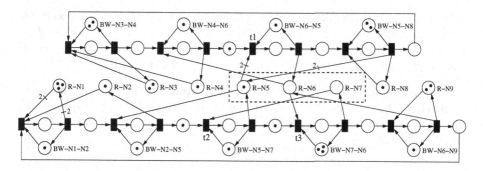

**Fig. 2.** A marked $S^4PR$ which models the system in figure 1. The system is deadlocked.

(one per each resource type, be it physical, e.g. available storage space or CPU slots, or logical, e.g. maximum number of simultaneous packets). Equivalently, there is a resource place per each node interconnection, modelling the available bandwidth and labelled BW-Ni-Nj.

All these resources can be shared among both concurrent processes. In this case, the local resources of the nodes N5 and N6 (held by resource places R-N5 and R-N6) are shared among both video streams. The resources are requested, used and freed when a packet (a token in the process net) is visiting the corresponding node. Finally, the idle places limit the number of potentially concurrent packets per video stream (it is assumed that this number is finite). Speaking in general terms, it is worth noting here that idle places can also be seen as special resource places, and then interpreted as the maximum number of process instances in concurrent execution for each process type.

**Definition 2.** *[13] Let $\mathcal{N} = \langle P_0 \cup P_S \cup P_R, T, C \rangle$ be an $S^4PR$. An initial marking $m_0$ is acceptable for $\mathcal{N}$ iff $||m_0|| = P_0 \cup P_R$ and $\forall p \in P_S, r \in P_R . m_0[r] \geq Y_r[p]$.*

Figure 4 depicts a marked $S^4PR$ with an acceptable initial marking. The marking shown in figure 2 is *not* an acceptable initial marking but, however, it *is reachable from* an acceptable initial marking, as the reader can check. This acceptable initial marking would correspond to the system state in which no video stream has begun to transmit yet (and hence every resource is available).

## 2.3 Non-liveness Characterization in the $S^4PR$ Class

During the paper, we will use the following definitions extensively. They will be used in several demonstrations and are basic for the non-liveness characterization that is stated in theorem 1. This well-known characterization will be the base for our first complexity result in section 3.

**Definition 3.** *[13] Let $\langle \mathcal{N}, m_0 \rangle$ be a marked $S^4PR$ with an acceptable initial marking, $\mathcal{N} = \langle P_0 \cup P_S \cup P_R, T, C \rangle$. Also, let $m \in RS(\mathcal{N}, m_0)$.*
*Then $t \in T$ is $m$-process-enabled iff $^\bullet t \cap P_S \neq \emptyset$ and $m[^\bullet t \cap P_S] > 0$. Otherwise, $t$ is $m$-process-disabled. Besides, $t$ is $m$-resource-enabled iff $\forall r \in {}^\bullet t \cap P_R, m[r] \geq Pre[r, t]$. Otherwise, $t$ is $m$-resource-disabled.*

**Theorem 1.** *[13] Let $\langle \mathcal{N}, m_0 \rangle$, $\mathcal{N} = \langle P, T, C \rangle$ be an $S^4PR$ with an acceptable initial marking. The system $\langle \mathcal{N}, m_0 \rangle$ is non-live iff exists a reachable marking $m \in RS(\mathcal{N}, m_0)$ such that the set $S_m \subseteq T$ of m-process-enabled transitions is non-empty and every transition in $S_m$ is m-resource-disabled.*

The system in figure 2 is non-live; indeed, it is a total deadlock. The reader can easily check that the set of $m$-process-enabled transitions is $\{t1, t2, t3\}$ and each one of those is $m$-resource-disabled: the resource places R-N5, R-N6 and R-N7 disallow their firing.

# 3    Complexity Results

In this paper, we will assume the reader is instructed on the basics of complexity theory [14] and particularly NP-completeness. Onwards, several problems will be proved either NP or co-NP-complete. All the problem reductions will be based on the well-known (general) satisfiability problem of boolean formulas in conjunctive normal form, commonly named SATISFIABILITY (SAT), which is NP-complete. A brief reminder is included in appendix B.

## 3.1    Non-liveness

The problem of optimal deadlock prevention requires determining whether a given system is non-live, in order to apply correction techniques to make the system live, such as those presented in [13]. Here we will devoted to the study of the complexity of the problem of non-liveness for a given acceptable initial marking. In particular, we will demonstrate that this problem is NP-complete. A couple of basic demonstrations are previously required, and hence will be introduced in the following. The studied problem is formally defined in this way:

*Problem 1.* **$S^4$PR-Non-Liveness ($S^4$PR-NL)**
*Given:* A marked $S^4$PR $\langle \mathcal{N}, m_0 \rangle$, being $m_0$ an acceptable initial marking.
*To decide:* Is $\langle \mathcal{N}, m_0 \rangle$ non-live?

**Proposition 1.** *Let $\langle \mathcal{N}, m_0 \rangle$, $\mathcal{N} = \langle P, T, C \rangle$, be a marked $S^4PR$ with an acceptable initial marking. Let $m$ be a reachable marking $m \in RS(\mathcal{N}, m_0)$. Then exists a firing sequence $\sigma$, $m_0[\sigma\rangle m$, such that there is no t-semiflow $X$ with $\sigma - X \geq 0$.*

*Proof.* Without loss of generality, let $X$ be a minimal t-semiflow such that $\sigma - X \geq 0$. Then we will prove that there exists a firing sequence $\sigma'$, $m_0[\sigma'\rangle m$, where $\sigma' - X \not\geq 0$, and $\sigma' = \sigma - k \cdot X$, with $k \in \mathbb{N} \setminus \{0\}$.

m is potentially reachable from $m_0$ with $\sigma'$ because of the net state equation:
$m = m_0 + C \cdot \sigma = m_0 + C \cdot (\sigma' + k \cdot X) = m_0 + C \cdot \sigma'$.

The sequence $\sigma'$ is also firable because a t-semiflow $X$ is a circuit of a state machine and the completion of X corresponds to the movement of a token in this state machine from the idle place throughout the circuit returning to the idle place. Taking into account that this token in the idle place does not use resources, while in the rest of the places of the circuit uses some resource, freezing this token in the idle place leaves a greater number of resources to fire the rest of transitions of $\sigma$. Therefore $\sigma'$ is also firable, reaching $m$.    □

**Lemma 1.** *Let* $\langle \mathcal{N}, m_0 \rangle$, $\mathcal{N} = \langle P, T, C \rangle$, *be a marked S$^4$PR with an acceptable initial marking, and let $m$ be a reachable marking from* $\langle \mathcal{N}, m_0 \rangle$, $m \in RS(\mathcal{N}, m_0)$. *Then exists a firing sequence $\sigma$ from $m_0$ to $m$, $m_0[\sigma\rangle m$, such that* $|\sigma| \leq K \cdot |T|$, *where* $K = \sum_{p \in P_0} m_0[p]$

*Proof.* By proposition 1, a firing sequence $\sigma_1$ exists, $m_0[\sigma_1\rangle m$, such that there is no t-semiflow $X$ with $\boldsymbol{\sigma_1} - X \geq \mathbf{0}$. Let us suppose that $|\sigma_1| > K \cdot |T|$. It is straightforward that there exists a transition $t \in T$ such that $t$ is fired at least $K + 1$ times in $\sigma_1$. Since the process subnets are conservative, and the process places are empty in $m_0$, for every reachable marking $m' \in RS(\mathcal{N}, m_0)$, $\sum_{p \in P_0 \cup P_S} m'[p] = K$.

This means that if we labelled each token in the process places with a unique identifier $i \in [1, K]$, at least one of them should visit twice the process place $p$, where $\{p\} = {}^\bullet t \cap (P_0 \cup P_S)$, i.e., the active process (the token) should travel through a circuit of the state machine. Since every circuit in a S$^4$PR induces a minimal t-semiflow ([8]) then exists a t-semiflow $X$, $\boldsymbol{\sigma_1} - X \geq \mathbf{0}$, contradicting the hypothesis.    □

The size of the firing sequence $\sigma$ in lemma 1 is polynomial in the size and population of the net. This will let us prove that S$^4$PR-NL is in NP.

**Theorem 2.** *S$^4$PR-NL is NP-easy.*

*Proof.* We will use the following problem for our demonstration:

*Problem 2.* **S$^4$PR-Bad-Marking (S$^4$PR-BM)**
*Given:* A marked S$^4$PR $\langle \mathcal{N}, m_0 \rangle$, being $m_0$ an acceptable initial marking, and a firing sequence $\sigma$ such that $(|\sigma| \leq K \cdot |T|)$, $(m_0[\sigma\rangle m)$ and $(m \neq m_0)$, where $K = \sum_{p \in P_0} m_0[p]$.
*To decide:* Does $\langle \mathcal{N}, m \rangle$ hold that every $m$-process-enabled transition is $m$-resource-disabled?

1. S$^4$PR-BM is in P. Given $\sigma$, $m$ can be easily computed using the net state equation. For every transition, $m$-process-enabledness and $m$-resource-disabledness can be checked in deterministic linear time in the size of $\mathcal{N}$.
2. Let $(\mathcal{N}, m_0, \sigma)$ be a valid input for S$^4$PR-BM, being $(\mathcal{N}, m_0)$ an input for S$^4$PR-NL. Since the length of $\sigma$ is polynomial in the size of the input, it is trivial to find two encodings $e_1(\mathcal{N}, m_0, \sigma)$ and $e_2(\mathcal{N}, m_0)$ such that $|e_1(\mathcal{N}, m_0, \sigma)| \leq c' \cdot |e_2(\mathcal{N}, m_0)|^c$, given $c, c'$.[1]
3. S$^4$PR-NL can be *verified* in deterministic polynomial time. By theorem 1, S$^4$PR-NL returns YES with input $(\mathcal{N}, m_0)$ iff exists a firing sequence $\sigma$, $m_0[\sigma\rangle m$ and $m \neq m_0$, such that every $m$-process-enabled transition is $m$-resource-disabled. In that case, by lemma 1, a firing sequence $\sigma$ can be found such that with $|\sigma| \leq K \cdot |T|$. Thus S$^4$PR-NL$(\mathcal{N}, m_0)$ returns YES iff exists $\sigma$ such that S$^4$PR-BM$(\mathcal{N}, m_0, \sigma)$ returns YES.    □

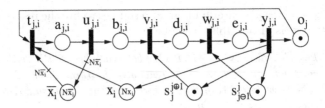

**Fig. 3.** SAT → S⁴PR-NL. Net $\mathcal{N}_i^j$ for each literal $x_i$ in $\mathcal{C}_j$.

Now we will devote to prove NP-hardness, reducing SAT to S⁴PR-NL. Let $\mathcal{F} = \mathcal{C}_1 \cdot \mathcal{C}_2 \cdot \ldots \cdot \mathcal{C}_{N_c}$ be a formula in conjunctive normal form, and let $X = \{x_1, \ldots x_k\}$ be the set of its variables. For every $x_i \in X$ let $N_{x_i}$ ($N_{\overline{x_i}}$) be the number of clauses of $\mathcal{F}$ in which the literal $x_i$ ($\overline{x_i}$) appears.

Also please note that, for every $j \in [1, N_c]$, we define the index $j \oplus 1$ as either $j + 1$ (iff $j < N_c$) or 1 (iff $j = N_c$). Similarly, we define the index $j \ominus 1$ as either $j - 1$ (iff $j > 1$) or $N_c$ (iff $j = 1$).

We will construct the net $\mathcal{N}_{\mathcal{F}}$ in the following compositional manner:

1. For every $x_i \in X$, $i \in [1, k]$, we add the place $x_i$ (in case $N_{x_i} > 0$) and the place $\overline{x_i}$ (in case $N_{\overline{x_i}} > 0$).
2. For every clause $\mathcal{C}_j$, $j \in [1, N_c]$, we add two places to $\mathcal{N}_{\mathcal{F}}$, called $o_j$ and $s_j^{j \oplus 1}$.
3. For every literal $x_i$ in $\mathcal{C}_j$, $i \in [1, k]$, $j \in [1, N_c]$, we add four places ($a_{j,i}$, $b_{j,i}$, $d_{j,i}$, $e_{j,i}$) and five transitions ($t_{j,i}$, $u_{j,i}$, $v_{j,i}$, $w_{j,i}$, $y_{j,i}$), and we connect them to the rest of the net as depicted in figure 3.
4. For every literal $\overline{x_i}$ in $\mathcal{C}_j$, $i \in [1, k]$, $j \in [1, N_c]$, we add the same places and transitions as in the last point, but we do not *exactly* connect them as depicted in figure 3. Instead, we must follow the same pattern of the figure but interchanging $x_i$ per $\overline{x_i}$, and $N_{x_i}$ per $N_{\overline{x_i}}$.

In order to avoid unnecessary confusions, we want to remark the fact that the place $s_{j \ominus 1}^j$ in figure 3 is the same place as $s_{j'}^{j' \oplus 1}$, for $j' = j \ominus 1$ ($j = j' \oplus 1$).

The initial marking $m_0$ of every place will be as shown in figure 3. The reader can check that the resulting net system $\langle \mathcal{N}_{\mathcal{F}}, m_0 \rangle$ is a marked S⁴PR with an acceptable initial marking, where $I_{\mathcal{N}_{\mathcal{F}}} = [1, N_c]$, every clause $\mathcal{C}_j$ results in a process net where $o_j$ is the idle place, and the resource places are every $x_i$, $\overline{x_i}$, and $s_j^{j \oplus 1}$.

In figure 4 it is depicted the resulting net $\mathcal{N}_F$ for the formula $F = x1(x1 + \overline{x2})(x2 + \overline{x3})$. In this example, SAT(F) returns YES since the formula is satisfiable, e.g. assigning $x1$="true", $x2$="false" and $x3$="false".

**Theorem 3.** *SAT → S⁴PR-NL*

*Proof.* We will prove that SAT(F) returns YES iff S⁴PR-NL($\mathcal{N}_{\mathcal{F}}, m_0$) returns YES. By theorem 1, $\langle \mathcal{N}_{\mathcal{F}}, m_0 \rangle$ is non-live iff exists a reachable $m$, $m \neq m_0$, such that every $m$-process-enabled transition is $m$-resource-disabled. The four necessary conditions defined by Coffman [1] establish that in this state a circular

---

[1] By $|e|$ we denote the length of the encoding $e$.

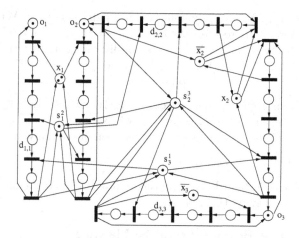

**Fig. 4.** SAT $\rightarrow$ S⁴PR-NL. Example: $F = x1(x1 + \overline{x2})(x2 + \overline{x3})$

wait exists. This is only possible with a circular wait on the resource places $s_j^{j\oplus1}$, since (by construction) the only transitions that can be $m$-process-enabled and $m$-resource-disabled are $v_{j,i}$ or $w_{j,i}$. Since it is also necessary that every locked process is in a "hold and wait" state on the blocking set of resources (as expressed by Coffman [1]), we can easily infer: $\langle \mathcal{N}_\mathcal{F}, m_0 \rangle$ is non-live iff exists $m \in RS(\mathcal{N}_\mathcal{F}, m_0)$ such that $\forall j \in [1, N_c]$ . $\exists | i \in [1, k]$ such that $m[d_{j,i}] = 1$ (thus, $m[s_j^{j\oplus1}] = m[a_{j,i}] = m[b_{j,i}] = m[e_{j,i}] = m[o_j] = 0$).

Now, $\forall j \in [1, N_c], i \in [1, k]$ such that $m[d_{j,i}] = 1$, there are two mutually exclusive alternatives: either (1) $Y_{x_i}[d_{j,i}] = 1$, $Y_{\overline{x_i}}[d_{j,i}] = 0$, or (2) $Y_{\overline{x_i}}[d_{j,i}] = 1$, $Y_{x_i}[d_{j,i}] = 0$. Note that $Y_{x_i}$ and $Y_{\overline{x_i}}$ are the minimal p-semiflows induced by the resource places $x_i$, and $\overline{x_i}$, respectively.

By construction, (1) is applied to $\mathcal{N}_\mathcal{F}$ when literal $x_i$ appears in the clause $\mathcal{C}_j$ of the formula $\mathcal{F}$. Equivalently, (2) is applied to $\mathcal{N}_\mathcal{F}$ when literal $\overline{x_i}$ appears in the clause $\mathcal{C}_j$ of the formula $\mathcal{F}$.

If (1) holds, then $\nexists j' \in [1, N_c], j \neq j'$, such that $Y_{\overline{x_i}}[d_{j',i}] = 1$ and $m[d_{j',i}] = 1$. Otherwise, $t_{j,i}$ and $t_{j',i}$ should have been fired to reach $m$. But the firing of $t_{j,i}$ requires that no token from $\overline{x_i}$ is taken, and the firing of $t_{j',i}$ requires that no token from $x_i$ is taken, so $t_{j,i}$ cannot be fired after $t_{j',i}$ and viceversa, leading to a contradiction. By an analogous reasoning, if (2) holds, then $\nexists j' \in [1, N_c]$, $j \neq j'$, such that $Y_{x_i}[d_{j',i}] = 1$ and $m[d_{j',i}] = 1$.

Let $f$ be a truth assignment for the set of boolean variables $X$, $f : X \rightarrow \{$true, false, don't care$\}$. For every $x_i \in X$ we define $f(x_i)$ as:

- $f(x_i)=$"true" iff $\exists j \in [1, N_c]$ such that $(m[d_{j,i}] = 1) \wedge (Y_{x_i}[d_{j,i}] = 1)$. This corresponds to case (1).
- $f(x_i)=$"false" iff $\exists j \in [1, N_c]$ such that $(m[d_{j,i}] = 1) \wedge (Y_{\overline{x_i}}[d_{j,i}] = 1)$. This corresponds to case (2).
- $f(x_i)=$"don't care", iff $\nexists j \in [1, N_c]$ such that $m[d_{j,i}] = 1$.

As we have seen, this assignments are mutually exclusive. Without loss of generality, we can finally redefine the non-liveness condition in the following way, which proves the hypothesis: $\langle \mathcal{N}_{\mathcal{F}}, m_0 \rangle$ is non-live iff exists a truth assignment $f$ such that $\forall j \in [1, N_c]$ . $\exists i \in [1, k]$ such that either $f(x_i) = $ "true" and $x_i$ appears in $\mathcal{C}_j$, or $f(x_i) = $ "false" and $\overline{x_i}$ appears in $\mathcal{C}_j$. □

Note that, as expected, the net system in figure 4 is non-live: the total deadlock $\langle \mathcal{N}_{\mathcal{F}}, m \rangle$ is reachable from $\langle \mathcal{N}_{\mathcal{F}}, m_0 \rangle$, where $m[d_{1,1}] = m[d_{2,2}] = m[d_{3,3}] = m[x_1] = m[x_2] = 1$, being the rest of the places empty. Finally, we can conclude:

**Theorem 4.** $S^4PR$-$NL$ *is NP-complete.*

*Proof.* $S^4$PR-NL is NP-hard since, by theorem 3, SAT is reducible to $S^4$PR-NL, and it is also NP-easy by theorem 2. □

### 3.2   Non-liveness Beyond the Initial Marking

The reader may have been left wondering why we chose to define the $S^4$PR problem beginning from an acceptable initial marking. Instead, we could have studied the more general problem of determining if, given $\langle \mathcal{N}, m \rangle$, $m \in RS(\mathcal{N}, m_0)$, the system is non-live. Indeed, the same complexity result applies: we can easily reduce this problem to $S^4$PR-NL. This is rather obvious from the fact that we can fire an arbitrary sequence from $m$ trying to lead every active process to the idle places. If we are able to reach $m_0$, then the reduction applies. If we are not able to reach $m_0$, we will have found a marking such that every $m$-process-enabled transition is $m$-resource-disabled, and the system is thus non-live.

Note that this is not true in general for every solution of the net state equation, $m = m_0 + C \cdot X, X \gneqq 0$. The problem resides in the fact that $S^4$PR nets may have killing spurious solutions, i.e., solutions of the net state equation that are not reachable and which are non-live while the system $\langle \mathcal{N}, m_0 \rangle$ is live. Note that the problem of determining if a given marking is a spurious solution is studied in subsection 3.4, and it is proven to be co-NP-complete.

### 3.3   Deadlock Avoidance and Detection

In previous works ([2,9,10]), the complexity of the deadlock avoidance problem has been determined for different classes of RAS, in some sense more restrictive than the $S^4$PR category, as explained in section 1. These seminal results are based on the study of safeness (as defined in the deadlock prediction problem [2], "the existence of a feasible sequence in which to allocate the remaining resource requirements of the processes"). However, the process structure in these earlier models was finite and acyclic: once a process had satisfied all the resource requirements, it was terminated and hence removed from the system. On the other hand, a marked $S^4$PR does not have a target state; instead, the processes are structurally repetitive. Hence, it is desirable to ensure that the *feasible sequence* is arbitrarily long. This leads us to the following definition:

**Definition 4.** *Let* $\langle \mathcal{N}, m_0 \rangle$, $\mathcal{N} = \langle P, T, C \rangle$ *be an* $S^4PR$ *with an acceptable initial marking, and let* $m$ *be a reachable marking,* $m \in RS(\mathcal{N}, m_0)$. *Then* $\langle \mathcal{N}, m \rangle$

*(or simply, m) is* doomed to deadlock *iff* $\exists k \in \mathbb{N}$ *such that for every firable sequence* $\sigma$, $m[\sigma\rangle$, *exists* $t \in T$ *such that* $t$ *is fired at most* $k$ *times,* $\sigma[t] \leq k$.

The negation of this property (i.e. $m$ is not doomed to deadlock) is somehow an extension of that concept of safeness and leads us to the optimal deadlock avoidance strategy: in our relaxed terminology, a resource allocation will be "safe" iff $m$ is not doomed to deadlock. Soon we will see that markings which are doomed to deadlock are well characterized in the S⁴PR class.

In contrast, an optimal deadlock detection strategy should detect iff a marking $m$ is doomed to deadlock, and apply recovery techniques in that case. It must be remarked that here we understand optimality in the strictest sense: the ability to detect the problem as soon as possible, i.e., as soon as a transition in the net is bound to die. Please note that other works define optimal detection as simply deciding iff there exists a transition which is effectively dead, i.e. no longer firable, in the current marking. The latter is less general and also computationally easier. The earlier will be proved co-NP-complete:

*Problem 3.* **S⁴PR-Deadlock-Detection (S⁴PR-DD)**
*Given:* A marked S⁴PR $\langle \mathcal{N}, m_0 \rangle$, being $m_0$ an acceptable initial marking,
    and a reachable marking $m$, $m \in RS(\mathcal{N}, m_0)$.
*To decide:* Is $\langle \mathcal{N}, m \rangle$ doomed to deadlock?

**Lemma 2.** *Let* $\langle \mathcal{N}, m_0 \rangle$, $\mathcal{N} = \langle P, T, C \rangle$ *be an* $S^4PR$ *with an acceptable initial marking, and let* $m$ *be a reachable marking,* $m \in RS(\mathcal{N}, m_0)$. *Then* $\langle \mathcal{N}, m \rangle$ *(or simply, m) is doomed to deadlock iff* $m_0 \notin RS(\mathcal{N}, m)$.

*Proof.* The necessary part ("only if") is rather obvious: every minimal t-semiflow is firable in isolation from $m_0$. This means that we can build a repetitive sequence in which we successively fire every minimal t-semiflow, hence firing every transition an arbitrarily large number of times. Regarding the sufficient part ("if"), let us proceed by reduction to absurd. Suppose that $m_0 \notin RS(N, m)$, and that exists an infinite finite sequence $\sigma$, $m[\sigma\rangle$ such that every transition is fired infinite times. In that case, every time a transition $t \in {}^\bullet P_0$ is fired in $\sigma$ (so the marking of an idle place is increased), we can freeze the token in the correspondent idle place (i.e. leave the token there). Since the idle places are the unique places in which no resource is used, this augments the number of resources available in the system, so the rest of active processes (i.e. tokens in the process places) can be moved in the same way as in the original sequence $\sigma$. Proceeding this way, we could construct a sequence $\sigma'$ that moves all the tokens to the idle places, reaching $m_0$, unless there exists a place $p \in P_S$ with frozen tokens in it $(m[\sigma'\rangle m'$, $m'[p] > 0)$. But this is impossible, since that would imply that $p^\bullet$ is $m'$-resource-disabled. Since the number of available resources has not been decreased, that would imply that $p^\bullet$ was not infinitely firable in $\sigma$, reaching a contradiction. □

Thus the problem of deadlock avoidance can be reduced to the problem of determining the reachability of the initial marking: a problem that is NP-complete, as we will see.

*Problem 4.* **S⁴PR-Reachable-Initial-Marking (S⁴PR-RIM)**
*Given:* A marked S⁴PR $\langle \mathcal{N}, m_0 \rangle$, being $m_0$ an acceptable initial marking,
     and a reachable marking $m$, $m \in RS(\mathcal{N}, m_0)$.
*To decide:* Is $m_0$ reachable from $\langle \mathcal{N}, m \rangle$?

**Theorem 5.** *S⁴PR-RIM is NP-complete.*

*Proof.* In order to prove NP-easiness, let us introduce the following problem:

*Problem 5.* **S⁴PR-Path-to-Initial-Marking (S⁴PR-PIM)**
*Given:* A marked S⁴PR $\langle \mathcal{N}, m_0 \rangle$, being $m_0$ an acceptable initial marking,
     a reachable marking $m \in RS(\mathcal{N}, m_0)$, and a firing sequence $\sigma$,
     $|\sigma| \leq K \cdot |T|$, where $K = \sum_{p \in P_0} m_0[p]$.
*To decide:* Is $m_0$ reached firing $m[\sigma\rangle$?

1. S⁴PR-PIM is in P (this is rather trivial: checking the firability of every transition in the sequence can be done in deterministic linear time).
2. Let $(\mathcal{N}, m_0, m, \sigma)$ be a valid input for S⁴PR-PIM, being $(\mathcal{N}, m_0, m)$ an input for S⁴PR-NL. As the size of $\sigma$ is polynomial in the number of transitions and population of the net, it is trivial to find two encodings $e_1(\mathcal{N}, m_0, m, \sigma)$ and $e_2(\mathcal{N}, m_0, m)$ such that $|e_1(\mathcal{N}, m_0, m, \sigma)| \leq c' \cdot |e_2(\mathcal{N}, m_0, m)|^c$, given $c, c'$.
3. S⁴PR-RIM can be *verified* in deterministic polynomial time. By lemma 1, but reasoning over the reverse net, if $m_0$ is reachable there is a firing sequence $\sigma$, $m[\sigma\rangle m_0$, with $(|\sigma| \leq K \cdot |T|)$. Hence, $S^4PR - NL$ returns YES with input $(\mathcal{N}, m_0)$ iff exists a firing sequence $\sigma$ such that S⁴PR-PIM returns YES.

Now that NP-easiness is proven, it is required to prove NP-hardness. But this part is rather straightforward, due to the fact that (as commented before) the problem of safeness in previous works ([2,9,10]) can be easily proven a subcase of S⁴PR-RIM. Since the problem was already NP-hard for this models, we conclude that the problem is NP-hard through restriction [14]. □

Summing up, S⁴PR-DD is co-NP-complete (i.e., optimal deadlock detection in the S⁴PR is co-NP-complete)[2]. The problem of optimal deadlock avoidance remains NP-complete for the S⁴PR class.

### 3.4   Spurious Markings

A spurious marking is a solution of the net state equation, $m = m_0 + C \cdot X$, $X \gneq \mathbf{0}$, that is not reachable from $m_0$. A killing spurious solution is a spurious marking such that $\langle \mathcal{N}, m \rangle$ is non-live. There exist Petri net subclasses, such as equal conflict (EQ) systems [15], for which killing spurious solutions are not possible. In those cases, the linear description provided by the net state equation can be used to determine the liveness of the system.

Unfortunately, the S⁴PR class is not one of those classes, and this limits the potential of the net state equation for this purpose. Unless that, noticeably,

---

[2] However, we remind the reader that there exists a reachable marking $m'$ such that it can be structurally characterized as a bad marking by theorem 1, but this does not affect the inherent computational complexity of the problem.

spurious solutions were efficiently detectable for a given $S^4PR$ system. As we will see, however, this is a co-NP-complete problem:

*Problem 6.* **$S^4$PR-Spurious-Detection ($S^4$PR-SD)**
*Given:* A marked $S^4PR$ $\langle \mathcal{N}, m_0 \rangle$, being $m_0$ an acceptable initial marking,
  and $m \in \mathbb{N}^{|P|}$, $m = m_0 + C \cdot X$, $X \geq 0$.
*To decide:* Is $m$ an spurious marking?

Intuitively, $m$ is an spurious marking iff $m_0$ is not reachable from $m$ in its reverse (note that there may be isolated spurious solutions, i.e. not connected to the reachability space). Meanwhile, the reverse net of a $S^4PR$ is another $S^4PR$. This is quite trivial, since the polarity inversion of the incidence matrix does not affect its (left or right) annullers, so the p and t-semiflows are preserved with respect to $\mathcal{N}$.

It is easy to see now that $S^4PR$-SD is co-NP-complete. This is bad news since, unless NP=P, this implies that we cannot *verify* that a marking is spurious in deterministic polynomial time using *solely* the structure of the net.

## 4  Conclusions

RAS is an abstraction of real systems allowing to concentrate on the study of problems such as deadlocks due to the sharing of resources used in mutual exclusion. Modelling RAS with Petri nets is particularly easy through the identification of processes with state machines and resources with monitor places representing the allocation of copies of resources. As a consequence, the $S^4PR$ subclass has already been proven specially useful and suitable for the RAS abstraction of Flexible Manufacturing Systems (FMS) [13]. For this reason, we have devoted an insight on the complexity of some problems related to handling with deadlocks using this kind of models.

As expected, many of the important problems are proven computationally intractable, and for this reason, the heuristics presented in [8,13] have special interest. Regarding optimal deadlock prevention, we have established that the problem of determining if a marked $S^4PR$ is non-live is NP-complete. Besides, we have provided evidence for NP-completeness of optimal deadlock avoidance for this class, generalizing earlier results for other types of RAS which were already proven NP-hard. This was accomplished thanks to proving the equivalence of this problem with that of deciding the reachability of the initial marking. The inverse problem (optimal deadlock detection, in the strictest sense) is co-NP-complete.

Moreover, because the mathematical methods presented in [13] are based on the net state equation, an insight on the complexity of the detection of spurious markings is also relevant. The intractability of the problem, along with the existence of killing spurious solutions, constrains the practicality of the net state equation for determining non-liveness.

Finally, a motivating example was also introduced, in order to depict the utility of our conceptual framework in the study and correction of deadlock problems in distributed systems and protocols, beyond the FMS context.

Obviously, the modelling power of the $S^4PR$ class is limited if we consider, e.g., certain applications coming from the world of distributed computing. The generalization of the S⁴PR subclass for modelling RAS hence emerges as an appealing future research direction. [16] is a first effort in this vein. For the generalized net classes, the problems here studied will fall, at best, within the same complexity classes. Nevertheless, their study will give us insight on more complex behaviours that can observed in these systems [16].

# References

1. Coffman, E.G., Elphick, M., Shoshani, A.: System deadlocks. ACM Computing Surveys **3**(2) (1971) 67–78
2. Gold, E.M.: Deadlock prediction: Easy and difficult cases. SIAM Journal on Computing **7**(3) (1978) 320–336
3. Murata, T.: Petri nets: Properties, analysis and applications. Proceedings of the IEEE **77**(4) (1989) 541–580
4. Lautenbach, K., Thiagarajan, P.S.: Analysis of a resource allocation problem using Petri nets. In Syre, J.C., ed.: Proc. of 1st European Conf. on Parallel and Distributed Processing, Toulouse, Cepadues Editions (1979) 260–266
5. Ezpeleta, J., Colom, J., Martínez, J.: A Petri net based deadlock prevention policy for flexible manufacturing systems. IEEE Trans. on Robotics and Automation **11**(2) (1995) 173–184
6. Xie, X., Jeng, M.D.: ERCN-merged nets and their analysis using siphons. IEEE Trans. on Robotics and Automation **29**(4) (1999) 692–703
7. Park, J., Reveliotis, S.A.: Deadlock avoidance in sequential resource allocation systems with multiple resource acquisitions and flexible routings. IEEE Trans. on Automatic Control **46**(10) (2001) 1572–1583
8. Tricas, F.: Deadlock analysis, prevention and avoidance in sequential resource allocation systems. PhD thesis, University of Zaragoza, Zaragoza (2003)
9. Lawley, M., Reveliotis, S.: Deadlock avoidance for sequential Resource Allocation Systems: Hard and easy cases. Int. Journal of Flexible Manufacturing Systems **13** (2001) 385–404
10. Sulistyono, W., Lawley, M.: Deadlock avoidance for manufacturing systems with partially ordered process plans. IEEE Trans. on Robotics and Automation **17**(6) (2001) 819–832
11. Brade, R., Zhang, L., Berson, S., Herzog, S., Jamin, S.: RFC 2205: Resource ReSerVation Protocol – Version 1 Functional Specification (1997)
12. Villapol, M., Billington, J.: Analysing properties of the resource reservation protocol. In Van der Aalst, W. and Best, E., eds.: Proc. of 24th Int. Conf. on Applications and Theory of Petri Nets. Vol. 2679 of LNCS. Springer–Verlag (2003) 377–396
13. Tricas, F., García-Vallés, F., Colom, J., Ezpeleta, J.: A Petri net structure-based deadlock prevention solution for sequential resource allocation systems. In: Proc. of IEEE Int. Conf. on Robotics and Automation, Barcelona, Spain (2005) 272–278
14. Garey, M., Johnson, D.: Computers and Intractability: A Guide to the Theory of NP-Completeness. W. H. Freeman & Co., New York, NY, USA (1979)
15. Teruel, E., Silva, M.: Liveness and home states in equal conflict systems. In Ajmone Marsan, M., ed.: Proc. of 14th Int. Conf. on Applications and Theory of Petri Nets. Vol. 691 of LNCS. Springer–Verlag (1993) 415–432
16. López-Grao, J.P., Colom, J.M.: Lender processes competing for shared resources: Beyond the S⁴PR paradigm. In: Proc. of IEEE Int. Conf. on Systems, Man and Cybernetics, Taipei, Taiwan (2006) To appear.

# A    Petri Nets: Basic Definitions

A *place/transition net* (P/T net) is a 3-tuple $\mathcal{N} = \langle P, T, W \rangle$, where $W$ is a total function $W : (P \times T) \cup (T \times P) \to \mathbb{N}$, being $P$, $T$ non empty, finite and disjoint sets. Elements belonging to the sets $P$ and $T$ are called respectively *places* and *transitions*, or generally nodes. P/T nets can be represented as a directed bipartite graph, where places (transitions) are graphically denoted by circles (rectangles): let $p \in P$, $t \in T$, $u = W(p,t)$, $v = W(t,p)$, there is a directed arc, labelled $u$ $(v)$, beginning in $p$ $(t)$ and ending in $t$ $(p)$ iff $u \neq 0$ $(v \neq 0)$.

The *preset (poset)* or set of input (output) nodes of a node $x \in P \cup T$ is denoted by $^\bullet x$ $(x^\bullet)$, where $^\bullet x = \{y \in P \cup T \mid W(y,x) \neq 0\}$ $(x^\bullet = \{y \in P \cup T \mid W(x,y) \neq 0\})$. The preset (poset) of a set of nodes $X \in bag(P) \cup bag(T)$ is denoted by $^\bullet X$ $(X^\bullet)$, where $^\bullet X = \{y \mid y \in {}^\bullet x, x \in X\}$ $(X^\bullet = \{y \mid y \in x^\bullet, x \in X\}$

A *generalized P/T net* is a net with positive arc weights. If the arc weights are unitary (i.e., $W$ can be defined as a total function $(P \times T) \cup (T \times P) \to \{0,1\}$) the net is called *ordinary*. A *state machine* is an ordinary net such that for every transition $t \in T$, $|^\bullet t| = |t^\bullet| = 1$.

Let $\mathcal{N} = \langle P, T, W \rangle$ be a P/T net. Its *reverse net* $\mathcal{N}^r = \langle P, T, W^r \rangle$ is the same net with its arcs inverted, i.e. $W^r(p,t) = W(t,p)$ and $W^r(t,p) = W(p,t)$.

A *self-loop place* $p \in P$ is a place such that $p \in p^{\bullet\bullet}$. A *pure P/T net* (also self-loop free P/T net) is a net with no self-loop places. In pure P/T nets, the net can be also defined by the 3-tuple $\mathcal{N} = \langle P, T, C \rangle$, where $C$ is called the *incidence matrix*, $C[p,t] = W(p,t) - W(t,p)$.

A *marking* $m$ of a P/T net $\mathcal{N}$ is a vector $\mathbb{N}^{|P|}$, assigning a finite number of marks $m[p]$ (called *tokens*) to every place $p \in P$. Tokens are represented by black dots within the places. The *support* of a marking, $\|m\|$, is the set of places which are marked in $m$, i.e. $\|m\| = \{p \in P \mid m[p] \neq 0\}$.

We define a *marked P/T net* (also P/T net system) as the duple $\langle \mathcal{N}, m_0 \rangle$, where $\mathcal{N}$ is a P/T net, and $m_0$ is a marking for $\mathcal{N}$, also called *initial marking*. $\mathcal{N}$ is said to be the structure of the system, while $m_0$ represents the system state.

Let $\langle \mathcal{N}, m_0 \rangle$ be a marked P/T net. A transition $t \in T$ is *enabled* (also *firable*) iff $\forall p \in {}^\bullet t$ . $m_0[p] \geq W(p,t)$, which is denoted by $m_0[t\rangle$. The *firing* of an enabled transition $t \in T$ changes the system state to $\langle \mathcal{N}, m_1 \rangle$, where $\forall p \in P$ . $m_1[p] = m_0[p] + C[p,t]$, and is denoted by $m_0[t\rangle m_1$. A *firing sequence* $\sigma$ from $\langle \mathcal{N}, m_0 \rangle$ is a non-empty sequence of transitions $\sigma = t_1 t_2 \ldots t_k$ such that $m_0[t_1\rangle m_1[t_2\rangle \ldots m_{k-1}[t_k\rangle$. The firing of $\sigma$ is denoted by $m_0[\sigma\rangle t_k$. We call the *firing count* vector $\boldsymbol{\sigma}$ of $\sigma$ to the Parikh mapping $\sigma \to \mathbb{N}^{|T|}$ (i.e. $\boldsymbol{\sigma}[t]$ is equal to the number of times $t$ appears in $\sigma$). The support of $\boldsymbol{\sigma}$ is denoted by $\|\boldsymbol{\sigma}\|$.

A marking $m$ is *reachable* from $\langle \mathcal{N}, m_0 \rangle$ iff there exists a *firing sequence* $\sigma$ such that $m_0[\sigma\rangle m$. The *reachability set* $RS(\mathcal{N}, m_0)$ is the set of reachable markings, i.e. $RS(\mathcal{N}, m_0) = \{m \mid \exists \sigma . m_0[\sigma\rangle m\}$.

The *net state equation* of a marked P/T net $\langle \mathcal{N}, m_0 \rangle$ is an algebraic equation defined as $m = m_0 + C \cdot \boldsymbol{\sigma}$, where $\boldsymbol{\sigma} \gneq \mathbf{0}$. Every reachable marking holds the net state equation, but there may exist solutions to the equation which are not reachable markings. Thus we will call $m$ a *potentially reachable marking*. The *potential reachability set* $PRS(\mathcal{N}, m_0)$ is defined as $PRS(\mathcal{N}, m_0) = \{m \mid \exists\,\boldsymbol{\sigma} \in \mathbb{N}^{|T|}.\ m = m_0 + C \cdot \boldsymbol{\sigma}, \boldsymbol{\sigma} \gneq \mathbf{0}\}$.

A transition $t \in T$ is *live* iff for every reachable marking $m \in RS(\mathcal{N}, m_0)$, $\exists m' \in RS(\mathcal{N}, m)$ such that $m'[t\rangle$. The system $\langle\mathcal{N}, m_0\rangle$ is *live* iff every transition is live. Otherwise, $\langle\mathcal{N}, m_0\rangle$ is *non-live*. A transition $t \in T$ is *dead* iff there is no reachable marking $m \in RS(\mathcal{N}, m_0)$ such that $m[t\rangle$. The system $\langle\mathcal{N}, m_0\rangle$ is a *total deadlock* iff every transition is dead, i.e. no transition is firable. A *home state* $m_k$ is a marking such that it is reachable from every reachable marking, i.e. $\forall m \in RS(\mathcal{N}, m_0)\ .\ m_k \in RS(\mathcal{N}, m)$. The net system $\langle\mathcal{N}, m_0\rangle$ is *reversible* iff $m_0$ is a home state.

A *p-semiflow* (*t-semiflow*) is a vector $Y \in \mathbb{N}^{|P|}$, $Y \neq \mathbf{0}$ ($X \in \mathbb{N}^{|T|}$, $X \neq \mathbf{0}$), which is a left (right) annuler of the incidence matrix, $Y \cdot C = \mathbf{0}$ ($C \cdot X = \mathbf{0}$). The support of a p-semiflow (t-semiflow) is denoted $\|Y\|$ ($\|X\|$), and its places (transitions) are said to be covered by $Y$ ($X$). The P/T net $\mathcal{N}$ is *conservative* (*consistent*) iff every place (transition) is covered by a p-semiflow (t-semiflow). A *minimal p-semiflow* (*minimal t-semiflow*) is a p-semiflow (t-semiflow) such that the g.c.d of its non-null components is one and its support $\|Y\|$ ($\|X\|$) is not an strict superset of the support of another p-semiflow (t-semiflow).

A *path* $\pi$ of a P/T net $\mathcal{N}$ is a sequence of nodes $\pi = x_1\ x_2\ ...\ x_n$ such that the odd components are places and the even components transitions, or viceversa, and for every pair $(x_i, x_{i+1})$, $W(x_i, x_{i+1}) \neq 0$. An *elementary path* is a path such that $\forall i, j \in [1, n]\ .\ x_i \neq x_j$, except for $x_1 = x_n$ (which is allowed). A *general circuit* is a path such that $x_1 = x_n$. An *elementary circuit* (or simply *circuit*) is both an elementary path and a general circuit.

# B    The Problem of Satisfiability(SAT)

Let $X = \{x_1, ..., x_n\}$ be a set of boolean variables. By the process of *truth assignment*, every variable in X is assigned one value: either true or false. Let $x_i \in X$, we call a *literal* to either $x_i$ or its negation, $\overline{x_i}$. Intuitively, if the variable $x_i$ is assigned the value true, the literals $x_i$ and $\overline{x_i}$ are true and false, respectively (and viceversa if false is assigned). We define a *clause* $\mathcal{C}_j$ as a non-empty set of literals. The value of a clause is the disjunction of its literals, i.e., it is true iff at least one literal is true; and false otherwise. Finally, a *formula* $\mathcal{F}$ is a non-empty set of clauses, and its value is the conjunction of them, i.e., it is true iff all its clauses are true; false otherwise.

Without loss of generality, we will assume that, given a formula $\mathcal{F} = \mathcal{C}_1 \cdot ... \cdot \mathcal{C}_k$ and the set of its variables $X$, every variable $x_i \in X$ appears in at least one clause, and also that $x_i$ appears at most once in each clause, be it negated or not.

*Problem 7.* **SATISFIABILITY (SAT)**
*Given:* A formula $F$ and the set of its variables $X$.
*To decide:* Is there a truth assignment for $X$ such that $\mathcal{F}$ is true?

# Optimized Colored Nets Unfolding

Fabrice Kordon, Alban Linard, and Emmanuel Paviot-Adet

Université P. & M. Curie - Paris 6, CNRS UMR 7606 - LIP6/MoVe
4, place Jussieu, F-75252 Paris CEDEX 05, France
Fabrice.Kordon@lip6.fr, Alban.Linard@lip6.fr, Emmanuel.Paviot-Adet@lip6.fr

**Abstract.** As some structural properties, like generative families of positive P-invariants, can only be computed in P/T nets, unfolding of Colored Petri Nets is of interest. However, it may generate huge nets that cannot be stored concretely in memory. In some cases, removing the dead parts of the unfolded net can dramatically reduce its size, but this operation requires the unfolded net to be represented anyway. This paper presents a symbolic representation of unfolded nets using Data Decision Diagrams. This technique allows to store very large models and manipulate them for optimization purpose.

## 1 Introduction

Colored Petri nets, introduced by K. Jensen in 1981 [8] are very convenient for modeling complex systems. However, basic structural properties of P/T nets [11] remain difficult to extend to Colored Petri Nets: a generative family of positive invariants can only be computed under restrictive conditions [5] and structural bounds are generally not available.

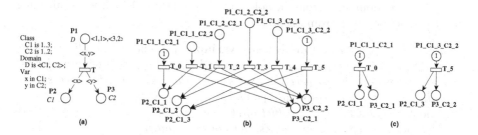

**Fig. 1.** Example of Net unfolding

To overcome this problem, modelers may transform the colored Petri net into an equivalent P/T net. This operation, called *unfolding*, generates for each original place, numerous P/T places instances according to its color domain. Moreover, one P/T transition is generated for any possible binding of each colored transition. This leads to huge unfolded net. As an example, the colored model (a in Figure 1) is unfolded into a P/T net (b in the figure). Hopefully, in many cases, simplifications can lead to a smaller unfolded net according to:

E. Najm et al. (Eds.): FORTE 2006, LNCS 4229, pp. 339–355, 2006.

1. the initial marking of places (here, place P1 in the colored model lacks some marking and thus, some of the corresponding P/T places are zero-marked),
2. false guards on transitions.

Model c in Figure 1 shows the unfolded Petri net after optimization.

Unfolding Colored Petri nets raises several problems when they become large because the result cannot be stored in memory. This is typically the case for Petri nets derived from higher level specification (such as UML as suggested in [1]). Optimization of the unfolded net, when possible, requires the unfolded net to be represented anyway before optimization.

In this paper, after a brief remainder of Well-Formed Petri Nets [3] in Section 2 and a presentation of Data Decision Diagrams (DDDs) [4] a shared structure we use to store huge P/T nets in Section 3, we present in Section 4 how P/T places and transitions are symbolically stored. P/T arcs, however, are not represented, they are computed on the fly from the colored description when needed. Section 5 describes the main contribution of this work: implementation of the optimization algorithms in this symbolic context. We end with experimentation on various types of specifications to assess when our technique is efficient in Section 6.

## 2   Well-Formed Colored Petri Nets

In this section we describe Well-Formed Petri Nets (WN) [3], the input formalism for our work. Originally designed to ease structural verification algorithms expression, this formalism is a subset of Colored Petri nets with a simple and rigorous syntax and is also used to exploit model symmetries. Definitions in this section are adapted from [12].

Classes and domains define the color structures used in WN models, allowing tokens to be identified from one another.

**Definition 1 (Classes, domains and variables).** *A* class *is a cyclicly ordered finite set of elements with successor (resp. predecessor) function defined. A class is an interval over the positive naturals $k_1..k_2$, where $k_1 < k_2$, the successor of $k_2$ is $k_1$ (resp. the predecessor of $k_1$ is $k_2$).*

*A* domain *is a Cartesian product of classes.*

*Variables are defined over classes, but not over domains.*

The next definition introduces basic expressions over variables. Those basic expressions are used in predicates and domain functions.

**Definition 2 (Basic color functions).** *A* basic color function $E(x)$ *is the identity function (noted x) or x++n or x--n the $n^{\underline{th}}$ successor and predecessor of variable x respectively or the constant function (denoted by the corresponding class member).*

**Definition 3 (Standard Predicates).** *A* standard predicate *is a Boolean expression of basic predicates. The allowed basic predicates are:* $E(x) = E(y)$,

$E(x) \neq E(y)$, $E(x) < E(y)$ where $x$ and $y$ are variables of same class and $E(x)$ and $E(y)$ are basic color functions.

**Definition 4 (Domain functions).** Let $D = \langle C_1, \dots C_n \rangle$ be a domain where $C_i$ are classes. Let $x_i$ be a variable defined over the class $C_i$.

A basic domain function $BF$ of $D$ is : $BF : \langle C_1, \dots C_n \rangle \to Bag(\langle C_1, \dots C_n \rangle)$ where $BF$ is a function of the form $BF = k.\langle E(x_1), \dots, E(x_n) \rangle$.

A Domain function $F$ of $D$ is: $F : \langle C_1, \dots C_n \rangle \to Bag(\langle C_1, \dots C_n \rangle)$ where $F$ is a function of the form $F = BF_1 + \cdots + BF_n$ where $BF_i$ is a basic domain function.

**Definition 5 (Well-Formed Colored Petri Nets).** A Well-Formed Net is a twelve-tuple $N = \langle P, T, Pre, Post, C, D, V, VDom, TVar, Dom, gd, M_0 \rangle$ where:

- $P$ and $T$ are disjoint finite non empty sets (respectively the places and transitions of $N$),
- $V$ is a set of variables,
- $C$ and $D$ are respectively sets of classes and domains,
- $VDom$ is a function that maps variables to classes,
- $TVar$ is a function that maps transitions to subsets of $V$,
- $Dom$ is a function defining the color domain of each place and transition, the domain of transition $t$ is a Cartesian product of the classes $VDom(v)$ for each $v$ in $TVar(t)$,
- $gd$ is a function defining for each transition $t$ its predicate (called guard), variables used in basic predicates belong to $Tvar(t)$,
- $Pre[p,t]$ (resp. $Post[p,t]$) is the pre-incidence (resp. post-incidence) function: a domain function over $Dom(p)$, variables used in each basic color functions belong to the corresponding class in the domain,
- $M_0 : M_0(p) \in Bag(Dom(p))$ is the initial marking of place $p$.

An equivalent P/T net can be assiociated to each WN. To a colored place P are associated $|Dom(P)|$ ordinay places. Equivalently,to a colored transition t are associated $|VDom(x_1)| * \cdots * |VDom(x_n)|$ ordinary transitions, where $x_i$ belongs to $TVar(t)$. Ordinary arcs link places to transitions according to $Pre$ and $Post$.

# 3   Data Decision Diagrams

Data Decision Diagrams represent assignment sequence sets of the form $e_1 = x_1; e_2 = x_2; \cdots e_n = x_n$ where $e_i$ are variables and $x_i$ are values. Like in Binary Decision Diagrams, common parts are shared at the beginning and the end of the sequences. No fixed order is needed over the assignments sequences and multiple reassignments are allowed. Moreover, no assumptions are done on the variables domains.

DDDs use three terminal nodes: 0, 1 and ⊤. As usual, a sequence ending with 1 is part of the set described by the DDD, a sequence ending with 0 is not part of this set and a sequence ending with ⊤ means that an error occurred in a previous operation. In the following, $E$ denotes a set of variables, and for any $e \in E$, $Dom(e)$ represents the domain of $e$. For more detailed information see [4].

**Definition 6 (Data Decision Diagram).** *The set $\mathbb{D}$ of DDDs is defined by $d \in \mathbb{D}$ if:*

- *$d \in \{0, 1, \top\}$ or*
- *$d = (e, \alpha)$ with:*
  - *$e \in E$*
  - *$\alpha : \mathrm{Dom}(e) \to \mathbb{D}$, such that $\{x \in \mathrm{Dom}(e) \,|\, \alpha(x) \neq 0\}$ is finite.*

*We denote $e \xrightarrow{a} d$, the DDD $(e, \alpha)$ with $\alpha(a) = d$ and for all $x \neq a$, $\alpha(x) = 0$.*

*We denote $e \xrightarrow{a..b} d$, the DDD $(e, \alpha)$ with $\alpha(a) = \ldots = \alpha(b) = d$ and for all $x \notin \{a, \ldots b\}$, $\alpha(x) = 0$.*

This definition allows multiple DDD representations of the empty set, therefore, each DDD can have multiple representations. An equivalence relation over the DDDs is thus needed. 0 denotes the empty set and each node equivalent to the empty set is replaced by 0. This induces a canonical representation.

Since DDDs represent sets, sets operators are defined over DDDs: *union* +, *intersection* $*$ and *difference* $\backslash$. DDDs also represent sets of sequences, the *concatenation* operator . is also defined: if $d_1$ and $d_2$ are two DDDs, then $d_1.d_2$ is composed of all possible sequences beginning with a sequence of $d_1$ while the remainder is a sequence of $d_2$.

The main feature of the DDDs that is attractive for our work is the notion of homomorphisms: an homomorphism $\Phi$ is a mapping on DDDs that maps the empty set to itself ($\Phi(0) = 0$) and that is linear with respect to the union ($\Phi(d_1 + d_2) = \Phi(d_1) + \Phi(d_2)$). The identity mapping $Id$ ($Id(d) = d$) is the easiest homomorphism one can define. Basic homomorphisms can be composed to create new homomorphisms: if $\Phi_1$ and $\Phi_2$ are homomorphisms, then $\Phi_1 \circ \Phi_2$ is a new homomorphism.

Another simple homomorphism is the one that takes a couple (variable, value) as parameters $Construct(e, x)$ and returns the DDD composed of a node labeled $e$ and an arc leading to terminal node 1, labeled $x$. Using predefined operators, DDDs can be created: $Construct(A, 1).(Construct(B, 2) + Construct(B, 4))$ returns the DDD $A \xrightarrow{1} B \xrightarrow{\{2,4\}} 1$. This DDD is depicted in Figure 2

Many operations on DDDs, like variable re-ordering or value modification, cannot be obtained via predefined operators only. A special set of homomorphisms is introduced: the *inductive homomorphisms*. Those homomorphisms associate a DDD to terminal node 1 and apply defined homomorphisms for each sub-DDD to each couple (variable, value).

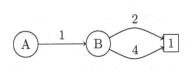

**Fig. 2.** Basic DDD creation

**Definition 7 (Inductive homomorphism).** *Let $I$ be an index set. Let $(d_i)_{i \in I}$ be a family of DDDs. Let $(\Phi_i(e, x))_{i \in I}$ be a family of homomorphisms.*

*Then the recursive definition of mappings $(\Phi_i)_{i \in I}$ in Figure 3 defines a family of homomorphisms called inductive homomorphisms.*

$$\forall d \in \mathbb{D}, \varPhi_i(d) = \begin{cases} 0 & \text{if } d = 0 \\ d_i & \text{if } d = 1 \\ \top & \text{if } d = \top \\ \sum_{x \in \mathrm{Dom}(e)} \varPhi_i(e, x)(\alpha(x)) & \text{if } d = (e, \alpha) \end{cases}$$

**Fig. 3.** Definition of inductive homomorphisms

# 4   Shared Structure

In this work, optimization algorithms are designed on P/T nets stored via decision diagrams. Since we chose to cut the unfolded net representation into several short decision diagrams, the symbolic structure must allow variable reordering locally to each set in order to compute P/T arcs. OBDDs [2] cannot, therefore, be used to store the unfolded net.

For this reason, we have chosen Data Decision Diagrams (DDDs) [4]: a structure that is not bound to any order, allows variable repetition and offers a large toolset to handle the structure. After a quick overview of the problem, a detailed description of the symbolic representation is given.

## 4.1   Partial Unfolding

Unfolding $P'_n$, if $n$ is a place (or $T'_n$ if $n$ is a transition), of a node $n$ with $Dom(n) = C_0 \times \ldots \times C_m$ is a set of $|C_0| * \ldots * |C_m|$ nodes $N'_n$ composed of unfolded nodes for all possible bindings for each component of $Dom(n)$. It results in a P/T net where all color classes have disappeared. Partial unfolding of the same node for color class $C_u$ is a set of $\prod_{c \in Dom(n)|c = C_u} |c|$ nodes, composed of all possible bindings for each component of $Dom(n)$ of color class $C_u$.

Full unfolding is a special case of partial unfolding, obtained by the successive partial unfoldings, in any given order, over all color classes. A colored net $N$ is fully unfolded to a net $N' = unfold(N) = \circ_{c \in C} unfold_c(N)$. Differences between full and partial unfolding are presented in algorithms of this paper.

## 4.2   Optimized Unfolding

The number of unfolded nodes in a net can be huge, especially when color classes contain a lot of elements, or when domains contain a lot of color classes. Unfolding of the Train [6] model generates more than $10^9$ transitions. Such a net cannot have a concrete representation in memory and is almost useless if its size is not reduced.

Optimizations can be applied to unfolded nets to reduce their size, but our previous unfolder needed a concrete representation of the unfolded net to perform these optimizations. When no concrete representation of the unfolded net was possible because of its size, the optimizations needed to reduce its size could not be applied.

The new unfolder described here offers a solution to this problem by the substitution of the concrete representation of the unfolded nets with a symbolic one for their places and transitions, and an implicit one for arcs. Optimizations can then be applied to huge unfolded nets and, in some cases, their size after optimization can be small enough for a concrete representation generation, usable by other tools.

## 4.3   Symbolic Unfolded Net

Symbolic representation of the unfolded net must be compact and allow fast operations. These two goals being more likely to be achieved using short decision diagrams, the representation chosen uses several decision diagrams, one for each colored place and one for each colored transition.

Symbolic representation of sets for unfolded places and transitions is done using DDD. This structure is well adapted to the representation of sets of integer vectors, and thus sets of vectors of color class values. Each sequence, in the representation of unfolded nodes from a node, is interpreted as one unfolded node. Integer vectors represent then, for an unfolded place or transition, the values in color classes associated to this particular object.

A **symbolic unfolded net** is defined above a Well-Formed Net by adding:

- $SVP : P \times (C \times \mathbb{N}) \rightarrow SV$ and $SVT : T \times V \rightarrow SV$ : functions returning for each couple (*place* $\times$ *domain component*) (the domain component being the color class and its occurrence number in the domain), resp. (*transition* $\times$ *valuation variable*), the DDD variable in the symbolic representation,
- $SP : P \rightarrow \mathbb{D}$ and $ST : T \rightarrow \mathbb{D}$ : for each $p \in P$ (resp. $t \in T$), its unfolded places (resp. transitions) represented using a DDD,
- $M_0' : P \rightarrow \mathbb{D}$ : for each $p \in P$, the DDD of initially marked unfolded places.

Let us note that arcs are not explicitly represented in a symbolic unfolded net. Therefore, there is no direct encoding of *Pre* and *Post* functions as usually: arcs are computed on the fly. To do so, four functions are defined to get pre-conditions or post-conditions of a node :

$$Pre_T(t) = \{p \in P | Pre[p, t] \neq \emptyset\} \qquad Post_T(t) = \{p \in P | Post[p, t] \neq \emptyset\}$$
$$Pre_P(p) = \{t \in T | Post[p, t] \neq \emptyset\} \qquad Post_P(p) = \{t \in T | Pre[p, t] \neq \emptyset\}$$

Partial unfolding is supported by this definition as the symbolic representation only gives an information about the presence of a node, still colored or not, in the unfolded net. Algorithms are presented for a full unfolding, because notations for partial unfolding can be less readable, but they also work for partial or are easily extended to achieve this goal.

We now introduce the notation $DDD_p = SP(p)$ (resp. $DDD_t = ST(t)$) for the symbolic representation of $P_p'$ (resp. $T_t'$) the unfolded places (resp. transitions) from $p$ (resp. $t$). A shorter notation is used for $SVP(p, c)$: it is the DDD variable for the component $c$, color class and occurrence number of it in $Dom(p)$, of place $p$.

The chosen representation only describes the presence of unfolded places or transitions and the structure of their DDD representation, and thus avoids a representation of unfolded arcs, because the operations on the net, $Pre$ and $Post$ matrices or guards, are represented using homomorphisms. As these homomorphisms are operations suited to only particular purposes, for example interpreting some guards or getting places pre-condition of several transitions, they are not part of the definition of the symbolic unfolded net.

The unfolder is basically divided in three parts : the translation from a Well-Formed Net to a symbolic unfolded net and the definition of operations on this symbolic unfolded net, the application of the operations on the symbolic representation, and the translation from a symbolic unfolded net to a Well-Formed or P/T Net.

### 4.4  Construction of Symbolic Representation

The symbolic representation $DDD_p$ of unfolded places $P'_p$ from a place $p$ is built recursively as shown in Algorithm 1. Unfolded places are initially represented with the DDD 1, meaning that an already non-colored place unfolded for some color class or a colored place unfolded for no color class is unfolded as itself. Then, for each component $c_i$ of $Dom(p)$ to unfold, its corresponding DDD variable $SVP(p, c_i)$ is added on top of place DDD, linked with one arc for each value in the color class of $c_i$ to previously built place DDD. The same applies to construction of unfolded transitions from a transition $t$, but each transition variable $v \in TVar(t)$ gives a corresponding DDD variable with $SVT(t, v)$.

This algorithm defines an order in the DDD, but this order has no influence on algorithms presented in this paper as only DDD variables are used in operations. However, the implementation deals with this problem by enabling other orders.

---

**Algorithm 1.** Symbolic unfolded net construction

---

| | |
|---|---|
| **Require:** $P \subset N$ | **Require:** $T \subset N$ |
| **Ensure:** $\forall p \in P, DDD_p$ | **Ensure:** $\forall t \in T, DDD_t$ |
| $\quad$ **for all** $p \in P$ **do** | $\quad$ **for all** $t \in T$ **do** |
| $\quad\quad DDD_p := 1$ | $\quad\quad DDD_t := 1$ |
| $\quad\quad$ **for all** $c \in Dom(p)$ **do** | $\quad\quad$ **for all** $v \in TVar(t)$ **do** |
| $\quad\quad\quad$ **if** $is\_unfolded(c)$ **then** | $\quad\quad\quad$ **if** $is\_unfolded(VDom(v))$ **then** |
| $\quad\quad\quad\quad DDD_p :=$ | $\quad\quad\quad\quad DDD_t :=$ |
| $\quad\quad\quad\quad \sum_{x \in c} SVP(p, c) \xrightarrow{x} DDD_p$ | $\quad\quad\quad\quad \sum_{x \in VDom(v)} SVT(t, v) \xrightarrow{x} DDD_t$ |
| $\quad\quad\quad$ **end if** | $\quad\quad\quad$ **end if** |
| $\quad\quad$ **end for** | $\quad\quad$ **end for** |
| $\quad$ **end for** | $\quad$ **end for** |

---

### 4.5  Reconstruction of Explicit Representation

Construction of an explicit unfolded net from a symbolic representation is done, as shown in Algorithm 2, by creating a place for each path in the decision diagrams of unfolded places, and creating a transition for each path in the DDD of unfolded transitions. The 0 DDD means no unfolded place or transition exists, 1 means the colored (or not) place or transition is kept identical in unfolded net, and other symbolic representations, except $\top$ which should never happen, mean unfolded places or transitions have to be created. The algorithm presented is valid only for full unfolding, but can be easily extended for partial unfolding. The algorithm is the same for transitions as for places, and the same for post arcs than for pre ones.

---

**Algorithm 2.** Concrete unfolded net construction

---

**Require:** $N$, the symbolic unfolded Net
**Ensure:** $N' = \langle P', T', Pre', Post', M0' \rangle$, the concrete unfolded net

Unfolded places
  **for all** $p \in P$ **do**
    **for all** $path \in DDD_p$ **do**
      $P'_p := P' \cup \{path\}$
    **end for**
    $P' := P' \cup P'_p$
  **end for**

Unfolded initial marking
  **for all** $p \in P$ **do**
    **for all** $p' \in P'_p$ **do**
      **if** $M_0(p)(p') \neq 0$ **then**
        $M'_0 := M0' \cup \{(p', M_0(p)(p'))\}$
      **end if**
    **end for**
  **end for**

Unfolded $Pre$ arcs
  **for all** $arc = {}^P\!\bigcirc\!\xrightarrow{valuation}\!\blacktriangleright\!\!\square^T \in Pre$ **do**
    **for all** $p' \in P'_p$ **do**
      **for all** $t' \in T'_t$ **do**
        $n := valuation(p', t')$
        **if** $n \neq 0$ **then**
          $Pre' := Pre' \cup \{ {}^P\!\bigcirc\!\xrightarrow{n}\!\blacktriangleright\!\!\square^T \}$
        **end if**
      **end for**
    **end for**
  **end for**

---

For each colored arc ${}^P\!\bigcirc\!\xrightarrow{valuation}\!\blacktriangleright\!\!\square^T \in Pre$, an unfolded arc ${}^P\!\bigcirc\!\xrightarrow{n}\!\blacktriangleright\!\!\square^T$ is created if the evaluation of *valuation* for unfolded values of $p'$ and $t'$ is non-zero. The same applies for colored arcs ${}^T\!\square\!\xrightarrow{valuation}\!\blacktriangleright\!\bigcirc^P \in Post$.

For each place $p \in P$, its initial marking has a symbolic representation $DDD_p^{marked}$ in the same way as $DDD_p$. For each unfolded place $p' \in P'_p$, its initial marking is created if a path in $DDD_p^{marked}$ corresponding to $p'$ is found.

## 5   Optimizations on the Unfolded P/T Net

Optimizations applied to the symbolic unfolded net are described in the next subsections. First of them is a simple one, the removal of **false** guarded transitions. Then, a more powerful but complicated one is presented, the removal of maximal unmarked syphon. A last optimization, the removal of marked orphaned places, is not presented in this paper as it uses the same operations as the maximal unmarked syphon.

Homomorphisms are not described in this paper because of lack of space, but are available to the reader on request to the authors.

## 5.1   Optimization Order

**Definition 8 (Partial order over optimizations).** $\prec$ *is a partial order operator over optimizations defined by* $o_i \prec o_j$ *iff* $o_j$ *applied on an unfolded net previously optimized by* $o_i$ *has a different result from* $o_j$ *applied on an unoptimized unfolded net.*

*Guard* $\prec$ *Syphon*, as maximal unmarked syphon reduces the unfolded net because some transitions can never be fired, either because one of their input places cannot be marked or because the bindings of the transition variables lead to a false guard.

*Guard* $\prec$ *Orphan* and *Syphon* $\prec$ *Orphan*, as removal of orphaned marked places has no effect until some transitions have been removed.

For each optimization *Opt*, the best result is obtained when the length of the path $Opt_0 \prec \ldots \prec Opt$ is maximal. Using this constraint and this partial order, the order for optimization application is : removal of false guarded transitions, removal of maximal unmarked syphon and removal of orphaned marked places.

## 5.2   Removal of false Guarded Transitions

A first optimization is to remove, from the unfolded net, the transitions that are false guarded. Guards are used in Well-Formed Nets to enable or disable unfolded transitions using unfold bindings of transition variables. Each unfolded transition has a unique set of bindings that can be used for guard evaluation to remove bindings leading to a false guard.

A guard is an expression tree, where nodes have different arities. Nodes and leaves do not cover all the range of syntactic tokens expressing guards, for example $x > y$ or $x \leq y$, as a reduced set of operators described in Figure 4 is sufficient.

| Name | Type | Arity | Meaning | |
|------|------|-------|---------|---|
| OR | node | 2 | $ltree \vee rtree$ | where $ltree, rtree$ are subtrees |
| AND | node | 2 | $ltree \wedge rtree$ | where $ltree, rtree$ are subtrees |
| NOT | node | 1 | $\neg tree$ | where $tree$ is a subtree |
| EQ | leaf | - | $lvar = rvar$ | where $lvar, rvar$ are variables |
| LT | leaf | - | $lvar < rvar$ | where $lvar, rvar$ are variables |
| IN | leaf | - | $var \in vals$ | where $var$ is a variable and $vals$ a set of values |
| TRUE | leaf | - | $true$ | |
| FALSE | leaf | - | $false$ | |

**Fig. 4.** Nodes and leaves in a guard tree

Application of a guard is an evaluation of the guard expression tree using bindings for all transition variables. The symbolic operation follows the same algorithm with one more indirection level, by creating for each guard an homomorphism to select sequences of bindings that evaluate to true. The same homomorphism is easily extended to select only non-false guards in partial unfolding, where some variables are not bound.

Creation of the homomorphism follows the guard expression tree, each node or leaf being translated to an homomorphism as described in the following paragraphs. One node, NOT raises a problem in its definition because its meaning is to keep all paths except selected ones. It thus translates to the difference between two symbolic representations, the full representation of all possible bindings and the representation of selected ones. We chose to avoid the difference operation by pushing negation down the tree using De Morgan's laws.

AND nodes are translated to the ∘ homomorphism operator. As the meaning of ∘ used here is ∧, evaluation of subtrees can be done in any order. OR nodes are as easy to translate, by the + homomorphism operator. Whereas two leaves, TRUE and FALSE have a direct translation by $Id$ and $Constant(0)$, which always returns the DDD 0, other leaves of the form $v_l$++$s_l = v_r$++$s_r$, $v_l$++$s_l < v_r$++$s_r$ and $v$++$s \in C$ have no predefined homomorphisms or operations corresponding and are thus translated to inductive homomorphisms.

In partial unfolding, a guard tree leaf applied on at least one unbound variable is considered always non-false, as later binding of the variable can still lead to true of false. The $Id$ homomorphism is used in this case instead of real leaf operation to keep the paths concerned with these special leaves.

### 5.3   Removal of Maximal Unmarked Syphon

The maximal unmarked syphon is a subset of the places of the unfolded net that cannot structurally be marked, and thus can be safely removed. Transitions post-condition of these places may be removed simultaneously because they can never be fired. Depending on the colored net, this syphon can be negligible, or almost cover the whole unfolded net.

**Algorithm for P/T Nets.** The algorithm for removal of the maximal unmarked syphon is based on an iterative construction, by removing places that can be marked from a superset $S$ of the syphon, until stability. It is composed of three steps, described below.

1. Initially, the considered set is composed of all the unfolded places except the initially marked ones.
   $S = \cup_{p \in P}(p' \in P'_p | M'_0(p') = \emptyset)$.
2. Until stability, reduction is applied on $S$. For each unfolded transition $t' \in T'_{t \in T}$, if all its input places are outside the syphon, $Pre_T(t') \cap S = \emptyset$, then the transition can structurally be fired and all its output places are removed from the syphon, $S \leftarrow S \setminus Post_T(t')$. If no place is removed from the syphon in one iteration, then stability has been reached and the algorithm comes to its ending step.
   $\forall t \in T, \forall t' \in T'_t, (Pre_T(t') \cap S = \emptyset) \implies S \leftarrow S \setminus Post_T(t')$
3. The algorithm is ended by removing the syphon from the unfolded net. All transitions post-condition of places in syphon are removed.
   $\forall p \in P, P'_p \leftarrow P'_p \setminus S$
   $\forall t \in T, T'_t \leftarrow T'_t \setminus \{t' \in T'_t | Pre_T(t') \cap S \neq \emptyset \vee Post_T(t') \cap S \neq \emptyset\}$

**Algorithm for Data Decision Diagrams.** The algorithm of the removal of maximal unmarked syphon can be easily extended to the manipulation of sets of nodes, and sets represented by DDDs. In the following paragraphs, we use the notation $DDD_n^i$ for the symbolic representation at step $i$ of unfolded node $n$, meaning that $SP(n) = DDD_n^i$ (for a place) in the symbolic unfolded net at this step. The three steps of the algorithm become :

1. $\forall p \in P, DDD_p^0 \leftarrow DDD_p \setminus M_0'(p)$
2. until stability :
   $\forall p \in P, DDD_p^i \leftarrow DDD_p^{i-1} \setminus \cup_{t \in T} HPost^T(DDD_t \setminus \cup_{p' \in P} HPost^P(DDD_{p'}^{i-1}))$
3. $\forall p \in P, DDD_p^n \leftarrow DDD_p \setminus DDD_p^{n-1}$
   $\forall t \in T, DDD_t^n \leftarrow DDD_t \setminus \cup_{p \in P}(HPre^P(DDD_p^{n-1}) \cup HPost^p(DDD_p^{n-1}))$

$HPre^P$, $HPre^T$, $HPost^P$ and $HPost^T$ are homomorphisms defined to apply respectively $Pre_P$, $Pre_T$, $Post_P$ and $Post_T$ on sets of places or transitions. These homomorphisms can be divided in two groups : $HPre^P$, $HPost^P$ and $HPre^T$, $HPost^T$, based on their input and output types, these group are described in the following paragraphs.

To ease reading of this paragraph, we take the example of $HPre^P$, but the same applies for the four homomorphisms. $HPre^P$ applies on all unfolded places $P'$ of the net. It is defined using sub-homomorphisms for each unfolded place set $P_p'|p \in P$ by the homomorphism $HPre_p^P$, which returns the set of unfolded transitions pre-condition of places unfolded from $p$. If not applied on places in $P_p'$, it returns 0. $HPre_p^P$ is itself divided into sub-homomorphisms for each arc $a$ from a transition $t$ to $p$, using a $HPre_a^P$ homomorphism. As the valuation of an arc is a sum of terms, $valuation = \sum_i v_i$, the latter homomorphism can be cut into smaller ones noted $HPre_v^P$, considering each valuation term as an arc. Operation for combination of sub-homomorphism is either $\circ$ or $\cup$, depending on the searched result.

$HPre^P = \cup_{p \in P} \cup_{t \in T|Post[t,p] \neq \emptyset} \cup_{v \in Post[t,p]} HPre_v^P$ is the homomorphism returning the set of unfolded transitions pre-condition of a set of unfolded places. If $Post[t,p] = \emptyset$, the unfolded arc does not exist and no set is returned, using the DDD 0, implicitly represented in the $\cup$ operators.

**Removal of Initially Marked Places.** For each colored place $p$, a DDD representing only its marked unfolded places $DDD_p^{marked}$ can be built, using the same symbolic representation as $DDD_p$. The operation to remove marked unfolded places is $DDD_p^0 = DDD_p \setminus DDD_p^{marked}$.

A colored mark is a tuple, $mark(p) = \langle c_1, \ldots, c_n \rangle$, with one $c_i$ value for each component of $Dom(p)$. In partial unfolding, if $c_i$ is of a non unfolded color class $C_j$, it is not used in the symbolic representation of unfolded places and thus not used in the marking representation.

For a place where no color class has to be unfolded, the unfolded marking is 0 for no marking, 1 for a marking.

$HPre_v^P$ and $HPost_v^P$ **Homomorphisms.** A colored arc is translated to an homomorphism $HPost_v^P$ if applied from $DDD_p^i$ to a subset of $DDD_t$, to get the transitions post-condition of places in $DDD_p^i$. Almost the same homomorphism $HPre_v^P$ is created for the reverse arc, to get transitions pre-condition of places, and only the small difference with $HPost_v^P$ is given.

These two operations are a composition of six homomorphisms, each one being a step in the transformation. Some steps can be grouped to improve efficiency by reducing the number of operations, but these optimizations are not presented here. The steps can be divided into two main groups : the selection of places that are valid inputs of the valuation (*1, 2*) and the conversion of these places to the symbolic representation of output transitions (*3, 4, 5, 6*).

Each step is itself composed of several homomorphisms, each one defined to be applied for only one color class, not the whole domain. The composition for several color classes is : $HPre_v^P = \circ_{term \in v} HPre_{term}^P$. We consider a colored arc from transition $t$ to place $p$ ($Pre_v^P$), or from place $p$ to transition $t$ ($Post_v^P$), valued with term *term*.

*Select valid places for valuation constants.* If $Dom(p) = c_0 \times \ldots \times c_n$, for each $v_i$ of $term = \langle v_0, \ldots, v_n \rangle$, if $c_i$ is an unfolded color class and $v_i$ is a constant, then the value of $v_i$ is compared to the unfold values of $P_p'$ for component $c_i$, assignment values of $SVP(p, c_i)$ DDD variable, to keep only the unfolded places matching the constant.

DDD variables involved in this step are useless in symbolic representation after the selection, because their values have no relation with values of valuation variables of $t$, and are thus removed.

*Select places consistent with valuation variables appearing several times.* A single variable can be referenced several times in one term. For each couple $c_i, c_j \in Dom(p)$ where $v_i = var + s_i$ and $v_j = var + s_j$ refer the same unfolded valuation variable *var*, only the unfolded places where $SVP(p, c_i)$ has the same value as $SVP(p, c_j)$ shifted with $s_i - s_j$ are kept in symbolic representation.

As values of $SVP(p, c_i)$ and $SVP(p, c_j)$ are linked, only one occurrence is necessary for the next steps, the other is removed.

*Remove successor ranks.* Successor ranks have been used in previous step to check consistency, but valuation variables do not use them. As each variable left in symbolic representation corresponds to a component $v_i = var + s_i$ of the term, an homomorphism transforms each value of $SVP(p, c_i)$ to its $s_i$ predecessor for the $HPost_{term}^P$ version, and to its $s_i$ successor for the $HPre_{term}^P$ one, to keep only the value without its successor rank.

*Transform place DDD to transition DDD.* In the previous steps, we considered the symbolic representation of $DDD_p$. From now one, we consider the one of $DDD_t$. The transformation begins in this step, by renaming for each remaining $v_i = var$ the variable $SVP(p, c_i)$ to $SVT(t, var)$.

*Reorder DDD variables to fit transition DDD order.* All transition variables in the valuation are in the symbolic representation, but their order differs of the order of transition variables in symbolic representation of the unfolded transitions. A reordering is thus done in this step to fit the order of the transition.

*Complete transition DDD.* For each variable $v \in TVar(t)|VDom(v)$ is unfolded, missing in symbolic representation, $SVT(t,v) \xrightarrow{x \in VDom(v)} 1$ is added in its right place in the symbolic representation.

**$HPre_v^T$ and $HPost_v^T$ Homomorphisms.** A colored arc is translated to an homomorphism $HPost_v^T$ if applied from $DDD_t$ to a subset of $DDD_p^i$, to get the places post-condition of transitions in $DDD_t$. Almost the same homomorphism $HPre_v^T$ is created for the reverse arc, to get places pre-condition of transitions.

As for $HPre_v^P$ and $HPost_v^P$, $HPost_v^T$ is a composition of four steps and divided in subhomomophisms for each term of $v$. We consider a colored arc from transition $t$ to place $p$ ($Post_v^T$), or from place $p$ to transition $t$ ($Pre_v^T$), valued with term *term*.

*Copy transition DDD variables to their bound place DDD variable.* For each unfolded transition variable $var \in TVar(t)|VDom(var)$ is unfolded, if $Dom(p) = c_0 \times \ldots \times c_n$, and $term = \langle v_0, \ldots, v_n \rangle$, for each $v_i \in term$, if $VDom(var)$ is $c_i$ then the DDD values for $SVT(t,var)$ are copied to the DDD variable $SVP(p,c_i)$.

*Remove unused DDD variables.* All valuation variables represented in DDD have been copied, if used in the term, to place DDD variables, and are thus useless. This step removes them from symbolic representation. For each $var \in TVar(t)|VDom(var)$ is unfolded, $SVT(t,var)$ is removed from DDD.

*Add successor ranks.* Successor ranks have not been used in previous steps. As each variable in symbolic representation corresponds to a component $v_i = var\text{++}s_i$ of the term, an homomorphism transforms each value of $SVP(p,c_i)$ to its $s_i$ predecessor for the $HPre_{term}^T$ version, and to its $s_i$ successor for the $HPost_{term}^T$ one.

*Insert constants of valuation.* As valuation can contain constants, new DDD variables are created to insert the constants in the symbolic representation. For each constant $v_i$ in the term, $SVP(p,c_i) \xrightarrow{v_i}$ is inserted in its right place.

# 6    Experimentation and Results

**Implementation.** Optimized unfolder has been implemented as a library and an executable built on top of this library. Unfolded net follows a pipe of optimizations, like those seen in sections 5.2 and 5.3. The symbolic to explicit net transformation presented in section 4.5 is also a component of this pipe.

**Experimentation.** We selected several models to validate our strategy:

- *PolyORB* : it comes from a cooperation with Telecom Paris to build Poly-ORB, a formally verified Middleware [7]. In our test, the model is parameterized according to the number of threads that are allocated in the system.
- *Peterson* : it models the Peterson's mutual exclusion algorithm for $N$ processes [10]. This model does not include any redundant information to test processes level. This fact explains the high number of transitions. In our test, the model is parameterized according to the number of processes.
- *Train* : It comes from a joint studies on the San Francisco area BART case study, that was presented in [6]. This model is not parametrized.

| Model | Initial | | Guards | | Syphon | | Orphans | | Optimized | | | |
|---|---|---|---|---|---|---|---|---|---|---|---|---|
| | Places | Transitions | % P | % T | % P | % T | % P | % T | Time | Memory | Places | Transitions |
| PolyORB_t20 | 4,964 | 3,392,800 | 0 | 100 | 0 | 0 | 0 | 0 | < 1 | 11 | 4,964 | 3,392,040 |
| PolyORB_t40 | 9,344 | 6,786,800 | 0 | 100 | 0 | 0 | 0 | 0 | < 1 | 20 | 9,344 | 6,784,860 |
| PolyORB_t60 | 13,724 | 10,182,400 | 0 | 100 | 0 | 0 | 0 | 0 | 1 | 29 | 13,724 | 10,178,480 |
| PolyORB_t80 | 18,104 | 13,579,600 | 0 | 100 | 0 | 0 | 0 | 0 | 1 | 41 | 18,104 | 13,572,900 |
| Peterson_05 | 1,150 | 58,850 | 0 | 55 | 100 | 45 | $\varepsilon$ | 0 | < 1 | 10 | 470 | 7,810 |
| Peterson_10 | 9,100 | 1,835,400 | 0 | 59 | 100 | 41 | $\varepsilon$ | 0 | 3 | 73 | 3,890 | 313,220 |
| Peterson_15 | 30,600 | 13,838,400 | 0 | 61 | 100 | 39 | $\varepsilon$ | 0 | 10 | 194 | 13,260 | 2,576,730 |
| Train | 10,620 | 1.4072e+09 | 0 | 61 | 99 | 39 | 1 | 0 | 5 | 111 | 343 | 202 |

**Fig. 5.** Execution results from our benchmark

Figure 5 summarizes the results we got on a 3.6 GHz Pentium-4 CPU with 2 GBytes of RAM. We provide the maximum number of places and transitions (columns *Initial Places* and *Initial Transitions*), the final number of places and transitions after optimizations (columns *Optimized Places* and *Optimized Transitions*). The explicit unfolded net is not generated, as for all examples but `Train` execution time would be hours or days. We also measure the execution time (in seconds) and the maximum amount of memory required to process the unfolding (in Mbytes). We also provide the ratio of deleted places and transitions for every listed optimizations (for example, 100% of deleted transition in one column means that all suppressed transitions are detected by this optimization).

Our first test (PolyORB) shows the capacity of our approach to take care of numerous objects in a very short time. This Petri net is very symmetric (all threads in the system can exchange their role) and that explains the very poor performances of the implemented optimizations (only the guard optimization is activated for a very small number of transitions). These symmetries also explain the very low amount of memory required to store that many Petri net objects (this is a typical advantage of decision diagram based representations).

Our second model (`Peterson`) only has two colored places (one for processes, another one for the level variables that store the last process to enter in each level). States of the processes are modelled as a class. Therefore, all classes of the domain place depicting the processes are not always useful (e.g. used to scan all processes), leading to never marked places in the unfolded net. For that types of specifications, optimization factor is excellent since up to 80% of dead transitions are eliminated.

Our last model (`Train`) provides spectacular performances on the optimization rate (99,99999985% of transitions as well as 99,995% of places are deleted). This is due to the presence of < and > in transition guards as well as the use of a modeling technique to express discretized non linear function (e.g. the braking distance according to a vehicle speed). A function $y = f(x_1, ..., x_N)$ is modeled with a place having a $N + 1$ product color class. This very large product, as well as that color domains usually are large, generates numerous P/T corresponding places for which only a few are marked (the initial marking only has a few of the possible values). As shown here, the corresponding P/T net model, before optimization, contains billions of places and transitions that do not remain after optimization.

The removal of orphaned marked places has poor results. It only removes a few places in the `Peterson` and `Train` models, and none in PolyORB. This optimization is only intended to clean the unfolded net after removal of the maximal unmarked syphon, and to inform the modeller about unused marked places, as these places might be a modelling error.

**Comparison with Maria.** We now compare our work to the unfolder included in Maria [9]. It is based on different principles : unfolding is viewed as related to the colored transition enabling test. Compact structures as BDDs or DDDs are not used : a unique explicit colored marking is built using the following rules:

- a place color is or is not in the marking, no cardinality is taken into account,
- all places colors in the initial marking are in the unique marking,
- if a transition is enabled with colors in the unique marking (here again, cardinalities are not taken into account), then all post-condition places colors are added to the unique marking.

Place colors in the unique marking are translated into ordinary places and corresponding transitions and arcs are computed. It can easily be shown that place colors not translated into ordinary places corresponds to our maximal unmarked syphon.

Performance differences between our symbolic unfolder and Maria have several explanations. Firstly, colored transition enabling test is more efficient than our symbolic manipulations : the latter one uses heavy DDD variable reordering. Secondly, our unfolder can use a lot of memory for some models, whereas Maria always keeps a very low memory usage, but maria is not able to extract information from huge optimized unfolded nets, like PolyORB, because Maria's strategy, in that case, leads to and explicit representation of the unfolded net.

The main difference between our unfolder and Maria is a consequence of the different chosen approaches : symbolic for our tool and explicit for maria. As expected, explicit approach has better results on small unfolded nets. For the `Train` model, Maria ends its execution after 20 seconds using less than 1 MBytes. This is equivalent in time (since Maria generates the output, which takes time) and much lower from the memory use than our symbolic approach. However, for the other examples, whereas no other operation can be done until the full unfolded net is generated for Maria, which can take hours, our symbolic unfolded net enables some operations without generation of its explicit representation. These new operations are to be defined in the future.

# 7    Conclusion

To complete some structural analysis of colored Petri nets, it is important to back-track to equivalent P/T nets and use structural techniques that are not yet available for colored Petri nets. This is important, especially when dealing with very large models deduced from higher specification languages. Our experiments show that it really supports very large unfolded models.

The technique presented in this paper relies on data decision diagram for a very compact internal representation. This is an original use of such techniques in a new application domain. It provides good perspectives in the handling of large system specifications.

Another advantage of our symbolic unfolding technique is that it is suitable for partial unfolding of a subset of the color domains. This is of interest to discard some useless color domains or increase the specification symmetry for analysis purpose. So far, no unfolder from High Level Petri Nets to P/T nets offers this possibility.

The presented technique is implemented and already available in CPN-AMI 3.0 as a beta version tool.

# References

1. S. Bernardi, S. Donatelli, and J. Merseguer. From UML sequence diagrams and statecharts to analysable Petri net models. In *WOSP '02: Proceedings of the 3rd int. workshop on Software and performance*, pages 35–45. ACM Press, 2002.
2. R. Bryant. Graph-based algorithms for boolean function manipulation. *IEEE Transactions on Computers*, 35(8):677–691, August 1986.
3. G. Chiola, C. Dutheillet, G. Franceschini, and S. Haddad. On Well-Formed Coloured Nets and their Symbolic Reachability Graph. *High-Level Petri Nets. Theory and Application, LNCS*, 1991.
4. J-M. Couvreur, E. Encrenaz, E. Paviot-Adet, D. Poitrenaud, and P-A. Wacrenier. Data decision diagrams for petri net analysis. In J. Esparza and C. Lakos, editors, *Applications and Theory of Petri Nets 2002*, number 2360 in LNCS, pages 101–120. Springer Verlag, June 2002.
5. J-M. Couvreur, S Haddad, and J. F. Peyre. Generative families of positive invariants in coloured nets sub-classes. In G. Rozenberg, editor, *Applications and Theory of Petri Nets, LNCS*, pages 51–70, 1991.
6. A. de Groot, J. Hooman, F. Kordon, E. Paviot-Adet, I. Vernier-Mounier, M. Lemoine, G. Gaudiere, V. Winter, and D. Kapur. A survey: Applying formal methods to a software intensive system. In *6th International Symposium on High-Assurance Systems Engineering*, pages 55–64. IEEE Computer Society, 2001.
7. J. Hugues, Y. Thierry-Mieg, F. Kordon, L. Pautet, S. Baarir, and T. Vergnaud. On the Formal Verification of Middleware Behavioral Properties. In *Proceedings of the 9th International Workshop on Formal Methods for Industrial Critical Systems (FMICS'04)*, volume ENTCS 133, pages 139 – 157. Elsevier, Sept. 2004.

8. K. Jensen. Coloured Petri nets and the invariant-method. *Theor. Comput. Sci.*, 14:317–336, 1981.

9. M. Mäkelä. Optimising enabling tests and unfoldings of algebraic system nets. In *Proceedings of the 22nd International Conference on Application and Theory of Petri Nets*, number 2075 in LNCS, pages 283 – 302. Springer-Verlag, 2001.

10. Gary L. Peterson. Myths about the mutual exclusion problem. *Information Processing Letters*, 12(3):115–116, June 1981.

11. R. Valk. *Basic definitions*, chapter 4, pages 41–51. Springer Verlag, Petri nets and system engineering (Claude Girault and Rudiger Valk Eds), first edition, 2003.

12. C. Dutheillet Y. Thierry-Mieg and I. Mounier. Automatic Symmetry Detection in Well-Formed Nets. In W. van der Aalst and E. Best, editors, *Applications and Theory of Petri Nets 2003: 24th International Conference, ICATPN 2003, Proceedings*, number 2679 in LNCS, pages 82–101. Springer Verlag, June 2003.

# Liveness by Invisible Invariants*

Yi Fang[1], Kenneth L. McMillan[2], Amir Pnueli[3], and Lenore D. Zuck[4]

[1] Microsoft, Redmond, Washington
yfang@microsoft.com
[2] Cadence Design Systems, Berkeley, California
mcmillan@cadence.com
[3] New York University, New York, New York
amir@cs.nyu.edu
[4] University of Illinois at Chicago
lenore@cs.uic.edu

**Abstract.** The method of Invisible Invariants was developed in order to verify safety properties of parametrized systems in a fully automatic manner. In this paper, we apply the method of invisible invariant to "bounded response" properties, i.e., liveness properties of the type $p \implies \diamondsuit q$ that are bounded – once a $p$-state is reached, it takes a bounded number of rounds (where a round is a sequence of steps in which each process has been given a chance to proceed) to reach a $q$-state – thus, they are essentially safety properties.

With a "liveness monitor" that observes certain behavior of a system, establishing "bounded response" properties over the system is reduced to the verification of invariant properties.

It is often the case that the inductive invariants for systems with "liveness monitors" contain assertions of a certain form that the original method of invisible invariant is not able to generate, nor to check inductiveness. To accommodate invariants of such forms, we extend the techniques used for invariant generation, as well as the small model theorem for validity check.

## 1 Introduction

*Uniform verification of parameterized systems* is one of the most challenging problems in verification. Given a parameterized system $S(N) : P[1] \parallel \cdots \parallel P[N]$ and a property $p$, uniform verification attempts to verify that $S(N)$ satisfies $p$ for every $N > 1$. One of the most powerful approaches to verification that is not restricted to finite-state systems is *deductive verification*. This approach is based on a set of proof rules in which the user has to establish the validity of a list of premises in order to validate a given temporal property of the system. The two tasks that the user has to perform are:

1. Provide some auxiliary constructs that appear in the premises of the rule;
2. Use the auxiliary constructs to establish the logical validity of the premises.

When performing manual deductive verification, the first task is usually the more difficult, requiring ingenuity, expertise, and a good understanding of the behavior of the

---

* This research was supported in part by NSF grant CCR-0205571 and ONR grant N00014-99-1-0131.

E. Najm et al. (Eds.): FORTE 2006, LNCS 4229, pp. 356–371, 2006.
© IFIP International Federation for Information Processing 2006

program and the techniques for formalizing these insights. The second task is often performed using theorem provers such as PVS [OSR93] or STEP [BBC+95], which require user guidance and interaction, and place additional burden on the user. The difficulties in the execution of these two tasks are the main reason why deductive verification is not used more widely.

A representative case is the verification of invariance properties using the proof rule INV of [MP95]: in order to prove that assertion $r$ is an invariant of program $P$, the rule requires coming up with an auxiliary assertion $\varphi$ that is *inductive* (i.e. is implied by the initial condition and is preserved under every computation step) and that strengthens (implies) $r$. The rule is described in Fig. 1, where $\Theta$ is the initial condition of program $P$.

$$
\begin{array}{l}
\text{I1.}\ \Theta \rightarrow \varphi \\
\text{I2.}\ \varphi \wedge \rho \rightarrow \varphi' \\
\text{I3.}\ \varphi \rightarrow r \\
\hline
\qquad \Box\, r
\end{array}
$$

**Fig. 1.** The proof rule INV

In [PRZ01, APR+01], we introduced the method of *invisible invariants*, that offers a method for automatic generation of the auxiliary assertion $\varphi$ for parameterized systems, as well as an efficient algorithm for checking the validity of the premises of INV. The generation of invisible auxiliary constructs is based on the following idea: it is often the case that an auxiliary assertion $\varphi$ for a parameterized system $S(N)$ has the form $\forall i : [1..N].q(i)$ or, more generally, $\forall i \neq j.q(i,j)$. We construct an instance of the parameterized system taking a fixed value $N_0$ for the parameter $N$. For the finite-state instantiation $S(N_0)$, we compute, using BDDs, some assertion $\psi$ that we wish to generalize to an assertion in the required form. Let $r_1$ be the projection of $\psi$ on process $P[1]$, obtained by discarding references to variables that are local to all processes other than $P[1]$. We take $q(i)$ to be the generalization of $r_1$ obtained by replacing each reference to a local variable $P[1].x$ by a reference to $P[i].x$. The obtained $q(i)$ is our candidate for the body of the inductive assertion $\varphi : \forall i.q(i)$. We refer to this generalization procedure as *project & generalize*. For example, when computing invisible invariants, $\psi$ is the set of reachable states of $S(N_0)$. The procedure can be easily generalized to generate assertions of the type $\forall i_1, \ldots, i_k.p(\vec{i})$.

Having obtained a candidate for the assertion $\varphi$, we still have to check the validity of the premises of the proof rule we wish to employ. Under the assumption that our assertional language is restricted to the predicates of equality and inequality between bounded-range integer variables (which is adequate for many of the parameterized systems we considered), we proved a *small-model* theorem, according to which, for a certain type of assertions, there exists a (small) bound $N_0$ such that such an assertion is valid for every $N$ iff it is valid for all $N \leq N_0$. This enables using BDD-techniques to check the validity of such an assertion. The cases covered by the theorem are those whose premises can be written in the form $\forall \vec{i} \exists \vec{j}.\psi(\vec{i}, \vec{j})$, where $\psi(\vec{i}, \vec{j})$ is a quantifier-free assertion that may refer only to the global variables and the local variables of $P[i]$ and $P[j]$ ($\forall \exists$-*assertions* for short).

Being able to validate the premises on $S[N_0]$ has the additional important advantage that the user never sees the automatically generated auxiliary assertion $\varphi$. This assertion is produced as part of the procedure and is immediately consumed in order to validate the premises of the rule. Being generated by symbolic BDD-techniques, the representation of the auxiliary assertions is often extremely unreadable and non-intuitive, and it usually does not contribute to a better understanding of the program or its proof. Because the user never gets to see it, we refer to this method as the "method of *invisible invariants*." As shown in [PRZ01, APR+01], embedding a $\forall \vec{i}.q(\vec{i})$ candidate inductive invariant in INV results in premises that fall under the small-model theorem.

In this paper we apply the method of invisible invariants to the second-most important properties of concurrent systems, namely, "response" properties. Response properties are properties of the type $q \Rrightarrow \Diamond r$ (i.e., $\Box(q \rightarrow \Diamond r)$), and they are the most common liveness properties. The most frequent form of response properties of parameterized systems is $\forall \vec{i}.(q(\vec{i}) \Rrightarrow \Diamond r(\vec{i}))$, where $q(\vec{i})$ and $r(\vec{i})$ are quantifier-free. Since the systems we are dealing with are finite-state, that is, for every value $N$, $S[N]$ is finite-state, every valid response property is *bounded* by some of the parameters of the system.

The ability to prove only *bounded* progress may seem like a limitation. However, note that we are dealing here only with finite-state systems. That is, for every $N$, $S[N]$ is finite-state. If a finite-state system satisfies a progress property, then it satisfies a corresponding bounded progress property, for a suitable bound. In the case of a simple transition system without fairness assumptions, the bound can be given in terms of the maximum number of transitions required to satisfy the progress condition. In the case of "justice" assumptions (of the form $\Box \Diamond p(i)$), the bound can be given in terms of the number of "rounds" in which every justice condition $p(i)$ is satisfied. Of course, the bound may be a rapidly increasing function of $N$. The main limitation of the present method is that it handles only the case when the bound increases linearly with $N$. We will show, however, that this condition is satisfied for several typical examples of parameterized protocols.

Roughly speaking, the bound determines "how fast" progress is achieved. In the case that the bound depends on the transition relation, the proof of progress can be replaced by a proof of a simpler safety property, *bounded progress*, that establishes that once $q(\vec{i})$ holds and enough transitions (where "enough" is determined by the bound) occur, $r(\vec{i})$ obtains. Since we are dealing with parameterized systems, the bound depends on the parameter $N$. For simplicity of notation, assume that $(\vec{i})$ is of size 1, i.e., the progress property at hand is $\forall i.q(i) \Rrightarrow \Diamond r(i)$. Let $z$ be some process. It suffices to show that $q(z) \Rrightarrow \Diamond r(z)$. Let $K$ range over *rounds*, in each of which each process is to take at least one step. Since we want to rule out stuttering rounds, we allow a process to take a stuttering step only if it has no non-stuttering step available to it. We show how to obtain $K$ and how to automatically construct a non-interfering "liveness monitor" such that, once (synchronously) composed with the original system, the method of invisible invariants can be used to show a ($K$-dependent) bounded progress (safety) property that establishes the liveness property of the parameterized system.

Often it is the case that the safety property obtained is too large for the model checker. Our experience has shown that splitting such individual proofs into two parts, livelock freedom and bounded overtaking, often helps to avoid those two obstacles. "Livelock freedom" establishes $\exists i.q(i) \Rightarrow \exists i. \Diamond r(i)$, and "bounded overtaking" establishes that once $\exists i.q(i)$, there is a bound $b$ such that for every $j \neq i$, the (regular) sequence $q(j)\Sigma^* r(j)\Sigma^* \neg r(j)$ can occur at most $b$ times before $r(i)$ becomes true. Bounded overtaking is a safety property, and, as we show, can be proved using the method of invisible invariants. Put together, livelock freedom and bounded overtaking establish individual liveness.

It is often the case that the invisible invariants we obtain contain $\exists \forall$-formulae, which are not covered under the small model theorem previously proven. We extend the small model theorem to deal with invariants that have $\exists \forall$-subformulae.

The paper is organized as follows: In Section 2, we give an informal overview of our method. In Section 3, we present the general computational model of FTS and the restrictions that enable the application of the invisible auxiliary constructs methods. We also review the small model theorem, which enables automatic validation of the premises of the various proof rules. In Section 4, we describe how to construct liveness monitors. In some cases, the inductive invariant requires $\exists \forall$-components, to which the invisible invariant method no longer applies. Section 5 shows an extended small model theorem that allows handling such invariants, as well as an enhanced *project & generalize* method that generates invariants with $\exists \forall$-components. In Section 6, we illustrate the method on an example of a BAKERY protocol.

*Related Work.* Proving "bounded liveness" properties by safety techniques was proposed in [BAS02]. There, the justice requirements are incorporated into the safety model. It is not clear whether the method can be extended to parameterized systems. Incorporating the justice of such systems into the safety model seems to be prohibitively costly.

A survey on the method of invisible invariants is in [ZP04]. A tool that allows automatic generation of invariants using the method is described in [BFPZ05].

The problem of uniform verification of parameterized systems is undecidable[AK86]. One approach to remedy this situation, pursued, e.g., in [EK00], is to look for restricted families of parameterized systems for which the problem becomes decidable. Unfortunately, the proposed restrictions are very severe and exclude many useful systems such as asynchronous systems where processes communicate by shared variables.

Another approach is to look for sound but incomplete methods. Representative works of this approach include methods based on: explicit induction [EN95], network invariants that can be viewed as implicit induction [LHR97], abstraction and approximation of network invariants [CGJ95], and other methods based on abstraction [GZ98]. Other methods include those relying on "regular model-checking" (e.g., [JN00]) that overcome some of the complexity issues by employing *acceleration* procedures, methods based on symmetry reduction (e.g.[GS97]), or compositional methods (e.g.[McM99]), combining automatic abstraction with finite-instantiation due to symmetry. Some of these approaches (such as the "regular model checking" approach) are restricted to particular architectures and may, occasionally, fail to terminate. Others, require the user to provide auxiliary constructs and thus do not provide for fully automatic verification of parameterized systems.

Most of the mentioned methods only deal with safety properties. Among the methods dealing with liveness properties, we mention [CS02], which handles termination of sequential programs, network invariants [LHR97], and *counter abstraction* [PXZ02].

Most relevant to the work here are [FPPZ04b, FPPZ04a] that extend the method of invisible invariants to *invisible ranking*, by applying the method for automatic genera-tion of auxiliary assertions to general assertions (not necessarily invariant), and propos-ing a rule for proving progress properties that embed the generated assertions in the rule's premises, and efficiently checks for their validity. As is well known to users of such rules, such a proof requires the generation of two kinds of auxiliary constructs: *helpful assertions* and *ranking functions*. To automatically generate ranking functions, we associate, with each potentially helpful transition an individual ranking function mapping states to integers in a small range. If the auxiliary constructs have no quan-tifiers, all the resulting premises are $\forall\exists$-premises and the small-model theorem can be used.

For protocols that cannot be proven with such restricted assertions, [FPPZ04a] ex-tends the method of invisible ranking by allowing helpful assertions (and ranking func-tions) belonging to transitions to be of the form $\forall j.H(i, j)$, where $H(i, j)$ is a quantifier-free assertion. (Substituted in the standard proof rules for progress properties, these as-sertions lead to premises that do not conform to the required $\forall\exists$ form, and therefore cannot be validated using the small model theorem.) To handle such premises the proof rule is extended by implementing a new mechanism for selecting a helpful transition based on the establishment of a *pre-order* among transitions in each state.

Similarly to the method of invisible ranking, the method proposed here is applica-ble to the same type of "bounded progress" properties. However, the invisible ranking method requires numerous auxiliary construct, some (especially the pre-order) are at times hard to compute. The method proposed here is much simpler. The bound is de-rived from a small instantiation of the system, and, once the bound is computed, the only auxiliary construct needed is the strengthening invariant, which is well studied.

## 2   From Bounded Progress into Safety

This section contains a somewhat intuitive overview of the method that will be formal-ized and detailed in the following sections.

Consider a parameterized system $S$ and a progress property $\phi\colon q \Rightarrow \Diamond r$. The prop-erty $\phi$ is bounded, if there is a bound $K$, independent of $N$, such that once a $q$-state is reached, after at most $K$ rounds in which each process takes at least one step, a goal $r$-state is reached.

Consider a "liveness monitor" $M_\phi$ that observes $S$. Once a $q$-state is reached, $M_\phi$ resets a counter of rounds. Once each process takes (at least) one step, $M_\phi$ increases the round counter. When there are no pending states – states on a $r$-free path that originates at a $q$-state – the monitor keeps the round count at zero and does not keep track of the processes. If $\phi$ is bounded by $K$, then in the monitored systems the round counter never exceeds $K$. Thus, proving $\phi$ is equivalent to proving that the $S\|M_\phi \models \Box(rnd < K)$ where $rnd$ is the round counter.

Of course, one has to choose $K$. One can either try to compute it (e.g., by instantiat-ing $S(N)$ for a small number of processes, say $N_0$, and considering the pending paths on the instantiation) or one may choose some small instantiation, try increasing values of $K$ until one succeeds, and then try the resulting $K$ on larger (yet small) instantiations.

Once $K$ is chosen, the method of invisible invariants can be used to show that for every $N$, $S \| M_\phi \models \Box (rnd < K)$. In fact, since the monitor needs to be finite-state, we construct it with the knowledge of (the assumed) $K$ and bound the round counter by $K$.

The method may fail for the following reasons:

1. For some $N$, $S(N) \not\models \phi$ or $\phi$ is not bounded;
2. The bound $K$ is too small;
3. The heuristics used for the generation of invisible invariants are not sufficient for the given system;

We cannot deal with the first case. As to the second case, a larger instantiation usually solves the problem. Hence, it makes sense to try $K$ on several instantiations before attempting to prove the property.

To deal with the third case, we present a new heuristic to generate candidate invariants with $\exists \forall$-assertions, and extend the small model theorem to accommodate invariants in such forms.

# 3   Preliminaries

As a computational model for parameterized bounded-data systems we use *bounded just transition systems*, that are a compassion-less variant of the model of *bounded fair transition system* of [FPPZ04a].

## 3.1   Just Transition Systems

We present a variant of the *just transition system* of [MP95]. A JTS is described by $S = \langle V, \Theta, \mathcal{T} \rangle$, with:

- $V = \{u_1, \ldots, u_n\}$ — A finite set of typed *system variables*. A *state* $s$ of the system provides a type-consistent interpretation of the system variables $V$, assigning to each variable $v \in V$ a value $s[v]$ in its domain. Let $\Sigma$ denote the set of all states over $V$. An *assertion* over $V$ is a first order formula over $V$. A state $s$ satisfies an assertion $\varphi$, denoted $s \models \varphi$, if $\varphi$ evaluates to T by assigning $s[v]$ to every variable $v$ appearing in $\varphi$. We say that $s$ is a $\varphi$-state if $s \models \varphi$.
- $\Theta$ — The *initial condition*: An assertion characterizing the initial states. A state is called *initial* if it is a $\Theta$-state.
- $\mathcal{T}$ — A finite set of transitions. Every transition $\tau \in \mathcal{T}$ is an assertion $\tau(V, V')$ relating the values $V$ of the variables in state $s \in \Sigma$ to the values $V'$ in an $S$-successor state $s' \in \Sigma$. Given a state $s \in \Sigma$, we say that $s' \in \Sigma$ is a $\tau$-*successor* of $s$ if $\langle s, s' \rangle \models \tau(V, V')$ where, for each $v \in V$, we interpret $v$ as $s[v]$ and $v'$ as $s'[v]$. We say that transition $\tau$ is *enabled* in state $s$ if it has some $\tau$-successor, otherwise, we say that $\tau$ is *disabled* in $s$. In the system we consider, every transition is disabled immediately after it is taken. Let $En(\tau)$ denote the assertion $\exists V'. \tau(V, V')$ characterizing the set of states in which $\tau$ is enabled.

Let $\sigma : s_0, s_1, s_2, \ldots$, be an infinite sequence of states. We say that transition $\tau \in \mathcal{T}^a$ is *enabled at position* $k$ of $\sigma$ if $\tau$ is enabled on $s_k$. We say that $\tau$ is *taken at position* $k$ if

$s_{k+1}$ is a $\tau$-successor of $s_k$. Note that several transitions can be considered as taken at the same position.

We say that $\sigma$ is a *computation* of $S$ if it satisfies the following requirements:

- *Initiality* — $s_0$ is initial, i.e., $s_0 \models \Theta$.
- *Consecution* — For each $\ell = 0, 1, ...$, state $s_{\ell+1}$ is a $\tau$-successor of $s_\ell$ for some $\tau \in \mathcal{T}$.
- *Justice* — for every $\tau \in \mathcal{T}$, there are infinitely many positions $k \geq 0$, such that $\tau$ is disabled or taken at position $k$. Since we assume that transition are disbled immediately after they are taken, this is equivalent to requiring that $\tau$ is disbaled infinitely many times.

*Composition of Just transition Systems.* Assume two JTS's $S_1 : \langle V_1, \Theta_1, \mathcal{T}_1 \rangle$ and $S_2 : \langle V_2, \Theta_2, \mathcal{T}_2 \rangle$. The *synchronous parallel composition* of $S_1$ and $S_2$, denoted by $S_1 ||| S_2$, is the JTS

$$\left( V_1 \cup V_2, \Theta_1 \wedge \Theta_2, \bigvee_{\tau_1 \in \mathcal{T}_1, \tau_2 \in \mathcal{T}_2} \tau_1 \wedge \tau_2 \right)$$

The *asynchronous parallel composition* of $S_1$ and $S_2$, denoted by $S_1 || S_2$, is the JTS

$$\left( V_1 \cup V_2, \Theta_1 \wedge \Theta_2, \mathcal{T}_1^+ \cup \mathcal{T}_2^+ \right)$$

where for every $i = 1, 2$, $\mathcal{T}_i^+$ includes, for every transition $\tau \in \mathcal{T}_i$, the transition $\tau$ with a conjunct requiring that all non-$V_i$ variable are presevered. Formally, for a set of variables $U$, let $pres(U)$ denote the assertion $\bigcup_{u \in U}(u' = u)$ stating that no $U$-variables is modified. Then $\mathcal{T}_i^+ = \{\tau \wedge pres(V_1 \cup V_2 \setminus V_i) : \tau \in \mathcal{T}_i\}$.

## 3.2  Bounded Just Transition Systems

To allow the application of the invisible invariants method, we further restrict the systems we study, leading to the model of *bounded just transition systems* (BJTS). For brevity, we describe here a simplified two-type model; the extension for the general multi-type case is straightforward.

Let $N \in \mathbf{N}^+$ be the *system's parameter*. We allow the following data types:

1. **bool**: the set of boolean and finite-range scalars;
2. **index**: a scalar data type that includes integers in the range $[1..N]$;
3. **data**: a scalar data type that includes integers in the range $[0..N]$; and
4. Any number of arrays of the type **index** $\mapsto$ **bool**. We refer to these arrays as *boolean arrays*.
5. At most one array of the type $b$ : **index** $\mapsto$ **data**. We refer to this array as the *data array*.

*Atomic formulas* may compare two variables of the same type. E.g., if $y$ and $y'$ are **index** variables, and $z$ is an **index** $\mapsto$ **data** array, then $y = y'$ and $z[y] < z[y']$ are both atomic formulas. For $z$ : **index** $\mapsto$ **data** and $y$ : **index**, we also allow the special atomic formula $z[y] > 0$. We refer to quantifier-free formulas obtained by boolean combinations of such atomic formulas as *restricted assertions*. As the initial condition

$\Theta$, we allow assertions of the form $\forall \vec{i}.u(\vec{i})$, where $u(\vec{i})$ is a restricted assertion. As the transitions $\tau \in \mathcal{T}$, we allow assertions of the form $\tau(i) : \forall j.\psi(i,j)$ for a restricted assertion $\psi(i,j)$.

*Example 1 (A Simple Mutual Exclusion Algorithm).*
Consider program SIMPLE in Fig. 2, which is a simple mutual exclusion algorithm that guarantees deadlock-freedom access to critical section for any $N$ processes.

$$
\begin{array}{l}
\textbf{in} \quad N : \textbf{natural where } N > 1 \\
\textbf{local} \ \ t \ : \textbf{bool where } t = 1 \\
\overset{N}{\underset{i=1}{\Big\|}} \ P[i] :: \left[
\begin{array}{l}
\textbf{loop forever do} \\
\quad \left[
\begin{array}{l}
0 : \textbf{NonCritical} \\
1 : \textbf{when } t = 1 \textbf{ do } t := 0 \\
2 : \textbf{Critical} \\
3 : t := 1
\end{array}
\right]
\end{array}
\right]
\end{array}
$$

**Fig. 2.** Program SIMPLE

In this version of the algorithm, location 0 constitutes the non-critical section which a process may non-deterministically exit to the trying section at location 1. Location 1 is the waiting location where a process waits until the token ($t$) is available and then takes it. Location 2 is the critical section, and location 3 is the exit section where the process returns the token. As we show, the program guarantees that if some processes are waiting to enter the critical section, eventually some process will succeed. Fig. 3 describes the BJTS corresponding to program SIMPLE.

$$
V : \begin{cases} \pi : \textbf{array}[1..N] \textbf{ of } [0..3] \\ t : \textbf{bool}; \end{cases}
$$
$$
\Theta : \forall i : \pi[i] = 0 \wedge t = 1
$$
$$
\mathcal{T} : \begin{cases}
\tau_0(i) : \forall j \neq i : \pi[i] = 0 \wedge \pi'[i] \in \{0,1\} \wedge pres(\{\pi[j], t\}) \\
\tau_1(i) : \forall j \neq i : \pi[i] = 1 \wedge t = 1 \wedge \pi'[i] = 2 \wedge t' = 0 \wedge pres(\{\pi[j]\}) \\
\tau_2(i) : \forall j \neq i : \pi[i] = 2 \wedge \pi'[i] = 3 \wedge pres(\{\pi[j], t\}) \\
\tau_3(i) : \forall j \neq i : \pi[i] = 3 \wedge \pi'[i] = 0 \wedge t' = 1 \wedge pres(\{\pi[j]\})
\end{cases}
$$

**Fig. 3.** BJTS for Program SIMPLE

As seen in the example of Fig. 3, the transition relation of process $P[i]$ is a disjunction of individual transitions of the form $\tau_0[i] \vee \tau_1[i] \vee \cdots \tau_k[i]$. We denote this disjunction by $\rho[i]$ and refer to it as the *process transition relation*. We denote by $dis[i] = \neg En(\rho[i])$ the assertion stating that the process transition is disabled, and by $dis\_or\_taken[i]$ the disjunction $dis[i] \vee \rho[i]$ claiming that process $P[i]$ is currently disabled.

### 3.3 The Small Model Theorem

Let $\varphi : \forall \vec{i} \exists \vec{j}.R(\vec{i}, \vec{j})$ be an AE-formula, where $R(\vec{i}, \vec{j})$ is a restricted assertion that refers to the state variables of a parameterized system $S(N)$ and to the quantified (**index**) variables $\vec{i}$ and $\vec{j}$. Let $N_0$ be the number of universally quantified, free **index** variables and **index** constants appearing in $R$. The claim below (stated in [PRZ01] and extended in [APR$^+$01]) provides the basis for automatic validation of the premises in the proof rules:

**Theorem 1 (Small model property).**
*An AE-formula $\varphi$ is valid iff it is valid over all instances $S(N)$ for $N \leq N_0$.*

The small model theorem allows to check validity of AE-assertions on small models and to derive from that their validity on arbitrary large instantiations. This can be accomplished using BDD techniques. The method of invisible invariants applies *project & generalize* to produce candidate inductive assertions for the set of reachable states that are A-formulae. Checking their inductiveness requires checking validity of AE-formulae. The method of invisible ranking applies *project & generalize* to produce candidate assertions for various assertions (pending, helpful, ranking), all A- or E-formulae and, the premises obtained using these assertions are again all AE-formulae. Thus, the theorem implies they can be verified on small instantiations.

## 4   Monitoring Liveness with Safety

Assume a progress property $\phi\colon q \Rightarrow \Diamond\, r$. It is often the case that such a progress property $\phi$ is "bounded", that is, there exists some bound $K$, such that after $K$ *rounds* where each process is given at least one chance to progress, a goal state is guaranteed to be reached. If $\phi$ is a bounded progress property with bound $K$, then, instead of showing that $S \models \phi$, we can construct a non-interfering *monitor* $M_\phi(K)$ which we synchronously compose with $S$, and show that the simple invariance property $\Box(rnd < K)$ holds over the new system $S\|M_\phi(K)$.

Thus, for the case of bounded progress, liveness can be reduced to safety. The process can be done automatically, since one can derive $K$ from the reachability graph of $S$.

Assume a BJTS $S\colon \langle V, \Theta, \tau \rangle$ and a progress property $\phi\colon q \Rightarrow \Diamond\, r$. The monitor $M_\phi(K)$ is a BJTS $M_\phi\colon \langle V_M, \Theta_M, \{\tau_M\} \rangle$, where:

$V_M$ – consists of $V$ and three new variables: a boolean *pend*, a variable *rnd* in the range $[0..K]$, and *moved* is an array $[1..N]$ of booleans. The variable *pend* is set when the system is in a state that follows a $q$-state on a $r$-less path. The variable *rnd* counts the number of rounds. The variable *moved*[$i$] is set when process $i$ is disabled.

$\Theta_M$ – $pend = (q \wedge \neg r) \wedge rnd = 0 \wedge \bigwedge_{i=1}^{N} \neg moved[i]$, i.e., initially the round is 0 and every *moved* is F.

$\tau_M$ – $\tau_M$ consists of three conjuncts, one for each of the variables (the *moved*-part is further composed of $N$ conjuncts). The transition $\tau_M$ consists of the following parts:

  1. $pend' = \neg r' \wedge (pend \vee q')$. This conjunct states that *pend* becomes true when it was false and $q \wedge \neg r$ is true, and that *pend* becomes false when $r$ is realized. In all other cases *pend* retains its previous value;

2. $\bigwedge_{i=1}^{N} moved'[i] = \left( \begin{array}{l} \textbf{if} \quad \neg pend' \vee \bigwedge_{j=1}^{N} moved[j] \textbf{ then } \textsc{f} \\ \textbf{else } dis\_or\_taken[i] \vee moved[i] \end{array} \right)$

This conjunct states that for every $i$, $moved[i]$ is true in pending states that are reached from $moved[i]$-states or when process $i$ is disabled, but only if the round is not over (since then all the $moved[i]$'s need be reset).

3. $rnd' = \left( \begin{array}{l} \textbf{if} \qquad \neg pend' \qquad\qquad\qquad\qquad \textbf{then } 0 \\ \textbf{else if } rnd < K \wedge \bigwedge_{j=1}^{N} moved[j] \textbf{ then } rnd + 1 \\ \qquad\qquad\qquad\qquad\qquad\qquad \textbf{else } \; rnd \end{array} \right)$

This conjunct states that a new round starts from pending states once all processes are were found disabled and a $r$-state was not reached. Similarly, $rnd$ becomes 0 when an $r$-state is reached. In all other cases it remains intact.

Note that none of the conjuncts update the variables in $V$, justifying our description of $M_\phi$ as "non constraining."

Thus, as long as $S$ is not in a pending state, $pend$, $rnd$, and all the $moved[i]$'s are $\textsc{f}$. Once $S$ is in a pending state, $pend$ is set. From thereon, whenever every process is found disabled, $rnd$ is incremented (as long as it is less than $K$). Obviously, if $rnd$ ever reaches $K$, than it means that the goal $q$ was not reached after $K$ rounds, thus refuting the assumption that $\phi$ is a bounded progress property with bound $K$. However, if $\square(rnd < K)$, we can be assured that $\phi$ holds over $S$. This is captured by following claim:

**Lemma 1 (Soundness).**

$$(S \| M_\phi(K)) \models \square(rnd < K) \implies S \models \phi$$

*Proof.* Assume that $S \not\models \phi$. Thus, there exists an $S$-computation $\sigma$ of the form $\Sigma^k q$ $(\Sigma - \{r\})^\omega$. Consider the behavior of $M_\phi(K) \| S$ when run on $\sigma$. Obviously, $\sigma \models \Diamond \square \, pend$. Since every process is guaranteed to be disabled infinitely many times, we have that $\sigma \models \square(\neg moved[i] \to \Diamond moved[i])$. We can therefore conclude that $\sigma \models \Diamond(rnd = K)$, thus $(S \| M_\phi(K)) \not\models \square(rnd < K)$.    $\square$

*Example 2 (Liveness Monitor for Program* SIMPLE*).*
Consider the program of Example 1, and suppose we want to establish the progress property $\phi: (\exists i.\pi[i] = 1) \Rightarrow \Diamond(\exists i.\pi[i] = 2)$. We guess $K = 2$, and run the program for instantiations of $N = 3, 4, 5$ to confirm that this is a reasonable bound. We then construct the progress monitor $M_\phi(2)$ as above, where $q: \exists i.\pi[i] = 1$ and $r: \exists i.\pi[i] = 2$. We instantiated Program SIMPLE to 4 processes and run it composed with $M_\phi$. We obtained the invariant

$\forall i \neq j. \; rnd < 2 \wedge (\neg pend \vee t = 1 \vee rnd = 0) \wedge$
$\qquad (\neg pend \to rnd = 0 \wedge \neg moved[i]) \wedge (pend \to \pi[i] \neq 2) \wedge$
$\qquad (rnd = 1 \to \pi[i] = 1 \wedge \neg moved[i]) \wedge$
$\qquad (\pi[i] = 0 \wedge t = 0 \vee \pi[i] = 3 \to \neg moved[i]) \wedge$
$\qquad (\pi[i] \geq 2 \to t = 0 \wedge \pi[j] < 2) \wedge (\pi[i] = 1 \wedge (t = 1 \vee \pi[j] = 3) \to pend) \wedge$
$\qquad (\pi[i] = 0 \wedge t = 1 \wedge moved[i] = 1 \to \pi[j] = 1 \vee \neg moved[j]) \wedge$
$\exists i. \; (rnd = 0 \wedge t = 0) \to (\pi[i] = 0 \wedge moved[i] \vee \pi[i] \geq 2)$

which is inductive and implies $rnd < 2$ over $(simple(4) ||| M_\phi(2))$. It follows Theorem 1 that $\square(rnd < 2)$ is valid over the composed program with every $N$, and, according to Lemma 1, this implies that $\phi$ is valid over every instantiation of Program SIMPLE.

## 5   Cases Requiring an EA-Invariant

The method of invisible invariants obtains auxiliary assertions that are boolean combination of $\forall$-formulae. Used in the proof rule INV, the premises to be proved are then (at most) $\forall\exists$- formulae, whose validity, as the small model theorem establishes, can be shown on small instantiations.

In some cases, however, the auxiliary assertions obtained can have $\exists\forall$-components (thus the proof rule has to establish validity of such formulae), to which the theorem no longer applies. For example, when attempting to establish the livelock freedom property of Program BAKERY in Section 6, we need an invariant that contains a clause:

$$\exists i : (at\_l_2[i] \land moved[i] = 0 \land \forall j \neq i : (y[j] = 0 \lor y[i] < y[j]))$$

claiming that (at the last round) some process has the lowest ticket and has not yet taken a step. This is an $\exists\forall$-assertion, the likes of which are quite common when establishing progress properties.

In this section we present a new small model theorem that applies to some cases where $\exists\forall$-premises need to be validated. To automatically obtain an $\exists\forall$-assertion as a component in invariant assertions, we divide the reachable states into $N$ symmetric subsets $D[1], \ldots, D[N]$, where each $D[i]$ can be over-approximated by an assertion of the type $D_\alpha(i) : \forall j.q(i, j)$, so that the disjunction of $D_\alpha(i)$'s is our desired $\exists\forall$-assertion. The body of the $\exists\forall$-assertion $q(i, j)$ is computed by the procedure *project & generalize*.

### 5.1   An Extended Small Model Theorem

Consider a parameterized BJTS $S(N)$ and a formula of the type $\forall\exists \lor \exists\forall$ that we want to show valid over all instantiations of $S$. The Small Model Theorem establishes that, when only the first disjunct exists, it suffices to show validity of the formula only on small instantiations whose size is bounded by the number of free and universally quantified variables. We extend it here for the case that the second disjunct exists, however, its scope is limited.

**Theorem 2 (Extended Small Model Theorem).** *Consider the formula*

$$\phi: \forall\vec{i}\exists\vec{j}.R(\vec{i}, \vec{j}) \lor \exists i \forall j.Q(i, j)$$

*where $R$ and $Q$ are restricted assertions, and, in addition, we have:*

$$\forall i, j, k.(\neg Q(i, j) \land \neg Q(j, k) \rightarrow (\neg Q(i, k) \lor \neg Q(j, j)))$$

*Let $N_0$ be the number of universally quantified, free **index** variables and **index** constants appearing in $R$. Then $\phi$ is valid over $S(N)$ for every $N \geq 2$ iff $\phi$ is valid over $S(N)$ for every $N \leq 2N_0$.*

*Proof Outline:*   We show that if $\neg\phi$ is satisfiable over a model of size $N_1 > 2N_0$, then it is satisfiable over a model of size $N_2 \leq 2N_0$. The formula $\neg\phi$ is equivalent to:

$$\psi\colon\ \exists\vec{i}\forall\vec{j}.\neg R(\vec{i},\vec{j})\ \wedge\ \forall i.\exists j.\neg Q(i,j)$$

and assume $s \models \psi$ for some state $s$ of $S(N_1)$ where $N_1 > 2N_0$. Following the proof of the original theorem ([APR$^+$01]), we take the (no more than $N_0$) values assigned to the constants, free, and existentially quantified **index** variables in the first conjuncts that $s$ assigns, say to $u_1, \ldots, u_L$ (where $L \leq N_0$). Obviously, if we project $s$ onto $U = \{u_1, \ldots, u_L\}$ (i.e., remove references to any **index** variables outside $U$), the resulting state satisfies the first conjunct, while adding back all the variables that refer to some particular **index** variable that is not in this set, will not change that.

We next add to $U$ at most $L$ other **index** variable that will guarantee the satisfiability of the second conjunct. Starting with $V_0 = \emptyset$, we iterate $L$ steps. At the $\ell^{th}$ step, we start with a set $V_{\ell-1}$ and a state $s_{\ell-1}$, such that $s_{\ell-1}$ is the projection of $s$ onto $V_{\ell-1}$, and $s_{\ell-1} \models \forall i \in V_{\ell-1}.\exists j \in V_{\ell-1}.\neg Q(i,j)$. We then add to $V_{\ell-1}$ the element $u_\ell$, and, possibly, another element, to obtain $V_\ell$.

Assume $1 \leq \ell < L$ and consider $u_\ell$. If $s \models \neg Q(u_\ell, v)$ for some $v \in V_\ell \cup \{u_\ell\}$, then $V_\ell = V_{\ell-1} \cup \{u_\ell\}$. Assume therefore that for all $v \in V_{\ell-1}$, $s \not\models \neg Q(u_\ell, v)$ and that $s \not\models \neg Q(u_\ell, u_\ell)$. Since $s \models \psi$, it follows that for some $j_1 \in [1..N_1]$, $s \models \neg Q(u_\ell, j_1)$. We continue along a $\neg Q$-chain in $[1..N_1]$ of the form $u_\ell = j_0, j_1, \ldots, j_m$ that the $j_i$'s are mutually distinct, for every $i = 0, \ldots, m$, $s \models Q(j_i, j_i)$, and for every $i = 1, \ldots, m$, $s \models \neg Q(j_{i-1}, j_i)$. (The finiteness of $[1..N_1]$ guarates that the chain is finite.) It thus follows that $s \models \neg Q(j_m, j_m) \wedge \neg Q(u_\ell, j_m)$. We then let $U_\ell = U_{\ell-1} \cup \{u_\ell, j_m\}$.

Note that the process adds at most $L$ new elements to $U$, thus the state attained is of size at most $2N_0$. Suppose $U_L = \{v_1, \ldots, v_{2L}\}$ where $v_1 < \ldots v_{2L}$. We can now contract the state to $1..2L$ and obtain a state $s'$ of $S(2L)$ such that $s' \models \psi$.     □

## 6   Example: BAKERY

Consider program BAKERY in Fig. 4, which is a variant of Lamport's original Bakery Algorithm that offers a solution to the mutual exclusion problem for any $N$ processes. In this version of the algorithm, location 0 constitutes the non-critical section which a process may non-deterministically exit to the trying section at location 1. Location 1 is the ticket assignment location – to guarantee the finiteness of the state-space, the ticket values are $[1..N]$; when a process $i$ takes a ticket, the tickets help by the other processes may be changed preserving their relative order, and process $i$ gets a ticket whose value is higher than the others. Location 2 is the waiting phase, where a process waits until it holds the minimal ticket. Location 3 is the critical section, and location 4 is the exit section. Note that $y$, the ticket array, is of type **index** $\mapsto$ **data**, and the program location array (which we denote by $\pi$) is of type **index** $\mapsto$ **bool**. In fact, $\pi$ is of type **index** $\mapsto [0..4]$, but it can be encoded by three boolean arrays. Note also that the ticket assignment statement at 1 is non-deterministic and may modify the values of all tickets.

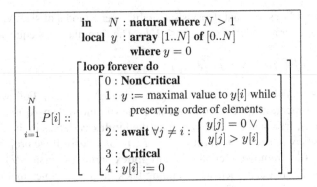

**Fig. 4.** Program BAKERY

The livelock freedom property of the program is:

$$\phi: (\exists z : at\_l_1[z]) \Rightarrow \Diamond(\exists z : at\_l_3[z])$$

The bound obtained for the property is $K = 2$.

Following are the results of our verification experiments applied to the BAKERY protocol.

1. We chose (arbitrarily) to instantiate the system to $N = 4$. We applied the enhanced *project & generalize* method [FPPZ04a] to BAKERY(4), generating candidate invariants in the forms of a boolean combinations of universal assertions. The best candidate obtained was $\varphi_1$ of the form

$$\phi_1: \forall i, j.\alpha_1(i,j) \wedge \exists i, j.\alpha_2(i,j) \vee \forall i, j.\alpha_3(i,j)^1$$

   The assertion $\phi_1$ failed to be inductive.
2. We used our invisible invariant generator to generate an $\exists\forall$-assertion $\phi_2\exists i\forall j\beta(i,j)$ over BAKERY(4). We then define $\phi: \phi_1 \wedge \phi_2$, which is both inductive and implies the safety property $\square(rnd < 2)$ over BAKERY(4).
3. We next checked whether $\neg\beta$ is reflexive or transitive. Since the test requires checking a universal assertion, we can apply Theorem 1 and derive that it suffices to check the reflexivity/transitivity of $\neg\beta$ over BAKERY($N_0$) for $N_0 \leq 4$ to derive that it is reflexive/transitive over BAKERY($N$) for every $N$.
4. By applying Theorem 2, we derived $N = 8$ as the size of the small model to establish the validity of the premises in INV using $\phi$ as the auxiliary invariant. The candidate invariant $\varphi_1 \wedge \varphi_2$ was reconstructed over BAKERY(8), and proved to be inductive and to imply the safety property $\square(rnd < 2)$. We can therefore conclude that the protocol satisfy the livelock freedom property for any instantiation.

The code for the programs can be found in *http://eeyore.cs.nyu.edu/acsys/forte06/*.

---

[1] We can "guide" our automated invisible invariant generator as to the form of the assertion to be produced; however, being invisible and produced by BDD techniques, the generated assertions cannot be neatly displayed.

We would like to point out that the proof obtained by the method proposed here is considerably simpler than the proof presented in [FPPZ04a] which calls for auxiliary constructs other than invariants, thus requires considerably more interaction with the user.

# 7  Discussion and Future Work

The paper presents a method for automatic verification of progress properties of parameterized systems based on the method of invisible invariants. The method is based on the observation that such progress properties are usually "bounded," and can thus be converted into safety properties. The heuristic proposed attempts to find a bound for the progress property, and use the method of invisible invariants to prove the resulting safety property.

There are several cases where the proposed method is bound to fail:

**Super-linear bounds:** As it is now, the method can only be successful when the bound is linear in the number of processes. Some protocols (e.g., Peterson's $N$-process mutual exclusion protocol) have bounds that are non-linear in the number of processes. We are currently working on extending the method to apply to cases where the bound is quadratic in the number of processes.

**Fairness-dependent bounds:** The method cannot be applied to cases where the bound depends on non-justice assumptions. Such non-justice fairness assumptions occur, for example, when using semaphores, the bound depends on the number of compassion (strong fairness) assumptions. However, compassion can be translated into justice, at the cost of adding some new variables to the system, hence our method can indirectly deal with such cases.

**Probability-dependent progress:** When protocols involve probabilistic choices among transitions, progress often depends on probabilistic arguments. As shown in [APZ03], one can often transform such protocols to non-probabilistic protocols by a "planner" that occasionally determines the results of some probabilistic choices, leaving the others non-deterministic. In fact, the projection used in the method of invisible invariants can be applied to obtain the planner automatically, and then the progress property can be bounded. Consequently, the method proposed here, in conjunction with the automatically obtained planner, can be applied to probabilistic protocols as well.

**Failure of invisible invariants:** The method of invisible invariant is heuristic in nature, and may sometimes fail. As we showed here, sometimes a $\forall\exists$ invariant is called for, which we can obtain only in certain cases. In some cases, there is no strengthening invariant of the type we can generate. For these cases, the method presented here is bound to fail.

As in the case of all BDD-based techniques, it is always possible that the invariant generated is too large for the model checker to handle. In fact, this may happen much faster than when checking "regular" safety properties, since those required here include the round counter.

# References

[AK86]     K. R. Apt and D. Kozen. Limits for automatic program verification of finite-state concurrent systems. *Info. Proc. Lett.*, 22(6), 1986.

[APR$^+$01]  T. Arons, A. Pnueli, S. Ruah, J. Xu, and L. Zuck. Parameterized verification with automatically computed inductive assertions. In *G. Berry, H. Comon, and A. Finkel, editors*, Proc. $13^{th}$ Intl. Conference on Computer Aided Verification (CAV'01), *volume 2102 of* Lect. Notes in Comp. Sci., *Springer-Verlag*, pages 221–234, 2001.

[APZ03]    T. Arons, A. Pnueli, and L. Zuck. Parameterized verification by probabilistic abstraction. In *6th International Conference on Foundations of Software Science and Computational Structures*, volume 2620 of *Lect. Notes in Comp. Sci.*, pages 87–102, Warsaw, Poland, April 2003. Springer-Verlag.

[BAS02]    A. Biere, C. Artho, and V. Schuppan. Liveness checking as safety checking. In Rance Cleaveland and Hubert Garavel, editors, *Electronic Notes in Theoretical Computer Science*, volume 66. Elsevier, 2002.

[BBC$^+$95]  N. Bjørner, I.A. Browne, E. Chang, M. Colón, A. Kapur, Z. Manna, H.B. Sipma, and T.E. Uribe. STeP: The Stanford Temporal Prover, User's Manual. Technical Report STAN-CS-TR-95-1562, Computer Science Department, Stanford University, November 1995.

[BFPZ05]   I. Balaban, Y. Fang, A. Pnueli, and L.D. Zuck. An invisible invariant verifier. In Proc. $17^{th}$ Intl. Conference on Computer Aided Verification (CAV'05), Springer-Verlage LNCS 3576, pp. 291–295, 2005.

[CGJ95]    E.M. Clarke, O. Grumberg, and S. Jha. Verifying parametrized networks using abstraction and regular languages. In *6th International Conference on Concurrency Theory (CONCUR92)*, volume 962 of *Lect. Notes in Comp. Sci.*, pages 395–407, Philadelphia, PA, August 1995. Springer-Verlag.

[CLP84]    S. Cohen, D. Lehmann, and A. Pnueli. Symmetric and economical solutions to the mutual exclusion problem in a distributed system. *Theor. Comp. Sci.*, 34:215–225, 1984.

[CS02]     M. Colon and H. Sipma. Practical methods for proving program termination. In *E. Brinksma and K. G.Larsen, editors*, Proc. $14^{th}$ Intl. Conference on Computer Aided Verification (CAV'02), *volume 2404 of* Lect. Notes in Comp. Sci., *Springer-Verlag*, pages 442–454, 2002.

[EK00]     E.A. Emerson and V. Kahlon. Reducing model checking of the many to the few. In *17th International Conference on Automated Deduction (CADE-17)*, pages 236–255, 2000.

[EN95]     E. A. Emerson and K. S. Namjoshi. Reasoning about rings. In *Proc. 22nd ACM Conf. on Principles of Programming Languages, POPL'95*, San Francisco, 1995.

[FPPZ04a]  Y. Fang, N. Piterman, A. Pnueli, and L. Zuck. Liveness with incomprehensible ranking. In *Proc. $10^{th}$ Intl. Conference on Tools and Algorithms for the Construction and Analysis of Systems (TACAS'04), volume 2988 of* Lect. Notes in Comp. Sci., *Springer-Verlag*, pages 482–496, April 2004.

[FPPZ04b]  Y. Fang, N. Piterman, A. Pnueli, and L. Zuck. Liveness with invisible ranking. In *Proc. of the $5^{th}$ conference on Verification, Model Checking, and Abstract Interpretation*, volume 2937 of *Lect. Notes in Comp. Sci.*, pages 223–238, Venice, Italy, January 2004. Springer-Verlag.

[GS97]     V. Gyuris and A. P. Sistla. On-the-fly model checking under fairness that exploits symmetry. In *O. Grumberg, editor, Proc.* Proc. $9^{th}$ Intl. Conference on Computer Aided Verification, (CAV'97), *volume 1254 of* Lect. Notes in Comp. Sci., *Springer-Verlag*, 1997.

[GZ98]     E.P. Gribomont and G. Zenner. Automated verification of szymanski's algorithm. In *B. Steffen, editor, Proc. $4^{th}$ Intl. Conference on Tools and Algorithms for the Construction and Analysis of Systems (TACAS'98), volume 1384 of* Lect. Notes in Comp. Sci., *Springer-Verlag*, pages 424–438, 1998.

[JN00]     B. Jonsson and M. Nilsson. Transitive closures of regular relations for verifying infinite-state systems. In *S. Graf and M. Schwartzbach, editors, Proc. $6^{th}$ Intl. Conference on Tools and Algorithms for the Construction and Analysis of Systems (TACAS'00), volume 1785 of* Lect. Notes in Comp. Sci., *Springer-Verlag*, 2000.

[LHR97]    D. Lesens, N. Halbwachs, and P. Raymond. Automatic verification of parameterized linear networks of processes. In *24th ACM Symposium on Principles of Programming Languages, POPL'97*, Paris, 1997.

[McM99]    K.L. McMillan. Verification of Infinite State Systems by Compositional Model Checking. In *Proc. Charme 1999*, volume 1703 of *Lect. Notes in Comp. Sci.*, Springer-Verlag, pages 219–234, 1999.

[MP95]     Z. Manna and A. Pnueli. *Temporal Verification of Reactive Systems: Safety.* Springer-Verlag, New York, 1995.

[OSR93]    S. Owre, N. Shankar, and J.M. Rushby. User guide for the PVS specification and verification system (draft). Technical report, Comp. Sci.,Laboratory, SRI International, Menlo Park, CA, 1993.

[PRZ01]    A. Pnueli, S. Ruah, and L. Zuck. Automatic deductive verification with invisible invariants. In *Proc. $7^{th}$ Intl. Conference on Tools and Algorithms for the Construction and Analysis of Systems (TACAS'01), volume 2031 of* Lect. Notes in Comp. Sci., *Springer-Verlag*, pages 82–97, 2001.

[PXZ02]    A. Pnueli, J. Xu, and L. Zuck. Liveness with $(0, 1, \infty)$-counter abstraction, 2002.

[VW86]     M.Y. Vardi and P. Wolper. An automata-theoretic approach to automatic program verification. In *Proc. First IEEE Symp. Logic in Comp. Sci.*, pages 332–344, 1986.

[ZP04]     L. Zuck and A. Pnueli. Model checking and abstraction to the aid of parameterized systems. *Computer Languages, Systems, and Structures*, Volume 30(3–4), pp. 139–169 2004.

# Extending EFSMs to Specify and Test Timed Systems with Action Durations and Timeouts*

Mercedes G. Merayo, Manuel Núñez, and Ismael Rodríguez

Dept. Sistemas Informáticos y Programación
Universidad Complutense de Madrid, 28040 Madrid, Spain
mgmerayo@fdi.ucm.es, {mn, isrodrig}@sip.ucm.es

**Abstract.** In this paper we introduce a timed extension of the extended finite state machines model. On the one hand, we consider that output actions take time to be performed. This time may depend on several factors such as the value of variables. On the other hand, our formalism allows to specify timeouts. In addition to present our formalism, we develop a testing theory. First, we define ten timed conformance relations and relate them. Second, we introduce a notion of timed test and define how to apply tests to IUTs.

## 1  Introduction

Formal testing techniques [2,9,14,3,5] allow to test the correctness of a system with respect to a specification. Formal testing originally targeted the functional behavior of systems, such as determining whether the tested system can, on the one hand, perform certain actions and, on the other hand, does not perform some non-expected ones. In the last years formal testing techniques also deal with non-functional properties such as the time that it takes to perform a certain action. In order to test timed systems, more precisely, the timed behavior of a system, we need a suitable language to formally specify these systems. The time consumed during the execution of a system falls into one of the following categories:

(a) The system consumes time while it performs its operations. This time may depend on the values of certain parameters of the system, such as the available resources.
(b) The time passes while the system waits for a reaction from the environment. In particular, the system can change its internal state if an interaction is not received before a certain amount of time.

A language focussing on temporal issues should allow the specifier to define how the system behavior is affected by both kinds of temporal aspects (e.g., a task is performed if executing the previous task took too much time, if the environment does not react for a long time, if the addition of both times exceeds a

---

* Research partially supported by the Spanish MCYT project TIC2003-07848-C02-01, the Junta de Castilla-La Mancha project PAC-03-001, and the Marie Curie project MRTN-CT-2003-505121/TAROT.

E. Najm et al. (Eds.): FORTE 2006, LNCS 4229, pp. 372–387, 2006.

given threshold, etc). In this paper we present a formalism, based on *extended finite state machines*, allowing to take into account the subtle temporal aspects considered before. Even though there exists a myriad of timed extensions of classical frameworks, most of them specialize only in one of the previous variants: Time is either associated with actions or associated with delays/timeouts. Our formalism allows to specify in a natural way both time aspects. While the definition of the new language is not difficult, mixing these temporal requirements strongly complicates the posterior theoretical analysis. In particular, the definition of timed conformance testing relations is more difficult than usually. The theoretical framework is also complicated by two additional features. First, we consider that variables may influence the timing aspects of the specification. Thus, the execution of an action may take different time values if the value of the variables change. Second, we do not impose any restriction on the deterministic behavior of our machines. This implies again that the same sequence of actions may take different time values to be executed.

We also propose a formal testing methodology allowing to systematically test a system with respect to a specification. Regarding functional conformance we have to consider not only that the sequences of inputs/outpus produced by the implementation must be considered in the specification. We have to take into account the possible timeouts. For example, a sequence of inputs/outputs could be accepted only after different timeouts have been triggered. Let us consider the machines depicted in Figure 1. In these diagrams we use the following notation: A transition labelled by '$i/o, t$' denotes that the execution of the output action $o$ takes time $t$ to be performed after the input $i$ is received; a transition with a label $t$ indicates that a timeout will be applied at time $t$. That is, if after $t$ time units no input is received then the timeout is executed. If we consider $M_1$ and $M_2$ we can observe that $M_1$ is not functionally conforming to $M_2$. The sequence $i_1/o_2$ that can be performed by $M_1$ is forbidden by $M_2$. On the other hand, if we consider the conformance of $M_2$ with respect to $M_1$ and we only check the possible sequences of inputs/outputs, $M_2$ would conform to $M_1$ due to the fact that the unique sequence that can be performed by $M_2$ is $i_1/o_1$. However, this sequence is allowed by $M_1$ only in the case that the input has been received after three time units. So, under our conformance framework, $M_2$ does not conform to $M_1$. We can say the same regarding the conformance of $M_3$ with respect to $M_1$. On the contrary, this is not the case when considering the conformance of $M_1$ with respect to $M_3$. The sequences performed by $M_1$ are accepted by $M_3$ at any time. So, $M_1$ functionally conforms to $M_3$.

Let us note that testing the temporal behavior of a system affected by nondeterminism requires to face some issues that are not considered by other testing approaches. In particular, contrary to usual approaches, providing an *incorrectness* diagnosis may require to consider the result of *all* tests in a test suite, because a single test result could be insufficient to claim the incorrectness of the IUT.[1] For instance, we may require that, among all the times the IUT may

---

[1] If we consider this statement the other way around then the resulting scenario is the usual one: Passing a test does not allow to claim that the IUT is correct.

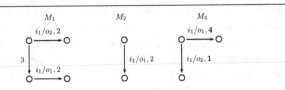

**Fig. 1.** Examples of functional conformance

consume to perform a task, one of them is smaller than the corresponding specification time for this task. Hence, if during the application of a test we observe that the IUT takes a long time, then it does not necessarily mean that the IUT cannot do it faster. Regarding temporal performance requirements, our testing methodology will take into account that the system is only responsible for the (a) type consumed time, not for that of (b) type. That is, we have to distinguish between time associated with the performance of tasks and passing of time due to the possible inactivity of the operator of the system.

Our *timed conformance relations* follow the standard pattern: An implementation is correct with respect to a specification if it does not show any behavior that is forbidden by the specification, where both the functional behavior and the temporal behavior are considered (and, implicitly, how they affect each other). In this paper we present ten different conformance relations. The differences among them come from the effect non-determinism causes in specifications/implementations. We will relate all these notions and propose alternative characterizations for some of them.

In terms of related work, our way to deal with time is completely different to that in *timed automata* [1]. As we said before, we can associate time with the performance of actions while timeouts can be easily represented. These features do not only improve the modularity of models, but they are also suitable for clearly identifying IUT requirements and responsibilities in a testing methodology. This paper continues the work in [12]. The main advantage with respect to this previous work is that we can now express timeouts, we remove all the restrictions regarding non-determinism of the machines, and we consider more conformance relations. Regarding testing of temporal requirements, there exist several proposals (e.g., [4,8,15,6]) but most of them are based on timed automata. Moreover, in these approaches tests are independent and the diagnosis of a test does not depend on other tests. By considering that tests are interrelated, we can relate non-determinism and temporal requirements, as well as define and apply several conformance relations where non-determinism is explicitly considered. There are also some time extensions of FSMs(e.g., [13,7]) but they do not deal with conformance.

The rest of the paper is structured as follows. In Section 2 we introduce our model. In Section 3 we give our timed conformance relations and provide several examples to show the differences among them. In Section 4 we show how tests are defined and applied to IUTs.

## 2    A Timed Extension of the EFSM Model

In this section we introduce our notion of *timed extended finite state machine*. As we have indicated in the introduction of the paper, we will add new features so that the timed behavior of a system can be properly specified. On the one hand, we consider that output actions take time to be executed. These time values will not only depend on the corresponding action to be performed and the state where the machine is placed. Actually, we will also consider that this time value takes into account the current value of the variables. In fact, with this approach we can simulate that the speed with which a task is performed depends on the available resources. On the other hand, we will also consider that the machine can evolve by raising *timeouts*. Intuitively, if after a given time, depending on the current state, we do not receive any input action then the machine will change its current state.

During the rest of the paper we will use the following notation. A tuple of elements $(e_1, e_2 \ldots, e_n)$ will be denoted by $\bar{e}$. $\hat{a}$ denotes an interval of elements $[a_1, a_2)$. A tuple of intervals is denoted by $\breve{t}$. Let $\breve{q} = (\hat{q}_1, \ldots, \hat{q}_n)$ and $\bar{t} = (t_1, \ldots, t_n)$. We write $\bar{t} \in \breve{q}$ if for all $1 \leq j \leq n$ we have $t_j \in \hat{q}_j$. We will use the projection function $\pi_i$ such that given a tuple $\bar{t} = (t_1, \ldots, t_n)$, for all $1 \leq i \leq n$ we have $\pi_i(\bar{t}) = t_i$. Let $\bar{t} = (t_1, \ldots, t_n)$ and $\bar{t}' = (t'_1, \ldots, t'_n)$. We write $\bar{t} = \bar{t}'$ if for all $1 \leq j \leq n$ we have $t_j = t'_j$. We write $\bar{t} \leq \bar{t}'$ if for all $1 \leq j \leq n$ we have $t_j \leq t'_j$. Finally, we will denote by $\sum \bar{t}$ the sum of all elements of the tuple $\bar{t}$, that is, $\sum_{j=1}^{n} t_j$.

**Definition 1.** Let Time be the domain to define time values, $D_1, \ldots, D_m$ be sets of values, and let us consider $\mathcal{D} = D_1 \times D_2 \times \cdots \times D_m$. A *Timed Extended Finite State Machine*, in the following TEFSM, is a tuple $M = (S, I, O, TO, Tr, s_{in}, \bar{y})$ where $S$ is a finite set of *states*, $I$ is the set of *input actions*, $O$ is the set of *output actions*, $TO : S \longrightarrow S \times (\text{Time} \cup \infty)$ is the *timeout function*, $Tr$ is the set of *action transitions*, $s_{in}$ is the *initial state*, and $\bar{y} \in \mathcal{D}$ is the tuple of initial values of the *variables*.

An *action transition* is a tuple $(s, s', i, o, Q, Z, C)$ where $s, s' \in S$ are the initial and final state of the transition, $i \in I$ and $o \in O$ are the input and output action associated with the transition, $Q : \mathcal{D} \longrightarrow \text{Bool}$ is a predicate on the set of variables, $Z : \mathcal{D} \longrightarrow \mathcal{D}$ is a transformation over the current variables, and $C : \mathcal{D} \longrightarrow \text{Time}$ is the time that the transition needs to be completed.

A *configuration* in $M$ is a pair $(s, \bar{x})$ where $s \in S$ is the current state and $\bar{x} \in \mathcal{D}$ is the tuple containing the current value of the variables.

We say that $M$ is *input-enabled* if for all state $s \in S$ and input $i \in I$ there exist $s', o, Q, Z, C$ such that $(s, s', i, o, Q, Z, C) \in Tr$.                    □

Given a configuration $(s, \bar{x})$, an action transition $(s, s', i, o, Q, Z, C)$ denotes that if the input $i$ is received and $Q(\bar{x})$ holds then the output $o$ will be produced after $C(\bar{x})$ units of time, and the configuration will be $(s', Z(\bar{x}))$. In this paper we consider that time can be discretized, that is, the time domain is isomorphic to $\mathbb{N}$. We will take advantage of this characteristic to simplify some definitions. In particular, we will sometimes enumerate the elements of Time simply as $0, 1, 2$ and so on.

For each state $s \in S$, the application of the timeout function $TO(s)$ returns a pair $(s', t)$ indicating the time that the machine can remain at the state $s$ waiting for an input action, and the state to which the machine evolves if no input is received on time. We assume that $TO(s) = (s', t)$ implies $s \neq s'$, that is, timeouts always produce a change of the state. We indicate the absence of a timeout in a given state by setting the corresponding time value to $\infty$.

**Definition 2.** Let $M = (S, I, O, TO, Tr, s_{in}, \bar{y})$ be a TEFSM and $c_0 = (s_0, \bar{x}_0)$ be a configuration of $M$. A tuple $(s_0, s, i/o, \hat{t}, t_o, \bar{v})$ is a *step* of $M$ for the configuration $c_0$ if there exist $k \geq 0$ states $s_1, \ldots, s_k \in S$ such that for all $1 \leq j \leq k$ we have $TO(s_{j-1}) = (s_j, t_j)$ and there exists a transition $(s_k, s, i, o, Q, Z, C) \in Tr$ such that $Z(\bar{x}_0) = \bar{v}$, $\hat{t} = \left[ \sum_{j=1}^{k} t_j, \sum_{j=1}^{k} t_j + \pi_2(TO(s_k)) \right]$, $t_o = C(\bar{x}_0)$ and $Q(\bar{x}_0)$ holds. We denote by $\mathtt{Steps}(M, s, \bar{x})$ the set of steps of $M$ for the configuration $(s, \bar{x})$.

We say that $(\hat{t}_1/i_1/t_{o1}/o_1, \ldots, \hat{t}_r/i_r/t_{or}/o_r)$ is a *timed evolution* of $M$ if there exist $r$ steps of $M$ $(s_{in}, s_1, i_1/o_1, \hat{t}_1, t_{o1}, \bar{y}_1), \ldots, (s_{r-1}, s_r, i_r/o_r, \hat{t}_r, t_{or}, \bar{y}_r)$ for the configurations $(s_{in}, \bar{y}), \ldots, (s_{r-1}, \bar{y}_{r-1})$, respectively. We denote by $\mathtt{TEvol}(M)$ the set of timed evolutions of $M$. In addition, we say that $(\hat{t}_1/i_1/o_1, \ldots, \hat{t}_r/i_r/o_r)$ is a *functional evolution* of $M$ and we denote by $\mathtt{FEvol}(M)$ the set of functional evolutions of $M$.    □

Intuitively, a step is an action transition preceded by zero or more timeouts. The interval $\hat{t}$ indicates the time values where the input action could be received. An evolution is a sequence of inputs/outputs corresponding to the action transitions of a chain of steps where the first one begins with the initial configuration of the machine. In addition, timed evolutions include time values which inform us about possible timeouts (indicated by the intervals $\hat{t}_j$) and the time consumed to execute each output after receiving each input in each step of the evolution.

*Example 1.* Consider the TEFSM depicted in Figure 2. We suppose that the variables of the TEFSM are given by a tuple $\bar{x} \in \mathbb{R}_+^4$ and we denote by $x_i$ the *i-th* component of $\bar{x}$. Let us assume that the value of the variables is $\bar{x} = (1, 2, 2, 1)$. Next, we give some of the *steps* that the machine can generate. For example, $(s_1, s_2, i_1/o_1, [0, 3), 3, (2, 2, 2, 0))$, represents the transition $t_{12}$ when no timeouts precede it. The input $i_1$ can be accepted before 3 units of time pass (this is indicated by the interval $[0, 3)$). In addition, $o_1$ takes $C_1((1, 2, 2, 1)) = 3$ time units to be performed and the new tuple of variables is $Z_1((1, 2, 2, 1)) = (2, 2, 2, 0)$. The second one, $(s_1, s_4, i_1/o_2, [3, 7), 4, (1, 3, 1, 1))$ is built from the timeout transition associated to the state $s_1$ and the action transition $t_{34}$. The step represents that if after 3 units of time no input is received, the timeout transition associated with that state will be triggered and the state will change to $s_3$. After this, the machine can accept the input $i_1$ before 4 units of time pass, that is, the timeout assigned to the state $s_3$. So during the time interval $[3, 7)$ if the machine receives an input $i_1$ it will emit an output $o_2$ and the state will change to $s_4$. Similarly,

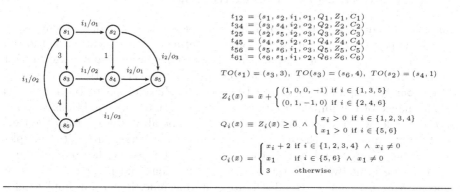

$$t_{12} = (s_1, s_2, i_1, o_1, Q_1, Z_1, C_1)$$
$$t_{34} = (s_3, s_4, i_2, o_2, Q_2, Z_2, C_2)$$
$$t_{25} = (s_2, s_5, i_2, o_3, Q_3, Z_3, C_3)$$
$$t_{45} = (s_4, s_5, i_2, o_1, Q_4, Z_4, C_4)$$
$$t_{56} = (s_5, s_6, i_1, o_3, Q_5, Z_5, C_5)$$
$$t_{61} = (s_6, s_1, i_1, o_2, Q_6, Z_6, C_6)$$

$$TO(s_1) = (s_3, 3), \quad TO(s_3) = (s_6, 4), \quad TO(s_2) = (s_4, 1)$$

$$Z_i(\bar{x}) = \bar{x} + \begin{cases} (1, 0, 0, -1) & \text{if } i \in \{1, 3, 5\} \\ (0, 1, -1, 0) & \text{if } i \in \{2, 4, 6\} \end{cases}$$

$$Q_i(\bar{x}) \equiv Z_i(\bar{x}) \geq \bar{0} \ \wedge \ \begin{cases} x_i > 0 & \text{if } i \in \{1, 2, 3, 4\} \\ x_1 > 0 & \text{if } i \in \{5, 6\} \end{cases}$$

$$C_i(\bar{x}) = \begin{cases} x_i + 2 & \text{if } i \in \{1, 2, 3, 4\} \ \wedge \ x_i \neq 0 \\ x_1 & \text{if } i \in \{5, 6\} \ \wedge \ x_1 \neq 0 \\ 3 & \text{otherwise} \end{cases}$$

**Fig. 2.** Example of TEFSMs

we can obtain the step $(s_1, s_1, i_1/o_2, [7, \infty), 1, (1, 3, 1, 1))$, using the timeout transitions corresponding to $s_1$ and $s_3$ and the action transition $t_{61}$. All the steps presented, correspond to the configuration $(s_1, (1, 2, 2, 1))$.

Now, we present an example of a temporal evolution built from two steps, and assuming that $s1$ is the initial state: $([7, \infty)/i_1/1/o_2, [3, 7)/i_1/3/o_2)$. The configuration that has been considered for the first step is again $(s_1, (1, 2, 2, 1))$. The configuration that corresponds to the second step is the one obtained after the first step has been performed, that is, $(s_1, (1, 3, 1, 1))$.                          □

Let us note that different instances of the same evolution may appear in a specification as result of the different configurations obtained after traversing the corresponding TEFSM.

In the following definition we introduce the concept of *instanced evolution*. Intuitively, instanced evolutions are constructed from evolutions by instanciating to a concrete value each timeout, given by an interval, of the evolution.

**Definition 3.** Let $M = (S, I, O, TO, Tr, s_{in}, \bar{y})$ be a TEFSM and let us consider a *timed evolution* $e = (\hat{t}_1/i_1/t_{o1}/o_1, \ldots, \hat{t}_r/i_r/t_{or}/o_r)$. We say that the tuple $(t_1/i_1/t_{o1}/o_1, \ldots, t_r/i_r/t_{or}/o_r)$ is an *instanced timed evolution of $e$* if for all $1 \leq j \leq r$ we have $t_j \in \hat{t}_j$. In addition, we say that the tuple $(t_1/i_1/o_1, \ldots, t_r/i_r/o_r)$ is an *instanced functional evolution* of $e$.

We denote by $\texttt{InsTEvol}(M)$ the set of instanced timed evolutions of $M$ and by $\texttt{InsFEvol}(M)$ the set of instanced functional evolutions.                          □

By abusing the notation, we will sometimes refer to instanced time evolutions such as $(t_1/i_1/t_{o1}/o_1, \ldots, t_r/i_r/t_{or}/o_r)$ as $(\bar{t}, \sigma, \bar{t}_o)$, where $t = (t_1, \ldots, t_r)$, $\sigma = (i_1/o_1, \ldots, i_r/o_r)$, and $t_o = (t_{o1}, \ldots, t_{or})$. Similarly, we will also refer to instanced functional evolutions as $(\bar{t}, \sigma)$.

*Example 2.* As example, if we consider the temporal evolution showed previously, $([7, \infty)/i_1/1/o_2, [3, 7)/i_1/3/o_2)$, we have that $(8, /i_1/1/o_2, 5/i_1/3/o_2)$ and $(12, /i_1/1/o_2, 3/i_1/3/o_2)$ are *instanced temporal evolutions*.                          □

## 3    (Timed) Implementation Relations

In this section we introduce our implementation relations. All of them follow the same pattern: An implementation $I$ *conforms* to a specification $S$ if for all possible evolution of $S$ the outputs that the implementation $I$ may perform after a given input are a subset of those for the specification. This pattern is borrowed from $\text{conf}_{nt}$ [10] and it is inspired in *ioco* [16]. In addition to the non-timed conformance of the implementation, we require some time conditions to hold. For example, we may ask an implementation to be always faster than the time constraints imposed by the specification. Additionaly, we require that the implementation always complies with the timeouts established by the specification.

Next, we formally define the sets of specifications and implementations. A specification is a timed extended finite state machine. Regarding implementations, we consider that they are also given by means of TEFSMs. In this case, we assume, as usual, that all the input actions are always enabled in any state of the implementation. Thus, we can assume that for any input $i$ and any state of the implementation $s$ there always exists a transition $(s, s, i, \text{null}, Q, Z, C)$ where $\text{null}$ is a special (empty) output symbol, the predicate $Q(\bar{x})$ is defined as $\neg \bigvee \{Q'(\bar{x}) \mid \exists$ a transition $(s, s', i, o, Q', Z', C')\}$, $Z(\bar{x}) = \bar{x}$, and $C(\bar{x}) = 0$. Let us note that such a transition will be performed when (and only if) no other transition is available for input $i$ (that is, either there are no transitions outgoing from $s$ labelled by $i$ or none of the corresponding predicates hold). Let us note that we do not restrict the machines to be deterministic. Thus, both implementations and specifications may present non-deterministic behavior. This is an important advantage with respect to previous work [12].

First, we introduce the implementation relation $\text{conf}_f$, where only functional aspects of the system (i.e., which outputs are allowed/forbidden) are considered while the performance of the system (i.e., how fast are actions executed) is ignored. Let us note that the time spent by a system waiting for the environment to react has the capability of affecting the set of available outputs of the system. This is because this time may trigger a change of the state. So, a relation focusing on functional aspects must explicitly take into account the maximal time the system may stay in each state. This time is given by the *timeout* of the state.

**Definition 4.** Let $S$, $I$ be TEFSMs. We say that $I$ *functionally conforms* to $S$, denoted by $I \text{ conf}_f S$, if for each functional evolution $e \in \text{FEvol}(S)$, with $e = (\hat{t}_1/i_1/o_1, \ldots, \hat{t}_r/i_r/o_r)$ and $r \geq 1$, we have that for all $t_1 \in \hat{t}_1, \ldots, t_r \in \hat{t}_r$ and $o'_r$, $e' = (t_1/i_1/o_1, \ldots, t_r/i_r/o'_r) \in \text{InsFEvol}(I)$ implies $e' \in \text{InsFEvol}(S)$.
□

The idea underlying the definition of $\text{conf}_f$ is that the implementation does not *invent* anything for those sequences of inputs that are *specified* in the specification. Let us note that if the specification has also the property of input-enabled then we may remove the condition "for each functional evolution $e \in \text{FEvol}(S)$, with $e = (\hat{t}_{t1}/i_1/o_1, \ldots, \hat{t}_{tr}/i_r/o_r)$ and $r \geq 1$". Next, we introduce our *timed* implementation relations. We will distinguish two classes of conformance relations: *Weak* and *strong*. The family of weak conformance relations demands conditions only over the total time associated to timed evolutions of the implementation with respect to the corresponding timed evolutions of the specification. In contrast, strong conformance relations establish requests over the time values corresponding to the performance of each transition separately. For each of these approaches we define five relations. In the $\text{conf}_a^s$ and $\text{conf}_a^w$ relations (conforms *always*) we consider, for any timed evolution $\sigma$ of the implementation, that if its associated functional evolution $\sigma'$ is a functional evolution of the specification then $\sigma$ is also a timed evolution of the specification. In the $\text{conf}_w^s$ and $\text{conf}_w^w$ relations (conformance in the *worst* case) the implementation is forced, for each timed evolution fulfilling the previous conditions, to be faster than the slowest instance of the same evolution in the specification. The $\text{conf}_b^s$ and $\text{conf}_b^w$ relations (conforms in the *best* case) are similar but considering only the fastest instance of the specification. Finally, the relations $\text{conf}_{sw}^s$ and $\text{conf}_{sw}^w$ (*sometimes worst*), and $\text{conf}_{sb}^s$ and $\text{conf}_{sb}^w$ (*sometimes best*), are similar to the previous relations, but in each case only *one* instance of each temporal trace of the implementation is required to be as fast as the worst/best instance in the specification.

**Definition 5.** Let $\bar{t}_o = (t_{o1} \ldots t_{or}) \in \text{Time}^r$. For all instanced functional evolution $insfevol = (t_1/i_1/o_1, \ldots, t_r/i_r/o_r) \in (\text{Time} \times I \times O)^r$, we denote by $insfevol \nabla \bar{t}_o$ the instanced timed evolution $(t_1/i_1/t_{o1}/o_1, \ldots, t_r/i_r/t_{or}/o_r)$. Let $S$ and $I$ be TEFSMs. The *timed conformance relations* are defined as follows:

- (*strong always*) $I \text{ conf}_a^s S$ iff $I \text{ conf}_f S$ and for all instanced functional evolution $insfevol \in \text{InsFEvol}(I) \cap \text{InsFEvol}(S)$ we have that $\forall \bar{t}_i$

$$insfevol \nabla \bar{t}_i \in \text{InsTEvol}(I) \implies insfevol \nabla \bar{t}_i \in \text{InsTEvol}(S)$$

- (*strong best*) $I \text{ conf}_b^s S$ iff $I \text{ conf}_f S$ and for all instanced functional evolution $insfevol \in \text{InsFEvol}(I) \cap \text{InsFEvol}(S)$ we have that $\forall \bar{t}_i$

$$insfevol \nabla \bar{t}_i \in \text{InsTEvol}(I) \implies \forall \bar{t}_s : \left( \begin{array}{c} insfevol \nabla \bar{t}_s \in \text{InsTEvol}(S) \\ \Downarrow \\ \bar{t}_i \leq \bar{t}_s \end{array} \right)$$

- (*strong worst*) $I \text{ conf}_w^s S$ iff $I \text{ conf}_f S$ and for all instanced functional evolution $insfevol \in \text{InsFEvol}(I) \cap \text{InsFEvol}(S)$ we have that $\forall \bar{t}_i$

$$insfevol \nabla \bar{t}_i \in \text{InsTEvol}(I) \implies \exists \bar{t}_s : \left( \begin{array}{c} insfevol \nabla \bar{t}_s \in \text{InsTEvol}(S) \\ \wedge \\ \bar{t}_i \leq \bar{t}_s \end{array} \right)$$

- (*strong sometimes best*) $I \text{ conf}_{sb}^s S$ iff $I \text{ conf}_f S$ and for all instanced functional evolution $insfevol \in \text{InsFEvol}(I) \cap \text{InsFEvol}(S)$ we have that $\exists \bar{t}_i$ such that

$$insfevol \nabla \bar{t}_i \in \text{InsTEvol}(I) \wedge \forall \bar{t}_s : \left( \begin{array}{c} insfevol \nabla \bar{t}_s \in \text{InsTEvol}(S) \\ \Downarrow \\ \bar{t}_i \leq \bar{t}_s \end{array} \right)$$

- *(strong sometimes worst)* $I \operatorname{conf}_{sw}^s S$ iff $I \operatorname{conf}_f S$ and for all instanced functional evolution $insfevol \in \mathtt{InsFEvol}(I) \cap \mathtt{InsFEvol}(S)$ we have that $\exists \, \bar{t}_i, \bar{t}_s$ such that

$$\begin{pmatrix} insfevol \nabla \bar{t}_i \in \mathtt{InsTEvol}(I) \\ \wedge \\ insfevol \nabla \bar{t}_s \in \mathtt{InsTEvol}(S) \\ \wedge \\ \bar{t}_i \leq \bar{t}_s \end{pmatrix}$$

- *(weak always)* $I \operatorname{conf}_a^w S$ iff $I \operatorname{conf}_f S$ and for all instanced functional evolution $insfevol \in \mathtt{InsFEvol}(I) \cap \mathtt{InsFEvol}(S)$ we have that $\forall \, \bar{t}_i$

$$insfevol \nabla \bar{t}_i \in \mathtt{InsTEvol}(I) \implies \exists \, \bar{t}_s : \begin{pmatrix} insfevol \nabla \bar{t}_s \in \mathtt{InsTEvol}(S) \\ \wedge \\ \sum \bar{t}_i = \sum \bar{t}_s \end{pmatrix}$$

- *(weak best)* $I \operatorname{conf}_b^w S$ iff $I \operatorname{conf}_f S$ and for all instanced functional evolution $insfevol \in \mathtt{InsFEvol}(I) \cap \mathtt{InsFEvol}(S)$ we have that $\forall \, \bar{t}_i$

$$insfevol \nabla \bar{t}_i \in \mathtt{InsTEvol}(I) \implies \forall \, \bar{t}_s : \begin{pmatrix} insfevol \nabla \bar{t}_s \in \mathtt{InsTEvol}(S) \\ \Downarrow \\ \sum \bar{t}_i \leq \sum \bar{t}_s \end{pmatrix}$$

- *(weak worst)* $I \operatorname{conf}_w^w S$ iff $I \operatorname{conf}_f S$ and for all instanced functional evolution $insfevol \in \mathtt{InsFEvol}(I) \cap \mathtt{InsFEvol}(S)$ we have that $\forall \, \bar{t}_i$

$$insfevol \nabla \bar{t}_i \in \mathtt{InsTEvol}(I) \implies \exists \, \bar{t}_s : \begin{pmatrix} insfevol \nabla \bar{t}_s \in \mathtt{InsTEvol}(S) \\ \wedge \\ \sum \bar{t}_i \leq \sum \bar{t}_s \end{pmatrix}$$

- *(weak sometimes best)* $I \operatorname{conf}_{sb}^w S$ iff $I \operatorname{conf}_f S$ and for all instanced functional evolution $insfevol \in \mathtt{InsFEvol}(I) \cap \mathtt{InsFEvol}(S)$ we have that $\exists \, \bar{t}_i$ such that

$$insfevol \nabla \bar{t}_i \in \mathtt{InsTEvol}(I) \, \wedge \, \forall \, \bar{t}_s : \begin{pmatrix} insfevol \nabla \bar{t}_s \in \mathtt{InsTEvol}(S) \\ \Downarrow \\ \sum \bar{t}_i \leq \sum \bar{t}_s \end{pmatrix}$$

- *(weak sometimes worst)* $I \operatorname{conf}_{sw}^w S$ iff $I \operatorname{conf}_f S$ and for all instanced functional evolution $insfevol \in \mathtt{InsFEvol}(I) \cap \mathtt{InsFEvol}(S)$ we have that $\exists \, \bar{t}_i, \bar{t}_s$ such that

$$\begin{pmatrix} insfevol \nabla \bar{t}_i \in \mathtt{InsTEvol}(I) \\ \wedge \\ insfevol \nabla \bar{t}_s \in \mathtt{InsTEvol}(S) \\ \wedge \\ \sum \bar{t}_i \leq \sum \bar{t}_s \end{pmatrix}$$

$\square$

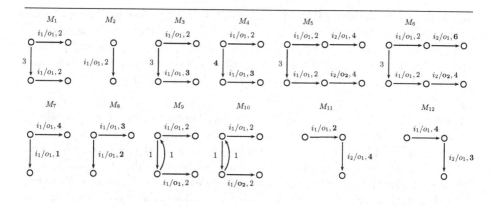

**Fig. 3.** Example of TEFSMs

## 3.1  Illustrating Examples

In this section we show how our implementation relations capture the functional and temporal behavior of systems. In particular, we give some examples where several TEFSMs are related. For the sake of simplicity, we will use some additional conformance binary operators. We will assume that $I$ conf$_*$ $S$ denotes that *all* implementation relations given in Definition 5 hold between $I$ and $S$. If *none* of these relations holds then we denote it by $I$ conf$_*$ $S$. Besides, $I$ conf$_\square$ $S$ denotes that all relations but conf$_a^s$ and conf$_a^w$ hold. We will consider the TEFSMs depicted in Figure 3. Finally, let us note that if a TEFSM is very similar to the ones presented before, then we stress the differences by using a boldface font.

*Equivalent machines.* We have $M_1$ conf$_*$ $M_2$. Actually, we also have $M_2$ conf$_*$ $M_1$. Let us note that the behavior of both machines is exactly the same regardless of whether 3 units of time pass: All transitions available for $M_1$ after taking a timeout are also available in $M_2$ from its first state. For similar reasons, we have $M_1$ conf$_*$ $M_9$, $M_9$ conf$_*$ $M_1$, $M_2$ conf$_*$ $M_9$, and $M_9$ conf$_*$ $M_2$.

*Non-Conformance due to different time values to perform output actions.* However, we have $M_3$ conf$_*$ $M_2$. Let us note that $M_3$ may take 3 time units to perform the output $o_1$ if it receives the input $i_1$ after 3 time units, $(3/i_1/3/o_1)$, while $M_2$ only needs 2 time units, $(3/i_1/2/o_1)$. Moreover, in these machines the only way to perform $i_1/o_1$ after a timeout 3 consists in taking these traces, respectively (the same applies for traces with a timeout higher than 3). Since $M_3$ is, in *any* case, slower than $M_2$ for these sequences of inputs/outputs, no conformance relation where $M_3$ is the IUT and $M_2$ is the specification holds. However, we have $M_2$ conf$_\square$ $M_3$: Despite $M_2$ does not take the same time values as $M_3$ for each sequence, its time is always smaller than (timeouts $\geq 3$) or equal to (timeouts $< 3$) the times of $M_3$.

*Non-conformance due to different timeouts.* As we have seen, reducing the time consumed by actions can benefit a TEFSM with respect to another. In spite of the fact that requirements on timeouts are *strict*, sometimes having different time-outs can benefit a TEFSM as well. Most traces in $M_3$ and $M_4$ take the same times. There is an exception: The trace with timeout 3. In $M_3$ we have $(3/i_1/3/o_1)$, but in $M_4$ we have $(3/i_1/2/o_1)$ because after 3 time units pass the state does not change yet in $M_4$. Hence, we have $M_4 \operatorname{conf}_\square M_3$ but $M_3 \operatorname{conf}_* M_4$.

*Non-conformance due to* $\operatorname{conf}_f$. Let us consider how the availability of outputs affects the relations. We have $M_5 \operatorname{conf}_* M_{11}$. Let us note that if $i_2$ is offered in $M_{11}$ after executing $i_1/o_1$ then only $o_1$ can be produced. However, $M_5$ can produce this output as well as $o_2$, which is forbidden by $M_{11}$. So, we do not have $M_5 \operatorname{conf}_f M_{11}$, and no temporal relation holds without fulfilling this condition. If $M_5$ is substituted by $M_6$ then the same considerations apply: We have $M_6 \operatorname{conf}_* M_{11}$. However, we have $M_{11} \operatorname{conf}_\square M_6$ because all sequences concerned by $M_{11}$ that appear in $M_6$ (in fact only the sequence $i_1/o_1, i_2/o_1$) are performed faster than or equal to the corresponding trace in $M_6$ (but we do not have that all are equal). Let us note that $M_9 \operatorname{conf}_* M_{10}$ and $M_{10} \operatorname{conf}_* M_9$. The reason is that $\operatorname{conf}_f$ does not hold, though, in this case, it does not hold in either direction. Let us note that, after 1 time units passes and the timeout is raised, if $i_1$ is offered then $M_9$ must answer $o_1$, and $o_2$ is forbidden. However, it is the other way around for $M_{10}$. Hence, their answers are mutually incompatible.

*Non-conformance due to different time requirements.* Let us consider a case where the IUTs and specifications can spent different time values in executing pairs of input/outputs included in traces. We consider $M_7$ and $M_8$. Since they only perform traces of length 1, any strong relation coincides with its respective weak version. Next we will refer to strong relations. Both $M_7$ and $M_8$ can execute $i_1/o_1$ in a time that cannot be taken in the other, so we do not have $M_7 \operatorname{conf}_a^s M_8$. The worst time values to execute $i_1/o_1$ in $M_7$ and $M_8$ are 4 and 3, respectively, while the best time values are 1 and 2, respectively. The worst time of $M_7$ is not better than the worst or the best time in $M_8$, so we have neither $M_7 \operatorname{conf}_w^s M_8$ nor $M_7 \operatorname{conf}_b^s M_8$. However, the best time in $M_7$ is better to both the worst and the best time of $M_8$. So, both $M_7 \operatorname{conf}_{sw}^s M_8$ and $M_7 \operatorname{conf}_{sb}^s M_8$ hold. On the other hand, the worst time in $M_8$ is better than the worst of $M_7$ but not than the best of $M_7$. Hence, $M_8 \operatorname{conf}_w^s M_7$ holds but $M_8 \operatorname{conf}_b^s M_7$ does not. Finally, the best time in $M_8$ is better than the worst of $M_7$, but not better than its best one. Thus, $M_8 \operatorname{conf}_{sw}^s M_7$ holds, but $M_8 \operatorname{conf}_{sb}^s M_7$ does not.

*Differences between weak and strong.* Next we show how temporal requirements are dealt by strong and weak relations. Let us consider $M_{11}$ and $M_{12}$. No strong relation holds between these TEFSMs in any direction. The reason is that $M_{11}$ performs, $i_1/o_1$, faster than $M_{12}$, but $M_{12}$ performs the next transition $i_2/o_1$ faster than $M_{11}$. The result is that none of these machines is always at least as fast as the other (concerning transitions). However, if we consider traces (i.e., weak relations) then some relations arise. Let us note that $M_{11}$ performs both available sequences of inputs/outputs ($i_1/o_1$ and $i_1/o_1, i_2/o_1$) faster than $M_{12}$: In $M_{11}$ they spend 2 and 6 time units, respectively, while these time values are 4 and 7, respectively, in $M_{12}$. So, all *weak* relations (but $\operatorname{conf}_a^w$) hold: We have

$M_{11} \operatorname{conf}_w^w M_{12}$, $M_{11} \operatorname{conf}_b^w M_{12}$, $M_{11} \operatorname{conf}_{sw}^w M_{12}$, and $M_{11} \operatorname{conf}_{sb}^w M_{12}$. None of them holds if we exchange the roles of both machines.

## 3.2 Relating Conformance Relations

**Theorem 1.** The relations given in Definition 5 are related as follows:

$$I \operatorname{conf}_{sw}^w S \Leftarrow I \operatorname{conf}_{sb}^w S$$
$$\Uparrow \qquad \Uparrow$$
$$I \operatorname{conf}_a^w S \Rightarrow I \operatorname{conf}_w^w S \Leftarrow I \operatorname{conf}_b^w S$$
$$\Uparrow \qquad \Uparrow \qquad \Uparrow$$
$$I \operatorname{conf}_a^s S \Rightarrow I \operatorname{conf}_w^s S \Leftarrow I \operatorname{conf}_b^s S$$
$$\Downarrow \qquad \Downarrow$$
$$I \operatorname{conf}_{sw}^s S \Leftarrow I \operatorname{conf}_{sb}^s S$$

Besides, we have $I \operatorname{conf}_{sw}^s S \Rightarrow I \operatorname{conf}_{sw}^w S$ and $I \operatorname{conf}_{sb}^s S \Rightarrow I \operatorname{conf}_{sb}^w S$. □

Let us remark that the implications inferred in the previous result are, obviously, transitive. For instance, we also have $I \operatorname{conf}_a^w S \Rightarrow I \operatorname{conf}_{sw}^w S$.

It is interesting to note that if specifications are restricted to take always the same time for each given evolution (independently from the possible derivation taken for such evolution) then, on the one hand, the relations $\operatorname{conf}_b^w$ and $\operatorname{conf}_w^w$ would coincide while, on the other hand, $\operatorname{conf}_b^s$ and $\operatorname{conf}_w^s$ also coincide. However these relations would be still different from the $\operatorname{conf}_a^w$ and $\operatorname{conf}_a^s$ relations. Similarly, if this property holds in implementations then all relations concerning the best temporal traces of the implementation (*sometimes* relations) coincide with the corresponding relation where all the temporal traces of the implementation are regarded.

**Lemma 1.** Let us consider two TEFSMs $I = (S_I, I_I, O_I, TO_I, Tr_I, s_{in_I}, \bar{y}_I)$ and $S = (S_S, I_S, O_S, TO_S, Tr_S, s_{in_S}, \bar{y}_S)$. If there do not exist different transitions $(s, s', i, o, Q, Z, C), (s, s'', i, o, Q', Z', C') \in Tr_I$ then

$$I \operatorname{conf}_b^s S \Leftrightarrow I \operatorname{conf}_{sb}^s S \qquad I \operatorname{conf}_w^s S \Leftrightarrow I \operatorname{conf}_{sw}^s S$$
$$I \operatorname{conf}_b^w S \Leftrightarrow I \operatorname{conf}_{sb}^w S \qquad I \operatorname{conf}_w^w S \Leftrightarrow I \operatorname{conf}_{sw}^w S$$

If there do not exist different transitions $(s, s', i, o, Q, Z, C), (s, s'', i, o, Q', Z', C') \in Tr_S$ then

$$I \operatorname{conf}_b^s S \Leftrightarrow I \operatorname{conf}_w^s S \qquad I \operatorname{conf}_{sw}^s S \Leftrightarrow I \operatorname{conf}_{sb}^s S$$
$$I \operatorname{conf}_b^w S \Leftrightarrow I \operatorname{conf}_w^w S \qquad I \operatorname{conf}_{sw}^w S \Leftrightarrow I \operatorname{conf}_{sb}^w S$$

□

The hierarchy of relations induced in Theorem 1 allows to compare implementations in the following way: $I_1$ is *preferable* to $I_2$ to implement $S$ if it meets with $S$ a relation that is *stricter* according to this hierarchy.

**Definition 6.** Let $I_1, I_2$ and $S$ be TEFSMs and $\operatorname{conf}_x$ and $\operatorname{conf}_y$ be timed conformance relations such that $I_1 \operatorname{conf}_x S$, $I_2 \operatorname{conf}_y S$, $\operatorname{conf}_x \Rightarrow \operatorname{conf}_y$, and $\operatorname{conf}_y \not\Rightarrow \operatorname{conf}_x$. We say that $I_1$ is *preferred* to $I_2$ to implement $S$ and we denote it by $I_1 >_S I_2$. □

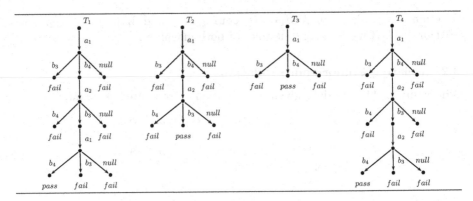

**Fig. 4.** Examples of Tests

## 4   Definition and Application of Tests

We consider that tests represent sequences of inputs applied to an IUT. Once an output is received, the tester checks whether it belongs to the set of expected ones or not. In the latter case, a fail signal is produced. In the former case, either a pass signal is emitted (indicating successful termination) or the testing process continues by applying another input. If we are testing an implementation with input and output sets $I$ and $O$, respectively, tests are deterministic acyclic $I/O$ labelled transition systems (i.e. trees) with a strict alternation between an input action and the set of output actions. After an output action we may find either a leaf or another input action. Leaves can be labelled either by *pass* or by *fail*. In addition to check the functional behavior of the IUT, test have also to detect whether wrong timed behaviors appear. Thus, tests have to include capabilities to deal with the two ways of specifying time. On the one hand, we will include *time stamps* to record the time that each sequence of output actions takes to be executed. The time values recorded from the IUT while applying the test will be compared with the ones expected by the specification. Each time stamp will contain a set of *time sequences* corresponding to the time values that the specification establishes for each transition of a trace. Since we do not restrict non-deterministic behavior, we will have as many time sequences as possible timed evolutions can exist for a trace. Moreover, depending on the number of inputs applied so far, we will have different lengths for the associated time sequences in the time stamps of the test. On the other hand, tests will include *delays* before offering input actions. The idea is that delays in tests will induce timeouts in IUTs. Thus, we may indirectly check whether the timeouts imposed by the specification are reflected in the IUT by offering input actions after a specific delay. Let us note that a tester can not observe when the IUT takes a timeout. However, she can check the IUT behavior after different delays.

**Definition 7.** A *test* is a tuple $T = (S, I, O, Tr, s_0, S_I, S_O, S_F, S_P, C, W)$ where $S$ is the set of states, $I$ and $O$ are disjoint sets of input and output actions, respectively, $Tr \subseteq S \times (I \cup O) \times S$ is the transition relation, $s_0 \in S$ is the initial state, and the sets $S_I, S_O, S_F, S_P \subseteq S$ are a partition of $S$. The transition relation and the sets of states fulfill the following conditions:

- $S_I$ is the set of *input* states. We have that $s_0 \in S_I$. For all input state $s \in S_I$ there exists a unique outgoing transition $(s, a, s') \in Tr$. For this transition we have that $a \in I$ and $s' \in S_O$.
- $S_O$ is the set of *output* states. For all output state $s \in S_O$ we have that for all $o \in O$ there exists a unique state $s'$ such that $(s, o, s') \in Tr$. In this case, $s' \notin S_O$. Moreover, there do not exist $i \in I, s' \in S$ such that $(s, i, s') \in Tr$.
- $S_F$ and $S_P$ are the sets of *fail* and *pass* states, respectively. We say that these states are *terminal*. Thus, for all state $s \in S_F \cup S_P$ we have that there do not exist $a \in I \cup O$ and $s' \in S$ such that $(s, a, s') \in Tr$.

Finally, we have two timed functions. $C : S_P \longrightarrow \bigcup_{j=1}^{\infty} \mathcal{P}(\texttt{Time}^j)$ is a function associating time stamps with passing states. $W : S_I \longrightarrow \texttt{Time}$ is a function associating delays with input states.

We say that a test $T$ is *valid* if the graph induced by $T$ is a tree with root at the initial state $s_0$.

We say that a test $T$ is an *instance* of the test $T'$ if they only differ in the associated timed functions $C$ and $W$.

Let $\sigma = i_1/o_1, \ldots, i_r/o_r$. We write $T \stackrel{\sigma}{\Longrightarrow} s$ if $s \in S_F \cup S_P$ and there exist states $s_{12}, s_{21}, s_{22}, \ldots s_{r1}, s_{r2} \in S$ such that $\{(s_0, i_1, s_{12}), (s_{r2}, o_r, s)\} \subseteq Tr$, for all $2 \leq j \leq r$ we have $(s_{j1}, i_j, s_{j2}) \in Tr$, and for all $1 \leq j \leq r - 1$ we have $(s_{j2}, o_j, s_{(j+1)1}) \in Tr$.

Let $T$ be a test, $\sigma = i_1/o_1, \ldots, i_r/o_r$, $s^T$ be a state of $T$, and $\bar{t}, \bar{t}_o \in \texttt{Time}^r$. We write $T \stackrel{\sigma}{\Longrightarrow}_{\bar{t}} s^T$ if $T \stackrel{\sigma}{\Longrightarrow} s^T$, $t_1 = D(s_0)$ and for all $1 < j \leq r$ we have $t_j = D(s_{j1})$. $\qquad\square$

Let us remark that $T \stackrel{\sigma}{\Longrightarrow} s^T$, and its variant $T \stackrel{\sigma}{\Longrightarrow}_{\bar{t}} s^T$, imply that $s$ is a terminal state. Next we define the application of a test suite to an implementation. We say that the test suite $\mathcal{T}$ is *passed* if for all test the terminal states reached by the composition of implementation and test are *pass* states. Besides, we give different timing conditions in a similar way to what we did for implementation relations.

**Definition 8.** Let $I$ be a TEFSM, $T$ be a valid test, $\sigma = i_1/o_1, \ldots, i_r/o_r$, $s^T$ be a state of $T$, $\bar{t} = (t_1, \ldots, t_r)$, and $\bar{t}_o = (t_{o1}, \ldots, t_{or})$. We write $I \parallel T \stackrel{\sigma}{\Longrightarrow}_{\bar{t}} s^T$ if $T \stackrel{\sigma}{\Longrightarrow}_{\bar{t}} s^T$ and $(\bar{t}, \sigma) \in \texttt{InsFEvol}(I)$. We write $I \parallel T \stackrel{\sigma}{\Longrightarrow}_{\bar{t}, \bar{t}_o} s^T$ if $I \parallel T \stackrel{\sigma}{\Longrightarrow}_{\bar{t}} s^T$ and $(\bar{t}, \sigma, \bar{t}_o) \in \texttt{InsTEvol}(I)$. Let $e = (\bar{t}, \sigma, \bar{t}_o) \in \texttt{InsTEvol}(I)$. We define the set $\texttt{Test}(e, \mathcal{T}) = \{T \mid T \in \mathcal{T} \wedge I \parallel T \stackrel{\sigma}{\Longrightarrow}_{\bar{t}, \bar{t}_o} s^T\}$.

We say that $I$ *passes* the set of valid tests $\mathcal{T}$, denoted by $\texttt{pass}(I, \mathcal{T})$, if for all test $T \in \mathcal{T}$ there do not exist $\sigma, s^T, \bar{t}$ such that $I \parallel T \stackrel{\sigma}{\Longrightarrow}_{\bar{t}} s^T$ and $s^T \in S_F$.

We say that $I$ *strongly passes* the set of valid tests $\mathcal{T}$ *for any time* if $\texttt{pass}(I, \mathcal{T})$ and for all $e = (\bar{t}, \sigma, \bar{t}_o) \in \texttt{InsTEvol}(I)$ we have that for all $T \in \texttt{Test}(e, \mathcal{T})$ such that $I \parallel T \stackrel{\sigma}{\Longrightarrow}_{\bar{t}, \bar{t}_o} s^T$ it holds $\bar{t}_o \in C(s^T)$.

We say that $I$ *strongly passes* the set of valid tests $\mathcal{T}$ *in the best time* if $\mathtt{pass}(I,\mathcal{T})$ and for all $e = (\bar{t},\sigma,\bar{t}_o) \in \mathtt{InsTEvol}(I)$ we have that for all $T \in \mathtt{Test}(e,\mathcal{T})$ such that $I \parallel T \overset{\sigma}{\Longrightarrow}_{\bar{t},\bar{t}_o} s^T$, for all $\bar{t}_c \in C(s^T)$ it holds $\bar{t}_o \leq \bar{t}_c$.

We say that $I$ *strongly passes* the set of valid tests $\mathcal{T}$ *in the worst time* if $\mathtt{pass}(I,\mathcal{T})$ and for all $e = (\bar{t},\sigma,\bar{t}_o) \in \mathtt{InsTEvol}(I)$ we have that for all $T \in \mathtt{Test}(e,\mathcal{T})$ such that $I \parallel T \overset{\sigma}{\Longrightarrow}_{\bar{t},\bar{t}_o} s^T$ there exists $\bar{t}_c \in C(s^T)$ such that $\bar{t}_o \leq \bar{t}_c$.

We say that $I$ *strongly passes* the set of valid tests $\mathcal{T}$ *sometimes in best time* if $\mathtt{pass}(I,\mathcal{T})$ and there exists $e = (\bar{t},\sigma,\bar{t}_o) \in \mathtt{InsTEvol}(I)$ such that for all $T \in \mathtt{Test}(e,\mathcal{T})$ with $I \parallel T \overset{\sigma}{\Longrightarrow}_{\bar{t},\bar{t}_o} s^T$ we have that for all $\bar{t}_c \in C(s^T)$ it holds $\bar{t}_o \leq \bar{t}_c$.

We say that $I$ *strongly passes* the set of valid tests $\mathcal{T}$ *sometimes in worst time* if $\mathtt{pass}(I,\mathcal{T})$ and there exists $e = (\bar{t},\sigma,\bar{t}_o) \in \mathtt{InsTEvol}(I)$ such that for all $T \in \mathtt{Test}(e,\mathcal{T})$ with $I \parallel T \overset{\sigma}{\Longrightarrow}_{\bar{t},\bar{t}_o} s^T$ we have that there exists $\bar{t}_c \in C(s^T)$ such that $\bar{t}_o \leq \bar{t}_c$.

We say that $I$ *weakly passes* the set of valid tests $\mathcal{T}$ *for any time* if $\mathtt{pass}(I,\mathcal{T})$ and for all $e = (\bar{t},\sigma,\bar{t}_o) \in \mathtt{InsTEvol}(I)$ we have that for all $T \in \mathtt{Test}(e,\mathcal{T})$ such that $I \parallel T \overset{\sigma}{\Longrightarrow}_{\bar{t},\bar{t}_o} s^T$ it holds $\sum \bar{t}_o = \sum \bar{t}_c$ for some $\bar{t}_c \in C(s^T)$.

We say that $I$ *weakly passes* the set of valid tests $\mathcal{T}$ *in the best time* if $\mathtt{pass}(I,\mathcal{T})$ and for all $e = (\bar{t},\sigma,\bar{t}_o) \in \mathtt{InsTEvol}(I)$ we have that for all $T \in \mathtt{Test}(e,\mathcal{T})$ such that $I \parallel T \overset{\sigma}{\Longrightarrow}_{\bar{t},\bar{t}_o} s^T$, for all $\bar{t}_c \in C(s^T)$ it holds $\sum \bar{t}_o \leq \sum \bar{t}_c$.

We say that $I$ *weakly passes* the set of valid tests $\mathcal{T}$ *in the worst time* if $\mathtt{pass}(I,\mathcal{T})$ and for all $e = (\bar{t},\sigma,\bar{t}_o) \in \mathtt{InsTEvol}(I)$ we have that for all $T \in \mathtt{Test}(e,\mathcal{T})$ such that $I \parallel T \overset{\sigma}{\Longrightarrow}_{\bar{t},\bar{t}_o} s^T$ there exists $\bar{t}_c \in C(s^T)$ such that $\sum \bar{t}_o \leq \sum \bar{t}_c$.

We say that $I$ *weakly passes* the set of valid tests $\mathcal{T}$ *sometimes in best time* if $\mathtt{pass}(I,\mathcal{T})$ and there exists $e = (\bar{t},\sigma,\bar{t}_o) \in \mathtt{InsTEvol}(I)$ such that for all $T \in \mathtt{Test}(e,\mathcal{T})$ with $I \parallel T \overset{\sigma}{\Longrightarrow}_{\bar{t},\bar{t}_o} s^T$ we have that for all $\bar{t}_c \in C(s^T)$ it holds $\sum \bar{t}_o \leq \sum \bar{t}_c$.

We say that $I$ *weakly passes* the set of valid tests $\mathcal{T}$ *sometimes in worst time* if $\mathtt{pass}(I,\mathcal{T})$ and there exists $e = (\bar{t},\sigma,\bar{t}_o) \in \mathtt{InsTEvol}(I)$ such that and for all $T \in \mathtt{Test}(e,\mathcal{T})$ with $I \parallel T \overset{\sigma}{\Longrightarrow}_{\bar{t},\bar{t}_o} s^T$ we have that there exists $\bar{t}_c \in C(s^T)$ such that $\sum \bar{t}_o \leq \sum \bar{t}_c$. $\qquad\square$

## 5   Conclusions and Future Work

In this paper we have introduced a new model to specify timed systems. In contrast with most approaches, our formalism allows to define time in two different ways: Duration of actions and timeouts of the system. Thus, by separating these two notions, it is easier to specify temporal properties of systems than if we use a formalism where only one of the possibilities is available. We have also developed a testing theory. On the one hand, we have defined ten conformance relations that take into account the influence of non-determinism in the behavior of systems. On the other hand, we have introduced a notion of test. In order to capture the timed behavior of the IUT, test can both delay the execution of the IUT and record the time that it took to perform a given action.

In terms of future work, we would like to take this paper as a first step, together with [11], to define a testing theory for systems presenting stochastic time together with timeouts.

# References

1. R. Alur and D. Dill. A theory of timed automata. *Theoretical Computer Science*, 126:183–235, 1994.
2. B.S. Bosik and M.U. Uyar. Finite state machine based formal methods in protocol conformance testing. *Computer Networks & ISDN Systems*, 22:7–33, 1991.
3. E. Brinksma and J. Tretmans. Testing transition systems: An annotated bibliography. In *4th Summer School, MOVEP 2000, LNCS 2067*, pages 187–195. Springer, 2001.
4. D. Clarke and I. Lee. Automatic generation of tests for timing constraints from requirements. In *3rd Workshop on Object-Oriented Real-Time Dependable Systems*, 1997.
5. K. El-Fakih, N. Yevtushenko, and G. von Bochmann. FSM-based incremental conformance testing methods. *IEEE Transactions on Software Engineering*, 30(7):425–436, 2004.
6. A. En-Nouaary and R. Dssouli. A guided method for testing timed input output automata. In *TestCom 2003, LNCS 2644*, pages 211–225. Springer, 2003.
7. M.A. Fecko, M.Ü. Uyar, A.Y. Duale, and P.D. Amer. A technique to generate feasible tests for communications systems with multiple timers. *IEEE/ACM Transactions on Networking*, 11(5):796–809, 2003.
8. T. Higashino, A. Nakata, K. Taniguchi, and A. Cavalli. Generating test cases for a timed I/O automaton model. In *12th Workshop on Testing of Communicating Systems*, pages 197–214. Kluwer Academic Publishers, 1999.
9. D. Lee and M. Yannakakis. Principles and methods of testing finite state machines: A survey. *Proceedings of the IEEE*, 84(8):1090–1123, 1996.
10. M. Núñez and I. Rodríguez. Encoding PAMR into (timed) EFSMs. In *FORTE 2002, LNCS 2529*, pages 1–16. Springer, 2002.
11. M. Núñez and I. Rodríguez. Towards testing stochastic timed systems. In *FORTE 2003, LNCS 2767*, pages 335–350. Springer, 2003.
12. M. Núñez and I. Rodríguez. Conformance testing relations for timed systems. In *5th Int. Workshop on Formal Approaches to Software Testing (FATES 2005), LNCS 3997*, pages 103–117. Springer, 2006.
13. J.C. Park and R.E. Miller. Synthesizing protocol specifications from service specifications in timed extended finite state machines. In *17th IEEE Int. Conf. on Distributed Computing Systems, ICDCS'97*, pages 253–260. IEEE Computer Society, 1997.
14. A. Petrenko. Fault model-driven test derivation from finite state models: Annotated bibliography. In *4th Summer School, MOVEP 2000, LNCS 2067*, pages 196–205. Springer, 2001.
15. J. Springintveld, F. Vaandrager, and P.R. D'Argenio. Testing timed automata. *Theoretical Computer Science*, 254(1-2):225–257, 2001.
16. J. Tretmans. Test generation with inputs, outputs and repetitive quiescence. *Software – Concepts and Tools*, 17(3):103–120, 1996.

# Scenario-Based Timing Consistency Checking for Time Petri Nets*

Li Xuandong, Bu Lei, Hu Jun, Zhao Jianhua, Zhang Tao, and Zheng Guoliang

State Key Laboratory of Novel Software Technology
Department of Computer Science and Technology
Nanjing University, Nanjing, Jiangsu, P.R. China 210093
lxd@nju.edu.cn

**Abstract.** In this paper, we solve the consistency checking problems of concurrent and real-time system designs modelled by time Petri nets for the scenario-based specifications expressed by message sequence charts (MSCs). The algorithm we present can be used to check if a time Petri net satisfies a specification expressed by a given MSC which requires that if a scenario described by the MSC occurs during the run of the time Petri net, the timing constraints enforced to the MSC must be satisfied.

## 1  Introduction

Scenarios are widely used as a requirements technique since they describe concrete interactions and are therefore easy for customers and domain experts to use. Scenario-based specifications such as message sequence charts offer an intuitive and visual way of describing design requirements. Message sequence charts (MSCs) [1] is a graphical and textual language for the description and specification of the interactions between system components. The main area of application for MSCs is as overview specification of the communication behavior of real-time systems, in particular telecommunication switching systems.

Time Petri nets [3] have been proposed as one powerful formalism for modelling concurrent and real-time systems because they can model both concurrency and real-time constraints in natural way. There are plenty of applications of time Petri Nets in modelling system specifications and designs.

Since Unified Modelling Language (UML) [2] became a standard in OMG in 1997, MSC-like diagrams (UML sequence diagrams) and time Petri nets-like models (UML activity diagrams) have become a main class of artifacts in software development processes. It follows that we often need to use MSCs and time Petri nets together in specification and design of software projects [4-6]. Usually, MSCs and time Petri nets are used in the different software development steps. Even used in the same step, e.g. requirements analysis, MSCs are used

* Supported by the National Natural Science Foundation of China (No.60425204, No.60233020), the National Grand Fundamental Research 973 Program of China (No.2002CB312001), and by the Jiangsu Province Research Foundation (No.BK2004080).

E. Najm et al. (Eds.): FORTE 2006, LNCS 4229, pp. 388–403, 2006.

usually to describe the scenario-based requirements provided directly by the customers, while time Petri nets are used to model the workflow synthesized by the domain and technical experts. So it is necessary and important to keep the consistency between these two kinds of models for software quality assurance.

In this paper, we introduce a more expressive mechanism in MSCs to describe timing constraints, and give the solution to the problem of checking concurrent and real-time system designs modelled by time Petri nets for the scenario-based specifications expressed by MSCs, which require that if a scenario described by a given MSC occurs during the run of a time Petri net, the timing constraints enforced to the MSC must be satisfied.

The paper is organized as follows. In next section, we introduce MSCs and the related timing constraints, and use them to represent the scenario-based specifications. In Section 3, we review the definition and some basic properties of time Petri nets. Section 4 gives the solution to checking time Petri nets for the scenario-based specifications expressed by MSCs. The related works and some conclusions are given in the last section.

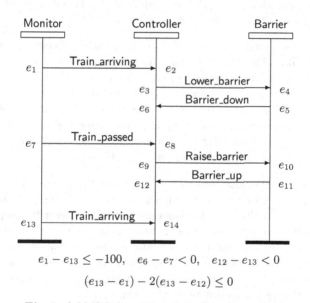

$$e_1 - e_{13} \leq -100, \quad e_6 - e_7 < 0, \quad e_{12} - e_{13} < 0$$

$$(e_{13} - e_1) - 2(e_{13} - e_{12}) \leq 0$$

**Fig. 1.** A bMSC describing the railroad crossing system

## 2   Message Sequence Charts with Timing Constraints

MSCs represent typical execution scenarios, providing examples of either normal or exceptional executions of the proposed system. The MSC standard as defined by ITU-T in Recommendation Z.120 [1] introduces two basic concepts: *basic MSCs* (bMSCs) and *High-Level MSCs* (hMSCs). A bMSC consists of a set of processes that run in parallel and exchange messages in a one-to-one, asynchronous fashion. A hMSC graphically combines references to bMSCs to describe parallel, sequence, iterating, and non-deterministic execution of the bMSCs. In this paper, we just use bMSCs to represent the scenario-based specifications, which are incomplete and usually specify the requirements provided directly by the customers. For example, a MSC is depicted in Figure 1, which describes a scenario about the well-known example of the railroad crossing system in [4,10]. This system operates a barrier at a railroad crossing, in which there are a railroad crossing monitor and a barrier controller for controlling the barrier. When the monitor detects that a train is arriving, it sends a message to the controller to lower the barrier. After the train leaves the crossing, the monitor sends a message to controller to raise the barrier.

The semantics of a MSC essentially consists of the sequences (of traces) of messages that are sent and received among the concurrent processes in the MSC. The order of communication events (i.e. message sending or receiving) in a trace is deduced from the visual partial order determined by the flow of control within each process in the MSC along with a causal dependency between the events of sending and receiving a message [1,6,7,9]. In accordance with [9], without losing generality, we assume that each MSC corresponds to a visual order for a pair of events $e_1$ and $e_2$ such that $e_1$ precedes $e_2$ in the following cases:

- **Causality:** A sending event $e_1$ and its corresponding receiving event $e_2$.
- **Controllability:** The event $e_1$ appears above the event $e_2$ on the same process line, and $e_2$ is a sending event. This order reflects the fact that a sending event can wait for other events to occur. On the other hand, we sometimes have less control on the order in which receiving events occur.
- **Fifo order:** The receiving event $e_1$ appears above the receiving event $e_2$ on the same process line, and the corresponding sending events $e_1'$ and $e_2'$ appear on a mutual process line where $e_1'$ is above $e_2'$.

For facilitating the specifications of real-time systems, the timers [1], interval delays [7,8], and timing marks [2] have been introduced to describe timing constraints in MSCs. All of these mechanisms are suitable to describe simple timing constraints which are only about the separation in time between two events. In this paper, we introduce more general and expressive timing constraints in MSCs. In a MSC, we use event names to represent the occurrence time of events. So, timing constraints can be described by boolean expressions on event names. Here we let any timing constraint be of the form

$$c_0(e_0 - e_0') + c_1(e_1 - e_1') + \ldots + c_n(e_n - e_n') \sim c,$$

where $e_0, e_0', e_1, e_1' \ldots, e_n, e_n'$ are event names, $c, c_0, c_1, \ldots, c_n$ are real numbers, and $\sim \in \{\leq, <\}$. For example, in the MSC depicted in Figure 1, the boolean expression $e_1 - e_{13} \leq -100$ represents the separation in time between the sending events $e_1$ and $e_{13}$ is not smaller than 100 time units. Furthermore, if we require that the separation in time between the sending event $e_{13}$ and the sending event $e_1$ is not greater than two times the one between the sending event $e_{13}$ and the receiving event $e_{12}$, we can describe the requirement by the timing constraint $(e_{13} - e_1) - 2(e_{13} - e_{12}) \leq 0$.

Compared to the timers, interval delays, and timing marks, the timing constraints we consider here can be used to describe more complex timing requirements in practical use. For the scenario of the railroad system depicted in Figure 1, we suppose that when a train has passed, a new train could come after at least 100 time units. Figure 1 depicts a specification for this system represented by a MSC in which we require that from the time one train is arriving to the time the next train is arriving, the barrier stay up for at least half of this period, which is represented by $(e_{13} - e_1) - 2(e_{13} - e_{12}) \leq 0$. Clearly, this timing constraint is about the relation between two separations in time between events (one is the separation in time between $e_{13}$ and $e_{12}$, and the other is the separation in time between $e_{13}$ and $e_1$), and the timers, interval delays, and timing marks can not be used to describe such a timing requirement since they are suitable to describe the simple timing constraints only about the separation in time between two events.

For checking the scenario-based specification expressed by MSCs, we formalize MSCs as follows.

**Definition 1.** A MSC is a tuple $D = (P, E, M, L, V, C)$ where

- $P$ is a finite set of processes. $E$ is a finite set of events corresponding to sending a message and receiving a message.
- $M$ is a finite set of messages. Each message in $M$ is of the form $(e, g, e')$ where $e, e' \in E$ corresponds to sending and receiving the message respectively, and $g$ is the message name which is a character string. For any message $(e, g, e') \in M$, we use $g!$ and $g?$ to represent the sending and the receiving for the message respectively if we just concern the message name, and let $\phi(e) = g!$ and $\phi(e') = g?$.
- $L : E \to P$ is a labelling function which maps each event $e \in E$ to a process $L(e) \in P$ which is the sender (receiver) while $e$ corresponds to sending (receiving) a message.
- $V$ is a finite set whose elements are a pair $(e, e')$ where $e, e' \in E$ and $e$ precedes $e'$, which is corresponding to a visual order.
- $C$ is a set of timing constraints on event names enforced on $D$. □

We use *event sequences* to represent the *traces* of MSCs which are corresponding to the untimed behavior of MSCs. Any event sequence is of the form $e_0\hat{\ }e_1\hat{\ }\ldots\hat{\ }e_m$, which represents that $e_{i+1}$ takes place after $e_i$ for any $i$ ($0 \leq i \leq m - 1$).

**Definition 2.** Let $D = (P, E, M, L, V, C)$ be a MSC. An event sequence of the form $e_0\hat{\ }e_1\hat{\ }\ldots\hat{\ }e_m$ is a *trace* of $D$ if and only if the following conditions hold:

- all events in $E$ occur in the sequence, and each event occurs only once, i.e. $\{e_0, e_1, \ldots, e_m\} = E$ and $e_i \neq e_j$ for any $i, j$ ($0 \leq i < j \leq m$); and
- $e_1, e_2, \ldots, e_m$ satisfy the visual order defined by $V$, i.e. for any $e_i$ and $e_j$, if $(e_i, e_j) \in V$, then $0 \leq i < j \leq m$. □

Corresponding to the sending or receiving for messages, we can transform the traces of a MSC into the *message trails* of the MSC.

**Definition 3.** Let $D = (P, E, M, L, V, C)$ be a MSC. For any trace of $D$ of the form $e_0{\char`\^}e_1{\char`\^} \ldots {\char`\^}e_m$, replacing each $e_i$ with $\phi(e_i)$ $(0 \leq i \leq m)$, we get a sequence $\phi(e_0){\char`\^}\phi(e_1){\char`\^} \ldots {\char`\^}\phi(e_m)$ of the sending or receiving for messages in $M$, which is a *message trail* of $D$.                                                                    □

Notice that for a MSC $D$, all events in a trace of $D$ are distinct, but there may be the same events in a message trail of $D$ which are corresponding to the message sending or receiving. For example, the events $e_1$ and $e_{13}$ are distinct in the MSC depicted in Figure 1, but $\phi(e_1) = \phi(e_{13}) =$ Train_arriving!.

We use *timed event sequences* to represent the behavior of MSCs. Any timed event sequence is of the form $(e_0, \delta_0){\char`\^}(e_1, \delta_1){\char`\^} \ldots {\char`\^}(e_m, \delta_m)$ where $e_i$ is an event and $\delta_i$ is a nonnegative real numbers for any $i$ $(0 \leq i \leq m)$, which describes that $e_0$ takes place $\delta_0$ time units after the system starts, then $e_1$ takes place $\delta_1$ time units after $e_0$ takes place, so on and so forth, at last $e_m$ takes place $\delta_m$ time units after $e_{m-1}$ takes place.

**Definition 4.** A timed event sequence $\omega = (e_0, \delta_0){\char`\^}(e_1, \delta_1){\char`\^} \ldots {\char`\^}(e_m, \delta_m)$ is a behavior of a MSC $D = (P, E, M, L, V, C)$ if and only if $e_0{\char`\^}e_1{\char`\^} \ldots {\char`\^}e_m$ is a trace of $D$ and $\delta_0, \delta_1, \ldots, \delta_m$ satisfy the timing constraints described by $C$, i.e. for any boolean expression $\sum_{i=0}^{n} c_i(f_i - f'_i) \sim c$ in $C$, $c_0\lambda_0 + c_1\lambda_1 + \ldots + c_n\lambda_n \sim c$ where for each $i$ $(0 \leq i \leq n)$, if $f_i = e_j$ and $f'_i = e_k$, then

$$\lambda_i = \begin{cases} \delta_{k+1} + \delta_{k+2} + \ldots + \delta_j & \text{if } j > k \\ -(\delta_{j+1} + \delta_{j+2} + \ldots + \delta_k) & \text{if } j < k \end{cases} .$$                    □

## 3    Time Petri Nets

Time Petri nets [3] are classical Petri Nets where to each transition $t$ a time interval $[a, b]$ is associated. The times $a$ and $b$ are relative to the moment at which $t$ was last enabled. Assuming that $t$ was enabled at time $c$, then $t$ may fire only during the interval $[c + a, c + b]$ and must fire at the time $c + b$ at the latest, unless it is disabled before by the firing of another transition. Firing a transition takes no time. The time Petri nets considered in this paper are 1-safe.

**Definition 5.** Let $\mathbf{N}$ be the set of natural numbers. A time Petri net is a six-tuple, $N = (P, T, F, Eft, Lft, \mu_0)$, where

- $P = \{p_1, p_2, \ldots, p_m\}$ is a finite set of *places*; $T = \{t_1, t_2, \ldots, t_n\}$ is a finite set of *transitions* $(P \cap T = \emptyset)$; $F \subset (P \times T) \cup (T \times P)$ is the *flow relation*; $\mu \subset P$ is the *initial marking* of the net.
- $Eft, Lft : T \rightarrow \mathbf{N}$ are functions for the *earliest* and *latest firing times* of transitions, satisfying that for any $t \in T$, $Eft(t) \leq Lft(t) < \infty$.

A *marking* $\mu$ of $N$ is any subset of $P$. For any transition $t$, ${}^\bullet t = \{p \in P | (p, t) \in F\}$ and $t^\bullet = \{p \in P | (t, p) \in F\}$ denote the *preset* and *postset* of $t$, respectively. A transition $t$ is *enabled* in a marking $\mu$ if ${}^\bullet t \subseteq \mu$; otherwise, it is *disabled*. Let *enabled*$(\mu)$ be the set of transitions enabled in $\mu$.                                                                    □

**Definition 6.** Let $\mathbf{T}$ be the set of nonnegative real numbers. A *state* of a time Petri net $N = (P, T, F, Eft, Lft, \mu_0)$ is a pair $s = (\mu, c)$, where $\mu$ is a marking of $N$, and $c : enabled(\mu) \rightarrow \mathbf{T}$ is called the *clock function*. The *initial state* of $N$ is $s_0 = (\mu_0, c_0)$ where $c_0(t) = 0$ for any $t \in enabled(\mu_0)$.    □

For the firing of a transition to be possible at a certain time, four conditions must be satisfied.

**Definition 7.** A transition $t$ may fire from state $s = (\mu, c)$ after delay $\delta \in \mathbf{T}$ if and only if (1) $t \in enabled(\mu)$, (2) $(\mu - {}^\bullet t) \cap t^\bullet = \emptyset$, (3) $Eft(t) \leq c(t) + \delta$, and (4) $\forall t' \in enabled(\mu) : c(t') + \delta \leq Lft(t')$.    □

The first condition is the normal firing condition for Petri nets. The second condition requires *contact-freeness*. The third condition specifies that the transition may only fire if its clock has reached the $Eft$ value of the transition. The last condition quantifies over all other enabled transitions, and makes sure that the delay $\delta$ doesn't cause any of the $Lft$ bounds to be invalidated. The new state is then calculated as follows.

**Definition 8.** When transition $t$ fires after delay $\delta$ from state $s = (\mu, c)$, the new state $s' = (\mu', c')$ is given as follows: $\mu' = (\mu - {}^\bullet t) \cup t^\bullet$, and for any $t' \in enabled(\mu')$, if $t' \neq t$ and $t' \in enabled(\mu)$, then $c'(t') = c(t') + \delta$ else $c'(t') = 0$. This is denoted by $s' = fire(s, (t, \delta))$.    □

The new marking is calculated normally. For clocks we have two cases: if a transition remains enabled in the new marking its clock value is incremented with $\delta$, while for newly enabled transition the clock value is 0. The behavior of a time Petri net is described in term of *runs*.

**Definition 9.** For any time Petri net, a *run*

$$\rho = s_0 \xrightarrow{(t_0, \delta_0)} s_1 \xrightarrow{(t_1, \delta_1)} \cdots \xrightarrow{(t_{n-1}, \delta_{n-1})} s_n \xrightarrow{(t_n, \delta_n)} \cdots$$

is a finite or infinite sequence of states, transitions, and delays such that $s_0$ is the initial state, and for every $i \geq 1$, $s_i$ is obtained from $s_{i-1}$ by firing a transition $t_{i-1}$ after delay $\delta_{i-1}$ which satisfies that $s_i = fire(s_{i-1}, (t_{i-1}, \delta_{i-1}))$.    □

As a tool used for modelling systems, time Petri nets are such that their transitions represent the potential events in the systems. Since in this paper we consider the problem of checking time Petri nets for the scenario-based specifications expressed by MSCs, for any time Petri net we consider in this paper, each transition $t$ is labelled with an event denoted by $\varphi(t)$, which may be corresponding to a message sending or receiving in a MSC. That is, for a MSC $D = (P, E, M, L, V, C)$, for a transition $t$ of a time Petri net, there may be a message $(e, g, e') \in M$ such that $\varphi(t) = g! = \phi(e)$ or $\varphi(t) = g? = \phi(e')$.

For example, for the railroad crossing system described in the above section, its design can be described by a time Petri net depicted in Figure 2. In the system, when the monitor detects that a train is arriving, it sends the message Train_arriving at once to the controller. The controller sends a message back for

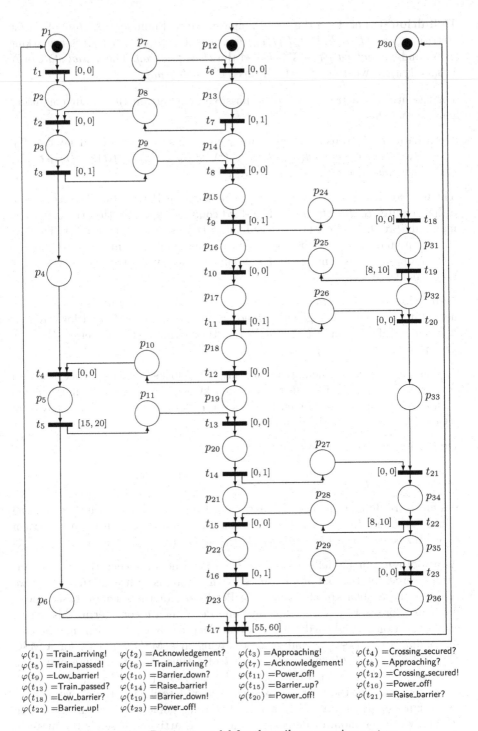

**Fig. 2.** Time Petri net model for the railway crossing system

acknowledgement in one time units, and the monitor gives a reply in one time units. Once the controller receives the confirmed message Approaching, it sends the message Low_barrier to the barrier in one time unit. The barrier is put down in $[8, 10]$ time units after receiving the message Low_barrier, and the message Barrier_down is sent to the controller. Then in one time unit the controller sends the message Power_off to the Barrier, and the message Barrier_secured to the monitor. It takes $[15, 20]$ time units for the train to pass the crossing after the monitor receives the message Barrier_secured. Once the train passes the crossing, the monitor sends a message to the controller, and after receiving the message the controller takes one time unit to send the message Raise_barrier to the barrier. The barrier becomes up in $[8, 10]$ time units after receiving the message from the controller, and the message Barrier_up is sent to the controller. Once receiving the massage Barrier_up, the controller takes one time unit to send a message to the barrier for turning off the power. The barrier holds up in the coming $[55, 60]$ time units, and then another train is arriving.

## 4   Checking Time Petri Nets for the Scenario-Based Specifications Expressed by MSCs

In this section, we give the solution to checking of time Petri nets for the scenario-based specifications represented by MSCs.

### 4.1   Definition of the Satisfaction Problem

Given a MSC $D = (P, E, M, L, V, C)$, we can get a scenario-based specification for timing consistency, denoted by $\mathcal{S}_T(D)$. For a time Petri net $N$, $\mathcal{S}_T(D)$ requires that whenever a scenario described by $D$ occurs in a run of $N$, the corresponding run segment must satisfy all the timing constraints in $C$. For example, Figure 1 depicts a timing consistency specification for the time Petri net in Figure 2, which requires that after a train has passed, a new train can come after at least 100 time units, and that from the time one train is arriving to the time the next train is arriving, the barrier stay up for at least half of this period.

The satisfaction problem of a time Petri net $N$ for a scenario-based specification $\mathcal{S}_T(D)$ is defined formally as follows. Let $D = (P, E, M, L, V, C)$ and

$$\rho = s_0 \xrightarrow{(t_0, \delta_0)} s_1 \xrightarrow{(t_1, \delta_1)} \ldots \xrightarrow{(t_{n-1}, \delta_{n-1})} s_n \xrightarrow{(t_n, \delta_n)} s_{n+1}$$

be a run of $N$. For any subsequence $\rho_1$ of $\rho$ which is of the form

$$\rho_1 = s_i \xrightarrow{(t_i, \delta_i)} s_{i+1} \xrightarrow{(t_{i+1}, \delta_{i+1})} \ldots \xrightarrow{(t_{j-1}, \delta_{j-1})} s_j \xrightarrow{(t_j, \delta_j)} s_{j+1} \quad (0 \leq i < j < n + 1),$$

since each transition $t_k$ is labelled with an event $\varphi(t_k)$ $(i \leq k \leq j)$, we get a sequence $\tau$ of events: $\tau = \varphi(t_i)\hat{\ }\varphi(t_{i+1})\hat{\ } \ldots \hat{\ }\varphi(t_j)$. By removing any $\varphi(t_k)$ $(i \leq k \leq j)$ from $\tau$ which is not corresponding to the sending or receiving for a message in $M$, we get an event sequence $\tau_1 = e_0\hat{\ }e_2\hat{\ } \ldots \hat{\ }e_m$ $(m \leq j - i)$. If $\tau_1$ is a message trail of $D$, $\varphi(t_i) = e_0$, and $\varphi(t_j) = e_m$, then we say that $\rho_1$ is an *image* of $D$ in $\rho$. If $\rho_1$ is an image of $D$, then there is a trace $f_0 \hat{\ } f_1 \hat{\ } \ldots \hat{\ } f_m$ of $D$ which is corresponding to $\tau_1$, and we can give a function

$$\theta : \{f_0, f_1, \ldots, f_m\} \rightarrow \{t_i, t_{i+1}, \ldots, t_j\}$$

which map each $f_k$ $(0 \le k \le m)$ in an incremental order to $t_l$ $(i \le l \le j)$ such that $\phi(f_k) = \varphi(t_l)$, that is, $\theta(f_0) = t_i$, $\theta(f_m) = t_j$, and if $\theta(f_a) = t_p$ and $\theta(f_b) = t_q$ $(a < b)$, then $p < q$. We define that the image $\rho_1$ of $D$ satisfies $\mathcal{S}_T(D)$ if $\delta_i, \delta_{i+1}, \ldots, \delta_j$ satisfy all the timing constraints in $C$, i.e. for any timing constraint $\sum_{k=0}^{n} c_k(g_k - g'_k) \sim c$ in $C$, $c_0\lambda_0 + c_1\lambda_1 + \ldots + c_n\lambda_n \sim c$ where for each $k$ $(0 \le k \le n)$, if $\theta(g_k) = t_a$ and $\theta(g'_k) = t_b$ $(i \le a, b \le j)$, then

$$\lambda_k = \begin{cases} \delta_{b+1} + \delta_{b+2} + \ldots + \delta_a & \text{if } a > b \\ -(\delta_{a+1} + \delta_{a+2} + \ldots + \delta_b) & \text{if } a < b \end{cases} .$$

We define that the run $\rho$ of $N$ satisfies $\mathcal{S}_T(D)$ if any image of $D$ in $\rho$ satisfies $\mathcal{S}_T(D)$, and that $N$ satisfies $\mathcal{S}_T(D)$ if any run of $N$ satisfies $\mathcal{S}_T(D)$.

## 4.2   Integer Time Verification Approach

According to the above definition, for solving the satisfaction problem of a time Petri net $N$ for a scenario-based specification $\mathcal{S}_T(D)$, we need to check all the runs of $N$. We know that for a time Petri net, its runs could be infinite and the number of its runs could be infinite. So we attempt to solve the problem based on a finite set of finite runs. In the following we present an integer time verification approach to solving the problem. A similar approach has been used by us to check time Petri nets for linear duration properties [17].

For a time Petri net $N$, a run $\rho$ of $N$ of the form

$$\rho = s_0 \xrightarrow{(t_0, \delta_0)} s_1 \xrightarrow{(t_1, \delta_1)} \ldots \xrightarrow{(t_{n-1}, \delta_{n-1})} s_n$$

is an *integral run* if all $\delta_i$s occurred in its combined steps are integers. It follows that any state $s = (\mu, c)$ occurring in an integral run satisfies $c(t)$ is an integer for any $t \in enabled(\mu)$, which is called *integral state*.

**Theorem 1.** A time Petri net $N$ satisfies a scenario-based specification $\mathcal{S}_T(D)$ if and only if any integral run of $N$ satisfies $\mathcal{S}_T(D)$.                           □

The proof of this theorem is presented in the appendix. According to the above theorem, when we check a time Petri net $N$ for a scenario-based specification $\mathcal{S}_T(D)$, we only need to consider the integral runs of $N$.

Since according to Definition 5 the upper bounds of the time intervals associated to transitions are finite, the number of the integral states in a time Petri net is finite. Therefore, for a time Petri net $N = (P, T, F, Eft, Lft, \mu_0)$, we can construct a *reachability graph* $G = (V, E)$ as follows, where $V$ is a set of nodes and $E$ is a set of edges:

1. The initial state $(\mu_0, c_0)$ of $N$ is in the set $V$, which is called *initial node*;
2. Let $s = (\mu, c)$ be in the set $V$, and $\kappa$ is the minimal value of the set $\{Lft(t) \mid t \in enabled(\mu)\}$. Then for any transition $t \in enabled(\mu)$, for any integer $\delta \geq 0$ such that $Eft(t) \leq c(t) + \delta \leq \kappa$, $s' = fire(s, (t, \delta))$ is in $V$, and $s \xrightarrow{(t,\delta)} s'$ is in the set $E$.

For a time Petri net $N$, a *path* in its reachability graph $G = (V, E)$ is a sequence of states, transitions, and delays $s_0 \xrightarrow{(t_0,\delta_0)} s_1 \xrightarrow{(t_1,\delta_1)} \ldots \xrightarrow{(t_{n-1},\delta_{n-1})} s_n$ such that $s_0$ is the initial node, $s_i \in V$ for every $i$ ($0 \leq i \leq n$), and $s_i \xrightarrow{(t_i,\delta_i)} s_{i+1} \in E$ for every $i$ ($0 \leq i < n$). It follows that any integral run of $N$ is a path in $G$, and any path in $G$ is an integral run of $N$. So we can solve the problem of checking a time Petri net $N$ for a scenario-based specification $\mathcal{S}_T(D)$ by checking if every path in the reachability graph $G$ of $N$ satisfies $\mathcal{S}_T(D)$.

## 4.3 Algorithm for Timing Consistency Checking

Since for a time Petri net whose reachability graph is $G$, a path in $G$ could be infinite and the number of paths in $G$ could be infinite, we need to solve the problem based on a finite set of finite paths in $G$ as follows.

First, for a time Petri net $N$, we define *loops* in its reachability graph $G$. Let $\varrho$ be a path in $G$ of the form $\varrho = s_0 \xrightarrow{(t_0,\delta_0)} s_1 \xrightarrow{(t_1,\delta_1)} \ldots \xrightarrow{(t_{n-1},\delta_{n-1})} s_n \xrightarrow{(t_n,\delta_n)} s_{n+1}$. If all $s_i$ ($0 \leq i \leq n$) are distinct and there are $s_k$ ($0 \leq k < n$) such that $s_k = s_{n+1}$, then we say that the subsequence

$$\varrho_1 = s_k \xrightarrow{(t_k,\delta_k)} s_{k+1} \xrightarrow{(t_{k+1},\delta_{k+1})} \ldots \xrightarrow{(t_{n-1},\delta_{n-1})} s_n \xrightarrow{(t_n,\delta_n)} s_k$$

is a *loop* in $G$, and $\delta_k + \delta_{k+1} + \ldots + \delta_n$ is the *elapsed time* on $\varrho_1$, denoted by $\zeta(\varrho_1)$. For a given MSC $D = (P, E, M, L, V, C)$, if there is $t_i$ ($k \leq i \leq n$) such that $\varphi(t_i) = \phi(e)$ ($e \in E$), then we say that the loop $\varrho_1$ is *related to* $D$.

Then, for a node $s$ in the reachability graph $G$ of a time Petri net, for a MSC $D$, we define recursively the set $\Theta(s, D)$ of the loops which are not related to $D$ as follows:

– any loop $\varrho$ in $G$ from $s$ to itself which is not related to $D$ is in $\Theta(s, D)$;

– for any loop in $\Theta(s, D)$ of the form $s_0 \xrightarrow{(t_0,\delta_0)} s_1 \xrightarrow{(t_1,\delta_1)} \ldots \xrightarrow{(t_{n-1},\delta_{n-1})} s_n$, any loop $\varrho$ in $G$ from $s_i$ ($0 \leq i < n$) to itself which is not related to $D$ is in $\Theta(s, D)$.

Let $N$ be a time Petri net with its reachability graph $G$. Now for a given scenario-based specification $\mathcal{S}_T(D)$ where $D = (P, E, M, L, V, C)$, we introduce the *violable points* in an image of $D$ in a path in $G$. Let $\varrho$ be a path in $G$, and $\varrho_1$ is an image of $D$ in $\varrho$ of the form

$$\varrho_1 = s_0 \xrightarrow{(t_0,\delta_0)} s_1 \xrightarrow{(t_1,\delta_1)} \ldots \xrightarrow{(t_{m-1},\delta_{m-1})} s_m \xrightarrow{(t_m,\delta_m)} s_{m+1}.$$

We have defined that $\varrho_1$ satisfies $\mathcal{S}_T(D)$ if $\delta_0, \delta_1, \ldots, \delta_m$ satisfy all the timing constraints in $C$, i.e. for any timing constraint $\sum_{k=0}^{n} c_k(g_k - g'_k) \sim c$ in $C$,

$c_0\lambda_0 + c_1\lambda_1 + \ldots + c_n\lambda_n \sim c$ where for each $k$ $(0 \le k \le n)$, if $\theta(g_k) = t_a$ and $\theta(g_k') = t_b$ $(0 \le a, b \le m)$, then

$$\lambda_k = \begin{cases} \delta_{b+1} + \delta_{b+2} + \ldots + \delta_a & \text{if } a > b \\ -(\delta_{a+1} + \delta_{a+2} + \ldots + \delta_b) & \text{if } a < b \end{cases}.$$

We say that $s_i$ $(0 \le i \le m)$ is a *violable point* in $\varrho_1$ if the following condition holds:

- $\varphi(t_i) \ne \phi(e)$ $(e \in E)$,
- there is a loop $\varrho' \in \Theta(s_i, D)$ whose elapsed time is greater than zero $(\zeta(\varrho') > 0)$, and
- $\delta_i$ occurs in $\lambda_k$ $(0 \le k \le n)$ and $c_k\lambda_k > 0$ (in this case, $c_k\lambda_k$ becomes larger while $\delta_i$ becomes larger).

Last, for a time Petri net $N$ with its reachability graph $G$, we define the finite set $\Delta(N, \mathcal{S}_T)$ of the finite paths in $G$ which we need to check for a given scenario-based specification $\mathcal{S}_T(D)$ where $D = (P, E, M, L, V, C)$. $\Delta(N, \mathcal{S}_T)$ is the set of the paths in $G$ which are of the form

$$s_0 \xrightarrow{(t_0,\delta_0)} s_1 \xrightarrow{(t_1,\delta_1)} \ldots \xrightarrow{(t_{k-1},\delta_{k-1})} s_k \xrightarrow{(t_k,\delta_k)} \ldots \xrightarrow{(t_{n-1},\delta_{n-1})} s_n \xrightarrow{(t_n,\delta_n)} s_{n+1}$$

where all $s_i$ $(0 \le i \le k)$ are distinct, $s_k \xrightarrow{(t_k,\delta_k)} \ldots \xrightarrow{(t_{n-1},\delta_{n-1})} s_n \xrightarrow{(t_n,\delta_n)} s_{n+1}$ is an image of $D$, and for any $s_i$ and $s_j$ $(k < i < j < n)$, if there is not any $t_l$ $(i \le l \le j)$ such that $\varphi(t_l) = \phi(e)$ $(e \in E)$ then $s_i \ne s_j$.

**Theorem 2.** A time Petri net $N$ satisfies a scenario-based specification $\mathcal{S}_T(D)$ if and only if any path $\varrho$ in $\Delta(N, \mathcal{S}_T(D))$ satisfies $\mathcal{S}_T(D)$ and no violable point occurs in the image of $D$ in $\varrho$.                                                            □

The proof of this theorem is presented in the appendix. For a timing Petri net $N$, for a scenario-based specification $\mathcal{S}_T(D)$, a path $\varrho$ in the reachability graph of $N$ is a *prefix* for $\Delta(N, \mathcal{S}_T(D))$ if it may be extended into a path which is in $\Delta(N, \mathcal{S}_T(D))$, i.e. there could be a sequence $\varrho_1$ of states, transitions, and delays such that $\varrho \xrightarrow{(t,\delta)} \varrho_1$ is in $\Delta(N, \mathcal{S}_T(D))$. Based on Theorem 2, we can develop an algorithm to check if a time Petri net $N$ satisfies a scenario-based specification $\mathcal{S}_T(D)$ (cf. Figure 3). The algorithm traverses the reachability graph $G$ of $N$ in a depth first manner starting from the initial node. The path in $G$ that we have so far traversed is stored in the list variable *currentpath*. The boolean variable *is_no_scenario* indicates if there is a scenario described by $D$ occurring in $N$ $(\Delta(N, \mathcal{S}_T(D)) \ne \emptyset)$. The set variable *loopset* is used to store all loops in $G$. The algorithm consists of two steps which are implemented by depth first search. In the first search, we traverse $G$ for getting all the loops in $G$, which are used for checking if no violable point occurs in the image of $D$ in any path in $\Delta(N, \mathcal{S}_T(D))$. Then we start a new depth first search to find out all the paths in $\Delta(N, \mathcal{S}_T(D))$ and to check them for $\mathcal{S}_T(D)$. For each new node we discover, we first check if it is such that the path corresponding to *currentpath* is in $\Delta(N, \mathcal{S}_T(D))$.

```
is_no_scenario :=true;

    currentpath := ⟨(μ₀, c₀)⟩; loopset := ∅;
    repeat
        node := the last node of currentpath;
        if node has no new successive node
        then delete the last node of currentpath
        else
          begin
            node := a new successive node of node;
            if node has occurred in currentpath (we find out a loop ϱ)
            then put ϱ into loopset
            else append node to currentpath;
          end
    until currentpath = ⟨⟩;

    currentpath := ⟨(μ₀, c₀)⟩;
    repeat
        node := the last node of currentpath;
        if node has no new successive node
        then delete the last node of currentpath
        else
          begin
            node := a new successive node of node;
            if node is such that the path ϱ corresponding to currentpath
                is in Δ(N, S_T(D))
            then
              begin
                check if ϱ satisfies S_T(D);
                if no, return false;
                is_no_scenario :=false;
                check if no violable point occurs in the image of D in ϱ;
                if no, return false;
              end
            if node is such that currentpath is corresponding to
                a prefix for Δ(N, S_T(D))
            then append node to currentpath;
          end
    until currentpath = ⟨⟩;

if is_no_scenario then return "No scenario of D occurs"
else return true.
```

**Fig. 3.** Algorithm for timing consistency checking

If yes, then we first check the path for $S_T(D)$ and assign *is_no_scenario* with **false**. Then we check if no violable point occurs in the image of $D$ in the path. If the new node is such that *currentpath* is not corresponding to a prefix for $\Delta(N, S_T(D))$, then the algorithm backtracks, otherwise the algorithm adds the new node to *currentpath*. The algorithm terminates because there is only a finite number of the paths in $\Delta(N, S_T(D))$. Since the algorithm is based on depth first search method, its complexity is proportional to the number of the prefixes for $\Delta(N, S_T(D))$ and to the size of the longest prefix for $\Delta(N, S_T(D))$.

The algorithm presented above has been implemented in a tool prototype. On a PentiumM/1.50GHz/512MB PC, the tool runs comfortably for several case studies including the railroad crossing system. The solution we give is based on investigating only the integer time state spaces of time Petri nets. But even for the integer time state spaces of time Petri nets, their sizes are often much large in the problems of practical interest so that more optimization and abstraction techniques are needed.

## 5   Related Work and Conclusion

To our knowledge, there has been few literature on consistency checking of time Petri nets for scenario-based specifications expressed by MSCs. A work closed to our own is described in [14] to verify whether the timed state machines in a UML model interact according to time-annotated UML collaboration diagrams, in which timed state machines are compiled into timed automata [16] and a collaboration diagram with time intervals is translated into an observer automaton, and the model checker UPPAAL [15] for timed automata is called for the verification, which is based on checking the automata inclusion. Compared to that work, the timing constraints considered in our work are more general and expressive than the timer, time intervals, and timing marks adopted in the existing works, which can be used to describe the relation among multiple separations in time between events. We know that for a clock constraint in a timed automaton, its corresponding timing constraint is about just the separation in time between two events. For describing timing constraints about the relation among multiple separations in time between events, we need to compare multiple clocks in a timed automaton, which will result in that the corresponding model checking problems are undecidable [16]. Thus, the scenario-based specifications expressed by MSCs considered in this paper cannot be verified by transferring to timed automata.

There have been a number of work on checking time Petri nets for the temporal logic based properties [11-13]. Compared to those works, on one hand, the problems considered in those works are to check if the behavior of time Petri nets satisfy the given temporal order of events specified by the temporal logics, while the problem we concern is to check if the behavior of time Petri nets satisfy not only the the given temporal order of events, but also the given timing constraints. On the other hand, the scenario-based specifications considered in this paper are a class of the original artifacts in software development processes, and often come directly from the requirements provided by the customers and domain experts. We know that it is not easy to use formal verification techniques directly in industry because the modelling languages in the verification tools are too formal and theoretical to master easily. For industry, it is much more acceptable to adopt MSCs as a specification language instead of the temporal logics in formal verification tools.

In this paper, since the specifications we concern usually come from the scenario-based requirements provided directly by the customers, which is incomplete, we just use bMSCs to describe the scenario-based specifications. For describing the more complete scenario-based specifications, we need to consider hMSC, which is one of our next works.

# References

1. ITU-T. Recommendation Z.120. ITU - Telecommunication Standardization Sector, Geneva, Switzerland, May 1996.
2. J. Rumbaugh and I. Jacobson and G. Booch. *The Unified Modeling Language Reference Manual*, Addison-Wesley, 1999.
3. B. Berthomieu and M. Diaz. Modelling and verification of time dependent systems using time Petri nets. In *IEEE Transactions on Software Engineering*, 17(3):259–273, March 1991.
4. Olaf Kluge. Modelling a Railway Crossing with Message Sequence Chatrs and Petri Nets. In H.Ehrig et al.(Eds.): *Petri Technology for Communication-Based Systems - Advance in Petri Nets*, LNCS 2472, Springer, 2003, pp.197-218.
5. van der Aalst, W.M.P. Interorganizational Workflows: An Approach based on Message Sequence Charts and Petri Nets. In *Systems Analysis - Modelling - Simulation*, Vol.34, No.3, pages 335-367. 1999.
6. Uwe Rueppel, Udo F. Meissner, and Steffen Greb. A Petri Net based Method for Distributed Process Modelling in Structural Engineering. In *Proc. International Conference on Computing in Civil and Building Engineering*, 2004.
7. R. Alur, G.J. Holzmann, D. Peled. An Analyzer for Message Sequence Charts. In *Software-Concepts and Tools* (1996) 17: 70-77.
8. Hanene Ben-Abdallah and Stefan Leue. Timing Constraints in Message Sequence Chart Specifications. In *Proceedings of FORTE/PSTV'97*, Chapman & Hall, 1997.
9. Doron A. Peled. *Software Reliability Methods*. Springer, 2001.
10. Constance L. Heitmeyer, Ralph D. Jeffords, and Bruce G. Labaw. Comparing Different Approaches for Specifying and Verifying Real-Time Systems. In *Proc. $10_{th}$ IEEE Workshop on Real-Time Operating Syatems abd Software*. New York, 1993. pp.122-129.
11. Andrea Bobbio, Andras Horvath. Model Checking Time Petri Nets using NuSMV. In *Proccedings of the Fifth International Workshop on Performability Modeling of Computer and Communication Systems (PMCCS2001)*, 2001.
12. Furfaro A. and Nigro L. Model Checking Time Petri Nets: A Translation Approach based on Uppaal and a Case Study. In *Proceedings of IASTED International Conference on Software Engineering(SE 2005)*, Innsbruck, Austria, Acta Press, 2005.
13. Tomohiro Yoneda, Hikaru Ryuba. CTL Model Checking of Time Petri Nets using Geometric Regions. In *IEICE Trans. INF. & SYST.*, Vol.E99-D, No.3, 1998, pp.1-11.
14. Alexander Knapp, Stephan Merz, and Christopher Rauh. Modelchecking Timed UML State Machines and Collaborations. In W. Damm and E.-R. Olderog (Eds.): *FTRTFT2002*, LNCS 2469, Springer, 2002, pp.395-414.
15. Kim Guldstrand Larsen, Paul Pettersson, and Wang Yi. UPPAAL in a Nutshell. In *International Journal of Software Tools for Technology Transfer*, 1(1-2): 134-152, 1997.
16. R. Alur and D. David. A theory of timed automata. In *Theoretical Computer Science* 126 (1994). pp.183-235.
17. Xuandong Li and Johan Lilius. Checking Time Petri Nets for Linear Duration Properties. In Peter Bucbolz, manuel Silva (Eds.), Petri Nets and Performance Models, IEEE Computer Society Press, 1999. pp.218-226.

## A    Proofs of Theorems

**Theorem 1.** A time Petri net $N$ satisfies a scenario-based specification $\mathcal{S}_T(D)$ if and only if any integral run of $N$ satisfies $\mathcal{S}_T(D)$.

**Proof.** Let $D = (P, E, M, L, V, C)$, and $\rho$ be a run of $N$ of the form

$$s_0 \xrightarrow{(t_0, \delta_0)} s_1 \xrightarrow{(t_1, \delta_1)} \ldots \xrightarrow{(t_{k-1}, \delta_{k-1})} s_k \xrightarrow{(t_k, \delta_k)} \ldots \xrightarrow{(t_{m-1}, \delta_{m-1})} s_m \xrightarrow{(t_m, \delta_m)} s_{m+1}$$

where $s_k \xrightarrow{(t_k, \delta_k)} \ldots \xrightarrow{(t_{m-1}, \delta_{m-1})} s_m \xrightarrow{(t_m, \delta_m)} s_{m+1}$ is an image of $D$. For a timing constraint $\xi \in C$ of the from $\sum_{i=0}^n c_i(g_i - g_i') \sim c$, let

$$\beta(\rho, \xi) = c_0 \lambda_0 + c_1 \lambda_1 + \ldots + c_n \lambda_n$$

where for each $i$ $(0 \le i \le n)$, if $\theta(g_i) = t_a$ and $\theta(g_i') = t_b$ $(k \le a, b \le m)$, then

$$\lambda_i = \begin{cases} \delta_{b+1} + \delta_{b+2} + \ldots + \delta_a & \text{if } a > b \\ -(\delta_{a+1} + \delta_{a+2} + \ldots + \delta_b) & \text{if } a < b \end{cases} .$$

The theorem follows immediately from the following claim: there is a run $\rho'$ of $N$ of the form

$$s_0' \xrightarrow{(t_0, \delta_0')} s_1' \xrightarrow{(t_1, \delta_1')} \ldots \xrightarrow{(t_{k-1}, \delta_{k-1}')} s_k' \xrightarrow{(t_k, \delta_k')} \ldots \xrightarrow{(t_{m-1}, \delta_{m-1}')} s_m' \xrightarrow{(t_m, \delta_m')} s_{m+1}'$$

such that it is an integral run of $N$ and that $\beta(\rho, \xi) \le \beta(\rho', \xi)$. This claim can be proved as follows.

Let $\alpha_i = \delta_0 + \delta_1 + \ldots + \delta_i$ $(0 \le i \le m)$. It is clear that if each $\alpha_i$ $(0 \le i \le m)$ is an integer, then $\rho$ is an integral run. Let $frac(\rho)$ be the set containing all fractions of $\alpha_i$ $(0 \le i \le m)$, 0, and 1, i.e.

$$frac(\rho) = \left\{ \gamma_i \ \middle| \ \begin{array}{l} 0 \le \gamma_i \le 1, 0 \le i \le m, \\ \text{and } \alpha_i - \gamma_i \text{ is an integer} \end{array} \right\} \cup \{0, 1\} .$$

Let $rank(\rho)$ be the number of the elements in $frac(\rho)$. Notice that if $rank(\rho) = 2$, then $\rho$ is an integral run. In the following, we show that if $rank(\rho) > 2$, we can construct a run $\rho_1$ of the form

$$s_0'' \xrightarrow{(t_0, \delta_0'')} s_1'' \xrightarrow{(t_1, \delta_1'')} \ldots \xrightarrow{(t_{k-1}, \delta_{k-1}'')} s_k'' \xrightarrow{(t_k, \delta_k'')} \ldots \xrightarrow{(t_{m-1}, \delta_{m-1}'')} s_m'' \xrightarrow{(t_m, \delta_m'')} s_{m+1}''$$

such that $rank(\rho_1) = rank(\rho) - 1$ and $\beta(\rho_1, \xi) \ge \beta(\rho, \xi)$. By applying this step repeatedly, we can get a run $\rho'$ which is an integral run of satisfying $rank(\rho') = 2$ and $\beta(\rho', \xi) \ge \beta(\rho, \xi)$ so that the claim is proved. Let

$$frac(\rho) = \{\gamma_0, \gamma_1, \ldots, \gamma_l\} \ (\gamma_0 = 0, \gamma_l = 1, \gamma_i < \gamma_{i+1} \ (0 \le i \le l - 1)),$$

and $index(\gamma_1) = \{i \mid 0 \le i \le m \text{ and } \delta_i - \gamma_1 \text{ is an integer}\}$. Let $\alpha_i'$ and $\alpha_i''$ defined as

$$\alpha_i' = \begin{cases} \alpha_i - \gamma_1 & \text{if } i \in index(\gamma_1) \\ \alpha_i & \text{if } i \notin index(\gamma_1) \end{cases} , \quad \alpha_i'' = \begin{cases} \alpha_i - \gamma_1 + \gamma_2 & \text{if } i \in index(\gamma_1) \\ \alpha_i & \text{if } i \notin index(\gamma_1) \end{cases} .$$

Let $\delta_0^I = \alpha_0'$ and $\delta_0^{II} = \alpha_0''$. For each $i$ $(1 \le i \le m)$, let $\delta_i^I = \alpha_i' - \alpha_{i-1}'$ and $\delta_i^{II} = \alpha_i'' - \alpha_{i-1}''$. Let

$$\rho_1' = s_0^I \xrightarrow{(t_0,\delta_0^I)} s_1^I \xrightarrow{(t_1,\delta_1^I)} \ldots \xrightarrow{(t_{k-1},\delta_{k-1}^I)} s_k^I \xrightarrow{(t_k,\delta_k^I)} \ldots \xrightarrow{(t_{m-1},\delta_{m-1}^I)} s_m^I \xrightarrow{(t_m,\delta_m^I)} s_{m+1}^I$$

$$\rho_1'' = s_0^{II} \xrightarrow{(t_0,\delta_0^{II})} s_1^{II} \xrightarrow{(t_1,\delta_1^{II})} \ldots \xrightarrow{(t_{k-1},\delta_{k-1}^{II})} s_k^{II} \xrightarrow{(t_k,\delta_k^{II})} \ldots \xrightarrow{(t_{m-1},\delta_{m-1}^{II})} s_m^{II} \xrightarrow{(t_m,\delta_m^{II})} s_{m+1}^{II}$$

It follows that $rank(\rho_1') = rank(\rho) - 1$ and $rank(\rho_1'') = rank(\rho) - 1$, and either $\beta(\rho_1',\xi) \ge \beta(\rho,\xi)$ or $\beta(\rho_1'',\xi) \ge \beta(\rho,\xi)$. Suppose $N = (P,T,F,Eft,Lft,\mu_0)$. Since $Eft(t)$ and $Lft(t)$ are a natural number for any $t \in T$, $\rho_1'$ and $\rho_1''$ are a run of $N$. Let $\rho_1 = \rho_1'$ when $\beta(\rho_1',\xi) \ge \beta(\rho,\xi)$, and $\rho_1 = \rho_1''$ when $\beta(\rho_1'',\xi) \ge \beta(\rho,\xi)$. By applying the above step repeatedly, the claim can be proved.                    □

**Theorem 2.** A time Petri net $N$ satisfies a scenario-based specification $\mathcal{S}_T(D)$ if and only if any path $\varrho$ in $\Delta(N,\mathcal{S}_T(D))$ satisfies $\mathcal{S}_T(D)$ and no violable point occurs in the image of $D$ in $\varrho$.

**Proof.** It is clear that the half of the claim holds: if $N$ satisfies $\mathcal{S}_T(D)$, then any path $\varrho$ in $\Delta(N,\mathcal{S}_T(D))$ satisfies $\mathcal{S}_T(D)$ and no violable point occurs in the image of $D$ in $\varrho$. The reason is that for a path $\varrho$ in $\Delta(N,\mathcal{S}_T(D))$, if there is a violable point $s$ in the image of $D$ in $\rho$, then we can construct a path $\varrho'$ from $\rho$ whose image of $D$ does not satisfy $\mathcal{S}_T(D)$ by repeating a loop $\varrho_1 \in \Theta(s,D)$ ($\zeta(\varrho_1) > 0$) many times such that $\zeta(\varrho_1)$ becomes large enough to violate the related timing constraint enforced to $D$. The other half of claim can be proved as follows. Let $D = (P,E,M,L,V,C)$. Suppose that there is a path $\varrho$ of the form

$$s_0 \xrightarrow{(t_0,\delta_0)} s_1 \xrightarrow{(t_1,\delta_1)} \ldots \xrightarrow{(t_{k-1},\delta_{k-1})} s_k \xrightarrow{(t_k,\delta_k)} \ldots \xrightarrow{(t_{n-1},\delta_{n-1})} s_n \xrightarrow{(t_n,\delta_n)} s_{n+1}$$

where $s_k \xrightarrow{(t_k,\delta_k)} \ldots \xrightarrow{(t_{n-1},\delta_{n-1})} s_n \xrightarrow{(t_n,\delta_n)} s_{n+1}$ is an image of $D$ which does not satisfy $\mathcal{S}_T(D)$. Since

- for any $s_i$ and $s_j$ $(0 \le i < j < k)$ such that $s_i = s_j$, by removing the subsequence $s_i \xrightarrow{t_i,\delta_i} s_{i+1} \xrightarrow{t_{i+1},\delta_{i+1}} \ldots \xrightarrow{t_{j-2},\delta_{j-2}} s_{j-1} \xrightarrow{t_{j-1},\delta_{j-1}}$ from $\varrho$ we can get a run of $N$, and

- for any $s_i$ and $s_j$ $(k < i < j < n)$ such that $s_i = s_j$ and that there is not any $t_l (i \le l \le j)$ such that $\psi(t_l) = \phi(e)$ $(e \in E)$, by removing the subsequence $s_i \xrightarrow{t_i,\delta_i} s_{i+1} \xrightarrow{t_{i+1},\delta_{i+1}} \ldots \xrightarrow{t_{j-2}} s_{j-1} \xrightarrow{t_{j-1},\delta_{j-1}}$ from $\varrho$ we can get a run of $N$,

we can construct a run $\varrho'$ from $\varrho$ which is in $\Delta(N,\mathcal{S}_T(D))$. Since there is no violable point in the image of $D$ in $\varrho'$, the sequences removing from $\varrho$ in the process of constructing $\varrho'$ do not related to any timing constraint in $C$. It follows that the image of $D$ in $\varrho'$ does not satisfy $\mathcal{S}_T(D)$, which results in a contradiction. Thus, the claim holds.                    □

# Effective Representation of RT-LOTOS Terms by Finite Time Petri Nets

Tarek Sadani[1,2], Marc Boyer[3],
Pierre de Saqui-Sannes[1,2], and Jean-Pierre Courtiat[1]

[1] LAAS-CNRS, 7 av. du colonel Roche, 31077 Toulouse Cedex 04, France
[2] ENSICA, 1 place Emile Blouin, 31056 Toulouse Cedex 05, France
[3] IRIT-CNRS/ENSEEIHT, 2 rue Camichel, 31000 Toulouse, France
tsadani@ensica.fr, mboyer@enseeiht.fr, desaqui@ensica.fr, courtiat@laas.fr

**Abstract.** The paper describes a transformational approach for the specification and formal verification of concurrent and real-time systems. At upper level, one system is specified using the timed process algebra RT-LOTOS. The output of the proposed transformation is a Time Petri net (TPN). The paper particularly shows how a TPN can be automatically constructed from an RT-LOTOS specification using a compositionally defined mapping. The proof of the translation consistency is sketched in the paper and developed in [1].

The RT-LOTOS to TPN translation patterns formalized in the paper are being implemented. in a prototype tool. This enables reusing TPNs verification techniques and tools for the profit of RT-LOTOS.

## 1 Introduction

The design of time-critical systems is a complex task. Given the risk to not detect transient errors by using conventional techniques such as simulation or testing, it is strongly recommended to use formal verification techniques such as model checking, that have been proven to facilitate early detection of design errors, and to contribute to produce systems at a correctness level that cannot be reached by using simulation and testing techniques.

The use of formal verification techniques is usually linked to the use of formal specifications. Among the wealth of formal specification techniques proposed in the literature, process algebras play a special role. Their compositional operators allow one to describe a system made up of components that communicate and operate concurrently. Besides its notion of compositionality, the capacity to model real-time mechanisms is an essential feature of RT-LOTOS [2,3], the timed process algebra addressed in this paper.

Several verification tools have been developed for timed process algebras. Few of them are really efficient. They usually implement translations into timed automata, which permits to reuse model checkers such as [4,5]. Petri nets verification tools may be considered as well. The possibility to reuse a Time Petri Nets analyzer for verifying RT-LOTOS specifications is one of the main motivation behind the work presented in this paper.

E. Najm et al. (Eds.): FORTE 2006, LNCS 4229, pp. 404–419, 2006.
© IFIP International Federation for Information Processing 2006

The RT-LOTOS to TPN translation approach discussed in this paper relies on the *TPN component* model first introduced in [6]. The model published in [6] is extended and improved. Discussion is not restricted to RT-LOTOS. The paper highlight difficulties and most important issues one might face while translating timed process algebras into Time Petri nets.

The paper is organized as follows. Section 2 introduces the RT-LOTOS language. Section 3 introduces the Time Petri net (TPN) model. Section 4 details RT-LOTOS to TPN translation patterns and explains the intuition behind the proof. In particular, it is shown how TPNs are embedded in components and composed. Section 5 surveys related work. We particularly compare our approach with the Petri Box Calculus [7]. Section 6 concludes the paper.

# 2   RT-LOTOS

The Language of Temporal Ordering Specifications (LOTOS[8]) is a formal description technique based on CCS [9] and extended by a multi-way synchronization mechanism inherited from CSP [10]. RT-LOTOS [2] extends LOTOS with three temporal operators: a *deterministic delay*, a *latency operator* which enables description of temporal indeterminism and a *time limited offer*. The main difference between RT-LOTOS and other timed extensions of LOTOS lies in the way a non-deterministic delay may be expressed. RT-LOTOS supports the so-called *latency* operator. Its usefulness and efficiency have been proved in control command applications and hypermedia authoring [11].

The following processes P and PL illustrate the use of the three temporal operators of RT-LOTOS.

```
Process P[a]: exit:=          Process PL[a]: exit:=
  delay(2)a{5}; exit            delay(2)latency(6)a{5}; exit
endproc                       endproc
```

Process P starts with a 2 time units delay. Once the delay expires, action a is offered to the environment during 5 time units. If the process's environment does not synchronize on a before this deadline, a time violation occurs and the process transforms into stop. Process PL differs from P, for it contains a *latency* operator. Action a is delayed by a minimum dealy of 2 units of time and a maximum delay of 8 units of time(in case the *latency* goes to its maximum value). From the environment's point of view, if the latency lasts $l$ time units, the process behaves like delay(2+$l$)a{5-$l$} (cf. the left part of Fig. 1). Of course, if the duration of the latency goes beyond 5 units of time, a temporal violation occurs and process PL transforms into stop(cf. the right part of Fig. 1).

The originality and interest of the latency operator is more obvious when one combines that operator with the *hiding* operator. In LOTOS, hiding allows one to transform an external *observable* action into an *internal* one. In RT-LOTOS, hiding has the form of a renaming operator which renames action a into i(a). In most timed extensions of LOTOS, hiding implies urgency. It thus removes any time indeterminism inherent to the limited time offering. In RT-LOTOS, a hidden action is urgent *as soon as it is no longer delayed by some latency operator.* Let us, e.g., consider the RT-LOTOS behavior **hide a in PL** where action **a** is hidden in process **PL**. If $l$ is the duration of the latency, **i(a)** will *necessarily* occur at date $2 + l$, if $l < 5$. (cf. Fig. 2). But, if $(l > 5)$, a temporal violation occurs (similarly to the situation where action **a** was an observable action).

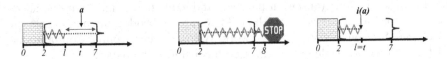

**Fig. 1.** Combining delay, latency and limited offering    **Fig. 2.** Adding hiding

Let us now point out some differences between RT-LOTOS and E-LOTOS [12]. In E-LOTOS, urgency may apply to observable actions as soon as the latter are defined as exceptions. Conversely, the RT-LOTOS semantics states that one cannot enforce urgency on visible events. The only way to introduce urgency in RT-LOTOS is to use the *hide* operator (cf Fig. 2). E-LOTOS further allows one to introduce temporal non-determinism by combining the operator used for non deterministic variable assignment with the deterministic delay operator (applied on the same variable). It is clear that E-LOTOS implements a data-oriented approach for specifying temporal non determinism (for example: **var t: time in ?t := any time [1<t<4]; wait (t) endvar; P**). Conversely RT-LOTOS implements a control oriented approach. In RT-LOTOS, the temporal non deterministic variable is a particular variable introduced by a specific operator. E-LOTOS and RT-LOTOS also use different ways to combine a non deterministic delay with a time limited offer. As depicted in Fig 1, the RT-LOTOS semantics states that the *latency* and the *time limited offer* start simultaneously. This makes it possible to express temporal violations when $t < l$. Conversely, for the E-LOTOS counterpart, the constraint on offering one action inside a time interval will not be active before the non deterministic delay elapses.

## 3   Time Petri Nets

To our knowledge, Petri nets were the first theoretical model augmented with time constraints [13,14], and the support of the first reachability algorithms for timed system [15,16].

The basic idea of time Petri nets (TPN [13,14]) is to associate an interval $I_s(t) = [a, b]$ (static interval) with each transition $t$. A transition *can* be fired if it has continuously been enabled during at least $a$ time units, and it *must* fire if continuous enabling time reaches $b$ time units. That is to say, once a transition is enabled $(M \lfloor t \rangle)$, a *firing interval* $I_f(t)$ is created with initial value $I_s(t)$. Time passing decreases the bounds of the interval. The transition may be fired once the lower bound reaches 0 and has to be fired when the upper bound reaches

0 (unless it conflicts with another transition). Figure 3 is a first example. In the initial marking, only $t_0$ and $t_1$ are enabled. After one time unit delay, $t_1$ is firable. Because $t_1$ reaches its upper interval always before $t_0$ becomes enabled $(3 > 2)$, then $t_0$ can never be fired. $t_2$ is fired five time units after the firing of $t_1$. Figure 4 illustrates the synchronization rule: $t_0$ (resp. $t_1$) is fired at an absolute date $\theta_0 \leq 2$ (resp. $\theta_1 \leq 2$), and $t_2$ is fired at $max(\theta_0, \theta_1) + 1$.

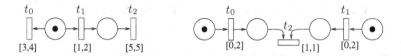

**Fig. 3.** Priority from urgency          **Fig. 4.** Synchronization

## 4    Translation from RT-LOTOS into TPN

The quality of a translation depends on its capability to guarantee a close relation between the properties that hold in the source and those that still hold in the target [17]. This is why we defined a one-to-one mapping of actions between RT-LOTOS and TPNs. Since we do not use auxiliary transitions, we ensure that the proposed translation patterns do not add any behavior. Moreover, RT-LOTOS is compositional by nature. It is then inevitable, during the translation procedure, to consider TPNs as composable entities. Unfortunately, TPNs in their original form miss a convenient way of composing or decomposing larger nets from or to smaller ones by means of a set of high level operators. We solve this problem by introducing the concept of *TPN component* as basic building block. We also define a set of operations on components (Section 4.2). These operations match the composition and temporal operators supported by RT-LOTOS.

### 4.1    Time Petri Net Component

A *Component* encapsulates a labeled TPN which describes its behavior. A component is endowed with interfaces and interactions points. It performs an action by firing the appropriate transition. A component has two sets of labels: *Act* the alphabet of the component and $Time = \{tv, delay, latency\}$. These three labels are introduced to represent the temporal behavior of components. The tv (for "temporal violation") label represents a time-limited offer expiration. A delay or latency label represents the expiration of some deterministic or non deterministic delay, respectively.

A component is graphically represented by a box containing one TPN. The black-filled boxes at the component boundary represent interaction points. For instance, the component $C_P$ in Figure 5 is built from some RT-LOTOS term P. During its execution, it may perform observable action a. The $in_i$ (initially marked places) represent the component input interface, and the *out* place denotes its output interface. A token in the *out* place of a component means that

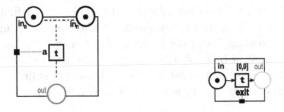

**Fig. 5.** Component example          **Fig. 6.** The exit pattern

the component has successfully completed its execution. A component is *activated* by filling its input places. A component is *active* if at least one of its transitions is enabled. Otherwise, the component is *inactive*.

**Definition 1 (Component).**

Let $Act = A_o \cup A_h \cup \{exit\}$ be an alphabet of actions, where $A_o$ is a set of observable actions *(with $i \notin A_o$, $exit \notin A_o$)*, $A_h = \{i\} \times A_o$ is the set of hidden actions *(If $a$ is an observable action, $i_a$ denotes a hidden action)*.

A component is a tuple $C = \langle \Sigma, Lab, I, O \rangle$ where

- $\Sigma = \langle P, T, Pre, Post, M_0, IS \rangle$ is a TPN.
- $Lab : T \to (Act \cup Time)$ is a labeling function which labels each transition in $\Sigma$ with either an action name (Act) or a time-event (Time = $\{tv, delay, latency\}$). Let $T^{Act}$ (resp. $T^{Time}$) be the set of transitions with labels in Act (resp. Time).
- $I \subset P$ is a non empty set of places defining the input interface.
- $O \subset P$ is the output interface of the component. A component has an output interface if it has at least one transition labeled by **exit**. If so, $O$ is the outgoing place of those transitions. Otherwise, $O = \emptyset$.

Moreover, a set of invariants is associated with the components:

**H1** There is no source transition in a component.

**H2** The encapsulated TPN is 1-bounded (cf. *safe* nets in [7]). H2 is called the "safe marking" property. It is essential for the decidability of reachability analysis procedure applied to TPNs.

**H3** If all the input places are marked, all other places are empty ($I \subset M \Rightarrow M = I$).

**H4** If the *out* place is marked, all other places are empty ($O \neq \emptyset \wedge O \subset M \Rightarrow M = O$).

**H5** For each transition $t$ such that $Lab(t) \in Act$, if the label is an observable action ($Lab(t) \in A_0$), its time interval is $[0, \infty)$, otherwise[1], it is $[0, 0]$.

Hypotheses H3–H4 are called *clean markings* in [7].

---

[1] $Lab(t) \in A_h \cup \{exit\}$.

## 4.2   Translation Patterns

When translating RT-LOTOS specifications into TPNs, we associate a specific operation (involving some component(s)) with each RT-LOTOS operator. These operations are graphically depicted through a set of patterns presented in next sections. To these graphical translation patterns, we add a complementary formal definition. For space reasons, the formalization of some patterns is not presented in this paper. A complete formal definition can be found in the extended version of this paper [1].

*Notation:* $f' = f \cup (a, b)$ denotes the function $f' : A \cup \{a\} \mapsto B \cup \{b\}$ such that $f'(x) = f(x)$ if $x \in A$ and $f'(a) = b$ otherwise.

*Low level Petri net operations.* The formal definition of the translation patterns uses the following low level Petri nets operators: $\cup, \backslash, \uplus$.
Let $N = \langle P, T, Pre, Post, M_0, IS \rangle$ be a TPN.

**Adding a place:** Let $p$ be a new place ($p \notin P$), $Pre_p$ and $Post_p$ two sets of transitions of $T$. $N' = N \cup \langle Pre_p, p, Post_p \rangle$ is the TPN augmented with place $p$ such that $^\bullet p = Pre_p$ and $p^\bullet = Post_p$.

$$N' = \langle P \cup \{p\}, T, Pre \cup \bigcup_{t \in Pre_p} (p, t), Post \cup \bigcup_{t \in Post_p} (t, p), M_0, IS \rangle$$

**Adding a transition:** Let $t$ be a new transition ($t \notin T$), and $I$ its time interval, $Pre_t$ and $Post_t$ two sets of places of $P$. $N' = N \cup \langle Pre_t, (t, I), Post_t \rangle$ is the TPN augmented with transition $t$ such that $^\bullet t = Pre_t$ and $t^\bullet = Post_t$.

$$N' = \langle P, T \cup \{t\}, Pre \cup \bigcup_{p \in Pre_t} (p, t), Post \cup \bigcup_{p \in Post_t} (t, p), M_0, IS \cup (t, I) \rangle$$

**Basic Components.** The $C_{\text{stop}}$ component is simply the empty net (no place, no transition). The $C_{\text{exit}}$ is a component which performs a successful termination. It has one input place, one output place, and a single transition labelled with exit and a static interval $[0, 0]$ (Fig.6).

**Patterns Applying to One Component.** Let us consider the component $C_P$ of Fig. 5. Fig. 7 depicts different patterns applied to $C_P$.

– $C_{\text{a;P}}$ (Fig. 7(a)) is the component resulting from prefixing $C_P$ with action a. $C_{\text{a;P}}$ executes a then activates $C_P$.
 $C_{\text{a;P}} = \langle \Sigma_{\text{a;P}}, Lab_{\text{a;P}}, \{in\}, O_P \rangle$ where the TPN $\Sigma_{\text{a;P}}$ is obtained by adding a place $in$ and a transition $t_0$ to $\Sigma_P$, $Lab_{\text{a;P}}$ associates a to transition $t_0$.

$$\Sigma_{\text{a;P}} = (\Sigma_P \cup \langle \emptyset, (t_0, [0, \infty)), I_P \rangle) \cup \langle \emptyset, in, t_0 \rangle$$
$$Lab_{\text{a;P}} = Lab_P \cup (t_0, \text{a})$$

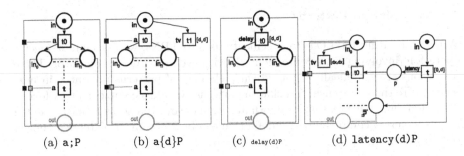

(a) a;P          (b) a{d}P          (c) delay(d)P          (d) latency(d)P

**Fig. 7.** Patterns applying to one component

- $C_{\mathtt{a}\{d\};P}$ (Fig. 7(b)) is the component resulting from prefixing $C_P$ with a limited offer of $d$ units of time on action a. If for any reason, a cannot occur during this time interval, the tv transition will be fired (temporal violation situation) and $C_{\mathtt{a}\{d\};P}$ will transform into an inactive component.
  The pattern is very similar to the one of $C_{\mathtt{a};P}$. Therefore, its definition reuses that of $C_{\mathtt{a};P}$.

$$C_{\mathtt{a}\{d\};P} = \langle \Sigma_{\mathtt{a}\{d\};P}, Lab_{\mathtt{a};P} \cup \{(t_1, \mathrm{tv})\}, \{in\}, O_P \rangle$$
$$\Sigma_{\mathtt{a}\{d\};P} = \Sigma_{\mathtt{a};P} \cup \langle \{in\}, (t_1, [d, d]), \emptyset \rangle$$

- $C_{\mathtt{delay(d)P}}$ (Fig 7(c)) is the component resulting from delaying the first action of P with a deterministic delay of d units of time. This is exactly the same pattern as $C_{\mathtt{a};P}$ except that the added transition has a delay label and a static interval equal to $[d, d]$.

$$C_{\mathtt{delay(d)P}} = \langle \Sigma_{\mathtt{delay(d)P}}, Lab_P \cup \{(t_0, \mathrm{delay})\}, \{in\}, O_P \rangle$$
$$\Sigma_{\mathtt{delay(d)P}} = (\Sigma_P \cup \langle \emptyset, (t_0, [d, d]) \rangle, I_P \rangle) \cup \langle \emptyset, in, t_0 \rangle$$

- $C_{\mathtt{latency(d)P}}$ (Fig 7(d)) is the component resulting from delaying the first actions of $C_P$ with a non deterministic delay of d units of time.
  Like the delay operator, the latency operator is defined by connecting a new transition to the input interface of $C_P$. This time, we add a static interval equal to $[0, d]$. The definition of the latency translation pattern must cope with the "subtle" situation where one (or several) action(s) among $C_P$'s first actions is (are) constrained with a limited offer (this set is denoted by $\mathcal{FA}_{lo}$). For instance, in Fig 7(d), action a is offered to the environment during $d_x$ units of time. The RT-LOTOS semantics states that the latency and the offering of a start simultaneously, which means that if the latency duration goes beyond $d_x$ units of time, the offer on a will expire. To obtain the same behavior, we add the input place $in_0$ of a to the input interface of the resulting component $C_{\mathtt{latency(d)P}}$. In the definition of the pattern, we denote $I_{lo}$ the set of these input places ($I_{lo} \subset I_P$). Thus $t_1$ and $t$ are enabled as soon as the component is activated (all its input places being marked). $C_{\mathtt{latency(d)P}}$ is able to execute a (fire $t_0$) if $t_0$ is enabled (i.e if $in_0$ and $p$ are marked) before $t_1$ is

fired (at $d_x$). Therefore, action a is possibly offered to the environment for no more than $d_x$ units of time, hence conforming to the RT-LOTOS semantics.

Let $\mathcal{FA}(C_P)$ be the set of transitions associated to the first actions of $P^2$, and $\mathcal{FA}_{lo}(C_P)$ be the set of first actions constrained by a time limited offer:

$$\mathcal{FA}_{lo}(C_P) = \{t_a \in \mathcal{FA}(C_P) \mid tv \in ({}^\bullet t_a)^\bullet\}$$

$$I_{lo} = {}^\bullet \mathcal{FA}_{lo}(C_P)$$

$$C_{\texttt{latency(d)P}} = \langle \Sigma_{\texttt{latency(d)P}}, Lab_P \cup \{(t, \text{latency})\}, I_{lo} \cup \{in\}, O_P\rangle$$

$$\Sigma_{\texttt{latency(d)P}} = \Sigma_P \cup \bigcup_{t_a \in \mathcal{FA}_{lo}(C_P)} \langle t, p_{t_a}, t_a\rangle \cup \langle \emptyset, in, \emptyset\rangle$$

$$\cup \left\langle \{in\}, (t, [0, d]), (I_P \backslash I_{lo}) \cup \bigcup_{t_a \in \mathcal{FA}_{lo}(C_P)} \{p_{t_a}\} \right\rangle$$

- $C_{\mu X.(P;X)}$ is the component which executes $C_P$'s actions ad infinitum. The recursion operator translation is mainly an untimed problem. It is not presented in this paper, since the focus is laid on timed aspects.
- $C_{\texttt{hide a in P}}$ is the component resulting from hiding action a in $C_P$. Hiding allows one to transform observable (external) actions into unobservable (internal) actions, then making the latter unavailable for synchronization with other components. In RT-LOTOS, hiding one or several actions induces a notion of urgency on action occurrence. Consequently, a TPN transition corresponding to one hidden action will be constrained by a time interval equal to $[0, 0]$. This implies that as soon as a transition is enabled, it is candidate for being fired.

**Patterns Applying to a Set of Components.** Each of the following patterns transforms a set of components into one component.

- $C_{\texttt{P|[a]|Q}}$ (Fig.8)
  The concept of handshake communication is an important feature of process algebras. It consists of a symmetric synchronization by which an action that is shared between $n$ processes can be executed only if all of them are ready to do so. In Petri nets, such a scenario is represented by a transition with $n$ input places. This transition can fire only if all its input places contain a token (cf. Fig. 4). At the PN level, the synchronization operation is achieved through transition merging. While transitions merging is straightforward in Petri nets, it turns to be a rather tricky issue in Time Petri nets. Indeed, it requires explicit handling of the time intervals assigned to transitions to be merged. These time intervals may be incompatible, which leads to express global timing constraints as a conjunction of intervals whose consistency is not guaranteed. This problem is not solved in [18](where each transition is assigned a time interval), as presented in Sect. 5.2.
  
  To solve this problem and make transition merging always a possible operation, we avoid assigning time intervals to action transitions. Instead, the

---

[2] Its formal definition is given in Def. 2, Sect. A.

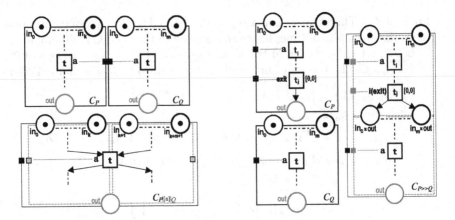

**Fig. 8.** Parallel synchronization pattern        **Fig. 9.** Sequential composition pattern

timing constraints are assigned to dedicated transitions (cf. time limited offer pattern).

The synchronization on a of $C_P$ and $C_Q$ is achieved by merging each a transition in $C_P$ with each a transition in $C_Q$, thus creating $n * m$ a transitions in $C_{P\,|\,[a]\,|\,Q}$ ($n$ and $m$ being the number of a transitions in $C_P$ and $C_Q$, respectively).

- $C_{P>>Q}$ (Fig. 9) depicts a sequential composition of $C_P$ and $C_Q$ which means that if $C_P$ successfully completes its execution then it activates $C_Q$. This kind of composition is possible only if $C_P$ has an output interface. The resulting component $C_{P>>Q}$ is obtained by merging the output interface of $C_P$ and the input interface of $C_Q$, and by hiding the `exit` interaction point of $C_P$.

$$C_{P>>Q} = \langle \Sigma_{P>>Q}, Lab_{\text{hide exit in P}} \cup Lab_Q, I_P, 0_Q \rangle$$
$$\Sigma_{P>>Q} = \langle P_P \backslash O_P \cup P_Q, T_{\text{hide exit in P}} \cup T_Q, Pre_P \cup Pre_Q, Post_{P>>Q}, IS_P \cup IS_Q \rangle$$
$$Post_{P>>Q} = (Post_P \backslash \{(t, O_P) \mid t \in {}^\bullet O_P\}) \cup \{(t, in_Q) \mid in_Q \in I_Q \wedge t \in {}^\bullet O_P\} \cup Post_Q$$

- $C_{P[]Q}$ (Fig. 10) is the component which behaves either as $C_P$ or $C_Q$.

We do not specify whether the choice between the alternatives is made by the component $C_{P[]Q}$ itself, or by the environment, but it should be made at the level of the first actions in the component. In other words, the occurrence of one of the first actions in either component determines which component will continue its execution and which one must be deactivated. The problem can be viewed as a competition between $C_P$ and $C_Q$. These two components compete to execute their first action. As long as the latter has not yet occurred, $C_P$ and $C_Q$ age similarly, which means that $Time$ transitions (labeled by tv, delay or latency) may occur in both components without any consequence on the choice of the wining component. Once one first action occurs, the control is irreversibly transferred to the winning component. The other one is deactivated, in the sense that it no longer contains enabled transitions. The *choice* operator is known to cause trouble in presence of initial parallelism. [19] defines a choice operator where each alternative has just one initial place. Therefore, none of the alternative allows any initial parallelism. We think that it is a strong restriction. We do not impose any constraint on the *choice* alternatives.

The solution we propose to define a choice between two components is as follows: to obtain the intended behavior, we introduce a set of special places, called *lock* places. Those places belong to the input interface of component $C_{P[]Q}$. Their function is to undertake control transfer between the two components. For each first action of $C_P$ we introduce one lock place per concurrent first action in $C_Q$ (for instance a has one concurrent action in $C_Q$: c, while c has two concurrent actions in $C_P$: a and b) and vice versa. A *lock* place interacts only with those transitions representing the set of initial actions and the time labeled transitions they are related with (delay for a and tv for b). *Time* transitions restore the token in the *lock* place, since they do not represent an action occurrence, but a time progression which has not to interfere with the execution of the other component (as long as the first action has not occurred, the two components age similarly). The occurrence of an initial action of $C_P$ (respectively $C_Q$) locks the execution of $C_Q$ (respectively $C_P$) by stealing the token from the *lock* places related to all $C_Q$'s (respectively $C_P$'s) first actions.

A unique *out* place is created by merging the *out* places of $C_P$ and $C_Q$.

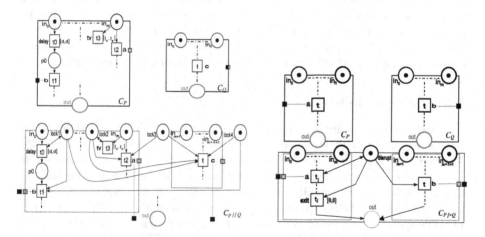

**Fig. 10.** Choice between $C_P$ and $C_Q$                **Fig. 11.** The disrupt pattern

- $C_{P[>Q}$ (Fig. 11) is the component representing the behavior where component $C_P$ can be interrupted by $C_Q$ at any time during its execution. It means that at any point during the execution of $C_P$, there is a choice between executing one of the next actions from $C_P$ or one of the first actions from $C_Q$. For this purpose, $C_Q$ *steals* the token from the shared place named disrupt (which belongs to the input interface of $C_{P[>Q}$). Thus the control is irreversibly transferred from $C_P$ to $C_Q$ (disrupt is an *input* place for $C_Q$ first action and exit transition of $C_P$; it is also an *input/output* place for all the others transitions of $C_P$). Once an action from $C_Q$ is chosen, $C_Q$ continues executing, and $C_P$'s transitions are no longer enabled.

### 4.3   Sketch of the Proof

We prove that the translation preserves the RT-LOTOS semantics and that the defined compositional framework preserves the good properties (H1–H5) of the components.

Intuitively an RT-LOTOS term and a component are timed bisimilar [20] iff they perform the same action at the same time and reach bisimilar states. For each operator, we prove that, from each reachable state, if the occurrence of a time progression (respectively an action) is possible in an RT-LOTOS term, it is also possible in its associated component, and conversely. Therefore, we ensure that the translation preserves the sequences of possible actions but also the occurrence dates of these actions. The entire proof may be found in [1].

## 5   Related Work

Much work has been done on translating process algebras into Petri Nets, by giving a Petri net semantics to process terms [21,19,22]. [22] suggests that a good net semantics should satisfy the retrievability principle, meaning that no new "auxiliary" transitions should be introduced in the reachability graph of the Petri net. [21,19] do not satisfy this criterion. In this paper, we define a one-to-one mapping which is compliant with this strong recommendation.

### 5.1   Untimed Models

A survey of the literature indicates that proposals for LOTOS to Petri net translations essentially address the untimed version of LOTOS [23,24,25,26,27,28]. The opposite translation has been discussed by [27] where only a subset of LOTOS is considered, and by [29] where the authors addressed the translation of Petri nets with inhibitor arcs into basic LOTOS by mapping places and transitions into LOTOS expressions. [26] demonstrated the possibility to verify LOTOS specifications using verification techniques developed for Petri nets by implementing a Karp and Miller procedure in the LOTOS world.

[23,28] operate a complete translation of LOTOS, handling both the control and data parts. Moreover, they just consider regular LOTOS terms. So do we. The LOTOS to PN translation algorithms of [23,28] were implemented in the CAESAR tool. Besides the temporal aspects addressed in this paper, a technical difference with [23,28] lies in the way we structure TPNs. Our solution is based on TPNs components. In our approach, a component may contain several tokens. Conversely, [23,28] structure Petri nets into units, each of them containing one token at most. This invariant limits the size of markings, and permits optimizations on memory consumption. The counterpart is that [23,28] use $\epsilon$-transitions.

The latter introduce non determinism. They are eliminated when the underlying automaton is generated (by transitive closure). The use of $\epsilon$-transitions may be inefficient in some particular cases (see the example provided in [6]).

The major theoretical study on taking advantage of both Petri nets and process algebras is presented in [7]. The proposed solution is Petri Box Calculus (PBC), a generic model that embodies both process algebra and Petri nets. The authors start from Petri nets to come up with a CCS-like process algebra whose operators may straightforwardly be expressed by means of Petri nets.

## 5.2 Timed Models

[30] pioneered work on timed enhancements of the control part of LOTOS inspired by timed Petri nets models. [31] defined a mapping from TPNs to TE-LOTOS which makes it possible to incorporate basic blocks specified as 1-bounded TPNs into TE-LOTOS specifications. However, because of the strong time semantics of TPNs (a transition is fired as soon as the upper bound of its time interval is reached unless it conflicts with another one) a direct mapping was not always possible.

Timed extensions of PBC have been proposed in [18,32]. Although the component model proposed in this paper is not a specification model but an intermediate model used as gateway between RT-LOTOS and TPNs, we find it important to compare our work with [18].

Of prime interest to us is the way [18] introduces temporal constraints in his framework by providing each action with two time bounds representing the earliest firing time and latest firing time. This approach is directly inspired by TPNs, where the firing of actions is driven by necessity. However, a well known issue with this strategy is that it is inappropriate for a compositional and incremental building of specifications. The main difficulty is to compose time intervals when dealing with actions synchronization. The operational semantics of [18] relies on intervals intersection to calculate a unique time interval for a synchronized transition. However, this approach is not always satisfactory, as shown in the following example.

Let us consider the following timed PBC term:
$E_1 = ((a[10, 10]; b[2, 2]) \parallel \hat{b}[12, 12]) \, sy\{b\}$. It expresses the parallel synchronization on $b$ (The synchronization of two conjugate actions $b$ and $\hat{b}$ gives rise to the silent action $i$) of the following terms:

- $a[10, 10]; b[2, 2]$ executes $a$ after 10 time moves (time has a discrete semantics), then it executes $b$, 2 time moves after the occurrence of $a$,
- $\hat{b}[12, 12]$ executes $\hat{b}$ after 12 time moves.

That is to say, $\hat{b}$ and $b$ occur at the same date (12 times units after the initial instant). Thus the synchronization on b should be possible. Nevertheless $E_1$ cannot execute the synchronization action $i$ since $[2, 2] \cap [12, 12] = \emptyset$. The synchronization rule of [18] states that the synchronization is possible only if it leads to a *well-defined* action, i.e. with consistent timing information. Therefore, the corresponding TPN (called *ctbox* in [18]) cannot be constructed.

To avoid this difficult interval composition, we do not assign any time interval to action transitions. In our framework, timed constraints are assigned to dedicated transitions (cf Fig. 7(b), 7(c) and 7(d)). Thus action transitions are free from any timing constraint. This way, the synchronization can be obtained by merging the action transitions without changing the timing constraints. Hence, we are able to straightforwardly construct the TPN of Fig. 12 (obtained by the application of the pattern of Fig 7(c), 7(a) and 8) corresponding to the following RT-LOTOS expression which is behaviorally equivalent to the above timed PBC expression:

```
P1= Hide a ,b in (      (delay(12)b; stop)
               |[b]| (delay(10)a; delay(2)b; stop))
```

Synchronization on b occurs indeed 12 time units after initial instant.

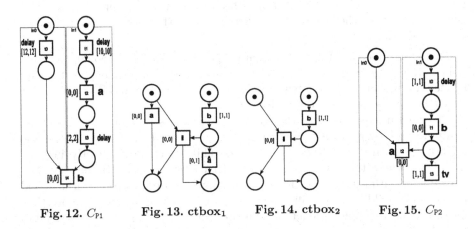

Fig. 12. $C_{P1}$          Fig. 13. ctbox$_1$          Fig. 14. ctbox$_2$          Fig. 15. $C_{P2}$

Moreover, even if the synchronization leads to a *well-defined* action. It was necessary to the author of [18] to enrich the semantics of the timed PBC with rules for allowing the firing of *illegal actions*. An action is said *illegal* if it has inconsistent timing information. For example, an action which has been enabled for an amount of time which exceeds its latest bound firing time.

As an illustration, let us now consider the following timed PBC expression taken from [18]: $E_2 = (a[0,0]||(b[1,1]; \hat{a}[0,1]))sy\{a\}$. $E_2$ cannot execute the synchronization action $i$ which is consistent with the TPN semantics (cf Fig 13 ). However, the situation changes for $E_2rs\{a\}$. The synchronization is enforced by the restriction operator. The corresponding net is obtained by removing $a$ and $\hat{a}$ transitions (cf Fig 14). Now it is possible to execute $b$ at $[1,1]$ followed immediately by $i$. However, rules based only on legal actions could not produce a similar result in the operational semantics since no legal action occurrence is possible for $a[0,0]$ after the elapsing of 1 time unit. Therefore, a rule permitting the firing of $a$ after one unit of time was introduced. The rules on allowing *illegal actions* were certainly unavoidable to ensure behavioural consistency between Timed PBC terms and their translation into Time Petri nets, but they badly impact on the simplicity of the operational semantics of [18].

The following RT-LOTOS expression which is behaviourally equivalent to $E_2 rs\{a\}$ : P2= Hide a,b in (a;stop)|[a]|(delay(1)b;a{1};stop) has to our opinion a more intuitive behavior. The consistency between the RT-LOTOS term and its corresponding TPN of Fig 15 is ensured without departing from the original RT-LOTOS semantics.

Finally, [32] extends PBC with actions durations. This model captures timing information in a different manner. In our framework, actions are taken to be indivisible. As a consequence it is difficult to compare [32] with the approach proposed in this paper.

## 6   Conclusions

The paper discusses an efficient transformational approach for the verification of RT-LOTOS specifications. Our intent is to use the reachability graph of a TPN to represent and analyze the behavior of real time systems described in RT-LOTOS. After taking a closer look at the semantics of the two timed models, we formally define the concept of TPN component, together with a set of a translation patterns which match the set of RT-LOTOS operators. These patterns are implemented in RTL2TPN, a prototype tool which takes as input an RT-LOTOS specification and generates a TPN in a suitable format. Thus, it becomes possible to integrate TINA[33], a powerful TPN analyzer tool, to our verification platform. First experimental results are promising and confirm the advantage of using TPNs as an intermediate model [6]. It worth to be noticed that the transformation gives RT-LOTOS a formal semantics in terms of TPNs. Thus, we start with a top level RT-LOTOS view, which describes the architecture of the system together with its desired communication behavior. We end up with a more detailed view at the TPNs level, which describes the operational machine behavior of the system and clarifies the use of some RT-LOTOS operators, such as the *latency* operator.

This work is not limited to the verification of real-time systems specified in RT-LOTOS. The ultimate goal is to provide a more powerful verification environment for real-time systems modeled in TURTLE [34], a real-time UML profile whose formal semantics is expressed in RT-LOTOS. The translation patterns may be reused for other timed extensions of LOTOS, in particular ET-LOTOS.

## References

1. Sadani, T., Boyer, M., de Saqui-Sannes, P., Courtiat, J.P.: Effective representation of regular RT-LOTOS terms by finite time petri nets. Technical Report 05605, LAAS/CNRS (2006)
2. Courtiat, J.P., Santos, C., Lohr, C., Outtaj, B.: Experience with RT-LOTOS, a temporal extension of the LOTOS formal description technique. Computer Communications **23**(12) (2000)

3. RT-LOTOS: Real-time LOTOS home page. (http://www.laas.fr/RT-LOTOS/)
4. Yovine, S.: Kronos: A verification tool for real-time systems. Software Tools for Technology Transfer **1**(123–133) (1997)
5. Bengtsson, J., Larsen, K.G., Larsson, F., Pettersson, P., Yi, W.: UPPAAL - a tool suite for automatic verification of real-time systems. In: Proc of the 4th DIMACS Workshop on Verification and Control of Hybrid Systems. Number 1066 in LNCS (1995) 232–243
6. Sadani, T., Courtiat, J., de Saqui-Sannes, P.: From RT-LOTOS to time Petri nets. new foundations for a verification platform. In: Proc. of 3rd IEEE Int Conf on Software Engineering and Formal Methods (SEFM). (2005)
7. Best, E., Devillers, R., Koutny, M.: Petri Net Algebra. Monographs in Theoretical Computer Science: An EATCS Series. Springer-Verlag (2001) ISBN: 3-540-67398-9.
8. ISO - Information processing systems - Open Systems Interconnection: LOTOS - a formal description technique based on the temporal ordering of observational behaviour. ISO International Standard 8807:1989, ISO (1989)
9. Milner, R.: Communications and Concurrency. Prentice Hall (1989)
10. Hoare, C.: Communicating Sequential Processes. Prentice-Hall (1985)
11. Courtiat, J.P.: Formal design of interactive multimedia documents. In H.Konig, M.Heiner, A., ed.: Proc. of 23rd IFIP WG 6.1 Int Conf on Formal Techniques for Networked and distributed systems (FORTE'2003). Volume 2767 of LNCS. (2003)
12. ISO/IEC: Information technology - enhancements to LOTOS (E-LOTOS). Technical Report 15437:2001, ISO/IEC (2001)
13. Merlin, P.: A study of the recoverability of computer system. PhD thesis, Dep. Comput. Sci., Univ. California, Irvine (1974)
14. Merlin, P., Faber, D.J.: Recoverability of communication protocols. IEEE Transactions on Communications **COM-24**(9) (1976)
15. Berthomieu, B., Menasche, M.: Une approche par énumération pour l'analyse des réseaux de Petri temporels. In: Actes de la conférence IFIP'83. (1983) 71–77
16. Berthomieu, B., Diaz, M.: Modeling and verification of time dependant systems using Time Petri Nets. IEEE Transactions on Software Engineering **17**(3) (1991)
17. Katz, S., Grumberg, O.: A framework for translating models and specifications. In: Proc. of the 3d Int. Conf. on Integrated Formal Methods. (Volume 2335 of LNCS.)
18. Koutny, M.: A compositional model of time Petri nets. In: Proc. of the 21st Int. Conf. on Application and Theory of Petri Nets (ICATPN 2000). Number 1825 in LNCS, Aarhus, Denmark, Springer-Verlag (2000) 303–322
19. Taubner, D.: Finite Representations of CCS and TCSP Programs by Automata and Petri Nets. Number 369 in LNCS. Springer-Verlag (1989)
20. Yi, W.: Real-time behaviour of asynchronous agents. In: Proc. of Int. Conf on Theories of Concurrency: Unification and Extension (CONCUR). Volume 458 of LNCS. (1990)
21. Goltz, U.: On representing CCS programs by finite Petri nets. In: Proc. of Int. Conf. on Math. Foundations of Computer Science. Volume 324 of LNCS. (1988)
22. Olderog, E.R.: Nets, Terms, and formulas. Cambridge University Press (1991)
23. Garavel, H., Sifakis, J.: Compilation and verification of LOTOS specifications. In Logrippo, L., et al., eds.: Protocol Specification, Testing and Verification, X. Proceedings of the IFIP WG 6.1 Tenth International Symposium, 1990, Ottawa, Ont., Canada, Amsterdam, Netherlands, North-Holland (1990) 379–394
24. Barbeau, M., von Bochmann, G.: Verification of LOTOS specifications: A Petri net based approach. In: Proc. of Canadian Conf. on Electrical and Computer Engineering. (1990)

25. Larrabeiti, D., Quelmada, J., Pavón, S.: From LOTOS to Petri nets through expansion. In Gotzhein, R., Bredereke, J., eds.: Proc. of Int. Conf. on Formal Description Techniques and Theory, application and tools (FORTE/PSV'96). (1996)

26. Barbeau, M., von Bochmann, G.: Extension of the Karp and Miller procedure to LOTOS specifications. Discrete Mathematics and Theoretical Computer Science **3** (1991) 103–119

27. Barbeau, M., von Bochmann, G.: A subset of LOTOS with the computational power of place/transition-nets. In: Proc. of the 14th Int. Conf. on Application and Theory of Petri Nets (ICATPN). Volume 691 of LNCS. (1993)

28. Garavel, H., Lang, F., Mateescu, R.: An overview of cadp 2001. European Association for software science and technology (EASST) Newsletter **4** (2002)

29. Sisto, R., Valenzano, A.: Mapping Petri nets with inhibitor arcs onto basic LOTOS behavior expressions. IEEE Transactions on computers **44**(12) (1995) 1361–1370

30. Bolognesi, T., Lucidi, F., Trigila, S.: From timed Petri nets to timed LOTOS. In: Protocol Specification, Testing and Verification X (PSTV), Proceedings of the IFIP WG6.1 Tenth International Symposium on Protocol. (1990) 395–408

31. Durante, L., Sisto, R., Valenzano, A.: Integration of time Petri net and TE-LOTOS in the design and evaluation of factory communication systems. In: Proc. of the 2nd IEEE Workshop on Factory Communications Systems (WFCS'97). (1997)

32. Marroquin Alonso, O., de Frutos Escrig, D.: Extending the Petri box calculus with time,. In: Proc. of the 22nd International Conference on Application and Theory of Petri Nets (ICATPN). Volume 2075 of LNCS. (2001)

33. Berthomieu, B., Ribet, P., Vernadat, F.: The TINA tool: Construction of abstract state space for Petri nets and time Petri nets. Int. Journal of Production Research **42**(14) (2004)

34. Apvrille, L., Courtiat, J.P., Lohr, C., de Saqui-Sannes, P.: TURTLE : A real-time UML profile supported by a formal validation toolkit. IEEE Transactions on Software Engineering **30**(4) (2004)

# A    First Actions

**Definition 2 (First actions set).** *Let $C$ be a component. The set of first actions $\mathcal{FA}(C_P)$ can be recursively built using the following rules*[3]:

$$\mathcal{FA}(C_{stop}) = \emptyset \quad \mathcal{FA}(C_{exit}) = \{t_{exit}\} \quad \mathcal{FA}(C_{a;P}) = \mathcal{FA}(C_{a\{d\}P}) = \{t_a\}$$
$$\mathcal{FA}(C_{\mu X.\,(P;X)}) = \mathcal{FA}(C_{delay(d)P}) = \mathcal{FA}(C_{latency(d)P}) = \mathcal{FA}(C_{P;Q}) = \mathcal{FA}(C_{P \gg Q}) = \mathcal{FA}(C_P)$$
$$\mathcal{FA}(C_{P\,|[A]|\,Q}) = \mathcal{FA}(C_{P[]Q}) = \mathcal{FA}(C_{P[>Q}) = \mathcal{FA}(C_P) \cup \mathcal{FA}(C_Q)$$
$$\mathcal{FA}(C_{hide\ a\ in\ P}) = h_a\,(\mathcal{FA}(C_P))$$

---

[3] Where $t_a$ is transition labelled by a. $h_a(\alpha) = \alpha$ if $\alpha \neq a$ and $h_a(a) = i_a$.

# Grey-Box Checking

Edith Elkind[1], Blaise Genest[1,2], Doron Peled[1], and Hongyang Qu[1,3]

[1] Department of Computer Science, Warwick, Coventry, CV4 7AL, UK
[2] CNRS & IRISA, Campus de Beaulieu, 35042 Rennes Cedex, France
[3] LIF, 39 rue Joliot Curie, 13453 Marseille Cedex 13, France

**Abstract.** There are many cases where we want to verify a system that does not have a usable formal model: the model may be missing, out of date, or simply too big to be used. A possible method is to analyze the system while learning the model (black box checking). However, learning may be an expensive task, thus it needs to be guided, e.g., using the checked property or an inaccurate model (adaptive model checking). In this paper, we consider the case where some of the system components are completely specified (white boxes), while others are unknown (black boxes), giving rise to a grey box system. We provide algorithms and lower bounds, as well as experimental results for this model.

## 1 Introduction

Tools for analyzing a system (e.g., model-checkers) usually require an accurate model of the system. However, such a model may be difficult to find: while some tools can perform the analysis based on a model constructed directly from the source code, there are few tools that can deal with a binary file or with a chip. A recent paper [12] proposed a method of checking black box systems, that is, systems for which we do not have a model. Later, it was extended to testing based on an approximately accurate model that can be automatically changed when discrepancies are found [9]. This approach is based on interactive learning of finite state systems [2] combined with conformance testing [14,6], and has many applications. For instance, [15] considers deriving a specification from observing a system, and [7,1] apply these techniques in order to guess an efficient property to be used as an interface in assume-guarantee reasoning.

In this paper, we extend the black box checking procedure of [12] to the case where some parts of the system in question are known. Specifically, we focus on the situation where we know the high level description of the system as well as some of its components, while the internal structure of the remaining components is unknown. We call such a system a *grey box*, and use the terms 'white box' and 'black box' to denote the known and the unknown parts, respectively. For instance, a component in a distributed system or a module in a hierarchical system can play the role of the (known) white box or the (unknown) black box. We propose the framework of grey box checking in a concurrent system, where several asynchronous components communicate with each other. We can easily extend our approach and get good complexity bounds for (sequential) hierarchical systems as well [8].

E. Najm et al. (Eds.): FORTE 2006, LNCS 4229, pp. 420–435, 2006.

In some settings, each component can be analyzed separately; in others, we can only test the system as a whole. In both cases, the information available about the white box can speed up the testing considerably. In the first case, the problem essentially reduces to learning the unknown components and thus its complexity does not depend on the size of the white box. For the more challenging case where all components have to be run together, we show that the complexity of checking the synchronous product $\mathcal{B} \times \mathcal{W}$ is substantially higher than the complexity of black box checking $\mathcal{B}$ (the increase in complexity is exponential in the size of the alphabet), but substantially lower than checking $\mathcal{B} \times \mathcal{W}$ as a black box (the savings are exponential in $|\mathcal{W}|$).

Our algorithms are based on the black box checking procedure of [12]. To decrease complexity, we use conformance testers that are better suited to our setup than the standard Vasilevskii-Chow algorithm [14,6]. Our first oracle relies on enumerating all finite automata up to a certain size and has an almost optimal worst case complexity. The second oracle combines the algorithm of [14,6] with ideas from partial order reduction and performs better in some of our experiments (see Section 6). Also, both algorithms use the information about the white box to speed up the learning algorithm of [2]. The experimental data provided by a new tool we are developing shows that the best compromise is to run both algorithms together, so that they help each other find discrepancies. This appears to speed up the process by several orders of magnitude.

While our goal is similar to that of adaptive model checking [9], we see our work as complementing the adaptive approach rather than replacing it. Indeed, adaptive model checking uses an inaccurate model to help the learner; here, we use partial but accurate information about the system being tested. The usefulness of the adaptive model checking has been argued by [9], which demonstrates that the learning algorithm is robust enough to deal with a partially wrong specification. However, there are small modifications to the system (e.g., adding a new state that separates two components of the system) that cannot be handled efficiently by this method. Our approach is likely to be successful if the changes can be limited to a small part of the system, which will then be treated as a black box. In particular, this applies to the case described above. Moreover, sometimes the two techniques can be combined. For instance, we may have an accurate model of a component, some old model of another component that was changed since the model was made, and another component that is totally unknown. Then we can use our approach for the product, and the adaptive approach when analyzing the second component.

## 2   Preliminaries

A *finite automaton* is a tuple $\mathcal{A} = (S, s_0, \Sigma, \rightarrow)$ where

- $S$ is the finite set of states,
- $s_0$ is the initial state of $\mathcal{A}$.
- $\Sigma$ is the finite set of letters (alphabet) of actions.
- $\rightarrow \subseteq S \times \Sigma \times S$ is the deterministic transition function, that is, for all $a \in \Sigma$ and $s, t, t' \in S$, if $s \xrightarrow{a} t$ and $s \xrightarrow{a} t'$ then $t' = t$.

We do not designate a set of accepting states; every state of $\mathcal{A}$ is considered to be accepting. A *run* $\rho$ of $\mathcal{A}$ is a finite or infinite sequence of transitions $(v_i, a_i, v_{i+1}) \in \to$ with $v_0 = s_0$. An *experiment* is any sequence of labels in $\Sigma^*$. Since every automaton that we consider is deterministic, any experiment is associated with at most one run. Abusing notation, we will identify a run with the corresponding sequence of labels. The language $\mathcal{L}(\mathcal{A})$ of $\mathcal{A}$ is the set of all maximal runs[1]. One can easily test whether an experiment $u$ is a prefix of a run: it suffices to feed the sequence $u$ to the system after a **reset**, letter by letter, and check that each time the next letter is enabled through executing a transition of the system.

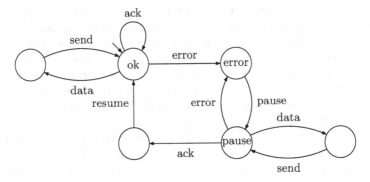

**Fig. 1.** The automaton *Interface*

## 2.1   The Black-Box Checking Procedure

Black-box checking was proposed in [12] for verification of (partially) unknown systems. It is based on interleaving learning and model checking. In what follows, we describe this approach in more detail.

**The Learning Algorithm.** In [2], Angluin describes an algorithm $L^*$ for learning the minimal deterministic automaton that corresponds to a given black box $\mathcal{A}$.

Angluin's learning algorithm builds a candidate automaton $\mathcal{A}^*$ by making experiments on the system $\mathcal{A}$, i.e., invoking a procedure $test(v)$ that returns 1 if $v$ is executable in the black box after a **reset**, and 0 otherwise. Once it has obtained a candidate solution $\mathcal{A}^*$ that is consistent with all experiments run so far, it calls an oracle that checks whether $\mathcal{L}(\mathcal{A}^*) = \mathcal{L}(\mathcal{A})$. If not, the oracle gives a minimal-size experiment $\sigma$ (discrepancy) distinguishing $\mathcal{A}^*$ from $\mathcal{A}$, i.e., a sequence $\sigma$ that is either in $\mathcal{L}(\mathcal{A}) \setminus \mathcal{L}(\mathcal{A}^*)$ or in $\mathcal{L}(\mathcal{A}^*) \setminus \mathcal{L}(\mathcal{A})$. The learning algorithm then uses $\sigma$ to refine the current solution. Later, we show how to build this oracle using Vasilevskii-Chow [14,6] algorithm.

To construct a candidate automaton, the algorithm keeps two sets of sequences: a prefix-closed set of *access sequences* $V \subseteq \Sigma^*$ and a suffix-closed set of

---
[1] A run is *maximal* if it is not a prefix of another run.

*distinguishing sequences* $W \subseteq \Sigma^*$. Each sequence $v$ in $V$ corresponds to reaching a state of $\mathcal{A}^*$ by executing $v$ from $s_0$. Different sequences may lead to the same state. Also, the algorithm keeps a table $T : (V \cup V.\Sigma) \times W \rightarrow \{0,1\}$ such that for any $v \in V \cup V.\Sigma$ we have $T(v,w) = 1$ if and only if $vw \in \mathcal{L}(\mathcal{A})$.

We define the equivalence $\sim \subseteq V \times V$ as $v \sim v'$ if $T(v,w) = T(v',w)$ for every $w \in W$. For $(V,W)$ to represent an automaton, it is necessary that $T$ is *closed*, i.e., for every $v \in V$ and $a \in \Sigma$ s.t. $T(v,a) = 1$, there exists $v' \in V$ with $v' \sim va$. If $T$ is not closed because $a$ is executable after $v$, but $va \not\sim v'$ for all $v' \in V$, we add $va$ to $V$. Also, we verify that the table $T$ is *consistent*, i.e., for all $v \sim v'$, if $T(v,a) = 1$, then $T(va,w) = T(v'a,w)$ for all $w \in W$. If this is not the case, the sequence $aw$ is added to $W$.

When the table $T$ is closed and consistent, we set $\mathcal{A}^* = ([V/\sim], \epsilon, \Sigma, \delta)$, where the transition relation $\delta$ is defined as follows. Let $[v]$ be a $\sim$ equivalence class of $v$. Set $\delta([v],a) = [v']$ when $v' \sim va$. This relation is well defined when the table $T$ is closed and consistent. We then invoke the oracle on $\mathcal{A}^*$. If the oracle returns a discrepancy $\sigma$, for each prefix $v$ of $\sigma$ that is not in $V$, we add $v$ to $V$ and update $T$ accordingly.

Here is the formal description of one phase of the algorithm $L^*$ after the oracle returned a discrepancy $\sigma$.

```
subroutine L*(V, W, T, σ) returns (V, W, T) =
      if T is empty then
            let V := {ε}, W := Σ;
            for each a ∈ Σ, set T(ε, a) according to test(a)
      else
            for each prefix v of σ do
                  add_rows(v);
      while T is inconsistent or not closed do
            if T is inconsistent then
                  find v₁, v₂ ∈ V, a ∈ Σ, w ∈ W,
                        such that v₁ ~ v₂ and T(v₁a, w) ≠ T(v₂a, w)
                  add_column(aw)
            else
                  find v ∈ V, a ∈ Σ,
                        such that va ∉ [u] for any u ∈ V
                  add_rows(va)
      end while
end L*
```

Here, the procedure $add\_rows(v)$ checks if $v \in V$, and if not, adds $v$ to $V$ and fills the new rows in $T$, i.e., makes the experiments **reset** $vaw$ for all $w \in W$ and all $a \in \Sigma \cup \{\epsilon\}$. Similarly, $add\_column(w)$ adds a new distinguishing sequence $w$ to $W$ and updates $T(v,w)$ for each $v \in V \cup V.\Sigma$ by making the experiment **reset** $vw$.

In our experiments, we use a modified version of $L^*$ algorithm proposed by Rivest and Schapire [13]. The algorithm of [13] adds an appropriately chosen *suffix* of the discrepancy to $W$ (instead of adding prefixes concatenated by a letter from $\Sigma$ to $V$, as in Angluin's algorithm). Also, Rivest and Schapire noticed that consistency check is also performed by the conformance algorithm. In fact, this is exactly what is done by Vasilevskii-Chow algorithm when $l = 1$ (see next subsection). Therefore, in their version of the learning algorithm they omit the consistency check.

Let $n$ be an upper bound on the number of states of the minimal deterministic automaton modeling the black box. Suppose that any counterexample returned by the oracle is of size $O(n)$ (this is indeed the case for all oracles considered in this paper). Then for the Rivest–Schapire version of the $L^*$ algorithm we have the following result.

**Proposition 1.** *[13] The $L^*$ algorithm makes $O(n^2|\Sigma|)$ membership queries and at most $n$ calls to the oracle. Its running time is $O(n^3|\Sigma|) + T_{oracle}$, where $T_{oracle}$ is the total time spent by the oracle.*

**Vasilevskii-Chow Algorithm.** The oracle is built using the Vasilevskii-Chow algorithm. This algorithm uses the sets $V, W$ and a known upper bound $n$ on the size of the minimal deterministic automaton modeling the black box. In order to check whether $\mathcal{A} = \mathcal{A}^*$, VC algorithm runs both automata on some sequences $y \in \Sigma^*$. We write check$(y) = 1$ if $y$ is either in $\mathcal{L}(\mathcal{A}) \setminus \mathcal{L}(\mathcal{A}^*)$ or in $\mathcal{L}(\mathcal{A}^*) \setminus \mathcal{L}(\mathcal{A})$. The sequences that are tested are those of the form $y = vxw$ with $v$ a selected representative per each equivalence class of $[V/\sim]$, $w \in W$ and $|x| \leq n - |[V\setminus\sim]|$. Intuitively, if two equivalent access sequences are not consistent, then one is not consistent with the actual black box and a new distinguishing sequence can be found.

```
VC(V,W,n):
  k =  sizeof([V/∼]);
  for l =  1,...,n − k
      for each word x of size l, c ∈ [V/∼], w ∈ W
          let v be an arbitrary representative of c;
          if check(vxw) then return vxw;
  return void;
```

**Proposition 2.** *[14,6] It is sufficient to test sequences of the form $y = vxw$ with $v$ selected as representative for each equivalence class of $[V/\sim]$, $w \in W$ and $|x| \leq n - k$ in order to find a difference between $\mathcal{A}^*$ and $\mathcal{A}$, where $k$ is the number of equivalent classes of $[V/\sim]$ and $n$ is a bound on the number of states of $\mathcal{A}$. The algorithm makes $k^2|\Sigma|^{n-k+1}$ membership queries. Its time complexity is $O(nk^2|\Sigma|^{n-k+1})$.*

Observe that the $L^*$ algorithm invokes Vasilevskii-Chow algorithm at most $n$ times, and after each call the value of $k$ increases by at least 1. Therefore, the total number of queries made by Vasilevskii-Chow algorithm during these calls is at most $|\Sigma|^n + 4|\Sigma|^{n-1} + \cdots + n^2|\Sigma| = O(n^2|\Sigma|^n)$, and the total time spent by Vasilevskii-Chow algorithm is $O(n^3|\Sigma|^n)$.

**Black Box Checking.** Finally, we describe the black box checking procedure [12], which is a way to test whether a given black box $\mathcal{A}$ satisfies a property $\varphi$. The property $\varphi$ describes a set of allowed (or *good*) runs. We assume that it is written in some formal notation such as LTL or Büchi automata, Let $\mathcal{L}(\varphi)$ be the set of runs (the *language* of) the specification $\varphi$. We denote by $\mathcal{A} \models \varphi$ ($\mathcal{A}$ satisfies $\varphi$) the fact that $\mathcal{L}(\mathcal{A}) \subseteq \mathcal{L}(\varphi)$.

Suppose that we are given a (partially) unknown system $\mathcal{A}$. Our goal is to check whether there exists a run of $\mathcal{A}$ that does not satisfy $\varphi$. Such a run is called a *counterexample*. To do so, we infer an automaton $\mathcal{A}^*$ by running experiments on $\mathcal{A}$. We begin by using the learning algorithm initialized with $V = \epsilon$ and $W = \Sigma$. Then we feed the model checker with the candidate automaton $\mathcal{A}^*$. The model checker tests whether $\mathcal{A}^*$ satisfies $\varphi$. If not, it outputs a counterexample $\sigma$ such that $\sigma \in \mathcal{L}(\mathcal{A}^*) \setminus \mathcal{L}(\varphi)$. We then test $\sigma$ on $\mathcal{A}$. If $\sigma \in \mathcal{L}(\mathcal{A})$, we have found a genuine counterexample. Otherwise, $\sigma$ is a discrepancy between $\mathcal{A}$ and $\mathcal{A}^*$ and can be used to change $\mathcal{A}^*$ so that it models $\mathcal{A}$ more accurately. If $\mathcal{A} \models \varphi$, we will have to repeat this procedure until $\mathcal{L}(\mathcal{A}^*) = \mathcal{L}(\mathcal{A})$. However, if $\mathcal{A} \not\models \varphi$, we may find a counterexample before we learn $\mathcal{A}$.

## 3  Our Model

We associate a set of components $(S^i, s_0^i, \Sigma^i, \rightarrow^i)$ with the automaton $\mathcal{G} = (\prod S^i, \prod s_0^i, \bigcup \Sigma^i, \rightarrow)$, where $\prod_{i=1,\ldots,n}(s_i) \xrightarrow{a} \prod_{i=1,\ldots,n}(t_i)$ iff for all $i$, either $a \notin \Sigma^i$ and $s_i = t_i$, or $a \in \Sigma^i$ and $s_i \xrightarrow{a} t_i$. We want to verify a property of the whole system $\mathcal{G}$, and we know the alphabet $\Sigma^i$ used by every component (if not we take $\Sigma^i = \Sigma$).

As a running example, we consider a data acquisition system (DAS) similar to the one used in [16]. It consists of three components *Interface*, *Command*, *Sensor*, which communicate as follows. The *Command* can **request** the *Sensor* to send a **data** to the *Interface*. The *Sensor* can inform the *Interface* that an **error** occurred. Finally, the *Interface* can **stop** and **resume** the *Command*, and **send** the data it received to the environment, receiving **acknowledgement** from it. Assume that the *Interface* is given by the automaton in Figure 1; the other two components are unknown. In the beginning, we assume that both *Sensor* and *Command* can always perform each of their internal actions. Alternatively, if we only have an old specification of these components, we can use it to initialize these components, as is done in adaptive model checking [9]. We want to verify that between one **pause** and one **send**, the system $\mathcal{G}$ always performs a **resume**. Of course, a bad sequence of actions seems possible with this *Interface*, with the trace **error pause data send**, but this error may not be possible in the system with the actual *Command* and *Sensor*.

The algorithm that we use depends on whether the components can be analyzed separately, or only as a whole. The latter case may occur if, for instance, the communication is coded in a special way, or if the system is on a chip.

## 4    Independent Components

In this section, we assume that we can perform a test $w$ on any black box $\mathcal{B}$. Our algorithm is a slight modification of the black box checking algorithm. Let $\mathcal{W}$ be the product of all white boxes. Our goal is to model check the system $\mathcal{G} = \mathcal{W} \times \prod_{i \leq l}(\mathcal{B}_i)$. Suppose $|\mathcal{W}| = m$, $|\mathcal{B}_i| \leq n$ for all $i = 1, \ldots, l$, i.e., $|\mathcal{G}| \leq mn^l$. We repeat the following steps until we find a counterexample or construct a product automaton $\mathcal{G}^*$ with $\mathcal{L}(\mathcal{G}^*) = \mathcal{L}(\mathcal{G})$.

- Execute the learning algorithm for each $\mathcal{B}_i$ separately to construct candidate automata $\mathcal{B}_i^*$.
- Model check the product $\mathcal{G}^* = \mathcal{W} \times \prod_{i \leq l}(\mathcal{B}_i^*)$.
- If no counterexample is found, call the conformance tester on every black box separately and feed the discrepancies to the learning algorithm.
- If a counterexample $\sigma$ is found, then for all $i$, set $\sigma_i = \pi_{\Sigma_i}(\sigma)$, where $\pi_{\Sigma_i}(\sigma)$ is the projection of $\sigma$ on the alphabet $\Sigma_i$, and test $\sigma_i$ on the black box $\mathcal{B}_i$. If each of these tests passes, then the algorithm terminates and returns $\sigma$ as a real counterexample. Otherwise, we have discrepancies (one per each component), which we then pass to the learner for each black box.

**Proposition 3.** *The maximal number of tests performed during the black box checking of a system* $\mathcal{W} \times \prod_{i \leq l} \mathcal{B}_i$ *is* $O(l\, n^2\, |\Sigma|^n)$. *The time complexity of this procedure is* $O(l\, n^3\, |\Sigma|^n)$.

Observe that the time complexity of running the black box testing procedure on $\mathcal{G}$ is $O(m^3 n^{3l}\, |\Sigma|^{mn^l})$. Thus, it is highly profitable to learn the components separately. For both algorithms, we can apply the method in an incremental way (increasing the size of the tested automata used by the Vasilevskii-Chow algorithm, up to $n$). In case that the checked system *does not* satisfy the specification, we typically find it much quicker than the worst case complexity (see [12]).

We now show how this algorithm behaves on the data acquisition example. We begin by model-checking the candidate system against our property (between one **pause** and one **send**, the system $\mathcal{G}$ always performs a **resume**), and find a first possible counterexample: **error pause data send**. We find out that *Sensor* never emits an **error** as its first execution (rather, it does nothing without receiving an action request). Thus, we learn that the current model for *Sensor* is wrong and we ask the learner to give a better approximation. The learner comes up with the following table (the rows contain the access sequences $V$, the columns contain the distinguishing sequences of $W$ initialized with $\Sigma$). A $\checkmark$ in the table means that $w \in W$ is executable after $v \in V$. This table can be interpreted as the following automaton for *Sensor*:

Then, the model-checker verifies the new system with the new *Sensor*, and finds no errors since the action **error** is not allowed in the current model of *Sensor*. Hence, the conformance tester checks both the *Sensor* and the *Command*. For *Sensor*, the conformance tester comes up with the distinguishing sequence **request error** which is fed to the learner.

| $T(v,w)$ | req | data | error |
|:---:|:---:|:---:|:---:|
| $\epsilon$ | ✓ | x | x |
| req | ✓ | ✓ | x |
| req,req | ✓ | ✓ | x |
| req,data | ✓ | x | x |

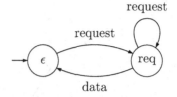

**Fig. 2.** First inferred black box *Sensor*: experiment Table and corresponding automaton

## 5   Testing a Grey Product

A more restrictive scenario is when we can only test whether $\sigma \in \mathcal{B} \times \mathcal{W}$. In what follows, we describe several new algorithms for this setting. Despite their simplicity, it turns out that our algorithms are almost optimal. We prove this by showing an (almost) matching lower bound. We focus on the case when there is one white box $\mathcal{W}$ of size $m$ and one black box $\mathcal{B}$ of size $n$. If there are several black boxes that cannot be tested separately, we consider $\mathcal{B}$ to be their product. In some cases, $\mathcal{B}$ cannot be learned exactly. For instance, if $b$ is in the intersection of both alphabets and $\mathcal{W}$ has no transition labeled by the letter $b$, then we cannot decide whether any state of $\mathcal{B}$ has a transition labeled by $b$. Therefore, our goal is to learn a black box $\mathcal{B}^*$ that satisfies $\mathcal{L}(\mathcal{B} \times \mathcal{W}) = \mathcal{L}(\mathcal{B}^* \times \mathcal{W})$. As $\mathcal{W}$ can be a machine that accepts every word of $\Sigma^*$, our problem is a generalization of black-box learning. This implies that one needs at least $n^2 \times |\Sigma|^n$ tests. We can also ignore what we know about $\mathcal{W}$ and treat $\mathcal{B} \times \mathcal{W}$ as a black box of size $mn$. This shows that it suffices to perform $O((mn)^2 \times |\Sigma|^{nm})$ tests of size $nm$. Clearly, if $m$ is much bigger than $n$, this approach does not seem attractive.

### 5.1   Lower Bounds

We start by proving two new lower bounds. They imply that testing a black box combined with a known white box is much more difficult than testing the black box alone. In particular, unlike in black box checking, the number of tests may have to be exponential in the size of the alphabet.

**Proposition 4.** *For any $n \in \mathbb{N}$, $|\Sigma|$ even, and $x, y \notin \Sigma$, there exists a family of black boxes $\mathcal{F} = (\mathcal{B}_r)_{r \in R}$ and a white box $\mathcal{W}$ with $|\mathcal{B}_r| \leq n+1, |\mathcal{W}| \leq n|\Sigma|^2$ such that $2^{\Omega(n|\Sigma|)}$ tests of size $\Omega(n|\Sigma|)$ are needed to distinguish between $\mathcal{B}_r \times \mathcal{W}$ and $\mathcal{B}_{r'} \times \mathcal{W}$.*

*Proof.* The automata in $\mathcal{F}$ are constructed as follows. Any automaton in this family has $n+1$ states $s_0, \ldots, s_n$ and uses the alphabet $\Sigma \cup \{x, y\}$. For each $1 \leq i \leq n$, let $\Sigma_i$ be a subalphabet of $\Sigma$ of size $|\Sigma|/2$. There is a transition $s_i \xrightarrow{a} s_i$ for every $a \in \Sigma_i$ and a transition $s_i \xrightarrow{a} s_0$ for every $a \in \Sigma \setminus \Sigma_i$. Also, for $i = 1, \ldots, n-1$ there is a transition $s_i \xrightarrow{x} s_{i+1}$. The only transition labeled by $y$ is $s_n \xrightarrow{y} s_0$. Finally, $s_0 \xrightarrow{a} s_0$ for every $a \neq y$. Every choice of subalphabets

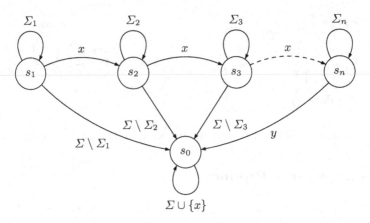

**Fig. 3.** A black box in $\mathcal{BB}$

$(\Sigma_1, \cdots, \Sigma_n)$ defines a black box in $\mathcal{F}$, which means that $|\mathcal{F}| = \binom{|\Sigma|}{|\Sigma|/2}^n$. Using Stirling's formula, we obtain $|\mathcal{F}| = 2^{\Omega(n|\Sigma|)}$.

To describe the white box $\mathcal{W}$, we fix a strict order $\prec \subseteq \Sigma \times \Sigma$ on letters. Intuitively, we want $\mathcal{W}$ to accept words that consist of $n$ blocks of $|\Sigma|/2$ letters from $\Sigma$ separated by $x$'s, followed by a $y$; within each block, the letters should be ordered according to $\prec$. More formally, $\mathcal{W}$ is the minimal deterministic automaton that accepts prefixes of the words $w_1 \cdots w_t$, $t = n(|\Sigma|/2 + 1)$, that satisfy the following: $w_t = y$, $w_{i(|\Sigma|/2+1)} = x$ for all $i = 1, \ldots, n-1$, and finally, for any $i$ such that $i \mod |\Sigma/2| + 1 \neq 0, 1$, we have $w_{i-1} \prec w_i$. It is not hard to see that $\mathcal{W}$ can be implemented using $n|\Sigma|^2$ states.

Clearly, any word of the form $w_1 \cdots w_t$ accepted by $\mathcal{W}$ is a word of the black box associated with $(\Sigma_1, \ldots, \Sigma_n)$, where $\Sigma_i$ consists of the letters in the $i$th block of $w$. On the other hand, all other black boxes do not accept this word. This implies that we need at least $2^{\Omega(n|\Sigma|)}$ tests of size $\Omega(n|\Sigma|)$ each.    □

Our second bound shows that the size of the counterexample cannot be bounded by a number lower than $nm$. Hence, the Vasilevskii-Chow approach of testing every sequence of a bounded size will require at least $|\Sigma|^{nm}$ tests.

**Proposition 5.** *Let $n \neq m$ be two prime numbers. There exists a white box $\mathcal{W}$ with $m + 1$ states and two black boxes $\mathcal{B}, \mathcal{B}'$ of size at most $n + 1$ such that a word of size $nm$ is needed to distinguish between $\mathcal{B} \times \mathcal{W}$ and $\mathcal{B}' \times \mathcal{W}$.*

*Proof.* For all $r > 0$, consider an automaton $\mathcal{A}_r$ with $r + 1$ states $s_1, \cdots, s_{r+1}$ and transitions $s_i \xrightarrow{a} s_{i+1}$ for all $i < r$, $s_r \xrightarrow{a} s_1$, and $s_r \xrightarrow{b} s_{r+1}$. The regular language accepted by $\mathcal{A}_r$ is $a^* + (a^{r-1})(a^r)^*b$.

If $\mathcal{W} = \mathcal{A}_m$ and $\mathcal{B} = \mathcal{A}_n$, it is easy to see that the smallest word of $\mathcal{G}$ that contains $b$ is $a^{mn-1}b$ because $m$ and $n$ are distinct primes. This is the smallest word that distinguishes $\mathcal{W} \times \mathcal{B}$ from $\mathcal{W} \times \mathcal{B}'$, where $\mathcal{B}'$ is the automaton with one state $s$ and $s \xrightarrow{a} s$.    □

## 5.2    An Almost Optimal Algorithm

It is not hard to identify the automaton that corresponds to the black box by considering all automata of size at most $n$.

**Proposition 6.** *Let $\mathcal{B}$ be a black box of size at most $n$ and $\mathcal{W}$ a known automaton of size $m$. One can learn $\mathcal{B} \times \mathcal{W}$ with at most $2^{n \times |\Sigma| \times \log n}$ tests of size at most $2nm - 1$.*

*Proof.* Let $(\mathcal{B}_r)_{r \in \{0, \cdots, l\}}$ be the family of all deterministic finite automata of size at most $n$. For all $r < l$, if $\mathcal{B}_r \times \mathcal{W}$ and $\mathcal{B}_{r+1} \times \mathcal{W}$ agree on all words of size at most $2nm - 1$, they are equivalent. Otherwise, they have a distinguishing sequence, i.e., a word $w$ of size at most $2nm - 1$ such that $w \in \mathcal{B}_r \times \mathcal{W}$ and $w \notin \mathcal{B}_{r+1} \times \mathcal{W}$ or vice versa. It suffices to test this word to make sure that $\mathcal{B} \neq \mathcal{B}_{r+1}$ or $\mathcal{B} \neq \mathcal{B}_r$. Observe that $w$ can be chosen as the smallest sequence in $(\mathcal{L}(\overline{\mathcal{B}_r^*}) \cap \mathcal{L}(\mathcal{B}_{r+1}^*) \cap \mathcal{L}(\mathcal{W})) \cup (\mathcal{L}(\overline{\mathcal{B}_{r+1}^*}) \cap \mathcal{L}(\mathcal{B}_r^*) \cap \mathcal{L}(\mathcal{W}))$. Moreover, since $\mathcal{B}_r^*$ is deterministic, computing its complement $\overline{\mathcal{B}_r^*}$ is easy. Hence, we have to perform at most $l$ tests of size at most $2nm - 1$ to find a $\mathcal{B}_r$ such that $\mathcal{B}_r \times \mathcal{W} = \mathcal{B} \times \mathcal{W}$. To finish the proof, note that the number of automata of size at most $n$ is bounded by $2^{n \times |\Sigma| \times \log n}$. $\qquad\qquad\square$

The worst-case running time of the algorithm described above is very close to the lower bound of Proposition 4. In other words, our algorithm is almost optimal. However, it is impractical since it has to test every possible automaton without learning anything before the very last test is performed. Thus, its average complexity is equal to its worst case complexity. On the other hand, if we apply the black box learning algorithm described in Section 2.1 to our grey box, the worst case complexity will be exponential in $m$, but the average complexity will be much lower. In what follows, we show how to combine the two approaches to construct an algorithm that needs at most $2^{n \times |\Sigma| \times \log n} + mn$ tests of size at most $2mn - 1$ in the worst case, but can be expected to do much better on average. The experiments in Section 6 show that this is indeed the case.

Our algorithm uses the learning algorithm $L^*$ on the grey box $\mathcal{G} = \mathcal{B} \times \mathcal{W}$. Whenever $L^*$ produces a candidate solution $\mathcal{G}^*$, we check that $\mathcal{G}^*$ does not accept sequences in $\overline{\mathcal{W}}$; any such sequence is a discrepancy and can be used to refine $\mathcal{G}^*$. Then, instead of using Vasilevskii-Chow algorithm for conformance testing, we use an oracle that only tests the candidate solution $\mathcal{G}^*$ proposed by $L^*$ on the distinguishing sequences considered in Proposition 6. More precisely, we generate automata of size up to $n$ one by one. Let $\mathcal{B}' = \mathcal{B}_i$ be the most recently generated such automaton. We compute a distinguishing sequence for $\mathcal{B}' \times \mathcal{W}$ and $\mathcal{G}^*$ and test it on the grey box. Clearly, either $\mathcal{B}' \times \mathcal{W}$ or $\mathcal{G}^*$ will behave differently from $\mathcal{G}$. If $\mathcal{B}' \times \mathcal{W} \neq \mathcal{G}$, we conclude that $\mathcal{B}' \neq \mathcal{B}$, so we set $\mathcal{B}' = \mathcal{B}_{i+1}$. If $\mathcal{G}^* \neq \mathcal{G}$, we have a discrepancy on $\mathcal{G}^*$ allowing refinement with $L^*$. Clearly, the first case can occur at most $2^{n \times |\Sigma| \times \log n}$ times, and the second case can occur at most $mn$ times (each time, the size of $\mathcal{G}^*$ increases). Therefore, the total number of tests is at most $2^{n \times |\Sigma| \times \log n} + mn$. Moreover, as $|\mathcal{G}^*| \leq mn$, the length of each experiment is at most $2mn - 1$.

For this algorithm to be efficient, we need to eliminate *early* many automata. To do so, we use the information about $\mathcal{B}$ provided by tests made by $L^*$. Namely, if $wa$ is executable in $\mathcal{B} \times \mathcal{W}$, then it is executable in $\mathcal{B}$. If $wa$ is executable in $\mathcal{W}$, but not in $\mathcal{B} \times \mathcal{W}$, then we know that it is not executable in $\mathcal{B}$. To generate the automaton, for each state and label we choose the destination of the transition from this state with this label. The number of automata generated depends heavily on the order in which we generate the transitions. Worse yet, the best ordering may change a lot with the choice of transition. Hence, we decide not to impose this order statically but to determine it dynamically: the next transition chosen is the one that makes the largest number of tests progress, so that hopefully a contradiction is reached and every extension of the current automaton is eliminated.

Another technique to speed up the algorithm is to use information about the white box in order to lower the number of distinguishing sequences per state of the candidate solution. We denote by $white(v)$ the state of $\mathcal{W}$ reached after reading the sequence $v \in V$, where $V$ is an access sequence for the grey box. We also denote by $W_s$ the distinguishing sequences needed to distinguish the states in $\{v \in V \mid white(v) = s\}$, for each state $s$ of $\mathcal{W}$. Recall that in Section 2.1 we defined an equivalence relation $\sim$ on $V \times V$. We can refine $\sim$ as follows: $v \sim v'$ iff $white(v) = white(v') = s$ and for all $w \in W_s$, $T(v, w) = T(v, w')$. Our closure and consistency checks are based on this new equivalence. The modified $L^*$ algorithm only fills those lines $T(v, w)$ with $w \in W_{white(v)}$. Notice that $|W_s| \leq n$. It may be the case that $white(v) = white(v')$ with $v$ and $v'$ accepting the same language, and hence we may have to apply a minimization procedure to get a minimal automaton.

## 5.3   An Algorithm Based on Partial Order Reduction

Another way to reduce the number of experiments in the conformance step is to use the information about the alphabet. This approach is inspired by partial order reduction [4]. Suppose that we know an independence relation $I$ given by $I = \Sigma^2 \setminus D$, with $(a, b) \in D$ iff $a, b \in \Sigma_i$ for some $i$. For instance, in the data acquisition example, $(\mathbf{request}, \mathbf{send}) \in I$.

**Definition 1.** *Let* $\sigma, \rho \in \Sigma^*$. *Define* $\sigma \overset{1}{\equiv} \rho$ *iff* $\sigma = uabv$ *and* $\rho = ubav$, *where* $u, v \in \Sigma^*$, *and* $a\,I\,b$.

That is, $\rho$ is obtained from $\sigma$ (or vice versa) by commuting an adjacent pair of letters.

**Definition 2.** *Let* $\sigma \equiv \rho$ *be the transitive closure of the relation* $\overset{1}{\equiv}$. *This relation is often called* trace equivalence *[10]*.

For example, for $\Sigma = \{a, b\}$ and $I = \{(a, b), (b, a)\}$ we have $abbab \overset{1}{\equiv} ababb$ and $abbab \equiv bbbaa$.

Let $\ll$ be a total order on the alphabet $\Sigma$. We call it the *alphabetic order*. We extend $\ll$ in the standard alphabetical way to words, i.e., $v \ll vu$ and $vau \ll vbw$ for $v, u, w \in \Sigma^*$, $a, b \in \Sigma$ and $a \ll b$.

**Definition 3.** *Let $\sigma \in \Sigma^*$. Denote by $\tilde{\sigma}$ the least string under the relation $\ll$ that is trace equivalent to $\sigma$. If $\sigma = \tilde{\sigma}$, then we say that $\sigma$ is in* lexicographic normal form *(LNF)* [11].

Our approach is based on using $L^*$ algorithm together with Vasilevskii–Chow conformance oracle. However, instead of checking all sequences of the form $vxw$, we only check the ones where $x$ is in LNF. Clearly, this preserves the correctness of our algorithm. In what follows, we show that by using appropriate data structures, we can ensure that the overhead due to generating sequences in LNF is not too big. This is also confirmed by our experimental results (see Section 6).

Denote by $\alpha(\sigma)$ the set of letters occurring in $\sigma$. Let $\prec_\sigma$ be a total order on the letters from $\alpha(\sigma)$ called the *summary* of $\sigma$. It is defined as follows:

**Definition 4.** *Define $a \prec_\sigma b$ if the last occurrence of $a$ in $\sigma$ precedes the last occurrence of $b$ in $\sigma$. That is, $a \prec_\sigma b$ if and only if $\sigma = vaubw$, where $v \in \Sigma^*$, $u \in (\Sigma \setminus \{a\})^*$, $w \in (\Sigma \setminus \{a, b\})^*$.*

**Lemma 1.** *Let $\sigma \in \Sigma^*$ be in LNF, and $a \in \Sigma$. Then $\sigma a$ is not in LNF exactly when we can decompose $\sigma = vu$, such that (a) $vau \equiv vua$ and (b) $vau \ll vu$.*

Intuitively, this means that we can commute the last $a$ in $vua$ backwards over $u$ to obtain a string that is smaller in the alphabetic order than $vu$. Note that it is not sufficient to check locally that $a$ does not commute with the previous letter, i.e., the case with $|u| = 1$. Consider $\Sigma = \{a, b, c\}$ and $I = \{(a,b), (b,a), (b,c), (c,b)\}$. Then $ca$ is in LNF, while $cab \equiv bca$, where $bca \ll ca$.

*Proof.* If the two conditions (a) and (b) hold, then obviously $vua$ cannot be in LNF since it is not minimal under the alphabetic order among sequences equivalent to it.

Conversely, let $\rho$ be the minimal string such that $\rho \equiv \sigma a$. Denote by $first(v)$ the first letter of a nonempty string $v$. Let $v$ be the maximal common prefix of $\rho$ and $\sigma$ (and thus also of $\sigma a$). Write $\sigma = vu$ (as in (i)), and $\rho = vw$. Consider the following cases:

1. $w$ starts with an $a$.
    (a) $u_1$ does not contain an $a$. Then $au \equiv ua$, satisfying (ii).
    (b) $u$ contains $a$. Write $u = u_1 a u_2$, where $u$ contains no $a$. Then $u = u_1 a u_2 \equiv a u_1 u_2$. Since $\rho = vw \ll vua$, we have that $a = first(w) \ll first(u_1) = first(u)$. Thus, $v a u_1 u_2 \ll v u_1 a u_2 = vu$, a contradiction to the fact that $\sigma$ is in LNF.
2. Write $w = w_1 a w_2$, where $w_2$ does not contain an $a$. Then, $w = w_1 a w_2 \equiv w_1 w_2 a \equiv ua$ and thus $w_1 w_2 \equiv u$. Since $vw \ll vu$, we have that $first(w_1) = first(w) \ll first(u)$. Thus, $v w_1 w_2 \ll vu = \sigma$ and $v w_1 w_2 \equiv vu$. This contradicts the fact that $\sigma$ is in LNF. $\quad\square$

The following Lemma shows how we can use a summary to decide whether $\sigma a$ is in LNF. Since $|\sigma|$ is usually quite larger than the size of the summary (essentially $|\Sigma|$), this makes the generation of normal forms much more efficient.

**Lemma 2.** *Let $\sigma \in \Sigma^*$ be in LNF with a summary $\prec_\sigma$ and $a \in \Sigma$. Then $\sigma a$ is not in LNF exactly when there is $b \in \alpha(\sigma)$ such that $a \ll b$ and for each $c$ such that $b \preceq_\sigma c$, $aIc$.*

In words, this means that it is sufficient to check the commutativity of $a$ with a suffix of the summary that commutes with $a$, and look among these letters for one that comes *after* $a$ in the alphabetic order. This replaces a similar check for an actual suffix of $\sigma$.

*Proof.* Suppose that $\sigma$ is in LNF and $\sigma a$ is not. Let $u$ be the shortest suffix of $\sigma$ according to the conditions of the previous lemma, i.e., $\sigma = vu$ and $vau \equiv vua$. Let $b$ be the head of $u$. Then $a \ll b$. Let $C = \alpha(u)$. We have $aIc$ for each $c \in C$, hence at least for each $b \preceq_\sigma c$.

Conversely, let $b \in \alpha(\sigma)$ a letter satisfying the conditions of the Lemma. Let $u$ be the shortest suffix of $\sigma$ that begins with $b$. Since $\prec_\sigma$ is the summary of $\sigma$, it follows that all the letters $c \in \alpha(u)$ satisfy $b \preceq_{\alpha(\sigma)} c$, hence $aIc$. This means that (a) and (b) from the previous lemma hold.     □

For instance, assume we have **request** $<$ **data** $<$ **error** $<$ **resume** $<$ **pause** $<$ **send** $<$ **ack**. Then if the action **error** is seen, the new order $<$ will be **request** $<$ **data** $<$ **resume** $<$ **pause** $<$ **send** $<$ **ack** $<$ **error**.

Like in other partial order approaches, this algorithm can provide us with a reduction that is at most exponential in the number of concurrent (e.g., independent black box) components. Conversely, in other extreme cases, there can be no reduction at all. It is worth noting that the same idea can be used to improve the learning algorithm. Namely, two equivalent (with respect to commutation) states will never be distinguished, hence the tests for one are copied from the other one.

## 6     Experimental Results

Our implementation prototype for grey box checking is written in SML and includes roughly 6000 lines of code. We use three kinds of examples: an artificially pathological example simple_$n$ with $n$ components, DAS (data acquisition system) with 4 components from [16] with every event observable, and finally, a system in which the memory is incremented and decremented by two processes through a COMA coherency protocol with unobservable actions (COMA was already used in [9], though modeled differently). The two different versions of COMA correspond to different initializations of the memory. Notice that we only include the learner/conformance part, since the model checking part is the same for all algorithms considered. The algorithms are based on Rivest–Schapire's version of the learning algorithm $L^*$, but call different conformance testers: VC for the usual Vasilevskii-Chow algorithm, LNF for VC generating only sequences in LNF, GBC for Grey Box Checking, i.e., generating distinguishing sequences from the possible automata, and LNFGBC, which uses mainly LNF with calls to GBC when no short sequences were found by LNF.

For each example, we indicated the number of states of the product $\mathcal{G}$ to learn, the number of letters of the alphabet, and the size 'leng.' of the largest experiment needed to distinguish two different states. Then for each algorithm, we give the number of experiments needed to learn the whole system (M indicates millions). We also give an indicative value of the time needed in parentheses, in minutes (or seconds if 's' is specified). All tests were realized on a P-M@1.2Ghz with 256MB of dedicated memory. In Grey Box Checking, we consider only one component as known, the other components being black boxes that cannot be tested separately. In COMA, the black box $\mathcal{B}$ and the white box $\mathcal{W}$ are close in size. In simple_2, $\mathcal{W}$ is much bigger than $\mathcal{B}$. For DAS and simple_4, $\mathcal{B}$ is much bigger than $\mathcal{W}$.

| example | states | letters | leng. | VC | LNF | GBC | LNFGBC |
|---------|--------|---------|-------|-----|-----|-----|--------|
| simple_2 | 19 | 2 | 18 | $.5M$ (9) | $.5M$ (9) | 388 (1s) | 444 (1s) |
| simple_4 | 82 | 6 | 9 | $7.2M$ (22) | $2.3M$ (3) | too long | $2.3M$ (4) |
| DAS | 73 | 12 | 4 | $.25M$ (13s) | $.13M$ (8s) | too long | $.13M$ (10s) |
| COMA(1) | 48 | 8 | 6 | $9.8M$ (33) | $5.7M$ (16) | 1821 (120) | $.4M$ (2) |
| COMA(2) | 48 | 8 | 7 | $46M$ (190) | $25M$ (75) | 1731 (170) | $.4M$ (2) |

**Partial Order**

– The overhead in time due to the computation of the lexicographic normal form (LNF) is negligible in all the tests we did.
– Apart from simple_2, which has no commutation, partial order results in a speedup by a factor of 2 to 7. While the speedup in DAS is due to the equivalence relation that we consider on states (the length of the distinguishing sequences is too small), the longer the distinguishing sequences are, the more commutations can be found and the better the speedup is.

**Grey Box Checking**

– GBC tests very few distinguishing sequences compared with LNF. However, the time taken is not linear in the number of tests performed.
– simple_2 is the pathological case for VC, which explains why Grey Box Checking succeeds. One is, however, unlikely to find such cases in real life.
– In many cases, a pure Grey Box Checking approach is unpractical. However, a distinction should be made between two cases: In Simple_4, no information guides the generation of automata. Even generating all automata with 3 states takes hours, and is useless. On the other hand, in the more realistic DAS example, the initialization gives a lot of information. Although the number of letters is high, every automaton of size 8 respecting the information can be generated within 90 seconds. There are roughly 430,000 such (partial) automata, compared to about $8^{96}$ if no information was known.
– When VC is efficient ('leng.' is small), Grey Box Checking is useless (DAS).
– Using LNFGBC, i.e., combining Grey Box Checking and LNF can be much more efficient than any of them separately in non-artificial cases (COMA).

Moreover, the overhead of GBC as a helper of LNF is small even in the case where GBC is useless, and can lead to impressive speedup (100 times in COMA(2)).

- Many improvements are possible, e.g., using some of the tests realized by LNF as information to guide the generation of automata.

## 7    Conclusion

Black box checking [12] was suggested as a way to directly verify a system when its model is not given but a way of conducting experiments is provided. In this paper we studied an extension of this problem, where our system is decomposed into a known part (white box) and unknown part (black box, or a collection of concurrently operating black boxes).

In particular, one of the most interesting cases that we address here is that of an unknown system (i.e., a black box) that is connected to a device whose specification is given (a white box), where both components are coupled, i.e., we can perform the experiments only on the combined system. We prove that the complexity of verifying such a system is strictly in between that of verifying the properties of the black box alone and that of considering the complete structure as a big black box for which no specification is given. We provide algorithms and heuristic methods for verifying such systems.

We implemented the proposed algorithms and showed that this approach can be practical. We performed several experiments verifying that the overhead of these techniques is small, while in some real life cases, the speedup over the black box checking algorithm can be up to two orders of magnitude.

## References

1. R. Alur, P. Madhusudan, and W. Nam. Symbolic Compositional Verification by Learning Assumptions. In *CAV'05*, LNCS, 2005.
2. D. Angluin. Learning Regular Sets from Queries and Counterexamples. *Information and Computation*, 75, 87-106 (1987).
3. R. Alur, R. Grosu and M. McDougall. Efficient Reachability Analysis of Hierarchical Reactive Machines In *CAV'00*, LNCS 1855, p.280-295, 2000.
4. E. M. Clarke, O. Grumberg, D. Peled, *Model Checking*, MIT Press, 1999.
5. E. Clarke, D. Long, K. McMillan. Compositional Model Checking. In *LICS'89*, IEEE , p.353-362, 1989.
6. T.S. Chow. Testing software design modeled by finite-states machines. In *IEEE transactions on software engineering*, SE-4, 1978, 178-187.
7. J. Cobleigh, D. Giannakopoulou, C. Pasareanu. Learning Assumptions for Compositional Verification. In *TACAS'03*, LNCS 2619, p.331-346, 2003.
8. E. Elkind, B. Genest, D. Peled and H. Qu. Grey-Box Checking. Internal Report, available at http://www.crans.org/~genest/EGPQ.ps.
9. A. Groce, D. Peled and M. Yannakakis. Adaptive Model Checking. In *TACAS'02*, LNCS 2280 , p.357-370, 2002.
10. A. Mazurkiewicz, Trace Semantics, Proceedings of Advances in Petri Nets, 1986, Bad Honnef, Lecture Notes in Computer Science, Springer Verlag, 279–324, 1987.

11. E. Ochmanski, Languages and Automata, in The Book of Traces, V. Diekert, G. Rozenberg (eds.), World Scientific, 167–204.
12. D. Peled, M. Vardi and M. Yannakakis. Black Box Checking. In *FORTE/PSTV'99*, 1999.
13. R. Rivest and R. Schapire. Inference of Finite Automata Using Homing Sequences. *Information and Computation*, 103(2), p.299-347, 1993.
14. M.P. Vasilevskii. Failure diagnosis of automata. *Kibertetika*, no 4, p.98-108, 1973.
15. W. Weimer and G. Necula Mining Temporal Specifications for Error Detection. In *TACAS'05*, LNCS 3440, p.461-476, 2005.
16. G. Xie and Z. Dang. Testing Systems of Concurrent Black-boxes - an Automata-Theoretic and Decompositional Approach. In *FATES'05*, LNCS, 2005.

# Integration Testing of Distributed Components Based on Learning Parameterized I/O Models

Keqin Li[1], Roland Groz[1], and Muzammil Shahbaz[2]

[1] LSR - IMAG
BP 72, F-38402 St Martin D'Hères Cedex, France
{Keqin.Li, Roland.Groz}@imag.fr
[2] France Telecom R&D
BP 98, 38243 Meylan Cedex, France
muhammad.muzammilshahbaz@orange-ft.com

**Abstract.** The design of complex systems, e.g., telecom services, is usually based on the integration of components (COTS). When components come from third party sources, their internal structure is usually unknown and the documentation is scant or inadequate.

Our work addresses the issue of providing a sound support to component integration in the absence of formal models. We consider components as black boxes and use an incremental learning approach to infer partial models. At the same time, we are focusing on the richer models that are more expressive in the designing of complex systems. Therefore, we propose an I/O parameterized model and an algorithm to infer it from a black box component. This is combined with interoperability testing covering models of the components.

## 1   Introduction

The design of new software systems, such as telecom services, is more and more based on the integration of components from third party sources (COTS), loosely coupled in a distributed architecture (e.g., web services). Testing the behavior of the assembly is important to build confidence in the system. In order to base testing on a sound and systematic basis, it has become common to use models. In reality, COTS are rarely provided with formal descriptions.

A general approach [4,2,3] is to generate formal models of COTS through their incremental learning. In [6], we proposed an approach to learn I/O models of COTS (using a slight modification of Angluin's Algorithm [1]), and define an Integration Testing Procedure based upon these models. Our current work addresses the issue of learning richer models that are more expressive in the design of complex systems. The goal is to help the integrator in deriving systematic tests to check component interactions. It is well known that typical interoperability problems are often related to incompatibility of data values that did not appear when components are tested in isolation, but are revealed by feeding the outputs of one component as inputs to another component. This is why we concentrate on a model where parameter values are taken into account. From those

E. Najm et al. (Eds.): FORTE 2006, LNCS 4229, pp. 436–450, 2006.

models, we compute systematic cross component interactions with classical test generation techniques for collections of automata.

## 1.1  Assumptions

Our basic assumptions are as follows.

- The components we deal with are viewed as black boxes. Only their interfaces are known, which means that we know at least their input types, although the actual parameter values may depend on the behaviors exercised.
- Although no global specification of the system is available, the integrator has a number of test scenarios for the global interaction of the system with its environment. Additionally, sample parameter values are provided for all interfaces of components.
- All internal and external interfaces can be observed in integration testing, but only external (non-integrated) interfaces are controllable, i.e. we can send input sequences through these interfaces to test the components. We assume our test harness makes it possible to observe connected interfaces.
- Inputs from the environment will only be provided on stable states of the system, viz. when all components are waiting for external stimuli and will not make any internal move. This corresponds to the notion of slow environment in system verification or quiescence in testing theory. We also assume that each input to a component triggers at most one output. Interaction between components is asynchronous, and at any time at most one "message in transit" holds in the system.
- We shall not attempt to derive a complete model of the components. COTS offer many functions. We shall just derive sub-models that correspond to the behaviors exercised in the integrated system. Even for that restricted part of the components, the models derived will be approximations in line with the testing goals (i.e., the level of confidence required).

## 1.2  Our Approach

In the absence of formal models for components, model inference from observations is a key point. Angluin [1] has proposed an algorithm that infers a Deterministic Finite Automaton (DFA) from observations of component's behavior. In [6], we proposed an extension of Angluin's algorithm that works with I/O automata. In this paper, we are dealing with a richer model that contains inputs and outputs along with the parameter values. These models are more applicable when the input set is typically very large. Then we can distinguish input types and their possible parameter values and model into a compact finite state machine, which we call PFSM (Parameterized Finite State Machines). Since existing algorithm for DFA inference uses number of queries, which grow polynomially with the size of alphabet, they are not well-suited for this situation. If some parameters are irrelevant or never used, the algorithm should not be disturbed by their presence. Certain adaptations of this algorithm have been tested for parameterized FSM e.g. in [2] but it does not cater for output parameters in the model.

Our approach is to further modify the above algorithms to conjecture a PFSM model of a component and also find a practical source for getting counterexamples when the conjecture is wrong or not suitable for integration. In requirements engineering approaches [7,8], the equivalence query used to get counterexamples is provided by an expert. Here we follow the approach used in [4,3] where the query is implemented by testing the integrated system which acts as an oracle. The outline of the integration methodology is as follows.

1. In the first step, an input alphabet is defined for each component $C$. This corresponds to the invocations on external interfaces with all the parameter values that are considered relevant (starting with those from scenarios or use cases defined for the system or provided for internal interfaces).
2. Each component is (unit) tested separately using the learning algorithm until balanced, closed and consistent observation tables for it are found. The output alphabet is determined along with output parameters. This provides the first model $C^{(1)}$ for $C$.
3. The components are integrated. This means that some of the outputs of one component will appear as inputs on the connected interface of another component. The assembly is tested in two stages.
4. In a first stage, we systematically test the provided system-wide scenarios expected from the assembly. In that stage, scenarios act as oracles. Faults can be detected, or a discrepancy with the inferred model may be identified, leading to incremental refinement of the model.
5. In a second stage, we generate (interoperability) tests from the models of the components. The actual outputs observed (both internal and to the environment) are recorded and compared to those provided by the models. Tests are performed until a discrepancy between predictions from the model is found or some coverage criteria on the model is achieved. Classifying discrepancies as faults may require expert input.
6. In both stages, discrepancies can lead to model refinement. The counterexamples found are injected in the learning algorithm to extend the models and the stage is iterated with the new $C^{(i+1)}$ components.

The rest of the paper is organized as follows. Section 2 presents unit testing of components and Section 3 presents their integration testing. An example is given in the Section 4. Finally, Section 5 concludes the paper.

## 2   Unit Testing

The first stage in our approach is unit testing, in which the components are tested individually. For each component $C$, its inputs are modelled as a set of input symbols $I_C^{(1)}$. This may be provided by the designer of the component, or abstracted from the informal descriptions or some preliminary testing of the component by the tester. With $I_C^{(1)}$, the tester performs unit testing using our learning algorithm and builds an initial model $C^{(1)}$. The model is an extension of FSM which incorporates inputs and outputs along with the parameter values. We call this model as Parameterized Finite State Machine (PFSM). At the same time, this extension can be considered as a restricted form of Extended Finite State Machine (EFSM), in the sense that all the context information are stored in states without the help of variables, and the knowledge of state and input can determine the transition. The next section describes PFSM formally and then its inferring algorithm is presented.

## 2.1  PFSM Model

A *Parameterized Finite State Machine* (PFSM) $M = \{Q, I, O, D_x, D_y, \delta, \lambda, \sigma, q_0\}$, where

- $Q$ is finite non-empty set of states,
- $I$ is finite set of input symbols,
- $O$ is finite set of output symbols,
- $q_0 \in Q$ is the initial state,
- $D_x$ is a set of possible values of input parameters,
- $D_y$ is a set of possible values of output parameters,
- $\delta : Q \times I \longrightarrow Q$ is a next state function,
- $\lambda : Q \times I \longrightarrow O$ is an output function,
- $\sigma : Q \times I \longrightarrow D_y{}^{D_x}$ is an output parameter function. $D_y{}^{D_x}$ is the set of all functions from $D_x$ to $D_y$.

When a PFSM model $M$ is in the state $q \in Q$ and receives an input $i \in I$ along with the parameter value $x \in D_x$, $M$ moves to the next state given by $q' = \delta(q, i) \in Q$, and produces an output given by $o = \lambda(q, i) \in O$, along with the output parameter value given by $f(x) = \sigma(q, i)(x)$.

In order to elaborate a complete parameterized output function for a state $q \in Q$, $i \in I$ and $x \in D_x$, we write $\lambda(q, i(x)) = o(f(x))$, where $o \in O$ is determined by $\lambda(q, i)$ and $f(x)$ is determined by $\sigma(q, i)(x)$.

Then, we extend the functions from input symbols to sequences as usual: for a state $q_1$, an input sequence $\alpha = i_1(x_1), ..., i_k(x_k)$ takes $M$ successively to the states $q_{j+1} = \delta(q_j, i_j), j = 1, ..., k$, with the final state $\delta(q_1, \alpha) = q_{k+1}$, and produces an output sequence $\lambda(q_1, \alpha) = o_1(f_1(x_1)), ..., o_k(f_k(x_k))$, where each $o_j(f_j(x_j)) = \lambda(q_j, i_j(x_j)), j = 1, ..., k$.

In the definition of PFSM $M$, in case $D_x$ and $D_y$ are obvious from context or trial, they can be omitted.

For input string $\alpha_i = i_1, ..., i_k(i_j \in I, 1 \leq j \leq k)$, and input parameter string $\alpha_p = x_1, ..., x_k(x_j \in D_x, 1 \leq j \leq k)$, we define their association as $\alpha_i \otimes \alpha_p = i_1(x_1), ..., i_k(x_k)$. The association of output string and output parameter string can be defined similarly.

We only consider *input enabled* PFSM, that is when $dom(\delta) = dom(\lambda) = Q \times I$. A machine can be made input enabled by adding loop back transitions on a state for all those inputs which are not acceptable for that state. Such transitions contain a special symbol $\Omega$ in place of an output from $O$. There may be some transitions in a PFSM model which contain no parameters, i.e., no input parameter value or output parameter value is associated with the respective inputs or outputs on the transitions. An example of PFSM model is given in the Figure 1.

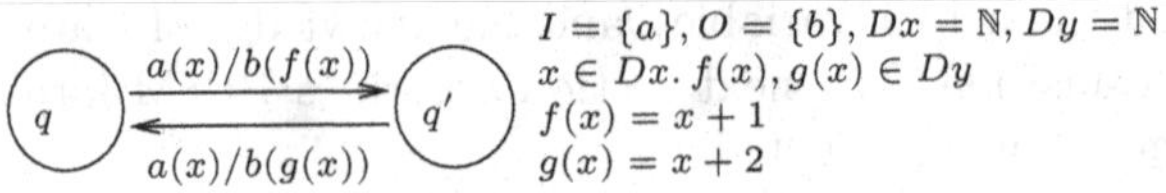

$I = \{a\}, O = \{b\}, Dx = \mathbb{N}, Dy = \mathbb{N}$
$x \in Dx.\, f(x), g(x) \in Dy$
$f(x) = x + 1$
$g(x) = x + 2$

**Fig. 1.** An example of PFSM model

## 2.2   Observation Tables

We assume that the reader is familiar with the original Angluin algorithm [1]. Here we explain our modifications with respect to PFSM inference.

In this work, an unknown PFSM $M = (Q, I, O, D_x, D_y, \delta, \lambda, \sigma, q_0)$ with known input symbols $I$ is used to model a component $C$. Since we can submit any input sequence with parameters to the component and observe the corresponding output sequence with parameters, for any input sequence $\alpha = i_1(x_1), ..., i_k(x_k)(i_j \in I, 1 \le j \le k)$, $\lambda(q_0, \alpha)$ is known. We also assume that each component can be reset to its initial state before each test.

**Basic Structure of Observation Tables.** In the testing procedure, the observed behavior of the component $C$ is recorded into two Observation Tables *Primary Table* (*PT*) and *Auxiliary Table* (*AT*), denoted by $(S, E, T)$ and $(S, E, T')$ respectively. The original Angluin's observation table is reflected in the Primary Table after being adapted in the way proposed in [6], the Auxiliary Table will record information on parameters. $S$ is a nonempty finite prefix-closed set of input strings (representing potential states of the PFSM). $E$ is a nonempty finite suffix-closed set of input strings (separating potential states of the PFSM), but the suffix $\varepsilon$ does not belong to $E$. $T$ is a finite function mapping $((S \cup S \cdot I) \times E)$ to $O^*$. $T'$ is a finite function mapping $((S \cup S \cdot I) \times E)$ to $2^{\{(\alpha_p, \beta_p) | \alpha_p \in D_x^+, \beta_p \in D_y^+\}}$.

In $PT$, for each $s \in (S \cup S \cdot I)$ and $e \in E$, $T(s, e) = t$, $t \in O^*$, such that $|t| = |e|$, and $\lambda(q_0, s \cdot e) = \lambda(q_0, s) \cdot t$.

In $AT$, for each $s \in (S \cup S \cdot I)$ and $e \in E$, if $(\alpha_p, \beta_p) \in T'(s, e), \alpha_p \in D_x^+, \beta_p \in D_y^+$, then $|\alpha_p| = |\beta_p| = |e|$, and $\forall \gamma_p \in D_x^{|s|}$, $\lambda(q_0, (s \cdot e) \otimes (\gamma_p \cdot \alpha_p)) = \lambda(q_0, s \otimes \gamma_p) \cdot (T(s, e) \otimes \beta_p)$.

Initially $S = \{\varepsilon\}$ and $E = I$. These sets are updated during the testing procedure.

Each table can be visualized as a two-dimensional array with rows labelled by the elements of $S \cup S \cdot I$ and columns labelled by the elements of $E$, with the entry for row $s$ and column $e$ equal to $T(s, e)$ and $T'(s, e)$ respectively. For $s \in S \cup S \cdot I$, $row_{PT}(s)$ denotes the finite function $f$ in $PT$ from $E$ to $O^+$ defined by $f(e) = T(s \cdot e)$, $row_{AT}(s)$ denotes the finite function $f'$ in $AT$ from $E$ to $2^{\{(\alpha_p, \beta_p) | \alpha_p \in D_x^+, \beta_p \in D_y^+\}}$ defined by $f'(e) = T'(s \cdot e)$.

**Properties of Observation Tables.** In the original Angluin's algorithm, the strings in $S$ represent candidate states of the automaton being learned. The rows in observation table are compared to differentiate the states in the conjecture. In this work, we follow the principle of Angluin's algorithm and adapt it.

In order to differentiate states in the conjecture, in addition to comparing rows in $PT$, we need to compare rows in $AT$. Since $T'(s,e)$ is a set of parameter string pairs, *compatibility*, rather than *equality*, is used in comparing rows in $AT$. Let $s_1, s_2 \in S \cup S \cdot I$ and $e \in E$, we say two sets $T'(s_1 \cdot e)$ and $T'(s_2 \cdot e)$ are *compatible*, denoted as $T'(s_1 \cdot e) \equiv T'(s_2 \cdot e)$ iff $\forall (\alpha_p, \beta_p) \in T'(s_1 \cdot e), \forall (\alpha'_p, \beta'_p) \in T'(s_2 \cdot e)$, if $\alpha_p = \alpha'_p$ then $\beta_p = \beta'_p$. Two rows in $AT$ are *compatible*, i.e., $row_{AT}(s_1) \equiv row_{AT}(s_2)$ iff $T'(s_1 \cdot e) \equiv T'(s_2 \cdot e), \forall e \in E$. We write $T'(s_1 \cdot e) \not\equiv T'(s_2 \cdot e)$ and $row_{AT}(s_1) \not\equiv row_{AT}(s_2)$ as sets and rows are *incompatible*. For example, $\{(1,2),(2,3)\} \equiv \{(5,6),(2,3)\}$, but $\{(1,2),(2,3)\} \not\equiv \{(2,4),(3,5)\}$.

we define $s_1 \cong s_2$, iff $row_{PT}(s_1) = row_{PT}(s_2) \land row_{AT}(s_1) \equiv row_{AT}(s_2)$.

Let us consider the following example: $s_1, s_2, s_3 \in S \cup S \cdot I$, $E = \{e\}$, and $T(s_1, e) = T(s_2, e) = T(s_3, e)$. $T'(s_1, e) = \{(1,2),(2,3)\}$, $T'(s_2, e) = \{(2,4),(3,5)\}$, and $T'(s_3, e) = \{(5,6)\}$. So, we have $s_1 \cong s_3$, $s_2 \cong s_3$, but $s_1 \not\cong s_2$. In this case, when deriving states from strings in $S$, we know $s_1$ and $s_2$ correspond to different states, e.g., $q_1$ and $q_2$, but we do not know which state $s_3$ corresponds to. This is because in $T'(s_3, e)$ there is not any element in the form of $(2, y)$.

Based on this observation, we introduce the concept of *balanced* observation tables. The observations tables are called *balanced* provided that $\forall s_1, s_2, s_3 \in S \cup S \cdot I$ and $e \in E$, such that $T(s_1, e) = T(s_2, e) = T(s_3, e)$, if $\exists \alpha_p \in D_x{}^+$, $\beta_{p1}, \beta_{p2} \in D_y{}^+$, s.t., $(\alpha_p, \beta_{p1}) \in T'(s_1, e)$, $(\alpha_p, \beta_{p2}) \in T'(s_2, e)$, and $\beta_{p1} \neq \beta_{p2}$, then $\exists \beta_{p3} \in D_y{}^+$, s.t., $(\alpha_p, \beta_{p3}) \in T'(s_3, e)$. In this previous example, if $T'(s_3, e) = \{(5,6),(2,3)\}$, the observation tables are balanced, and $s_1 \cong s_3$, $s_2 \not\cong s_3$, and $s_1 \not\cong s_2$.

Now, we have the following lemma:

**Lemma 1.** *In balanced observation tables, $\cong$ is an equivalence relationship.*

The proof of the lemma can be found in [5].

For $s_1, s_2 \in S \cup S \cdot I$, if $s_1 \cong s_2$ then $s_1$ is in the equivalence class of $s_2$. So we can define $[s]$, $s \in S$ an equivalence class of rows where each row is equivalent to $s$.

Like in original Angluin's algorithm, the observation tables $PT$ and $AT$ are called *closed* if for each $t$ in $S \cdot I$ there exists an $s$ in $S$ such that $t \cong s$. The observation tables $PT$ and $AT$ are called *consistent* if for every $s_1, s_2 \in S$, such that $s_1 \cong s_2$, it holds that $s_1 \cdot i \cong s_2 \cdot i$, for all $i \in I$.

**Making Conjecture from Observation Tables.** When the observation tables $(S, E, T)$ and $(S, E, T')$ are balanced, closed and consistent, a conjectured PFSM $M(S, E, T, T') = (Q, I, O, \delta, \lambda, \sigma, q_0)$ can be made from the tables as follows:

- $Q = \{[s] | s \in S\}$,
- $q_0 = [\varepsilon]$,
- $\delta([s], i) = [s \cdot i]$,

- $\lambda([s], i) = T(s \cdot i)$,
- $\sigma([s], i) = \bigcup_{t \in [s]} T'(t \cdot i)$.

The property of the conjecture is stated in a theorem below. A full proof of the theorem can be seen in the technical report [5].

**Theorem 1.** *If $(S, E, T)$ and $(S, E, T')$ are balanced, closed and consistent observation tables, then the PFSM $M(S, E, T, T')$ is consistent with the primary table $(S, E, T)$ and auxiliary table $(S, E, T')$. Any other PFSM consistent with $(S, E, T)$ and $(S, E, T')$ but inequivalent to $M(S, E, T, T')$ must have more states.*

### 2.3 Unit Testing (Learning) Procedure

The unit testing (learning) procedure is described as follows:

1. Start with $S = \{\varepsilon\}$ and $E = I$. All elements in $PT$ are unknown, and all elements in $AT$ are empty sets.
2. Construct test cases for unknown elements in $PT$, and record the outputs in $PT$ and $AT$. For $s = i_1, ..., i_m \in S \cup S \cdot I$ and $e = i_{m+1}...i_{m+n} \in E$, choose input parameter values from $D_x$ to construct input parameter string $\alpha_p = x_1, ..., x_{m+n}(x_j \in D_x, 1 \leq j \leq m+n)$, provide $(s \cdot e) \otimes \alpha_p$ to the component as test case, and obtain the output $o_1(y_1), ..., o_m(y_m), ..., o_{m+n}(y_{m+n})$. Set $T(s, e) = o_{m+1}, ..., o_{m+n}$, and include $(x_{m+1}, ..., x_{m+n}, y_{m+1}, ..., y_{m+n})$ in $T'(s, e)$.
3. Make $PT$ and $AT$ balanced. Whenever they are not balanced, find $s_1, s_2, s_3 \in S \cup S \cdot I$, $e \in E$, $T(s_1 \cdot e) = T(s_2 \cdot e) = T(s_3 \cdot e)$, $\alpha_p \in D_x^+$, $\beta_{p1}, \beta_{p2} \in D_y^+$, such that $(\alpha_p, \beta_{p1}) \in T'(s_1 \cdot e)$, $(\alpha_p, \beta_{p2}) \in T'(s_2 \cdot e)$, $\beta_{p1} \neq \beta_{p2}$, but $\nexists(\alpha_p, \beta_{p3}) \in T'(s_3 \cdot e)$. Construct $(s_3 \cdot e) \otimes (\gamma_p \cdot \alpha_p)$ as test case in which $\gamma_p$ is any input parameter string of length $|s_3|$. Provide the test case to the component and record the output in $PT$ and $AT$.
4. Check whether $PT$ and $AT$ are closed. If not, find $s_1$ in $S$ and $i$ in $I$ such that $s_1 \cdot i \not\cong s$ for all $s \in S$. Add the string $s_1 \cdot i$ to $S$ in both tables and go back to step 2 to fill missing elements.
5. Check whether $PT$ and $AT$ are consistent. If not, find $s_1$ and $s_2$ in $S$, $e$ in $E$, and $i$ in $I$ such that $s_1 \cong s_2$, but $T(s_1 \cdot i \cdot e) \neq T(s_2 \cdot i \cdot e)$ or $T'(s_1 \cdot i \cdot e) \not\equiv T'(s_2 \cdot i \cdot e)$. Add the string $i \cdot e$ to $E$ in both tables and go back to step 2 to fill missing elements.
6. Now, $PT$ and $AT$ are balanced, closed and consistent. Make conjecture PFSM $M = (S, E, T, T')$.

Balanced, closed and consistent observation tables of the example in the Figure 1 are shown in the Figure 2. In the example, $row_{PT}(\varepsilon) = row_{PT}(a) = row_{PT}(aa)$ because of same output symbol in all rows. On the other hand, $row_{AT}(\varepsilon) \not\equiv row_{AT}(a)$ because of $\alpha_p = 2$ that makes $T'(\varepsilon, a) \neq T'(a, a)$. We also have $row_{AT}(aa) \equiv row_{AT}(\varepsilon)$ and $row_{AT}(aa) \not\equiv row_{AT}(a)$.

| $PT$ | | $AT$ | |
|---|---|---|---|
| | a | | a |
| $\varepsilon$ | b | $\varepsilon$ | (1,2)(2,3) |
| a | b | a | (2,4)(3,5) |
| aa | b | aa | (5,6)(2,3) |

$$f'(x) = \begin{cases} 2, & x = 1 \\ 3, & x = 2 \\ 6, & x = 5 \end{cases}, \quad g'(x) = \begin{cases} 4, & x = 2 \\ 5, & x = 3 \end{cases}$$

**Fig. 2.** Balanced, closed and consistent observation tables of PFSM example in the Figure 1 are shown (left). The learned output parameter functions $f'$ and $g'$ are also shown (right).

So, $\varepsilon \cong aa \not\cong a$, i.e., $[\varepsilon]$ and $[a]$ are two different states. The conjecture from the table corresponds to the PFSM model in the Figure 1. The learned output parameter functions $f'$ and $g'$ are in Figure 2, too.

In integration testing, counterexamples and new input symbols can be identified. The process of dealing with them is similar as described in [6].

## 3 Integration Testing

At the end of unit testing, a conjecture PFSM is obtained for each component. Then the integration testing procedure begins. In this procedure, the components are integrated, and their joint behaviors are tested. Normally, several components can be integrated. The integration testing procedure of two components is illustrated in the following.

Suppose there are two components $M$ and $N$. Their internal structures are not known, so they are considered as two black boxes. Initially, their sets of input symbols are known as $I_M$ and $I_N$, respectively. In the unit testing (learning) of them, the initial models $M^{(1)} = (Q_M, I_M, O_M, \delta_M, \lambda_M, \sigma_M, q_{M0})$ and $N^{(1)} = (Q_N, I_N, O_N, \delta_N, \lambda_N, \sigma_N, q_{N0})$ are constructed.

### 3.1 Integration Testing Procedure

In [6], the integration testing architecture and procedure are described in which the model is Finite State Machine (FSM). In this paper, we follow the principle of [6] and adapt to the PFSM model.

For PFSM $M = (Q_M, I_M, O_M, \delta_M, \lambda_M, \sigma_M, q_{M0})$, we define the projection operator $\downarrow$, which projects $M$ to an FSM $M \downarrow = (Q_M, I_M, O_M, \delta_M, \lambda_M, q_{M0})$. It can be proved that if $M$ is input deterministic and input enabled, $M \downarrow$ is input deterministic and input enabled, too.

In integration testing, a test case is a sequence of tuples in which external input symbol and parameter value, and the expected external output symbol and parameter value are specified. According to the architecture described in [6], when we execute a test case, the external interfaces can be controlled, and all the interfaces can be observed. Thus in addition to comparing the external output symbols and parameter values with expected ones, we also obtain the input and output sequences with parameter values of the two components respectively.

The integration testing procedure can be divided into two stages.

The first stage is similar to Scenario Testing in [6], in which test cases are constructed according to test scenarios. In this work, since a range of input parameters and constraints on output parameter values are specified in test scenarios, the input parameter values are selected according to the ranges during constructing test cases.

In executing the test case, in addition to checking whether the test scenario has been respected, we check whether the observed behaviors conform to the models of components. If there is a discrepancy between the observed behavior of one component and its model, we go back to the unit testing procedure to refine the model with the input sequence as counterexample.

In order to achieve a certain coverage of the ranges specified in test scenarios, each test scenario can yield several test cases. When all the test cases have successfully been executed, we begin the second stage.

In the second stage, test cases are constructed one by one according to a certain test generation strategy. First, following the Integration Testing procedure for FSMs specified in [6], test cases are generated based on $M^{(1)} \downarrow$ and $N^{(1)} \downarrow$. Then, input parameters are selected according to a certain policy to form a complete test case.

Whenever one test case has been generated, we execute it. We check whether the observed behaviors conform to the models of components, and go back to unit testing procedure if counterexample has been found.

This stage and thus the integration testing procedure terminate when the coverage criterion chosen by the test generation strategy is satisfied.

In both stages of the integration testing procedure, after executing a test case and obtaining the real parameterized output string, there are several possibilities:

- The real parameterized output string is exactly the expected one. In this case, we continue to construct and execute the next test case.
- The real parameterized output string is the expected one except for some transitions the executed input parameter values have not been specified in the models. In this case, we record these input/output parameter value pairs in the corresponding cells in $AT$, and update the corresponding output parameter functions in the models. Then, we continue to construct and execute the next test case.
- The real output symbols are the expected ones, but there are some output parameters which are different from expected ones. In this case, we have found a parameter counterexample. We record these input/output parameter value pairs in the corresponding cells in $AT$, go back to unit testing to make the observation tables balanced, closed and consistent, and make another conjecture.
- The real output symbols are different from expected ones. In this case, we have found an I/O counterexample. Or For a certain component, some new input symbols have been produced by other components. For the two cases, we go back to unit testing and follow the process specified in [6].

## 3.2   The Relationship Between Unit Testing and Integration Testing

In unit testing, some input sequences have been executed on a component. Based on the output sequences observed, the closed and consistent observation table has been constructed, and a conjecture of the PFSM has been made.

In integration testing, from the point of view of the component, e.g. $M$, more input sequences are checked. There are several possibilities to introduce "new" information into these sequence:

- Symbols produced by the other component. When being integrated, some outputs of component $N$ are given to component $M$ as inputs. And these symbols may have not been included in $I_M$. So, new input symbols are identified. In our approach, this "mismatch" is identified during integration testing, rather than comparing $O_N$ and $I_M$ directly. Thus, only those symbols which appear in the interaction are considered.
- Parameter values produced by the other component. These values are generated in the integration, and may have not been tried in unit testing.
- Test scenario. In a test scenario, along with the pairs of input and output symbols, the parameter values being interested are provided. And some of the values may have not been used in unit testing.
- The second stage of integration testing. In this stage, more new parameter values are used to uncover the behaviors of the integrated system.

With all these "new" information, more behaviors of the components and the integrated system can be observed in the integration testing procedure.

## 3.3   Result of Integration Testing

At the end of integration testing, for each component, we have a model, which is consistent with all the tests that have been passed. And as stated by Theorem 1, If the component and the model have the same numbers of states, they are equivalent to each other. At the same time, the joint behavior of these components have been systematically tested. Using the approach described in [6], a transition coverage is achieved. Faults could be discovered during integration test execution.

# 4   Example

We illustrate our component integration strategy using a simple example. Suppose an integrator is developing a travel agency web application, in which two components have been identified, i.e., Room Reservation and Travel Agent.

## 4.1   Room Reservation Component

The simplified behavior of the component Room Reservation is as follows. The component starts working when a name of the place is given from the external enviornment. It provides a list of residences depending upon the place it is given. The residence can be either a Hotel or a Guest House. Then it takes one residence as input and outputs a list of room types particular for that residence. When one of the room types is given, the component responds with the list of luxury types offered with the room. When one of the luxury type is provided, the components gives out its corresponding price. Finally, it confirms reservation upon an OK signal.

The component can be described as a PFSM model. The inputs, outputs and associated parameter functions are shown in Figure 3. For simplicity, not all the transitions are shown. For each state, if there is no transition for certain input, the machine outputs $\Omega$ and stays in the state. Also, $D_x$ and $D_y$ may be infinite but the figure shows some of the possible input parameter values and their corresponding output parameter values. The abbreviations used in the example are also given in the figure.

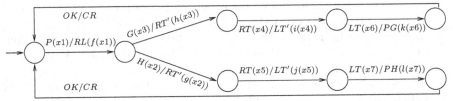

P: Place, H: Hotel, G: Guest House, RT: Room Type, LT: Luxury Type, OK: OK, RL: Residence List, RT': Room Types, LT': Luxury Types, PH: Price for Hotel, PG: Price for Guest House, CR: Confirm Reservation, PAR: Paris, LDN: London, Htn: Hilton Hotel, Sh: Sherton Hotel, YR: Youth Residence (Guest House), Vil: Villa (Guest House), Sgl: Single, Dbl: Double, Std: Standard, Dlx: Delux, Exe: Executive, Stu: Studio, Dor: Dormitory.

x1: Place Name as PAR, LDN, ...       f(x1): List of Residencies for place x1 as {Htn,Sh,YR,Vil,...}
x2: Hotel Name as Htn, Sh, ...         g(x2): List of Room Types for Hotel x2 as {Sgl,Dbl,...}
x3: Guest House Names as YR, Vil ...    h(x3): List of Room Types for Guest House x3 as {Sgl,Dbl,Dor,...}
x4: Guest House Room Type as Sgl, Dor, ...  i(x4): List of Luxury Types for Guest House Room Type x4 as {Std,Dlx,Stu,...}
x5: Hotel Room Type as Sgl, Dbl, ...    j(x5): List of Luxury Types for Hotel Room Type x5 as {Std,Dlx,Exe,...}
x6: Guest House Luxury Type as Std, Dlx, Stu, ...  k(x6): Cost for Guest House Luxury Type x7 as 50$,60$,...
x7: Hotel Luxury Type as Std, Dlx, Exe, ...   l(x7): Cost for Hotel Luxury Type x7 as 50$,60$,...

**Fig. 3.** PFSM model of Room Reservation Component

## 4.2    Unit Testing of Room Reservation Component

In the unit testing procedure, the component Room Reservation is considered as a black box and $I_M^{(1)}$ is known as $\{P, H, G, RT, LT, OK\}$. The *Learner* constructs tables $PT$ and $AT$ for the component. Initially $S = \{\varepsilon\}$, $E = I_M^{(1)}$. The tester execute several test cases with different input parameter values from $D_x$ to fill the tables. Finally when the observation tables are balanced, closed and consistent, a conjecture is made. The Figure 4 shows $PT$ for Room Reservation component. The corresponding $AT$ is shown in the Figure 5. For sake of simplicity, the rows which contain $\Omega$ in all columns of the table are omitted. The figure 6 (right) shows the conjecture accompanied by the input and output parameter values used during the unit testing.

|  | P | H | G | RT | LT | OK |
|---|---|---|---|---|---|---|
| ε | RL | Ω | Ω | Ω | Ω | Ω |
| P | Ω | RT' | RT' | Ω | Ω | Ω |
| P-H | Ω | Ω | LT' | Ω | Ω |  |
| P-H-RT | Ω | Ω | Ω | Ω | PH | Ω |
| P-H-RT-LT | Ω | Ω | Ω | Ω | Ω | CR |
| P-G | Ω | Ω | LT' | Ω | Ω | Ω |
| P-H-RT-LT-OK | RL | Ω | Ω | Ω | Ω | Ω |

**Fig. 4.** Primary Table $(PT)$ for Room Reservation Component

|  | P | H | G | RT | LT | OK |
|---|---|---|---|---|---|---|
| ε | (PAR,{Htn,YR}) (LDN,{Sh,Vil}) | Ω | Ω | Ω | Ω | Ω |
| P | Ω | (Htn,{Sgl}) (Sh,{Sgl,Dbl}) | (YR, {Sgl,Dor}) | Ω | Ω |  |
| P-H | Ω | Ω | Ω | (Sgl,{Std,Dlx}) (Dbl,{Std,Exe}) | Ω | Ω |
| P-G | Ω | Ω | Ω | (Sgl,{Std,Dlx}) | Ω | Ω |
| P-H-RT | Ω | Ω | Ω | Ω | (Std,50$) (Dlx,70$) | Ω |
| P-H-RT-LT | Ω | Ω | Ω | Ω | Ω | Ω |
| P-H-RT-LT-OK | (PAR,{Htn,YR}) | Ω | Ω | Ω | Ω | Ω |

**Fig. 5.** Auxiliary Table $(AT)$ corresponding to Primary Table in figure 4

### 4.3  Travel Agent Component

The component $N$ of the web application is a Travel Agent. On one side, it accepts inputs from the user and on the other side, it communicates with some back end system. The simplified behavior of the Travel Agent component is as follows. It takes a place name from user and transmits it to the back end. Later, it takes the list of residences from the back end and displays it to the user. The user inputs one of the residences, i.e., Hotel or Guest House, which is then transmitted to the back end. The back end responds with the list of room types for the provided residence. The component selects and resends one of the room types to the back end which then provides the list of luxury types associated with that room type. Once the luxury type is selected, the Travel Agent asks the back end for its price. It shows the corresponding price to the user after increasing it by 10% for its commission. When the user selects OK, the component asks the back end for confirmation, and finally the confirmation message is sent to the user.

The unit testing of Travel Agent component is performed with $I_N^{(1)} = \{UI\_P, RL, UI\_H, UI\_G, RT', LT', PH, PG, UI\_OK, CR\}$. The symbols starting with "UI_" are inputs from user, and symbols starting with "UO_" are outputs to user. A conjecture in the Figure 6 (left) is made when observation tables of the component are found balanced, closed and consistent. The input parameters used in the unit testing and their corresponding output parameters are also given in the figure.

### 4.4 Integration Testing

In the integration testing, the two components are connected to each other. In this case, all the inputs of component Room Reservation come from component Travel Agent. The component Room Reservation is considered as a back end for Travel Agent which also accepts the inputs from the user. The integration of the learned models of the two components is shown in the Figure 6.

In the procedure, the test input $P(LDN)$ is given to the component Travel Agent, which transmits it to the component Room Reservation. The component produces a list of residences as $RL(\{Htn, YR\})$ and sends back to Travel Agent component, which shows the list to user. The user selects a guest house $YR$ from the list and provides a second input to the integrated system. The component Travel Agent then sends input $G(YR)$ to the component Room Reservation, and it continues working according to the models in the Figure 6. According to the real component of Room Reservation in the Figure 3, the output sequence produced from an input sequence $P(PAR) - G(YR) - RT(Sgl) - LT(Std)$ is $RL(\{Htn, YR\}) - RT'(\{Sgl, Dor\}) - LT'(\{Std, Dlx\}) - PG(50\$)$, but the learned model does not show the output symbol $PG$. Hence, a divergence is found between the real component and its conjecture. In this case, the above input sequence is treated as a counterexample for Room Reservation component which will be learned again with the help of unit testing. When the observation tables are found balanced, closed and consistent, a new conjecture is made which is equivalent to that in the Figure 3. The conjecture is then integrated with Travel Agent component to complete integration testing.

Apart from the counterexample explained above, the example has other counterexamples with respect to the parameter values. For instance, the component Travel Agent contains some parameter values which can be input from the component Room Reservation, but the learned parameter functions of component Room Reservation are unable to produce those values. As an example, the component Travel Agent expects a guest house named $Vil$ from user, when the list of residences from component Room Reservation is provided. The testing proceeds with the list of room types provided from component Room Reservation, from which $RT(Dbl)$ is selected by the component Travel Agent. The response from the actual component of Room Reservation can be $RT'(\{Std, Stu\})$, which is seen in the output parameter function $q$ of the learned model of Travel Agent component, but function $v$ of the learned model of Room Reservation component is unable to produce. This is because, the component Room Reservation is never tested with residence $Vil$ in its unit testing. Thus, the input sequence $P(LDN) - G(Vil) - RT(Dbl)$ can be treated as a counterexample for this component. In the following unit testing, observation tables will be updated and a new conjecture will be made.

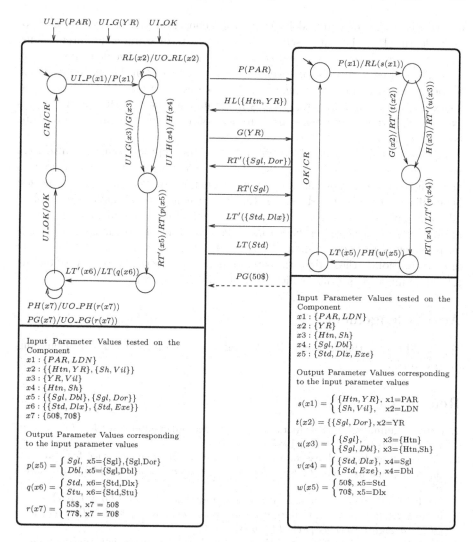

**Fig. 6.** Integration of PFSM Models of Travel Agent (left) and Room Reservation (right) Components - The dotted line between the components shows missing output from Room Reservation Component

## 5   Conclusion

In this paper, we propose to use automata learning algorithms as a means to alleviate the absence of models for components, in a model-based testing approach. As in previous related work [3,4], we adapt Angluin's algorithm [1] to a testing context, in an incremental approach. Our contribution extends this approach in two directions. First, we use the models to drive integration testing. Since the models are derived from testing observations, they cannot by themselves constitute oracles or a sound basis for the generation of tests for the components learnt. But they are used to drive the tests of component interactions: partial models learnt for isolated components provide a convenient abstraction that can be used as a basis for covering the sequences of component interactions. Secondly, we extend the learning algorithm to a model where we deal with parameterized inputs and outputs. This is motivated by the fact that actual values exchanged during interactions are a major source of interoperability problems between components.

[2] proposes an extension to Angluin's algorithm where actions can also have parameters, represented by a combination of boolean values. Our algorithm does not include any bound on the domain of parameters, and we introduce the notion of auxiliary table in the algorithm to deal with it without having to explore all combinations. However, in contrast, our model does not include guards on parameters. We are currently working on an extension to include predicates on parameters to trigger different transitions. We are also working towards an implementation of these algorithms to adapt to the practical problems of testing telecommunication services which provided our framework.

## Acknowledgement

We would like to thank Alexandre Petrenko (CRIM) for our fruitful discussions on this topic.

## References

1. Dana Angluin. Learning regular sets from queries and counterexamples. *Information and Computation*, 2:87–106, 1987.
2. Therese Berg, Bengt Jonsson, and Harald Raffelt. Regular inference for state machines with parameters. *Lecture Notes in Computer Science*, 3922:107–121, March 2006.
3. Edith Elkind, Blaise Genest, Doron Peled, and Hongyang Qu. Grey box checking. In *26th IFIP WG 6.1 International Conference on Formal Models for Networked and Distributed Systems (FORTE 2006)*, 2006.
4. Hardi Hungar, Oliver Niese, and Bernhard Steffen. Domain-specific optimization in automata learning. In *CAV*, pages 315–327, 2003.
5. Keqin Li, Roland Groz, and Muzammil Shahbaz. Inference of parameterized finite state machine - technical report. Technical report, Laboratoire Logiciels Systèmes Réseaux, http://www-lsr.imag.fr/Les.Groupes/VASCO/publi-2006.htm, 2006.
6. Keqin Li, Roland Groz, and Muzammil Shahbaz. Integration testing of components guided by incremental state machine learning. In *Testing: Academic & Industrial Conference - Practice And Research Techniques (TAIC PART)*, 2006.
7. Erkki Mäkinen and Tarja Systä. Mas - an interactive synthesizer to support behavioral modelling in uml. In *ICSE '01: Proceedings of the 23rd International Conference on Software Engineering*, pages 15–24, Washington, DC, USA, 2001. IEEE Computer Society.
8. Stephane S. Somé. Beyond scenarios: generating state models from use cases. In *Proceedings of SCESM'02*, 2002.

# Minimizing Coordination Channels in Distributed Testing

Guy-Vincent Jourdan[1], Hasan Ural[1], and Hüsnü Yenigün[2]

[1] School of Information Technology and Engineering (SITE)
University of Ottawa
800 King Edward Avenue
Ottawa, Ontario, Canada, K1N 6N5
{gvj, ural}@site.uottawa.ca
[2] Faculty of Engineering and Natural Sciences
Sabancı University
Tuzla, Istanbul, Turkey 34956
yenigun@sabanciuniv.edu

**Abstract.** Testing may be used to show that a system under test conforms to its specification. In the case of a distributed system, one may have to use a distributed test architecture, involving $p$ testers in order to test the system under test. These $p$ testers may under some circumstances have to coordinate their actions with each other using external coordination channels. This may require the use of up to $p^2 - p$ unidirectional coordination channels in the test architecture, which can be an extensive and expensive setup. In this paper, we propose a method to generate checking sequences while minimizing the number of required coordination channels, by adapting existing methods that generate checking sequences to be applied in a centralized test architecture. We consider the case of unidirectional and bidirectional coordination channels, and the case of transitive coordination.

## 1 Introduction

One way to check the conformance of an implementation to a specification is to employ a *checking sequence* [1, 2]. Several methods have been proposed over the last two decades to reduce the length of these checking sequences, e.g. [3, 4, 5, 6], but all of these methods focus on centralized systems. When testing distributed systems, a tester is placed at each port (interface) of the system to form a distributed test architecture. During the application of a checking sequence within a distributed test architecture, the existence of multiple remote testers brings out the possibility of two types of coordination problems among testers: *controllability* and *observability* problems. These problems occur if a tester cannot determine either when to apply a particular input to a system under test (SUT), or whether a particular output from a SUT is generated in response to a specific input, respectively.

*Controllability* refers to the ease of affecting the specified outputs. A *controllability (synchronization) problem* exists when a tester is required to send an

E. Najm et al. (Eds.): FORTE 2006, LNCS 4229, pp. 451–466, 2006.

input in the current transition, and because it is not *involved* in the previous transition, i.e., it did not send the input or receive the output in the previous transition, it does not know when to send the input to the SUT.

*Observability* refers to the ease of determining if specified inputs affect the outputs. An *observability problem* exists when a tester is expecting to receive an output from the SUT in response to either the previous input or the current input and because it did not send the current input, it does not know when to start or stop waiting for the output.

Several possible venues have been explored to deal with these problems. Some authors have provided necessary and sufficient conditions to avoid controllability and/or observability problems [7, 8]. When these problems cannot be avoided, coordination among the remote testers is required through external coordination message exchanges [9, 10, 11, 12, 13, 14, 15, 16, 17, 18, 19]. Other authors have proposed techniques to minimize these coordination messages necessary to facilitate the application of a checking sequence in a distributed test architecture [14, 20, 21].

In this paper, we look at the use of external coordination messages from a different point of view: we adapt the algorithm of [4] to distributed testing and attempt to minimize the *number* of coordination channels required to perform the test. If $p$ testers are involved in a distributed test architecture, potentially every pair of testers will need to exchange a coordination message at one point or another, thus leading to a need of $p^2 - p$ unidirectional coordination channels to be added to the test environment. This can potentially require an extensive and expensive setup just to run the test. Our goal is thus to require as few coordination channels as possible, in contrast to exchanging as few external coordination messages as possible. Once a channel has been set up, one would use it for exchanging as many external coordination messages as necessary rather than incurring the cost of setting up additional channels.

The rest of the paper is organized as follows: Section 2 gives the preliminaries. Section 3 reviews the checking sequence generation algorithm that will be modified to generate a checking sequence while minimizing the number coordination channels required. Section 4 presents the proposed approach. Section 5 gives the concluding remarks.

## 2    Preliminaries

A multiport deterministic FSM $M$ is defined by a tuple

$$(S, s_1, p, X_1, X_2, \ldots, X_p, \delta, Y_1, Y_2, \ldots, Y_p, \lambda_1, \lambda_2, \ldots, \lambda_p)$$

in which $S$ is a finite set of *states*, $s_1 \in S$ is the *initial state*. The number of states of $M$ is denoted $n$ and the states of $M$ are enumerated, giving $S = \{s_1, \ldots, s_n\}$. $p \geq 1$ is an integer which gives the number of ports of $M$, and the set of ports of $M$ is denoted $[p]$ to denote the set $\{1, 2, \ldots, p\}$.

$X_i$ is the set of input symbols on port $i$ such that for $j \in [p]$ and $j \neq i$, $X_i \cap X_j = \emptyset$. In other words, the input sets of the ports are disjoint. We use $X = \cup_{i \in [p]} X_i$ to denote the set of all input symbols.

$\delta : S \times X \rightarrow S$ is the *next state function*. If $s' = \delta(s, x)$ for states $s, s' \in S$ and $x \in X_i$ for some $i \in [p]$, this means that, when the machine $M$ is in state $s$, and input $x$ is applied at port $i$, then the machine will transfer to state $s'$.

$Y_i$ is the set of output symbols on port $i$ such that for $i, j \in [p]$ if $i \neq j$ then $Y_i \cap Y_j = \{-\}$, where $-$ is null output.

$\lambda_i : S \times X \rightarrow Y_i$ is the *output function on port $i$*. Intuitively, if $M$ is at a state $s$, and an input $x \in X$ is applied to $M$, then the output $\lambda_i(s, x)$ is observed at port $i$, unless $\lambda_i(s, x) = -$. Let $Y$ denote the set $Y_1 \times Y_2 \times \cdots \times Y_p \setminus (-, -, \ldots, -)$. We will also use the *output function* $\lambda : S \times X \rightarrow Y$, which is defined as $\lambda(s, x) = (\lambda_1(s, x), \lambda_2(s, x), \ldots, \lambda_p(s, x))$. We use $y|_i$ to denote the output at port $i \in [p]$ in $y \in Y$. The functions $\delta$ and $\lambda$ can be extended to input sequences in a straightforward manner.

An FSM, that will be denoted $M_0$ throughout this paper, is shown in Figure 1. Here, $S = \{s_1, s_2, s_3, s_4, s_5\}$, $X_1 = \{a\}$, $X_2 = \{b\}$, $X_3 = \{c\}$ and $Y_1 = \{1\}$, $Y_2 = \{2\}$, $Y_3 = \{3\}$.

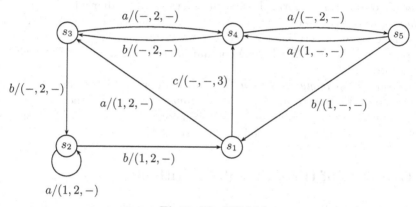

**Fig. 1.** The FSM $M_0$

Throughout the paper, we use barred symbols (e.g. $\bar{x}, \bar{P}, \ldots$) to denote sequences, and juxtaposition to denote concatenation. In an FSM $M$, $s_i \in S$ and $s_j \in S$, $s_i \neq s_j$, are *equivalent* if, $\forall \bar{x} \in X^*$, $\lambda(s_i, \bar{x}) = \lambda(s_j, \bar{x})$. If $\exists \bar{x} \in X^*$ such that $\lambda(s_i, \bar{x}) \neq \lambda(s_j, \bar{x})$ then $\bar{x}$ is said to *distinguish* $s_i$ from $s_j$. An FSM $M$ is said to be *minimal* if none of its states are equivalent. A *distinguishing sequence* for an FSM $M$ is an input sequence $\bar{D}$ for which each state of $M$ produces a distinct output. More formally, for all $s_i, s_j \in S$ if $s_i \neq s_j$ then $\lambda(s_i, \bar{D}) \neq \lambda(s_j, \bar{D})$. Thus, for example, $M_0$ has distinguishing sequence $ab$.

An FSM $M$ can be represented by a directed graph (*digraph*) $G = (V, E)$ where a set of vertices $V$ represents the set $S$ of states of $M$, and a set of directed edges $E$ represents all transitions of $M$. Each edge $e = (v_j, v_k, x/y) \in E$ represents a transition $t = (s_j, s_k, x/y)$ of $M$ from state $s_j$ to state $s_k$ with input $x$ and output $y$ where $s_j, s_k \in S$, $x \in X$, and $y \in Y$ such that $\delta(s_j, x) = s_k$, $\lambda(s_j, x) = y$. For a vertex $v \in V$ and $E' \subseteq E$, *indegree*$_{E'}(v)$ denotes the number of edges from $E'$ that enter $v$ and *outdegree*$_{E'}(v)$ denotes the number of edges from $E'$ that leave $v$.

A sequence $\bar{P} = (n_1, n_2, x_1/y_1)(n_2, n_3, x_2/y_2) \ldots (n_{k-1}, n_k, x_{k-1}/y_{k-1})$ of pairwise adjacent edges from $G$ forms a *path* in which each *node* $n_i$ represents a vertex from $V$ and thus, ultimately, a state from $S$. Here $initial(\bar{P})$ denotes $n_1$, which is the *initial node* of $\bar{P}$, and $final(\bar{P})$ denotes $n_k$, which is the *final node* of $\bar{P}$. The sequence $\bar{Q} = (x_1/y_1)(x_2/y_2) \ldots (x_{k-1}/y_{k-1})$ is the *label* of $\bar{P}$ and is denoted $label(\bar{P})$. $\bar{Q}$ is said to be a *transfer sequence* from $n_1$ to $n_k$. The path $\bar{P}$ can be represented by the tuple $(n_1, n_k, \bar{Q})$ or by the tuple $(n_1, n_k, \bar{x}/\bar{y})$ in which $\bar{x} = x_1 x_2 \ldots x_{k-1}$ is the *input portion* of $\bar{Q}$ and $\bar{y} = y_1 y_2 \ldots y_{k-1}$ is the *output portion* of $\bar{Q}$. The *cost* of a path is given as the number of pairs of input/output symbols in its label. Two paths $\bar{P}_1$ and $\bar{P}_2$ can be concatenated as $\bar{P}_1 \bar{P}_2$ only if $final(\bar{P}_1) = initial(\bar{P}_2)$.

A *tour* is a path whose initial and final nodes are the same. Given a tour $\bar{\Gamma} = e_1 e_2 \ldots e_k$, $\bar{P} = e_j e_{j+1} \ldots e_k e_1 e_2 \ldots e_{j-1}$ is a path formed by *starting* $\bar{\Gamma}$ with edge $e_j$, and hence by *ending* $\bar{\Gamma}$ with edge $e_{j-1}$. An *Euler Tour* of $G$ is a tour that contains each edge of $G$ exactly once. A set $E'$ of edges from $G$ is *acyclic* if no tour can be formed using the edges in $E'$. A digraph $G = (V, E)$ is *symmetric* if for each vertex $v \in V$, $indegree_E(v) = outdegree_E(v)$. A *minimum-cost symmetric augmentation* $G' = (V, E')$ of a graph $G = (V, E)$ is a symmetric digraph where $E' = E \cup \Delta$, where $\Delta$ contains a minimum number of replications of some edges in $E$.

A digraph is *strongly connected* if for any ordered pair of vertices $(v_i, v_j)$ there is a path from $v_i$ to $v_j$. An FSM is *strongly connected* if the digraph that represents it is strongly connected. It will be assumed that any FSM considered in this paper is deterministic, minimal, and strongly connected.

## 3    Overview of the Original Algorithm

In this section, we will present an existing approach for generating reduced length checking sequences [4]. The method, in its original form, does not take into account the fact that the resulting checking sequence will be applied in a distributed test architecture. To apply it on a distributed test architecture, external coordination messages must be inserted into the checking sequence. Hence, it may be used to generate a checking sequence applicable within a distributed test architecture which uses more coordination channels than it may actually be needed. We will show in the next section how to modify the method to generate checking sequences minimizing the number of coordination channels required.

Let $M$ be an FSM and let $N$ be an implementation of $M$. A *checking sequence* is a sequence of inputs to be applied to $N$ that will help determine whether $N$ is a correct implementation of $M$ or not, i.e. whether $N$ is isomorphic to $M$ or not [1]. If $M$ has a distinguishing sequence $\bar{D}$, then $\bar{D}$ can be used in the checking sequence to help to identify the states. Let us call $\bar{T}_i = \bar{D}/\lambda(s_i, \bar{D})\bar{B}_i$ a *T–sequence*, where $\bar{B}_i = \bar{I}_i/\lambda(\delta(s_i, \bar{D}), \bar{I}_i)$ for a possibly empty input sequence $\bar{I}_i$ (i.e. the input portion of a transfer sequence). We call $initial(T)$ (resp. $final(T)$) the first (resp. last) state of the sequence $T$. An $\alpha'$–*sequence* is a sequence $\bar{T}_{k_1} \bar{T}_{k_2} \ldots \bar{T}_{k_{r_k}}$, for some $1 \le k_1, k_2, \ldots, k_{r_k} \le n$, such that $\forall i \in \{1, 2, \ldots, r_k - 1\}$, $initial(\bar{T}_{k_{i+1}}) =$

$final(\bar{T}_{k_i})$. A $T$-set is a set of $T$-sequences, and an $\alpha'$-set is a set of $\alpha'$-sequences $\{\bar{\alpha}'_1, \bar{\alpha}'_2, \dots, \bar{\alpha}'_q\}$ satisfying the following condition [4]: for all $i \in \{1, 2, \dots, n\}$, there exists $j \in \{1, 2, \dots, n\}$ and $k \in \{1, 2, \dots, q\}$, such that $\bar{T}_i \bar{T}_j$ is a subsequence of $\bar{\alpha}'_k$.

In [4], the following method is explained to produce a checking sequence. Given a digraph $G = (V, E)$ corresponding to an FSM $M$, a $T$-set $T = \{\bar{T}_1, \bar{T}_2, \dots, \bar{T}_n\}$, and an $\alpha'$-set $A = \{\bar{\alpha}'_1, \bar{\alpha}'_2, \dots, \bar{\alpha}'_q\}$, first another digraph $G' = (V', E')$ is produced by augmenting the digraph $G$ as follows (Figure 2 is the digraph $G'$ corresponding to the digraph $G$ of FSM $M_0$ given in Figure 1, where the input portion of $\bar{T}_1, \bar{T}_2, \bar{T}_3, \bar{T}_4$ and $\bar{T}_5$ is $ab$):

a) $V' = V \cup U'$ where $U' = \{v' : v \in V\}$, i.e. for each vertex $v$ in $G$, there are two copies of $v$ in $G'$. In Figure 2, the nodes at the bottom are the nodes in $V$, and the nodes at the top are the nodes in $U'$.

b) $E' = E_C \cup E_T \cup E_{\alpha'} \cup E''$ where
   i) $E_C = \{(v'_i, v_j, x/y) : (v_i, v_j, x/y) \in E\}$. The solid edges leaving the nodes at the top in Figure 2 are the edges in $E_C$.
   ii) $E_T = \{(v_i, v'_j, \bar{T}_i) : \bar{T}_i \in T, s_i = initial(\bar{T}_i), s_j = final(\bar{T}_i)\}$. In Figure 2, these edges are shown with dashed lines.
   iii) $E_{\alpha'} = \{(v_i, v'_j, \bar{\alpha}'_k) : \bar{\alpha}'_k \in A, \bar{\alpha}'_k = \bar{T}_i \dots \bar{T}_j, initial(\bar{T}_i) = s_i, final(\bar{T}_j) = s_j\}$. For example, in Figure 2 we consider an $\alpha'$-set $A = \{\bar{\alpha}'_1 = \bar{T}_4 \bar{T}_1 \bar{T}_2 \bar{T}_1, \bar{\alpha}'_2 = \bar{T}_5 \bar{T}_3 \bar{T}_3\}$. The bold solid edges in Figure 2 are the edges of $E_{\alpha'}$.
   iv) $E'' \subseteq \{(v'_i, v'_j, x/y) : (v_i, v_j, x/y) \in E\}$. $E''$ is a subset of the copies of the edges in $E$ placed between the corresponding nodes in $U'$. $E''$ is selected in such a way that, $G'' = (U', E'')$ does not have a tour and $G'$ is strongly connected. These edges are shown in Figure 2 with dotted lines.

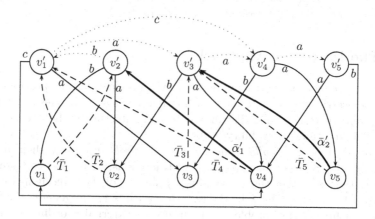

**Fig. 2.** $G'$ for $M_0$, with outputs omitted. The edges in $E_{\alpha'}$, $E_C$, $E_T$, and $E''$ are shown as bold solid lines, solid lines, dashed lines, and dotted lines, respectively.

In [4], it is shown that the input portion of the label of a path $\bar{P}$ in $G'$ that starts from $v_1$ and ends at $v_1$, that includes all the edges in $E_{\alpha'}$, and all the edges in $E_C$ (that is, the solid lines in Figure 2) and that is followed by $\bar{D}$ is a checking sequence of $M$.

In order to reduce the length of the resulting checking sequence, an optimization algorithm may be used. The method given in [4] forms a minimum-cost symmetric augmentation $G^*$ of the digraph induced by $E_{\alpha'} \cup E_C$ by adding replications of edges from $E'$. If $G^*$, with its isolated vertices removed, is connected, then $G^*$ has an Euler tour. Otherwise, a heuristic such as the one given in [3] is applied to make $G^*$ connected and an Euler tour of this new digraph is formed to find a path from $v_1$ to $v_1$. A checking sequence is then constructed based on the Euler tour as the input portion of the label of the path from $v_1$ to $v_1$ followed by $\bar{D}$.

$(s_1, s_3, a/(1, 2, -))$ $\quad$ $(s_3, s_2, b/(-, 2, -))$ $\quad$ $(s_2, s_1, b/(1, 2, -))$ $\quad$ $(s_1, s_3, a/(1, 2, -))$
$(s_3, s_2, b/(-, 2, -)) \star (s_2, s_2, a/(1, 2, -))$ $\quad$ $(s_2, s_2, a/(1, 2, -))$ $\quad$ $(s_2, s_1, b/(1, 2, -)) \star$
$(s_1, s_4, c/(-, -, 3)) \star (s_4, s_5, a/(-, 2, -))$ $\quad$ $(s_5, s_1, b/(1, -, -))$ $\quad$ $(s_1, s_3, a/(1, 2, -))$
$(s_3, s_2, b/(-, 2, -)) \star (s_2, s_2, a/(1, 2, -))$ $\quad$ $(s_2, s_1, b/(1, 2, -))$ $\quad$ $(s_1, s_3, a/(1, 2, -))$
$(s_3, s_2, b/(-, 2, -))$ $\quad$ $(s_2, s_1, b/(1, 2, -))$ $\quad$ $(s_1, s_3, a/(1, 2, -))$ $\quad$ $(s_3, s_2, b/(-, 2, -)) \star$
$(s_2, s_2, a/(1, 2, -))$ $\quad$ $(s_2, s_1, b/(1, 2, -))$ $\quad$ $(s_1, s_3, a/(1, 2, -))$ $\quad$ $(s_3, s_4, a/(-, 2, -))$
$(s_4, s_3, b/(-, 2, -)) \star (s_3, s_4, a/(-, 2, -))$ $\quad$ $(s_4, s_5, a/(-, 2, -))$ $\quad$ $(s_5, s_1, b/(-, 2, -)) \star$
$(s_1, s_4, c/(-, -, 3)) \star (s_4, s_3, b/(-, 2, -)) \star (s_3, s_4, a/(-, 2, -))$ $\quad$ $(s_4, s_3, b/(-, 2, -)) \star$
$(s_3, s_4, a/(-, 2, -))$ $\quad$ $(s_4, s_5, a/(-, 2, -))$ $\quad$ $(s_5, s_4, a/(1, -, -)) \star (s_4, s_3, b/(-, 2, -)) \star$
$(s_3, s_4, a/(-, 2, -))$ $\quad$ $(s_4, s_3, b/(-, 2, -)) \star (s_3, s_4, a/(-, 2, -))$ $\quad$ $(s_4, s_3, b/(-, 2, -)) \star$
$(s_3, s_4, a/(-, 2, -))$ $\quad$ $(s_4, s_5, a/(-, 2, -))$ $\quad$ $(s_5, s_4, a/(1, -, -))$ $\quad$ $(s_4, s_5, a/(-, 2, -))$
$(s_5, s_1, b/(1, -, -)) \star (s_1, s_4, c/(-, -, 3)) \star (s_4, s_5, a/(-, 2, -))$ $\quad$ $(s_5, s_1, b/(1, -, -))$
$(s_1, s_3, a/(1, 2, -))$ $\quad$ $(s_3, s_2, b/(-, 2, -))$

**Fig. 3.** The transition sequence on FSM $M_0$ (given in Figure 1) corresponding to the checking sequence produced from $G'$ (given in Figure 2). Two consecutive transitions with a $\star$ between them have a synchronization problem.

## 4   The Proposed Approach

A checking sequence constructed by the method reviewed in the previous section requires insertion of the external coordination message exchanges to be applicable by remote testers in a distributed test architecture without encountering controllability and observability problems.

Formally, a (controllability) synchronization problem occurs when, in the labels $x_i/y_i$ and $x_j/y_j$ of any two adjacent transitions, there exists a tester $l$ that sends $x_j$ that is neither the one sending $x_i$ nor one of those receiving an output belonging to $y_i$. Let tester $k$ be the tester that sends $x_i$. In general, the solution to the synchronization problem is to insert an external coordination message exchange relating to controllability between $x_i/y_i$ and $x_j/y_j$ from tester $k$ to tester $l$ to notify tester $l$ to send its input to the SUT [15].

Any two consecutive transitions $t_{ij}$ and $t_{jk}$ whose labels are $x_i/y_i$ and $x_j/y_j$ in a sequence of transitions form a synchronizable pair of transitions if $t_{jk}$ can follow $t_{ij}$ without generating a synchronization problem. Any sequence of transitions in which every pair of consecutive transitions is synchronizable is called a *synchronizable transition sequence*. An input/output sequence is said to be *synchronizable* if it is the label of a synchronizable transition sequence.

The observability problem manifests itself as an undetectable *output shift fault*. Formally, given a synchronizable transition sequence $t_1 \ldots t_k$ of $M$ with label $x_1/y_1 \; x_2/y_2 \ldots x_k/y_k$, an *output shift fault* in an implementation $N$ of $M$ exists if one of the following holds for some $1 \le i < j \le k$:

1. There exists $m \in [p]$ and $y_i|_m = o \in Y_m \setminus \{-\}$ in $M$, for all $i < l \le j$ we have that $y_l|_m = -$ in $M$, for all $i \le l < j$ we have that $N$ produces output $-$ at $m$ in response to $x_l$ after $x_1 \ldots x_{l-1}$, and $N$ produces output $o$ at $m$ in response to $x_j$ after $x_1 \ldots x_{j-1}$. Here the output $o$ shifts from being produced in response to $x_i$ to being produced in response to $x_j$ and the (forward) shift is from $t_i$ to $t_j$.
2. There exists $m \in [p]$ and $o \in Y_m \setminus \{-\}$ such that $y_j|_m = o$ in $M$, for all $i \le l < j$ we have that $y_l|_m = -$ in $M$, for all $i < l \le j$ we have that $N$ produces output $-$ at $m$ in response to $x_l$ after $x_1 \ldots x_{l-1}$, and $N$ produces output $o$ at $m$ in response to $x_i$ after $x_1 \ldots x_{i-1}$. Here the output $o$ shifts from being produced in response to $x_j$ to being produced in response to $x_i$ and the (backward) shift is from $t_j$ to $t_i$.

An instance of the observability problem manifests itself as a *potentially undetectable output shift fault* if there is an output shift fault related to $o \in Y_m$ in two transitions with labels $x_i/y_i$ and $x_j/y_j$, such that $x_{i+1} \ldots x_j \notin X_m$. The tester at $m$ will not be able to detect the faults since it will observe the expected sequence of interactions in response to $x_i \ldots x_j$. Let tester $h$ be the tester that sends $x_j$. In general, the solution to the observability problem is to insert an external coordination message exchange relating to observability between $x_i/y_i$ and $x_j/y_j$ from tester $h$ to tester $m$:

- Case 1: $(y_i|_m = o$ in $M)$ By this exchange, tester $h$ informs tester $m$ that it must have received an output from the SUT by now.
- Case 2: $(y_j|_m = o$ in $M)$ By this exchange, tester $h$ informs tester $m$ to expect receiving an output from the SUT [15].

In most cases, insertion of an external coordination message exchange relating to observability can be avoided by appending additional input/output subsequences to the label of the path whose input portion will be used as a checking sequence [8]. Therefore, we will focus only on the controllability problem in the rest of the paper.

The algorithm in [4] is intended for a centralized test architecture, and hence in a distributed test architecture, some portions of the sequence generated by the algorithm may lead to synchronization problems. We thus need to adapt the algorithm to the distributed test architecture by modifying it in two ways: on one hand, we try to select checking sequences that do not cause synchronization problems (recognizing the fact that they might then be longer than the ones requiring synchronization); on the other end we need to add some coordination channels, when a synchronization problem cannot be avoided directly.

Note that there can be different types of coordination channels (unidirectional or bidirectional) and the relaying of coordination messages through other testers using available coordination channels (transitive coordinations between testers) may or may not be allowed. We will first examine the case of unidirectional coordination channels without transitive communications. The other cases will be explored in Section 4.3.

## 4.1  Modifying the Digraph $G'$

Briefly, our approach consists of modifying the digraph $G'$ being built so that only possible (synchronizable) transition sequences are available, and use that modified digraph to build a checking sequence in which no controllability problem exists. If it is not possible to generate a checking sequence with the current form of the digraph, then additional coordination channels are added (which in turn modifies the digraph and allows more consecutive pairs of transitions to be executed without synchronization problems), until a digraph is formed that allows building a checking sequence without any synchronization problem.

We first modify the digraph $G'$ by replacing each edge
$(v_i, v'_j, x_1 x_2 \ldots x_k / y_1 y_2 \ldots y_k) \in E_T \cup E_{\alpha'}$ with a sequence of edges $(v_i, u^i_1, x_1/y_1)$, $(u^i_1, u^i_2, x_2/y_2), (u^i_2, u^i_3, x_3/y_3), \ldots, (u^i_{k-2}, u^i_{k-1}, x_{k-1}/y_{k-1}), (u^i_{k-1}, v'_j, x_k/y_k)$ where $u^i_1, u^i_2, \ldots, u^i_{k-1}$ are new nodes introduced into the digraph. Let us call this new digraph as $G''$. Note that any path in $G'$ will have a corresponding path in $G''$ and vice versa. In fact the only difference between $G'$ and $G''$ is that, we have inserted explicit nodes along the edges in $G'$ whose labels are not single input/output symbols. Therefore, in $G''$ all the edges will have a single input/output symbol pair as their labels.

Note the algorithm in Section 3 finds a tour over the edges $E_{\alpha'} \cup E_C$. Let us call these edges *the essential edges in $G'$*. We also call an edge in $G''$ an *essential edge in $G''$*, if it is an edge in $E_C$, or it is an edge that we insert into $G''$ as we create the edges corresponding to the individual steps along an edge in $E_{\alpha'}$.

Let $e_1 = (u_1, u, x_1/y_1)$ and $e_2 = (u, u_2, x_2/y_2)$ be two edges in $G''$. Note that the algorithm given in Section 3 may produce a checking sequence in which $e_1$ is immediately followed by $e_2$ since $e_1$ ends at and $e_2$ starts at vertex $u$. However, we would like to allow the possibility of having $e_1$ being followed by $e_2$ only if it is possible to do so without creating a synchronization problem.

In order to set up the digraph in such a way that, $e_1$ can be followed by $e_2$ only without creating a synchronization problem, we derive another digraph $G''' = (V''', E''')$ which is the *interchange graph* (or *line graph*) of $G''$. In other words, each edge $(u_1, u_2, x/y)$ in $G''$, becomes a vertex $(u_1, u_2, x/y) \in V'''$. For two nodes $(u_1, u_2, x/y)$ and $(u'_1, u'_2, x'/y')$ in $V'''$, $((u_1, u_2, x/y), (u'_1, u'_2, x'/y'), \epsilon) \in E'''$ if and only if $u'_1 = u_2$. We also have the mapping $R : E''' \to 2^{[p] \times [p]}$ that maps an edge in $E'''$ to a set of coordination channels. Intuitively, for an edge $((u_1, u, x/y), (u, u'_2, x'/y'), \epsilon) \in E'''$, $R((u_1, u, x/y), (u, u'_2, x'/y'), \epsilon)$ is the set of coordination channels such that if any one of these coordination channels exist, then $(u, u'_2, x'/y')$ can follow $(u_1, u, x/y)$ without a synchronization problem.

A vertex $(u_1, u_2, x/y) \in V'''$ is called an *essential vertex in $G'''$* if the edge $(u_1, u_2, x/y)$ in $G''$ is an essential edge in $G''$.

A subset $C \subseteq [p] \times [p]$ of coordination channels induces a digraph $G'''_C = (V''', E'''_C)$ where $E'''_C \subseteq E'''$, such that for an edge $((u_1, u, x/y), (u, u'_2, x'/y'), \epsilon) \in E'''$, $((u_1, u, x/y), (u, u'_2, x'/y'), \epsilon) \in E'''_C$ iff $R((u_1, u, x/y), (u, u'_2, x'/y'), \epsilon) = \emptyset$ (no coordination channel is required) or $R((u_1, u, x/y), (u, u'_2, x'/y') \cap C \neq \emptyset$ (at least one of the required coordination channels is available).

Then, our problem can be formulated as to find a set $C \subseteq [p] \times [p]$ of coordination channels with minimal cardinality such that $G'''_C$ has a strongly connected component which includes all the essential vertices in $G'''$. When $G'''_C$ has a strongly connected component which includes all the essential vertices in $G'''$, we can find a tour in this strongly connected component that visits all these essentials vertices. Thanks to the way we constructed $G'''$, this tour indeed corresponds to a tour in $G''$ that includes all the essential edges of $G''$, and therefore corresponds to a tour in $G'$ which includes all the edges in $E_C$ and $E_{\alpha'}$ that can thus be used to generate a checking sequence.

Thus we need to build a set $C \subseteq [p] \times [p]$ of coordination channels. If $(i, j) \in C$, for $i, j \in [p]$, this means that a coordination channel exists from the tester at port $i$ to the tester at port $j$. Two successive transitions with labels $x_1/y_1$ and $x_2/y_2$, where $x_1 \in X_i$ and $x_2 \in X_j$ for some $i, j \in [p]$, are *synchronizable* if and only if:

1. $i = j$; or
2. $y_1|_j \neq -$; or
3. $(i, j) \in C$; or
4. $\exists k \in [p]$ such that $y_1|_k \neq -$ and $(k, j) \in C$

In the first two cases, the synchronization is achieved without using any external coordination message exchanges. In the last two cases, the synchronization is done externally, either by having the tester at port $i$ (the sender of the input of the first transition) send an external coordination message to the tester at port $j$, or by having the tester at some port $k$, which receives a non–null output due to the first transition, send an external coordination message to the tester at port $j$.

## 4.2  A Heuristic to Find the Coordination Channels

As explained in Section 4.1, the original problem has been reformulated as finding a set $C \subseteq [p] \times [p]$ of coordination channels with minimal cardinality such that $G'''_C$ has a strongly connected component which includes all the essential vertices in $G'''$.

Initially, $C = \emptyset$. If $G'''_\emptyset$ has a strongly connected component which includes all the essential vertices in $G'''$, then we are done and by using $G'''_\emptyset$ we can construct a checking sequence that does not require any coordination channels at all. If that is not the case, then coordination channels must be added in order to add more edges in $G'''_C$, until such a strongly connected component can be found (note that if $C_1 \subseteq C_2$ then the edges of $G_{C_1}'''$ are included in the edges of $G_{C_2}'''$, that is, by adding new coordination channels we add edges to $G'''$). In the worst case scenario, we will add coordination channels between every pair of testers, which will in effect put us back in the case studied in [4].

In order to decide which coordination channels to add, we propose the following heuristic, that converges to a solution while trying to add as few channels as possible. We start from the digraph $G_C'''$, with $C = \emptyset$. We first create the *condensation* of $G_C'''$: the condensation of $G_C'''$ is a graph $\widehat{G}_C'''$ containing one vertex for each strongly connected component of $G_C'''$. Two vertices representing components are joined by an edge in $\widehat{G}_C'''$ if there is an edge in $G_C'''$ from a vertex in one component to a vertex in the other. Such an acyclic condensation can be built in $O(V''' + E''')$ [22]. In [23], it is shown that finding a graph augmentation (that is, adding new edges) that strongly connects $\widehat{G}_C'''$ is equivalent to finding an augmentation that strongly connects $G_C'''$, by using a mapping between a vertex of $\widehat{G}_C'''$ and any vertex of the corresponding strongly connected component in $G_C'''$. It is also pointed out in [23] that in order to strongly connect a condensed graph we necessarily need to add outgoing edges to each of its sink and isolated vertices, and incoming edges to each of its source and isolated vertices.

We proceed as follows, starting with $C = \emptyset$:

- Condense the current graph $G_C'''$ into $\widehat{G}_C'''$.
- Identify the set $\Phi$ of sources, sinks and isolated vertices in $\widehat{G}_C'''$ that are issued from the condensation of strongly connected components of $G_C'''$ containing essential vertices. If $\Phi$ is not empty, then let $\Phi_1$ be the set of such sources, $\Phi_2$ be the set of such sinks and $\Phi_3$ be the set of such isolated vertices. Otherwise ($\Phi$ is empty), let $\Phi_1$ be the set of sources, $\Phi_2$ be the set of sinks and $\Phi_3$ be the set of isolated vertices in $\widehat{G}_C'''$.
- For each possible new coordination channel: count the number of elements from $\Phi_1$ and $\Phi_3$ that will have at least one outgoing edge added to them by the inclusion of the channel to $C$, and the number of elements of $\Phi_2$ and $\Phi_3$ that will have at least one incoming edge added to them by the inclusion of the channel to $C$; identify the coordination channel $c$ that will maximize this number (that is, identify the coordination channel $c$ that would remove the most sources, sinks and isolated vertices from $\widehat{G}_{C \cup \{c\}}'''$).
- Add this coordination channel $c$ to $C$.
- Re-calculate the digraph $G_C'''$ based on the new set $C$. If $G_C'''$ still has not a strongly connected component which includes all the essential vertices in $G'''$, then re-iterate the process. Else, stop.

It is clear that the above process converges toward a solution, since in the worst case we end up adding every pair to $C$. The solution found will be correct according to [4], will not contain any synchronization issues by construction and may require the addition of fewer coordination channels than simply synchronizing the original solution found in [4] (the solution may however be longer than the one found originally).

We illustrate our approach with the example given in Figure 4. This figure shows a digraph which stands for an example of $G''$ (although we do not show the labels of the transitions for simplicity). Assume that in this example, the transition $d$ has a synchronization problem with the transition $e$, and that transition $f$ has a synchronization problem with the transition $g$; every other transition pair is synchronizable. Without adding any coordination channel, the graph $G_\emptyset'''$ shown in Figure 6 is obtained; note that $d$ is not connected to $e$, and $f$ is not connected to $g$. The digraph is then condensed into $\widehat{G}_\emptyset'''$ shown in Figure 7. It has four vertices, showing that $G_\emptyset'''$ is not strongly connected.

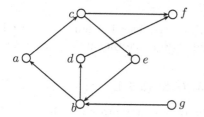

**Fig. 4.** A sample graph $G''$, with $i/o$ labels not shown. Assume that transition pairs $(d, e)$ and $(f, g)$ have synchronization problems.

**Fig. 5.** The graph $G'''$ corresponding to $G''$ of Figure 4

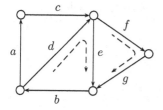

**Fig. 6.** The graph $G_\emptyset'''$ corresponding to $G''$ of Figure 4

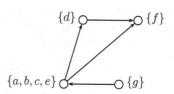

**Fig. 7.** The graph $\widehat{G}_\emptyset'''$ corresponding to $G_\emptyset'''$ of Figure 6

Assume now that the addition of the coordination channel $c_1$ allows the synchronization of $(d, e)$ (Figure 8). Adding such a coordination channel would not add any outgoing edges from sinks nor incoming edges to sources of $\widehat{G}_\emptyset'''$. The digraph $\widehat{G}_{\{c_1\}}'''$ is shown in Figure 9.

Assume that the addition of the coordination channel $(c_2)$ allows the synchronization of $(f, g)$ (Figure 10). This time, adding such a coordination channel would add an outgoing edge from sink $\{f\}$ and an incoming edge to source $\{g\}$ in $\widehat{G}_\emptyset'''$. Thus $c_2$ will be chosen over $c_1$, and the resulting digraph $\widehat{G}_{\{c_2\}}'''$ is shown in Figure 11: everything collapses in a single vertex, showing that $G_{\{c_2\}}'''$ is now strongly connected, and an Euler path can be found.

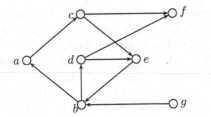

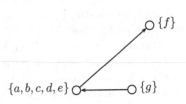

**Fig. 8.** The graph $G'''_{\{c_1\}}$: the coordination channel $c_1$ resolves the synchronization problem in transition pair $(d, e)$

**Fig. 9.** The graph $\widehat{G}'''_{\{c_1\}}$ corresponding to $G'''_{\{c_1\}}$ of Figure 8. Sources and sinks are not impacted by the addition

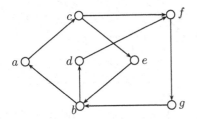

**Fig. 10.** The graph $G'''_{\{c_2\}}$: the coordination channel $c_2$ resolves the synchronization problem in transition pair $(f, g)$

**Fig. 11.** The graph $\widehat{G}'''_{\{c_2\}}$ corresponding to $G'''_{\{c_2\}}$ of Figure 10: the graph is now strongly connected

Going back to the example related to FSM $M_0$ (given in Figure 1), the following set of coordination channels is required to make the checking sequence given in Figure 3 synchronized:

$$C = \{(1, 2), (2, 1), (2, 3), (3, 2), (3, 1)\}$$

However, for the same FSM, applying the proposed approach to the digraph $G'$ given in Figure 2 will yield the following set of coordination channels to make the checking sequence given in Figure 12 synchronized:

$$C = \{(1, 2), (2, 1), (3, 1), (3, 1)\}$$

Note that, the length of the checking sequence given in Figure 3 is 50. The checking sequence given in Figure 12 requires one less coordination channel, but one more input symbol, making its length 51. Also note that, the number of coordination messages exchanged is reduced by 1. However this reduction is only coincidental, as the method proposed does not aim at reducing the number of coordination messages.

## 4.3   Different Types of Synchronization Strategies

In the discussion presented so far, it is assumed that coordination channels are unidirectional, and thus coordination occurs only in one direction over a single

$(s_1, s_3, a/(1,2,-))$  $(s_3, s_2, b/(-,2,-))$  $(s_2, s_1, b/(1,2,-))$  $(s_1, s_3, a/(1,2,-))$
$(s_3, s_2, b/(-,2,-)) \star (s_2, s_2, a/(1,2,-))$  $(s_2, s_2, a/(1,2,-))$  $(s_2, s_1, b/(1,2,-)) \star$
$(s_1, s_4, c/(-,-,3)) \star (s_4, s_5, a/(-,2,-))$  $(s_5, s_1, b/(1,-,-))$  $(s_1, s_3, a/(1,2,-))$
$(s_3, s_2, b/(-,2,-)) \star (s_2, s_2, a/(1,2,-))$  $(s_2, s_1, b/(1,2,-))$  $(s_1, s_3, a/(1,2,-))$
$(s_3, s_2, b/(-,2,-))$  $(s_2, s_1, b/(1,2,-))$  $(s_1, s_3, a/(1,2,-))$  $(s_3, s_2, b/(-,2,-)) \star$
$(s_2, s_2, a/(1,2,-))$  $(s_2, s_1, b/(1,2,-))$  $(s_1, s_3, a/(1,2,-))$  $(s_3, s_4, a/(-,2,-))$
$(s_4, s_3, b/(-,2,-)) \star (s_3, s_4, a/(-,2,-))$  $(s_4, s_5, a/(-,2,-))$  $(s_5, s_1, b/(-,2,-)) \star$
$(s_1, s_3, a/(1,2,-))$  $(s_3, s_4, a/(-,2,-))$  $(s_4, s_3, b/(-,2,-)) \star (s_3, s_4, a/(-,2,-))$
$(s_4, s_3, b/(-,2,-)) \star (s_3, s_4, a/(-,2,-))$  $(s_4, s_5, a/(-,2,-))$  $(s_5, s_4, a/(1,-,-)) \star$
$(s_4, s_3, b/(-,2,-)) \star (s_3, s_4, a/(-,2,-))$  $(s_4, s_3, b/(-,2,-)) \star (s_3, s_4, a/(-,2,-))$
$(s_4, s_3, b/(-,2,-)) \star (s_3, s_4, a/(-,2,-))$  $(s_4, s_5, a/(-,2,-))$  $(s_5, s_4, a/(1,-,-))$
$(s_4, s_5, a/(-,2,-))$  $(s_5, s_1, b/(1,-,-)) \star (s_1, s_4, c/(-,-,3)) \star (s_4, s_5, a/(-,2,-))$
$(s_5, s_1, b/(1,-,-))$  $(s_1, s_3, a/(1,2,-))$  $(s_3, s_2, b/(-,2,-))$

**Fig. 12.** The transition sequence on FSM $M_0$ (given in Figure 1) of the checking sequence produced from $G'''$. Two consecutive transitions with a $\star$ between them have a synchronization problem.

channel. In other words, $C$ contains *ordered* pairs of testers $(i,j)$, allowing an external coordination message to be sent from $i$ to $j$ but not from $j$ to $i$. Also having $(i,j)$ and $(j,k)$ in $C$ does not insure that a pair of transitions involving testers $i$ and $k$ can necessarily be synchronized.

It is however possible to modify our approach to accommodate for both cases.

**Bidirectional Synchronization Channels.** If coordination channels are bidirectional, then once a pair of testers $(i,j)$ is added to $C$, any pair of transitions involving testers $i$ and $j$ can be synchronized, be it from $i$ to $j$ or from $j$ to $i$ (in both directions). Thus, in that scenario, two successive transitions with labels $x_1/y_1$ and $x_2/y_2$, where $x_1 \in X_i$ and $x_2 \in X_j$, $i,j \in [p]$, are synchronizable if and only if (let $C^s$ denote the symmetric closure of $C$ below):

1. $i = j$; or
2. $y_1|_j \neq -$; or
3. $(i,j) \in C^s$; or
4. $\exists k \in [p]$ such that $y_1|_k \neq -$ and $(k,j) \in C^s$

Adapting the algorithm to this new definition is straightforward. We only need to consider $G'''_{C^s}$ instead of $G'''_C$ while checking if all the essential nodes are in a single strongly connected component.

**Transitive Synchronizations.** It is possible for the testers to organize a synchronization strategy allowing the coordination of two testers in the absence of direct coordination channels between them, by using a chain of external coordination messages involving other testers. Such a transitive synchronization strategy can be considered both with unidirectional and bidirectional coordination channels.

When we consider unidirectional channels with transitive strategy, two successive transitions with labels $x_1/y_1$ and $x_2/y_2$, where $x_1 \in X_i$ and $x_2 \in X_j$,

$i, j \in [p]$, are synchronizable if and only if (let $C^t$ denote the transitive closure of $C$ below) :

1. $i = j$; or
2. $y_1|_j \neq -$; or
3. $(i, j) \in C^t$; or
4. $\exists k \in [p]$ such that $y_1|_k \neq -$ and $(k, j) \in C^t$

When we consider bidirectional channels with transitive strategy, two successive transitions with labels $x_1/y_1$ and $x_2/y_2$, where $x_1 \in X_i$ and $x_2 \in X_j$, $i, j \in [p]$, are synchronizable if and only if (let $C^{st}$ denote the symmetric and transitive closure of $C$ below) :

1. $i = j$; or
2. $y_1|_j \neq -$; or
3. $(i, j) \in C^{st}$; or
4. $\exists k \in [p]$ such that $y_1|_k \neq -$ and $(k, j) \in C^{st}$

Adapting the algorithm to this new definition is also straightforward. We only need to consider $G'''_{C^t}$ or $G'''_{C^{st}}$ instead of $G'''_C$ while checking if all the essential nodes are in a single strongly connected component.

Note that if establishing new coordination channel is considered costly, then following such a transitive synchronization strategy is certainly worthwhile, since it can significantly lower the number of coordination channels required.

## 5    Conclusions

We have presented an approach to minimize the number of coordination channels in a distributed test architecture for the application of a checking sequence. The proposed approach is presented as a modification of an existing method for constructing a checking sequence, but can be adapted to work with any other method that constructs a checking sequence by finding a tour on an auxiliary graph derived from a finite state machine specification of the application.

The heuristic algorithm explained above finds a set of coordination channels $C$ such that $G'''_C$ has the required property (i.e. having all the essential vertices in a single strongly connected component). However, since it is a greedy heuristic algorithm, it may accumulate a set of coordination channels which may have a subset $C'$ that will yield $G'''_{C'}$ with the required property. To find such a subset of $C$, will require a post–processing phase. The nature of this processing phase is explained as follows:

Note that inclusion of a coordination channel $(i, j) \in [p] \times [p]$ in $C$ inserts a set of edges in $G'''_C$. Namely, an edge $e \in E'''$ is inserted in $G'''_C$ due to the inclusion of $(i, j)$ in $C$, if $(i, j) \in R(e)$. The same edge $e$ can be inserted by the inclusion of some other coordination channels in $R(e)$ into $C$ as well.

Let $R^{-1}(i, j) = \{e \in E''' \mid (i, j) \in R(e)\}$, i.e. $R^{-1}(i, j)$ is the set of edges inserted by the coordination channel $(i, j)$. Given a set of coordination channels

$C$, let $R^{-1}(C) = \cup_{(i,j) \in C} R^{-1}(i,j)$. For two sets of coordination channels $C'$ and $C$ such that $C' \subseteq C$ but $R^{-1}(C') = R^{-1}(C)$, it is obvious that $G'''_{C'}$ has all the essential vertices in a single strongly connected component iff $G'''_C$ does, because both $C'$ and $C$ insert the same set of edges. This is an instance of the set cover problem, which is known to be NP–complete. An existing heuristic algorithm for the set cover problem can be used to find a minimal subset $C'$ of $C$ such that $R^{-1}(C') = R^{-1}(C)$.

## Acknowledgments

This work is supported in part by the Natural Science and Engineering Research Council of Canada under grants RGPIN 976 and RGPIN 312018, CITO/OCE of the Government of Ontario, and a grant by Sabancı University.

## References

1. Lee, D., Yannakakis, M.: Principles and methods of testing finite state machines - A survey. In: Proceedings of the IEEE. Volume 84. (1996) 1090–1126
2. Gill, A.: Introduction to The Theory of Finite State Machines. McGraw Hill, New York (1962)
3. Ural, H., Wu, X., Zhang, F.: On minimizing the length of checking sequences. IEEE Transactions on Computers **46** (1997) 93–99
4. Hierons, R.M., Ural, H.: Reduced length checking sequences. IEEE Transactions on Computers **51** (2002) 1111–1117
5. Tekle, K.T., Ural, H., Yalcin, M.C., Yenigun, H.: Generalizing redundancy elimination in checking sequences. In: ISCIS 2005, LNCS 3733. (2005) 915–926
6. Yao, M., Petrenko, A., v. Bochmann, G.: Conformance testing of protocol machines without reset. In: Protocol Specification, Testing and Verification. Volume XIII. (1993) 241–256
7. Chen, J., Hierons, R., Ural, H.: Conditions for resolving observability problems in distributed testing. In: FORTE 2004, LNCS 3235. (2004) 229–242
8. Chen, X.J., Hierons, R.M., Ural, H.: Resolving observability problems in distributed test architecture. In: IFIP FORTE 2005, LNCS 3731. (2005) 219–232
9. Sarikaya, B., v. Bochmann, G.: Synchronization and specification issues in protocol testing. IEEE Transactions on Communications **32** (1984) 389–395
10. Luo, G., Dssouli, R., Bochmann, G.V., Venkataram, P., Ghedamsi, A.: Test generation with respect to distributed interfaces. Comput. Stand. Interfaces **16** (1994) 119–132
11. Tai, K., Young, Y.: Synchronizable test sequences of finite state machines. Computer Networks and ISDN Systems **30** (1998) 1111–1134
12. Hierons, R.M.: Testing a distributed system: Generating minimal synchronised test sequences that detect output-shifting faults. Information and Software Technology **43** (2001) 551–560
13. Khoumsi, A.: A temporal approach for testing distributed systems. Software Engineering, IEEE Transactions on **28** (2002) 1085–1103
14. Wu, W.J., Chen, W.H., Tang, C.Y.: Synchronizable for multi-party protocol conformance testing. Computer Communications **21** (1998) 1177–1183

15. Cacciari, L., Rafiq, O.: Controllability and observability in distributed testing. Inform. Software Technol. **41** (1999) 767–780
16. Boyd, S., Ural, H.: The synchronization problem in protocol testing and its complexity. Information Processing Letters **40** (1991) 131–136
17. Dssouli, R., von Bochmann, G.: Error detection with multiple observers. In: Protocol Specification, Testing and Verification. Volume V., Elsevier Science (North Holland) (1985) 483–494
18. Dssouli, R., von Bochmann, G.: Conformance testing with multiple observers. In: Protocol Specification, Testing and Verification. Volume VI., Elsevier Science (North Holland) (1986) 217–229
19. Rafiq, O., Cacciari, L.: Coordination algorithm for distributed testing. The Journal of Supercomputing **24** (2003) 203–211
20. Hierons, R.M., Ural, H.: Uio sequence based checking sequence for distributed test architectures. Information and Software Technology **45** (2003) 798–803
21. Chen, J., abd H. Ural, R.M.H.: Overcoming observability problems in distributed test architectures. (Information Processing Letters) to appear.
22. Tarjan, R.E.: Depth-first search and linear graph algorithms. SIAM J. Comput. **1** (1972) 146–160
23. Eswaran, K.P., Tarjan, R.E.: Augmentation problems. SIAM J. Comput. **5** (1976) 653–665

# Derivation of a Suitable Finite Test Suite for Customized Probabilistic Systems[*]

Luis F. Llana-Díaz, Manuel Núñez, and Ismael Rodríguez

Dept. Sistemas Informáticos y Programación
Universidad Complutense de Madrid, 28040 Madrid, Spain
{llana, mn, isrodrig}@sip.ucm.es

**Abstract.** In order to check the conformance of an IUT (implementation under test) with respect to a specification, it is not feasible, in general, to test the whole set of IUT available behaviors. In some situations, testing the behavior of the IUT assuming that it is stimulated by a given usage model is more appropriate. Specifically, if we consider that specifications and usage models are defined in probabilistic terms, then by applying a finite set of tests to the IUT we can compute a relevant metric: An upper bound of the probability that a user following the usage model finds an error in the IUT. We also present a method to find an *optimal* (with respect to the number of inputs) set of tests that minimizes that upper bound.

## 1 Introduction

In order to test the behavior of an IUT (*implementation under test*) sometimes it is preferable to check only some functionalities that are specially relevant or critical. In this line, we can consider that the IUT is analyzed in the context of a specific usage model or, more generally, in terms of its interaction with a (probably abstract) *user* that represents some manners to interact with the IUT. Let us note that if only the functional behavior of systems is considered (that is, we just check what must or must not be done), then this kind of *user-customized* approach consists in testing a *subset* of the behaviors defined by the specification. However, if other kinds of features are taken into account then this approach might provide some interesting possibilities. In particular, if specifications and *user models* are defined in *probabilistic* terms then we can calculate a measure that cannot be computed otherwise: After a finite set of tests is applied to the IUT, we can calculate a measure of the probability that a user behaving according to the user model finds a *wrong* behavior in the IUT. That is, after a finite subset of the infinite set of relevant behaviors is analyzed, we will be provided with a *global* measure of correctness of the IUT.

We can do it as follows. First, we choose some tests that exercise some behaviors concerned by the user model. Then, we apply the tests to the IUT to check

---

[*] Research partially supported by the Spanish MCYT project TIC2003-07848-C02-01, the Junta de Castilla-La Mancha project PAC-03-001, and the Marie Curie project MRTN-CT-2003-505121/TAROT.

E. Najm et al. (Eds.): FORTE 2006, LNCS 4229, pp. 467–483, 2006.

whether the behaviors exercised by these tests are *correct* with respect to the specification. Basically, tests induce some stimuli (sequences of inputs) and we observe the response (sequences of outputs) produced by the IUT. We cannot observe if the IUT produces $a$ with probability 0.5; what we can observe is the fact that $a$ is produced or not, but not the value 0.5. In fact, our process to assess the IUT will be probabilistic. For each specific *behavior case* (i.e., sequence of inputs) analyzed by tests, we apply a *hypothesis contrast* to check whether we can claim, for a given level of *confidence* $\alpha$, that the answers (i.e., sequences of outputs) produced by the IUT behave as required by the specification. For instance, if the specification says that $a$ and $b$ are produced with 0.5 probability each, then the confidence will be high if they are observed 507 and 493 times, respectively. However, if they are produced 614 and 386 times then the confidence will be lower.

Let us suppose that, after a suitable hypothesis contrast is applied, a given IUT behavior case is *validated* with confidence $\alpha$. Then we can assume, with that confidence, that the probability of each IUT response (in that behavior case) is actually defined as in the specification. Under this confidence, we can calculate the probability that a sequence of inputs/outputs *whose behavior was validated* is produced during the interaction of the IUT and the user model. By using this information we will calculate our correctness metric: An *upper bound* of the probability that a wrong probabilistic behavior is observed when the user model and the IUT interact. In the *worst* case all behaviors that have not been either validated or observed are wrong. Hence, after a finite test suite is applied, we can compute the probability of taking a non-validated behavior, which is incorrect in the worst case (with confidence $\alpha$).

Let us note that this measure cannot be computed in other testing frameworks. In particular, if the probabilistic behavior of systems is not considered (or it is, but user models are not regarded), then after a finite test suite is applied the coverage of all relevant cases is null in general: Among an infinite set of behavior cases to be analyzed, an infinitesimal part of them are tested. Thus, without any additional assumptions, nothing about the correctness of this IUT can be claimed. Though the capability of a finite test suite to detect errors in an IUT can be assessed, it is done either in heuristic terms [8,10,2] or by adding some hypotheses about the IUT behavior that allow to reduce the number of cases to be tested [1,11,21,17,18]. On the contrary, our metric provides a (probabilistic) non-heuristic correctness measure without reducing the *testing space*.

In this paper we continue a previous work [12]. In that approach, the behavior of the composition of the IUT and the user model is probabilistically compared to the behavior of the composition of the specification and the user model. A *single* hypothesis contrast is used to compare the former (denoted by means of a single random variable) and the latter (represented by a sample denoting all observations). Though this approach is simple and elegant, it has a drawback: Even if we assume that user models are correct by definition, their probabilistic behavior may be a source of *sampling noise*. For instance, let us suppose that the user model chooses between $a$ and $b$ with equal probability. Then, in both cases, the specification answers $c$ and $d$, again with equal probabilities. Though it is not very probable, the interaction of the user model and a *correct* IUT could produce $a/c$ 100 times and $b/c$ 100 times. In this case, we would (wrongly) deduce that the IUT is incorrect, because the specified probability of both $a/c$ and $b/c$ is $0.5 \cdot 0.5 = 0.25 \not\simeq \frac{100}{200}$. Similarly, $a/c$ and $a/d$ could be produced 100 times each, which again is not accepted. However, the latter sample is rejected due to a (rare) behavior of the user model. On the contrary, in this paper we will apply a hypothesis contrast for each *behavior case* (i.e., sequence of inputs). Each hypothesis contrast application checks whether responses (i.e., sequences of outputs) are properly given for the considered sequence of inputs. In the previous example, the correctness of the IUT when $a$ or $b$ are produced is independently checked. Hence, the sample cannot be ruined by a rare behavior of the user model (of course, it can still be ruined by a rare behavior of a correct IUT). Besides, in this paper we will use the metric of error probability of the IUT to find *optimal* sets of tests. Let us note that our metric does not only provide a correctness measure, but it also can be used to guide the testing process: If we compute that *passing* a given test suite $\Omega_1$ would provide an error measure 0.3, while passing another suite $\Omega_2$ would provide an error measure 0.2, then the suite $\Omega_2$ is preferable.

In terms of other related work, there is significant work on testing preorders and equivalences for probabilistic processes [4,16,19,5,3,20,14,13]. Most of these proposals follow the *de Nicola and Hennessy's style* [6,9], that is, two processes are equivalent if the application of any test belonging to a given set returns the same result. Instead, we are interested in checking whether an implementation conforms to a specification. In particular, our relations are similar to the ones introduced in [21,15].

The rest of the paper is structured as follows. In the next section we present some basic notions; in Section 3 we introduce tests and we define the interaction between machines and users; in Section 4 we present the relations that allow to relate specifications and implementations; next, in Section 5 we describe our method to calculate an upper bound of the error probability of an IUT after it is tested, and we use this notion to find optimal test suites; finally, in Section 6 we present our conclusions and some lines of future work.

## 2   Basic Notions

First, we introduce some statistics notions. An *event* is any reaction we can detect from a system or environment; a random variable is a function associating each event with its probability.

**Definition 1.** Let $\mathcal{A}$ be a set of events and $\xi : \mathcal{A} \to [0, 1]$ be a function such that $\sum_{\alpha \in \mathcal{A}} \xi(\alpha) = 1$. We say that $\xi$ is a *random variable* for the set of events $\mathcal{A}$.

If we observe that the event $\alpha \in \mathcal{A}$ is produced by a random source whose probabilistic behavior is given by $\xi$ then we say that $\alpha$ *has been generated by $\xi$*. We extend this notion to sequences of events as expected: If we observe that the sequence of events $H = \langle \alpha_1, \ldots, \alpha_n \rangle$ is consecutively produced by a random source whose probabilistic behavior is given by $\xi$ then we say that $H$ *has been generated by* $\xi$ or that $H$ is a *sample* of $\xi$.

Given the random variable $\xi$ and a sequence of events $H$, we denote the *confidence* that $H$ is *generated by* $\xi$ by $\gamma(\xi, H)$.     □

This definition introduces a simple version of discrete random variable where all the events are independent. The actual definition of a *random variable* is more complex but it is pointless to use its generality in our setting. In the previous definition, the application of a suitable *hypothesis contrast* is abstracted by the function $\gamma$. We have that $\gamma(\xi, H)$ takes a value in $[0, 1]$. Intuitively, a sample will be *rejected* if the probability of observing that sample from a given random variable is low. Due to lack of space we do not present here an actual definition of the function $\gamma$. An interested reader can find it in [12]. It is worth to point out that the results of this paper do not depend on the formulation of $\gamma$, being possible to *abstract* the actual definition.

Next we present the formalism we will use to define *specifications* and *implementations*. A *probabilistic finite state machine* is a finite state machine where each transition is equipped with a probability. Thus, a transition $s \xrightarrow{i/o}_p s'$ denotes that, if the machine is in state $s$ and the input $i$ is received then, with probability $p$, it moves to the state $s'$ and produces the output $o$. We will assume that the environment stimulates the machine with a single input at any time. Thus, given $s$ and $i$, the addition of all values $p$ such that there exist $o$, $s'$ with $s \xrightarrow{i/o}_p s'$ must be equal to 1. In contrast, there is no requirement binding the probabilities departing from the same state and receiving different inputs because each one describes (part of) a different probabilistic choice of the machine. In other words, we consider a *reactive* interpretation of probabilities (see [7,16]).

**Definition 2.** A *Probabilistic Finite State Machine*, in short PFSM, is a tuple $M = (S, I, O, \delta, s_0)$ where

- $S$ is the finite *set of states* and $s_0 \in S$ is the *initial state*.
- $I$ and $O$, with $I \cap O = \varnothing$, denote the sets of *input* and *output* actions, respectively.
- $\delta \subseteq S \times I \times O \times (0, 1] \times S$ is the *set of transitions*. We will write $s \xrightarrow{i/o}_p s'$ to denote $(s, i, o, p, s') \in \delta$.

Transitions and states fulfill the following additional conditions:

- For all $s \in S$ and $i \in I$, the probabilities associated with outgoing transitions add up to 1, that is, $\sum \{p \mid \exists o \in O, s' \in S : s \xrightarrow{i/o}_p s'\} = 1$.
- PFSMs are *free of non-observable non-determinism*, that is, if we have two transitions $s \xrightarrow{i/o}_{p_1} s_1$ and $s \xrightarrow{i/o}_{p_2} s_2$ then $p_1 = p_2$ and $s_1 = s_2$.
- In addition, we will assume that implementations are *input-enabled*, that is, for all state $s$ and input $i$ there exist $o, p, s'$ such that $s \xrightarrow{i/o}_p s'$.     □

Although PFSMs will be used to define specifications and implementations, a different formalism will be used to define *user models*. Specifically, we will use *probabilistic labeled transition systems*. A user model represents the external environment of a system. User models actively produce inputs that stimulate the system, while passively receive outputs produced by the system as a response. The states of a user model are split into two categories: *Input states* and *output states*. In input states, all outgoing transitions denote a different input action. Since inputs are probabilistically chosen by user models, any input transition is endowed with a probability. In particular, $s \xrightarrow{i}_p s'$ denotes that, with probability $p$, in the input state $s$, the input $i$ is produced and the state is moved to $s'$. Given an input state $s$, the addition of all probabilities $p$ such that there exists $i, s'$ with $s \xrightarrow{i}_p s'$ must be *lower* than or equal to 1. If it is lower then we will consider that the remainder up to 1 implicitly denotes the probability that the interaction with the system *finishes* at the current state. Regarding output states, all transitions departing from an output state are labeled by a different output action. However, output transitions do not have any probability value (let us remind that outputs are chosen by the system). Input and output states will strictly alternate, that is, for any input state $s$, with $s \xrightarrow{i}_p s'$, $s'$ is an output state, and for any output state $s$, with $s \xrightarrow{o} s'$, $s'$ is an input state.

**Definition 3.** A *probabilistic labeled transition system*, in short PLTS, is a tuple $U = (S_I, S_O, I, O, \delta, s_0)$ where

- $S_I$ and $S_O$, with $S_I \cap S_O = \varnothing$, are the finite sets of *input* and *output* states, respectively. $s_0 \in S_I$ is the *initial state*.
- $I$ and $O$, with $I \cap O = \varnothing$, are the sets of *input* and *output* actions, respectively.
- $\delta \subseteq (S_I \times I \times (0, 1] \times S_O) \cup (S_O \times O \times S_I)$ is the *transition relation*. We will write $s \xrightarrow{i}_p s'$ to denote $(s, i, p, s') \in S_I \times I \times (0, 1] \times S_O$ and $s \xrightarrow{o} s'$ to denote $(s, o, s') \in S_O \times O \times S_I$.

Transitions and states fulfill the following additional conditions:

- For all input states $s \in S_I$ and input actions $i \in I$ there exists at most one outgoing transition from $s$: $|\{s \xrightarrow{i}_p s' \mid \exists\, p \in (0, 1], s' \in S_O\}| \leq 1$.
- For all output states $s \in S_O$ and output actions $o \in O$ there exists exactly one outgoing transition labeled with $o$: $|\{s \xrightarrow{o} s' \mid \exists\, s' \in S_I\}| = 1$.
- For all input state $s \in S_I$ the addition of the probabilities associated with the outgoing transitions is lower than or equal to 1, that is, $\mathtt{cont}(s) = \sum\{p \mid \exists s' \in S_O : s \xrightarrow{i}_p s'\} \leq 1$. So, the probability of stopping at that state $s$ is $\mathtt{stop}(s) = 1 - \mathtt{cont}(s)$.                                             □

By iteratively executing transitions, both PFSMs and PLTSs can produce sequences of inputs and outputs. The probabilities of these sequences are given by the probabilities of the transitions. Next we introduce some *trace* notions.

**Definition 4.** A *probability trace* $\pi$ is a finite sequence of probabilities, that is, a possibly empty sequence $\langle p_1, p_2, \ldots, p_n \rangle \in (0, 1]^*$. The symbol $\epsilon$ denotes the empty probability trace. Let $\pi = \langle p_1, p_2, \ldots, p_n \rangle$ be a probability trace. We define its *sef-product*, denoted by $\prod \pi$, as $\prod_{1 \leq i \leq n} p_i$. Since $\prod_{a \in \varnothing} = 1$, we have $\prod \epsilon = 1$. Let $\pi = \langle p_1, p_2, \ldots, p_n \rangle$ and $\pi' = \langle p'_1, p'_2, \ldots, p'_m \rangle$ be probability traces. Then, $\pi \cdot \pi'$ denotes their concatenation that is, $\langle p_1, p_2, \ldots, p_n, p'_1, p'_2, \ldots, p'_m \rangle$, while $\pi * \pi'$ and $\pi / \pi'$ denote their pairwise product and division respectively, that is, $\langle p_1 * p'_1, p_2 * p'_2, \ldots, p_r * p'_r \rangle$ and $\langle p_1 / p'_1, p_2 / p'_2, \ldots, p_r / p'_r \rangle$, where $r = \min(n, m)$.

A *trace* $\rho$ is a finite sequence of input/output actions $(i_1/o_1, i_2/o_2, \ldots, i_n/o_n)$. The symbol $\epsilon$ denotes the empty trace. Let $\rho$ and $\rho'$ be traces. Then, $\rho \cdot \rho'$ denotes their concatenation. A *probabilistic trace* is a pair $(\rho, \pi)$ where $\rho$ is a trace $(i_1/o_1, i_2/o_2, \ldots, i_n/o_n)$ and $\pi = \langle p_1, p_2, \ldots, p_n \rangle$ is a probability trace. If $\rho$ and $\pi$ are both empty then we have the *empty probabilistic trace*, written as $(\epsilon, \epsilon)$. Let $(\rho, \pi)$ and $(\rho', \pi')$ be probabilistic traces. Then, $(\rho, \pi) \cdot (\rho', \pi')$ denotes their concatenation, that is, $(\rho \cdot \rho', \pi \cdot \pi')$.

An *input trace* $\varrho$ is a finite sequence of input actions $(i_1, i_2, \ldots, i_n)$. We extend the previous notions of empty trace and concatenations to input traces in the expected way. If $\rho = (i_1/o_1, i_2/o_2, \ldots, i_n/o_n)$ then we denote by $\mathrm{i}(\rho)$ the input trace $(i_1, i_2, \ldots, i_n)$. A *probabilistic input trace* is a pair $(\varrho, \pi)$ where $\varrho$ is an input trace $(i_1, i_2, \ldots, i_n)$ and $\pi = \langle p_1, p_2, \ldots, p_n \rangle$. We also consider the concepts of concatenation and empty probabilistic input traces.     □

Next we define how to extract traces from PFSMs and PLTSs. First, we consider the reflexive and transitive closure of the transition relation, and we call it *generalized* transition. Then, probabilistic traces are constructed from generalized transitions by considering their sequences of actions and probabilities.

**Definition 5.** Let $M = (S, I, O, \delta, s_0)$ be a PFSM. We inductively define the *generalized* transitions of $M$ as follows:

- We have that $s \overset{\epsilon}{\Longrightarrow}_\epsilon s$ is a generalized transition of $M$ for all $s \in S$.
- If $s \overset{\rho}{\Longrightarrow}_\pi s'$ and $s' \overset{i/o}{\longrightarrow}_p s_1$ then $s \overset{\rho \cdot i/o}{\Longrightarrow}_{\pi \cdot \langle p \rangle} s_1$ is a generalized transition of $M$.

We say that $(\rho, \pi)$ is a *probabilistic trace* of $M$ if there exists $s \in S$ such that $s_0 \overset{\rho}{\Longrightarrow}_\pi s$. In addition, we say that $\rho$ is a *trace* of $M$ and that $\mathrm{i}(\rho)$ is an *input trace* of $M$. The sets $\mathrm{pTr}(M), \mathrm{tr}(M), \mathrm{iTr}(M)$ denote the sets of *probabilistic traces*, *traces*, and *input traces* of $M$, respectively.     □

The previous notions can also be defined for PLTSs. In order to obtain sequences of paired inputs and outputs, traces begin and end at input states.

**Definition 6.** Let $U = (S_I, S_O, I, O, \delta, s_0)$ be a PLTS. We inductively define the *generalized* transitions of $U$ as follows:

- We have that $s \overset{\epsilon}{\Longrightarrow}_\epsilon s$ is a generalized transition of $U$ for all $s \in S_I$.
- If $s \in S_I$, $s \overset{\rho}{\Longrightarrow}_\pi s'$, and $s' \overset{i}{\longrightarrow}_p s'' \overset{o}{\longrightarrow} s_1$ then $s \overset{\rho \cdot i/o}{\Longrightarrow}_{\pi \cdot \langle p \rangle} s_1$ is a generalized transition of $U$.

We say that $(\rho, \pi)$ is a *probabilistic trace* of $U$ if there exists $s \in S_I$ such that $s_0 \overset{\rho}{\Longrightarrow}_\pi s$. In that case we will also say that $(\mathbf{i}(\rho), \pi)$ is a *probabilistic input trace* of $U$. In addition, we say that $\rho$ is a *trace* of $U$ and that $\mathbf{i}(\rho)$ is an *input trace* of $U$. We define the probability of $U$ to stop after $\rho$, denoted by $\mathbf{stop}_U(\rho)$, as $\mathbf{stop}(s)$. The sets $\mathbf{pTr}(U)$, $\mathbf{piTr}(U)$, $\mathbf{tr}(U)$ and $\mathbf{iTr}(U)$ denote the set of *probabilistic traces, traces,* and *input traces* of $U$ respectively.    □

Next we identify PLTS that *terminate*, that is, such that all infinite traces have probability 0.

**Definition 7.** Let $U$ be a PLTS. We say that $U$ is a *terminating* PLTS if for all $s$ such that there exists $\rho$ and $\pi$ with $s_0 \overset{\rho}{\Longrightarrow}_\pi s$ we have that there exists $s', \rho', \pi'$ such that $s \overset{\rho'}{\Longrightarrow}_{\pi'} s'$ and $\mathbf{stop}_U(\rho \cdot \rho') > 0$.    □

**Proposition 1.** A PLTS $U$ is terminating iff $\sum_{(\rho,\pi)\in\mathbf{pTr}(U)} (\prod \pi) * \mathbf{stop}_U(\rho) = 1$.    □

As we will see, PLTS will be used to denote user models. In particular, any user model will be supposed to be a *terminating* PLTS.

# 3   Tests and Composition of Machines

In this section we define our tests as well as the interaction between the notions introduced in the previous section (PFSMs and PLTSs). As we said before, we will use PLTSs to define the behavior of the external environment of a system, that is, a user model. Moreover, PLTSs are also appropriate to define the *tests* we will apply to an IUT. Tests are PLTSs fulfilling some additional conditions. Basically, a test defines a finite sequence of inputs; we will use them to check a given secuence of inputs. Since tests consider a single sequence of inputs, each intermediate input state of the sequence contains a single outgoing transition labeled by the next input and probability 1. Output states offer transitions with different outputs.

**Definition 8.** A test $T = (S_I, S_O, I, O, \delta, s_0)$ is a PLTS such that for all $s \in S_I$ there is at most one transition $s \overset{i}{\longrightarrow}_p s'$ (and if it exists then $p = 1$), and for all $s \in S_O$ there is at most one *next input state* $s \overset{o}{\longrightarrow} s'$ with a *continuation*, that is, $|\{s'' \mid \exists\, i \in I,\, o \in O,\, s''' \in S_O,\, p \in (0,1]:\, s \overset{o}{\longrightarrow} s'' \overset{i}{\longrightarrow}_p s'''\}| \leq 1$.    □

Let us note that, contrarily to other frameworks, tests are not provided with diagnostic capabilities on *their own*. In other words, tests do not have fail/success states. Since our framework is probabilistic, the requirements defined by specifications are given in probabilistic terms. As we will see in the next section, deciding whether the IUT conforms to the specification will also be done in probabilistic terms. In particular, we will consider whether it is *feasible* that the IUT *behaves* as if it were defined as the specification indicates. We will check this fact by means of a suitable *hypothesis contrast*.

Our testing methodology consists in testing the behavior of a system under the assumption that it is stimulated by a given user model. Thus, tests will be extracted from the behavior of the user model. Next we show how a test is constructed from a probabilistic trace of a user model. The input and output states of the test are identified with natural numbers. All the input states (but the first one) are also endowed with an output action. In order to distinguish between input and output states we decorate them with • and ⋆, respectively. Tests extracted from user model sequences fulfill an additional condition: All input states reached from a given output state (via different outputs) are connected with the *same* output state through the same input, up to the end of the sequence. A single test can process *any* answer to a given sequence of inputs, that is, it detects any sequence of outputs produced by the IUT as response.

**Definition 9.** Let $\varrho = (i_1, i_2, \ldots, i_r)$ be an input trace, $I$ be a set of input actions such that $\{i_1, \ldots i_r\} \subseteq I$, and $O$ be a set of output actions. We define the *test associated* to $\varrho$, $\mathtt{assoc}(\varrho)$, as the test $(S_{IT}, S_{OT}, I, O, \delta_T, 0^\bullet)$, where

- $S_{IT} = \{0^\bullet, r^\bullet\} \cup \{(j, o)^\bullet | o \in O, 1 \leq j \leq r\}$ and $S_{OT} = \{j^\star | 1 \leq j \leq r\}$.
- For all $1 \leq j < r, o \in O$: $(j, o)^\bullet \xrightarrow{i_{j+1}}_1 (j+1)^\star$ , $j^\star \xrightarrow{o} (j, o)^\bullet \in \delta_T$. We also have $0^\bullet \xrightarrow{i_1}_1 0^\star$. $\qquad\qquad\square$

Next we define the composition of a PFSM (denoting either a specification or an IUT) with a PLTS (denoting either a user model or a test) in terms of its behavior, that is, in terms of traces and probabilistic traces. The set of traces is easily computed as the intersection of the traces produced by both components. In order to define the set of probabilistic traces, the ones provided by both components are considered. For a given input/output pair $i/o$, the probability of producing $i$ will be taken from the corresponding transition of the PLTS, while the probability of producing $o$ as a response to $i$ will be given by a transition of the PFSM. Let us note that the states of a specification do not necessarily define outgoing transitions for all available inputs, that is, specifications are not necessarily *input-enabled*. So, a PFSM representing a specification could not provide a response for an input produced by a PLTS. Since the specification does not define any behavior in this case, we will assume that the PFSM is allowed to produce *any* behavior from this point on. The composition of a PLTS and a PFSM will be constructed to check whether the traces *defined* by the specification are correctly produced by the implementation. Hence, undefined behaviors will not be considered relevant and will not provide any trace to the composition of the PLTS and the PFSM. In order to appropriately represent the probabilities of the relevant traces, their probabilities will be *normalized* if undefined behaviors appear. We illustrate this process in the following example.

*Example 1.* Let us suppose that a user model can produce the inputs $i_1, i_2$, and $i_3$ with probabilities $\frac{1}{2}, \frac{1}{4}$ and $\frac{1}{4}$, respectively. At the same time, the corresponding specification provides outgoing transitions with inputs $i_1$ and $i_2$, but not with $i_3$. Since the specification does not define any reaction to $i_3$, the probabilities of taking inputs $i_1$ or $i_2$ in the composition of the specification and the user model are normalized to denote that $i_3$ is not considered. So, the probability of $i_1$ becomes $\frac{1/2}{3/4} = \frac{2}{3}$ while the probability of $i_2$ is $\frac{1/4}{3/4} = \frac{1}{3}$.     □

The next definition finds an appropriate normalization factor when these situations appear (in the previous example, this factor is $\frac{3}{4}$). Besides, we show how to recompute the probabilities of all traces in a PLTS when only sequences of inputs that are accepted by a a given PLTS are considered. Finally, we consider the behavior of the composition of a PFSM and a PLTS. The set of traces of this composition is provided by the intersection of the set of traces of each machine. In order find the probabilistic traces we consider, on the one hand, the probabilistic traces of the PFSM and, on the other hand, the probabilistic traces of the PLTS *normalized to* this PFSM.

**Definition 10.** Let $M = (S_M, I, O, \delta_M, s_{0M})$ be a PFSM and let us consider a PLTS $U = (S_{IU}, S_{OU}, I, O, \delta_U, s_{0U})$ such that $s_{0M} \overset{\rho}{\Longrightarrow}_{\pi_1} s_1$ and $s_{0U} \overset{\rho}{\Longrightarrow}_{\pi_2} s_2$. We define:

– The sum of the probabilities of *continuing together after* $\rho$ as

$$\mathsf{cont}_{M \| U}(\rho) = \sum \left\{ p \; \middle| \; \begin{array}{l} \exists i \in I, \, o \in O, \, s_2' \in S_{OU}, \, s_1' \in S_M, \, r \in (0,1] : \\ s_2 \xrightarrow{i}_p s_2' \; \wedge \; s_1 \xrightarrow{i/o}_r s_1' \end{array} \right\}$$

– The *normalization factor of* $M \| U$ *after* $\rho$ as the sum of the previous probability plus the probability of $U$ to stop after $\rho$, that is $\mathsf{norm}_{M \| U}(\rho) = \mathsf{cont}_{M \| U}(\rho) + \mathsf{stop}_U(\rho)$.

We inductively define the probabilistic traces of $U$ *normalized* to $M$ as follows:

– $(\epsilon, \epsilon)$ is a normalized probabilistic trace.
– Let $(\rho, \pi)$ be a normalized probabilistic trace. Let us suppose that we have $s_{0M} \overset{\rho}{\Longrightarrow}_{\pi_1} s_1' \xrightarrow{i/o}_{p_1} s_1$ and $s_{0U} \overset{\rho}{\Longrightarrow}_{\pi_2} s_2' \, s_2' \xrightarrow{i}_{p_2} s'' \xrightarrow{o} s_2$. Then, $(\rho \cdot i/o, \pi \cdot \langle p \rangle)$ is a normalized probabilistic trace, where $p$ is the product of $p_1$ and $p_2$ *normalized* with respect to the normalization factor of $M \| U$ after $\rho$, that is, $p = \frac{p_1 \cdot p_2}{\mathsf{norm}_{M \| U}(\rho)}$.

Let $(\rho, \pi)$ be a normalized probabilistic trace where we have $s_{0U} \overset{\rho}{\Longrightarrow}_{\pi'} s$ for some $\pi', s$. We say that $(\mathsf{i}(\rho), \pi)$ is a *normalized probabilistic input trace*. In addition, we say that $\rho$ is a *normalized trace* and that $\mathsf{i}(\rho)$ is a *normalized input trace*. We define the probability of $U$ to stop after $\rho$ normalized to $M$, denoted by $\mathsf{nstop}_{U,M}(\rho)$, as $\frac{\mathsf{stop}(s)}{\mathsf{norm}_{M \| U}(\rho)}$. The sets $\mathsf{npTr}_M(U)$, $\mathsf{npiTr}(U, M)$, $\mathsf{ntr}(U, M)$ and $\mathsf{niTr}(U, M)$ denote the set of *normalized probabilistic traces, normalized traces,* and *normalized input traces* of $U$ to $M$ respectively.

The *set of traces* generated by the *composition* of $M$ and $U$, denoted by $\mathsf{tr}(M \| U)$, is defined as $\mathsf{tr}(M) \cap \mathsf{tr}(U)$. The *set of probabilistic traces* generated by the *composition* of $M$ and $U$, denoted by $\mathsf{pTr}(M \| U)$, is defined as

$$\{(\rho, \pi_1 * \pi_2) | (\rho, \pi_1) \in \mathsf{pTr}(M) \; \wedge \; (\rho, \pi_2) \in \mathsf{npTr}_M(U)\}$$

The *set of input traces* generated by the *composition* of $M$ and $U$, denoted by $\text{iTr}(M \parallel U)$, is defined as the set $\{\text{i}(\rho) \mid \rho \in \text{tr}(M \parallel U)\}$. $\qquad\square$

**Proposition 2.** Let $M$ be a PFSM and let $U$ be a PLTS, then

$$\text{tr}(M \parallel U) = \{\rho \mid \exists p \in (0,1] : (\rho, p) \in \text{pTr}(M \parallel U)\} \qquad\square$$

Let us remark that the probabilistic behavior of the traces belonging to the composition of PFSMs and PLTSs is completely specified: The probabilities of inputs are provided by the PLTS while the probabilities of outputs are given by the PFSM. Since our method consists in testing the behavior of the IUT for some sequences of inputs, we will be interested in taking those traces that share a given sequence of inputs. Next we develop these ideas for sequences and sets of sequences.

**Definition 11.** Let $Tr$ be a set of traces and $\varrho$ an input trace. We define the *set of traces of $Tr$ modulo $\varrho$*, denoted by $\text{tr}_\varrho(Tr)$, as the set $\{\rho \mid \text{i}(\rho) = \varrho, \ \rho \in Tr\}$. If $M$ is a PFSM and $U$ is a PLTS, for the sake of clarity, we write $\text{tr}_\varrho(M)$, $\text{tr}_\varrho(U)$, and $\text{tr}_\varrho(M \parallel U)$ instead of $\text{tr}_\varrho(\text{tr}(M))$, $\text{tr}_\varrho(\text{tr}(U))$, and $\text{tr}_\varrho(\text{tr}(M \parallel U))$, respectively. Let $Tr$ be a set of traces and $iTr$ a set of input traces. We define the *set of traces of $Tr$ modulo $iTr$*, denoted by $\text{prob}_{pTr}(iTr)$, as the set $\{\text{tr}_\varrho(Tr) \mid \varrho \in iTr\}$. $\qquad\square$

We will construct a random variable denoting the probability of each trace in the composition of a specification and a user. Unfortunately, taking the probability associated to each trace in the composition is not appropriate. In fact, the sum of the probabilities of all traces may be higher than 1. This is because traces denote events such that some of them *include* others. For instance, if the event $(a/b, c/d)$ is produced then we know that $(a/b)$ is also produced. We solve this problem by taking into account a factor that is not explicitly considered in the traces: The choice of a user to stop in a state. In particular, the event representing that $(a/b, c/d)$ is produced *and*, afterwards immediately, the user finishes does not imply that $(a/b)$ is produced and then the user stops.

**Proposition 3.** Let $M$ be a PFSM and let $U$ be a terminating PLTS. We have

$$\sum_{(\rho,\pi)\in\text{pTr}(M\parallel U)} \left(\prod \pi\right) * \text{nstop}_{U,M}(\rho) = 1 \qquad\square$$

By the previous result, we can use traces *up to termination* to construct a random variable denoting the probability of observe any trace in the composition of a specification and a user.

**Definition 12.** Let $M$ be a PFSM and let $U$ be PLTS. We define the *traces random variable of the composition of $M$ and $U$* as the function $\xi_{M\parallel U} : \text{pTr}(M \parallel U) \longrightarrow (0,1]$ such that for all $(\rho, \pi) \in \text{pTr}(M \parallel U)$ we have

$$\xi_{M\parallel U}(\rho) = \left(\prod \pi\right) * \text{nstop}_{U,M}(\rho) \qquad\square$$

# 4   Probabilistic Relations

In this section we introduce our probabilistic conformance relations. Following our user customized approach, they relate an IUT *and* a user model with a specification *and* the same user model. These three elements will be related if the probabilistic behavior shown by the IUT when stimulated by the user model appropriately follows the corresponding behavior of the specification. In particular, we will compare the *probabilistic traces* of the composition of the IUT and the user with those corresponding to the composition of the specification and the user. Let us remind that IUTs are input-enabled but specifications might not be so. So, the IUT could define probabilistic traces including sequences of inputs that are not defined in the specification. Since there are no specification requirements for them, these behaviors will be ignored by the relation. In order to do it, an appropriate subset of the traces of the composition of the IUT and the user must be taken. The probability of each trace belonging to this set will be recomputed by considering a suitable normalization. Later we will see another relation where, due to practical reasons, this requirement will be relaxed.

**Definition 13.** Let $S, I$ be PFSMs and $U$ be a PLTS. We define the *set of probabilistic traces generated by the implementation $I$ and the user model $U$ modulo the specification $S$*, denoted by $\mathtt{pTr}(I \parallel U)_S$ as the set

$$\{(\rho, \pi_i * \pi_o) \mid \mathtt{i}(\rho) \in \mathtt{iTr}(S) \ \wedge \ (\rho, \pi_i) \in \mathtt{npTr}_S(U) \ \wedge \ (\rho, \pi_o) \in \mathtt{pTr}(I)\}$$

Let $S, I$ be PFSMs and $U$ be a PLTS. We say that $I$ *conforms to $S$ with respect to $U$*, denoted by $I \mathtt{\,conf}_U S$, if $\mathtt{pTr}(I \parallel U)_S = \mathtt{pTr}(S \parallel U)$.  □

The previous result provides a diagnostic by comparing the complete set of traces of the composition of the specification and the user with the full set of traces of the implementation and the user (up to the specification). We can also perform local comparisons: A local diagnostic is obtained by comparing only those traces that have a given sequence of inputs. Though we can compare these traces by comparing their corresponding probabilities, we will manipulate these probabilities before. In particular, we will divide the probability of each of them by the probability its sequence of inputs. These values will denote the probability of performing the sequence of outputs of the trace *provided that* the sequence of inputs is the considered one. Though this transformation is not needed to perform the current comparison, using these probabilities will be useful in further analyses.

**Definition 14.** Let $A$ be a set of probabilistic traces and $(\varrho, \pi)$ be a probabilistic input trace. We define *the restriction $A$ to $(\varrho, \pi)$*, denoted by $A \backslash (\varrho, \pi)$, as the set $\{(\rho, \pi'/\pi) \mid (\rho, \pi') \in A \ \wedge \ \mathtt{i}(\rho) = \varrho\}$.  □

**Definition 15.** Let $S, I$ be PFSMs, $U$ be a PLTS, and $(\varrho, \pi) \in \mathtt{npiTr}(U, S)$ such that $\varrho \in \mathtt{iTr}(S)$. We say that $I$ *conforms to $S$ with respect to $U$ in the input trace $\varrho$*, denoted by $I \mathtt{\,conf}_{U, \varrho} S$, if $\mathtt{pTr}(I \parallel U)_S \backslash (\varrho, \pi) = \mathtt{pTr}(S \parallel U) \backslash (\varrho, \pi)$.  □

Next we relate our notions of conformance and conformance for a given sequence of inputs. If we have local conformance for all sequences of inputs, then the global conformance is met.

**Proposition 4.** Let $S, I$ be PFSMs, and $U$ and be a PLTS, then $I \operatorname{conf}_U S$ iff for any probabilistic input trace $(\varrho, \pi) \in \operatorname{piTr}(U)$ such that $\varrho \in \operatorname{iTr}(S)$ we have $I \operatorname{conf}_{U,\varrho} S$.            $\square$

Our tests are designed to check any input trace. The parallel composition of the test with the specification $S \parallel T$ performs traces that are not present in the parallel composition of the user and the specification $S \parallel U$. However, if we remove the probabilities associated to the input trace in the user model then the probability of the traces that are in both compositions is the same. Thus, if the implementation conforms the specification with respect to the test $T$ (i.e. $I \operatorname{conf}_T S$), then it also conforms the specification with respect to the user in the trace (i.e. $I \operatorname{conf}_{U,\varrho} S$).

**Proposition 5.** Let $S$ be a PFSM, $U$ and be a PLTS, $(\varrho, \pi) \in \operatorname{npiTr}(U, S)$ such that $\varrho \in \operatorname{iTr}(S)$, and $T = \operatorname{assoc}(\varrho)$. Then

- For all $\rho \in \operatorname{tr}(S \parallel U) \cap \operatorname{tr}(S \parallel T)$ we have $\xi_{S\parallel T}(\rho) * \prod \pi = \xi_{S\parallel U}(\rho)$
- if $I \operatorname{conf}_T S$ then $I \operatorname{conf}_{U,\varrho} S$.            $\square$

Although the previous relation properly defines our probabilistic requirements, it cannot be used in practice because we cannot *read* the probability attached to a transition in a black-box IUT. Let us note that even though a single observation does not provide valuable information about the probability of an IUT trace, an *approximation* to this value can be calculated by interacting a high number of times with the IUT and analyzing its reactions. In particular, we can compare the empirical behavior of the IUT with the ideal behavior defined by the specification and check whether it is *feasible* that the IUT would have behaved like this if, internally, it were defined conforming to the specification. Depending on the empirical observations, this feasibility may be different. The feasibility degree of a set of samples with respect to its ideal probabilistic behavior (defined by a random variable) will be provided by a suitable contrast hypothesis. We will rewrite the previous relation $I \operatorname{conf}_T S$ in these terms.

**Definition 16.** Let $M$ be a PFSM and $U$ be a PLTS. We say that a sequence $\langle \rho_1, \rho_2, \ldots, \rho_n \rangle$ is a *trace sample* of $M \parallel U$ if it is generated by $\xi_{M\parallel U}$.            $\square$

**Definition 17.** Let $S$ be a PFSM and $H = \langle \rho_1, \rho_2, \ldots, \rho_n \rangle$ be a sequence of traces. $H_S$ denotes the sub-sequence $\langle \rho_{r1}, \rho_{r2}, \ldots, \rho_{rn} \rangle$ of $H$ that contains all the probabilistic traces whose input sequences can be produced by $S$, that is, $\operatorname{i}(\rho_{ri}) \in \operatorname{iTr}(S)$.

Let $S$ and $I$ be PFSMs, and $U$ be a PLTS. Let $\varrho \in \operatorname{iTr}(S)$, $T = \operatorname{assoc}(\varrho)$, and $H = \langle \rho_1, \rho_2, \ldots, \rho_n \rangle$ be a trace sample of $I \parallel T$, and $0 \le \alpha \le 1$. We write $S \operatorname{conf}_H^\alpha I$ if $\gamma(\xi_{S\parallel T}, H_S) \ge \alpha$.            $\square$

# 5   Optimal Test Suites

In this section we will focus on two aspects: How to find a suitable test suite and how to provide a metric that allows us to measure the *quality* of test suites. Test suites will we be chosen when they have a *good value* in that metric.

## 5.1   Testing Quality Measurement

Let us suppose that we have a test suite. We apply each test to validate a single trace. By iterating the process for each test, we can get a set of *validated* input traces. Since not all the traces are checked, we have to know how accurate is our judgment about the correctness of the specification. We will measure this accuracy in probabilistic terms. We assume that only the tested and validated input traces are correct and that all the others are incorrect. So, the probability of executing one of those untested traces gives us an *upper bound of the probability that the user finds an error in the implementation*. In order to compute this upper bound, we have to calculate the probability with which the user executes one of the validated traces. The complementary of that probability will be the upper bound we are looking for. In order to compute those probabilities we use the random variable $\xi_{S\|U}$. For any tested input trace $\varrho$, its probability is equal to the probability of the set of traces of $S \| U$ whose input traces are those of $\varrho$.

**Definition 18.** Let $S$ be a PFSM and $U$ be a PLTS. Then,

1. If $\varrho \in \mathtt{iTr}(S \| U)$ then we denote by $\mathbf{prob}_{S\|U}(\varrho)$ the probability of the set of events $\mathtt{tr}_\varrho(\mathtt{tr}(S \| U))$ assigned by the random variable $\xi_{S\|U}$.
2. For any set $iTr \subseteq \mathtt{iTr}(S \| U)$, we denote by $\mathbf{prob}_{S\|U}(iTr)$ the probability of the set of events $\mathtt{tr}_{iTr}(\mathtt{pTr}(S \| U))$ assigned by $\xi_{S\|U}$.     □

In the random variable $\xi_{S\|U}$ we consider only full execution of traces, i.e. until the user decides to stop. For that reason we have that all events are independent.

**Proposition 6.** Let $S$ be a PFSM and $U$ be a PLTS. If $\varrho \in \mathtt{iTr}(S \| U)$ then

$$\mathbf{prob}_{S\|U}(\varrho) = \sum \left\{ \left( \prod \pi \right) * \mathtt{nstop}_{U,S}(\rho) \mid \mathtt{i}(\rho) = \varrho \wedge (\rho, \pi) \in \mathtt{pTr}(S \| U) \right\}$$

For any set $iTr \subseteq \mathtt{iTr}(S \| U)$, $\mathbf{prob}_{S\|U}(iTr) = \sum \left\{ \mathbf{prob}_{S\|U}(\varrho) \mid \varrho \in iTr \right\}$.     □

Next we show how to compute the aforementioned upper bound. The scenario is the following. We have applied tests corresponding to some input traces and we have obtained some samples. Then, we consider only those traces such that the corresponding sample passes the hypothesis contrast. The *upper bound that the user finds a error* is calculated by considering that the rest of input traces behaves incorrectly. So, we calculate the probability to execute one of the validated traces, that is $\mathbf{prob}_{S\|U}(iTr)$, being the complementary probability the bound we are looking for. Let us remark that the IUT does not appear in the expression $\mathbf{prob}_{S\|U}(iTr)$. The reason is that we have already tested the implementation in the input traces of the set $iTr$. Thus, we can assume that the implementation behaves for those traces as indicated by the specification. Besides, we cannot compute that probability from the implementation since it is a *black box*: We can only test it and take samples from it.

**Definition 19.** Let $S, I$ be PFSMs and $U$ be a PLTS.

– Let $\varrho$ be an input trace, $H$ be a sample of $I \parallel \texttt{assoc}(\varrho)$, and $\alpha$ be a feasibility degree. We say that $\varrho$ is $(H, \alpha)$-*tested* if $I \texttt{ conf}_H^\alpha S$.
– Let $iTr$ be a set of input traces and $\mathcal{H}$ be the set of samples $\{H_\varrho \mid \varrho \in iTr,\ H_\varrho \text{ is a sample of } I \parallel \texttt{assoc}(\varrho)\}$. We say that $iTr$ is $(\mathcal{H}, \alpha)$-*tested* if $I \texttt{ conf}_{H_\varrho}^\alpha S$ for all $\varrho \in iTr$.

Let $iTr \subseteq \texttt{iTr}(S \parallel U)$ be a $(\mathcal{H}, \alpha)$-*tested* set of input traces for a set of samples $\mathcal{H}$ and a feasibility degree $\alpha$. Then, the *upper bound of error probability of the user* $U$ *to find and error in* $I$ *with respect to the input trace set* $iTr$, $\texttt{ubErr}_{iTr}^{\mathcal{H}, \alpha}(I, U)$, is the probabity of executing a trace $\rho$ such that $\texttt{i}(\rho) \notin iTr$:

$$\texttt{ubErr}_{iTr}^{\mathcal{H}, \alpha}(I, U) = 1 - \texttt{prob}_{S \parallel U}(iTr) \qquad \square$$

## 5.2  Obtaining a Good Test Suite

Now we give a criteria to choose the *best test suite*. This criteria will be equivalent to the *0/1 knapsack problem*. Due to its intrinsic complexity, *good enough* test suites will be obtained by applying one of the known suboptimal algorithms.

Since each test checks a single input trace, our test suite will try to minimize the upper bound introduced in Definition 19. So, to find a good test suite is equivalent to find an input trace set $iTr$ that maximizes $\texttt{prob}_{S \parallel U}(iTr)$. This will be our first criterium to choose our test suite. Obviously, the set that maximizes that probability is the whole set of input traces, that is usually infinite. We need another criteria to limit the number of tests to be applied. It will consist in minimizing the size of tests. Since each tests consists in a sequence of $n$ pairs input/output, it sends and receives exactly $n$ input/output actions. Then, we consider $n$ as the size of the test.

**Definition 20.** Let $\varrho = (i_1, i_2, \ldots i_n)$ be an input trace. We say that the *length* of the test $T = \texttt{assoc}(\varrho)$ is $n$ and we write $\texttt{length}(T) = n$. Let $iTr$ be a set of input traces. We define the *length* of the set $\mathcal{T} = \{\texttt{assoc}(\varrho) \mid \varrho \in iTr\}$, denoted by $\texttt{length}(\mathcal{T})$, as $\sum\{\texttt{length}(T) \mid T \in \mathcal{T}\}$

Let $S$ be a PFSM and $U$ be a PLTS. Let $n \in \mathbb{N}$ and $iTr \subseteq \texttt{iTr}(S \parallel U)$. We say that the set of tests $\mathcal{T} = \{\texttt{assoc}(\varrho) \mid \varrho \in iTr\}$, with $\texttt{length}(\mathcal{T}) \leq n$, is $n$-*optimum* if there does not exist another set of traces $iTr' \subseteq \texttt{iTr}(S \parallel U)$ and a set of tests $\mathcal{T}' = \{\texttt{assoc}(\varrho) \mid \varrho \in iTr'\}$ with $\texttt{length}(\mathcal{T}') \leq n$ such that $\texttt{prob}_{S \parallel U}(iTr') > \texttt{prob}_{S \parallel U}(iTr)$. $\qquad \square$

Let us note that, since each trace is independent from the others, the problem to find an $n$-optimum test suite is equivalent to the 0/1 knapsack problem: The total size of the knapsack is $n$; the elements are the input traces $\varrho = (i_1, \ldots, i_r) \in$ $\mathtt{iTr}(S \parallel U)$ such that $r \leq n$; the cost of the trace $\varrho = (i_1, \ldots, i_r)$ is $r$; the value of a trace $\varrho$ is $\mathtt{prob}_{S\parallel U}(\varrho)$. Due to the intrinsic complexity of that problem, it is not feasible to find an $n$-optimum test suite. However, we can consider one of the suboptimal well-known algorithms to solve the problem (see for example [22]).

## 5.3    Testing Methodology

Finally, let us briefly sketch our testing methodology:

1. We fix $n$, the combined size of tests belonging to the suite, and $\alpha$, the feasibility degree to pass the hypotheses contrast.
2. We find a suboptimal test suite $\mathcal{T}$, corresponding to a set of input traces, for the size $n$.
3. We generate the trace sample $H_T$ for all test $T \in \mathcal{T}$.
4. We consider the set of input traces whose samples pass the hypotheses contrast with the required feasibility degree $\mathcal{H} = \{H_T \mid \exists T \in \mathcal{T} : I\, \mathtt{conf}^{\alpha}_{H_T}\, S\}$, $iTr = \{\varrho \mid \exists T \in \mathcal{T} : H_T \in \mathcal{H} \wedge T = \mathtt{assoc}(\varrho)\}$.
5. We calculate the probability of error $\mathtt{ubErr}^{\mathcal{H},\alpha}_{iTr}(I, U)$.

# 6    Conclusions and Future Work

In this paper we have presented a formal methodology to test probabilistic systems that are stimulated according to a given user model. In particular, we compare the behavior of a specification when it is stimulated by a user model with the behavior of an IUT when it is stimulated by the same model. By taking into account the probabilities of systems we have that, after a finite test suite is applied to the IUT, we can measure, for a given confidence degree, an upper bound of the probability that a user behaving as the user model finds an error in the IUT. Though a previous work [12] introduces a first approach to compute this metric, this method lies in the idea of comparing a single random variable denoting *all* the behaviors in the composition of the specification and the user with a sample denoting the behavior of the IUT when the user stimulates it. On the contrary, in this paper we separately study the behavior of the IUT for each sequence of inputs. Hence, the frequency of sequences of inputs is not part of the sampled information. This approach requires to use a specific random variable for each sequence of inputs (instead of a single random variable for all traces), as well as separately validating each sample with respect to its corresponding random variable. We use the method to find, for a given number of input actions, a optimal finite test suite, that is, a suite such that if it is passed then the upper bound of error probability is lower that the value obtained with any other test suite of the same size.

As future work, we plan to *compact* the information collected by samples. Let us suppose that a sample $(a/x, b/y, c/z)$ is obtained. This implies that if the sequence of inputs $(a, b)$ would have been offered instead of $(a, b, c)$, then the sequence of outputs $(x, y)$ would have obtained. That is, if the sample

$(a/x, b/y, c/z)$ is obtained then the sample $(a/x, b/y)$ is also obtained, as well as $(a/x)$. Hence, by considering all prefixes of a sample, the number of observations for some sequences of inputs increases. Since the precision of hypothesis contrasts is higher when the size of samples is higher, this approach would allow us to improve the precision of our probabilistic method.

# References

1. B.S. Bosik and M.U. Uyar. Finite state machine based formal methods in protocol conformance testing. *Computer Networks & ISDN Systems*, 22:7–33, 1991.
2. L. Bottaci and E.S. Mresa. Efficiency of mutation operators and selective mutation strategies: An empirical study. *Software Testing, Verification and Reliability*, 9:205–232, 1999.
3. D. Cazorla, F. Cuartero, V. Valero, F.L. Pelayo, and J.J. Pardo. Algebraic theory of probabilistic and non-deterministic processes. *Journal of Logic and Algebraic Programming*, 55(1–2):57–103, 2003.
4. I. Christoff. Testing equivalences and fully abstract models for probabilistic processes. In *CONCUR'90, LNCS 458*, pages 126–140. Springer, 1990.
5. R. Cleaveland, Z. Dayar, S.A. Smolka, and S. Yuen. Testing preorders for probabilistic processes. *Information and Computation*, 154(2):93–148, 1999.
6. R. de Nicola and M.C.B. Hennessy. Testing equivalences for processes. *Theoretical Computer Science*, 34:83–133, 1984.
7. R. van Glabbeek, S.A. Smolka, and B. Steffen. Reactive, generative and stratified models of probabilistic processes. *Information and Computation*, 121(1):59–80, 1995.
8. R.G. Hamlet. Testing programs with the aid of a compiler. *IEEE Transactions on Software Engineering*, 3:279–290, 1977.
9. M. Hennessy. *Algebraic Theory of Processes*. MIT Press, 1988.
10. W.E. Howden. Weak mutation testing and completeness of test sets. *IEEE Transactions on Software Engineering*, 8:371–379, 1982.
11. D. Lee and M. Yannakakis. Principles and methods of testing finite state machines: A survey. *Proceedings of the IEEE*, 84(8):1090–1123, 1996.
12. L.F. Llana-Díaz, M. Núñez, and I. Rodríguez. Customized testing for probabilistic systems. In *18th Int. Conf. on Testing Communicating Systems, TestCom 2006, LNCS 3964*, pages 87–102. Springer, 2006.
13. N. López, M. Núñez, and I. Rodríguez. Specification, testing and implementation relations for symbolic-probabilistic systems. *Theoretical Computer Science*, 353(1–3):228–248, 2006.
14. M. Núñez. Algebraic theory of probabilistic processes. *Journal of Logic and Algebraic Programming*, 56(1–2):117–177, 2003.
15. M. Núñez and I. Rodríguez. Encoding PAMR into (timed) EFSMs. In *22nd IFIP Conf. on Formal Techniques for Networked and Distributed Systems, FORTE 2002, LNCS 2529*, pages 1–16. Springer, 2002.
16. M. Núñez and D. de Frutos. Testing semantics for probabilistic LOTOS. In *Formal Description Techniques VIII*, pages 365–380. Chapman & Hall, 1995.
17. A. Petrenko. Fault model-driven test derivation from finite state models: Annotated bibliography. In *4th Summer School, MOVEP 2000, LNCS 2067*, pages 196–205. Springer, 2001.

18. I. Rodríguez, M.G. Merayo, and M. Núñez. A logic for assessing sets of heterogeneous testing hypotheses. In *18th Int. Conf. on Testing Communicating Systems, TestCom 2006, LNCS 3964*, pages 39–54. Springer, 2006.

19. R. Segala. Testing probabilistic automata. In *CONCUR'96, LNCS 1119*, pages 299–314. Springer, 1996.

20. M. Stoelinga and F. Vaandrager. A testing scenario for probabilistic automata. In *ICALP 2003, LNCS 2719*, pages 464–477. Springer, 2003.

21. J. Tretmans. Test generation with inputs, outputs and repetitive quiescence. *Software – Concepts and Tools*, 17(3):103–120, 1996.

22. V. V. Vazirani. *Approximation Algorithms*. Springer-Verlag, 2001.

# Author Index

# Lecture Notes in Computer Science

For information about Vols. 1–4142

please contact your bookseller or Springer

Vol. 4190: R. Larsen, M. Nielsen, J. Sporring (Eds.), Medical Image Computing and Computer-Assisted Intervention – MICCAI 2006, Part I. XXXVVIII, 949 pages. 2006.

Vol. 4189: D. Gollmann, J. Meier, A. Sabelfeld (Eds.), Computer Security – ESORICS 2006. XI, 548 pages. 2006.

Vol. 4188: P. Sojka, I. Kopeček, K. Pala (Eds.), Text, Speech and Dialogue. XIV, 721 pages. 2006. (Sublibrary LNAI).

Vol. 4187: J.J. Alferes, J. Bailey, W. May, U. Schwertel (Eds.), Principles and Practice of Semantic Web Reasoning. XI, 277 pages. 2006.

Vol. 4186: C. Jesshope, C. Egan (Eds.), Advances in Computer Systems Architecture. XIV, 605 pages. 2006.

Vol. 4185: R. Mizoguchi, Z. Shi, F. Giunchiglia (Eds.), The Semantic Web – ASWC 2006. XX, 778 pages. 2006.

Vol. 4184: M. Bravetti, M. Núñez, G. Zavattaro (Eds.), Web Services and Formal Methods. X, 289 pages. 2006.

Vol. 4183: J. Euzenat, J. Domingue (Eds.), Artificial Intelligence: Methodology, Systems, and Applications. XIII, 291 pages. 2006. (Sublibrary LNAI).

Vol. 4182: H.T. Ng, M.-K. Leong, M.-Y. Kan, D. Ji (Eds.), Information Retrieval Technology. XVI, 684 pages. 2006.

Vol. 4180: M. Kohlhase, OMDoc – An Open Markup Format for Mathematical Documents [version 1.2]. XIX, 428 pages. 2006. (Sublibrary LNAI).

Vol. 4179: J. Blanc-Talon, W. Philips, D. Popescu, P. Scheunders (Eds.), Advanced Concepts for Intelligent Vision Systems. XXIV, 1224 pages. 2006.

Vol. 4178: A. Corradini, H. Ehrig, U. Montanari, L. Ribeiro, G. Rozenberg (Eds.), Graph Transformations. XII, 473 pages. 2006.

Vol. 4177: R. Marín, E. Onaindía, A. Bugarín, J. Santos (Eds.), Current Topics in Aritficial Intelligence. XIII, 621 pages. 2006. (Sublibrary LNAI).

Vol. 4176: S.K. Katsikas, J. Lopez, M. Backes, S. Gritzalis, B. Preneel (Eds.), Information Security. XIV, 548 pages. 2006.

Vol. 4175: P. Bücher, B.M.E. Moret (Eds.), Algorithms in Bioinformatics. XII, 402 pages. 2006. (Sublibrary LNBI).

Vol. 4174: K. Franke, K.-R. Müller, B. Nickolay, R. Schäfer (Eds.), Pattern Recognition. XX, 773 pages. 2006.

Vol. 4173: S. El Yacoubi, B. Chopard, S. Bandini (Eds.), Cellular Automata. XV, 734 pages. 2006.

Vol. 4172: J. Gonzalo, C. Thanos, M. F. Verdejo, R.C. Carrasco (Eds.), Research and Advanced Technology for Digital Libraries. XVII, 569 pages. 2006.

Vol. 4169: H.L. Bodlaender, M.A. Langston (Eds.), Parameterized and Exact Computation. XI, 279 pages. 2006.

Vol. 4168: Y. Azar, T. Erlebach (Eds.), Algorithms – ESA 2006. XVIII, 843 pages. 2006.

Vol. 4167: S. Dolev (Ed.), Distributed Computing. XV, 576 pages. 2006.

Vol. 4166: J. Górski (Ed.), Computer Safety, Reliability, and Security. XIV, 440 pages. 2006.

Vol. 4165: W. Jonker, M. Petković (Eds.), Secure, Data Management. X, 185 pages. 2006.

Vol. 4163: H. Bersini, J. Carneiro (Eds.), Artificial Immune Systems. XII, 460 pages. 2006.

Vol. 4162: R. Královič, P. Urzyczyn (Eds.), Mathematical Foundations of Computer Science 2006. XV, 814 pages. 2006.

Vol. 4161: R. Harper, M. Rauterberg, M. Combetto (Eds.), Entertainment Computing - ICEC 2006. XXVII, 417 pages. 2006.

Vol. 4160: M. Fisher, W.v.d. Hoek, B. Konev, A. Lisitsa (Eds.), Logics in Artificial Intelligence. XII, 516 pages. 2006. (Sublibrary LNAI).

Vol. 4159: J. Ma, H. Jin, L.T. Yang, J.J.-P. Tsai (Eds.), Ubiquitous Intelligence and Computing. XXII, 1190 pages. 2006.

Vol. 4158: L.T. Yang, H. Jin, J. Ma, T. Ungerer (Eds.), Autonomic and Trusted Computing. XIV, 613 pages. 2006.

Vol. 4156: S. Amer-Yahia, Z. Bellahsène, E. Hunt, R. Unland, J.X. Yu (Eds.), Database and XML Technologies. IX, 123 pages. 2006.

Vol. 4155: O. Stock, M. Schaerf (Eds.), Reasoning, Action and Interaction in AI Theories and Systems. XVIII, 343 pages. 2006. (Sublibrary LNAI).

Vol. 4154: Y.A. Dimitriadis, I. Zigurs, E. Gómez-Sánchez (Eds.), Groupware: Design, Implementation, and Use. XIV, 438 pages. 2006.

Vol. 4153: N. Zheng, X. Jiang, X. Lan (Eds.), Advances in Machine Vision, Image Processing, and Pattern Analysis. XIII, 506 pages. 2006.

Vol. 4152: Y. Manolopoulos, J. Pokorný, T. Sellis (Eds.), Advances in Databases and Information Systems. XV, 448 pages. 2006.

Vol. 4151: A. Iglesias, N. Takayama (Eds.), Mathematical Software - ICMS 2006. XVII, 452 pages. 2006.

Vol. 4150: M. Dorigo, L.M. Gambardella, M. Birattari, A. Martinoli, R. Poli, T. Stützle (Eds.), Ant Colony Optimization and Swarm Intelligence. XVI, 526 pages. 2006.

Vol. 4149: M. Klusch, M. Rovatsos, T.R. Payne (Eds.), Cooperative Information Agents X. XII, 477 pages. 2006. (Sublibrary LNAI).

Vol. 4148: J. Vounckx, N. Azemard, P. Maurine (Eds.), Integrated Circuit and System Design. XVI, 677 pages. 2006.

Vol. 4147: M. Broy, I.H. Krüger, M. Meisinger (Eds.), Automotive Software – Connected Services in Mobile Networks. XIV, 155 pages. 2006.

Vol. 4146: J.C. Rajapakse, L. Wong, R. Acharya (Eds.), Pattern Recognition in Bioinformatics. XIV, 186 pages. 2006. (Sublibrary LNBI).

Vol. 4144: T. Ball, R.B. Jones (Eds.), Computer Aided Verification. XV, 564 pages. 2006.

Vol. 4143: R. Lämmel, J. Saraiva, J. Visser (Eds.), Generative and Transformational Techniques in Software Engineering. X, 471 pages. 2006.